THE POLITICAL ECONOMY OF
POVERTY, EQUITY, AND GROWTH

THE POLITICAL ECONOMY OF POVERTY, EQUITY, AND GROWTH

A Comparative Study

DEEPAK LAL and H. MYINT

CLARENDON PRESS · OXFORD

1996

Oxford University Press, Walton Street, Oxford OX2 6DP

Oxford New York
Athens Auckland Bangkok Bombay
Calcutta Cape Town Dar es Salaam Delhi
Florence Hong Kong Istanbul Karachi
Kuala Lumpur Madras Madrid Melbourne
Mexico City Nairobi Paris Singapore
Taipei Tokyo Toronto
and associated companies in
Berlin Ibadan

Oxford is a trade mark of Oxford University Press

Published in the United States by
Oxford University Press Inc., New York

British Library Cataloguing in Publication Data
Data available

Library of Congress Cataloging in Publication Data
Data available
ISBN 0–19–828863–8

1 3 5 7 9 10 8 6 4 2

Typeset by Best-set Typesetter Ltd., Hong Kong

Printed in Great Britain
on acid-free paper by
Bookcraft (Bath) Ltd., Midsomer Norton, Avon

PREFACE

THIS book provides a synthesis of the findings of a multi-country compara-tive study financed by the World Bank. The Introduction describes the nature and scope of the project, as well as its intellectual design. Here we need only note the division of labour involved in writing this book, and our acknowledgements to the many individuals without whose help this study could not have been completed.

The book consists of ten chapters. Lal is primarily responsible for Chap-ters 1–2, 5–7, 9, and 10, Myint for Chapters 3, 4, and 8. We have sought to make the book intelligible to the general reader with some knowledge of economics, say a reader of *The Economist*. Technical discussions are put in starred sections which can be skipped by such readers without losing the thread of the argument.

Our major debt is to the authors of our country studies, without whom obviously this book could not have been written. They are: David Bevan, Henry Bruton, Mauricio Carrizosa Serrano, Paul Collier, Gus Edgren, Edgardo Favaro, Ronald Findlay, Claudio Gonzales-Vega, Jan Gunning, Bent Hansen, Angus Maddison, Oey A. Meesook, Frederic Pryor, Douglas Rimmer, Simon Rottenberg, Antonio Urdinola, Richard Webb, and Stanislaw Wellisz. They worked with various associates, who contributed to the country studies. These are: Claudio R. Contador, Annibal V. Villela, Sonia Maria Rodrigues da Rocha, Luis A. Villela, Victor Urquidi, Jesus Reyes Heroles, Rafael Izquierdo (Brazil and Mexico); Alwyn Young, Linda Lim, Pang Eng Fong, Carl Stone, Philippe Lan Shin Saw (Five Small Open Economies); Pranee Tinakorn, Chayan Vaddhanaphuti, Martin D. Chrisney, Ukrist Pathmanond (Thailand); and Victor Hugo Cespedes (Costa Rica). In addition a number of special studies were comissioned on cross-sectional aspects of our subject. We are grateful to the authors of these: George Psacharopoulos, Gary Fields, Jandhyala B. G. Tilak, Jere R. Behrman, Harold Alderman, Alexander Berg, Elliot Berg, and Zafitis Tzannatos.

Next we owe an immense debt to Anne Krueger, the then Vice-President of Economics and Research, and the Vice-Presidents on the Research Policy Council of the time (1985), *viz.* Shahid Hussain, David Knox, and Joe Wood, who approved this large and risky project, to be funded as part of the World Bank's comparative studies programme. We hope that their trust has been justified. We would also like to thank the Swedish Inter-national Development Agency for providing partial funding for the study, and Bo Kalstrom for arranging this.

The project was overseen throughout its life of four years by an external panel consisting of Dharma Kumar, Gerald Meier, Guido di Tella, Perry Anderson, and Shegiro Ishikawa. Their inputs, at the periodic conferences we held to co-ordinate this vast project, were indispensable both in maintaining the intellectual integrity of the various country studies and in monitoring the progress of the project. The draft of this synthesis volume was discussed at a conference in Washington in September 1989, with the principal authors and members of the external panel.

In addition Sir Alan Walters and Professors T. N. Srinivasan and Jean Waelbroek provided comments on this first draft, whilst Professor Mark Blaug has provided detailed comments on Sections II–III in the Introduction. The revised second draft was discussed at seminars in Japan, Malaysia, Singapore, and Thailand, and at a conference organized by the International Centre for Economic Growth in Mexico. The comments by the discussants at these seminars were most useful, as were those by the anonymous reviewers for the World Bank's publications committee. This led to a revised third draft in early 1992. By October 1992, the committee decided not to publish the book as a World Bank publication. We are grateful to Andrew Schuller, two anonymous reviewers for the Clarendon Press, and the delegates of Oxford University Press for their support in seeing this book in print. We are particularly pleased that, unlike the other volumes in the series arising from the comparative study, this is the only one to meet the market test of not requiring a World Bank subsidy towards its publication! The detailed comments from one of the OUP reviewers were particularly valuable in redrafting this final version. Given the long delay between the first and final drafts of the book, and the explosion in research on various aspects of the subject, this final revision has meant a virtual rewriting of parts of the book. This we hope in fact strengthens the basic argument, which, based as it was on the country studies, has not changed. But both of us have grown older during the lengthy process of completing this study, with Myint retiring completely from academic life in 1993, and Lal moving to UCLA. As our subject matter is one of the grand themes of economics, we still hope that, even though the period of study of our countries was the end of 1985, the general conclusions drawn will still be of relevance, particularly as in this final revision (mostly to Lal's chapters) we have tried to take account of the other literature on our subject-matter which has appeared to date.

This final revision, which has taken nearly another year, would not have been possible without Lal's being granted leave of absence for the 1993–4 academic year by UCLA. He is also grateful to Professor Richard Layard, who provided an academic home at the Centre for Economic Performance, at the LSE, during this period.

The help of various World Bank staff members has also been indispensable in the initiation and completion of this project. We would particularly like to thank Armeane Choksi, Stephen O'Brien, and Surjit Bhalla (who later joined our external panel on leaving the Bank) for their support of the project.

The project was administered from the World Bank by Oey Meesook (until 1986), and Deepak Lal (1985–7). Thereafter (October 1987–June 1990) George Psacharapolous directed the project for the World Bank and most ably saw it through its inevitably stormy final phases.

The day-to-day administration of the project has been conducted by five full-time project administrators, who have been most efficient, and without whose contribution this project would never have been completed. They are Sappho Harrambolous, Josie Basinette, Jeannine Timmins, the late Celina Bermudez, and Susan Tamondong-Helin.

We have also been ably assisted by three research assistants who have worked full-time with us on the project. Successively they were Martin Chrisney, Ahmad Ebrahimi, and Carole Willis.

For the final draft Joon-Mo Yang of UCLA ably assisted in the statistical time-series analysis of our growth series.

Finally, but not the least, we owe an immense debt to the four secretaries to the project, who apart from keeping our daily lives in order have also efficiently undertaken the various organizational and production tasks in producing this and the other volumes in the series with cheerfulness and efficiency. They are Leela Thampy, Janet Roddy, Monique Caldwell, and Jane Halville. The final draft of this synthesis volume was put together with great efficiency by Lorraine Grams at UCLA.

We are most grateful to all these individuals and to the World Bank for making this book possible. It is for our readers to judge whether the effort and resources spent have been worthwhile.

D. L. and H. M.

London and Los Angeles
October 1994

CONTENTS

LIST OF FIGURES

LIST OF TABLES

Introduction

THIS book synthesizes the findings emerging from a comparative analysis of 'The Political Economy of Poverty, Equity, and Growth' of twenty-one developing countries, sponsored by the World Bank. The country studies themselves are being published as part of a series in ten volumes, of which this is the last.

I. DESIGN OF THE COMPARATIVE STUDY

The aim of the study was to provide a critical evaluation of the economic history of these twenty-one developing countries during the period 1950–85. It explored the *processes* which contributed to different outcomes in terms of growth, poverty, and equity in these countries in relation to: (*a*) the initial conditions—resource endowment and economic structure; (*b*) national political institutions and forms of economic organization; and (*c*) economic policies (including those which might have been undertaken).

A coherent story of the growth and income distribution experiences of each country based on the methods of what may be termed 'analytical economic history' and 'political economy' (see Sections II–III below) are the basic building-blocks of the project. Each country study provided both a historical narrative and an exploration of deeper questions of how and why things happened. The 'political economy' dimension of each country study sought to identify the role of ideology and interest groups in shaping policy.

Our comparative approach involved an initial pairing of countries which seemed to show significant similarities or contrasts of initial conditions or policies. Whilst initial impressions of similarity or difference were not borne out on closer inspection in every case (see Chapter 3), nevertheless we feel that this binary approach offered a novel and promising way of reconciling in-depth case study with a broader comparative study approach. The second comparative stage is contained in the synthesis of the political and economic determinants of growth and poverty outcomes contained in the rest of the chapters of this book.

In order to provide an in-depth study of individual cases, a smaller number of countries (21) was selected than is conventional in comparative *statistical* studies. We have serious doubts about the validity of inferences drawn from such cross-sectional regression studies about historical processes (see below and Chapter 2). Therefore this project has aimed instead to interpret the nature and significance of the usual quantifiable variables for each country in its historical and institutional context, by combining qualitative with quantitative analysis.

To provide some unifying elements to the project, the authors of the country studies were presented by the co-directors (Lal and Myint) with a number of provisional hypotheses to be considered in the course of their work. These concern the determinants of growth; the importance of historical and organizational factors in determining alternative feasible paths of poverty-redressing growth; and the relative roles of ideas, interests, and ideology in influencing decision-making. This book discusses the extent to which these were substantiated.

The following is the list of the country volumes and their principal authors, each containing separate studies of particular countries and their comparative analyses.

1. Malawi and Madagascar   Frederic Pryor (Oxford, 1990)
2. Egypt and Turkey   Bent Hansen (Oxford, 1991)
3. Sri Lanka and Malaysia   Henry Bruton (Oxford, 1992)
4. Indonesia and Nigeria   David Bevan, Paul Collier, and Jan Gunning (Oxford, forthcoming)
5. Thailand and Ghana   Oey A. Meesook and associates (Thailand) (mimeo, 1987); Douglas Rimmer (Ghana) (Pergamon, 1992); and Gus Edgren (twin study) (mimeo, 1987)
6. Brazil and Mexico   Angus Maddison and associates (Oxford, 1992)
7. Costa Rica and Uruguay   Simon Rottenberg, Claudio Gonzales-Vega, and Edgardo Favaro (Oxford, 1993)
8. Colombia and Peru   Antonio Urdinola, Mauricio Carrizosa Serrano, and Richard Webb (mimeo, 1987)
9. Five small economies: Ronald Findlay, Stanislaw
   Hong Kong, Singapore   Wellisz, and associates
   Malta, Jamaica, and   (Oxford, 1993)
   Mauritius

In addition there is a specially commissioned volume of essays on cross-country themes which has been edited by George Psacharopoulous (1991).

The two relatively novel features of our method of analysis in the comparative study were 'analytical economic history' and 'political economy'.

The following two sections outline and defend these methods that we have used to derive our qualitative—but not unanalytical—judgements of the determinants of growth and poverty alleviation in our sample of countries. Busy readers may wish to skip these sections, and move directly to the synopsis of the volume which ends this introduction.

II. ANALYTICAL ECONOMIC HISTORY

In this section we briefly outline the justification for the method of analytical economic history that we adopted in our country case-studies. We also relate it to other 'methods' in economics, and see why in practice it may be persuasive.

1. The Logic of Comparative Studies

Comparative studies, of which ours is an example, are a form of comparative historical analysis which has a distinguished pedigree in social science.[1] J. S. Mill sets out the logic of these studies explicitly in his *A System of Logic* (especially book III, ch. VIII), and this comparative method was applied with great skill by Alexis de Tocqueville in his *Democracy in America*, and by Marc Bloch in *Feudal Society*.

The method is particularly suited to the empirical study of problems of growth and development, as J. N. Keynes noted at the turn of the century.[2] The evolution of institutions is likely to be central in explanations of differing growth performances,[3] for the present decisions of economic agents which impinge on the development process will be constrained in part by their past, through various cultural and ideological norms and organizational structures. These institutional aspects which have evolved historically will constrain the feasible set of choices of current decision-makers. We need to understand the different 'rules of the game' and the different incentive structures relating to alternative organizational forms, and how they evolve. Also we need to know how people react to changes in the set of choices facing them when either the informal constraints of cultural norms or the more purposive ones embodied in particular organizational structures alter. In short, we need to understand dynamic institutional changes if we are ultimately to find deeper answers to the question of why some countries have grown and developed and others have not. However, as there is no rigorous model defining dynamic institutional change, and even if there were it would be unlikely to be amenable to econometric analysis, our approach must be eclectic. It must also connect the present with the past. This is one major aim of the historical comparative studies method.

A major difference between the comparative study method and statistical (econometric) analysis can be seen in terms of the two forms of induction distinguished by J. N. Keynes, namely quantitative induction and 'qualitative induction'.[4] Quantitative induction is based purely on statistical analysis, qualitative on the historical or comparative method. It is the latter which concerns us.

The logical status of this experimental method was clearly set out by Mill. He distinguished between what he called the 'Method of Agreement' and the 'Method of Difference' (as two of his five methods of experimental enquiry). The method of difference is the normal method used in the experimental sciences. By this method 'one can try to establish that several cases have in common a set of causal factors, although they vary in other ways that might have seemed causally relevant'. The method of agreement, by contrast, compares 'cases in which the phenomenon to be explained and the hypothesized cause are both present to other cases in which the phenomenon and the causes are both absent, but which are otherwise as similar as possible to the positive cases'.[5] Mill emphasized that the method of difference is by itself a more powerful method for establishing valid causal connections, but that

on those subjects where artificial experimentation is impossible . . . our only recourse of a directly productive nature [is the method of agreement], while in the phenomena which we can produce at pleasure, the method of difference generally affords a more efficacious process which will ascertain causes as well as mere laws.[6]

In practice, on the comparative historical method, it is possible to combine both types of comparative method. 'This is done by using at once several positive cases along with suitable negative cases as contrasts.'[7]

The method, like any other method of multivariate analysis, must depend upon some prior theoretical structure. It also has the usual problem concerning the selection of the relevant sample, and the appropriate *ceteris paribus* conditions used in the identification of relevant causal links, as well as in drawing robust inferences about the relative strength of various supposed causes leading to the effects which are of interest. If statistical analysis is broadly defined as the arrangement of quantitative data into patterns, together with the attachment of some measure of the confidence that can be attached to the correctness of the pattern that is inferred, it is clear that statistical analysis, whenever it is feasible, is not only complementary but can form an important part of the comparative method. However, as Keynes emphasized, this comparative method is wider than the purely statistical inquiry by which

social science and political economy are spoken of as branches or departments of the science of statistics, a science which studies social and economic phenomena in the only satisfactory way, namely, by the accumulation of facts and generalizations from them.[8]

He rightly argues that this view is too narrow, as the economic methods used in practice by economists embody not only this form of quantitative induction, but also qualitative induction and, of course, deduction.

This is also the place to emphasize Hayek's distinction between *specific* and *pattern* predictions, and between the sciences of 'simple' and of 'complex' phenomena, with their associated simple and complex orders.[9] He argues that in simple orders, as in physics, specific predictions are possible, but in the complex orders studied by the social sciences and biology, 'where the elements which have to be taken into account are neither few enough that you can know them all nor a sufficiently large number that you can substitute probabilities for the new information', the scope for specific predictions is very limited, and 'that at most [what can be achieved is] . . . pattern predictions, or predictions of the principle'.[10] This prediction of patterns, namely 'the recurrent associations of a range of effects with limited causes', is possible for complex phenomena as studied in this book, even when it is not possible to predict 'individual events within those patterns'[11] This pattern-prediction—based on our historical country studies—is one of our primary tasks in this book.

The comparative studies method is thus by and large the classical method of economic analysis applied to comparative history. As such it is best termed 'analytical economic history', which combines the deductive analysis of economic theory with both the quantitative inductive analysis of statistics (to the extent that this is possible) and the qualitative inductive analysis of comparative history.[12]

2. Forensic Story-Telling

The comparative studies method, which is largely based on the classical method, can also be looked upon as a form of story-telling. Moreover, as a story-teller tries to tell a story which is both interesting and persuasive, so the method is attuned to the multifaceted aspects of persuasion.[13] These concern the selection of 'facts', the crafting of the story, and choosing from amongst a number of competing stories the one which fits the 'facts' better than another.[14]

In our stories we are attempting to establish plausible causal links. Two different forms of causation are distinguished by philosophers. One is based on statistical regularities, the other in terms of counterfactual analysis. It is the latter form of causal analysis which underlies analytical economic history.

This analysis of causation in economics in terms of counterfactuals has been most ably outlined and defended by Sir John Hicks,[15] who distinguishes between three types of causality in relationship to time: 'Sequential (in which cause precedes effect), contemporaneous (in which both relate to the same period) and static (in which both are permanencies)'.[16] Much economic analysis is concerned with contemporaneous and static causation. Whilst this is useful and illuminating in many areas—demand analysis, welfare economics, international trade theory—it is not much use in answering the types of questions concerning the *processes* of development which are concerned with sequential causation.

As Hicks notes:

The more characteristic economic problems are problems of change, or growth and retrogression, and of fluctuation. The extent to which these can be reduced into scientific terms is rather limited; for at every stage in an economic process new things are happening, things which have not happened before—at the most they are rather like what has happened before. We need a theory that will help us with these problems; but it is impossible to believe that it can ever be a complete theory. It is bound, by its nature, to be fragmentary. It is commonly called 'dynamic' in contrast to 'static'; but that is a name which now seems to me to be better avoided. For 'dynamics', in its original sense, is a branch of mechanics; and *the problem to which the economic counterpart (if it is a counterpart) refers, is not mechanical.* As economics pushes on beyond 'static' it becomes less like science, and more like history.[17]

But the resulting 'historical' method is different from that conventionally used by historians, largely because in economics it must include the application of the theoretical apparatus (the 'tool kit', in Joan Robinson's felicitous phrase) of the economist.[18] As Hicks notes: 'When theory is applied it is being used as a means of explanation: we ask not merely what happened, but why it happened. That is causation; exhibiting the story, so far as we can, as a logical process.'[19]

The resulting method of analytical economic history is then a composite of the characteristics of two different types of economic history. According to Hicks,

One of the standard ways of writing economic history (much practised by political historians in their economic chapters) is to survey the state of the economy under consideration, as it was in various historical periods, comparing one state with another. This is comparative statics. It is when the economic historian tries to throw his work into the form of a narrative that it becomes, in our sense, dynamic.[20]

Moreover, the method is essentially forensic. As Hicks notes:

Take the field which is common to economics and history; the study of the past, with the object of finding out, not only what happened, but why it happened. That is causality; if the study is successful, it should enable us to state a cause; we should be able to say that A caused B . . . There is clearly an analogy with the proceedings of a court of law. Someone was murdered; who was the murderer?[21]

The resulting answer will not be infallible, but should still meet the requirement that the jury arrives at a conclusion that is 'beyond reasonable doubt'.

But, of course, there will always be debate about what is reasonable doubt, and in that sense it is unlikely that any important empirical issue in economics will ever be finally settled. This applies to the method of analytical economic history as to any of the other methods of empirical social science.

3. Conclusion

In summary, the method of analytical economic history involves using theoretical constructs to order whatever evidence is available to tell as plausible a 'story' as the facts will bear, using Mill's principles of agreement and difference in a comparative analysis of different countries' historical experience. The theoretical constructs required to order the facts are Joan Robinson's economist's 'box of tools'. They are:

economic theory in its verbal and mathematical forms, statistical theory and practice, familiarity with certain accounting conventions, statistical sources, and a background of stylized historical fact and worldly experience. The use of such tools to fashion sturdy little arguments is the metier of the economist, the economists' 'method'.[22]

What we are seeking are pattern predictions in the sense of Hayek. Finally, the comparative studies method is essentially forensic. We need to persuade the jury of our professional peers. And, because the method recognizes the importance of persuading a sceptical jury, if successfully applied it *is* persuasive!

III. POLITICAL ECONOMY

In this section we provide an outline of another central aspect of our study—political economy.

We have used the term 'political economy' to direct attention to the political, institutional, and historical factors affecting economic growth and income distribution. In particular, it was hoped that analysis could be broadened in two ways:

  (i) by taking account of the organizational factors affecting the workings of the market mechanism and the administrative and fiscal machinery of the government; and

 (ii) by taking account of the political factors affecting economic decision-making.

  (i) The organizational and institutional factors may be considered at two levels. First, there are the factors indicating the incomplete development of the market system for products and for the factors of production (land, labour, and capital funds), paralleled by the incomplete development of the government administrative and fiscal system. Ideally, in order to study the functional efficiency of the market and the non-market economic mechanisms, we should have information about their relative transactions and administrative costs, and their initial patterns and changes over time. This type of information is, of course, very difficult to come by.

These country studies have been able to find only fragmentary or indirect information concerning transactions costs, for instance the inter-regional price differentials for agricultural products (Colombia) or retail–wholesale price margins. Some interesting information regarding the administrative costs of the state agricultural board is given in the Ghana study.[23] Another indirect source of information concerning the organizational developments may be obtained from the national accounts showing the 'structural changes' in production.[24] The share of agriculture in GDP declines as expected in most countries over time, but frequently the most rapidly expanding sector appears to be, not the manufacturing sector, but the ancillary sectors, such as transport and communications, trade and finance. This may be regarded as reflecting the development of the *'invisible'* organizational infrastructure of the economy, the 'textural' development in the fabric of the economy reducing the transactions costs, as distinct from the 'structural change'.

Secondly, at a deeper level below the functional efficiency of the market and the government mechanisms, we have the factors affecting the 'political stability', i.e. the capacity of whatever government is in power to carry out its basic functions of maintaining law and order, administering justice, protecting property rights, and enforcing contracts. The far-reaching effects of a breakdown in political stability on growth, poverty, and income distribution are all too clear to see in the case of a number of countries which have gone through violent revolutions, such as Ghana during the 1972–83 period or Peru during 1968–75, not to speak of the civil war in Nigeria or many coups in the Latin American countries. But, apart from these upheavals, it is also necessary to keep in mind the importance of political stability in situations in which it is endemically eroded by high inflation rates, sporadic insurgency, or communal tensions. These endemic conditions of political instability[25] may be found in many of the countries included in our study.

The general problem, irrespective of the political system, is to create some effective administrative structure to provide the essential public goods required for economic stability. This administrative structure has to be given suitable incentives to perform efficiently. These incentives are generally either based on patronage and rewards or some norms and values (ideology) which ensure that public servants behave in ways which are consistent with the objectives of the system.

(ii) The second aspect of 'political economy' which we had in mind was the study of the political factors behind economic decision-making. The authors of *Five Small Open Economies*, Findlay and Wellisz, have suggested a schematic picture to assist this type of analysis. Conventional economic analysis is concerned with the mutual interactions between the 'government' and the 'economy' of a country, the economy responding to the policies and parameters set by the government, and the government policies in their turn constrained by the flows of revenue from the economy. In an open-economy framework we then introduce the influence of the 'world' on the economy and the government of a country through foreign trade, foreign investment, and the influence of the international organizations, such as the World Bank and the IMF. Findlay and Wellisz then introduce an additional entity into the picture: the 'polity' of a country, which is influenced by the economy and in its turn exerts political pressures on the government (see chapter 1 of *Five Small Open Economies*).

Our country studies cover a wide variety of polities, ranging at one extreme from those approximating to Western-style parliamentary democracies, to oligarchies based on dominant political parties or a single party, to out-and-out military dictatorships at the other extreme (not to speak of a surviving case of colonial government in Hong Kong). A very common pattern is the alternation of civilian administrations, whether democratic or oligarchical, with military administrations, whether right-wing or left-wing. Normally, we should expect the influence of the polity on the government to be reduced at the advent of military take-overs. But military dictatorships or civilian oligarchies, however strong, cannot entirely dispense with political support. Some military or civilian rulers have sought support by populist policies appealing to students and trade unions, while others have consolidated their power through a network of patron–client relationships, or by organizing different interest groups as 'wings' of a one-party state.

The network of patron–client relationships, sometimes with regional political bases, has been vividly described in some country studies, notably for Colombia and Egypt. The organization of the wings of the ruling party is widespread and can be seen, for example, in Nkrumah's CPP; in the legacy of Sukarno's 'Guided Democracy' in Indonesia; or in Mexico's PRI. Strong military governments have been able to suppress political pressures and control domestic inflation, introducing stabilization policies, for instance in Brazil and in Turkey. On the other hand, 'political trade cycles' in the form of increased government expenditures before parliamentary elections can be observed in various countries (e.g. Mexico and Jamaica), although few of them approximate to the 'political exchange model' in which 'political entrepreneurs' compete for votes in terms of well-articulated party programmes in a setting of a stable political framework.

The variety of political systems shown by the countries in our study raises the question of how far the political factors behind economic policy decision-making can be satisfactorily explained by some analytical models of political economy. This task is attempted in Chapter 6. But as much of what is termed the 'new' political economy is unfamiliar to many development economists, it might be useful to provide a brief outline of the various approaches which underlie this type of analysis, and which have been found useful in various ways in our country studies.

1. The 'New' Political Economy

The essence of the new political economy is the application of the economic principle to areas which were previously considered to be the province of political science. This has been done in two distinct ways.

(a) Social Choice

The first strand can be viewed as normative, in so far as it sought to determine whether a democratic polity wedded to majoritarian decision-making could generate a social welfare function satisfying some seemingly innocuous assumptions. This led to Arrow's famous Impossibility Theorem.[26] The vast literature on social choice it has generated is not strictly relevant for our more positive purposes.[27] We need only note that it undercuts any beliefs that a majoritarian democratic state can be the benevolent state assumed in much of the technocratic writings on economic policy.

(b) Public Choice

The second strand is part of positive economics. It is based on a number of different and distinct contributions. Its central feature is the claim that the scope of economics should not be defined in terms of subject-matter (and so apply only to the production and exchange of goods and services) but by its method, namely 'the logic of choice'. Thus, as Mancur Olson put it:

Economic theory is, indeed, relevant whenever actors have determinate wants or objectives and at the same time do not have such an abundance of the means needed to achieve these ends that all of their desires are satisfied. The ends in question may be social status or political power, and the means will be anything that is in fact conducive to the attainment of the ends, whether or not these means can fetch a price on the market. This means that economic (or more precisely micro-economic) theory is in a fundamental sense more nearly a theory of rational behavior than a theory of material goods.[28]

The resulting application of price theory to various aspects of politics has come to be known as public choice. Much of this theory, and in fact much of the new political economy, has been conceived with contemporary Western representative democracies in mind. As this institutional form is rare in most developing countries (despite their adoption of some formal trappings and some of the rhetoric of democracy), the *direct* applicability of much of the existing public-choice theory to developing countries is limited. However, since some interest or pressure group activity can be expected in all polities, the factors identified in the success or failure of particular groups by public-choice theorists are relevant, too, in developing countries. Hence we provide a highly condensed summary in the next few paragraphs of those areas ('rent-seeking', 'political business cycles', and 'pressure-group equilibrium') where the insights developed within public choice can be (and have been) applied to developing countries.

The main interest of the new political economy for our purposes is in the processes by which policies may be determined, the effects of policies, and the dynamics of interaction between policy formulation and its effects.[29]

A fundamental distinction in approaches to the formulation of policy is whether the government is regarded as being a cipher for the interests of private agents (the Factional State—see Chapter 6) or as an entity having and pursuing interests of its own (the Autonomous State—see Chapter 6). On the former, government-as-cipher view, the problem is to model the process by which competing interests of private agents are resolved into policy outcomes, and to delineate endogenously the constraints upon power-gaining agents in their appropriation of resources from other agents. On the latter, government-as-dictator view, the problem is to specify the objective function of the government and to delineate the constraints upon it imposed by the behaviour of private agents. Each of these approaches in turn subdivide.

If atomistic agents bargain with no constraints upon coalition formation, no blocking coalition exists and the 'core' is the competitive outcome.[30] The government-as-cipher literature escapes from this result by constraining coalition formation in various ways. One approach focuses upon the formulation of policy as the outcome of political parties (generally two parties) competing for a plurality of votes from an atomistic electorate.

This is the *first* area in which public-choice theorists have applied microeconomic principles to politics for the understanding of political institutions—such as the existence of political parties, voting behaviour under different 'rules of the game', and practices such as log-rolling (vote-trading) and the outcome of competitive elections.[31] We shall be using one of the results, the so-called 'median voter' theorem that emerged from this literature, in Chapter 6.

The second type of result generated by the 'parties–voters' model of the factional state is of cyclical time preference. This *second* strand in the new political economy literature leads to so-called models of the political business cycle.[32] These deal with the determinants of a democratic government's macroeconomic policies and aim to show how governments time their spending and taxation decisions with an eye to the election date. These models rest on the idea of myopia on the part of the electorate in assessing government performance, combined with the discrete timing of assessments resulting from periodic elections. The consequences of this combination are a permanent bias in policy decisions toward the short run and a cycle of policy changes which anticipates elections. The assumption of myopia on the part of private agents is questionable, but may be valid given the very low incentive to devote effort to assessing government performance resulting from acute free-rider problems. The approach may therefore be of some interest in that subset of developing countries which have genuinely contested elections and where intertemporal decisions appear defective (for example, excessive inflation or foreign debt).

An alternative to the parties–voters model of the factional state is the competing-pressure-groups model. This leads to the *third* area of public choice, which concerns the evolution of pressure groups and the characteristics of a pressure-group equilibrium. As this is an area whose insights have been of importance in analysing developing countries, we discuss it at slightly greater length.

For the political economy of pressure groups, there are three different sets of insights which are relevant. The first was explicitly used by Peter Bauer,[33] a pioneer of the economics of developing countries, but was set out formally most clearly by Mancur Olson.[34] He argued that small concentrated interest groups are more likely to form and to succeed in their aim of influencing the democratic political process to their ends than larger, more diffused groups. For the pay-off from any given benefit acquired through the political process for any individual member of a pressure group diminishes with the size of the group. Also the larger the group, the more difficult it becomes for it to coalesce to subserve its aims, because of the ubiquitousness of the free-rider problem in organizing collective action. An example is the stylized fact that in developing countries with a preponderance of farmers, agriculture is taxed for the benefit of urban consumers, whilst in developed countries they are subsidized at the cost of the much larger number of urban consumers.

The pressure-group model has been recently formalized by Gary Becker in a form which does not depend upon the institution of voting and hence is applicable to the majority of non-democratic polities found in the Third World.[35] Economic agents are assigned to groups with similar interests. The control of the membership of each group varies because of differences in their ability to control free riding. The purpose of the group is to exert pressure on the polity to obtain policies which imply a redistribution of income in their favour. The competition for influence is a zero-sum game, but for the transfers (which are the pay-offs of the pressure-group game) it is a negative-sum game, because of the dead-weight losses to society associated with transfers. Becker shows that successful pressure groups (measured in transfers per member) have the following characteristics:

(i) means of controlling free riding, such as group loyalty or exclusion from benefits;

(ii) a favourable influence function, such that a given expenditure of effort or funds on lobbying generates a large change in policy;

(iii) a transfer mechanism which is efficient in the sense that dead-weight costs, and spill-over benefits to other groups, are a small proportion of the total cost of making the transfers (since it is the total cost which generates resistance);

(iv) small size, so that large transfer benefits per capita imply only small costs per capita from other agents (resistance is more likely to be a function of the total cost per capita, because free-rider problems inhibit losers from colluding);

(v) opponent interest groups (competing for influence) with the opposite characteristics.

The second area in which the pressure-group model has been found most useful is in the recent literature on the endogenous determination of tariffs.[36] As this literature is directly applicable to developing countries, we shall outline its contributions when we make use of them later in Chapter 6.

The third area in which the pressure-group model has been most usefully deployed is in the analysis of so-called 'rent-seeking'.[37] One of the seminal contributions in this area was an analysis of rent-seeking in India and Turkey by Anne Krueger.[38] Rent-seeking is defined as political activity by individuals and groups who devote scarce resources to obtain the 'rents' associated with monopoly rights granted by the government.[39] Apart from the traditional dead-weight loss associated with any artificial restriction of supply, there are in addition the costs incurred by economic agents associated with securing the rents, which in the limit (if there is competitive rent-seeking) will imply costs incurred being exactly equal to the rents sought.[40] Thus, whereas the pressure-group equilibrium model of Becker focuses primarily upon competing groups, the rent-seeking and 'directly unproductive activities' (DUP) literature is concerned with the resource costs of lobbying activities. Both approaches seem useful. Previous history yields an inheritance of interest groups (including élites). The ability of these groups to exert influence can then be assessed in terms of the above characteristics and compared with policy decisions.

The pressure-group and parties–voters models of the factional state need not be mutually exclusive. For example, the need of a governing party to be re-elected may act as a constraint upon powerful pressure groups. Parties provide a cheap way in which a majority can collude to thwart a small but influential group. Alternatively, they may apply to different domains of policy. The parties–voters model, with its emphasis upon time preference, has as a natural focus monetary and debt policies, while the pressure-group model, with its emphasis on transfers, focuses upon relative price interventions and government expenditure.

The fourth area of public-choice theory of interest to us is the study of bureaucracy,[41] which shows how modern bureaucracies will tend not to serve the general weal but their own (by reducing the amount of time worked, expanding the size of the bureau, expanding perks attached to their jobs), and will tend towards a system in which there is attenuation of control by their elected superiors (because of the absence of any obvious accounting system). Some of the insights from this literature will be useful in our subsequent model of a bureaucrat-maximizing predatory state.

The final strand in public choice is what has been termed the theory of constitutions. This seeks to 'design . . . improved governmental methods based on the positive information about how governments actually function'.[42] As most of the positive analyses on which these constitutional prescriptions are based refer mainly to the United States, this theory is not directly relevant for our purpose.[43] However, as one of the purposes of this theory is to devise a constitution which establishes and maintains a set of property rights which promotes economic efficiency, it leads on to various other components of the new political economy which *are* relevant for constructing political economy models applicable to developing countries.

The most relevant of these other components of the new political economy is the new economics of institutions and organizations.[44]

(c) Economics of Institutions and Organizations

This is a burgeoning field which seeks to provide endogenous theories of institutions. It seeks to explain the existence of organizations such as firms and joint-stock companies and the use of various non-market methods of transacting. It encompasses the literature on property rights and transactions costs, as well as the so-called principal-agent problem, which has been particularly useful in the discussion of various institutions in developing countries such as sharecropping and in the analysis of interrelated factor markets.

There are two major strands in this literature. One can be called the transactions costs school, which encompasses the work on property rights (briefly discussed above) and the 'new economic history' (discussed below). The other is based on the theory of imperfect information.[45]

The major insight underlying the transactions costs strand of the literature[46] has been well summed up by Stephen Cheung as follows:

When transaction costs are defined to include all costs not found in a Crusoe economy [where neither property rights, nor transactions, nor any kind of economic organization can be found], and economic organizations are defined equally broadly to include any arrangement requiring the service of a visible hand, a corollary appears: all organization costs are transaction costs, and vice versa. That is why during the past two decades economists have striven to interpret the various forms of organizational arrangements in terms of the varying costs of transactions.[47]

As North, amongst others, has emphasized, the key to economic performance is the cost of transacting. In a small autarkic peasant village the costs of transactions, which include those of information (concerning negotiations and monitoring and enforcement of contracts), are low. But as the extent of the market and hence the division of labour in such communities is limited, productivity is low. With increasing specialization and the division of labour (seen since Adam Smith as an essential part of the growth process), interdependence increases and contracts become more impersonal. This increases the cost of transacting, because of the increasing scope for opportunistic behaviour on the part of economic agents, in the form of cheating, shirking, and moral hazard. In order to garner the productivity gains from the widening of the market and the increased specialization it entails, modern economies have evolved various institutional structures which effectively define and enforce property rights. They constrain the opportunistic behaviour of economic agents, and limit the uncertainties associated with the more extended and impersonal social interactions associated with a widening of the market. Thus, according to North, there has been a trade-off in the historical growth process between the greater productivity gains to be had from specialization and the accompanying economies of scale, and the higher transactions costs involved in the spread of impersonal contracts.[48]

2. Economics of Imperfect Information

The literature on imperfect information and the principal-agent problem examines different institutional and contractual forms as ways of providing incentive-compatible means of conducting economic activity. Problems of incentive compatibility arise when individual actions cannot be perfectly observed or inferred or be monitored in the face of uncertainty, which leads to the well-known problems of moral hazard and adverse selection.[49] It should be noted that the classical debate about the feasibility of national planning between Lange–Lerner and Mises–Hayek[50] was essentially about the incentive-compatibility of central planning.[51] The application of this literature to institutional structures in developing countries is vast.[52] To give some flavour of this literature, in a recent book[53] one of the present authors suggests that the Indian caste system provided an incentive-compatible solution to the Aryan problem of maintaining a cheap rural labour supply without the need for central political enforcement. The castewise division of labour, enforced through social ostracism, lowered the income which any single caste could obtain from leaving the Aryan economy and also inhibited collusive exits by several castes.

3. Implications

One of the major implications of the new institutional economics which is of relevance to our study is that one of the main pillars of Walrasian neo-classical economics—the separability of equity and efficiency—breaks down when transaction costs and imperfect information are important; the terms and conditions of contracts in various transactions, which directly affect the efficiency of resource allocation, now crucially depend on ownership structures and property relations.[54]

Thus, unlike the institution-free traditions of technocratic economics, which assume that any desired distribution of income and endowments can be chosen with only minor deleterious effects on the efficiency and productivity of the economy, the new institutional economics suggests that particular institutional structures, and hence the property rights and distribution of income streams flowing from them, cannot be separated from the growth and productivity outcomes they entail. We cannot, in the manner of technocratic economics, devise a Pareto-efficient productive structure, and then implement the social-welfare-maximizing distribution of national income to yield a Pareto optimum—not even if this were done through lump-sum taxes and subsidies.

This is a subject to which we will return in the concluding chapters of this book.

IV. SYNOPSIS OF THE SYNTHESIS VOLUME

Readers may find it useful to have a brief synopsis of the structure of this synthesis volume. It is in ten chapters.

The first chapter deals with the interrelationships between poverty, equity, and growth. It deals in the first section with various measurement issues, and provides a discussion of the reasons why we have taken a positive rather than the usual normative approach in studying questions of growth, poverty, and equity. It also explains why we have eschewed the usual concern with statistical measures of inequality of incomes in this study. The next three sections of the chapter deal with the question of whether growth can be expected to alleviate poverty. This is answered by distinguishing between three different types of poverty, and two differing ethical perspectives on questions of poverty alleviation. The final section summarizes the evidence from our country studies on whether growth can be expected to alleviate mass structural poverty.

Chapter 2 begins our comparative analysis of the determinants of the divergent growth outcomes in our sample of countries. This is based on an implicit organizing framework, which distinguishes between the different factor endowments (threefold, in terms of the relative endowments of land, labour, and capital), organizational structures (twofold), and polities (fivefold) in our sample of countries. The framework is introduced and applied in successive chapters.

In Chapter 2 we first examine what can be learnt from the aggregate growth outcomes of our sample of countries in terms of conventional statistical cross-country regressions, to see how far they confirm the qualitative conclusions from our country studies. The next three sections take account of the vast explosion in research surrounding the so-called 'new' growth and trade theories, which are supposed to have ushered in a counter-revolution in development thought, and which are at odds in many ways with the conclusions of this book. We show that the counter-revolutionaries have not made a persuasive case for overturning the major conclusion of our country studies that the level of investment and its efficiency are the proximate causes of growth, and that the policy regime (particularly the degree of 'openness' and the absence of policy-induced distortions in the working of the price mechanism) is the primary determinant of the efficiency of investment. After this necessary deconstruction, which the general reader may find scholastic and hence choose to skip, we begin our constructive tasks in the final section of the chapter.

These are to go behind the proximate causes of growth. In searching for the deeper causes for the growth and poverty redressal outcomes in our countries we show how a threefold classification of countries by their initial factor endowments, in terms of a three-factor trade-theoretic framework due to Anne Krueger and extended by Edward Leamer, is a useful starting-point. Unlike the two-factor (labour and capital) case, the three-factor (land, labour, and capital) framework yields a richer menu of alternative efficient development paths, depending upon a country's initial endowments of land, labour, and capital, and how these change with capital accumulation and population growth. Of the multiplicity of possible changing endowment and hence development paths, we concentrate for heuristic purposes on two possible paths of a 'typical' land-abundant and labour-abundant country, and show that whilst the factor price implications (and *mutatis mutandis* the political economy pressures) of the two-factor case (with real wages rising monotonically with rising capital–labour ratios) are applicable to the labour-abundant case, they may not hold in the case of a land-abundant country. We then show how this model provides an illuminating classificatory device in synthesizing our country studies.

Chapter 3 explains the thinking behind the method of pairing countries for the purpose of comparative historical analysis, and brings out the salient outcomes of economic growth, poverty alleviation, and income distribution which may have emerged from the pairwise country comparisons.

Chapter 4 attempts to provide a framework for interpreting the longer-run aspects of these different economic outcomes. Organizational and institutional factors are introduced in the conventional framework of international trade, in the hope of obtaining a better understanding of the relationship between exports and economic growth and the role of different types of economic policy.

Chapter 5 deals with questions of macroeconomic stability and growth.

It identifies a number of countries in which growth collapsed during the more turbulent post-1973 international economic environment. It then examines the economic causes of the growth collapses that have occurred in some of the countries, and finds them to be due to an over-expansion in public expenditures, linked by and large either to 'big push'-type investment expenditures, or to unsustainable social expenditures.

The next two chapters (Chapter 6 and 7) bring in the deeper political and ideological factors which can help in explaining different policies and growth and poverty-alleviation outcomes in our sample of countries. Chapter 6 introduces a fivefold classification of the polity, and shows how two models of the 'autonomous' and 'factional' state can be applied to these subdivisions. It then identifies the importance of the interaction between different factor endowments and polities in generating macroeconomic crises which lead to growth collapses, as well as the role of these crises in the political economy of reform.

Chapter 7 introduces the interplay of ideas and ideology in the formulation of economic policy in our countries. The dominant ideology of economic nationalism is put into historical perspective as reminiscent of the nation-building sought by the absolutist monarchies of Renaissance Europe. The similarities between their mercantilist systems of government control and the *dirigiste* economic policies of developing countries are highlighted. The impetus for reform in both cases is shown to be the paradoxical promotion of economic disorder by attempts to increase the span of government control. The process of economic liberalization in the nineteenth-century Age of Reform and the current wave in the Third (and Second) World are shown to stem from the same desire of nation-builders to reassert control over economies made increasingly ungovernable by past *dirigisme*.

The next two chapters of the book are on policy. The first of these (Chapter 8) analyses the empirical policy lessons for promoting growth arising from our country studies. It emphasizes, in particular, the importance of the classical prescription for providing an economic environment with stable property rights which favours the promotion of productivity, thrift, and above all entrepreneurship. It also takes a sceptical look at various strategies of development that have been proposed.

The next chapter (Chapter 9) does the same for various redistributive programs for poverty alleviation. It also looks explicitly at the political economy of public income transfers, and finds that both in theory and practice the role of direct transfers in alleviating poverty is likely to be limited.

The final chapter (Chapter 10) provides a highly condensed summary (in the first section) of the patterns we have discovered in the determinants of policies and outcomes analysed in the previous chapters. All readers are asked to read this, as it provides a quick summary of our findings. The final section of the chapter outlines and defends a 'classical' framework for economic policy to promote poverty-redressing growth, which we believe is supported by the arguments and evidence presented in this book.

Throughout the book, we have been conscious of the fact that the mode of analysis employed may appear novel and controversial. So we have been at pains to link this work with the evolution of thought on a wide variety of economic and political issues relating to growth and development. The notes at the end of each chapter thus form an essential part of the book. Besides containing simple references relevant to the text, they also include references to the relevant literature as well as extended comments and explanations on various subjects. It is unavoidable that any general interpretation, however hedged by qualifications, of the obviously heterogeneous and, in an important sense, unique evolution of particular economies and polities, must be controversial. Also, given the ambitious nature of our interdisciplinary task, readers may require Coleridge's 'willing suspension of disbelief for the moment'[55] on individual bits of arguments and evidence that we present (neither of which can, by the very nature of our subject-matter, be decisive), and wait to see if the whole adds up to a recognizable and persuasive mosaic of explanation.

Any novelty that readers may discern in our approach, or in our findings, is probably largely due to the current amnesia about the nineteenth-century classical tradition of political economy. If this book is seen as an application, however refurbished by modern artifacts, of that tradition, as well as, in large part, an analytical and empirical validation of many of its prescriptions, our analytical purposes will have been well served. Our readers alone can judge whether this helps them to understand how the world works as well as ways to change it.

NOTES TO INTRODUCTION

1. A good account and justification of this method is in Skopcol (1979: 33–40).
2. He wrote (1890: 283–4):

> There are in fact few departments of political or social science in which the *a priori* method avails less than in economic development. . . . In more general problems relating to economic growth and progress the part played by abstract reasoning is reduced to a minimum, and the economist's dependence upon historical generalizations is at a maximum. . . . For only by the direct comparison of successive stages of society can we reasonable hope to discover the laws, in accordance with which economic states tend to succeed one another or to become changed in character.

3. See North (1990).

4. J. N. Keynes (1890: 334).
5. Skopcol (1979: 36).
6. Mill (1843: 219).
7. Skopcol (1979: 36).
8. J. N. Keynes (1890: 334).
9. Hayek (1952b, 1994).
10. Hayek (1994: 142–3).
11. Ibid. 28.
12. For a discussion of the relationship of this classical comparative historical method with the positivist methodologies associated with Milton Friedman (1953), Samuelson (1952), Hutchinson (1938, 1977, 1978), and Popper (1959), see Lal (1994b), which also contains references to the literature. Useful discussions of methodology are contained in Blaug (1980), I. M. T. Stewart (1979), and Hausman (1992).

One of the salient differences between the classical and positivist viewpoints is the role of statistical tests, which are considered to be the hallmark of economics as a science by the positivists. The rise and fall of 'testing' in economics has been valuably surveyed by de Marchi (1988), in terms of the revolt against the leading contemporary proponent of the classical viewpoint, Lionel Robbins, which was led at the LSE by the group of 'Young Turks' surrounding Richard Lipsey. Robbins and Maynard Keynes took the view that 'in economics the parameters are themselves in the most important cases quickly changing variables' (Robbins, 1938: 351), so that they were both skeptical about quantification. The above quotation was also cited by Popper (1957: 143) when 'nearly' exempting economics as a subject requiring testability.

But as de Marchi notes, amongst Robbins's younger colleagues there was growing dissatisfaction that 'there must be something more to economic science than (as Steuer has nicely put it . . .) "the discovery of irresistible truth through logical manipulation of a few self-evident postulates"' (1988: 144). He surveys their subsequent discovery of Popper and the twists and turns in their final disenchantment with Popperian falsificationism, epitomized by Lipsey's statement in the second edition of his famous textbook: 'I have abandoned the Popperian notion of refutation' (Lipsey, 1966: xx). But the tradition lives on in US graduate schools! However, Solow (1985) has questioned this belief amongst 'the best and brightest in the profession . . . [that] economics is the physics of society' (p. 330). He argues that 'the attempt to construct economics as an axiomatically based hard science is doomed to fail . . . [as] the classical hard science devices for discriminating between competing hypotheses are closed to us. The main alternative device is the statistical analysis of historical time-series. But then another difficulty arises. In order to distinguish between complex and subtle competing hypotheses, many of which 'are capable of fitting the data in a gross sort of way . . . we need long time-series observed under stationary conditions. . . . [But] much of what we observe cannot be treated as the realization of a stationary stochastic process without straining credulity' (p. 328). He then 'recommends' marrying the tools of the economist with 'the ability [of the economic historian] to imagine how things might have been before they became as they now are' (p. 331). This is close to the classical method of analytical economic history we have adopted in this comparative study.

13. Clower (1972: 87) has put the point nicely:

> Contrary to popular opinion and the pretensions of some scientists, the bulk of all knowledge commonly regarded as 'scientific' is expressed in terms of stories that differ little from stories told by writers of serious novels. The resemblance is not accidental. The aim of the novelist is to persuade us that his story might almost be true, while that of the scientist is to persuade us that outwardly chaotic sense data fall into meaningful patterns. We might argue that the two situations differ in that the scientist doesn't invent his facts (at least, he is not supposed to) whereas the novelist is not so constrained. On further reflection, however, the two cases seem to be indistinguishable. Although the scientist does not invent his facts, he does choose them. More precisely, he selects from an infinity of possible facts collections in which (for reasons best known to him) he is able to 'recognize' interesting patterns. In exactly the same manner, the novelist chooses from an infinity of possible characters and situations just that combination about which he thinks a good story can be told. In both cases, therefore, it is strictly true to say that the artist 'invents' his story. We need not be surprised, therefore, to find 'order' in economic or social phenomena any more than we are surprised to find 'order' in natural phenomena—or in any good novel. Scientists would not bother to write about 'nature' or 'society' any more than novelists would bother to write about 'life' unless they were first convinced that what they had to say made a story that was worth telling.

14. Blaug's doubts on such an enterprise may be noted (1980: 127):

> Story-telling makes use of the method of what historians call colligation, the binding together of acts, low-level generalization, high-level theories, and value judgments in a coherent narrative, held together by a glue of an implicit set of beliefs and attitudes that the author shares with his readers. In able hands, it can be extremely persuasive, and yet it is never easy to explain afterwards why it has persuaded.
>
> How does one validate a particular piece of story-telling? One asks, of course, if the facts are correctly stated; if other facts are omitted; if the lower-level generalizations are subject to counter examples; and if we can find competing stories that will fit the facts. In short, we go through a process that is identical to the one that we regularly employ to validate the hypothetic deductive explanations of orthodox economics. However, because story-telling lacks rigor, lacks a definite logical structure, it is all too easy to verify and virtually impossible to falsify. It is or can be persuasive precisely because it never runs the risk of being wrong.

15. This is noted by Elster (1983: 240, n. 23): 'Hicks (1979, Ch. 2) rests his whole analysis of causation on the purported counterfactual implications.'

16. Hicks (1979: xi).

17. Ibid., p. xi (emphasis added).

18. Also Hayek (1949: 71) has emphasized:

If our historical fact is such a complex as a language or a market, a social system or a method of land cultivation, what we call a fact is either a recurrent process or a complex pattern of persistent relationships which is not 'given' to our observation but which we can only laboriously reconstruct— and which we can reconstruct only because the parts (the relations from which we build up the structure) are familiar and intelligible to us. To put it paradoxically, what we call historical facts are really theories which, in a methodological sense, are of precisely the same character as the more abstract or general models which the theoretical sciences of society construct. The situation is not that we first study the 'given' historical facts and then perhaps can generalize about them. We rather use a theory when we select from the knowledge we have about a period certain parts as intelligibly connected and forming part of the same historical fact.

19. Hicks (1979: p. xi).
20. Hicks (1965: 11).
21. Hicks (1979: 5). Also see McCloskey (1985: 289). In this McCloskey also deals with the fear that many have of this forensic approach. Thus he notes:

> The positivist philosopher will claim that using such a rhetorical forensic approach to science would not have standards. But he is wrong. On the contrary, the standards of 'consistent theory' or 'good prediction' presently in use are low, to the point of scientific fraud . . . Consider this. Is it more difficult for a Chicago economist to produce still another regression consistent with the hypotheses of peasant rationality or, on the other hand, to produce a set of arguments, drawn from all the evidence he can find and his audience thinks relevant, that can actually persuade an economist from Yale?

22. Ibid. 24.
23. Useful additional information covering the price differentials for agricultural exports is given in Krueger, Schiff, and Valdes (1988). This paper is the output of the World Bank Comparative Study on the 'Political Economy of Agricultural Pricing Policies'.
24. It should be noted that most national accounts have very incomplete coverage of the informal sector, which is often the most dynamic sector in developing countries. This means that this study and the country studies on which it is based have to be treated with some caution.
25. Political instability is not synonymous with government instability. Thus Italy since the Second World War and France under the Fourth Republic had political and economic stability even though their governments were unstable.
26. Strictly speaking, Arrow's theorem was originally called the *general possibility* theorem, and was concerned about aggregating individual preferences into social preferences, with majority rule being only one of the possible procedures of aggregation.
27. An accessible survey is provided in Sen (1987a).
28. Olson (1967: 9) cited in Barry (1978: 5–6).
29. The following paragraphs incorporate Appendix B by Paul Collier in the original research proposal: Myint and Lal (1985).
30. Of course, it is important to note that the theory of the 'core' merely provides the characteristic properties of the core. It does not as yet specify how a

particular outcome within the core is to be attained through a *process* that is consistent with rational behaviour.

31. The seminal works are Downs (1957) and Black (1958).
32. The major works here are: Nordhaus (1975), Lindbeck (1976), and Frey (1978). See also Alt and Chrystal (1983) for a critique of these models.
33. Bauer (1954).
34. Olson (1965).
35. Becker (1983).
36. See in particular Mayer (1984) which also contains references to the earlier literature.
37. The first outline of rent-seeking was in Tullock (1967).
38. Krueger (1974).
39. As individuals can engage in rent-seeking activity, there is obviously no *necessary* connection between the 'pressure group' and 'rent-seeking' literature.
40. This theory has been rechristened and further developed in a series of articles by Bhagwati on directly unproductive activities. See, for instance, Bhagwati (1982). Also see Buchanan, Tollison, and Tullock (1980) for a collection of major articles on this theme.
41. The important contributions here are by Niskanen (1971), Tullock (1965), and Downs (1967).
42. Tullock (1987).
43. The important works in this area, besides the seminal book by Buchanan and Tullock (1962), are Brennan and Buchanan (1980 and 1985). An excellent concise survey is provided in Buchanan (1987).
44. Others are the economic analysis of the law and regulation: see D. Friedman (1987), Peltzman (1975), the Coase theorem in Coase (1960), and Posner (1981). On regulation, the seminal contributions are by Demsetz (1968), Posner (1975), Stigler (1971), and Peltzman (1976). These articles and various others on specific industrial regulations by members of the Chicago School, which has pioneered this field, are included in Stigler (1988).
45. The major works in this strand are Akerloff (1984), Spence (1974), and various writings by Stiglitz, of which an accessible account can be found in Stiglitz (1986). Also see the articles in the special issue of *World Development* (1989).
46. The major contributions are by Coase (1937), Cheung (1969), Alchian and Demsetz (1972), Arrow (1974), and Williamson (1975). Also the recent literature on so-called 'contestable markets' can be placed in the lineage despite its technocratic apparatus. See Baumol *et al.* (1982).
47. Cheung (1987).
48. The literature on the economics of property rights and the new economic history fits into its place in this context.

    Economics of Property Rights: The seminal contributions are by Coase (1960) and Demsetz (1967), whilst Feeny (1988) is an application of this approach to developing countries. Coase showed that in an economy with an appropriately defined and legally enforced system of property rights and no transactions costs, voluntary exchanges in goods with externalities would lead to a Pareto-efficient allocation. Demsetz showed why property rights develop, what economic factors create a need to change and redefine property rights, and how these changes in the economic environment are translated into a restructuring of property rights.

The major source of changes in property rights and hence in institutions is, usually, major alteration in relative prices, which forces agents to see that they would benefit from a change in contractual arrangements. The new set of property rights then allows further gains from trade by reducing the transactions costs previously associated with a widening of the market.

New Economic History: This is also the basic insight underlying a major work in the new economic history (which relies increasingly on the use of formal economic theory in formulating models and historical hypotheses), of concern to us, namely the work of North (1981) and North and Thomas (1973). Also of relevance are Hicks (1969) and Lal (1988a, 1989a). In this context Rostow (1960) and Gerschenkron (1962) should also be mentioned, though their 'grand' theses of take-off and backwardness are no longer found to be persuasive. For detailed recent critiques see Crafts (1984, 1985).

The North–Thomas approach to the economic history of the West is particularly relevant for our purposes, as it

> relates to the period prior to the onset of modern economic growth and sees *the* pre-requisite as the establishment of an appropriate set of property rights which ensure a reasonable degree of equality between the social and private rates of return on innovation. The key novelty of this approach relates to the attempt to endogenize institutional structure and in particular to relate institutional innovations to population growth, changing land/labour ratios and relative prices. Crucial however in the outcome was the strength of the State and its response to fiscal problems and the degree of political collusion between lords.   (Crafts, 1987)

Finally, in an older comparative tradition are the two works by E. L. Jones (1981, 1988).

49. A lucid survey of the vast literature is provided in Stiglitz (1987).
50. Hayek (1935).
51. See Lal (1983, 1987a).
52. For a wide-ranging survey and integration of much of the literature concerning rural institutions in land-scarce developing countries, see Binswanger and Rosenzwig (1986). On interrelated factor markets see Basu (1984).
53. Lal (1988a).
54. Bardhan (1989b: 1389).
55. Samuel Taylor Coleridge, *Biographia Literaria*, ch. 14.

1

Poverty, Equity, and Growth

OUR subject-matter encompasses the title of the most famous book of classical political economy, Adam Smith's *An Inquiry into the Nature and Causes of the Wealth of Nations*. For Smith,

Wealth is production; the wealth of a nation is what we now call the National Product. Adam Smith is to tell us what the Social Product of a Nation is; what is meant by its being large or small; what is meant by its growing. That is 'nature'. . . . Then he tells us why the Social Product is large or small, and why it grows; that is 'causes'.[1]

We will primarily be concerned in this book with the second of Smith's general subjects, concerning the causes of the wealth of nations. But we still need to say something about the first, the measurement of the social product, which has been a primary concern of the past literature on poverty, equity, and growth in developing countries. This is done in the Section I.

The next three sections deal with the question of whether growth can be expected to alleviate poverty. This is answered in the context of a threefold classification of poverty distinguished by its causes, outlined in Section II; whilst Section III outlines two differing ethical perspectives which continue to be at odds on the question of poverty alleviation. In the final section we summarize the evidence from our country studies and others on whether growth can be expected to alleviate mass structural poverty.

I. WEALTH AND WELFARE

There are four interrelated stances on issues of measurement adopted in our comparative study, which require some justification. First, it is concerned with changes in real income or wealth. Second, it eschews any distributional norms, and hence is not concerned with social welfare as conventionally defined. Third, it uses a more subjective notion of equity than that represented by statistical measures such as the Gini coefficient. The notion of equity tries to articulate particular relative income differences in our countries, whose alleviation has motivated public policy in some of them. Fourth, we adopt a fairly eclectic measure of poverty. Readers who find all this uncontroversial should skip this section.

1. Real Income

Although measurement of the social product or real income appears to be a purely objective enterprise, it is by no means uncontroversial,[2] as is shown by the immense literature on the subject. This is because of the normative significance attached to it, as a measure of the standard of living (including its growth) in different countries at different times.

The classics measured the heterogeneous flow of goods which make up the social product by valuation in terms of 'cost'. Pigou's innovation in his *Economics of Welfare* was to change the method of valuation to marginal utility—the hallmark of the neoclassical marginalist revolution.[3] The subsequent development and wide application of national-income accounting now provides at least one measure based on reasonably consistent definitions of this neoclassical concept of the social product. As Hicks noted,[4] the measure can be interpreted either as a measure of 'real output', if it is looked at as being derived from the relevant rates of transformation of the production possibility set (the 'cost' approach), or as a 'welfare' measure if it is looked at as being derived from the marginal rates of substitution of consumer indifference sets (the 'utility' approach).[5]

Conventional national income accounting proceeds mostly in terms of factor costs, and it is this 'cost' interpretation of the social product, in terms of resources applied, that we will be primarily concerned with in this study. In this sense our approach is more classical than most recent writings on growth and development.

But some justification is required for our eschewing a 'utility' measure of the social product, particularly as it has been the subject of most of the theoretical controversy in measuring economic performance.

2. Equality or Equity?

As is well known, the conventional national income concept of the social product[6] does not take account of any distributional preferences of either a particular observer, or the relevant society; and for egalitarians that has always been one of its major shortcomings.

Though there is much on distribution issues in Adam Smith, classical writers believed he had underemphasized their importance. Ricardo's prime objective was to correct this apparent neglect. He stated in his preface to *The Principles of Political Economy and Taxation* that 'to determine the laws which regulate this distribution [between rent, profit, and wages] is the principal problem of Political Economy'.[7] However, in the modern discussion of distributional issues it is the personal distribution of income, rather than its functional distribution (discussed by Ricardo and the classics), which is considered to be of relevance. But in nineteenth-century Britain it was possible to assume, as it still is in many developing countries, that there was a close correspondence between the functional and personal distribution of income. For there was a purer differentiation of income 'classes' on the basis of the ownership of one or the other of the primary factors of production—capital, labour, and land. In our subsequent discussion of distributional issues, we too will, therefore, be adopting the classical focus on the functional rather than the personal distribution of income, particularly on the course of wages, profits, and rents on alternative development paths (see Chapter 2). As we show in subsequent parts of the book, this also allows us to link the purely economic effects from changing factor proportions and thence relative factor prices to broader questions of political economy concerning the interactions between the polity and the economy (see Chapter 6).

With John Stuart Mill, distribution is well in the forefront of the analysis of the nature of the wealth of nations. Following on from him (and with further contributions from Marx and his followers) the classical and modern national-income accounting measures of the standard of living, which (following Adam Smith) have recently been labelled measures of 'opulence' by Sen,[8] have constantly been under attack. This is primarily because they do not take account of the distribution of the social product between 'classes' or 'individuals'.

Pigou sought to deal with this problem by applying the utilitarian calculus to the declining marginal utility schedules of different individuals. He obtained a measure of Marshall's 'maximum satisfaction' through his (own) definition that 'the economic welfare of a community consists in the balance of satisfactions derived from the use of the national dividend over the dissatisfactions involved in the making of it'.[9] This attempt at incorporating distributional effects in the measurement of the social product was criticized by Robbins and the new welfare economists on the grounds that it involved illegitimate and meaningless interpersonal comparisons of utility.[10] The continuing divide between this classical liberal position and what can be called distributivist egalitarianism, in dealing with poverty, is discussed further in Section III.

It would, however, take us well beyond our remit to survey the resulting voluminous literature on attempts to provide welfare judgements based on a single normative measure of the size and distribution of national income.[11] Their usefulness in judging performance across our sample of countries, with great differences in political systems and ethical beliefs, is open to one fatal objection. Their use must be based upon accepting egalitarianism as either a self-evident or universally accepted moral imperative. Neither position is tenable.[12] Therefore we eschewed the use of these indices in our country studies, as they cover a diverse number of countries, few of which have embraced egalitarianism.

This is not to deny that any measure of welfare must involve ethical judgements—not only about the distributions of income and wealth but also about the existing legal (property-rights) and political system which generates them. What we do deny is that there is some universal egalitarian moral code to which we can appeal in defining social justice.[13] Moreover, in making ethical judgements, it is insufficient merely to examine the existing distribution of income and assets and recommend its alteration purely on the basis of its divergence from some egalitarian norm. It is equally important to judge whether the resulting coercive redistribution of incomes or assets is in consonance with other moral ends, such as liberty and equity.[14]

We would therefore accept Ian Little's double welfare criterion in his famous *Critique of Welfare Economics*,[15] by which the real-income comparisons based on the arts of the national income statistician provide one part of the double criterion for judging changes in economic welfare. The second part is a supplement based on 'distributional' judgements. These ethical judgements, for our purposes, are contingent, since they cannot (for the reasons briefly discussed above) be based on any *universal* moral principles. It is this much more nebulous notion of what we term 'equity', which differs in different time and places and which seems to be relevant in assessing economic outcomes in the perceptions of the citizens of the different countries, which our country studies tried to elcit. But as this notion differs from country to country, so will its statistical proxies (if any). No universal and mechanical index, such as the distributional indices on offer, can therefore be used as part of the set of indicators of comparative aggregate performance.

Our country studies suggest that 'equity', defined in the sense of income equality between the richer and the poorer sections of the population, has not been a major concern of the governments of these countries. What has really concerned them is distributional problems between groups which cut across the conventional concept of income equality.[16] Thus 'economic nationalism', which is pervasive in most of our countries, is concerned with the problem of the distribution of incomes, wealth, or economic assets and economic activities between the nationals of a country and foreigners. Further, in many countries, the nationals are made up of different ethnic, regional, and tribal groupings. In such plural societies, equity or fairness is primarily perceived—by both the State and the majority of its citizens—in terms of the relationships between these different internal groups, for example between the Sinhalese and Tamils in Sri Lanka[17] and between the Malays and the Chinese in Malaysia and Indonesia. The problem of income inequality within the Malay community is regarded as a secondary matter by the Malaysian government, compared with the problem of income inequality between the Malays and the Chinese.

In large and geographically extensive countries such as Indonesia and Nigeria, the problem of equity is aggravated by regional jealousies, for example those between Java and the outer islands, and those between the different regions and tribal groupings of Nigeria which boiled over in a bitter civil war.

Finally, the Latin American countries with their historical legacy of concentrated land-ownership from the days of the original Spanish and Portuguese colonization, reinforced by the land policies during the nineteenth-century, present their own rich regional variants of the equity problem. In addition to unequal land-ownership and an unequal burden of the inflation tax on various sections of the population, among the bitterly felt issues of equity in the Latin American context have been the unequal treatment of the original Indian population where they exist in large numbers, as in Peru and Mexico; the stark contrasts in the living styles between the shanty-town dwellers and the affluent urban middle class; and the wide regional income disparities, such as those existing between the north-east and southern regions of Brazil.

Thus, the general evidence of our country studies suggests that the promotion of income equality as measured by conventional statistical methods has not been a major concern of governments in these countries. What has really concerned them is not income distribution between the rich and the poor as such, but between the nationals and foreigners and among the various ethnic, tribal, and regional groups within the domestic population, which cut across statistical indices of income equality. Some of the burning issues of fairness and equity, for example the question of a national language in a plural society, may be motivated by the question of job distribution among the various communities, but they may be deeply rooted in non-economic factors such as the desire to preserve ethnic identities and traditional cultures and religions.[18]

3. Poverty

Whilst egalitarianism's moral force may not be as potent as many believe, the objective of redressing abject absolute poverty or destitution would seem to be accepted by most moral codes. Certainly all existing religions would accept it, as would those on widely differing points of the secular political spectrum.[19]

As with equity, defining absolute poverty and hence the 'poor' may seem to be an objective exercise. It has been thought that some minimum nutritional standard based on the objective calorific needs of an individual could provide the basis of such an objective measure, and international organizations vied with each other in the 1970s to provide estimates of international poverty linked to malnutrition.[20] But these estimates have been questioned, largely on the grounds that, since they are based on supposed genetically determined norms, they do not take account of individual variability and adaptability. They therefore substantially overestimate the extent of malnutrition and poverty in developing countries.[21]

Hence they are controversial. But to the extent that the effects of malnutrition are likely to affect various social indicators, such as infant mortality and life expectancy at birth, we have preferred to incorporate these health and nutritional aspects in our discussion of social indicators in our sample countries.[22]

Another index of poverty that has been derived is the so-called 'headcount' index of persons below some national or international poverty line. In their well-known study, *Redistribution with Growth*, Chenery *et al.* set the international poverty line at two arbitrary levels of 'annual *per capita* incomes of U.S. $50 and U.S. $75 (in 1971 prices)'. Subsequently Ahluwalia *et al.* set an international poverty line at 'the income per head accruing to the forty-fifth percentile of the Indian population', valued in terms of 1970 Kravis dollars.[23]

As these authors themselves realized,[24] however, there are two problems with their resulting estimates of 'international poverty'—one theoretical, which, given the paucity of data, cannot be overcome; the other interpretative, which makes any international poverty line meaningless. The theoretical problem is that the headcount measure of poverty ignores the degree of poverty below the poverty line.[25] But the data requirements for estimating more appropriate poverty indices, like the Sen index, are rarely met in developing countries. So, *faute de mieux*, a headcount index of those below some minimum level of income/consumption was used, wherever possible, in our country studies.

The second problem with previous World Bank estimates of poverty concerns the use of an international poverty line. As Ahluwahlia *et al.* rightly noted:

Not only is the notion of a biologically determined absolute poverty level imprecise, it is in any case wrong to think that poverty should be defined solely in terms of biological requirements. . . . Once we recognize that acceptability by contemporary social standards is a key requirement, it follows that poverty lines used in national policy debates will vary across countries, reflecting differences in levels of economic, social and political development. By the same token, they will also change over time.[26]

That poverty must be defined with reference to the living standards in particular countries, at a particular time, is again accepted by most creeds, from classical liberal (in the nineteenth-century English sense) to socialist.[27] But this necessary relativity of the poverty lines *across* countries has often been confused with the assertion that poverty within a country must also always be a relative notion, in the sense that, say, the lowest 20 per cent of individuals in the distribution of income are considered to be poor. In the latter sense, except with complete equality in the distribution of income, the poor *by definition* must always be with us, as there will always be the two lowest deciles in the income distribution. It is from this relativist view of poverty within a country, that it is easy to slip into identifying poverty redressal with egalitarianism. But, as for instance Sen and many others have pointed out, this is illegitimate.[28] Given some nationally determined standard for defining poverty—which is unlikely to change within a decade or two—the question whether absolute poverty (defined with reference to this nationally invariant real-income standard) has altered is separable from whether inequality of income has changed. Clearly, alleviating poverty is not synonymous with reducing the inequality of income.[29]

We therefore asked our country authors to judge the changes in the extent of poverty in their countries by considering the numbers below a fixed national poverty line corresponding to the real income per capita of the bottom 20 per cent in the base year (1950). Given the paucity of data, even this assessment was not possible for many of our countries, and in some the authors chose a particular country-specific poverty line which they deemed to be relevant (see Chapter 3).

But for our comparative purposes, once the relevance of different national poverty lines is accepted in forming judgements on the association of poverty redressal with economic growth, it is merely the direction of the change in poverty redressal which is relevant. For in the absence of any international standard of poverty, it is not possible to relate changes in the *extent* of poverty redressal with growth rates across different countries. It is only possible to determine whether poverty increased or decreased, rather than to measure the extent of the change.[30] In many cases, lacking data on the changes in income of the poorest groups, the authors of our country studies have had to rely on other supplementary information, largely on various social indicators, to judge the direction of the change in poverty in their respective countries.

These supplementary indices, on health, nutrition, education, housing, sanitation, clean water, and so on, also form the centre-piece of the so-called 'basic needs' approach,[31] as well as what has been labelled the Physical Quality of Life Index (PQLI), which is a simple average of three indices derived from life expectancy, infant mortality, and literacy rates.[32] The 'basic needs' advocates are right, in our view, in setting up an objective of poverty redressal in contrast with the distributivist objective underlying, for instance, *Redistribution with Growth*. However, it is difficult to provide a rationale for the concern with the commodities and services included in the basic-needs bundles as ends in themselves. They are better looked at as being '*instrumentally* (rather than intrinsically) important'.[33] One way of looking at them is in utilitarian terms—as in Pigou's phrase 'a national minimum standard of real income', which he

conceived, not as a subjective minimum of satisfaction, but as an objective minimum of conditions. . . . Thus the minimum includes some defined quantity and quality of house accommodation, of medical care, of education, of food, of leisure, of the apparatus of sanitary convenience and safety where work is carried on, and so on. Furthermore, the minimum is absolute. If a citizen can afford to attain it in all departments, the State cares nothing that he would prefer to fail in one. It will not allow him, for example, to save money for a carouse at the cost of living in a room unfit for human habitation.[34]

This paternalism was justified by Pigou on the utilitarian grounds that even if these public provisions to the poor led to the 'national dividend' (national income in modern terms) being lower, these transfers were profitable in 'maximizing satisfaction'. Furthermore, Pigou argued that in judging the correct level of the minimum standard,

the correct formal answer . . . is that economic welfare is best formulated by a minimum standard raised to such a level that the direct good resulting from the transference of the marginal pound transferred to the poor just balances the indirect evil brought about by the consequent reduction of the dividend.[35]

There is a direct link between this Pigovian minimum standard and the so-called critical consumption level estimated in some methods of project analysis,[36] which provides the level of income at which income/consumption accruals are considered by the government to be socially as valuable as public income. Given some notion of the egalitarian bias, if any, of a particular government, this critical consumption level has been estimated for a number of countries within a second-best 'optimal' growth framework which takes account of the effects on both growth and poverty redressal, amongst contemporaries and as between generations (intra- and inter-temporally).[37]

However, whilst such an inter-temporally consistent poverty line would take account of the inter-temporal trade-offs that have not been faced in the basic-needs literature,[38] it will not help us to advance on our comparative measurement problems beyond the crude poverty lines we have adopted for our country studies.

Nor does this Pigovian justification of the basic-needs-type minimum-standards approach tell us how to define the quantities of the various basic-needs goods corresponding to this minimum *consumption* standard. Paternalism, as suggested by Pigou, is the only recourse. As many proponents of the welfare state have argued, the specific quantities of the various goods must be bureaucratically provided to the poor. (We discuss the alternative policies of direct versus indirect poverty-redressal more fully in Chapter 9.) This paternalism is best summed up in Douglas Jay's immortal words that

Housewives on the whole cannot be trusted to buy all the right things, where nutrition and health are concerned. This is really no more than an extension of the principle according to which the housewife herself would not trust a child of four to select the week's purchases. For in the case of nutrition and health, just as in the case of education, the gentleman in Whitehall really does know better what is good for people than the people themselves.[39]

Neither the paternalism involved in the Pigovian (and modern welfare-state) approach to basic needs, nor the utilitarian ethic on which it is based, is acceptable. For instance, it is difficult to believe that all the world's citizens adhere to utilitarianism, when even in the Western countries of its provenance so many have discounted this ethic.[40] Hence the paternalistic, utilitarian justification for being concerned with the basic-needs goods *per se* will not be acceptable.

Recently, Sen has sought to provide a conceptual basis for these basic-needs indicators, in terms of more nebulous notions such as 'functionings' and 'capabilities'.[41] It is beyond our remit to go into their validity. Suffice it to note that they remain controversial,[42] and we would not wish to use them in justifying the supplemental use of 'basic needs' or 'social indicators' in judging poverty redressal in our sample of countries.

A simpler and more straightforward justification would be provided by answering in the affirmative to two rhetorical questions that Sen asks about these indicators:

Are they best seen in terms of *commodities* that people may be reasonably expected to possess (typically the chosen form in the basic needs literature)? This would relate nicely to some extended sense of opulence and to a justification in terms of the value of popular opulence. But is that justification easy to accept?[43]

We will therefore be using social indicators relating to infant mortality, life expectancy, and literacy as supplementary indices to judge the extent of poverty redressal (Chapter 9). Though the attempts at providing a rationale for some aggregate of these social indicators have not been successful, we will also for illustrative purposes present the one aggregate—the physical quality of life index (PQLI)—which has found some favour, at least amongst laymen.[44]

4. Conclusions

In conclusion, therefore, in this study we will be unashamedly classical and judge economic performance by its promotion of opulence, but in the extended sense which takes account of the opulence of the 'poor'. Ian Little in his *A Critique of Welfare Economics* noted that

Dr. Myint in his book *Theories of Welfare Economics* traces the development of what he calls welfare economics from Adam Smith to the present day. We would prefer to say that welfare economics began with Pigou. Before that we had 'happiness' economics; and before that 'wealth' economics. After all, Smith wrote of the wealth, not the welfare, of nations. I do not think this is a trifling distinction. The suggestive force, and the implications of the three phrases, 'This would increase the welfare of society', 'This would increase the happiness of society', and 'This would increase the wealth of the nation' are not the same.[45]

For the reasons briefly outlined, lacking any universal ethical standards, comparative statements about the welfare of different countries will remain problematic, but the classical measures of the wealth of nations will still form an important part of this evaluation. Sir John Hicks entitled the first volume of his collected essays dealing with these basic measurement questions *Wealth and Welfare*. What we are saying is that positive classical measures of wealth retain a primacy, general acceptance, and applicability across a diverse set of countries that normative neoclassical measures of welfare can never attain. We will therefore understandably be concerned in this book with wealth rather than with welfare.[46]

II. THREE TYPES OF POVERTY

We are, however, for the reasons given above, concerned with the alleviation of poverty, and in particular with the extent to which this accompanies the growth process. In assessing the evidence from our country studies it is useful to distinguish between three types of poverty: structural mass poverty, destitution, and conjunctural poverty.

1. Structural Mass Poverty

For most of our history poverty has been the natural state of humanity. Until the end of the nineteenth century when the power of the unbound Prometheus was at last becoming manifest with the rolling Industrial Revolution, few economists held out the prospect of alleviating mass poverty. Classical economics with its law of diminishing returns and the Malthusian principle of population predicted a long-run stationary state where the mass of people languished at a subsistence standard of living. This, as Wrigley has shown in a brilliant book, was due to their belief that they were still concerned with the age-old problem of the development of an 'organic' economy, which Wrigley defines as 'an economy bounded by the productivity of land'.[47] In such an economy—and historically this has been the dominant type over the globe—there is a universal dependence on organic raw materials for food, clothing, housing, and fuel. Their supply is in the long run inevitably constrained by the fixed factor, land. This was also true of traditional industry and transport. Most metal-working industries were dependent upon charcoal (a vegetable substance) for smelting and working crude ores; whilst

since many branches of industry, most mining ventures and almost all forms of transport, as well as agriculture, made extensive use of animal muscle as a source of mechanical energy, the productivity of land was crucial to the supply of power as well as heat. Woodland and pasture were as necessary to English industry as her arable land was to the family table. A recognition of the significance of the productivity of land to the whole range of productive activities of society is both implicit and explicit in the writings of the classical economists, and the leverage which the application of the principle of declining marginal returns thus exacted was very powerful.[48]

The system of capitalism and free trade outlined and defended by Adam Smith could increase the productivity of the organic economy somewhat over what it was under mercantilism. It would also help the poor by lowering the cost of their consumption bundle, whilst boosting their wages as producers, but if this increase in popular opulence led to excessive breeding, the land constraint would inexorably lead back to subsistence wages. Technical progress could hold the stationary state at bay, but the land constraint would ultimately prove binding.

The Industrial Revolution led to the replacement of this organic economy by a mineral-based energy economy. But this fundamental change was only becoming apparent towards the middle of the nineteenth century in England, and it was not until Marx was writing that it had become manifest. This new economic regime 'escaped from the problem of the fixed supply of land and of its organic products by using mineral raw materials'—in particular coal. It began to provide most of the heat energy of industry, and, with the development of the steam-engine, virtually unlimited supplies of mechanical energy. 'The prospects for growth both in aggregate output and in output per head were entirely transformed from those which had always previously obtained.'[49]

Thus the Industrial Revolution in England was based on two forms of 'capitalism'. One was institutional, namely that defended by Adam Smith—because of its productivity-enhancing effects, even in an organic economy; and the other physical: the capital stock of stored energy represented by the fossil fuels, which allowed mankind to create a

world that no longer follows the rhythm of the sun and the seasons; a world in which the fortunes of man depend largely upon how he himself regulates the economy and not upon the vagaries of weather and harvest; a world in which poverty has become an optional state rather than a reflection of the necessary limitations of human productive powers.[50]

Not only the subsequent experience of the First World, but that of many countries in the Third World has borne this out. It is possible, as many countries in south-east Asia, for instance, have shown, to eradicate mass poverty within a generation, because neither of the twin foundations of the gloomy classical prognostications, diminishing returns (see Scott, 1989) and the Malthusian principle (see Birdsall, 1989 on the demographic transition), are secure. In Section IV we examine if these inferences are also valid for our sample of countries. Historically, there have been concerns about two other sources of poverty: that of destitution, and that of those who, due to conjunctural problems, find themselves temporarily in poverty.

Both these sources of poverty have existed over millennia, though the sources of conjunctural problems have changed.

2. Destitution

It is worth noting that, in the past, when mass structural poverty was the norm for mankind, the poblem of poverty was seen as being confined essentially to destitution (see Himmelfarb, 1983, and Iliffe, 1987). As until fairly recently most organic economies have also been labour-scarce and land-abundant economies, the primary cause for people falling into destitution was a lack of labour power (either their own, because for instance of physical disabilities, or that of family members, if they have no families) to work the land. This remains a major source of destitution in land-abundant parts of Africa.[51] In this world the 'poor' are the destitute, who are recognized as 'deserving', whilst, as the Elizabethan poor law noted, any able-bodied poor were to be classified as vagrants.[52]

With population expansion and the emergence of land-scarce economies in Europe and in many parts of Asia, there arose 'the poverty of the able-bodied who lacked land, work, or wages adequate to support the dependents who were partly responsible for their poverty'.[53] Their poverty merges with the mass structural poverty we had discussed before, and growth will, as it has, lead to its amelioration.

3. Conjunctural Poverty

This leaves conjunctural poverty. For most of history, as economies have been organic agrarian economies, this form of poverty was linked to climatic crises or political turmoil. Its most dramatic manifestation was in the form of a famine. Since the Indian Famine Code was devised by the British Raj in the late nineteenth century, it has been known that, to deal with what Sen (1982) labels 'entitlement failures' which precipitate a famine, it is necessary for the government to provide income directly (through public works or food-for-work schemes, for instance) to those who have suffered this temporary loss of income-generating employment. As the Indian example shows (except for one wartime exception), this administrative solution can eliminate famines. But this solution does require political stability and a relatively competent administration. Without these it is not feasible.[54]

Hence, nowadays, famines are caused by politics. This is supported by examining the major post-war famines: the one in China followed the political Great Leap Forward, and has been described as the worst in human history, costing 63 million lives (actual and prospective—through lost or postponed births; see Lin, 1990); the Sudanese and Eritrean famines were due to civil wars in which famine was a political weapon used by the state against secessionists; and the Somali famine has resulted from the collapse of that country into a Hobbesian state of nature.

Finally, the Industrial Revolution has introduced its own source of conjunctural poverty in the form of the trade cycle and the unemployment that ensues in its downturns.

4. Alleviating Destitution and Conjunctural Poverty

Historically, the destitute poor survived through four means. The first was through institutions like the Church, which took one of its primary tasks to be the care of the poor. Individual charity provided a second means, whilst a third was organization by the poor themselves, either by underworld groupings or by self-help organizations like rotating credit associations. 'Finally, historians have stressed that the poor relied less on institutions or organizations than on their own efforts, devious, ugly, cruel, and dishonest as these might be.'[55]

Various implicit forms of insurance, embodied in interlinked contracts in factor markets, have historically been the major way of dealing with conjunctural poverty in traditional village economies (see Platteau (1991) for a survey and references to this literature). They are still of importance in the highly risky environment faced by rural agents in many parts of south Asia (see Bardhan (1980) for a survey).

III. TWO ETHICAL TRADITIONS AND POVERTY ALLEVIATION

All these traditional ways of dealing with destitution and conjunctural poverty were gradually superseded in most Western societies by the evolution of the welfare state. As the socialist impulse, strengthened by the appeal of Marxism in the late nineteenth century, provided an important intellectual impetus to these developments (see Himmelfarb), not surprisingly the socialist ethic of egalitarianism got muddled with the age-long impulse to alleviate absolute poverty. Its apotheosis was the socialist economies that were set up in the Soviet Union, China, and Eastern Europe, and which sought to subserve this end by socializing the *means* of production. The Western socialists who advocated welfare states, by contrast, sought to socialize the *results* of production. This has led to essential ethical and thence policy differences, which underlie the continuing tension between Western socialists seeking to equalize people, albeit within the context of a market economy, and classical liberals who see the two ends of poverty alleviation and egalitarianism as distinct.

1. Classical Liberalism

For the classical liberal it is a contingent fact that there is no universal consensus on what a just or fair income distribution should be, despite the gallons of ink spilt by moral philosophers on trying to justify their particular prejudices as the dictates of reason. Egalitarianism is therefore to be rejected as the norm for deriving principles of public policy.[56]

This does not mean that classical liberals are immoral! The greatest of them all, Adam Smith, after all wrote *The Theory of Moral Sentiments*. Both of the great moral philosophers of the Scottish Enlightenment—Smith and Hume—recognized benevolence as the primary virtue, but they also noted its scarcity. However, as Smith's other great work *The Wealth of Nations* showed, fortunately, a market economy which promotes opulence does not depend on this virtue for its functioning. It only requires a vast number of people to deal and live together, even if they have no personal relationships, as long as they do not violate the 'laws of justice'. The resulting commercial society promotes some virtues (what Shirley Letwin (1992) has labelled the 'vigorous virtues')—hard work, prudence, thrift, and self-reliance—which, as they benefit the agent rather than others, are inferior to altruism. But, by promoting general prosperity, these lower-level virtues do unintentionally help others. Hence the resulting society is neither immoral or amoral.

Thus a good government is one which promotes opulence through a policy of promoting natural liberty by establishing laws of justice which guarantee free exchange and peaceful competition, the improvement of morality being left to non-governmental institutions.[57] But since Smith, down to Friedman and Hayek, classical liberals have also recognized that society or the state should seek to alleviate absolute poverty.[58]

On the classical liberal view, there could be an externality, whereby 'the recipient's consumption of particular goods or services (food, education, medical care, housing) or his attainment of certain states (being better nourished, better educated, healthier, better housed) that are closely correlated with an adequate consumption of such goods'[59] enters the *donor's* utility function. As it is the specific consumption of these commodities, not the recipient's utility, which enters the donor's utility function, there is no utility 'handle' which can be used, as on the alternative distributivist view, to allow distributional considerations to be smuggled into the analysis of poverty alleviation programmes.

Thus the indigent and the disabled are to be helped through targeted benefits. For various merit goods—health, education, and possibly housing—these involve in-kind transfers. This is very much the type of social-policy package that was implemented in Pinochet's Chile, and which succeeded not only in protecting the poor during Chile's arduous transformation to a liberal market economy, but also led to dramatic long-term improvements in its various social indicators.[60]

2. Distributivist Egalitarianism

The alternative, technocratic approach to poverty alleviation is by contrast necessarily infected with egalitarianism because of its lineage. At its most elaborate it is based on some Bergson–Samuelson-type social welfare function. Given the ubiquitous assumption of diminishing marginal utility underlying the approach, any normative utility weighting of the incomes of different persons or households leads naturally to some form of egalitarianism. But this smuggling in of an ethical norm which is by no means universally accepted leads to a form of 'mathematical politics'.[61] Poverty alleviation becomes just one component of the general problem of maximizing social welfare, where, given the distributional weighting schema, all the relevant trade-offs between efficiency and equity, including inter-temporal ones, can be derived in terms of the appropriate distribution-cum-efficiency shadow prices (see Little and Mirrlees, 1974, and Lal, 1980*b*). If the concern is solely with those falling below some normative 'poverty line', this merely implies a different set of weights, with the weight of unity, say, to changes in consumption (income) above the line, and increasing weights to those who fall progressively below the line (see Ravallion (1992) for a full explication of this approach in the design and evaluation of poverty alleviation programmes in the Third World).

But this is a thin edge of a very big wedge. Besides leading to recommendations for all sorts of redistributive schemes, it also leads to a vast increase in *dirigisme*. To alleviate poverty, an end embraced by classical liberals, on this route they are being led to endorse the creation of a vast Transfer State, which in the long run could be inimical to the growth and poverty-redressing effectiveness of a market economy (see Chapter 9).

IV. GROWTH, INEQUALITY, AND POVERTY ALLEVIATION

A usual riposte to the classical liberal position of separating questions of alleviating absolute poverty from egalitarianism is that, in theory, a market-based growth process could lead to such a worsening of the income distribution that instead of the poor seeing a rise in their incomes as part of the growth process, they could be impoverished. This view was strengthened by the so-called Kuznets hypothesis, which stated that inequality was likely to worsen in the early stages of development, before it declined, with per capita incomes rising towards current developed-country levels.

All the empirical evidence, to date, is against the Kuznets hypothesis, and its corollary that growth might not alleviate absolute mass poverty. Table 1.1 summarizes the changes in the incidence of poverty and income inequality as judged by the country authors for our sample of countries. It also shows the GDP growth rates per capita over the relevant periods. From

Table 1.1. Growth, poverty, and inequality

Country		GDP per capita growth rate (%)	Poverty	Income inequality
(I)		Positive		
Labour-abundant				
Hong Kong		6.6	↓	↑↓
Singapore		6.5	↓	↑↓
Malta		5.2	↓	↓
Land-abundant				
Malaysia		4.3	↓	↑↓
Thailand		4.0	↓	↓
Brazil		3.9	↓	↑
Turkey		3.1	↓	↓
Mexico		2.6	↓	↑
Costa Rica		1.8	↓	↓
Columbia		2.1	↓	↓
Intermediate				
Egypt		3.0	↓	n.c.
Indonesia		3.1	↓	↓
Sri Lanka		2.6	↓ 53–70	↓ 53–69
			↑ 70–77	↑ 70–77
			↑ 77–	↓ 77–
Malawi		1.5	↑ 64–84	↑
Mauritius		0.7	n.a.	n.a.
(II)		Mixed		
Land-abundant				
Uruguay	↓ 55–67	−1	n.a.	↑
	↑ 67–85	1.2	n.c.	↑
	(67–84)			
Nigeria	↑ 60–73	3.4	↓ n.c.	↑
	↑ 73–9	0.6	n.c.	↑
	↓ 79–84	−5.9	↑	↑
Intermediate				
Peru	↑ 50–81	2.1	n.c.	↑
	↓ 81–5	−3.9	n.c.	n.a.
Jamaica	↑ 50–72	4.7	↓	↑
	↓ 72–86	−2.9	↑	↑
Madagascar	↑ 50–69	1.0	↑	↑
	↓ 69–84	−2.2	↑	↑
(III)		Falling		
Ghana	60–81	−1.0	↑	↑

↓ less poverty/declining inequality; ↑ more poverty/growing inequality; ↑↓ no clear overall trend.

n.c.: no change.

Source: I, GDP per capita growth rates are taken from Table 2.1, col. 3. II, III, GDP per capita growth rates are calculated from country study data, and in the case of Nigeria and Ghana from World Bank data files. Poverty and income inequality trends are taken from the country studies.

this it is evident that there is a clear positive correlation between income growth per capita and poverty redressal, but *not* on reductions in income inequality (where the pattern is extremely mixed). For the reasons given above, we are concerned about the movements in the poverty indices but not in those for inequality.

Further evidence of the positive association between poverty redressal and growth is provided in Psacharopoulos (1991) by Fields, who has put together the available data on poverty redressal and inequality for all the developing countries for which it is available, subject to three minimal criteria of consistency. These are that the data are national, that they are based on an actual household survey or census, and that the income concept used and the recipient unit identified should be constant over time. His results are summarized in Tables 1.2 (for poverty) and 1.3 (for inequality). On the relationship between poverty and growth he concludes, first, that it is true in most but not all cases that poverty tends to decrease with growth, and that poverty tends to decrease more often the more rapid is economic growth. Second, he finds that growth has *not* had a demonstrably

Table 1.2. Change in poverty and rates of growth, spell analysis

(A) Change in poverty and growth rate of GNP

Spell	Growth rate of GNP	Change in poverty
Jamaica, 1973–1979	−4.3%	↑
Bangladesh, 1966/67–1973/74	−2.1	↑↓
Pakistan, 1969/70–1979	1.7	↓
Sri Lanka, 1963–1973	2.2	↓
Bangladesh, 1976/77–1981/82	2.4	↑↓
Sri Lanka, 1978/79–1981/82	2.8	↑↓
Sri Lanka, 1973–1978/79	3.3	↓
Korea, 1976–1980	3.5	↓
Thailand, 1968/69–1975/76	4.0	↓
Thailand, 1975/76–1981	4.1	↓
Mexico, 1963–1968	4.3	↓
Indonesia, 1978–1980	4.5	↑
Bangladesh, 1973/74–1976/77	4.8	↑
Indonesia, 1970–1976	4.8	↓
Jamaica, 1968–1973	4.9	↑
Indonesia, 1976–1978	4.9	↓
Malaysia, 1976–1979	4.9	↓
Malaysia, 1970–1976	5.0	↓
Thailand, 1962/63–1968/69	5.2	↓
Hong Kong, 1966–1971	5.4	↓
Singapore, 1975–1980	5.8	↓
Hong Kong, 1971–1976	7.3	↓
Korea, 1965–1970	7.6	↓
Korea, 1970–1976	7.8	↓
Singapore, 1966–1975	8.8	↓

Table 1.2. *Continued*

(B) Change in poverty and growth rate of ICP

Spell	Growth Rate of ICP	Change in poverty
Jamaica, 1973–9	−3.5%	↑
Sri Lanka, 1963–73	−2.1	↓
Bangladesh, 1966/67–1973/4	−0.7	↑↓
Pakistan, 1969/70–1979	1.5	↓
Bangladesh, 1973/74–1976/7	2.6	↑
Jamaica, 1968–73	3.0	↑
Sri Lanka, 1973–1978/9	3.3	↓
Thailand, 1968/69–1975/6	3.5	↓
Mexico, 1963–8	4.5.	↓
Malaysia, 1970–6	4.6	↓
Thailand, 1962/63–1968/9	5.3	↓
Hong Kong, 1966–71	5.9	↓
Indonesia, 1970–6	6.0	↓
Singapore, 1975–80	6.3	↓
Indonesia, 1976–8	6.5	↓
Korea, 1970–6	6.6	↓
Hong Kong, 1971–6	6.7	↓
Indonesia, 1978–80	7.2	↓
Korea, 1965–70	8.6	↓
Singapore, 1966–75	8.8	↓
Malaysia, 1976–9	9.7	↓

↓ poverty decreased.
↑ poverty increased.
↑↓ poverty increased using one poverty line and decreased using another.

Sources: Fields (1991: table 8).
For change in poverty, ibid., table 2.
Growth rates of GNP calculated by the author from data in *IMF Financial Statistics Supplement no. 8*, pp. 18–21. Growth rates of ICP calculated by the author from data in Summers and Heston (1984).

greater effect in reducing poverty in Asia than in Latin America, but rather the available evidence supports the opposite conclusion.

On inequality, he finds that, first, there is no systematic tendency for inequality to increase with economic growth. For in his sample inequality increased in as many growth episodes as it decreased. However, growth tends to increase inequality more often in Latin America than in Asia. Second, he finds no relationship between inequality in the initial distribution of income and subsequent growth rates. Nor does more rapid growth increase inequality—rather the converse seems to hold. Third, he concluded that there is no tendency for inequality to increase more in the early than in the later stages of development (this refutes the Kuznets hypothesis).

Table 1.3. Change in Gini coefficient and rates of growth, spell analysis

(A) Low-income countries

Growth spells in which Gini coefficient increased ($n = 10$):	Growth spells in which Gini coefficient decreased ($n = 11$):
Bangladesh, 1973/4–1976/7	Bangladesh, 1976/7–1981/2
Indonesia, 1970–6	Egypt, 1964/65–1974/5
Indonesia, 1976–8	Indonesia, 1967–70
Pakistan, 1971/2–1979	Indonesia, 1978–80
Pakistan, 1979–84	Pakistan, 1963/4–1966/7
Sri Lanka, 1973–1978/9	Pakistan, 1966/7–1968/9
Sri Lanka, 1978/9–1981/2	Pakistan, 1968/9–1969/70
Thailand, 1962/3–1968/9	Pakistan, 1969/70–1970/1
Thailand, 1968/9–1975/6	Philippines, 1965–71
Thailand, 1975/6–1981	Philippines, 1971–75
	Sri Lanka, 1963–73

(B) High-income countries

Growth spells in which Gini coefficient increased ($n = 9$):	Costa Rica, 1977–1979
Bahamas, 1977–1979	Hong Kong, 1966–1971
Brazil, 1970–1972	Korea, 1976–1982
Costa Rica, 1971–1977	Malaysia, 1976–1979
Hong Kong, 1976–1981	Mexico, 1969–1977
Jamaica, 1968–1973	Singapore, 1972/73–1977/78
Korea, 1970–1976	Trinidad and Tobago, 1971/72–1975/76
Malaysia, 1970–1976	Turkey, 1968–1973
Mexico, 1958–1963	
Mexico, 1963–1969	Growth spells in which Gini coefficient was unchanged ($n = 3$):
Growth spells in which Gini coefficient decreased ($n = 10$):	Brazil, 1978–80
Bahamas, 1975/1977	Chile, 1968–1971
Brazil, 1976–1978	Hong Kong, 1971–1976

Note: The dividing line between high income and low income is US $728.
Source: Fields (1991), table 9.

From this it is evident that there is by and large a clear positive corre-lation of income growth per capita with poverty redressal, but not with reduction in income inequality (where the pattern is extremely mixed). Finally, Squire (1993) reports on a 21-country study for which comparable data on income distribution were available for two points of time. Using a headcount index based on a common poverty line in 1985 Kravis dollars of $370 per person a year, an ordinary least-squarts regression of the change in the headcount index (*CHHI*), the growth in mean expenditure (*G*), and the initial headcount index (*HI*), yielded:

$$CHHI = -0.24G - 0.01HI \qquad \bar{R}^2 = 0.70$$
$$(t = -4.06) \quad (t = -2.90) \qquad N = 21$$

A one per cent increase in the growth rate of mean income increases the annual rate of decline in the headcount index by 0.24 percentage points. Also, the negative sign on *HI* refutes the Kuznets hypothesis. 'At least for this sample it appears that changes in inequality worked on average in favor of the poor . . . and that this effect was stronger in situations where poverty was greater at the start of the period of observation.'[62]

The distributivist objections (based on the Kuznets curve) to the classical liberal presumption that growth would alleviate poverty thus seem to have little empirical support. On the existing evidence, mass poverty can be alleviated by rapid, efficient (labour-intensive) growth, and we need not worry about the distributional consequences. That leaves problems of destitution and conjunctural poverty, to which we return in Chapter 9. But before that we need to see how growth, which indubitably relieves mass poverty, can be fostered.

NOTES

1. Hicks (1981).
2. See Sen (1979).
3. See Hicks (1981).
4. Hicks (1940, 1958).
5. As Sen (1979: 19) notes:

> For neither approach is it necessary to assume that the marginal conditions of optimality prevail in the form of the substitution rates equalling the corresponding transformation rates; nor is it necessary to require the convexity of *both* substitution and transformation surfaces. . . . [Thus] the Samuelson-Graaf approach to comparing social welfare based on convex indifferent substitution surfaces . . . carried the excess baggage of assuming that 'diminishing returns prevail and prices equal marginal cost'.

> The references are to Samuelson (1950) and Graaf (1957: 162).

> It should also be noted that more recently, as part of the development of so-called Little–Mirrlees shadow-pricing rules (see Little and Mirrlees, 1974), in many second-best situations (where the government maximizes social welfare subject to constraints—in particular, the absence of lump-sum taxes and subsidies) social welfare maximization still requires productive efficiency. For marginal changes, the appropriate weights for obtaining a measure of economic welfare (irrespective of the form of the social welfare function) are the 'relative weights on the different commodities given by the marginal rates of transformation' (Sen, 1979: 26). That is, assuming constrained optimality, marginal-

welfare judgements can still be based on transformation rates in production, that is, the cost approach to the social product. But these transformation rates have to be the Little–Mirrlees (LM) shadow prices. But as Mirrlees shows (1969), changes in national income at these LM shadow prices will also reflect changes in actual social welfare if '(a) some commodity taxes are chosen optimally, (b) all polices not chosen optimally, and all market prices not determined optimally, remain constant'. If these unlikely assumptions do not hold, then 'if a measure of the changes in social welfare is wanted, it will have to be constructed directly from information about the changes in consumption of different income groups'. However, national income measured in terms of the 'optimal' social prices

> can be given an important interpretation . . . a small change in income at these prices shows the change in *maximum attainable social welfare*, even when the government is not pursuing policies that allow social welfare to be maximized (given the instruments at its disposal) . . . [then] we may imagine that we are decomposing the *actual* change in social welfare into two parts: the change that results from a change in *attainable* welfare; and the change that is attributable to changes in the extent to which actual taxes, tariffs, quotas, and controls reduce social welfare below the maximum.   (Mirrlees, 1969: 8–9)

Also see Lal (1980b).

6. Recent noteworthy refinements are the attempts by Kravis and his team to provide internationally comparable estimates which correct for differences in purchasing power between different countries because of differences of actual exchange rates from purchasing-power parity, due to tariffs, etc., and in differences in the relative prices of non-traded goods in different countries (see Kravis, Heston, and Summers, 1978, and Summers and Heston, 1988).
7. Ricardo (1951).
8. Sen (1987b).
9. Pigou (1932). Pigou's 'national dividend' is the same as what would now be called real national income.
10. Cf. Robbins (1932).
11. But cf. Sen (1979) for a lucid survey.
12. Lal (1976, 1987a). Recently an egalitarian political philosopher has stated: 'As a basic premise of all political thinking, the proposition of fundamental equality cannot be derived from anything else' (Barry, 1989). That is, egalitarianism is like a 'taste'. As the above two articles by one of the present authors show, this taste is certainly not universalizable! For a trenchant philosophical critique of egalitarianism, cf. Raz (1986), especially ch. 9. Also see the essays in W. Letwin (1983), particularly the introductory essay by Letwin and that by Flew.
13. Cf. also Hayek (1976, 1988).
14. Cf. Sen (1982). Also the justice of the process which determined the existing endowments may be questioned; see Nozick (1974).
15. Little (1957).
16. However, many traditional analyses of income inequality often show that the major proportion of national inequality arises from 'between-groups' rather than from 'within-groups' inequality. If this is generally the case, then a concern

with reducing between-group inequality may also be appropriate in reducing aggregate or national inequality.

17. But in Sri Lanka there is a further subdivision within the Tamils: the native Tamils, who have lived in Sri Lanka almost as long as the Sinhalese, and the Indian Tamils on the estates, who came in as immigrant labour much later. The interests of these two groups have not been coterminous.

18. The study of Malaysia and Sri Lanka by Henry Bruton lays particular emphasis on these aspects.

19. Most socialists would of course accept this as an axiom of their creed, but even libertarian thinkers such as Smith, Hayek, and Milton Friedman would also accept it. See Smith [1776] (1910), Hayek (1960), and M. Friedman (1962).

20. See e.g. Reutlinger and Selowsky (1976), and Berg (1973).

21. See e.g. Srinivasan (1981). A balanced survey and evaluation of the literature on nutrition and health issues is provided by Behrman in the Special Studies volume of this series edited by Psacharopoulos (1991).

22. But see Behrman (1991) for the pitfalls in linking nutritional and health status to changes in social indicators.

23. Chenery et al. (1974); Ahluwalia et al. (1979).

24. See Chenery et al. (1974: 10 n. 11) and Ahluwalia et al. (1979: 301).

25. See Sen (1976) and Kakwani (1980).

26. Ahluwalia et al. (1979: 301). But they nevertheless went on to lay down an international poverty line and to estimate the extent of world poverty.

27. Thus Smith (book V, ch. II) stated: 'By necessaries I understand, not only the commodities which are indispensably necessary for the support of life, but whatever the custom of the country renders it indecent for creditable people, even of the lowest order, to be without' (Smith, 1910: 691). In the 19th-century liberal tradition, more recently Hayek has noted: 'It can hardly be denied that, as we grow richer, that minimum of sustenance which the community has always provided for those not able to look after themselves, and which can be provided outside the market, will gradually rise, or that government may, usefully and without doing any harm, assist or even lead in such endeavors' (Hayek, 1960: 257).

28. See Sen (1985b).

29. That reducing absolute poverty continues to be *identified* with egalitarianism can be seen from the following passage from the ILO's recent volume surveying their research on distributional issues: 'Poverty is a concept with which economists—and not only economists—are now more concerned than they are with wealth. In other words, thinking in terms of wealth and poverty, rich and poor—in terms of *economic equality*—is more prevalent than two centuries ago' [emphasis added] (Lecaillon et al., 1984). The rest of the book is about inequality, not poverty!

30. Also see Fields (1991) who applies the same criterion in examining the available data from a larger sample of developing countries.

31. See ILO (1977) and Streeten et al. (1981).

32. Morris (1979).

33. Sen (1987b: 25).

34. Pigou (1932: 759).

35. Ibid. 761.

36. See Little and Mirrlees (1974) and Scott (1976); also Lal (1980*b*).
37. This poverty line, estimated as a percentage of the average consumption levels per capita of industrial-wage households, was 48% in India (Lal, 1977*a*); 50% in Jamaica (Lal, 1979); 52% in Korea (Lal, 1977*b*).
38. See Srinivasan (1977).
39. As quoted in Howarth (1985: 30).
40. See for instance Sen and Williams (1982), Raz (1986), and the various rights-based theories of Dworkin (1977), Nozick (1974), and Rawls (1972).
41. Sen (1985*a*, 1987*b*).
42. See in particular the contribution by Bernard Williams in Sen (1987*b*). There are two important points made by Williams. The first concerns the identification of 'capabilities'; he raises four questions:

> Do capabilities entail the opportunity or ability to choose? The answer seems to be that at least some of them do. The second question is: Do *all* capabilities entail the opportunity or ability to choose? The answer to that may well be 'no', as Sen is using the idea . . . The third question is: How do we count capabilities? There is a danger of trivialisation here, in particular if one simply generates capabilities from commodities. It may be said that every time we multiply commodities, we multiply capabilities. . . . My fourth question is: How is the capability of doing X related to the actual ability to do X now? (Ibid. 97–8)

The other point made by Williams is equally serious and conerns us more directly—namely, that

> Sen is discussing [the notion] . . . of somebody's interests or well-being rather than some narrower class of his economic interests. However, we have to bear in mind here a question . . . namely, what the practical relevance of the idea of the standard of living is, . . . we need to put into the argument the connection between the concept of the standard of living and the concept of government action, or other forms of public action. One thing we may have in mind, when we talk about the standard of living, as a notion narrower than that of a whole set of people's individual interests, is the matter of which interests can be effectively and legitimately affected, in a direct way by government policy. . . . Reflections on these questions might, indeed, help us to see why a particular subclass of peoples' interests—roughly, their economic interests—should be naturally picked out by the phrase 'the standard of living'. (Ibid. 96)

43. Sen (1987*b*: 25). The passage continues:

> Why should we be concerned—not just strategically but fundamentally—with opulence, rather than with what people succeed in doing or being? And if it is accepted that the concern is basically with the kind of lives people lead or can lead, then this must suggest that the 'basic needs' should be formulated in line with functionings and capabilities. . . . The main issue is the goodness of the life that one can lead.

The answer to this line of reasoning is provided by the second passage from Williams in n. 42 above.

48 POVERTY, EQUITY, AND GROWTH

44. See Streeten and associates (1981: 86–90) for a discussion of the limitations of the various aggregative social indicators that have been proposed.
45. Little (1957: 79).
46. This should not be taken to imply that the so-called theory of the optimum allocation of resources, which forms part of modern welfare economics, is irrelevant for our purposes. It is not, and we shall be making use of it. But the so-called 'efficiency' aspects of welfare can be readily separated from the normative 'equity' aspects. These positive aspects of the theory are, as Little pointed out, 'the logical conclusions of a set of consistent value axioms which are laid down for the welfare economist by some priest, parliament or dictator' (ibid. 80). Thus they do not depend upon accepting a particular ethical viewpoint.
47. Wrigley (1988: 5).
48. Ibid. 18–19.
49. Ibid. 5–6.
50. Ibid. 6.
51. Iliffe (1987: 4).
52. Himmelfarb notes that by the end of the 18th century the distinction between the indigent and the poor had become clearly established, and cites a succinct formulation by Patrick Colloquhon in 1799:

> Indigence therefore and not poverty, is the evil. It is that condition in society which implies want, misery, and distress. It is the state of anyone who is destitute of the means of subsistence, and is unable to labor or procure it to the extent nature requires. The natural source of subsistence is the labor of the individual; while that remains with him he is denominated poor; when it fails in whole or in part he becomes indigent.   (cited in Himmelfarb, 1983: 78)

53. Iliffe (1987: 5).
54. Increasing destitution has been due to political violence in post-colonial Africa, and not to the cyclical climatic factors which have always put some Africans (particularly pastoralists) at risk. The various civil wars in Africa have created 12 million 'mass distress migrants' between 1964 and 1984 (Olivier, 1987).
55. Iliffe (1987: 7).
56. See the essays in W. Letwin (1983) for reasons why egalitarianism is incoherent, and Hayek (1988) for why it is incompatible with a sustainable market order.
57. Some *dirigistes* have invoked Adam Smith to their cause by pointing to the so-called 'Adam Smith problem', where the individualism underlying *The Wealth of Nations* is contrasted with the altruism extolled as the supreme virtue in his *Theory of Moral Sentiments*, it being claimed that Smith the moral philosopher seems to condemn the very society that Smith the economist conmended. In an important book Muller (1992) has shown that there is no such incoherence in Smith's work.
58. Milton Friedman (1962: 19), has argued that the alleviation of absolute poverty has a public-goods aspect to it. But Sugden (1982, 1983) cogently argues that this position, which predicts an insufficient supply of private charity, leads to unacceptable conclusions, e.g. if there is a $1 decrease in a charity's income and

a $1 increase in the philanthropist's, the latter's charitable gifts would rise by $1!

59. Harberger (1984).

60. See Castaneda (1992) for a detailed account of these social-policy reforms and their outcome.

61. The technocratic approach to public policy has been based on the welfare economics pioneered by Bergson and Samuelson and which Sen has labelled 'welfarism'. But the trouble with this has always been: how are the judgements about the social good which form the social welfare function to be derived? As Sugden (1993: 1949) notes: 'most welfarists think of social welfare judgements as being made by a particular individual, but from a neutral standpoint. This basic idea can be found, for example, in Arrow's (1963, p. 107) ethically neutral "public official" . . . it can be traced back to Adam Smith's "impartial spectator".' In classical utilitarianism, pleasure provided the measure of goodness. But this view founders on the impossibility of finding a metric for pleasure, in particular one which is interpersonally comparable. Nor, as Sen (1982) has shown in his penetrating critique of welfarism, is the revealed-preference version any more coherent. He has then attempted to argue for his own conception of the social good based on 'capabilities' and 'functionings, which, unlike revealed-preference welfarism, 'does not automatically assert that whatever the individual chooses is good for him. Then, by aggregating in some way the good of all individuals, we can arrive at a conception of the social good' (Sugden, 1993: 1951). But as Sugden notes, 'given the rich array of functionings that Sen takes to be relevant, given the extent of disagreement among reasonable people about the nature of the good life, and given the unresolved problem of how to value sets', it is not operational, and provides no alternative to the measurements of real national income and practical cost-benefit analysis based on Marshallian consumer theory that are the bread and butter of applied economics.

The alternative to this attempt to define the social good—which Platonic Guardians then maximize—is an alternative vision of public policy where 'society is seen as a system of cooperation among individuals for their mutual advantage. On this view, the primary role of government is not to maximize the social good, but rather to maintain a framework of rules within which individuals are left free to pursue their own ends' (ibid. 1948). This is the classical liberal vision of the state as a civil association, in Oakeshott's terms (see Ch. 7). Its contemporary exponents are the Virginia public-choice school and the neo-Austrians like Hayek. Amongst philosophers it is reflected in the contractarian tradition of the American liberal Rawls, and the libertarian Nozick. It is the viewpoint we find most congenial. But it should be noted that Sen (1992) has claimed that even this tradition can be subsumed into his own and that its proponents are also egalitarians—with respect to the good 'liberty'. But, as Sugden argues convincingly, this is a misreading of this contractarian and classical liberal position, which cannot be subsumed, as Sen suggests, into a theory of the social good.

62. Squire (1993: 378).

2

Aggregate Growth Outcomes

IF growth alleviates mass structural poverty, the determinants of growth are of considerable importance. Much of the rest of this book is concerned with forming judgements on these determinants on the basis of our country studies and others. This is done in successive stages. First, in this chapter we examine what can be learnt from the aggregate growth outcomes of our sample of countries in terms of the conventional statistical cross-country type of analysis, to see how far they confirm the broad judgements that we have arrived at on the basis of the detailed country studies (Section I below). Chapter 3, besides providing a summary of the country studies, moves to the next stage of the analysis by examining what can be learnt from our process of 'twinning' countries. Chapters 4–7 then attempt to go behind the proximate causes to see if there are any patterns in the interplay of initial conditions, organizations, interests, and ideas which can help to explain the policies which we have found are important influences on the proximate determinants of growth. As, for the reasons mentioned in the Introduction, there can be no ultimate 'test' or 'proof' in our enterprise, this successive peeling of our onion will, we hope, provide mutually reinforcing support at different levels for the story we think emerges from our comparative study.

Faute de mieux, we have to paint our canvas with a very broad brush, and hence many of the nuances and the richness of the country studies, on which our judgements are based, will inevitably be lost in this synthesis volume. As all our country authors have seen and concurred with the broad judgements derived from their studies, they share the responsibility for the country-specific interpretations we have made. But readers of this synthesis volume are urged to read at least some of the accompanying country volumes to find the detailed corroboration for various qualitative statements that appear in this volume.

In the inductive process in deriving a 'story' from our country studies— particularly the policies and their determinants which affect the proximate causes of growth—we have found the framework of a three-factor open-economy model, introduced in the last section of this chapter, particularly useful. But before that, we need to take account of the vast explosion of research on the so-called 'new' growth and 'new' trade theories and the statistical exercises they have given rise to since this comparative study was designed and executed. These researches are claimed to have led to a counter-revolution in development thinking (Krugman, 1992) about the policies which influence the proximate causes of growth. As the empirical framework is largely that of cross-section regression analysis, they are usefully considered in this chapter in Sections II and III below. The general reader impatient with such scholastic debates can move directly from the first to the final section of this chapter.

Measurement Issues: Before summarizing the aggregate growth perform-ance of our sample of 21 developing countries during the period 1950–85, it will be useful to emphasize the fragility of the underlying data as well as noting the representativeness of our sample of countries.

We measure growth performance in terms of GNP growth rates. Note that the available GNP figures (including those published by the World Bank) are subject to significant measurement errors, and are incomplete in their coverage, especially of the informal sector, which forms a major part of the economies of many developing countries. Hence they must be treated with extreme caution.[1] The ranking of countries by their per capita GNPs, whether in World Bank or Kravis dollars, could differ from the 'true' value because of these measurement errors. Moreover, when converted into growth rates, the errors in measuring GNP can become compounded if they are multiplicative and serially correlated over time.

Furthermore, our sample of 21 of these countries is 'small' with reference to all those countries collectively referred to as the Third World. There are two classification schemes which might be useful in giving some idea of the representativeness of the sample.

First, the World Bank divides its countries into three groups: low-in-come, lower-middle-income, and upper-middle-income countries. In its 1987 *World Development Report* it listed 37 low-income countries with an income per capita of $400 or less in 1985, and 59 middle-income countries, of which 23 were upper-middle-income with incomes per capita above $1,600 and 36 lower-middle-income with incomes between $400 and $1,600 in 1985. In our sample of 21 countries,[2] four (Malawi, Madagascar, Ghana, Sri Lanka) are low-income; ten (Indonesia, Egypt, Thailand, Nigeria, Jamaica, Peru, Turkey, Mauritius, Costa Rica, Colombia) are lower-middle-income, and six (Brazil, Uruguay, Malaysia, Mexico, Hong Kong, Singapore) are upper-middle-income countries. Malta is not in-cluded in the World Bank list, but with a 1985 income per capita of $3,280, it would rank as in the upper-middle-income group. Thus compared with the World Bank's full listing of developing countries our sample is biased towards the lower-middle-income countries, largely by the relative under-representation of the World Bank's low-income countries.[3]

However, classifying countries by different ranges of income per capita is not very useful for our purposes.[4] Thus Fig. 2.1 shows the estimates made by Irving Kravis and associates of GDP per capita in our 21 countries

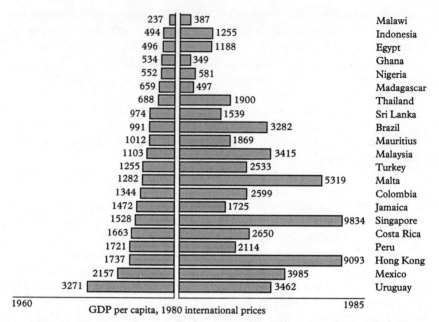

237	387		Malawi
494	1255		Indonesia
496	1188		Egypt
534	349		Ghana
552	581		Nigeria
659	497		Madagascar
688	1900		Thailand
974	1539		Sri Lanka
991	3282		Brazil
1012	1869		Mauritius
1103	3415		Malaysia
1255	2533		Turkey
1282	5319		Malta
1344	2599		Colombia
1472	1725		Jamaica
1528	9834		Singapore
1663	2650		Costa Rica
1721	2114		Peru
1737	9093		Hong Kong
2157	3985		Mexico
3271	3462		Uruguay

1960   GDP per capita, 1980 international prices   1985

Fig 2.1. Real GDP per capita in 1980 international prlces, 1960 and 1985
Source: Summers and Heston March (1988).

(adjusting for purchasing-power parity differences, using Kravis dollars) for 1960 and 1985. Table 2.1 provides data on the real growth rates for our countries in Kravis dollars for 1960–85.

As is apparent, the income categories of our countries in terms of GDP in Kravis dollars altered markedly between the two years. Suppose we classify countries as low-income at below $500 in 1980 Kravis dollars, lower-middle-income between $500 and $2,000, and upper-middle-income above $2,000. Then Ghana and Madagascar, which were lower-middle-income in 1960 on this definition, were now (1985) low-income. Indonesia and Egypt had moved from the low to the lower-middle income group, whilst Brazil, Malaysia, Turkey, Malta, Colombia, Singapore, Costa Rica, Peru, and Hong Kong had become upper-middle-income countries.[5]

These changes in income in terms of GDP per capita are obviously related to differences in GDP growth rates, which we are trying to explain in this study. So, for our purposes, a classification of our sample countries based on relative growth performance per capita would appear to be more suitable.

In his recent survey of the historical growth record of 37 countries, Lloyd Reynolds divides them into four tiers depending upon their growth rate of real GNP per capita between 1960 and 1980. In the first tier are ten high-

Table 2.1. Real GDP per capita in 1980 International Prices, 1950–85

	1950	1955	1960	1985	Growth rate 1960–85
Malawi		212	237	387	2.0
Indonesia			494*	1,255	3.8
Egypt	427	433	496	1,188	3.6
Ghana		511	534	349	−1.7
Nigeria	478	543	552	581	0.2
Madagascar			659	497	−1.1
Thailand	638	516	688	1,900	4.1
Sri Lanka	787	868	974	1,539	1.8
Brazil		832	991	3,282	4.9
Mauritius	1,253	1,145	1,012	1,869	2.5
Malaysia		1,006	1,103	3,415	4.6
Turkey	822	1,132	1,255	2,533	2.8
Malta		1,087	1,282	5,319	5.9
Colombia	1,188	1,376	1,344	2,599	2.7
Jamaica		1,117	1,472	1,725	0.6
Singapore			1,528	9,834	7.7
Costa Rica	1,175	1,541	1,663	2,650	1.9
Peru	1,235	1,501	1,721	2,114	0.8
Hong Kong			1,737	9,093	6.8
Mexico	1,652	1,905	2,157	3,985	2.5
Uruguay	2,864	3,523	3,271	3,462	0.2

*Figure for 1962.

Source: Summers and Heston (1988).

growth economies with a median growth rate of 4.5% per annum, in the second tier are nine modest-growth economies with a median growth rate of 2.8% per annum, the third tier contains nine low-growth economies with a median growth rate of 1.6%, and the fourth tier another nine economies with no growth (median growth rate 0.0%).[6] Twelve of our sample of 21 countries are also part of Reynolds's set, and of these, seven (Brazil, Thailand, Malaysia, Nigeria, Indonesia, Turkey, Egypt) are classified by Reynolds as high-growth, two (Colombia and Mexico) as moderate-growth, two (Sri Lanka and Peru) as low-growth, and one (Ghana) as no-growth.

To show that such relative indices of economic performance do not always provide a robust classification, we provide (in Table 2.2, column 3) the estimated GDP growth rates per capita from our country studies. In the rest of our study we have relied entirely on these data, rather than the Kravis–Summers–Heston (KSH) data set, partly because our country stories are based on them, and for some countries (e.g. Sri Lanka) the KSH trends differ significantly from those derived by our authors. In many cases the country studies have found World Bank data to be the most reliable.

Table 2.2. Comparative statistical profile

	1 GDP growth rate 1950–85	2 Population growth rates 1950–85	3 GDP growth rate per capita 1950–85	4 GNP per capita 1985 (US $)	5 AV I:GDP Rate 1950–85
A. *Labour-abundant*					
Hong Kong	8.9 (60–85)	2.3 (60–85)	6.6	6,120	26.1 (66–86)
Singapore	8.3 (60–86)	1.8 (60–86)	6.5	7,590	34 (60–87)
Malta	5.6 (50–84)	0.4	5.2	3,280	26.1 (55–87)
Median	8.3	1.8	6.5	6,120	26.1
Mean	7.6	1.5	6.1	5,663.3	28.7
Variance	2.1	0.6	0.4	3,200,289	13.9
B. *Land-abundant*					
Malaysia	6.9 (60–85)	2.6	4.3	1,980	23 (60–85)
Thailand	6.7	2.7	4	800	22.9 (50–87)
Brazil	6.6	2.7	3.9	1,660	21.4
Mexico	5.7	3.1	2.6	2,100	18.2
Turkey	5.6	2.5	3.1	1,080	18.9 (50–81)
Costa Rica	5	3.2	1.8	1,310	22 (67–84)
Colombia	4.7	2.6	2.1	1,320	19
Nigeria	3.7	2.6	1.1	820	16.6
Ghana	1.3 (66–86)	2.5 (66–85)	−1.2	370	11.7 (55–85)
Uruguay	1.1 (55–84)	0.8	0.3	1,670	12.9 (55–87)
Median	5.6	2.6	2.6	1,320	19
Mean	4.7	2.5	2.2	1,311	18.7
Variance	4.4	0.4	3	306,877	15.7
C. *Intermediate*					
Egypt	5.4	2.4	3	660	19.4 (53–84)
Indonesia	5.3 (52–85)	2.2	3.1	530	15.2 (60–83)
Sri Lanka	4.7	2.1	2.6	380	17.2
Malawi	4.3 (54–86)	2.8 (54–85)	1.5	170	23.4 (64–86)
Peru	4.1 (50–84)	2.6	1.5	1,010	19.1 (50–83)
Jamaica	3.3	1.3	2	910	22.1 (50–86)
Mauritius	2.9	2.2	0.7	1,100	22.3 (55–87)
Madagascar	2 (50–86)	2.4	−0.4	240	14.3 (50–84)
Median	4.1	2.4	1.5	660	19.1
Mean	4	2.3	1.7	646.7	18.8
Variance	1.4	0.2	1.4	125,805	11.1

6	7	8	9				
Distortion Index	Total Factor Productivity Gwth %	% VA	DDR In PQLI 1960–80	1960–70	1970–80	1980–85	1960–85
n.a.	4.28	47	5.7	12.7	9.4	9.4	10.71
n.a.	−0.01	−0.1	n.a.	4.2	12	5.9	7.6
n.a.	n.a.	n.a.	n.a.	n.a.			
	2.1	23.5	5.7	8.5	10.7	7.7	9.2
	2.1	23.5	5.7	8.5	10.7	7.7	9.2
	4.6	554.6	0	18.1	1.7	3.1	2.4
1.57	n.a.	n.a.	2.8	5.8	7.4	10.7	7.4
1.43	1	n.a.	3.1	5.2	11.8	8.4	8.44
1.86	2	53.7 21.9	1.9	5.1	7.5	6.6	6.4
1.86	2	28.3 37.5	2.8	2.8 (65–80)	13.4	10.1	8.4
2.14	2.23	34.8	2.8		5.5	25.3	10.14 (65–85)
n.a.	n.a.	n.a.	4.8	9.6	3.5	0.4	5.3
1.71	2.1	20.7	3	2.2	1.9	1.6	1.96
2.71	n.a.	n.a.	1.5	6.6	2.6	−9.9	1.5
2.86	n.a.	n.a.	1.1	0.2	−8.4	−7.9	−4.9
2.29	n.a.	n.a.	1.9	2.2	4.8	n.a.	2.8
1.86	2	34.8	2.8	5.1	5.5	6.6	6.4
1.92	1.87	33.5	2.6	4.5	5	4.5	4.7
0.3	0.2	127.9	1.1	7.3	36.2	103.2	20.6
2.14	1.66	n.a.	1.8	3.2	−0.7	3.9	1.8
1.86	0.6	n.a.	2.4	4	8.7	1.1	5.3
1.86	n.a.	n.a.	2.9	4.7	−2.4	7.3	2.3
1.14	n.a.	n.a.	0.8	11.6	5.7	2.9	7.4
2.29	1.5	28.3	2.4	2	3.9	1.4	2.6
2.29	n.a.	n.a.	4.9	4.7 (65–80)	−6.8	−7.3	−2.5
n.a.	n.a.	n.a.	n.a.		3.4	7.4	4.4
n.a.	n.a.	n.a.	n.a.	5.3	−1.2	−2.8	1.02
2.14	1.5	28.3	2.4	4.7	2.6	1.4	2.3
2	1.3	28.3	2.4	5.1	1.5	0.4	2.6
0.19	0.32	0	0.50	8.2	14.2	32.2	4.9

Table 2.2 *Continued*

	10			11	12
	Ratio X:GDP 1950	Ratio X:GDP 1985	% change in ratio	Agricultural product growth rate 1950–85	Population density 1965 (Thou. per sq. km)
A. *Labour-abundant*					
Hong Kong	79.3 (1960)	106.6	34.4	−1.1 (60–84)	27.7
Singapore	163 (1960)	196 (1982)	20.2	1.3 (60–85)	14.5
Malta	65.4 (1955)	72.5	10.9	n.a.	2.3
Median	79.3	106.6	20.2	0.1	
Mean	102.6	125	21.8	0.1	
Variance	1,858.3	2,711.9	93.4	1.4	
B. *Land-abundant*					
Malaysia	54.8 (1955)	54.8	0	3.7	0.26
Thailand	21.8	26	19.3	4.3	0.23
Brazil	9.6	12	25	4.1	0.05
Mexico	14.1	16.1	14.2	4.1	0.04
Turkey	8.2	20.6	151.2	3.2	0.08
Costa Rica	27.4	31.5	15	3.4 (60–85)	0.1
Colombia	10.9	14.7	34.9	3.3	0.05
Nigeria	20.7	16.7	−19.3	2.2	0.12
Ghana	33.5	9.6	−71.3	3.2	0.13
Uruguay	3.7	23.5	535.1	0.7	0.02
Median	14.1	20.6	19.3	3.4	
Mean	20.5	20.5	65	3.2	
Variance	231.1	168.4	28,752.7	1	
C. *Intermediate*					
Egypt	19.5 (1960)	21.5	10.3	2.9	1.1
Indonesia	13.3 (1960)	22.9	72.2	3.5	0.35
Sri Lanka	38.9	25.6	−34.2	3.1	0.52
Malawi	20.8 (1955)	23.5	13	3.5 (60–85)	0.1
Peru	20.8	21.6	3.9	2.1	0.04
Jamaica	30.5	58.2	90.8	1.3	0.36
Mauritius	46	53.5	16.3	0.09 (60–85)	0.72
Madagascar	11.9 (1960)	14.5	21.8	2.3	0.02
Median	20.8	22.9	13	2.3	
Mean	24.7	28.7	19.4	2.3	
Variance	117.4	222.6	1,404.3	1.1	

Sources:
Column
1 From country studies, except Ghana (World Bank) and Indonesia: Gillis (1984).
2 Calculated from World Bank data files.
3 Estimated as difference between 1 and 2.
4 World Tables 1987.
5 From country studies, IFS Yearbook 1988, and World Tables 1987 for Hong Kong.
6 World Development Report 1982 and Agarwala (1983).
7 From Chenery *et al.* (1986), and Tilak (1991).
8 Estimated using standard equations in Morris (1979).

13 % labour force in agriculture 1965	14 Urban Population (% total) 1965	15 Industrial growth rate 1965–80	1980–5	16 Government consumption, average % GDP 65–85	17 Primary school enrolment 1965	1984
6	89	n.a.	n.a.	7	103	105
6	100	12.2	5.9	11.5	105	115
10	72	n.a.	n.a.	15	126	n.a.
59	26	n.a.	6.7	15	90	97
82	13	9.5	5.1	11.5	78	97
49	50	10	0.3	10	108	103
50	55	7.6	0.3	8.5	92	116
75	32	7.2	6	10.5	101	113
47	38	8.7	−0.1	14.5	106	101
45	54	5.5	2.9	9	84	119
72	15	13.4	−5.8	8	32	92
61	26	1.4	−5.5	11.5	69	67
20	81	3.1	−7.2	13.5	106	109
55	41	7	7	21	75	84
71	16	11.9	1	8.5	72	118
56	20	5.1	4.2	11	93	103
92	5	n.a.	1.3	15.5	44	62
50	52	4.4	−3	10.5	99	116
37	38	−0.1	−1.6	12	109	106
37	37	n.a.	4.3	12.5	101	106
85	12	n.a.	−6.8	18	65	121

9a WDR 1982.
9b WDR 1982.
9c WDR 1987.
9d Estimated from 9a, 9b, and 9c.
10a Calculated from World Bank Tables 1976, except Singapore, from WDR 1984.
10b Calculated from World Tables 1987.
10c Calculated from 10a and 10b.
11–17 Compiled from World Tables 1980/7.

Table 2.2 shows that using the Reynolds criteria, Nigeria can no longer be called a high-growth country. Instead, we have the following classification of our 21 countries for growth rates per capita between 1950 and 1985:[7]

(i) high-growth economy (median of Reynolds's category 4.5%): Singapore, Hong Kong, Malaysia, Thailand, Brazil, Malta.
(ii) moderate-growth economy (median 2.8%): Indonesia, Sri Lanka, Egypt, Mexico, Turkey, Colombia.
(iii) low-growth economy (median 1.6%): Malawi, Peru, Nigeria, Jamaica, Costa Rica.
(iv) no growth economy (median 0.0%): Uruguay, Madagascar, Ghana, Mauritius.[8]

GDP growth rates per capita can be interpreted in terms of the opulence measure of welfare (see Chapter 1), and hence they are an important index of relative economic performance. However, in exploring this strongly divergent performance of our 21 countries it is the growth rate of GDP or output that primarily concerns us, as we assume (not unrealistically) that population growth rates (whose determinants are outside the scope of this study) are exogenously determined in our various economies.

I. THE PROXIMATE CAUSES OF GROWTH

The factors which determine the growth of the national product are our main concern in this study.

In his famous book, *The Theory of Economic Growth*.[9] Arthur Lewis wrote:

The growth of output per head depends on the one hand on the natural resources available, and on the other on human behaviour. This book is primarily interested in human behaviour, and concerns itself with natural resources only in so far as they affect human behaviour.

Our purpose is similar, though we will be more concerned than was Lewis with explaining the difference that differing relative resource endowments make to human behaviour.

Lewis then went on to write that 'The enquiry into human actions has to be conducted at different levels, because there are proximate causes of growth, as well as causes of these causes.' He identified three proximate causes of growth, as has much of the subsequent literature on growth and development, namely, allocative efficiency, the investment rate, and the rate of technical progress.

The major qualitative conclusion from our country studies is that relative differences in both the efficiency and level of investment are the proximate causes of the differences in growth performance of the countries in our sample. Furthermore, the policy regime was crucial in explaining the differences in the efficiency of investment. Like past comparative studies which have examined the role of foreign trade policy in explaining differences in economic performance in developing countries,[10] our country studies, too, emphasized the importance of so-called 'outward-looking' trade regimes in fostering better growth performance, with, as we shall see, some important exceptions. Our country studies also confirm the importance of the extent of policy-induced distortions in the working of the price mechanism as an important determinant of the differences in the growth outcomes in our countries.

Finally, and most important, some of our studies (in particular that of Hong Kong) have shown the importance of entrepreneurship for growth performance. Those countries which have created institutions and an economic environment which have fostered entrepreneurship, largely by reducing the costs of doing business (transaction costs), and a stable system of property rights, have also been able to create more flexible economies. They have weathered the squalls in the world economy since 1973 much better than those economies which, through their attempts to repress private entrepreneurship, have limited their economies' 'capacity to transform'.[11]

Crude statistical representations of some of these conclusions of our analytical economic histories, which some may find more persuasive than a perusal of the country studies, are provided by the cross-section two-stage least-squares (TSLS) regression we have run on the summary data of economic performance of our sample of countries,[12] provided in Table 2.2. These regression estimates are summarized in Table 2.3, whose Part A has the GDP growth rate between 1950 and 1985 (from the country studies) as the dependent variable, whilst that in Part B is the growth rate (1960–85) in Kravis dollars given in Table 2.1. The two independent variables—investment rate and export growth rate (used as a proxy for the 'openness' of the economy)—are both taken as endogenous variables which are both affected by and affect the growth rate (the dependent variable). Various structural and policy variables (listed in the notes to the table) were used to form instruments for these endogenous variables.

The investment rate is invariably positively correlated with the growth rate at a highly significant level. Table 2.4 summarizes the changes in investment rates and growth rates in each country over the 1950–85 period. Again, except for some exceptions (Malta 1970–7, Nigeria 1973–9, Indonesia 1979–84, Manritins 1960–5, Jamaica 1960–70 and 1977–86, and Turkey 1977/9–1983/5), periods of rising investment rates were associated with a rise in the growth rate and vice versa.

Of the proxies tried for openness, the export growth rate performed best and was always positively correlated with growth, often at a highly signifi-

Table 2.3. Growth regressions: TSLS

Endogenous Variables: INV EXPGRT

Instruments: CLAB EXPCHG DUMTR GOVC PRIMED LITAD AGRLAB URBP

(A) Dependent variable: GRTH; no. of observations = 21.

Regressions	C	INV	LAB	EXPGRT	EXPCHG	GOVC	PRIMED	LITAD	R^2
R.I		0.13** (2.31)	0.85* (1.93)						0.94
R.II		0.11** (2.44)	0.67* (2.00)	0.22** (2.39)					0.97
R.III		0.06 (0.75)	1.31** (2.46)		0.05 (1.51)				0.94
R.IV	-0.02 (1.7)	0.23*** (2.94)	0.97** (2.35)						0.67
R.V	-0.02 (1.26)	0.18** (2.5)	0.79** (2.22)	0.17 (1.65)					0.79
R.VI	-0.02 (0.82)	0.15 (1.12)	1.84** (2.23)		0.03 (0.68)				0.66
R.VII	-0.06 (0.75)	0.20** (2.53)	0.68 (1.72)	0.15 (1.35)		-0.05 (0.75)			0.79
R.VIII	-0.01 (0.63)	0.18* (1.83)	0.76 (1.6)	0.14 (1.26)		-0.05 (0.6)	0.005 (0.34)		0.79
R.IX	-0.005 (0.29)	0.22** (2.44)	0.60 (1.38)	0.15 (1.33)		-0.07 (0.85)		-0.007 (0.53)	0.79

EXPGRT   growth rate of exports 1960–85
EXPCHG   change in ratio of exports to GDP, 1985 and 1960
DUMTR   trade regime dummy (1 outward, 0 inward-oriented)
PRIMED   percentage age groups in primary education 1965
LITAD   adult literacy rate in 1960
AGRLAB   percentage of labour force in agriculture 1965
URBP   urban population as percentage of total 1965

Notes: *** significant at 1%; ** significant at 2.5%; * significant at 5%.
Figures in brackets are *t* ratios.
GRTH annual GDP growth rated 1950–85 (country studies).
INV average share of investment in GDP 1950–85.
LAB labour force growth rates 1960–85.
GOVC govt. consumption as share of GDP, average 1965–85.

Table 2.3. *Continued*

(B) Dependent variable: GRTK; no. of observations = 21.

Regressions	C	INV	LAB	EXPGRT	EXPCHG	GOVC	PRIMED	LITAD	R^2
R.I		0.16** (2.29)	0.70 (1.29)						0.92
R.II		0.13** (2.36)	0.43 (1.08)	0.32*** (2.97)					0.96
R.III		0.08 (0.78)	1.22* (1.83)		0.05 (1.37)				0.92
R.IV	−0.04** (2.52)	0.33*** (3.57)	0.91* (1.86)						0.68
R.V	−0.03** (2.2)	0.26*** (3.21)	0.66 (1.64)	0.22* (1.91)					0.81
R.VI	−0.04* (1.91)	0.34* (2.08)	0.88 (1.40)		−0.003 (0.07)				0.67
R.VII	−0.03 (1.51)	0.27*** (3.00)	0.61 (1.35)	0.21 (1.71)		−0.03 (0.30)			0.81
R.VIII	−0.03 (1.33)	0.26** (2.32)	0.66 (1.20)	0.21 (1.63)		−0.02 (0.10)	0.003 (0.16)		0.81
R.IX	−0.02 (0.99)	0.31*** (2.99)	0.46 (0.91)	0.22 (1.66)		−0.05 (0.55)		−0.01 (0.91)	0.80

Notes: Significance levels as in previous note. Figures in brackets are *t* ratios.
GRTK: annual growth rates of GDP (Kravis dollars) from Table 4.1
The other variables are as in previous footnote.
All the regressions in this table have been estimated by the GIVE procedure in the statistical package ECOS.

Table 2.3. *Continued*

(C) Instruments: C LAB EXPCHG DUMTR GOVC PRIMED AGRLAB URBP POPDEN LABLAN; Dependent Variable: no. of observations: 21.

	C	AGRGRT	EXPGRT	POPDEN	LABLAN	INV	Rsq
GRTH							
R.I	-1.31	0.66	0.23**	0.16*		0.15	0.75
	(0.61)	(1.67)	(2.10)	(2.07)		(1.56)	
R.II	-1.48	0.69	0.23*		0.05*	0.15	0.75
	(0.69)	(1.69)	(2.01)		(2.09)	(1.63)	
GRTK							
R.III	-1.17	0.35	0.29**		0.03	0.18*	0.82
	(0.54)	(0.85)	(2.52)		(1.39)	(1.93)	
R.IV	-1.00	0.33	0.29**	0.11		0.17	0.82
	(0.46)	(0.83)	(2.57)	(1.41)		(1.83)	

Notes: Significance levels as in previous note. Figures in brackets are *t* ratios.
AGRGRT Agricultural growth rates from Table 2.2.
POPDEN Population density (1,000 per sq km of agricultural land, from Table 2.2).
LABLAN labour to land ratio from Table 2.9.
The other variables are as in previous footnote.

Table 2.4. Investment: GDP analysis

I: GDP and GDP growth trends are split into periods to illustrate how and if GDP growth trends are related to I: GDP trends:

Periods which correspond to each author's division of their country's economic history			Those periods more appropriate to the I: GDP time series patterns (i.e. taking account of sharp changes in the I: GDP level)		
Period	I: GDP trend	AV annual real GDP growth rate %	Period	I: GDP trend	AV annual GDP growth
Columbia					
1950–67	↑	4.6	1950–87	Fairly	4.7
1968–74	—	6.7		steady	
1975–85	↑	3.3			
Peru				1950–55	6.2
1950–66	↑	6	1955–70	↓	5.2
1967–85	—	2.5	1970–85	↑	2.4
Nigeria					
1950–60	↑	3.6	1950–75	↑	6.1
1960–73	↑	6.4	1975–83	↓	0.7
1973–79	↑	3.6		1960–75	
1979–84	↓	−2.9			
Indonesia					
1960–66	—	2.1	1960–67	—	2.0
1966–73	↑	6.3	1967–75	↑	8.9
1973–79	—	7.0	1975–80	—	7.9
1979–84	↑	6.0	1980–83	↑	4.8
Sri Lanka				1950–56	2.3
1950–60	↑	3.4	1956–77	—	5.0
1960–70	↑	4.8	1977–80	↑	6.4
1970–77	↓	2.9	1980–85	↓	5.0
1977–85	↑	5.7			
Malaysia				1960–62	6.9
1957–69	—	6.5	1962–69	—	6.4
1970–80	↑	7.9	1969–82	↑	7.6
1980–85	↓	5.8	1982–85	↓	4.3
Malawi				1954–64	3.0
1964–79	↑	5.9	1964–79	↑	6.6
1979–86	↓		1979–86	↓	1.2
Madagascar				1950–52	0.04
1950–60	↓	2.4	1952–62	↓	3.2
1960–72	↑	3.1	1962–71	↑	3.1
1972–84	—	0.2	1972–77	—	0.1
			1977–79	↑	3.5
			1979–84	↓	−1.1
Ghana					
1950–58	n.a.	4.1	1960–83	↓	0.9
1959–65	↓	1.6			
1966–71	↑	4.3			
1972–83	↓	−1.3			
1983–present	↑	6.0			

Table 2.4. *Continued*

I: GDP and GDP growth trends are split into periods to illustrate how and if GDP growth trends are related to *I* : GDP trends:

Periods which correspond to each author's division of their country's economic history			Those periods more appropriate to the *I*: GDP time series patterns (i.e. taking account of sharp changes in the I: GDP level)		
Period	I: GDP trend	AV annual real GDP growth rate %	Period	*I* : GDP trend	AV annual GDP growth
Brazil			1940–50		5.3
1950–64	—	6.6	1950–74	↑	7.6
1964–80	↑	8.1	1974–85	↓	4.4
1980–87	↓	2.8			
Mexico			1950–60		6.1
1958–70	↑	6.7	1960–81	↑	6.6
1970–80	↑	6.6	1981–85	↓	0.1
1980–87	↓	0.8			
Costa Rica					
1950–63		5.3	1967–80	↑	5.7
1963–73	↑	7.2	1980–84	↓	0.04
1973–85	—	2.9			
Malta			1950–55		2.2
1960–65	↑	0.3	1955–70	↑	4.8
1965–70	↑	9.0	1970–73	↓	6.0
1970–77	↓	11.4	1973–82	↑	10.2
after 77	↑		1982–87	↓　1982–84	0.4
Mauritius			1950–60		0.1
1960–65	↓	5.4	1960–70	↓	2.9
1965–70	↓	−0.3	1970–76	↑	7.7
1970–77	↑	8.2	1976–83	↓	2.7
after 77	↓		1983–87	↑　1983–86	3.4
Jamaica					
1950–60	↑	8.0	1950–69	↑	6.0
1960–70	↑	4.0	1969–77	↓	1.3
1970–77	↓	0	1977–86	↑	−0.9
Singapore					
1960–65	↑	5.7	1960–72	↑	9.9
1966–73	↑	12.3	1972–77	↓	7.4
1974–77	↓	6.4	1977–84	↑	8.7
1978–83	↑	8.8	1984–87	↓　1984–86	0.1
Turkey					
1951/3–1961/3	↑	4.9	1950–81	↑	5.7
1961/3–77/9	↑	6.4			
1977/9–83/5	↑	2.9			
Uruguay			1950–60		2.1
1955–73	↓	1.0	1960–68	↓	0.6
1973–84	↓	1.5	1968–79	↑	3.8
			1979–87	↓　1979–84	−3.0

Table 2.4. *Continued*

I: GDP and GDP growth trends are split into periods to illustrate how and if GDP growth trends are related to *I* : GDP trends:

Periods which correspond to each author's division of their country's economic history			Those periods more appropriate to the *I*: GDP time series patterns (i.e. taking account of sharp changes in the I: GDP level)		
Period	I : GDP trend	AV annual real GDP growth rate %	Period	*I* : GDP trend	AV annual GDP growth
Thailand					
1953–58	↑	4.4	1950–79	↑	6.6
1959–72	↑	7.7	1979–87	↓ 1979–85	5.4
1973–85	↓	6.6			
Hong Kong				1960–66	11.2
1965–80	↑	8.5	1966–69	↓	5.5
1980–86	↓	6.0	1969–80	↑	9.4
			1980–86	↓ 1980–85	5.7
Egypt				1950–60	3.4
1960–65	↑	6.1	1960–64	↑	6.4
1965–73	↓	3.1	1964–73	↓	3.9
1973–81/2	↑	8.1	1973–79	↑	8.6
after 81/2	↓		1979–87	↓ 1979–85	7.2

Notes: I : GDP trends taken from IFS data except in the cases of Indonesia, Costa Rica, Madagascar, Malawi, Malaysia, Sri Lanka (country study data), and Hong Kong (World Tables).
Average annual GDP growth rates are taken from the country studies. Figures for the first GDP column concerning authors' country divisions are taken directly from the text, whilst the second GDP column, concerning periods more appropriate to the I : GDP trends (and Colombia 1975–85, Madagascar 1972–84, and Uruguay 1973–84) are calculated from GDP figures in the country studies. There is a slight discrepancy between the two but this does not affect the general patterns.

cant level. By contrast, of two other proxies, the change in the export share between 1960 and 1985 did not perform as well, whilst the last, a trade regime variable based on a classification contained in the World Bank's *World Development Report 1987*, was statistically insignificant and the results are not reported in Table 2.3.[13]

Our country studies did not find differences in educational levels (or their rates of change) important in explaining growth performance in their respective countries. Thus our writers on the five small economies, which include two of the south-east Asian newly industrializing countries (NICs), concluded:

Nor do the differences in human capital formation and education account for the variation in growth outcomes. The population of Hong Kong may be more energetic and enterprising, on average, than that of Jamaica, but it is not noticeably better educated in a formal sense. In fact, when it comes to education, the multilingual Maltese and Mauritians have the most impressive record, while Jamaica also holds its own quite well in health and literacy.[14]

This runs counter to the findings of many recent cross-sectional statistical analyses of the real growth rates data put together by Kravis and his associates, and also of various recent theoretical growth models (discussed below).

The most comprehensive cross-section statistical analysis of the determinants of growth is by Barro.[15] It is based on the data in Summers and Heston (1988) for 98 countries (in all three worlds) between 1960 and 1985, and on other variables mainly from the World Bank's data base. He finds that a higher rate of investment, a lower share of government consumption spending, higher school enrolment rates, greater political stability, and lower fertility are all correlated with a faster rate of growth of GDP. We have serious doubts about the index used for political stability, and have not included it in our regressions. But we have run TSLS regressions incorporating two alternative measures for human capital (used by Barro) as well as the share of government consumption spending in our regressions in Table 2.3. None of these variables is statistically significant for our sample of countries, and one of the human capital variables (adult literacy in 1960) consistently had the wrong sign (in the numerous regressions run incorporating it but not reported here). Clearly, these statistical results confirm the qualitative conclusion of our country studies that, at least for our sample of countries, differences in human capital or the share of government consumption cannot explain their growth rate differences.

Next, in Table 2.3 (C) we have run TSLS regressions incorporating the variables which Reynolds found were of importance in explaining growth performance in his cross-sectional statistical study of growth differences. He found that four variables—the agricultural production growth rate (AG), the export growth rate (EG), the investment/GDP growth rate (I:GDP), and population density in 1960 (P)—provided the best explanation.[16] We ran a similar regression for our sample of countries, but using instrumental variables to take account of the endogeneity of export, agricultural growth, and investment rates. Also the sample periods of our country studies are different from Reynolds. The export growth variable was invariably highly significant, whilst population density in two regressions and the investment rate in one were mildly significant.

Next, to provide some cross-sectional statistical counterpart to the findings of our country studies that the relative level of policy-induced distortions is an important proximate cause for differences in the efficiency of investment and hence in growth performance, we have used a composite distortion index developed by Agarwala (1983) for the World Bank's *World Development Report 1983* as a rough measure of these differences in the level of distortion. The index was formed from a classification of distortions in foreign exchange pricing (exchange rate, protection of manufacturing, protection or taxation of agriculture), factor prices (capital, labour), and product pricing (power tariffs, inflation), based on the judgement of World Bank country economists. The distortions were classified as low, medium, and high for each country. The composite distortion index was then derived by replacing these categories by the numbers 1, 2, 3, and taking a simple unweighted average of the individual distortions. Clearly it is a highly imperfect and subjective indicator, but it should nevertheless pick up the gross differences between countries in policy-induced distortions as judged by World Bank staff.

The Agarwala index is available for only 15 of the 21 countries[17] (see Table 2.2). Table 2.5 classifies our countries into categories jointly determined by their growth rates and the value of the distortion index.

From Table 2.5 (A) it is evident that for the 1960–85 period, whereas all the low-distortion countries had growth rates above 4%, the high-distortion countries (except for Peru) had growth rates below 4%. Moreover, as the classification for two sub-periods, 1960–73 and 1973–85, in Parts B and C shows, the effects of the policy distortion on the growth rates was much more marked in the post-1973 period, when all the high-distortion countries had growth rates below 4%.

Table 2.6 gives the OLS regression for the distortion index, and the growth rates of GDP, agricultural output, exports, and industrial output. These confirm that the policy-induced distortions affected growth performance particularly in the post-oil-shock period of turbulence in the world economy, and were a significant determinant of various sectoral aspects of economic performance.

Finally, we need to note the third of Lewis's proximate causes of growth-rate differences, namely differences in the rate of technical progress. To estimate these is the purpose of statistical computations of the sources of growth pioneered by Solow and further refined and developed by Denison.[18] This growth accounting has recently been applied to many developing countries. Chenery et al.[19] provide a useful summary of the resulting estimates of total factor productivity (TFP). Assuming that technical progress is neutral in the Hicksian sense,[20] and that along with capital and labour it is the only source of growth, that factor prices equal marginal products, and that output is produced by the usual neoclassical production function, allows the growth in aggregate output (value added) to be disaggregated into the growth of labour and capital weighted by their respective factor shares in total output, and a residual which gives the growth of total factor productivity.[21]

The TFP growth rate, and its share in explaining the growth of output for the ten countries in our sample for which it is available, are reported in column 7 of Table 2.2, whilst Fig. 2.2 (reproduced from Chenery et al.)

Table 2.5. Growth and distortions

Growth rate	Distortion index value		
	Below 1.8	1.8–2.2	above 2.2
(A) 1960–85			
Above 6%	Malaysia Thailand	Brazil	
4–6%	Malawi Colombia	Mexico Turkey Egypt Indonesia Sri Lanka	Peru
Below 4%			Uruguay Nigeria Jamaica Ghana
(B) 1960–73			
Above 6%	Malaysia Thailand	Brazil Mexico Turkey (	Jamaica
4–6%	Malawi Colombia	Sri Lanka	Peru Nigeria
Below 4%		Indonesia Egypt	Uruguay Ghana
(C) 1973–85			
Above 6%	Malaysia Thailand	Indonesia Egypt	
4–6%	Colombia	Brazil Sri Lanka	
Below 4%	Malawi	Mexico Turkey	Uruguay Peru Nigeria Ghana Jamaica

illustrates the estimates of total factor inputs (capital and labour) and TFP growth in the growth of output for the 39 developed and developing countries for which they had TFP estimates.[22]

Of our six countries included in the Chenery study, it is apparent from Fig. 2.2 that, except for Hong Kong, they all fall in the cluster marked B

Table 2.6. Regressions (OLS): Growth and Distortions (No. of observations = 15)

Regressions	Dependent variable	C	DISTRTN	Rsq
R.I	GRTH5085	9.56*** (5.8)	−2.47*** (3.04)	0.42
R.II	GRTH5073	7.57*** (4.08)	−1.36 (1.56)	0.15
R.III	GRTH7385	10.38*** (3.37)	−3.14* (2.09)	0.25
R.IV	AGRGRT	5.56*** (5.3)	−1.27** (2.20)	0.32
R.V	EXPGRT	16.66*** (4.39)	−6.36*** (3.4)	0.48
R.VI	IND6585	10.84*** (2.97)	−2.98 (1.67)	0.18
R.VII	IND6580	8.92* (1.97)	−1.25** (2.21)	0.24
R.VIII	IND8085	13.69*** (3.08)	−6.45*** (2.97)	0.41

Notes: ***significant at 1% level; **significant at 2.5%; *significant at 5%.
Figures in brackets are *t* ratios.
DISTRTN Agarwala's distortion index, see Table 2.2.
GRTH5085 GDP growth rate 1950–85.
GRTH5073 GDP growth rate 1950–73.
GRTH7385 GDP growth rate 1973–85.
AGRGRT agricultural growth rate 1950–85.
EXPGRT export growth rate 1960–85.
IND6585 growth rate industry 1965–85.
IND6580 growth rate industry 1965–80.
IND8085 growth rate industry 1980–85.

which has TFP growth rates between 0.5 and 2.0, and much of the growth in output between 4 and 6% per annum is accounted for by the increase in total factor inputs. Hong Kong alone, with its much higher growth rate of output, has both higher factor inputs and higher factor productivity. By contrast, developed countries (except Japan), which are in cluster A in Fig. 2.2, tend to have a much larger share of TFP growth rather than total factor input growth in their growth rates of output, which are typically lower than those for both sets of developing countries to be found in clusters B and C.

There have also been various attempts to 'unpack "technical progress in

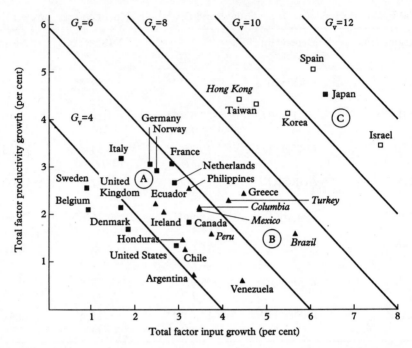

Fig 2.2. Relationship between total factor productivity growth and total factor input growth

Source: Chenery *et al.* (1986), fig. 2.5, p. 25.

the broadest sense" into a number of constituents, of which various human-capital variables and "technological change in the narrow sense" are the most important.[23] In Denison's most recent estimates for the sources of US growth between 1929 and 1982,[24] about 12% of the growth of output is attributed to the growth of capital, about 25% to the growth of labour of a constant educational level, and another 16% to the increased education of an average worker. The rest is allocated by Denison to improved allocation (11% through the transference of workers from low productivity agriculture to higher productivity industry, 11% to economies of scale, and 34% to technological progress in the narrow sense). There is a negative contribution of various miscellaneous factors (such as environmental protection measures) of 9%.

Similar growth accounting studies were done for a number of developing countries in the 1950s and 1960s.[25] The additional insight they provide is the potential contribution of education to economic growth. Psacharopoulos[26] has provided a survey table (Table 2.7) based on these studies.

As he himself notes:

Table 2.7. The contribution of education to economic
growth (percentage)

Country	Growth rate explained
NORTH AMERICA	
Canada	25.0
United States	15.0
EUROPE	
Belgium	14.0
Denmark	4.0
France	6.0
Germany	2.0
Italy	7.0
Greece	3.0
Israel	4.7
Netherlands	5.0
Norway	7.0
United Kingdom	12.0
USSR	6.7
LATIN AMERICA	
Chile	4.5
Argentina	16.5
Colombia	4.1
Brazil	3.3
Equador	4.9
Honduras	6.5
Peru	2.5
Mexico	0.8
Venezuela	2.4
ASIA	
Japan	3.3
Malaysia	14.7*
Philippines	10.5
South Korea	15.9*
AFRICA	
Ghana	23.2*
Kenya	12.4*
Nigeria	16.0*

*Estimates based on 'Schultz-type' growth accounting.

Note: Unless otherwise noted, estimates are based on Denison-
type growth accounting.

Source: Psacharopoulos (1973: 116) and Nadiri (1972: 138).

No easy generalizations can be made on the basis of this table. Education seems to
have contributed substantially to the growth rate of some highly advanced countries—such as the U.S., Canada and Belgium—as well as to the growth rate of
African and Asian countries (with the exception of Japan). In Latin America,

Argentina notably stands out from the rest with a much higher contribution of education to growth.[27]

As the last is hardly an example of a fast-growing country, whilst Japan as the fastest-growing has one of the lowest contributions of education to growth, it is difficult to believe on this evidence that it is differences in the growth of 'educational capital' which primarily explains differences in growth rates, a conclusion which is confirmed both by the qualitative and quantitative evidence for our sample of countries.[28]

The robustness of the statistical cross-section exercises reported in this section can be questioned. But at least their results are in conformity with the qualitative inferences derived from our country studies. To that extent the conclusions to be derived are likely to be more robust than those based on the purely statistical analyses of the Kravis *et al.* data set which have exploded in recent years. For as Solow has remarked on these exercises: 'I do not find this a confidence-inspiring project. It seems altogether too vulnerable to bias from omitted variables, to reverse causation, and above all to the recurrent suspicion that the experiences of very different national economies are not to be explained as if they represented "points" on some well defined surface.'[29] This fragility of the inferences drawn from these econometric exercises is highlighted by Levine and Renault's analysis of 41 cross-section regression studies in which econometric linkages are sought between long-run growth rates and a host of economic policy, political, and institutional indicators. They find that 'almost every particular policy indicator considered by the profession are fragile: small alterations in the "other" explanatory variables overturn past results'.[30] They do, however, 'identify a positive, robust correlation between growth and the share of investment in GDP and between the investment share and the ratio of international trade to GDP'.[31] But

when controlling for the share of investment in GDP, [they] could not find a robust relationship between any trade or international price-distortion indicator and growth . . . [this] indicates that the relationship between trade and growth may be based on enhanced resource accumulation and not necessarily on the improved allocation of resources.[32]

But as no causal mechanism is specified for the increased accumulation resulting from better trade policy, this conclusion must itself be fragile! In fact, Sala-i-Martin states that

Levine and Renault always find some group of *policy variables* that matter. The problem is that since policies are so highly correlated with each other, the data cannot always tell them apart. . . . Hence the main message from the Levine and Renault study is not that nothing matters, but that policy matters. The data cannot really tell exactly which policy is bad.[33]

A conclusion which will not surprise any development economist, and, which is the justification for our methodology in this book.

Our conclusions after this statistical wild-goose chase will seem very meagre to the general reader who has stayed through this section. Broadly, the qualitative conclusions of our country studies, that the proximate causes of growth are the rate of investment and its efficiency and that the latter is influenced by policy (in particular trade policy), still stand.

II. NEOCLASSICAL GROWTH MODELS

The proximate causes of growth in our sample of countries in the previous section emphasize the importance of policy (which determines the efficiency of investment) and of preferences (which determine the level of investment). In the standard neoclassical (Solow–Swan) model of steady-state growth, neither should affect the rate of growth. Increasing the savings/investment rate and removing policy-induced distortions raises the steady-state level of income per capita but does not affect its growth rate. The steady-state growth rate of an economy—its 'natural rate of growth'—is determined by the exogenously given growth rate of population, plus the rate of labour-augmenting (Harrod-neutral) technical progress, which falls like manna from heaven (see Fig. 2.3).

However, historically it is unlikely that any country has had steady-state growth. This has led to the notion of the traverse.[34] Improving allocative efficiency and/or varying the investment rate leads to a steady-state growth path with a higher income per capita but with an unchanged steady-state growth rate. However, during this transition from one steady-state path to another, along the so-called 'traverse', the growth rate will be transitionally above the steady-state natural rate of growth.[35] Our evidence on the positive correlation between growth rates and measures of allocative efficiency and investment could thus be rationalized in principle within the neoclassical model.[36]

Growth in the neoclassical model can thus be ascribed to two main sources. First is the growth of population and productivity on the steady-state growth path. Second is the transitional growth associated with moving from one steady-state growth path to another, which is associated with improved efficiency and increased investment. Earlier numerical experiments by Sato and Atkinson[37] found that the neoclassical model's transitional dynamics involved very slow adjustment towards a steady state—up to 100 years—and could account for a large part of the rise in growth rates (not explained by the rise in the 'natural rate of growth'). However, King and Rebelo have recently shown that, based on estimates of structural

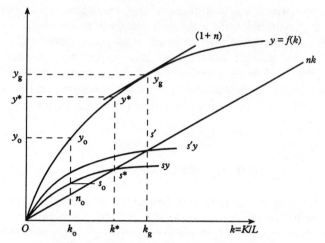

Fig 2.3. The neoclassical growth model

Note. The standard one-sector neo-classical growth model depicts. Oy is the neoclassical production function showing output perhead as a function of capital per head. The curve s'y shows the savings available, which are proportional to output per head. The ray nk shows the investment required to maintain any given capital–labour ratio constant, when the sum of the rate of population growth (p) and labour-augmenting technical progress (t) is equal to n ($n = p + t$). Assume the economy begins with capital per head of k_0 and hence output per capita of y_0. Then, savings per capital are $s_0 k_0$, of which $n_0 k_0$ are required to equip the new entrants into the labour force (at the rate n) to keep the capital/head constant. This leaves a surplus of $s_0 n_0$ savings available for capital deepening. The consequent rise in the capital and output/head continues until the steady-state capital–labour ratio of k^* is reached, with steady-state output per capita output of y^* and of per capita consumpton of $y^* s^*$. In this steady state the output *per capita* and and capital stock will remain constant, and hence the rate of growth of output and capital will be equal to the exogenously determined growth of the effective labour force, namely to, the natural rate of growth.

The economy can achieve a higher steady-state output and consumption per capita by raising the savings rate (the sy line). The savings rate which yields the highest steady-state consumption per capita is given by s'y, which gives the steady-state output per head y_g, where the slope of the produciton function is the same as the nk line (that is, the marginal product of capital is equal to the natural rate of growth n). This maximizes consumption per head ($s'y_g$)—the distance between the production function y and the nk line. This yields the so-called Golden Rule of Accumulation. A savings rate higher than s' would be sub-optimal. But because raising savings incurs costs in terms of consumption forgone, the optimal savings rate, which balances these costs against the benefits of the higher consumption per head on the new steady-state path, will be lower than that given by the Golden Rule of Accumulation. Raising the savings rate raises the steady-state level of output per head from y^* to y_g, but the steady-state rate of growth remains unchanged at n, the natural rate of growth.

parameters which are consistent with the Maddison (1991) and Summers and Heston data sets, transitional dynamics can explain only a small part of observed growth experience.[38]

A major stylized fact about this growth experience is that it is not in concordance with one of the implications of the neoclassical model, namely that, with access to the same technology, there should be convergence of growth rates, wage rates, and capital stocks per capita, across countries. But whilst there is some evidence of such convergence amongst developed countries (see Scott, 1989), for developing countries Romer (1989) and Barro (1991) find divergence rather than convergence in growth rates on analysing the Summers and Heston data sets. If transitional dynamics cannot account for these differences in growth performance, differences in the rate of exogenous technical progress would be one recourse within the standard Solow–Swan growth model. This seems implausible. It could, however, be argued that the policy-induced distortions in developing countries have obstructed the diffusion of new technology (from the common pool available to all countries). Hence the assumption of the exogeneity of technical change in the neoclassical model is not applicable to these countries.

This leads to the notion of *conditional convergence* within the Solow–Swan framework. Each country is then seen to be approaching its own particular target of steady-state income per capita (y_i^*), which is determined by 'the level of technology and attitudes about saving, work, and fertility, but also government polices in regard to taxation, maintenance of property rights, and provision of infrastructure services'.[39] An economy will then grow faster if its initial income per capita (y_i) is further away from its target steady-state level (y_i^*).

Regions of large countries such as the USA, or countries within a regional block such as the EEC, can be expected to have similar underlying conditions and hence y_i^*s. For them there should be, as there is (see Barro and Sala-i-Martin, 1991 and 1992), an inverse relationship between their initial income per capita and its subsequent growth. The speed of convergence between the US regions, the regional economies of Europe, and the provinces of Japan turns out to be between 2 and 3 per cent per year.[40] Barro's cross-country regressions[41] can then be used to control for the differing underlying determinants of each country's target steady-state growth rate (y_i^*). When this is done then for the 114 countries in the Summers–Heston data set, 'the estimated rate of convergence for real per capita GDP turns out to be statistically highly significant and of a magnitude, about 1.5% per year, that is only slightly below that found for the U.S. states and the regions of Europe and Japan'.[42] This conditional convergence does not imply absolute convergence, because of the divergences in target growth rates, for which Barro concludes 'the main source of divergence is likely to be government policies that affect the incentives to invest and to operate efficiently.'[43] This conclusion is in consonance with the evidence from our country studies.

III. ENDOGENOUS GROWTH THEORIES

Though the theory of the traverse and conditional convergence can provide a theoretical and statistical justification for the importance of policy within the Solow–Swan framework in determining growth rates, the ultimate determinants of steady-state growth within the framework still remain exogenous.

Several authors, starting with Kaldor (1957), Kaldor and Mirrlees (1962), and Arrow (1962),[44] have sought to introduce the rate of investment (which in the neoclassical model only affects the level and not the rate of steady-state growth) as an endogenous determinant of technical progress. However, in their models too, neither improvements in allocative efficiency nor rises in the savings rate affect the economy's natural rate of growth.[45]

More recently, a so-called 'new' growth theory—whose pioneers are Romer and Lucas—has arisen in the USA, which seeks to endogenize what the neoclassical model takes to be the exogenous determinants of steady-state economic growth. But whilst asking the right questions, these new theories have not taken us much further than the standard Solow–Swan model. Nor have theorists (see Solow, 1994, and Stern, 1991), nor development economists (see Pack, 1994) found these new theories persuasive. This is partly because of their implausible assumption that there are externalities from physical or human capital, so that there are strictly constant returns to capital (see Pack, 1994, for the evidence against such externalities), and partly because they involve merely mathematical tinkering within the standard Solow–Swan model without any fundamental rethinking of its building-blocks.[46] A totally new endogenous growth model which does this, and which we find more persuasive, is due to Scott.[47]

1. Scott's Growth Framework

The Scott model is best placed within what Harry Johnson (1964) called the 'generalized capital accumulation approach' deriving from Irving Fisher (1930). This sees capital accumulation as broadly defined to include all forms of investment which yield a stream of income over time:

'Investment' in this context must be defined to include such diverse activities as adding to material capital, increasing the health, discipline, skill and education of the human population, moving labor into more productive occupations and locations and applying new knowledge to increase the efficiency of productive processes. All such activities involve incurring costs, in the form of current resources, and investment in them is socially worthwhile if the rate of return over costs exceeds the general rate of interest, or the capital value of the additional income they yield exceeds the cost of obtaining it.[48]

This wider notion of investment as the prime mover of the growth process also makes growth endogenous, 'and is a potent simplification of the analytical problem of growth, and one which facilitates the discussion of problems of growth policy by emphasizing the relative returns from alternative investments or currently available resources'.[49]

Scott's endogenous neoclassical growth model is the fullest working out of this approach. It is neoclassical in so far as it assumes profit and utility maximization. But there are three important departures from the Solow–Swan framework.

First, he argues that

for all practical purposes, depreciation in a progressive economy should be regarded as essentially a transfer of income from capitalists to workers. The latter benefit from rising wages which result in appreciation which is omitted from the conventional accounts. Were it included, it would offset depreciation on capital assets. It would then be clear that net investment for society as a whole is (approximately) equal to *gross* investment as conventionally measured, and not to gross investment minus depreciation.[50]

Second, Scott argues that there are no diminishing returns to cumulative gross investment (that is, the capital stock measured as the sum of all past gross investment), but there could be diminishing returns to the *rate* of investment.

Third, he maintains that there is no need to invoke any independent or exogenous technical progress to explain growth. He argues that 'investment is . . . by definition . . . the cost of change, and so will cover all activities associated with growth', and that 'growth due to capital and technical progress are both the result of investment' in the sense of 'the cost, in terms of consumption foregone, of propelling the economy forward instead of leaving it in a stationary state'.[51]

Incurring capital expenditure leads to a rearrangement of the things of this world. It does not lead to there being any more of some substance 'capital'. There is then simply change which is due to investment, and to population growth. We cannot separate change which is 'more capital' from change which is 'technical progress'. We must abandon the attempt to distinguish between movements along a production function whose arguments are labor, land and all capital, and a shift in that function due to technical progress.[52]

Within his proposed framework, 'the rate of increase of static income is a function of only two variables: total savings and labor force growth. There is no independent technical progress'.[53] Scott provides a detailed empirical analysis of the conformity of the growth experience of currently developed countries in terms of his model. All his statistical tests show that his model can explain a very large part of their differences in growth performance.

Scott assumes that the economy is like a giant firm, that

Undertaking investments alters the investment opportunities, not just by removing some, but also by creating others. The firm is always selecting the best opportunities it is aware of, but undertaking investments makes it aware of new opportunities since it learns by experience and by investing. Some of its investment consists of the cost of searching for opportunities. This is the case for research and development expenditures, which must be widely interpreted to include market research, investigation of new sources of supply, hire of business consultants and efficiency experts, etc. But almost any investment expenditure, by changing the world, enables something new to be learned. There is therefore no reason why investment opportunities should become exhausted. At any one time it is true the firm will be aware of a limited number of opportunities, some better than others. Hence increasing the rate of investment can be expected to worsen its average quality: more means worse. But there is no reason to suppose that the set of opportunities gets worse (or better) on average as time passes.[54]

Instead of the usual production function, Scott argues that the economy's technology is best depicted by a set of inexhaustible investment opportunities. He envisages the investment opportunities available as a cake, which is 'continually remade'.

But there are two qualifications to this assumption of a constant set of investment opportunities which may be relevant. First is the possibility of catch-up:

What may happen in such cases is that both the favorable stream of new inventions, etc. and the adverse stream of competitive pressures are shut off from a particular country for various reasons. Subsequently, the country is opened up to such influences. Investors in that country then reap the benefits of access to the new inventions, etc. Since competition will not have forced up wage rates, investment opportunities will on balance be enhanced, although the lack of investment in the past will limit this enhancement. As investment proceeds, and the country catches up, wage rates will be bid up and eventually the set of opportunities will become normal.[55]

The second is that the set can shrink or expand. There is no law that requires a constant set. 'Some have claimed to be able to detect long waves of invention which should show up as expansions and contractions in the set of opportunities. My own investigation suggests a movement in one direction only—happily that of expansion.'[56]

But as a working hypothesis, an inexhaustible constant set of investment opportunities seems plausible.

His model then leads to a simple linear equation to explain growth:

$$g = aQs + b \cdot g_{L},$$ (1)

where g = growth rate of output,
  a and b are constants,
  Q is an index of the quality of investment,
  s = investment/savings rate,
  g_{L} = growth rate of quality-adjusted labour force.

By contrast, in the standard neoclassical model in which growth depends only upon the exogenous growth of quality-adjusted employment and technical progress, the relevant growth equation would be, in Scott's notation,

$$g = a + bg_{\mathrm{L}}. \tag{2}$$

Scott then tests his model against the standard neoclassical one on data for ten countries over a number of subperiods from the nineteenth century to 1973. He finds the results are close to the predictions of the model. The investment–output ratio and the growth of quality-adjusted labour each explain about half of the growth of output. The term which would capture exogenous technical progress is statistically insignificant and not different from zero.

Moreover, he finds that a 'catch-up' variable (in a disaggregation of Q) explains a small but significant portion of growth performance since the Second World War. He also finds that the efficiency of investment increased significantly after the Second World War (the value of Q increased). It is this changed efficiency of investment which requires explanation.[57]

Thus as Scott concludes, unlike the Solow–Swan model, which says 'no technical change, no growth', his model reasserts the importance of the economic aspects of economic growth:

The determinants of the volume and efficiency of investment are restored to the center of attention, and both have long been the concern of economists. We can, with renewed confidence in their importance, study the behavior of firms, project appraisal, the working of capital markets, the determinants of saving, systems of taxation, and their impact on savings and the volume and pattern of investment, all of which are very relevant to economic growth in the long run. We do not have to abdicate to scientists and engineers or even to those economists who specialize in the study of technical change. I do not deny for a moment their interest and importance but I do assert the importance of the economic aspects of economic growth.[58]

We have attempted a similar regression exercise to Scott's to see whether his model fits the aggregate facts about our countries better than the neoclassical model. The two reduced-form equations arising from Scott's model are given by equations (1) and (2). Data on the growth rates of output and the average gross investment rate were given in Table 2.2. The data on the growth rate of the labour force are given in Table 2.8. Ideally we need a measure of the growth rate of the quality-adjusted labour force. As we do not have data to derive this, we have used the growth rate of the labour force as a whole between 1960 and 1985 in our sample countries, as a proxy for our variable g_L.

The regressions were run on both the GDP growth rates from the country studies (g) and the real GDP growth rates of output as given by Kravis *et al.* (g_K). All the regression estimates are given in Table 2.8 (B).

Table 2.8. Determinants of growth

(A) Growth of labour force (g_L), share of wages (w) and average rates of return to investment (r)

Country	g_L	w	r
A. *Labour-abundant*			
Hong Kong	0.0363	0.616	0.255
Singapore	0.0386	0.467	0.190
Malta	0.0135	n.a.	n.a.
B. *Land-abundant*			
Malaysia	0.0339	n.a.	n.a.
Thailand	0.0309	0.520	0.222
Brazil	0.0325	0.647	0.210
Mexico	0.0355	0.647	0.187
Turkey	0.018	0.570	0.240
Costa Rica	0.0365	0.585	0.130
Colombia	0.0249	0.530	0.178
Nigeria	0.0293	0.520	0.131
Ghana	0.0258	>1.000	−0.109
Uruguay	0.0066	0.347	0.068
C. *Intermediate*			
Egypt	0.0229	0.434	0.227
Indonesia	0.0262	n.a.	n.a.
Srilanka	0.0231	0.690	0.181
Malawi	0.0251	0.501	0.130
Peru	0.0293	n.a.	n.a.
Jamaica	0.0197	n.a.	
Mauritius	0.0260	n.a.	n.a.
Madagascar	0.0179	n.a.	n.a.

Notes: g_L growth of labour force (1960–85)—estimated from *World Tables* and *Social Indicators of Development*, 1988.

w share of wages. From country studies and D. Anderson (1990). For Sri Lanka, from Lal (1979).

r estimated from $r = (g - w \cdot g_L)/s$, where the values of g and s are from Table 2.2 for the growth rate of GDP and the average investment rate respectively, and g_L is as given above.

Table 2.8. *Continued*

(B) Regression results—testing alternative growth models

Dependent variable	Constant	g_L	s	R^2
I. Scott model (OLS)				
R.I/g		0.71	0.15	0.94
		(1.82)	(2.99)	
R.II/g_k		0.56	0.18	0.92
		(1.15)	(2.8)	
II. Neoclassical model (OLS)				
R.III/g	0.0056	1.63		0.42
	(0.464)	(3.68)		
R.IV/g_k	0.0008	1.86		0.37
	(0.051)	(3.4)		

g growth rate of GDP (1950–85).
g_k growth rate of real GDP (Kravis) (1960–85).
g_L growth rate of labour force (1960–85).
s average investment (gross) rate 1950–85.
Figures in brackets are t ratios.

From this it is evident that the Scott growth equation provides a much better fit to our data than the equation for the neoclassical model. Equation R.I explains 94% of the variance in growth rates in our sample of countries. Also, as the theory predicts, the coefficient a in (2) is not significantly different from zero. From the regression R.IV in Table 2.3 (A) and (B), which nests the two competing models, the neoclassical model would expect the constant and the coefficient on labour to be positive and significant, and that on investment to be insignificant, whereas Scott would predict an insignificant constant close to zero, and significant positive coefficients on the other two terms. For the regression reported in Table 2.3 (A), based on our country study data, the Scott model fares better than the neoclassical, whilst in Table 2.3 (B), based on the Summers–Heston data, the coefficients on both labour and investment are positive and significant (contrary to the neoclassical view), and the constant is significant but negative.

However, not too much should be read into this. After all, it is implausible that any of our sample of countries has been on a steady-state growth path over the period considered (see Chapter 5).

More relevant for our purposes is that Scott's growth model implies that the rate of return to investment in the steady state will also be constant. This rate of return (r) is derived as

$$r = \left(g - w \cdot g_{\mathrm{L}}\right)/s, \tag{3}$$

where, in addition to the previous notation, w is the share of labour incomes in output.

The data on w (the share of labour incomes in output) are virtually non-existent in developing countries, in large part because it is difficult to separate the share of labour from that of capital in the earnings of the self-employed who are a predominant part of the labour force. Nevertheless, some of our country authors were able to provide some estimates for w. Moreover, Anderson has obtained some indirect estimates of w for a number of developing countries.[59] From both these sources, we have data on w for 14 of our countries. The computed values of the average rate of return (r) in these countries, during the period for which GDP growth rates are reported in column 1 of Table 2.2, is also shown in Table 2.8 (A). These returns are available for some countries in all three of the broad resource-endowment categories we will be using (see below): labour-abundant, land-abundant, and intermediate. The average return for all the countries in our sample for which we have data (and excluding Ghana which has a negative rate of return) is 18%. This is also roughly the average of the returns to the countries in the land-abundant and intermediate resource-endowment groups. The large variation from this average of course reflects the differences that result from the relative effectiveness and efficiency of investment in our different countries. It is these differences in efficiency which will be an important determinant of the difference in growth rates in our countries. For, apart from any differences in the growth of the quality-adjusted labour force, the Scott model emphasizes that, in line with common sense, it is differences in the level and returns to investment which are the proximate determinants of differences in growth rates. Much of the rest of this book seeks to find deeper reasons in terms of initial endowments and organizational and political factors which have led to these differences in the returns to investment in our countries.

2. Entrepreneurship

But it should be noted, even at this stage, that the key aspect of Scott's analysis is its emphasis on the 'importance of allocation' for the growth rate. Scott argues that if

investment is essentially a matter of incurring costs to reallocate resources then the efficiency with which this is done must affect the yield of investment, and so the proportionate rate of growth in the long run. So long as investment is occurring, reallocation is occurring. It is not once-and-for-all, but a continuing process, and, indeed, the principal source of growth in many countries.[60]

Moreover, he argues,

investment at any given time is undertaken in a state of ignorance about the future. We make changes whose consequences we cannot wholly foresee, and, simultaneously, others are making changes of which we can only become aware after they are made. In the light of these changes we are then in a better position to make the next round of changes.[61]

This implies 'that there is an externality to investment'.[62] But 'if the externality exists just because we are ignorant of the future effects of investment, it may be impossible to discover very much about the characteristics of investment that produce the externality'.[63]

The argument needs to be extended. It suggests the importance of an economic environment that is conducive to this ignorance-based, externality-creating form of investment. Scott notes:

The very slow rates of growth experienced [in developed countries] before the Industrial Revolution may be explained by poor communications and low rates of investment by others, which reduced the supply of investment opportunities to any individual, while high rates of discount caused by insecurity meant that few opportunities were taken up. There were many anti-growth factors, with lack of freedom to pursue and improve one's own business, and lack of confidence that one could keep most of the gains perhaps the most important of these.[64]

This would also seem to be of importance in explaining the divergent growth performance amongst our sample of currently developing economies.

This is also the place for the neo-Austrian insights concerning the role of the entrepreneur in an economic environment characterized by ignorance.[65] The entrepreneur is redundant in neoclassical economics, which assumes an environment of purely actuarial Knightian risk.[66] But he is at the centre of the neo-Austrian stage—creating and searching out investment opportunities and gambling on the future. Like the speculator and middleman, the entrepreneur is an economic agent who lives by making money out of irreducible Knightian uncertainty. This entrepreneurial function must, for reasons to do with incentives and information, be decentralized. To the extent that an outward-orientated trade stragegy has to rely on this entrepreneurial function (as export markets cannot be ensured by local mandarins), it will induce the creation of that economic framework in which Scott's externality-creating investments will lead to faster growth.[67] This would provide a preliminary explanation for the positive effect on growth of an outward orientation in trade, which also emerges from the aggregate outcomes of our studies discussed above.

One promising model from the new growth theory stable, which incorporates some of these neo-Austrian insights, is that of Murphy, Shleifer, and Vishny (1991). This endogenizes growth by assuming that there are increasing returns to ability (talent): 'Talented people typically organize production by others, so they can spread their ability advantage over a larger scale.'[68] The economic environment then determines whether a country's talented people start firms, innovate and foster growth, or become rent-seekers aiming merely to redistribute wealth, thereby reducing growth.

Nor, as Schultz (1990) has recently emphasized, should the entrepreneurial function be seen as confined to what Leibenstein has called N-entrepreneurship, that is, 'the activities necessary to carry on an enterprise where not all the markets are well established or clearly defined and/or in which the relevant parts of the production function are not completely known'.[69] Instead, most economic agents are involved in entrepreneurial activity at some time. Despite the picture portrayed by theorists of equilibrium growth, most actual growth occurs as a disequilibrium phenomenon.[70] For it is the result of agents learning to deal speedily with those emerging disequilibria which are a necessary concomitant of economic change. Whilst the textbook perfect-competition model assumes that changes in the econmic environment, say changing relative prices, lead to instantaneous shifts in resources along the production function, with the economy moving from one equilibrium position to the next, in practice such flexibility of response is rarely to be found. The responses to these emergent disequilibria are entrepeneurial, and the more sluggish the entrepreneurial response in effecting a new equilibrium, the more likely that the economy, instead of moving smoothly along its production possibility frontier, will instead move inside it. This will imply unemployment of capital and labour, because the responses of economic agents are not flexible enough to deal with the resource shifts which are required (and which are profitable) in the light of changing relative prices.

As Schultz has emphasized, one of the most noticeable and remarkable demonstrations of the entrepreneurial capacity of ordinary people was provided by the response to the emergence of a new technology (the new high-yielding seeds) by Third World peasants, which led to what is called the Green Revolution.

There seems to be some evidence that human capital variables (such as literacy) are related to this entrepreneurial function. Thus, in South Asia, for instance, the earliest adopters of the Green Revolution technology tended to be the most educated farmers. In his analysis of Hong Kong's entrepreneurs, Young in our country study cites survey evidence that 'they were somewhat more highly educated than the average production worker or "man on the street"!' As Young notes, 'if educational levels in a rough sense reflect an individual's training in the process of learning, then entrepreneurs were better prepared than the average person to adapt and fill in gaps in their knowledge.'[71] But, as the example of the mainly illiterate entrepreneurial Marwaris in India shows,[72] it would be facile to conclude that raising the educational level of the population will necessarily make it more entrepreneurial. Unfortunately, theory is not much help in explaining the three classical mainsprings of growth: thrift, productivity, and entrepreneurship.

Thus, we are inexorably led—as was Lewis—beyond the three proximate causes of growth as formalized in neoclassical growth theory, as well as the two causes (the level and efficiency of investment) in the more plausible growth theory of Scott, in explaining the different growth outcomes in our sample countries. As Lewis wrote:

The second stage of the analysis takes us behind these proximate causes to ask why it is that they are found strongly operating in some societies but not in others, or at some stages of history but less so in others. What environmnets are most favourable to the emergence of these forces which promote growth? This stage of the equiry subdivides itself. First we must enquire which kinds of institutions are favourable to growth, and which are inimical to effort, to innovation or investment. Then we must move into the realm of beliefs and ask what causes a nation to create institutions which are favourable, rather than those which are inimical to growth.[73]

We too will be exploring the role of ideas and institutions in explaining the different outcomes in our sample countries, but in addition, unlike Lewis, we shall also be looking at interests in explaining why human actions (in the large) which ultimately determine these growth outcomes were what they were. That one must go beyond beliefs and attitudes is exemplified by the meagre gleanings that Lewis obtained from the sociological and anthropological literature. Perhaps the extension of the standard economist's logic based on interest can usefully be deployed to explain why some countries have succeeded in creating institutional frameworks which are favourable for growth, whilst others have not? At least that is the hope of the so-called 'economic imperialists' who have recently shown the value of *The Economic Approach to Human Behavior*,[74] as the title of one of the most famous books in this new tradition has it! We examine these institutional and political factors in Chapters 4 and 6.

IV. DOES OPENNESS MATTER?

But before we can do so, we need to take account of a stream of revisionist literature which seems to controvert one of the major qualitative findings of our country studies, as well as of past comparative studies, that the degree of openness of an economy is an important determinant of its growth rate.

It is important to note more precisely what the country studies have established. They show that *changes* in policy which affect a country's degree of participation in international trade affect its economic performance. Studies such as Wade (1990) which argue that protection was rife even in the export-oriented NICs are therefore beside the point, for past comparative studies as well as our own country studies only establish that reducing the degree of protection raised the rate of growth of the relevant country—and even then, as we shall see below, there are important nuances. From this one can infer that the neoclassical theory of trade is of relevance for developing countries, and that moving to free trade would lead to an even higher growth rate, as that theory predicts. But as, apart from Hong Kong, there is no entirely free-trading nation, there can be no conclusive empirical evidence provided to confirm this inference.

Against this view the revisionists have mounted a three-pronged attack. One prong is theoretical, the second is statistical, and the third is based on country studies of the prime exhibits in the past in the 'outward-oriented' cupboard (Korea and Taiwan), being converted into shining examples of *dirigiste* trade and industrial policies. We discuss each in turn.

1. Theory

A self-styled 'new trade' theory (Helpman and Krugman, 1985) has been taken by some (see F. Stewart, 1982, and Helliner, 1985)—though not, one should add, by its progenitors (see Krugman, 1987)—to provide theoretical justification for departing from openness through the adoption of activist trade and industrial policies. Baldwin (1992) has neatly encapsulated this theory in a refurbished 'Baldwin envelope'. This shows that part of the new trade theory's case for intervention is the classic terms-of-trade type of argument for trade intervention, and the other part is a variant of the infant-industry argument for the domestic promotion of industry. Both are based on replacing the constant returns to scale and perfect competition assumption by increasing returns to scale and imperfect competition.

The classical terms-of-trade argument assumed that a country had some monopoly power in foreign trade. As this was a 'distortion' in international trade, standard theory accepted that an 'optimum tariff' would be its first best cure from the viewpoint of the national weal. However, a country would still be unwise to levy the optimum tariff, as it could lead to retaliation by its trading partners. In the ensuing trade war, as H. G. Johnson (1954) showed, the country could be worse off than in the pre-tariff situation. The wrinkle which has been added by the new trade theory is to replace the monopoly in international markets by oligopoly or monopolistic competition in the world market for a particular good. They then show that an appropriate trade policy response by the home country government could shift the super-normal profits earned in the international monopolistically competitive industry to the national firm. As with the classical terms-of-trade argument, though theoretically valid, its practical relevance is limited by the threat of retaliation. Moreover, even in the absence of retaliation, the few empirical studies that have been done to estimate the potential gains from trade intervention find them to be small (see Dixit, 1988, and Baldwin and Krugman, 1988a, b). Moreover, econometric studies of trade liberalization under imperfect competition and scale economies (see Richardson, 1989) have in fact strengthened the case for liberalization, as they show even larger gains from trade than under the assumption of perfect competition, because of 'the reductions in markups of price above marginal costs brought about by greater international competition and the increase in the average size of firms as competition eliminates small inefficient firms'.[75]

The second theoretical argument being mooted is a resurrection of a Listian type of argument emphasizing increasing returns and pecuniary externalities for infant industry protection (see Pack and Westphal, 1986). As is well known (see Corden, 1974, and Baldwin, 1969), if these exist, there could be grounds for government intervention.[76] But the first best policy will be some appropriate domestic subsidy rather than protection from foreign trade, following the central tenet of the modern theory of trade and welfare that in dealing with domestic distortions it is best to deal directly with the distortion; intervention in foreign trade being at best a third or fourth best policy.

A necessary condition for infant industry intervention to be justified is that the inputs per unit of outputs decrease more rapidly in that industry (or in other words, its total factor productivity increases) both relatively to (a) its foreign competitors, and (b) other industries in the country. But this condition is not sufficient, for in addition it is necessary that the discounted net present value of the losses incurred during the high-cost phase is recouped during the post-infancy phase to earn at least the social rate of return to investment in the economy (see Krueger and Tuncer, 1982, and Bell et al., 1984).

The TFP test, which provides only the necessary conditions for justifying infant industry promotion, was applied by Krueger and Tuncer to a sample to Turkish industry for 1963–76. They found there was no tendency for input per unit of output to fall more rapidly in more protected industries. Similarly, in a survey of the productivity performance of infant industries in a number of developing countries, Bell et al. concluded:

There is little evidence about productivity growth among infant industries in today's less developed countries. But the evidence does suggest that many infant firms have failed to reach international competitiveness—or if they have once reached it, have failed to maintain it. This inference is consistent with the record of overall industrial performance in these countries. It is also consistent with findings from various studies of the costs of protection in developing countries.[77]

However, as Bell et al. note, none of studies in their survey explicitly estimated any externalities generated by the relevant firms for other firms (and vice versa). One of the more important externalities that is adduced in support of the infant industry case is labour training. Assuming that workers cannot borrow against the returns to prospective human capital, they will be unable to finance the costs of any on-the-job training that develops general skills. If firms are to bear the cost of training in general skills, they may suffer a loss, and hence they may be unwilling to provide the training, which nevertheless is socially (at shadow prices) desirable. A social cost-benefit study of labour training in the public sector in India (Chakravarti, 1972) did find that the social rate of return to training was positive (and greater than the social discount rate), even though the private rate of return (to the firm) was negligible or negative. Public subsidization of labour training in industrial enterprises may thus be a valid form of industrial promotion, even though protection of industry (for the usual reasons of 'getting to the heart of the matter') will not be.

But it is important to note that the presumed externality—often labelled a pecuniary externality—in the case of labour training, actually turns out to be a case of a distortion in the working of the capital market. It is the correction of this distortion which requires government intervention, and not the existence of a pecuniary externality *per se*.

This illustrates the slippery notion of externalities as the uncompensated side-effects of a producer's or consumer's activity on other economic agents. Two theoretical points need to be kept in mind in their identification.

The first is a distinction made by James Buchanan and Craig Stubblebine between Pareto-relevant and Pareto-irrelevant externalities. Pareto-relevant externalities are said to be present when, in a competitive equilibrium, the marginal conditions for optimal resource allocation and hence for Pareto efficiency are violated. Then government intervention may be required. But not all the side-effects on consumers and producers in a highly interdependent market economy will result in Pareto-relevant externalities.

The second distinction, due to Jacob Viner, is between pecuniary and technological externalities. Pecuniary externalities are those in which one individual's activity level affects the financial circumstances of another. But this does not imply any resulting misallocation of resources. Consider, for example, a perfectly competitive economy in which there are continuous shifts in tastes and technology. Suppose that some group increases its consumption of whisky; the price rises, and this affects the welfare of other consumers of whisky. This has no significance for the efficiency of the economy, which *ex hypothesi* is perfectly competitive and hence (in the jargon) Pareto-efficient. Or suppose there is a cost-saving invention by one producer. He increases his output and reduces his price. Through market interdependence other producers lose rents and are hurt, and consumers gain (consumer's surplus). It is readily shown that the consumer gains and those of the cost-reducing producer are always greater than the losses of the inefficient producers. What is more, the cost-reducing producer must not take account of the losses of the inefficient producers, for if he did he would restrict output and would therefore be behaving as a quasi-monopolist; thus the industry's output level would be suboptimal.

Pecuniary externalities are therefore synonymous with market interdependence and the price system. They must be Pareto-irrelevant. By contrast, technological externalities are interdependencies between economic agents which are not mediated through the market, and hence not reflected in relative prices. A well-known example is the smoke emitted by a factory which raises the costs of a nearby laundry.

The pecuniary externalities associated with increasing returns were used by Scitovsky and Rosenstein-Rodan to advocate programmes of 'balanced growth' and 'big pushes' in the 1950s. The arguments being advanced for industrial strategies by, for instance, Pack and Westphal (1986) are of the same kind. But these pecuniary externalities are Pareto-irrelevant. If they were Pareto-relevant, then, as Scitovsky noted, 'the complete integration of all industries would be necessary to eliminate all divergences between private profit and public benefit',[78] or, as Rosenstein-Rodan advocated, 'the whole of industry to be created is to be treated and planned like one huge firm or trust'.[79] This so-called co-ordination of investment plans is, of course, nothing else but the planning syndrome—the search for a centrally determined investment plan which takes account not merely of current changes but of all future changes in the demand/supply of a myriad of goods. It is now known that because of imperfect information and irreducible uncertainty no market economy can ever attain the inter-temporal Pareto-efficient outcome of the Utopian Arrow–Debreu theoretical construct, where there are markets for all 'commodities' indexed by date and state of nature till kingdom come. But neither can the planners achieve this outcome, as Hayek and Mises pointed out years ago in the debate about the efficiency of Soviet-type central planning.[80] The recent collapse of this system world-wide is a resounding empirical confirmation of the validity of the Austrian insight that in the real world imperfect markets are superior to imperfect planning.

2. Cross-Country Regressions

Establishing a conclusive econometric causal link between openness and growth is the Holy Grail for the positivist temperament of many contemporary economists. This search has been bedeviled by two lacunae. The first is the lack of a properly specified theoretical model which would predict the effects of openness on growth (the issue discussed in the previous section). Lacking such a model, various *ad hoc* justifications have been provided for econometric exercises that have hitherto been undertaken to link various measures of openness to growth. The second is that it has proved very difficult to provide a statistical measure of openness. What is required is a measure which in, say, the standard diagram of a 'two by two' open economy facing constant terms of trade, shows the deviation of the economy's actual production and trade equilibrium point from what it would have been under free trade. Apart from Hong Kong no country has been a complete free trader, nor is any country completely autarkic, so statistical tests looking at changing trade regimes over time in one country, or at differences in trade regimes across countries, must have some summary measure of these differences. The earlier studies (e.g. Little, Scitovsky, and Scott, 1970, and Balassa, 1971) used measures of average effective protection (EPR) or domestic resource costs (DRC). But it is immensely time-consuming to obtain decent EPR estimates, particularly when protection in developed and developing countries increasingly takes the form of non-tariff barriers of growing complexity. Hence EPR estimates are few and far between,[81] so that they cannot be used to conduct a conclusive time-series or cross-section econometric analysis of openness and growth. Two alternative measures used are, first, subjective indices of trade bias (World Bank, 1987; Papageorgiou et al. 1991), and second, rates of export growth (or some variant) as a proxy for different degrees of anti-export bias. They are taken to be the independent variables in regressions testing the effects of openness on growth. Neither has been found persuasive by the sceptics, as there seems to be no agreement on the subjective indices, while the studies using the exports route are subject to a fatal criticism recently levelled by Sheehy. He shows that similar bivariate tests between the growth rate and other components of GDP also support the promotion of *all* major components of GDP. As he rightly concludes, 'These results in no way overturn the case for an export promotion strategy. They merely indicate that a large body of evidence that is supposed to demonstrate the superiority of this strategy has no bearing on the controversy.'[82]

Dollar (1992) has constructed an openness index for the period 1976–85 based on the distortions in real exchange rates and in their variability, derived from the Summers and Heston (1991) data on relative price levels and corrected for the effects of differing factor endowments (proxied by GDP per capita) on the price of non-traded goods. As he himself notes, there are serious anomalies in the rankings. Thus Hong Kong, which is as 'outward-oriented' an economy as you can get, is found to be less outward-oriented than Sri Lanka, Pakistan, and a whole host of other countries. Taiwan is nearly at the bottom of the most open quartile (and more closed than Peru), Korea is in the middle! Nevertheless, using this index, he finds it 'highly correlated with per capita GDP growth in a large sample of developing countries'.[83]

The most serious attempt at a rigorous derivation of an openness index is by Leamer (1988). He estimates the net trade flows and trade intensities from a Heckscher–Ohlin model with nine factors of production, calibrated for one year, 1982. The residuals between the predicted and actual trade intensity ratios are taken as an indicator of trade barriers. Two indices are produced, one for 'openness', which measures the effects of trade restrictions, and another for 'intervention', which also includes the effects of export subsidies.

Leamer provides a detailed critique of his own indices. The most credible are his 'adjusted trade intensity measures'. But as he concludes, 'What seems clear is that in the absence of direct measures of barriers, it will be impossible to determine the degree of openness for most countries with much subjective confidence.'[84]

Nevertheless, Edwards argues that 'the Leamer indexes are imperfect proxies (although I think the best available ones) of the theoretical trade intervention and trade distortions index.'[85] He finds a robust positive relationship in a cross-section of 30 developing countries (for which the Leamer indices are available), between growth rates of GDP per capita for 1970–82 (and also 1960–82), and the Leamer openness and trade intervention indices. However, as one emerging law is that 'all econometric evidence is equivocal', I doubt if the die-hard positivists with different prior beliefs will be persuaded by this.[86]

As the case for openness ultimately depends upon its effects on the efficiency of investment, ideally we would need to estimate the social rates of return to investment in different countries, with the presumption that they would vary positively with openness. The Little–Scitovsky–Scott study was in part based on the social rates of return calculated on Little–Mirrlees (1974) lines for a sample of projects in the countries they studied. Unfortunately we do not have such rates of return available for a large number of countries and over time to provide the conclusive case in favor of openness and growth that the sceptics seem to want. However, the *1991 World Development Report* correlates the rates of return, estimated on the basis of Squire and van der Tak (1975), with a measure of trade orientation based on an index of tariff and non-tariff barriers in 32 countries for projects financed by the World Bank and the International Finance Corporation. The estimated *ex post* rates of return fall systematically with the restrictiveness of the trade regime (World Bank, 1991: 82–3). The same is true of various other measures of distortions such as the black-market premium on foreign exchange. But these conclusions are heavily dependent, as we have seen, upon the classification of countries by differing degrees of 'openness'.

Finally, it maybe noted that Riedel (1994) has incorporated this rate-of-return channel into the cross-country regression framework by estimating a regression which assumes a linear relationship between openness and the return to investment, with the growth rate of exports g^x as the proxy for openness, given by

$$g = a_0 + \left[a_1 + a_2 g^X\right] \cdot \left(I/Y\right) + a_3 g^L.$$

Fitting World Bank data for the 75 developing countries for which it is available for these variables, averaged over 1965 to 1978, yields a relationship (where the constant term was omitted as it was not found to be significantly different (from zero):

$$g = \left[0.07 + 1.17 g^X\right]\left(I/Y\right) + 0.75 g^L.$$
$$\left(3.05\right) \left(7.00\right) \qquad \left(4.56\right)$$
$$\left(\ \right)\text{-}t \text{ statistics}; \quad R^2 = 0.61; \quad F = 58.26.$$

That a_0 was not significantly different from zero provides further support, as Riedel notes, 'for Scott's view that investment and labor force growth provide a complete explanation of growth, leaving no residual to be attributed to exogenous changes in technology. These results suggest that the return to investment rises about one percent for every percentage point increase in the rate of export growth.'[87]

3. Case-Studies of Asian Miracle Economies

The most audacious of the revisionists have, however, sought to use the case-study method to challenge what Little (1982) called the neoclassical consensus on trade and growth. It is the qualitative evidence produced by three counter-revolutionaries concerning Japan, Korea, and Taiwan (Johnson, 1982, Amsden, 1989, and Wade, 1990) which has been found the most persuasive by many in questioning neoclassical orthodoxy.[88]

We therefore turn to two of these studies. The most cogent is the book by Wade on Taiwan. He concedes that

It is clear that many of the conditions prescribed by neoclassical development theory were present in Taiwan by the early 1960s. Since then, the real exchange rate has been kept roughly equal . . . Effective protection has been low . . . Wages have been at market-clearing levels, bank interest rates have been kept relatively high, government has run budget surpluses, savings and investment have been very high, the labor force has been well trained, the industrial structure includes a sizeable sector of small firms unable to exercise oligopoly power, and the domestic environment has been stable . . . In short Taiwan seems to meet the neoclassical growth conditions unusually well. Yet other evidence shows that the government has been intervening for decades, often quite aggressively, to alter the trade and industrial profile of the economy in ways that it judges to be desirable. We then face a formidable identification problem. How can we decide to what extent Taiwan's exceptional economic performance is due to the presence of many of the neoclassical growth conditions and to what extent to the government's selective promotion policies? Ultimately I cannot resolve the issue.[89]

But he believes that neoclassical economists have overlooked the fact that 'the government has indeed been guiding the market on a scale much greater than is consistent with neoclassical prescriptions or with the practice of Anglo-American economics'.[90] It is this fact about the undoubted *dirigisme* to be found in Taiwan, Korea, and Japan which seems to be at the heart of the dispute (reflecting their prior beliefs) between those who believe that interventionist trade and industrial policies are desirable and those who do not. The question boils down to, what were their governments doing which was different from what was done in many other developing countries, for instance India, and was their stellar growth performance due to or despite this *dirigisme*?

This view of the 'market governance' school, that industrial policy was responsible for the success of the Asian miracle economies, has also found some support in the World Bank's recent study *The East Asian Miracle* (1993). But Little (1994), in a persuasive critique of both the case-studies and the *Miracle* study, shows that their case is far from established.

The revisionism of both Amsden (Korea) and Wade (Taiwan), as well as that supported by the *Miracle* study, is based on the infant industry argument. As noted above, to establish this case it must be shown that industrial *dirigisme* yielded social rates of return equal to or above the social discount rate in the industries sought to be protected or promoted. No such evidence is provided by Wade or Amsden.

Little provides estimates for rates of return based on the Scott method, for Korea for the period of 1963–82. He compares the returns in the period 1963–73, when the Korean economy was opened up, with those during 1974–9 when it adopted a policy of promoting heavy industry. These were 31% and 19.2% respectively. 'These figures', he claims, 'are bad news for heavy industry fundamentalists, and those who stress the importance and value of the government's industrial policies.'[91] Moreover, they unequivocally show that the effects of changes in policy, towards openness in the earlier period and towards *dirigisme* in the second, had the effects predicted by the neoclassicals.

Further support for this position is provided by the World Bank's *Miracle* study, which has used the roundabout route of total factor productivity growth to assess the value of industrial policy in eight high-performing Asian economies (HPAEs), of which five—Hong Kong, Singapore, Indonesia, Malaysia, and Thailand—are in our sample, the other three being Japan, Korea, and Taiwan. It first asks whether the policies were effective, by examining whether sectoral growth at the two-digit ISIC level departed from the predictions of the standard Heckscher–Ohlin model—that is, from the pattern which would have occurred with a reliance purely on market forces. For Korea, the prime exhibit in the revisionist cupboard, it concluded: 'the quantitative importance of government intervention to alter the structure of production is not confirmed at the sectoral level.'[92] For Japan, Singapore, and Hong Kong the results are inconclusive, whilst for Taiwan 'growth was market-conforming; government intervention did little to alter the structure of production at the sectoral level'.[93]

But perhaps selective promotion of infant industries led to faster TFP growth rates in the favoured sectors? Data on sectoral growth rates was only available for Korea. Here the *Miracle* study finds 'no simple correlation between TFP and promoted sectors',[94] and that 'the major reason for Korea's manufacturing success lay in high individual values [for TFP growth] for most sectors in most periods'.[95] Moreover, Dollar and Sokoloff have estimated that TFP growth in light labour-intensive industry in Korea (during 1963–79) was 7.4% per annum, as compared with only 3.3% for the capital-intensive heavy industries promoted by Korean industrial policy.[96]

The *Miracle* study also runs a regression using the Dollar openness index (discussed above) as the explanatory variable for the growth of TFP in 51 countries, and finds it highly significant.[97] Little remarks:

This was taken as a measure of openness. It could also be taken as a measure of the efficiency of the use of resources. Neoclassical authors and common-sense would, of course, claim it was both. The proportion of manufactured exports in total exports was also significant. On the above bases what does the Miracle conclude concerning selective intervention? The most selective intervention in the HPAE's—the commitment to manufactured exports—was also the most general (p. 325). Eliminating the double-talk, this should read 'The least selective intervention in the HPAE's—the commitment to manufactured exports—was the most successful.'[98]

If the spectacular performance of the Asian HPAEs (whose miraculous nature is questioned by Little, as it can be explained in conventional terms of a high rate of investment efficiently deployed) was despite rather than because of the undoubted *dirigiste* policies followed in many of them, the question arises what was the real purpose of these industrial policies? Some theoretical aspects of the recent theory of industrial organization are helpful in providing an explanation.

While much of the recent marriage between trade theory and industrial organization has been concerned with various price-theoretic aspects of monopolistic competition, little use has been made of the aspects which cover problems of corporate governance when there is a separation of ownership and control. The relevant issue is what Demsetz calls the control function of private wealth, and the inequality in its distribution.[99]

This role is based on the problem of maintaining beneficial control over resources in the presence of economies of size. I do not refer here to the wealth required to pay for inputs on a scale demanded by large firms, but, rather to the wealth required to reduce the degree to which ownership is separated from the control of these resources. The maintenance of such control requires large amount of *individual, private* wealth in settings where large-scale enterprise would be efficient except for resolving the problem of control. The large-scale enterprise requires an ownership interest sufficiently large to encourage the owner(s) to undertake the task of overseeing management and other inputs, and of setting a proper course for the enterprise.

A diffuse ownership structure discourages this undertaking because of well-known free rider problems. No owner of a trivial fraction of equity has enough interest or power to take the problem of control seriously; leaving this task to someone else makes more sense. However, this someone, if he or she is to exist, must own a large personal stake in the firm. An undivided large equity stake requires considerable personal wealth when the efficient size of the firm is large.

Collectively owned assets, whether owned by the state through socialism or through diffuse corporate shareholdings, do not offer a practical substitute for a large private and personal equity stake. The collective characteristic of such alternatives frustrates the resolution of the free rider problem. Neither nationalization nor diffuse private shareholdings can be expected to establish the beneficial control that is characteristic of a large, private, individual equity stake. Hence, if large enterprises are to be maintained efficiently, it is important that many individuals hold enough private wealth to finance large equity stakes in these firms. Resolution of the control problem is a productive function of the having of wealth.[100]

Furthermore, in a later article he notes that 'For U.S. companies as large as the Fortune 500, the aggregate fraction of equity owned by the five largest shareholders is about one-quarter. For Japanese and several important European countries this fraction is much larger.'[101]

The implications for the theory of trade and growth are that, within the two-factor HOS model, as a county's dynamic comparative advantage shifts up the ladder of comparative advantage with capital–labour ratios rising with capital accumulation and growth, this control problem will become worse. To effectuate their emerging comparative advantage in more capital-intensive and *ipso facto* larger-scale enterprises, they will have to solve the control problem. A comparison of the four South-East Asian NICs (two of which, Hong Kong and Singapore, are also in our sample) and India provides contrasting examples of how this effectuation can come about. It also provides an explanation for the different outcomes from the alternative types of *dirigiste* industrial policies adopted in, for instance, Korea and India.

Essentially there are three ways in which 'controllable' investment can be made to overcome the agency problem in large capital-demanding enterprises. The first is through sufficient concentration of private wealth, and some institutional means for it to be spread over a number of enterprises while maintaining control by some concentrated owners.[102] The second is by allowing foreign equity to control local large-scale firms. The third is for the 'government to gather the net wealth of its citizens into a tax supported fund that can be large enough to make investments in a large capital-demanding enterprise, while maintaining concentrated ownership positions in these enterprises'.[103] This last is likely to be ineffective and inefficient for the usual reasons of 'bureaucratic failure', as the functioning of numerous public enterprises in developing countries attests, as compared to the other two forms, where the self-interest of the owner is more clearly tied to the profitability of the enterprise.

The differences in industrial policies (or lack of them) and their relative efficiency in the four clearly outward-oriented NICs—Korea, Taiwan, Hong Kong, and Singapore—and the inward-oriented India can now be assessed. The most striking feature of the effects of the *dirigiste* industrial policies in Korea was their promotion of the *chaebol*, a diversified business group on the pattern of the Japanese *zaibatsu*. The major instrument was long-term subsidized credits. Amsden (1989) provides details of how the government used this instrument to favour a select number of industrial groups, once the industrial structure evolved away from light to medium and heavy industry. The selection was based on being ruthless in allowing the exit of badly managed or bankrupt groups, and using the attainment of export targets as a monitoring device for continuing the subsidies. Given that, by and large, the net effect of Korea's trade policies was neutral (as even the counter-revolutionaries accept), the export success of a group was a pretty good index of its efficiency. Moreover, while 'Korea's stock market remained moribund . . . the chaebol remained closely held family concerns'.[104] Moreover, they controlled a highly diversified set of enterprises (a pattern also found in many other developing countries—see below), and gradually accounted for a large share of the national product. 'In 1984 the three largest chaebol alone accounted for a staggering 36% of national product.'[105]

Given the relative poverty of Korea in the 1960s, as well as the relative equality in its wealth distribution when it embarked on its spectacular industrialization, the industrial policies of Korea can be seen as creating highly concentrated private holdings of wealth, whose owners were chosen by a relatively efficient dynamic monitoring process based on export success (under a relatively neutral overall trade regime). The state transferred wealth from the rest of the citizens to the *chaebol* (through its credit subsidies), which they then multiplied through their spectacular growth performance.[106]

On the Demsetz theory, it was the creation of this inequality in wealth holdings through its industrial policy which allowed the problem of control to be solved when Korea's dynamic comparative advantage shifted away from light towards more large-scale industry in the 1970s and 1980s. But openness was crucial both in providing a simple monitor of the relative efficiency of the new wealth holders and in ensuring that this industrial promotion did not go against the grain of the country's comparative advantage.[107] That this was the aim of Korea's *dirigisme* is given further strength by the explicit statement by President Park Chung Hee (who oversaw the Korean miracle) in his book *The Country, the Revolution and I*, 'of allowing "millionaires who promoted the reform" to enter the central stage, "thus encouraging national capitalism" '.[108] 'The millionaires were envisioned by Park to have created large-size plants to realize economies of scale. He saw the government's role as one of overseeing the millionaires to avoid any abuse of power.'[109]

In Taiwan, by contrast, the Nationalist government 'has been much concerned to prevent large-scale capital from acquiring enough autonomy to shape the regime'.[110] This is in part because of its past ideological 'anti-big capitalist conviction reinforced by fear of the political potential of native Taiwanese economic power'.[111] The industrial structure has therefore been allowed to evolve more 'naturally', with a preponderance of small firms mainly in light industry. The capital-intensive industries when they were developed, 'like steel, shipbuilding and petrochemicals', were kept in the public sector.[112] This is the second route to effectuating emerging comparative advantage in more capital-intensive lines. Once again it is the *dirigisme* involved in the latter which, it is suggested by Wade, goes against the neoclassical policy paradigm on openness. But once again it is better seen as a response to the agency problem in large-scale capital-intensive firms, outlined by Demsetz. Moreover, as one would expect, the efficiency of this solution compared to that based on the private sector is questionable. Wade reports:

A recent study compared the performance of 12 public manufacturing enterprises with that of the 300 top private firms in terms of financial indicators such as rate of return on sales and assets, over the 1976–84 period. By all indicators the public enterprises' average performance was worse. The study went on to compare the performance of the four public enterprises which face the most competition from private firms against that of their competitors. The result was the same.[113]

However, in Taiwan, outside the public sector there has been a growing importance of business groups[114] and in the concentration of industrial assets,[115] which suggests that, if the government had not pre-empted the 'basic industries' for itself, the emerging concentration of industrial wealth could have been expected to solve the Demsetz control problem.

Singapore represents an example of an open economy which has solved the control problem of effectuating its dynamic comparative advantage by relying on foreign equity investment (see Findlay, Wellisz, and associates, 1993). In 1963, 'foreign investment contributed 57% of value added and exports and 32% of employment in the manufacturing sector. . . . In 1980 these ratios had risen to 81% of value added, 72% of employment and no less than 93% of exports.'[116] The government has been *dirigiste*, 'involved in selective intervention into the pattern of production, consciously attempting to "pick winners" and to promote "high tech" projects that are supposed to represent the wave of the future'.[117] But, given the neutrality of its trade regime, it has not attracted the 'tariff jumping' type of direct investment which in other countries has led to low or negative social rates of return (see Lal, 1975, and Streeten and Lall, 1977). But, as in Korea in the late 1970s and early 1980s, this *dirigisme* has occasionally come unstuck. For instance, when the government raised mininum wages in the 1980s to induce investment in industries that were a couple of rungs up its 'ladder of comparative advantage', it led the country into a serious recession. But, as in Korea, these mistakes in resource allocation in labour-abundant and land-scarce small economies are easily recognized (see Chapter 10), and they have been speedily reversed.

By contrast, Hong Kong has been a virtual *laissez-faire* economy. As a result, its industrial structure is dominated by

small plants owned and operated by local residents, using relatively little capital and unsophisticated technology. These small firms have been extremely adaptable and flexible, adept at moving into profitable lines and out of unprofitable ones very quickly. The early dependence on cheap clothing, footwear, plastic toys and so on has been replaced by more expensive clothing with higher value added including fashion items, and electronics.[118]

Before we conclude that the Singapore outcome is 'better' than the Hong Kong one, we need to consider the productivity of capital in the two countries. If, *faute de mieux*, we measure it by the incremental capital-output ratio, in Hong Kong this ranged from 2.4 in 1961–73 to about 3 in the 1970s and 1980s. In Singapore, by contrast, it has risen from about 2.6 in the 1960–73 period to 6.2 in 1974–7 and about 5.0 in 1978–83.[119] Hong Kong has therefore been able to maintain a higher growth rate of consumption per capita than Singapore 'with a relatively modest investment rate of 25% through efficient allocation of capital to labour intensive industry'.[120]

Finally we consider India, whose history of industrialization provides a vivid illustration of the importance for efficiency of openness, as well as the Demsetz control problem. India was one of the pioneers of industrialization in the Third World. The first modern textile factory was set up with Indian enterprise and capital in 1851, the first jute mill whose output was exported in 1854; the first steel mill was in 1911. As this was a period when the British Raj followed the policies of free trade and *laissez-faire* of the metropolitan power, these industries could not have had social rates of return below their private ones. Moreover, they clearly reflected India's comparative advantage. India's industrial performance and manufacturing export performance were among the best in the world (Lal, 1988*a*). The form of business organization that evolved to take account of the Densetz problem (particularly in the more capital-intensive industries) was the business group, and the managing agency system. This allowed family businesses to exercise control over a number of industries by having a strategic equity holding in each (see Rungta, 1970). As Hazari noted in his detailed study of the structure of the corporate private sector in the 1950s (that is, soon after Independence), 'the Tata's seem to hold only about 5% of the equity of Tata Steel, while the total controlling block (most of it, held by a trust), in Indian Iron equity is only 17%.'[121] He estimated that in 1951 the 13 largest business groups accounted for 33.09% of the share capital and 38–41% of the gross capital stock of all non-governmental companies.

With Independence, India turned its back on an open economy, and also, on ideological grounds, sought to counter the 'economic power' of corporate business by reserving the so-called commanding heights of the economy—capital-intensive heavy industry—for the public sector. As could be expected, even in industries like steel, where India had a comparative advantage (see W. A. Johnson, 1966), the substitution of the public-sector mode of dealing with the control problem rather than private-sector one based on business groups led to inevitable inefficiencies and lower, even negative rates of return on the investments made (see Lal, 1988b). India, of course, also placed onerous controls on foreign equity on grounds of economic nationalism; while the reversal of openness led to declining and eventually negative total factor productivity (TFP) growth rates in much of Indian industry (see Ahluwalia, 1985).

Enough has been said to suggest that, the success of the industrial policies of some of the NICs as compared with India was due to their working with the grain of their comparative advantage, and in not preventing, or in actively promoting, an efficient private-sector-based solution (except for Taiwan-with the usual dire results) to the Demsetz control problem. If this interpretation is correct, then even the *dirigiste* policies of the Asian NICs can be looked upon as supporting the neoclassical case rather than that of the self-styled market governance school deriving from Chalmers-Johnson and others.

It is also worth noting one important feature of the differences in response to the control problem in Singapore and Korea on the one hand and India and Taiwan on the other. It was the confidence of the state in itself in the former group that allowed it to foster what in the latter were considered to be rival centres of economic and thence political power, while Hong Kong followed the natural evolution of its comparative advantage and its effectuation without any obvious political mediation. Enough has been said to show that in terms of its citizens' welfare the Hong Kong route was certainly no worse and probably better than that of the comparators. This leads naturally to questions concerning political economy.[122]

V. THE THREE-FACTOR OPEN-ECONOMY GROWTH
FRAMEWORK

It is surprising that the revisionists have attempted to base their case on the Far Eastern NICs, in which, as we have seen above, it cannot be supported. A much better case is made, at least indirectly, by some of the authors of our case-studies. Thus Maddison (Brazil and Mexico) finds that neither *dirigiste* polices nor changes in them can explain the spectacular growth performance of both economies till 1980. As he notes for Brazil:

> generally, foreign analysts have taken a benign view of the dynamic impact of this dirigiste protectionist system. [They] have pointed to the successful transformation from a relatively simple manufacturing structure in 1929 and high concentration on one agricultural export crop to a much more sophisticated economy in the 1980s, with great flexibility in producing new export products.[123]

Both countries 'had respectable growth in TFP in 1950-80. Brazil 2.2% a year and Mexico 2.3%.'[124]

For Sri Lanka and Malaysia, Bruton argues that, despite remaining relatively open economies, they both failed in 'finding a new source of support and dynamism if they were not to suffer a decline'.[125] He argues that they both needed to build up their transformation capacity, which would have 'eased dependence on the traditional sector', by a move

> to new activities. Some protection would have been necessary. Such protection would then constitute a form of investment—investment in the creation of a more flexible, responsive economy. . . . The trick, of course is to protect without imposing severe distortions on the system and to ensure that during the protection, capacity in new activities emerges. It is no small trick, and our basic criticism of the policies in both countries is that they failed to achieve it.[126]

His preferred policy to achieve this transformation capacity is the maintenance of an undervalued exchange rate.

Hansen (Egypt and Turkey) is even more blunt. 'Conventional stereotypes do not apply', he writes. 'Market orientation (Egypt in the 1930s and Turkey in the 1980s) has not generally been accompanied by high growth or equity; import substitution and etatism have not generally been accompanied by low growth and improved equity.'[127]

How can these judgements be reconciled with those of our other authors, whose countries seem to fit the neoclassical story much better, as well as the other evidence we have noted which supports the link between openness, the efficiency of investment, and thence growth performance? Clearly, neither the aggregative neoclassical growth model (even in the more useful amended form due to Scott) nor the framework of the statistical cross-section regression studies is very useful for this purpose. For these approaches suggest that there is a unilinear path to development, whereas the above examples from our country studies show that even with the seemingly robust policy of openness this is not necessarily always the case.

The problem is clearly highlighted by the two-factor neoclassical growth model. Within this model a poor, developing country starts from an initial position of a low capital stock per capita, and hence low income per capita.

As the economy accumulates capital, it progresses on the traverse to the relevant equilibrium growth path. The real wage will be rising and the rental rate on capital falling.[128] The long–run movement in the two key factor prices which emerges from this model is clear. But even a cursory examination of the undoubtedly patchy data on these variables for developing countries (both past and present)[129] will show that these predictions are by no means borne out. For many countries, as they have grown, returns on capital have not fallen nor real wages risen markedly.

Moreover, the neglect of land as a factor of production is particularly serious in developing countries, for whom agriculture and primary-product-producing activities remain of importance. Two theoretical routes are available out of this conundrum. The first is the celebrated Lewis model of surplus labour[130] and its extension into a two-sector dualistic model by Ranis and Fei.[131] In these models, during the surplus labour phase, the modern sector grows through capital accumulation and the transference of labour from the traditional sector at a constant real wage. Thus, during this early phase of development, the rise in real wages and fall in profits predicted by the neoclassical model will not occur. Once the surplus labour has been absorbed the model reverts to the standard neoclassical model.[132]

However, the plausibility of the surplus labour phase of the Lewis model has been questioned on both theoretical and empirical grounds;[133] as such, it is not a very useful framework for us to order the different development patterns emerging in our country studies.

The second route, and the one we adopt, is to combine the neoclassical growth model with an extension of the Heckscher–Ohlin model which has three factors of production: capital, labour, and land. This has been done in a model by Anne Krueger.[134] Countries start off with different endowments of the three factors of production, which can be depicted in a triangular resource-endowment simplex (due to Leamer)[135] that has the three factors of production—land, labour, and capital—as its three vertices (see Fig. 2.4).

Assume for simplicity that all goods are produced through fixed-proportions techniques, so that there is a single input vector corresponding to each commodity. The production functions are the same all over the world, in keeping with the Heckscher–Ohlin tradition. Free trade is assumed. For simplicity we also assume that all goods are traded.[136]

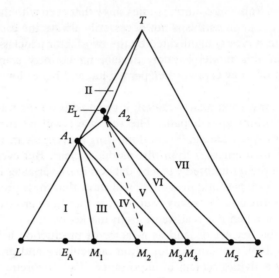

	Outputs Produced	Wage Rate
Region I	A_1, M_1	W_1
Region II	A_1, A_2	$W_2 > W_1$
Region III	A_1, M_1, M_2	$W_3 > W_1$
Region IV	A_1, M_2, M_3	$W_4 > W_3$
Region V	A_1, A_2, M_3, M_4	$W_5 > W_4$
Region VI	A_2, M_4, M_5	$W_6 > W_5$
Region VII	A_2, M_5	$W_7 > W_6 > W_2$

Fig 2.4. The three-factor, n-good model

Let us assume that in the World Economy there are five manufactured goods indexed from 1 to 5, produced with only labour and capital. They are of increasing capital intensity, and their input vectors are shown as $M_1, \ldots, M_5$ along the labour (L) and capital (K) edge of the resource endowment triangle in Fig. 2.4. In addition there are two agricultural goods. The first, A_1, is produced with only labour and land, and lies on the labour and land (T) edge of the endowment triangle. The second, A_2, uses all three factors of production, but it is more land-intensive than the agricultural good A_1.

The seven points representing the input vectors and the three axis coordinates are connected by line segments, to divide the endowment triangle into seven 'regions of diversification'[137] for a given set of commodity prices for the seven commodities. The factor endowment vectors of different countries can also be represented by points in land–labour–capital space in the endowment triangle. Then it can be shown that countries with endowment points in the same region of diversification will have the same factor prices and produce the same commodities with the vector inputs given by the vertices of the regions of diversification. The commodities produced in the seven regions are listed in the note to Fig. 2.4. Given commodity prices, relative factor intensities determine factor prices in each of these regions.

Unlike the case of the two-good, two-factor open economy, once we have three factors and a number of commodities being produced, then there are a multiplicity of efficient development paths, which depend upon (a) the initial factor endowment (and changes in it), (b) technology (which will be changing over time), (c) relative commodity prices (which will also be altering), and, most important, (d) the relative rates of growth of labour and capital, which will determine the path of the economy's endowment ratio in the Leamer triangle. To see the mechanics of the model, consider two alternative paths of a country's endowment in Fig. 2.4. The first is of, say, a land- and capital-scarce but labour-abundant country, whose initial endowment point E_A is on, or close to, the labour–capital axis. With capital accumulating faster than the growth of the labour force, assume the country which we label labour-abundant moves from region I to region III to IV. In this process it moves up the ladder of comparative advantage with respect to manufactured goods, with rising capital intensity. Hence on this development path the wage rises and the rental on capital falls. Moreover, with land scarcity, the rents on land will rise as the economy moves along the labour–capital axis, with both the capital stock and labour force growing. Moreover, as the scarcity of land is likely to make agriculture uncompetitive, most land will be progressively urbanized.

The second path is for a land-abundant but labour- and capital-scarce country, whose initial endowment point E_L is assumed to lie in the region of diversification II, where it produces both the relatively labour-intensive agricultural good A_1 and the land- and-capital-intensive good A_2. We label this country as land abundant. Assume, as in the previous case, that both capital and labour are growing. The economy's land-to-labour ratio will be falling, and its capital–labour and capital–land ratios rising over time. Suppose this path of the economy's changing factor endowment is given by the dashed line from E_L. The economy will then move from region II through VII and then from VI through V to IV. In this process it will begin to industrialize as soon as it moves into region VII, but in the most capital-intensive manufacture. Over time it will move into regions which require specialization in increasingly more labour-intensive goods. The factor price consequence of this development path (in line with the emerging and changing comparative advantage of the economy) will be a falling wage rate and, from the time the economy moves into region VII, rising rental rates on capital and land. Clearly, the functional distributional (and *ipso facto* political) implications of the required path of wages on this stylized land-abundant open economy's development path (with a falling wage) would be very different from those of the stylized labour-abundant case (with rising wages), as predicted by the standard two-factor models. But note that, even though the wage might be falling for some time in the course of the land-abundant country's development, it will still be higher than for the labour-intensive country until both wage paths converge on the region of specialization in region IV.[138]

This is the basis for Krueger's statement that

First, the distinction between poor and underdeveloped countries emerges clearly from the model. A 'poor' country is one with an unfavorable land-man endowment. An underdeveloped country is one with a relatively small endowment of capital per person. An underdeveloped country, however, could conceivably have a higher *per capita* income and real wage than a 'more developed' but poor country. Second, a country abundantly endowed with land and therefore with a relatively high wage would not necessarily have a comparative advantage in labor-intensive manufactures even in its early stages of capital accumulation: the real wage at which persons would leave agriculture might be too high. In such an instance, the capital-labor ratio in manufacturing would be higher in the early stages of development than in a poorer country, while the output per unit of capital and the rate of return on capital would be lower than in a lower-wage country.[139]

Thus the three-factor model of trade and growth provides us with a useful organizing framework for thinking about our sample of countries. First, by emphasizing the initial resource endowments, it provides an obvious anchor, for the initial conditions which we had hypothesized (see the Introduction) would be a major determinant of the different outcomes concerning poverty and growth in our countries. Second, by yielding a number of alternative 'efficient' development paths, it would help to explain the odd departures from the viewpoint of standard two-factor neo-classical growth theory with its unilinear development path in terms of movements in the key factor prices, as well as deleterious effects of protection on resource allocation. Third, this framework should also help to explain poverty and growth outcomes, in so far as both the redressal of poverty and various aspects of equity are related to movements in real wages.

Finally, and most important, in assessing the reasons for government actions impinging on growth and poverty in our different countries, interest-based explanations may be expected to have some validity. If the effects on factor rewards of public policies are reflected in interest-group pressures on the polity, there will be some links between the changing factor-price implications of the different development paths and policy. These factor-proportion-based influences on the polity must not, however, be taken to provide a deterministic explanation of the politics of our different countries.

Ideas, ideologies, hysteresis, and chance (Machiavelli's *fortuna*) must obviously play an important part in the actual historical outcomes. Nevertheless, we have found the three-factor framework of the development of an open economy to be the most useful in making comparisons from our country studies.

To this end, Fig. 2.5 shows the location of our countries in the endowment triangle for which data was available (from Leamer, 1984) for 1958 and the end of 1978. In the Leamer data set, the capital stock variable was derived as the accumulated and discounted gross domestic investment flows since 1948, assuming an average life of 15 years. It includes

residential capital and capital used in the service sector. Furthermore, the figure is translated into dollars at the current exchange rate and is consequently excessively sensitive to exchange rate fluctuations. In addition, it includes no human capital, though this is probably unimportant since investments in physical and human capital maybe almost proportional, and if they are, the total capital figure would be a constant multiple of the physical capital figure that is used.[140]

The labour variable was derived as the number of economically active population. 'It fails to distinguish parttime and seasonal workers fron full time workers. It excludes non-market work such as employment on family-owned farms and work in the home. No adjustment is made for differences in weekly hours worked or vacation time'.[141]

The land variable is the permanent cropped and arable land area adjusted for climatic conditions, following a quantitative schema given by Trewartha.[142] But this concept of 'arable' land 'does not adequately address the vast differences in fecundity in different parcels of land'.[143] Nor is there any adjustment for the mineral natural resources to be found in the land endowments of different countries.[144]

There are thus obvious measurement problems associated with this data set, and hence our classification of our countries into the various groups on its basis should not be taken as being any more than heuristic. Nevertheless, we believe that the classification is illuminating.

We need to classify these countries in terms of relative factor scarcities (based on the physical definitions of these endowments), as these will determine their changing comparative advantage. In a three-factor framework, this factor scarcity is not unambiguous. Relative factor abundance and scarcity, and hence comparative advantage, must be judged against that of their trading partners, which, as most of our countries are 'small', can be taken to be in relation to the whole of the free trading world. Leamer (1987) provides an estimate of the aggregate endowments of capital, labour, and land for 38 countries which account for most of the free world's trade.

From these we can derive the 'world endowment' point (WE in Fig. 2.5) as described in the note to Table 2.9.

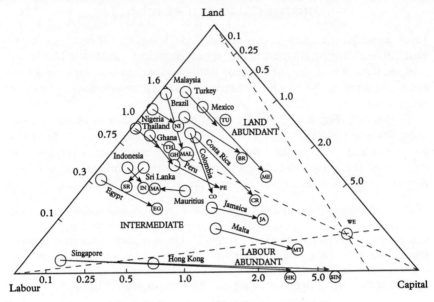

Fig 2.5. Resource endowments, 1958–78

Data for Fig. 2.5, from Leamer (1984), Table B.1

Derivation of ratios for 1958

	Capital	Active labour	Land, permanent crop and arable	K/L	K/land	land/L
	current million dollars 1958	thousands 1958	thousand hectares 1960			
Brazil	13,395	21,430	30,254	0.63	0.44	1.41
Columbia	3,153	4,500	5,051	0.70	0.62	1.12
Costa Rica	338	350	484	0.97	0.70	1.38
Egypt	545	7,380	2,548	0.07	0.21	0.35
Ghana	664	2,630	2,541	0.25	0.26	0.97
Hong Kong	747	1,190	14	0.63	53.36	0.01
Indonesia	4,381	32,740	16,740	0.13	0.26	0.51
Jamaica	718	610	233	1.18	3.08	0.38
Madagascar			2,770			
Malawi			1,971			
Malaysia	275	2,730	4,287	0.10	0.06	1.57
Malta	121	100	16	1.21	7.56	0.16
Mauritius	177	200	93	0.89	1.90	0.47
Mexico	9,153	10,260	24,908	0.89	0.37	2.43
Nigeria	1,606	18,520	22,199	0.09	0.07	1.20
Peru	1,966	3,000	2,351	0.66	0.84	0.78
Singapore	80	540	13	0.15	6.15	0.02
Sri Lanka	885	3,190	1,737	0.28	0.51	0.54
Thailand	400	13,540	12,639	0.03	0.03	0.93
Turkey	5,815	12,800	25,755	0.45	0.237	2.01
Uruguay			1,779			

Data for Fig. 2.5, from Leamer (1984), Table B.1 (*Continued*)

Derivation of ratios for 1978

	Year	Capital	Labour	Land: permanent crop and arable	K/L	K/land	land/L
		millions in 1958 prices	thousands	thousand hectares			
Brazil	1978	82,579	37,656.0	51,706	2.19	1.60	1.37
Columbia	1978	11,488	8,464.0	5,407	1.36	2.12	0.64
Costa Rica	1978	1,640	715.0	497	2.29	3.30	0.70
Egypt	1975	5,401	10,037.0	2,825	0.54	1.91	0.28
Ghana	1978	2,438	4,024.1	2,730	0.61	0.89	0.68
Hong Kong	1978	6,629	2,015.0	9	3.29	736.56	0.00
Indonesia	1978	18,139	50,503.9	19,087	0.36	0.95	0.38
Jamaica	1978	1,507	718.0	263	2.10	5.73	0.37
Madagascar			3,668.0	2,759	0.00	0.00	0.75
Malawi			2,382.0	2,278	0.00	0.00	0.96
Malaysia	1975	5,075	4,451.0	4,198	1.14	1.21	0.94
Malta	1978	403	124.9	14	3.23	28.79	0.11
Mauritius	1975	138	280.0	106	0.49	1.30	0.38
Mexico	1978	55,005	18,898.0	25,025	2.91	2.20	1.32
Nigeria	1975	11,757	27,385.0	30,000	0.43	0.39	1.10
Peru	1978	5,925	4,911.9	2,723	1.21	2.18	0.55
Singapore	1978	5,795	924.1	8	6.27	724.40	0.01
Sri Lanka	1978	1,094	5,189.0	1,979	0.21	0.55	0.38
Thailand	1975	9,373	20,491.0	16,680	0.46	0.56	0.81
Turkey	1978	22,405	17,467.0	28,590	1.28	0.78	1.64
Uruguay			1,106.0	1,437	0.00	0	1.30

This allows us to divide the resource endowment triangle into six regions, by drawing the three endowment ratio lines for the world endowment passing through *WE*. We then classify our countries, in Table 2.9, into groups based on their initial factor-endowment comparisons with that for the trading world as a whole, in 1958.

From Fig. 2.5 and Table 2.9, it is clear that all our countries had 1958 capital–labour ratios which were lower than that at the world endowment point. So in terms of the capital–labour ratio all our countries were capital-scarce. But in the three-factor case, we also need to judge capital scarcity by the ratio of capital to land. Only if this ratio, too, is higher than that for the world endowment can we unambiguously say that the country is labour-abundant. Otherwise the classification (in our terms) is ambiguous. Hong Kong has a higher capital-to-land ratio than the world endowment, as do Singapore and Malta in 1978, and these are therefore the only labour-abundant countries in our sample.

Table 2.9. Factor endowments in 1958 and 1978

	K/L		K/Land		Land/L	
	1978	1958	1978	1958	1978	1958
Brazil	2.19	0.63	1.60	0.44	1.37	1.41
Colombia	1.36	0.70	2.12	0.62	0.64	1.12
Costa Rica	2.29	0.97	3.30	0.72	0.70	1.38
Egypt	0.54	0.74	1.91	0.21	0.28	0.35
Ghana	0.61	0.25	0.89	0.26	0.68	0.97
Hong Kong	3.29	0.63	736.56	53.36	0.00	0.01
Indonesia	0.36	0.13	0.95	0.26	0.38	0.51
Jamaica	2.10	1.18	5.73	3.08	0.37	0.38
Madagascar						
Malawi						
Malaysia	1.14	0.11	1.21	0.06	0.94	1.57
Malta	3.23	1.21	28.79	7.56	0.11	0.16
Mauritius	0.49	0.89	1.30	1.90	0.38	0.47
Mexico	2.91	0.89	2.20	0.37	1.32	2.43
Nigeria	0.43	0.09	0.39	0.07	1.10	1.20
Peru	1.21	0.66	2.18	0.84	0.55	0.78
Singapore	6.27	0.15	724.40	6.15	0.01	0.02
Sri Lanka	0.21	0.28	0.55	0.51	0.38	0.55
Thailand	0.46	0.03	0.56	0.03	0.81	0.93
Turkey	1.28	0.45	0.78	0.23	1.64	2.01
Uruguay						
Ratios based on total world endowment*	12.00	12.00	13.00	13.00	0.9	0.9

*These have been derived from the data given in Leamer (1987: 965) that the aggregate capital per man was $12,000, capital per hectare was $13,000, and land per man was 0.9 hectares, for 38 countries for which data was available from around the world in 1978. Lacking any other information we have used this to derive the common world endowment ratio in terms of our units (capital per thousand men; capital per thousand hectares; and hectares per man) for both 1958 and 1978, as shown.

In Table 2.10, therefore, we show the resulting classification of our countries' endowments in 1958, first in columns 1–3 in terms of their threefold factor proportions in relation to those in the world endowment compared with the three-factor ratios. We next classify our countries with respect to the abundance or scarcity of one factor in relation to *both* other factors whenever possible. As a result, we get a classification of our countries into three groups. First, *land-abundant* countries are those for which capital is scarce relative to both labour and land, labour is scarce relative to capital, and land is abundant relative to both capital and labour. Second, *labour-abundant* countries are those in which labour is abundant in relation to both capital and land, and in which land is scarce relative to both labour

Table 2.10. Factor supplies in 1958 relative to average world endowment (WE)

Country	Factor proportions		Classification relative to WE			Factor endowment classification
	Capital/labour	Capital/land	Land/labour	Labour	Land	Capital	
Brazil	S	S	A	scarce*	abundant	scarce	Land-abundant
Colombia	S	S	A	scarce*	abundant	scarce	Land-abundant
Costa Rica	S	S	A	scarce*	abundant	scarce	Land-abundant
Egypt	S	S	S	abundant	?	scarce	Intermediate
Ghana	S	S	A	scarce*	abundant	scarce	Land-abundant
Hong Kong	S	A	S	abundant	scarce	scarce	Labour-abundant
Indonesia	S	S	S	abundant	?	scarce	Intermediate
Jamaica	S	S	S	abundant	?	scarce	Intermediate
Malaysia	S	S	A	scarce*	abundant	scarce	Land-abundant
Malta	S	S/A	S	abundant	scarce?	scarce	Labour-abundant
Mauritius	S	S	S	abundant	?	scarce	Intermediate
Mexico	S	S	A	scarce*	abundant	scarce	Land-abundant
Nigeria	S	S	A	scarce*	abundant	scarce	Land-abundant
Peru	S	S	S	abundant	?	scarce	Intermediate
Singapore	S	S/A	S	abundant	scarce?	scarce	Labour-abundant
Sri Lanka	S	S	S	abundant	?	scarce	Intermediate
Thailand	S	S	A	scarce*	abundant	scarce	Land-abundant
Turkey	S	S	A	scarce*	abundant	scarce	Land-abundant

Derived from the data in Table 2.9.

Notes: S numerator scarce (ratio is less than the WE ratio in Table 2.9) and denominator abundant.

A numerator abundant (ratio is greater than WE ratio in Table 2.9) and denominator scarce.

* in relation only to land.

? intermediate.

scarce? on edge of scarcity.

and capital. The third are *intermediate* groups of countries, where labour is abundant in relation to both capital and land, but land is not un-ambiguously abundant or scarce relative to capital and labour, as they have both capital/land and land/labour ratios which are lower than those for the world endowment. These three regions are labelled as such in Fig. 2.5. On this basis we have divided our countries into three broad groups (as is done in Table 2.2) based on their initial factor endowments in the 1950s: labour-abundant (Hong Kong, Singapore, and Malta); land-abundant (Malaysia, Thailand, Brazil, Turkey, Mexico, Costa Rica, Colombia, Ghana, Nigeria, and Uruguay);[145] and intermediate (which are the rest, namely Egypt, Indonesia, Sri Lanka, Malawi, Peru, Jamaica, Mauritius, and Madagascar). Table 2.2 also lists the median, mean, and variance for the various aggregate indicators for each of these three groupings of countries.

It should be noted that fig. 1 of Leamer (1987) shows the endowment ratios for 1978 for 38 countries, of which 20 are developing countries. In the labour-abundant segment, apart from our three sample countries, the only other one is Korea.[146] No data are available for Taiwan of for China, and India, which many think of as a labour-abundant country, is clearly in the intermediate category. Thus our three labour-abundant countries are not an unrepresentative sample.

Furthermore, this classification based on endowments neglects the size of a country as a relevant variable. This is as it should be. For our hypothesis is that initial factor endowments, rather than the size of a country, are a more relevant determinant of both economic policy and the political economy of our countries. These initial endowments are analogous to the genetic endowments of individuals, which partly (but not wholly) deter-mine their behaviour. Countries with similar endowments are expected, at a first cut, to behave in similar ways, irrespective of their size. This was the purpose of our study of five small economies (Findlay, Wellisz, and associ-ates), which whilst being similar in size had differing resource endow-ments—three labour-abundant, and the other two in the intermediate category. As we hope to show in subsequent parts of this book, the latter behaved more like their comparators in the intermediate resource endow-ment category than like the former with which they shared the attribute of being small open economies.[147]

In addition to the indices concerning growth, discussed in earlier sections of this chapter, we have also included an index reflecting the extent of poverty redressal as measured by the annual percentage reduction in the deficit between the maximum of 100 and the actual value of Physical Quality of Life Index (PQLI) between 1960 and 1980.

The following stylized facts emerge from comparing these three groups of countries. First, the growth performance of the labour-abundant countries was better than that of the land-abundant ones, while those in the intermediate group of economic endowments had the worst performance. However, the variance in growth performance within the groups was highest in the land-abundant countries. Basing ourselves on the qualitative judgements in our country studies, the average level of distortions in our labour-abundant countries was much lower and returns to investment higher than that of the other two groups. It would appear that both higher investment rates and lower allocative inefficiencies were related to the better growth performance of the labour-abundant countries compared to the other groups. The average investment rates did not differ markedly between the land-abundant and intermediate groups of countries, but total factor productivity growth (for the countries for which this was available) tended to be higher in the land-abundant than the intermediate group of countries, though it was lower than the star performer, Hong Kong. The returns to investment were about the same on average (18%) for both the intermediate and land-abundant groups (for which we had data), excluding Ghana which is an exceptional case. In the labour-abundant group Hong Kong had the highest rate of return (25.5%), while Singapore (19%) was close to the average of the land-abundant and intermediate groups. There is not much difference in the average performances in poverty alleviation between the land-abundant and intermediate groups, which were not as good as that for Hong Kong.

It might also be useful to look at the movements in real wages in our sample countries to see whether they are broadly in consonance with our expectations from the three-factor open-economy framework. The available real wage trends are depicted in Fig. 2.6 (I–III) for our three groups of countries. It should be noted that great caution is needed in interpreting wage data for developing countries.[148]

The charts in each group have been rank-ordered in terms of the income growth per capita in the relevant countries during the period. Best-fit trend lines have been fitted to the wage data, and the corresponding equations appear beside each graph with t-ratios. Against each country's chart we also show the percentage change in the capital–labour ratio (K/L) between 1958 and 1978 as depicted in Fig. 2.5. This gives a rough measure of how far each country has moved towards the capital vertex in the resource endowment triangle. Our expectations are:

(1) We expect that real wages will rise almost automatically in the labour-abundant countries with capital accumulation. This is borne out by Fig. 2.6 (I).

(2) We would expect that a very high rate of capital accumulation is required to provide a rising real wage trend in land-abundant countries. But if this rate falls below some critical (and country specific) level,[149] there could be periods of falling wages. These expectations again seem to be broadly confirmed by Fig. 2.6 (II). Thus the two land-abundant countries

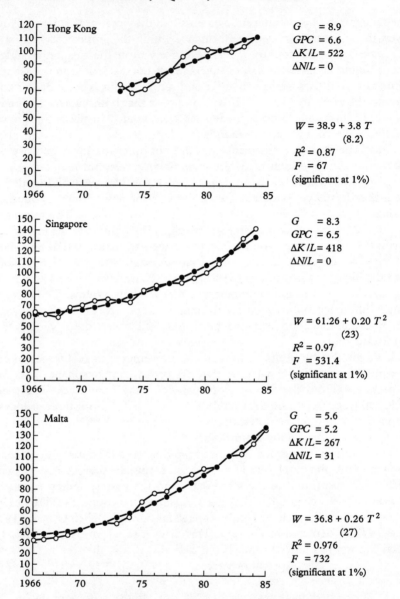

Fig 2.6. Real wages: (I) labour-abundant countries

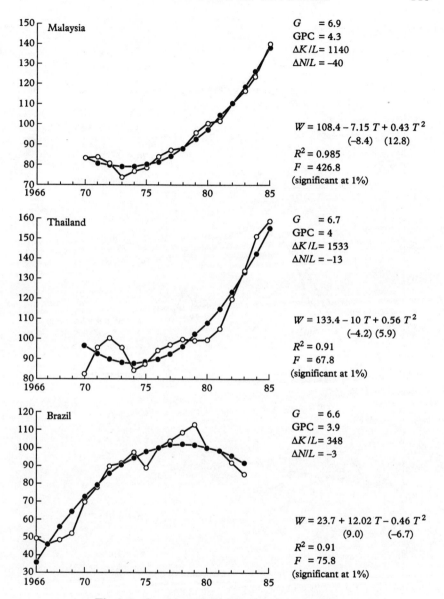

Fig 2.6. *Continued*: (II) land-abundant countries

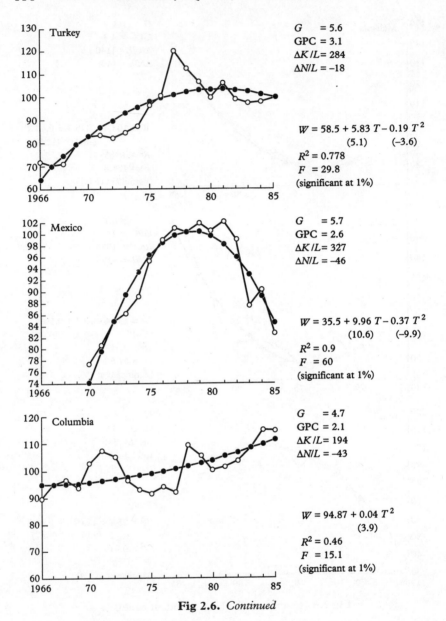

Turkey

G = 5.6
GPC = 3.1
$\Delta K/L$ = 284
$\Delta N/L$ = –18

$W = 58.5 + 5.83\,T - 0.19\,T^2$
$\qquad\qquad (5.1) \qquad (-3.6)$
$R^2 = 0.778$
$F = 29.8$
(significant at 1%)

Mexico

G = 5.7
GPC = 2.6
$\Delta K/L$ = 327
$\Delta N/L$ = –46

$W = 35.5 + 9.96\,T - 0.37\,T^2$
$\qquad\qquad (10.6) \qquad (-9.9)$
$R^2 = 0.9$
$F = 60$
(significant at 1%)

Columbia

G = 4.7
GPC = 2.1
$\Delta K/L$ = 194
$\Delta N/L$ = –43

$W = 94.87 + 0.04\,T^2$
$\qquad\qquad\qquad (3.9)$
$R^2 = 0.46$
$F = 15.1$
(significant at 1%)

Fig 2.6. *Continued*

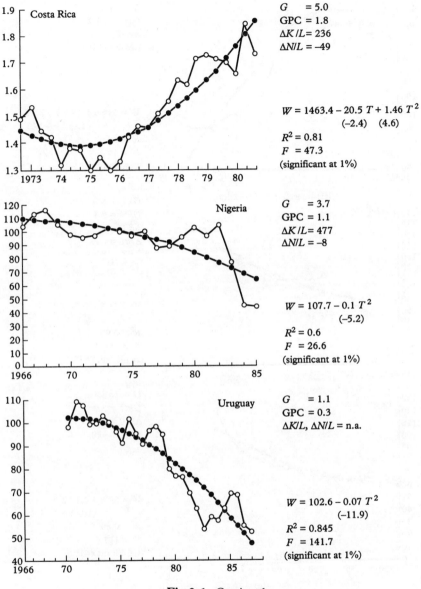

G = 5.0
GPC = 1.8
$\Delta K/L$ = 236
$\Delta N/L$ = −49

$$W = 1463.4 - 20.5\,T + 1.46\,T^2$$
$$\quad\quad\quad (-2.4)\quad (4.6)$$
$R^2 = 0.81$
F = 47.3
(significant at 1%)

G = 3.7
GPC = 1.1
$\Delta K/L$ = 477
$\Delta N/L$ = −8

$$W = 107.7 - 0.1\,T^2$$
$$\quad\quad\quad (-5.2)$$
$R^2 = 0.6$
F = 26.6
(significant at 1%)

G = 1.1
GPC = 0.3
$\Delta K/L$, $\Delta N/L$ = n.a.

$$W = 102.6 - 0.07\,T^2$$
$$\quad\quad\quad (-11.9)$$
$R^2 = 0.845$
F = 141.7
(significant at 1%)

Fig 2.6. *Continued*

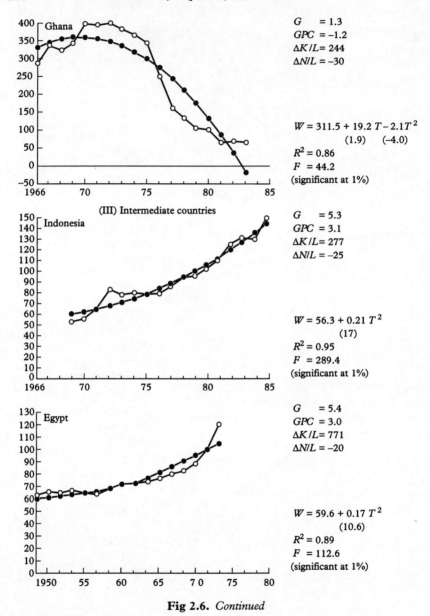

Ghana

$G = 1.3$
$GPC = -1.2$
$\Delta K/L = 244$
$\Delta N/L = -30$

$W = 311.5 + 19.2\,T - 2.1T^2$
$\qquad\qquad (1.9)\quad (-4.0)$
$R^2 = 0.86$
$F = 44.2$
(significant at 1%)

(III) Intermediate countries

Indonesia

$G = 5.3$
$GPC = 3.1$
$\Delta K/L = 277$
$\Delta N/L = -25$

$W = 56.3 + 0.21\,T^2$
$\qquad\qquad (17)$
$R^2 = 0.95$
$F = 289.4$
(significant at 1%)

Egypt

$G = 5.4$
$GPC = 3.0$
$\Delta K/L = 771$
$\Delta N/L = -20$

$W = 59.6 + 0.17\,T^2$
$\qquad\qquad (10.6)$
$R^2 = 0.89$
$F = 112.6$
(significant at 1%)

Fig 2.6. *Continued*

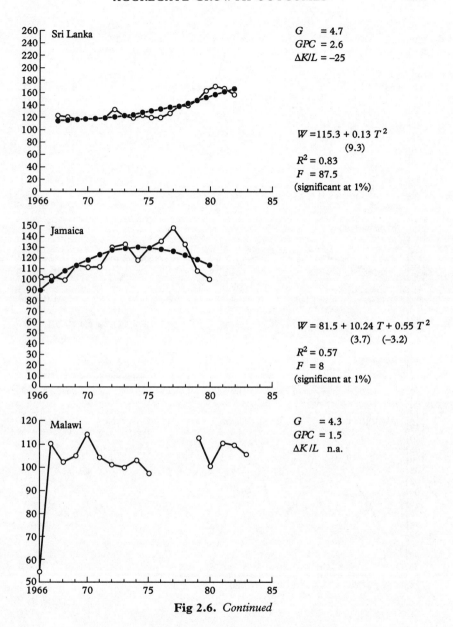

Sri Lanka

$G \quad = 4.7$
$GPC = 2.6$
$\Delta K/L = -25$

$W = 115.3 + 0.13\ T^2$
$\qquad\qquad (9.3)$
$R^2 = 0.83$
$F \ = 87.5$
(significant at 1%)

Jamaica

$W = 81.5 + 10.24\ T + 0.55\ T^2$
$\qquad\qquad\quad (3.7) \quad (-3.2)$
$R^2 = 0.57$
$F \ = 8$
(significant at 1%)

Malawi

$G \quad = 4.3$
$GPC = 1.5$
$\Delta K/L$ n.a.

Fig 2.6. *Continued*

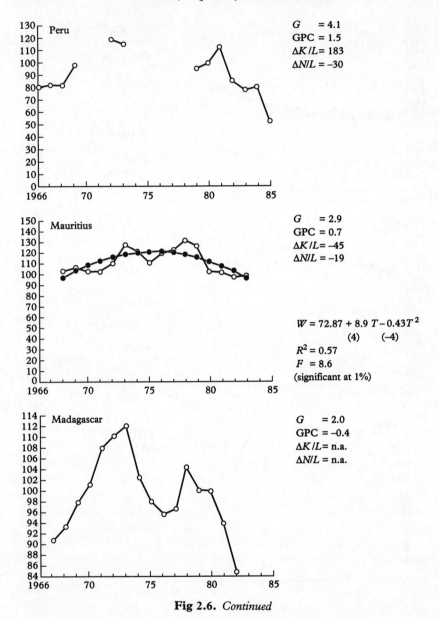

$$W = 72.87 + 8.9\,T - 0.43T^2$$

$R^2 = 0.57$

$F = 8.6$

(significant at 1%)

Fig 2.6. *Continued*

Explanatory notes to Fig. 2.6

☐   real earnings per employee
+   best-fit line

except: Costa Rica ☐ real average monthly wage, thousands of 1975 colones
         Uruguay   ☐ real industrial wage in terms of consumer prices
         Sri Lanka ☐ industry and commerce real wage rate index

Real wage indices are mainly taken from *World Tables* World Bank (1987). The data for Uruguay and Costa Rica are taken from the country studies, and the Sri Lankan data are taken from the Review of the Economy, Central Bank of Sri Lanka (1981).

G = GDP growth rate
GPC = GDP growth rate per capita
$\Delta K/L$ = change in capital/labour ratio, 1958–78
$\Delta N/L$ = change in land/labour ratio

Best-fit regression lines (+) were obtained by fitting 3 forms of equation to the wage index time series data:

$$W = \alpha + \beta T,$$
$$W = \alpha + \beta T^2,$$
$$W = \alpha + \beta T + \delta T^2,$$

where W = wage index,
       T = time (represented by 1, 2, 3, 4, . . .).

Figures in brackets are t-ratios.
Malawi and Peru have broken wage series and so no regression could be fitted. Madagascar seems to have a '2-hump' pattern, and so does not fit the 3 types of line applied here.

with clearly rising trends of real wages, Malaysia and Thailand, have also had phenomenal increases in their ratios of capital to labour between 1958 and 1978. The remaining countries (Brazil, Turkey, Mexico, Costa Rica, Colombia, Nigeria, Uruguay, and Ghana) have all had marked periods of falling real wages, with their trends conforming to either a U or inverted U shape. Two of these, Brazil and Mexico, also had marked positive real wage trends during the 1958–78 period for which we have comparable factor-proportion data, but have subsequently seen declining real wages as the rate of capital accumulation fell in the 1980s. But it is notable that these rising real wage trends were associated with larger percentage increases in the capital–labour ratio than in Malta, the labour-abundant country for which this ratio increased the least. Moreover Turkey, despite raising the capital–labour ratio by a larger percentage than in Malta, had some decline in real wages (unlike Malta).

(3) For intermediate-group countries we would not expect any simple relationship between changing aggregate capital–labour ratios and real wage trends. This too is confirmed by Fig. 2.6 (III), which shows a mixed picture. Thus, despite a large rise in its capital–labour ratio, Nigeria has had a declining real wage trend, whereas Mauritius, which saw its capital–labour ratio fall, had virtually stagnant real wages.

Thus, by and large, there seens to be some tentative support for the applicability[150] of the three-factor-proportion open-economy framework that we have adopted to classify our sample countries.

Looking at the effects on poverty of growth in terms of our threefold classification of countries, it is apparent from Table 1.1 that, of our 21 countries, 15 have had increases in income per capita over the 1950–85 period. Of these, all the labour- and land-abundant countries have seen mass structural poverty reduced. It is within the intermediate resource endowment class of countries that there is some evidence that in Sri Lanka and Malawi there may have been some increase in the incidence of mass structural poverty despite income growth per capita. But it should be noted that the evidence for this increase in poverty is fragile.[151]

There are five countries which have had periods of rising and falling income growth rates per capita. Except for the land-abundant Uruguay and Nigeria, all the others (Peru, Jamaica, and Madagascar) are in the intermediate resource endowment class. Except for Uruguay and Peru, these countries have seen an increase in poverty associated with their declining income per capita. Finally, there is one country in our sample, Ghana (a land-abundant country), which is *sui generis* in having declining income per capita over most of our period and, not surprisingly, increasing poverty.

We hope this is sufficient to convince our readers that even at this preliminary stage one building-block in the construction of our overall comparative story—the three-factor model based classification of our countries into three broad resource endowment groups—is of some interest. But to delve any deeper we need to go beyond the gross features of performance emphasized in this chapter to take a closer look at the stories our country authors have provided about their respective countries.

NOTES

1. Also see Srinivasan (1994) for a devastating critique of the serious lacunae in the data which have been so cavalierly used in various cross-sectional comparisons and regressions.
2. The countries are listed in ascending order of their 1985 *per capita* income according to the World Bank's *World Development Report*, Table 1, pp. 202–3.
3. Thus, if we exclude Malta (as it does not appear in the World Bank's list), the World Bank's percentage shares and ours in the three income categories are: low income, 39 and 20; lower middle, 38 and 50; upper middle, 24 and 30.
4. The justification for an aid agency of using such a classification is of course based on the implicit judgement that aid flow should be matched to the relative poverty (measured by per capita income) of the recipient. It has also been used for statistical exercises by Chenery and Syrquin (1975) to analyse the patterns of growth. But the usefulness of these exercises is at least ques-

tionable. See, for instance, the review of Chenery *et al.* (1986) by Moykr (1988: 1755–6).

5. The Kravis data on GDP per capita, as we would expect, generally differ from the World Bank data, but this difference is particularly marked for Sri Lanka. At our request the authors of the Kravis figures checked the unusual Sri Lankan figures, but found no fault in the methodology. The general picture told by World Bank data seems to provide a reasonable account of the path of GDP per capita in Sri Lanka, as outlined in our country study by Bruton.

6. Reynolds (1985: table 2, pp. 390–1).

7. Thus in Reynold's sample 27% are high-growth, 24% are moderate-growth, 24% low-growth, and 24% no-growth. In our sample and for the longer period considered, 29% are high-growth, 29% are moderate-growth, 23% are low-growth, and 19% are no-growth economies. So our sample again contains more high- and moderate-growth cases than Reynolds's.

8. In terms of Kravis dollars, the implicit growth rates between 1960 and 1985 (from Table 2.1) yield a classification in which Indonesia becomes a high-growth economy from a moderate-growth economy, Mauritius moves from a no-growth to a moderate-growth economy, Sri Lanka from a moderate to low, and Nigeria, Jamaica, and Peru move from low to no growth.

9. W. A. Lewis (1955).

10. The most important of these are Little, Scitovsky, and Scott (1970), Donges (1976), Bhagwati (1979), and Krueger (1978). For a survey of these and subsequent studies on the links between trade regimes and growth, see Lal and Rajapatirana (1987).

11. The phrase is due to Kindleberger (1962).

12. As the investment rate and export growth rate (as a proxy for the degree of openness of the economy to foreign trade) are both endogenous variables in regressions where they are the independent and the growth rate is the dependent variable, instrumental-variables estimation methods like TSLS are required to take account of this endogeneity. For growth is likely to have an impact both on the investment rate and on export performance, as well as being determined by them.

13. Two justifications have been provided for cross-section regressions which use the rate of export growth (EXPGRT) or else the export growth rate adjusted for export share (EXPGRT/EXPSHR) as the proxy variable for confirmation of the importance of outward orientation for growth performance. The first is the claim by Balassa (1978) that as export- and import-substituting production represent competing uses of given resources, a positive coefficient on an export growth variable provides evidence that the shift of resources to this use led to a net addition to GDP. The second is based on Feder (1983), who argued that in a two-sector model with exports and non-exports, the former were a factor of production in the latter, assuming that export production provides positive externalities to non-export production.

Recently Sheehy (1990) has questioned these statistical approaches to establishing the presumptions in favour of an outward-orientated policy, by showing that similar bi-variable tests between the growth rate and other components of GDP also support the promotion of *all* major components of GDP.

Equally seriously flawed are the statistical studies based on so-called Granger causality (essentially tests of precedence) which seek to show that 'many of the countries most famous for the miraculous growth rates that appeared to arise from export promotion policies (e.g. Korea, Taiwan, Brazil) provide no statistical support for the export promotion hypothesis' (Jung and Marshall, 1985: 10). A critique of this and the similar study by Darratt (1986) is provided in Lal and Rajapatirana (1987). The essential point is that in terms of elementary trade theory, in the Jung and Marshall study, for instance, the cases in which output growth Granger-causes export growth should also be counted as outward orientated. Once this is done their paradoxical conclusion disappears. This is apart from the obvious epistemological doubts that Leamer (1985), for instance, has voiced about the notion of Granger causality. As emphasized in the text, the robustness of the link between outward orientation and growth performance is based on the detailed analytical economic histories of a large number of countries contained in a series of comparative studies, including our own. That it is sought to controvert these by dubious statistical tests is another sign of the methodological degeneration we deplored in the introduction.

14. Findlay and Wellisz (1994: 296).

15. Barro (1991); also see Romer (1990b), who also finds human capital variables statistically significant in explaining cross-country growth differences.

16. This estimated regression equation for his sample of countries for 1960–80 was

$$G = -0.5 + 0.8AG + 0.09EG$$
$$(2.4) \qquad (2.4)$$
$$-0.005P + 0.01(I : GDP)$$
$$(-0.8) \qquad (1.7)$$

$R^2 = 0.7$ (significant at 1.2% level); figures in brackets are t statistics.

It should be noted, however, that since in these regressions one endogenous variable (the growth rate) is regressed against another set of endogenous variables (e.g. export growth and agricultural growth), the interpretation and inferences drawn from the coefficients may be dubious.

17. For its details see Rampogal Agarwala (1983). These are obvious problems in associating this index with allocative efficiency, which in an open economy we identify with the allocation of inputs and outputs, which maximizes the value of output at world prices. This definition of allocative efficiency is to be distinguished from two other senses in which the term is used. The first is in terms of technical efficiency, which means that the economy is operating on its production possibility frontier (PPF). A tariff, whilst it leads to allocative inefficiency (in the above sense), need not lead to technical inefficiency if the economy operates on the PPF but not at the free-trade point. Secondly, there could be allocative inefficiency if producers' choice of the input–output mix

does not maximize profits at the given prices they face. A tariff-distorted set of prices need not lead to this form of inefficiency either.

18. Solow (1957); Denison (1985).
19. Chenery *et al.* (1986).
20. Hicks's neutral technical progress raises the output produced from a given combination of labour and capital without changing their relative marginal products.
21. Thus if

Y_t is output in year t, whose growth rate is g_y;

K_t is the capital stock in year t, whose growth rate is g_k;

L_t is the labour supply in year t, whose growth rate is g_l;

A_t is the Hicks neutral technical progress factor, whose growth rate is g_A;

w is the wage rate;

r is the profit (rental) rate on capital;

p is the price of output;

then

$$Y_t = A \cdot F(K_t, L_t). \tag{1}$$

Differentiation with respect to time and dividing through by P_Y yields

$$\frac{\dot{Y}}{Y} = \frac{\dot{A}}{A} + A \cdot \frac{\delta Y}{\delta K} \cdot \frac{\dot{K}}{pY} + A \cdot \frac{\delta Y}{\delta L} \cdot \frac{\dot{L}}{pY}. \tag{2}$$

Marginal productivity factor pricing implies

$$\frac{r}{p} = \frac{\delta Y}{p \delta K}; \quad \frac{w}{p} = \frac{\delta Y}{p \delta L}. \tag{3}$$

The shares of labour and capital are given by:

$$a_K = \frac{rK}{pY},$$
$$a_L = \frac{wL}{pY}, \tag{4}$$

and with $g_X = \dfrac{\dot{X}}{X}$

we have from (4) and (2) that

$$g_Y = g_A + a_K g_K + a_L g_L, \tag{5}$$

which is the basic growth accounting equation.

22. See Chenery *et al.* (1986: ch. 1) for details.
23. Solow (1988: 313).
24. Denison (1985).

25. A survey of their results can be found in Nadiri (1972).
26. Psacharopoulos (1973; see also 1984).
27. Psacharopoulos (1984: 336–7).
28. Also see Pack and Page (1994) and Behrman (1990). Pack (1994: 61), summarizing these studies, notes: 'By 1960, most of the newly industrializing economies already had a higher level of education than would have been predicted by their national income—but many other poor countries that did not grow had similarly high levels. . . . Although there was substantial investment in education in these nations [the NICs], growth in educational levels has not greatly exceeded that in many other less developed countries which have failed to grow.' However, as we emphasize in Ch. 10, subsidizing primary and secondary education may be of importance for poverty alleviation.
29. Solow (1994: 51).
30. Levine and Renault (1992: 943).
31. Ibid. 942.
32. Ibid. 954.
33. Sala-i-Martin (1994: 742–3).
34. See Hicks (1965).
35. Thus Solow (1988: 308–9) notes:

> I remember that writings on economic development often asserted that the key to a transition from slow growth to fast growth was a sustained rise in the savings rate. The recipe sounded implausible to me . . . it turned out [in the neoclassical growth model] to be an implication of diminishing returns that the equilibrium rate of growth is not only not proportional to the saving (investment) rate, but is independent of the saving (investment) rate. A developing economy that succeeds in permanently increasing its saving (investment) rate will have a higher level of output than if it had not done so, and must therefore grow faster for a while. But it will not achieve a permanently higher rate of growth of output. More precisely, the permanent rate of growth of output per unit of labor input is independent of the saving (investment) rate and depends entirely on the rate of technological progress in the broadest sense.

36. For a sophisticated statistical examination of various theories about the phases of growth (e.g. the Kondratieff cycle) which takes this perspective of the traverse in explaining the historical record of growth rates in developed countries, see Solomon (1990).
37. See Sato (1966), Atkinson (1969), and Morishima (1973).
38. King and Rebelo (1993).
39. Barro (1994: 9).
40. Ibid. 4–5.
41. Barro (1991).
42. Barro (1994: 12).
43. Ibid. 23.
44. For a fuller survey, see Hahn and Matthews (1965).
45. Also see Eltis (1973).
46. There are two broad types of models in this genre. One strand abandons the assumption of diminishing returns to capital of the Solow–Swan model, and postulates constant returns to capital. They have been labelled AK models,

and it is instructive to see why. The starting-point for modern growth theory was the Harrod Domar model whose basic equation for steady state growth was:

$$g = s/k = n \qquad (2.1)$$

where
g = growth rate of output (Y),
s = the ratio of savings to national income (S/Y),
k = the capital output ratio (K/Y),
n = the growth rate of the labour force (L).

The production function had constant returns to scale with fixed coefficients. As s, k, and n were thus exogenously determined, it was only by chance that they could satisfy equation (2.1), to yield steady-state growth. The neoclassical model replaced the fixed coefficient technology with a neoclassical production function represented by

$$Y = A\mathrm{f}(K, L) \qquad (2.2)$$

(A is total factor productivity). This yields the well-known growth accounting identity,

$$g = t + a \cdot (dK/K) + b \cdot n, \qquad (2.3)$$

where t is the rate of technical progress, and a and b are the elasticities of output with respect to capital and labour. In the constant returns to scale Cobb–Douglas case; $a + b = 1$.

With perfect competition, a and b will also be the share in income of capital and labour. From (2.3), since in the steady state $dK/K = g$, the determinants of growth rates per capita $(g - n)$ in the steady state are

$$g - n = \frac{t + n(a + b - 1)}{(1 - a)}. \qquad (2.4)$$

With constant returns to scale $(a + b = 1)$, steady-state growth rates are determined entirely by exogenous technical progress (t) and labour force growth (n). But even within this framework, increasing returns to scale $(a + b > 1)$ will lead to positive income growth per capita in the steady state, even if there is no technical progress $(t = 0)$. Endogenous growth theorists' main contribution is to show that within the Solow–Swan framework, even without increasing returns to scale there can be positive income growth per capita if there are constant returns to capital $(a = 1)$, and (with $t = 0$) non-reproducible raw labour is assumed away, because it is argued that what is important for growth is not the numbers working but the human capital embodied in them. If all these reproducible inputs are put into a composite good called 'capital', then the production function becomes

$$Y = AK^a. \qquad (2.5)$$

But then we are back, as Solow (1994: 49) has remarked, 'to generalized Domar, but with bells and whistles'. For from (2.5) we can derive its growth accounting identity:

$$g = t + a(dK/K);\qquad(2.3a)$$

if there is no technical progress ($t = 0$), and $a = 1$, this reduces to the Harrod–Domar identity, $g = s/k$. Theoretically, we seem to be back where we started. Moreover, to avoid explosive growth there have to be strict constant returns to capital ($a = 1$) (see Solow, 1994).

Moreover, two of our sample countries provide counter-evidence for the empirical implications of these linear AK models. There are two types of justifications for the constant returns to capital assumption provided. One emphasizes externalities (Romer, 1986, and Lucas, 1988), the others do not, but generate a linear production function by bounding the marginal product of accumulable factors away from zero (Jones and Manuelli, 1990), or making sectors of the economy linear in accumulable factors. The implication of the models which emphasize externalities in accumulation is that countries with a higher rate of accumulation of physical and human capital will also have higher TFP growth. But as Young—who was associated with our Hong Kong study—has shown in a comparison of Hong Kong and Singapore, the former had an investment rate which fluctuated around 20% of GDP between 1960 and 1985, whilst Singapore's rate rose from 9% in 1960 to 43% in 1984. Despite this, 'Hong Kong has experienced rapid TFP growth, while Singapore has, on average, experienced slightly negative growth in factor productivity' (Young, 1992: 37): exactly the opposite of the predicted outcome. Nor is the implication of these models, that the share of the unaccumulable factor (raw labour) should be falling over time, borne out. 'In Singapore it is almost constant, although in Hong Kong it has fallen dramatically. Nevertheless, with a share of raw labor equal to approximately one-third of national income in both economies in the mid-1980s, there appears to be considerable aggregate concavity in accumulable factors' (ibid. 17).

The other broad class of models in the new growth theory endogenizes technical change, with an emphasis on human capital as a critical input in acquiring knowledge (Romer, 1990a; Stokey, 1991; Young 1991, 1993; Grossman and Helpman, 1991). But as Solow (1994) notes, there is as yet little empirical content to these theories.

47. Scott (1976, 1989).
48. H. G. Johnson (1964: 221).
49. Ibid.
50. Scott (1989: 92).
51. Scott (1976: 317, 330, 318).
52. Ibid. 331.
53. Ibid.
54. Scott (1989: 150–1).
55. Ibid. 161.
56. Ibid. 162.
57. As McCombie in his review of Scott's book notes (1990: 273): 'It is also found that the efficiency of investment increased substantially in the post-war period, and this becomes in fact the new residual that requires explanation.'
58. Scott (1989: 100).
59. See D. Anderson (1990).

60. Scott (1976: 332–3).
61. Ibid. 334.
62. Ibid. The central element of Lucas's model (1988) is an externality in human capital investment. Many of his insights would seem to complement those of Scott, and so would those of Romer (1986).
63. Scott (1976: 325).
64. Ibid., p. xl.
65. See Lal (1987a).
66. This has also been emphasized in an important recent book by Schultz (1990).
67. One view of the importance of investment in growth is based on Solow's embodiment hypothesis about technical progress, which would suggest that the rate of technical progress would be positively correlated with the speed of investment. However, Denison (1985) has found no explanatory value in the embodiment hypothesis. More recently Solow (1988: 315) reports unpublished work by Wolff, which shows that on the basis of historical data for Canada, France, Germany, Italy, Japan, the UK, and the USA, covering 1880–1979, there is a strong positive correlation between the average growth rate of total factor productivity and various measures of the speed of investment (such as the growth rate of the capital stock, growth rate of the capital-labour ratio, the average investment quota). Solow takes this as support for the embodiment hypothesis. However, from our Table 2.2 above, which charts the average investment ratio (a proxy for the speed of investment) and lists the TFP estimates for the seven countries in our sample for which it is available, there does not appear to be any such correlation (at least for the short time-periods considered). So the embodiment link between investment and technical progress would also seem to be weak. But Solow offers two alternative explanations for the embodiment hypothesis (ibid.):

> For example, it could be the case that some countries are better able to exploit the common pool of technological progress than others, for reasons that have nothing to do with the rate of capital formation; but in exactly those technologically progressive countries investment is most profitable, so naturally the rate of investment is higher. Or else rapid technical progress *and* high investment could both be the result of some third factor, like the presence of conditions that encourage entrepreneurial activity. High investment and fast technical progress will then go together.

It is this last interpretation (which is close to Scott's) that we favour, and which is the starting-point, in a sense, of this study.

68. Murphy, Shleifer, and Vishny (1991: 503).
69. Leibenstein (1968: 73).
70. See Schultz (1990).
71. Young, *Hong Kong*, p. 78, see Findlay and Wellisz (1993: 45).
72. See Timberg (1978).
73. W. A. Lewis (1955: 11).
74. Becker (1976).
75. Baldwin (1992: 41).
76. In an important paper, Markusen and Melvin (1984) synthesize the results on

the gains from trade (GFT) in the presence of increasing returns and differentiated products (a summary of the various models is available in Helpman (1981), whilst Srinivasan (1989) provides a survey which looks in particular at the relevance of these models for developing countries). They identify three types of models that have been developed. The first are with homogeneous goods and with increasing returns to scale (IRS) external to individual firms; the second are with homogeneous goods and with IRS internal to individual firms; and the third are models with differentiated products produced under monopolistic competition. They show that in all three cases GFT may not occur for the same two reasons. As is well known, in the standard neoclassical trade model with constant returns to scale and perfect competition, the free trade price line is tangential to the economy's production frontier (implying marginal cost pricing) and also forms a separating hyperplane to the production set. In all the three type of new trade theory models, the IRS goods have marginal costs lower than price, so the tangency condition breaks down, with the free trade price line cutting the production set at the free trade point. Second, even if the tangency condition is satisfied (that is, marginal costs equal price), IRS could lead to non-convexities in the production set, so that even a price plane which is tangential may not form a separating hyperplane to the production set. They then show that

> With respect to the tangency conditions, results (generally well known) show that losses from trade may occur if trade contracts the IRS industries. The intuition is fairly straightforward. With prices greater than marginal costs in autarky, the economy is already under-producing the IRS goods. If trade reduces production further, the economy may be moving away rather than towards its optimal production mix. We suggested that a sufficient condition for GFT is that trade have a certain rationalizing effect on production. This is a rather crude notion to the effect that surviving industries expand output more than in proportion to the number of IRS industries lost due to the opening of trade. We argued that this is in fact a reasonable outcome (although hard to define rigorously) provided that trade does not decrease the total resources devoted to the IRS industries. Non-convexities present a more difficult problem. On the one hand, we are able to show that the same expansion of all IRS industries that is sufficient for GFT in the convex case continues to be sufficient in the presence of non-convexities. Further, this result does not rely on restrictive functional forms, specialization in production, or on average-cost pricing in the IRS industries. On the other hand, the weighted increase in the outputs of the IRS industries that is sufficient in the convex case is no longer sufficient with non-convexities. We are thus still without a sufficient condition for GFT in the realistic case in which trade expands some IRS industries and contracts others. (Markusen and Melvin, 1984: 30–1)

77. Bell *et al.* (1984: 123).
78. Scitovsky (1969: 249).
79. Rosenstein-Rodan (1943: 204).
80. For the continuing sceptics one need only note that recent estimates of TFP

growth in the USSR show that from 1970 TFP (which was never more than 1.6% p.a.) became stagnant, and from 1975 was negative (see Ofer, 1987). This is increasingly seen both by the Soviets themselves and by outside observers as a systemic problem flowing in large part from that *dirigiste* form of industrial planning whose justification was the 'co-ordination failure' highlighted by Scitovsky and Rosenstein-Rodan. Desai and Martin (1983) have, moreover, estimated the inefficiency arising from inter-branch misallocation of capital and labour deployed in Soviet industry, and find that it ranges from a low of about 3–4% to a high of 10% of efficient factor use. Moreover, this inefficiency is rising over time. For China, another command economy, also presumably capable of overcoming the co-ordination failure, Chow (1985) found that the increase in industrial output was mainly due to an increase in capital inputs, rather than of improvement in technology or efficiency.

81. See Sampson and Yeats (1977), and Cline *et al.* (1978). Also, as Leamer (1988) notes, the usual method of computing tariff equivalents, of non-tariff barriers by comparing domestic with international prices, is only accurate for the case when the products are standardized and there is no market power.

82. Sheehy (1990: 115).

83. Dollar (1992: 540).

84. Leamer (1988: 198–9).

85. Edwards (1992: 16).

86. Another route to investigating the openness–growth link is to examine the effects of recent World Bank structural adjustment programmes, whose major aim is to influence the growth rate by reducing policy-induced distortions and thereby improve the supply side of the economy. It is encouraging that a study by Mosley *et al.*, whose authors' prior beliefs are clearly not in consonance with the neoclassical consensus, concludes from the statistical and qualitative evidence of nine cast studies that 'the evidence in favour of the proposition that *compliance with conditions* caused an improvement in GDP and export performance is stronger than the evidence in favour of the proposition that the *finance* associated with policy based lending caused such an improvement' (Mosley *et al.*, 1991: p. i. 228).

87. Riedel (1994: 47).

88. Witness the favourable review that Wade (1990), the most economically literate of these three, received in *The Economist*.

89. Wade (1990: 89).

90. Ibid.

91. Little (1994: 19).

92. World Bank (1993: 333).

93. Ibid. 334.

94. Ibid. 335.

95. Ibid. 336.

96. Dollar and Sokoloff (1990: 318).

97. World Bank (1993: table A6.3).

98. Little (1994: 16).

99. Demsetz (1988).

100. Ibid. 231.

101. Demsetz (1992: 6).

102. But there are different ways in which this can be done, with different implications for equity. The state could tax and supply the proceeds to persons it favours. Alternatively, it could use the taxes to provide a fund from which all could borrow. Thirdly, it could provide capital for large ownership stakes simply by favouring policies that tolerate inequality in the distribution of wealth. Finally, financial institutions (banks) could own enough equity in such enterprises to overcomes this control problem, as in Germany and Japan.

103. Demsetz (1992: 6).

104. Amsden (1989: 131).

105. Ibid. 116.

106. Amsden reports: 'private firms in Korea contributed very little of their own capital to most investment projects . . . internal financing in 1963–73 accounted on average for only 20% of total financing (compared with 32–35% for Japan (1954–67) and 65% for the U.S. (1947–63). . . . In 1983 the manufacturing sector in Korea . . . financed only 9.9% of its business through retained earnings and capital increases' (ibid. 85).

107. But it should not be inferred from this that this policy was necessarily ideal in effectuating Korean comparative advantage. Amsden has estimated gross rates of return for the period 1971–82 for four classes of manufacturing outputs, two labour-intensive and two capital-intensive. She concludes: 'The data support three interrelated conclusions. First the most labor intensive industries have the highest profit rates. Second, the youngest industries [the capital-intensive ones which were promoted during Korea's *dirigiste* 'Big Push' in the 1970s] have the lowest profit rates . . . Third, the capital intensive industries have the highest export growth rates, besides having the highest overall rates of subsidization (measured by the loan to value added ratio)' (ibid. 85).

108. Park (1963: 120).

109. Amsden (1989: 14).

110. Wade (1990: 270).

111. Wade (1990: 296).

112. Scitovsky (1990: 136).

113. Wade (1990: 81).

114. A number of authors (e.g. Leff, 1978, 1979) have noted that 'big business groups have evolved into critical factors in late industrializing countries' (Amsden, 1989: 119). But, as she notes, no satisfactory explanation has been provided for this. The Demsetz hypothesis may well provide the answer.

115. See Wade (1990: 68 ff.).

116. Findlay *et al.* (1993: 301).

117. Ibid.

118. Ibid. 300.

119. Ibid. 301.

120. Ibid. 302.

121. Hazari (1966: 8). That the founder of the 'house of Tata' was aware of maintaining the concentration of private wealth in exercising control over the enterprises he had created is shown by his creation of a family trust 'which was indivisible from the beginning because of its objective of preserving jointly owned assets in perpetuity' (Yasuoka, 1984: 28).

122. One final worry that has been aired about the promotion of openness can be readily cleared. It has been argued by Cline (1982) and Streeten (1982) that

if all developing countries tried to follow the export-led growth strategy of the Far Eastern NICs the developed countries would not allow this surge of Third World imports into their economies. It was claimed that there was a fallacy of composition in generalizing the East Asian experience to the rest of the developing world. Ranis (1985), in a robust response, argues that as an increase in the South's exports enables it to finance larger imports they will provide larger markets for Northern exporters. This is already happening with the opening up of China and India. Hence there is no prima-facie reason why developed country tolerance of Third World imports should decrease. International trade, after all, is *not* a zero-sum game.

123. Maddison *et al.* (1992: 62).
124. Ibid. 6.
125. Bruton (1992: 362).
126. Ibid. 363.
127. Hansen (1992: p. xiv).
128. The similarity of development paths emerging from the standard two-factor model does not imply that the time paths of their capital–labour ratios or their pattern of comparative advantage in the final steady state will be the same across all countries.
129. For the past, see Adelman and Morris (1988: tables A.22, A.23). For the present, see Squire (1981).
130. W. A. Lewis (1954).
131. Ranis and Fei (1961).
132. See Dixit (1973).
133. We are ignoring the second stage, between the so-called Lewis turning-point and the commercialization point in the Fei–Ranis model, where there is still 'dualism' in the labour market, as the marginal product of labour in agriculture is still less than the real wage in industry, which is determined by the *average* product of labour in agriculture, until the 'commercialization point'— where the average and marginal products of labour in agriculture are equalized. See Lal (1989*a*) for a detailed critique and references to the surplus labour literature.
134. The seminal contribution here is R. Jones (1971). Its extension to the model outlined in the text is due to Krueger (1977). Also see Deardoff (1984) for a geometric version of Krueger's model.
135. Leamer (1987). The endowment triangle

represents graphically the relative endowments of three factors (physical capital, labor, arable land). In the three-dimensional factor space, straight lines emanating from the origin contain all endowment vectors with the same ratio of factors. These lines in three dimensions can be represented by points in two dimensions by intersecting the positive orthant with a plane to form the endowment triangle. The three co-ordinates in the three-dimensional factor space are represented by the corners of an endowment triangle, and the endowments vectors of each of the countries are represented by points . . . The main point to keep in mind is that *every endowment point on a straight line emanating from one corner of the triangle has the same ratio of the other two factors.* For this reason the scales of the three factor ratios can be placed on the edges of the triangle. (pp. 963–4)

136. For a model that includes non-traded goods see Leamer (1987) and Lal (1989c).

137. These regions of specialization will depend upon commodity prices, and will alter as commodity prices change.

138. It might seem paradoxical that, whilst the economy's capital–labour ratio is rising, it is falling in manufacturing. But remember that the rate of growth of labour for the economy is not the same as in manufacturing only. Then it is possible for the agricultural labour force to grow more slowly (because of fixed land) than for the economy as a whole, thereby allowing and requiring the labour force in the manufacturing sector to grow more rapidly than for the economy as a whole. Thus a rising capital–labour ratio for the economy as a whole can be associated with a falling capital–labour ratio in manufacturing. Of course, there will be some rate of capital growth at which the capital–labour ratio for manufacturing would also be rising along with that for the economy as a whole, and this paradoxical development path would not occur.

139. Krueger (1977: 15).

140. Leamer (1987: 986).

141. Ibid.

142. Trewartha (1943).

143. Leamer (1987: 985).

144. Leamer (1984) does provide some estimates of the annual production in 1958 and 1978 of three major natural resource industries: oil, coal, and minerals. But whereas the other factor endowments, however imperfect, are for the relevant stocks of factors, the flow of output of these natural resource industries cannot be taken to be a measure of the corresponding stocks of natural resources. However, from an examination of the Leamer natural resource output data and the land–labour ratios for our sample of countries, it appears that apart from Peru, Indonesia, Jamaica, and Egypt, all the other major natural-resource-rich countries are also land-abundant. These four countries are in the intermediate endowment category. In subsequent chapters we will be concerned with the behavioural consequences of the differing natural resource endowments of our countries. But as a heuristic device, identifying land-abundant with natural-resource-rich may not be too misleading.

145. Though not listed in Leamer's set of data, and hence in Fig. 2.5, Uruguay is clearly a land-abundant country.

146. Jamaica is on the edge of the labour-abundant segment in fig. 1 of Leamer (1987). But if account is taken of the abundant natural resources of Jamaica then it would clearly be in the intermediate category (see n. 144 above).

147. Srinivasan (1986) provides a lucid discussion of the notion of size of country as a variable determining economic performance, and finds it wanting.

148. See Squire (1981).

149. Depending on the country's initial position in the resource endowment triangle, and the areas of specialization it traverses (in Fig. 2.5).

150. For the relevance and outline of this notion of 'applicability' within the classical methodology, see Lal (1994b). However, one general caveat should be noted about all the empirical comparisons we have made in terms of our threefold classification. This is that we only have three small island economies in our labour-abundant group, whereas the other two groups are more hetero-

geneous and also there are more countries in each group. So there are problems concerning both the relative sample sizes and the degrees of relative heterogeneity within the three groups, which require some caution about the generalization we are able to draw from the empirical comparisons we will be making in this study.

151. See Bruton (1992: ch. 15), and Pryor (1990: ch. 16).

3

Country Profiles

In this chapter we shall begin by explaining the general thinking behind the method of pairwise comparisons used for the purpose of comparative historical analysis. We shall then outline the salient relationships between economic policies and the outcomes of economic growth, income distribution, and poverty alleviation which have emerged from the country studies based on pairwise comparisons.

I. THE METHOD OF PAIRING COUNTRIES

The starting-point of our study is the economic history of individual countries covering the period 1950–85. We begin in each country around 1950, with the initial conditions being defined broadly to include not only its income level per capita, resource endowments, and other quantifiable economic characteristics but also the qualitative organizational and institutional factors which enter into the initial historical setting. We next try to trace the general dimensions of a country's growth and the broad direction of changes in its income distribution and poverty alleviation which have taken place during the period, taking into account significant turning-points where they occurred. We thus arrive at the salient economic outcomes in that country at the end of our period, around 1985. The analytical economic history of each country then attempts to explain these outcomes in terms of the initial conditions, the policies pursued, and other relevant exogenous factors, such as the disturbing factors from the world market, to obtain a coherent story for each country.

We selected pairs of countries which seemed to have significant similarities or differences to each other in their initial conditions, in their policies, and in the relevant exogenous factors, to conduct our comparative historical analysis.

An austere-minded historian can take the position that the economic history of a country should be treated as a unique manifestation of its particular circumstances and conjuncture of events. On the other hand, like many economists, we have taken the position that in this kind of subject, embracing a large number of developing countries, some sort of comparative analysis is indispensable for a more satisfactory understanding of their economic development.

For the purpose of a comparative study of the relationship between economic growth, income distribution, and poverty alleviation, the question of obtaining a representative sample is somewhat problematical. Since only a very limited number of developing countries possess usable and comparable statistical data on income distribution and the incidence of poverty, we are likely to end up in any case with a relatively small sample of countries, whether we choose a comparative statistical approach or a comparative historical approach.

This can be seen from a systematic cross-section statistical study by G. Fields which we commissioned for our project.[1] Fields has adopted purely statistical criteria, such as the nation-wide coverage of data and the consistency of definitions over time, to select countries with usable statistical data. On this basis he has excluded some of the countries in our study and has added others. He has also divided the history of each country into phases or 'spells' covering a medium period, and has treated each of these spells as a sample for his cross-section analysis. Even so, the total number of samples which he considers eligible for the purpose of a comparative statistical study is not much larger than our sample of 21 countries, which have been selected not on the chance availability of usable statistics but in the hope that they might yield useful comparisons from the standpoint of economic analysis and policy.

We may now explain the thinking behind our method of pairing countries for economic analysis. Historically, this may be traced to the 'method of difference' in J. S. Mill's *System of Logic* (Book III, ch. VIII). More familiarly, we may think of it in terms of a judicious use of the assumption of 'other things being equal' widely used in economic analysis. The method of pairing we have adopted may be illustrated in terms of a number of 'stylized' cases with variants and mixtures.

The simplest case is that of a pair of countries which, starting from similar initial conditions and pursuing similar policies, have arrived at similar outcomes in growth, income distribution, and poverty alleviation. The clearest example of such near-laboratory conditions of similarity is given by Hong Kong and Singapore.

Next, we may take the case of a pair of countries which, starting from similar initial conditions, have pursued different policies and have arrived at different economic outcomes. Here, if we can use the assumption of other things being equal with regard to exogenous factors from the outside world market, we can reasonably trace the link between different policies and different outcomes. If we use the initial conditions around 1950 as our reference point, Thailand and Ghana provide a good example of two peasant export economies which, starting from the similar initial conditions of abundant land accessible to peasant farmers, have now developed into two very different types of economy, mainly attributable to the different policies they have pursued.

An important variant of this case is that of two countries which, starting from similar initial conditions, have pursued different policies towards economic growth, with similar policies towards income distribution, arriving at different outcomes. We shall find that income distribution policies in practice are motivated, not so much by the desire to equalize incomes between the rich and the poor as such, but to favour politically important groups, such as the electorally powerful urban population or certain favoured ethnic groups. The Sri Lanka–Malaysia pair illustrates the case where similar income distribution policies have been pursued to favour the indigenous Sinhalese and Malay peasant rice farmers, combined with different policies towards the plantations and mining export sector. Malaysia's greater success in achieving growth and a more sustained ability to pursue her income distribution objective than Sri Lanka may be traced to different policies towards international trade and foreign investment in the plantation and mining sector.

Next, we have to take account of the influence of the exogenous outside 'disturbing factors' on the economic outcomes in the pair of countries we are comparing. This has been a fertile source of debate on how far a country's economic performance is attributable to its own policies or to the exogenous factors beyond its control. In general, we should expect buoyant world market conditions, such as those during the 1960s, to have a favourable effect on a country's export expansion and economic growth. But we have exceptional cases such as Ghana which show poor growth performance even during the 1960s due to inappropriate domestic economic policies. Conversely, we should expect the turbulent world economic environment following the oil shock to have an unfavourable effect on growth. Here again we have exceptions, such as Hong Kong and Singapore, which made quick recoveries from external shocks, and Uruguay, which showed an improvement in growth performance during the 1973–80 period due to reforms in domestic economic policies.

The most dramatic cases where the exogenous factors made a significant modification of the initial conditions is provided by two major oil-exporting countries, Nigeria and Indonesia. This pair illustrates the different outcomes in growth, income distribution, and poverty alleviation due to different policy responses to the windfall gains from the oil boom.

So far we have been concerned with the pairs of countries which have started from similar initial conditions or have been subject to similar exogenous disturbances but have ended up with different outcomes attributable to different policies. To complete the schema, we may think of a pair of countries which started from different initial conditions, but have followed similar policies. Here the outcomes will depend on what type of similar economic policies have been pursued. At the macroeconomic level we should expect inappropriate policies, such as failure to keep budget deficits under control, or maintaining official interest rates below the market-clearing level, to result in similar outcomes of domestic inflation and balance-of-payments difficulties, irrespective of the differences in the initial conditions. This will be true whether the failure to maintain macroeconomic stability is motivated by a desire to finance ambitious investment programmes to promote rapid economic development (frequently misnamed as 'growth-orientated' policies) or by a desire to finance ambitious social welfare programmes (the equity-orientated policies). But implications of the policies to promote highly capital-intensive import-substituting manufacturing industries may be different for two countries which start from different initial conditions. The promotion of capital-intensive industries will be more out of line with the initial factor endowments for a labour-abundant country than for a resource-abundant country. In a resource-abundant country, a higher wage level reflecting a higher initial land–man ratio may to some extent justify the adoption of capital-intensive methods in manufacturing industry, provided the productivity of labour in manufacturing can be raised to match the initial higher wage level. The method of pairing countries which we have outlined departs from the conventional methods in two ways.

First, a commonly used method in cross-section statistical analysis is to rank countries according to their *current* income levels per capita and judge the economic performance of a country in relation to the norm for its 'peer group' with a similar income level per capita. Our method of starting from the 'initial conditions' takes account, not only of the current income levels, but also of the initial levels of income for the two countries at the beginning of the period of comparisons. This avoids a misleading foreshortening in historical perspective when we are comparing pairs of countries such as Thailand and Ghana, or Sri Lanka and Malaysia, whose ranking in income levels per capita has drastically changed between 1950 and 1985.

Another commonly used method is to compare a country's economic performance by its 'peer group' belonging to the same regional grouping, such as Asia, Africa, or Latin America. But our approach suggests that useful comparisons may be made between countries belonging to different regions, as in the cases of Jamaica and Mauritius, Thailand and Ghana, and Nigeria and Indonesia. Conversely, countries belonging to the same geographical region may turn out to be more different than they appear at first sight. This is illustrated in the case of Colombia and Peru, which seem to provide a natural pair as two adjacent middle-sized Latin American countries well endowed with natural resources, but which turn out to have significant differences in their social setting and the nature of their major exports. A similar difference can be found between Egypt and Turkey, despite their regional and historical affinities.

The contrast we have drawn between the comparative historical ap-

proach and the comparative statistical approach should not, however, obscure the fact that the two approaches are complementary and can be used
as a way of cross-checking each other's results. The results of the cross-
section statistical analysis are strengthened if they can be backed by more
detailed historical studies of individual countries, while the results of a
comparative historical analysis are strengthened if they agree with the
findings of the cross-section statistical analyses based on a larger or a
different sample of countries.

The two salient findings of our comparative historical analysis of the 21
countries included in our project are:

(1) that there is a close relationship between a country's success or
    failure in pursuing policies to expand exports and its rate of econ-
    omic growth; and
(2) that the growth in income per capita of a country tends to reduce
    poverty in an absolute sense, although income distribution in a
    relative sense may become more equal or less equal with economic
    growth.

The first conclusion is consistent with the relationship between export and
economic growth found in Chapter 2 (p. 59), and can also find support in
many other cross-section studies showing the statistical association between
exports and economic growth,[2] and the second conclusion is in line with
Fields's cross-section analysis of the relationship between economic
growth, poverty alleviation, and income distribution.[3]

The building-blocks of our comparative studies are the analytical economic histories of individual countries, written by authors who combine
considerable specialist knowledge with general analytical skills. These individual case-studies can stand on their own as independent contributions,
whatever the value which may be attached to our comparative analysis. But
the richness of these contributions cannot really be appreciated without
reading the country volumes themselves. In what follows, we shall limit
ourselves only to the *comparative* aspects of pairwise studies, focusing on the
broad economic outcomes which have emerged from the respective country
studies.

II. FIVE SMALL OPEN ECONOMIES

We may start with the country volume which is concerned not with a
single pair but with a cluster of five countries. This consists of Hong
Kong and Singapore forming a pair, Jamaica and Mauritius forming
another pair, and Malta as a fifth country serving as a link between the two
pairs.

1. Hong Kong and Singapore

Hong Kong and Singapore provide almost laboratory conditions for comparing two economies which started from similar initial conditions of abundant labour with no natural resources and which, having pursued similar outward-looking policies of labour-intensive exports, have achieved similar outcomes in the form of phenomenally high and sustained rates of economic growth, raising their incomes per capita five- to sixfold between 1960 and 1985. These high rates of growth have been accompanied by rapidly expanding demand for labour and rising wages, leading to favourable changes in income distribution and poverty alleviation.

The basic relationship between export expansion and economic growth in Hong Kong and Singapore is not open to dispute. It is more interesting to consider a salient point of contrast: Hong Kong's economic growth has taken place under the colonial *laissez-faire* conditions, whereas government intervention in the labour and capital markets and in the attraction of foreign investment has played a major role in Singapore's policies for promoting economic growth.

This takes us beyond the conventional debate on 'planning versus market' to the deeper question concerning the factors governing the effectiveness of the economic mechanisms which have been chosen to implement policy. It will then be seen that both Hong Kong and Singapore possess a stable economic and political framework based on conservative fiscal and monetary policies, the provision of adequate social infrastructure, and an 'autonomous' polity able to resist political pressures from interest groups. As city states they enjoy the advantages of compactness, reducing transaction, administrative, and information costs. Given these underlying similarities, it is not too surprising that the two economies should have been able to pursue the outward-looking policies of expanding manufactured exports with comparable success, the vigour of Hong Kong's Chinese private entrepreneurs paralleled by the well-recognized administrative and managerial capabilities of the Singapore government.

There is, however, a further interesting point of contrast. Both Hong Kong and Singapore started by specializing in the exports of the labour-intensive type of 'simple manufactures', to take advantage of their initial conditions of abundant labour.[4] The subsequent tightening of the labour market led both to climb the ladder of comparative advantage, helped by moving from more labour-intensive to more capital-intensive types of manufactures. But Hong Kong's exports still continue to be dominated by small-scale producers with extensive subcontracting, despite diversification into new lines of exports such as electronics, digital watches, and toys. In contrast, in Singapore an increasingly important role in exports is played by large-scale capital-intensive producers and multinational corporations employing advanced technology. This difference in the type of manufactured products may be attributed to Hong Kong's free-market policies contrasted with Singapore's deliberate policy of encouraging capital-intensive high-technology industries. Singapore has been able to finance her policy of forcing the natural pace of climbing the ladder of comparative advantage by her ability to extract a very high rate of domestic savings through compulsory contributions to the Common Provident Fund (CPF) levied on the whole of her labour force. But Hong Kong's free-market policies have enabled her to adjust more flexibly to changing external conditions. In the unsettled conditions of the world economy following the recession in the early 1980s, Hong Kong has been able to maintain a steadier growth rate than Singapore.

2. Jamaica and Mauritius

Our next pair of countries, Jamaica and Mauritius, have similar antecedents as sugar plantation economies in which the bulk of the population has descended from the slaves and indentured workers originally brought from outside to work on the plantations. With independence and the introduction of majority rule, the policies of both countries came to be dominated by trade-union-based political parties, whether moderate or radical, concerned with higher wages and better social conditions and generally with the redistribution of income from the plantation owners to the workers. In the initial conditions of the 1950s, many economists would look on these two countries as typical monoculture export economies which, in view of unfavourable world market demand for primary exports and growing population pressure, would have to seek economic salvation through domestic industrialization based on import-substitution policies.

As it turned out, the actual courses of development in the two countries diverge from the conventional expectation in their different ways.

Jamaica enjoyed a 20-year boom during 1952–72, propelled by a rapid expansion of bauxite/alumina exports. Unfortunately, this turned out to be a 'precious bane' in that it provided Jamaica with the resources to pursue in an undisciplined manner not only import-substitution policies under the aegis of highly inefficient government development corporations, but also labour legislation and social welfare policies which pushed up wage costs, thus negating the advantage offered by an abundant labour supply. In the rival bids for electoral favours through the expansion of government expenditure on education, health, low-cost housing, and jobs in the civil service and para-statal organizations, political power passed to the 'radical', People's National Party (PNP) under Michael Manley in 1972. The underlying economic weaknesses of the political setting came to the surface. Jamaica plunged into economic difficulties, marked by heavy budget deficit and foreign exchange crisis with intensification of quantitative import controls. During the period 1972–9, Jamaica suffered from negative rates of increase in income per capita of –3.5% a year in Kravis dollars and an increase in the proportion of the population below a fixed poverty line. Jamaica has only slowly recovered from this economic debacle. (See Tables 3.1 and 3.2.)

Mauritius also started after independence with a dominant Labour Party concerned with the redistribution of income from the Franco-Mauritius owners of the sugar estates to the Indian estate workers through labour legislation and increase of social welfare expenditure, combined with the usual import-substitution policies. But Mauritius took a dramatic step away from the Jamaican path in the early 1970s, when the sugar estate owners

Table 3.1. Jamaica: Government earnings from the bauxite industry (millions of US $)

	Taxes and royalties		Levy earnings*
1964	20.52	1974	179.99
1965	22.09	1975	150.43
1966	27.53	1976	139.40
1967	24.29	1977	180.99
1968	24.33	1978	194.25
1969	29.49	1979	190.29
1970	35.95	1980	205.71
1971	30.21	1981	192.99
1972	28.42	1982	135.51
1973	26.95	1983	121.34
Total:	269.78	Total:	1,690.89

*Does not include royalty payments.
Source: Findlay and Wellisz (1993: table 4.31, p. 184).

Table 3.2. Jamaica: Contribution to GDP (millions of 1974 Jamaican dollars)

Year public	'Material' production (agriculture, mining, manufacturing and construction)	Defence and administration
1972	983.3	207.2
1973	954.9	250.9
1974	950.9	251.4
1975	920.0	265.1
1976	829.7	307.3
1977	793.0	328.3
1978	800.8	344.1
1979	763.8	360.2
1980	692.7	350.4

Source: Findlay and Wellisz (1993: table 7.4, p. 308).

took advantage of a large sugar boom to invest in the production of labour-intensive manufactured exports, made possible by the government's introduction of the Export Processing Zone (EPZ) free from government import controls. The trade unions acquiesced in a relaxation of minimum wage regulations for female workers. With the infusion of foreign capital and entrepreneurs from Hong Kong, and access to EEC markets under the Lomé and Yaoundé Conventions, Mauritius succeeded in expanding labour-intensive manufactured exports. Helped also by her notable success in reducing birth rates, Mauritius has enjoyed a high but fluctuating growth rate.

3. Malta

The study on the five small open economies is completed by the addition of Malta, which has similar initial economic conditions to Hong Kong and Singapore combined with similar political conditions to Jamaica and Mauritius. Just as in Jamaica, a radical Labour Party under Dom Mintoff came to dominate politics from 1971 and pursued policies of controlling the 'commanding heights of the economy' by nationalization, quantitative controls on foreign trade, and minimum-wage legislation. But unlike Jamaica, Malta recorded an unexpectedly high rate of economic growth (though the official figures showing higher growth than even Hong Kong and Singapore appear to be biased upwards). There seem to be three reasons for this contrasting experience.

- First, Malta managed to expand labour-intensive manufactured exports, notably textiles, during the 1970–80 decade.
- Second, while the Manley government in Jamaica lost control over public expenditure, the Mintoff government kept a strict control over budget deficits, sharing with Hong Kong, Singapore, and Mauritius the legacy of British colonialism in the form of 'Gladstonian finance'.
- Third, unlike Manley, Mintoff was also very successful in acquiring foreign aid from all sides, including Libya and Italy, and orders for ship construction from the Soviet Union and Communist China, thus consolidating the government's power base provided by the dock workers.

It will be seen that the salient points which have emerged from the study on the five small open economies are: (i) the clear relationship between economic growth and export expansion according to the comparative advantage determined by the initial conditions, and (ii) the importance of keeping budget deficits under control to maintain macroeconomic stability. These provide the common factors in explaining the economic successes not only of Hong Kong and Singapore but also of Mauritius and Malta. They also explain the poor economic record of Jamaica, which, starting in 1960 as one of the richer among the five countries, now has the lowest income level per capita in the group (see Table 3.3).

Table 3.3. Five Small Economies: Real GDP per capita in 1980 international prices, selected years, 1960–85 (US dollars)

Year	Jamaica	Mauritius	Malta	Hong Kong	Singapore
1960	1,472	1,012	1,282	1,737	1,528
1965	1,807	1,153	1,355	2,704	1,753
1970	2,422	1,025	2,068	3,555	2,869
1975	2,293	1,367	3,099	4,521	4,130
1980	1,857	1,484	4,630	7,268	5,817
1985	1,725	1,869	5,319	9,093	9,834

Source: Findlay and Wellisz (1993: table 7.1, p. 294).

III. SRI LANKA AND MALAYSIA

Sri Lanka and Malaysia have somewhat similar initial conditions of abundant land, with Malaysia possessing a larger reserve of uncultivated land in the 1950s. After independence, both countries followed a similar policy of redistributing incomes in favour of their respective peasant farmers, but they have followed different policies towards their plantation and mining export sectors on which their pre-war economic prosperity had been based. In general, Sri Lanka has pursued inward-looking policies towards foreign trade and investment whereas Malaysia has pursued outward-looking policies, maintaining an open economy underpinned by conservative fiscal and monetary policies. Malaysia has enjoyed a much higher rate of economic growth than Sri Lanka and has been able to follow her income distribution and social welfare policies in a more sustainable manner.

When these two countries were first opened up by foreign investment to produce plantation and mining exports, their peasant farmers were comfortably off in the traditional agricultural sector because of abundant land and were not willing to work as wage labourers in the estates and the mines. Thus, large inflows of immigrant labour from India and China were necessary for the expansion of primary exports. This has created the 'plural societies' in which equity is perceived not simply in terms of income distribution between the rich and the poor or between estate owners and estate workers, as in Jamaica and Mauritius, but in a triangular relationship between the foreign investors in the mines and plantations, the Indian and Chinese immigrant workers and their descendants, and the indigenous Sinhalese and Malay peasant farmers, mainly devoted to subsistence rice production with some production of export crops.

Both Sri Lanka and Malaysia have pursued policies to help their peasant rice farmers by embarking on large-scale irrigation projects, combined with subsidies and price support programmes to increase domestic self-sufficiency in rice. Both countries have also devoted public expenditure to improving social infrastructure and the provision of social services in health and education in the rural areas. In addition, Malaysia vigorously pursued a land settlement programme in which the Federal Land Development Agency (FELDA) cleared up land, planting it with young rubber trees and oil-palms, constructed low-cost housing, and handed over the individual smallholdings to selected Malay peasant farmers ready-made.

There are, however, two salient differences in the policies pursued by Sir Lanka and Malaysia. Firstly, as a continuation of the wartime rationing system, Sri Lanka became committed to an extensive and indiscriminate system of consumer rice subsidies, providing a specified quantity of free or subsidized rice to each consumer. This has proved to be a serious burden on her budget and foreign exchange supply, since a large proportion of rice has to be imported. In the face of political opposition to the abolition of the subsidies, it was not until 1980 that Sri Lanka was able to replace them by a Food Stamp Scheme which limited government subsidies to a certain value. Secondly, Sri Lanka's inward-looking policies discouraged the expansion of the plantation exports, notably tea and rubber, which have been the mainstay of her government revenues and foreign exchange earnings. The exports from the plantation sector have languished through heavy taxation, threats of further nationalization, restrictions on profit remittances, and import controls on inputs.

In contrast, Malaysia's exports from the plantation and mining sector have expanded rapidly in the setting of her open economy and stable economic conditions providing a favourable investment climate. Malaysia pioneered research in high-yielding rubber clones to meet the competition of synthetic rubber. There has also been diversification into new lines of primary exports, notably in oil-palm and hardwood and some oil exports. Like other South-East Asian countries, such as Thailand, Malaysia is now well on its way in the expansion of manufactured exports.

We now briefly touch on some of the significant turning-points in the stories of Sri Lanka and Malaysia. Sri Lanka's turning-point occurred in 1977, when there was a distinct shift from an inward to an outward orientation of policies, followed by a marked expansion in exports, employment, and economic growth. This has improved poverty alleviation, with no observable effects on income distribution and social indicators for health and education.[5] But since 1983 the government has been obliged to slow down its reform programmes in the face of formidable macroeconomic imbalances arising from its inability to reduce public expenditure and close down loss-making state enterprises.[6] Sri Lanka has also been plagued by armed insurgency, not only from the Tamil minority community but also from radical groups from within the Sinhalese community itself, which her social welfare policies have been unable to defuse.

Malaysia's problem of armed insurgency has been fortunately left behind since the days of the 'emergency' in the 1950s. Her turning-point occurred in May 1969 with violent racial riots between the Malays and Chinese. This has impelled the Malaysian government to abandon its traditional non-interventionist policies and to assume a vastly expanded role in running state-owned enterprises to implement the New Economic Policy (NEP). The stated aim of the NEP is to redistribute incomes and assets among the three groups, the Malays, the Chinese, and the Foreigners, according to a formula of 30%:40%:30% respectively of the total commercial and industrial assets of the country, the target to be achieved over a twenty-year period.

However, the world recession of the early 1980s delivered a short sharp shock to the Malaysian economy when its balance of payments became unfavourable for the first time, and its foreign exchange reserves suffered a sharp reduction. This induced the government to cut back public expenditure and privatize many state-owned enterprises. Thus the priority in government policies was shifted from equity to growth and stability. More accurately, this may be regarded as a shift from the policies of redistributing income to the Malay population directly by government action to an indirect policy of promoting growth instead.

Sri Lanka has been frequently cited as an example of a country which has achieved a high degree of income equality and impressive standards of health and education through direct social welfare policies and consumer subsidies. It has been argued that Sri Lanka's rate of growth is no worse than the average judged by the norms of a low-income country, and that at this normal rate of growth, it would take a 'long haul' for Sri Lanka to achieve her present standards of health and education by relying on growth policies alone.[7]

Our method of comparing Sri Lanka with Malaysia, starting from their initial conditions around the 1950s, provides us with a different perspective. Sri Lanka and Malaysia started out in 1960 with roughly similar income levels per capita (in terms of IPC/Kravis dollars, Sri Lanka's income per capita of $961 was higher than that of Malaysia, $888).[8]

Since then Sri Lanka's growth in income per capita has been about 2.5% a year (around the average for low-income countries), whereas Malaysia's income per capita has grown at 4.3% a year. Because of this difference in growth rates, Sri Lanka still remains a low-income country whereas Malaysia has progressed to the ranks of upper-middle-income countries. It is, therefore, misleading to judge Sri Lanka's growth performance over time by the norms for her present status as a low-income country. As we have said, the main factor contributing to this difference in growth rates may be found in the different policies which Sri Lanka and Malaysia have adopted towards the plantation and mining sectors, affecting their export performance.

Both Sri Lanka and Malaysia have been concerned with redistributing incomes in favour of their indigenous Sinhalese and Malay peasant farmers on grounds of equity. Malaysia's expanding exports have provided her government with expanding revenues to pursue this objective in a sustainable manner, whereas the stagnation of Sri Lanka's exports has resulted in balance-of-payments difficulties and 'stop-go' policies in her social welfare programmes. It may nevertheless be asked whether there is an inherent conflict between the policy of promoting exports from the plantation sector and the policy of agricultural import-substitution to promote domestic self-sufficiency in rice produced in the peasant sector. Such a conflict would arise if all the available land were fully utilized, and if there were no difference in the quality of land suitable for plantation exports and for rice cultivation. Malaysia's large reserve of unused land relaxed the land constraint, and even in Sri Lanka the difference in the type of land suitable for tea and rubber and for rice prevented a sharp conflict between the competing uses for land. In so far as capital investment in plantations and mines comes from abroad, there also need not be a sharp conflict between the competing uses of domestic capital resources.

In both Sri Lanka and Malaysia, the growth in income per capita has been associated with a reduction of poverty, the main incidence of poverty being in the rural areas. In Sri Lanka, food subsidies have alleviated the most severe effects of poor nutritional standards among the poor, but the costs of unselective subsidies became increasingly heavy over time.[9] According to Bruton,[10] poverty in Sri Lanka declined from Independence to 1973 but did not change very much over the decade 1973 to 1981/2, the incidence being around 20 to 25 per cent of the population.

In Malaysia, with a much faster rate of economic growth, there has been a sharper decline in poverty. Before 1970, roughly half the Malay population was estimated to be living in poverty. After that date, there has been a marked decline in poverty, most significantly among the Malay paddy farmers, fishermen, and rubber smallholders who formed the poorest section of the community. (See Table 3.4.)

We now come to the changes in income distribution: the available information concerning changes in income shares over time is given in Tables 3.5 and 3.6.

But in 'plural' societies such as Sri Lanka and Malaysia, income distribution among different ethnic groups looms larger than income distribution between the rich and the poor as such. Income distribution by ethnic groups is set out in Tables 3.7 and 3.8.

In terms of broad outcomes, Malaysia, with her more open economy and favourable policies towards foreign investment in the mining and plantation sector and later in the manufacturing sector, seems to be able to help her

Table 3.4. Malaysia: Incidence of poverty by activity and rural/urban area (per cent)

Sector and area	Poverty incidence		
	1970	1976	1984
Rural	58.7	47.8	24.7
Rubber smallholders	64.7	58.2	43.4
Paddy farmers	88.1	80.3	57.7
Estate workers	40.0	—	19.7
Fishermen	73.2	62.7	27.7
Coconut smallholders	52.8	64.7	46.9
Other agriculture	89.0	52.1	34.2
Other	35.2	27.3	10.0
Urban	21.3	17.9	8.2
Manufacturing	23.5	17.1	8.5
Construction	30.2	17.7	6.1
Transport and utilities	30.9	17.1	3.6
Trade and services	18.1	13.9	4.6
Agriculture	—	40.2	23.8
Mining	33.3	10.1	3.4
Other		22.4	17.1
Total	49.3	39.6	18.4

Source: Bruton (1992: table 12.3, p. 220).

Table 3.5. Sri Lanka: Decile Shares of Total Monthly Income (Spending Units)

Decile	1953	1963	1973	1978/79	1981/82
First	1.90	1.50	2.79	2.12	2.16
Second	3.30	3.95	4.38	3.61	3.55
Third	4.10	4.00	5.60	4.65	4.35
Fourth	5.20	5.21	6.52	5.68	5.24
Fifth	6.40	6.27	7.45	6.59	6.35
Sixth	6.90	7.54	8.75	7.69	7.02
Seventh	8.30	9.00	9.91	8.57	8.69
Eighth	10.10	11.22	11.65	11.22	10.71
Ninth	13.20	15.54	14.92	14.03	14.52
Tenth	40.60	36.77	28.03	35.84	37.29
Gini co-efficients	0.46	0.45	0.35	0.44	0.45

Source: Bruton (1992: table 5.4, p. 65).

Malay peasants in a more effective and sustainable manner than Sri Lanka has been able to help her Sinhalese peasants by the 'direct approach' of expanding social welfare in a setting of generally inward-looking policies. It is true that Sri Lanka's social indicators for life expectancy, infant mortality, and the proportion of children in primary and secondary schools remained

Table 3.6. Malaysia: Income Share of Households by Deciles

Decile	1957/58	1970	1976	1979	1984
Lowest	2.2	1.2	1.2	1.3	1.4
Second	3.5	2.8	2.1	2.4	2.8
Third	4.6	3.2	3.2	3.6	3.8
Fourth	5.4	4.5	4.6	4.6	4.8
Fifth	6.5	5.5	5.1	5.5	6.0
Sixth	7.7	6.8	6.7	7.0	7.2
Seventh	9.2	9.1	8.4	8.6	9.3
Eighth	11.1	10.7	11.4	11.2	11.5
Ninth	15.0	15.1	15.7	16.5	16.6
Highest	34.8	41.1	42.9	39.3	36.6
Mean income	220	275	513	693	1,095
Median income	156	170	313	436	723
Gini coefficient	0.42	0.50	0.53	0.51	0.48

Source: Bruton (1992: table 12.1, p. 215).

Table 3.7. Sri Lanka: Income for Income Receiver by Ethnic Group

Ethnic group	1963		1973		Ratio of median income to mean income	
	Mean income*	Percentage of all island	Mean income	Percentage of all island	1963	1973
	1	2	3	4	5	6
Sinhalese:						
Kandyan	218	81	422	93	0.65	0.89
Low Country	292	109	520	114	0.68	0.82
Tamils:						
Ceylon	327	122	470	103	0.60	0.82
Indian	148	55	225	49	0.80	0.80
Moors and Malays	414	155	670	147	0.60	0.70
Other	819	306	982	215	0.57	0.64
All island	267	100	455	100	0.62	0.79

*Rupees per two months.

Note: The table divides the Sinhalese population into the 'Kandyan' (the poorer sector of the population) and the 'Low Country' Sinhalese.

Source: Bruton (1992: table 7.3, p. 115).

Table 3.8. Peninsular Malaysia: Household income by ethnic group, 1979 and 1984 ($ per month)

Ethnic group	Constant 1970 prices			Current prices		
	Average annual growth rate			Average annual growth rate		
	1979	1984	1980–4	1979	1984	1980–4
Bumiputera						
Mean	296	384	5.3	492	852	11.6
Median	197	262	5.9	237	581	19.6
Chinese						
Mean	565	678	3.7	938	1,052	9.8
Median	373	462	4.4	620	1,024	10.6
Indian						
Mean	455	494	1.7	756	1,094	7.7
Median	314	347	2.0	521	770	8.1
All ethnic groups						
Mean	417	494	3.4	693	1,095	9.6
Median	263	326	4.4	493	723	8.0
Urban						
Mean	587	695	3.4	975	1,541	9.6
Median	361	463	5.1	600	1,027	11.3
Rural						
Mean	331	372	2.4	550	824	8.4
Median	222	269	3.9	369	596	10.1

Source: Bruton (1992: table 15.4, p. 319).

very high in comparison with other countries in the region during the 1960s and 1970s. But as Bhalla and Glewwe have taken pains to point out, Sri Lanka started from very favourable initial conditions concerning health and education in the 1950s.[11]

IV. THAILAND AND GHANA

At first sight, Thailand and Ghana seem to be an unlikely pair to choose. At present, Thailand is firmly established as a middle-income country with rapid economic growth, belonging to the exceptionally dynamic group of South-East Asian and 'Pacific Rim' countries. Ghana, on the other hand, is a low-income country belonging to the sub-Saharan group of African countries, notable for their poor economic performance and stagnation.

Yet, historically speaking, the two countries have gone through a similar process of economic growth through the expansion of peasant exports. This has been based on the familiar 'vent for surplus' process of extending cultivation into an abundant supply of unused land brought about by the spread of the exchange economy into subsistence agriculture, facilitated by improvements in transport and communications and the introduction of a modern administrative framework.

The initial conditions in the 1950s in the two countries were quite similar. Ghana's real income per capita of $1,009 in terms of the IPC/ Kravis dollars (1975 prices) was more than twice as high as Thailand's $446,[12] but they both still possessed a considerable amount of unused land to permit the continuation of their pre-war process of economic growth through peasant export expansion. Further, they both operated under traditional land tenure systems which provided a fairly equal distribution of land ownership or access to land. In Ghana the traditional tribal land tenure system has been reinforced by the British colonial policy of excluding large land concessions to plantations. With this fairly equal distribution of access to land, the expansion of peasant exports based on the traditional labour-intensive technology may be expected to promote not only economic growth but also the reduction of poverty and the improvement of income distribution.

Thus Thailand and Ghana fit into our general comparative scheme as an example of two countries which started from similar initial conditions but have pursued different economic policies, ending up with different outcomes in growth, poverty alleviation, and income distribution. Taking the period 1965–83 (before Ghana's recent economic recovery), the World Bank figures for income growth per capita are 4.3% a year for Thailand and −2.1% a year for Ghana. Ghana's peasant farmers are, however, as responsive to economic incentives as the Thai peasant farmers. Thus the striking difference in economic outcomes must be attributed to differences in government policies.

Thailand early abandoned the Marketing Board system and adopted a moderate export tax on rice, allowing sufficient economic incentives to her rice farmers. Supported by improvements in infrastructure, irrigation, and above all transport and communications, Thailand not only succeeded in maintaining the expansion of her traditional export of rice from her central plain but also in developing new peasant export crops, such as maize, tapioca, and sugar from her North and North-East regions. This export expansion, which continued well into the 1970s, resulted not only in a reduction of poverty through the rapid rise in incomes per capita, but also in a reduction of regional income inequalities between the richer central plains and the peripheral regions.

Ghana, on the other hand, held on to the Cocoa Marketing Board system long after she has found it possible to raise the bulk of her revenues from a graduated export tax. The combined burden of the Cocoa Marketing Board and the export tax seriously discouraged her cocoa exports. Moreover, the marketing board system imposed additional burdens in the form of dead-weight losses from inefficient administration and corruption, and repressed the growth of a private trading and credit network. Thus while the Thai peasant farmers benefited from the development of a private network of traders and middlemen effectively linking them with the world market, the Ghanaian farmers became increasingly cut off from world market conditions, receiving only a fraction of the world market price for their produce. They had no alternatives except to smuggle cocoa to neighbouring countries and to retreat into subsistence agriculture.

Thailand's export expansion policies were underpinned by conservative fiscal and monetary policies, enabling her to control domestic inflation and maintain an equilibrium rate of exchange and to attract a considerable inflow of foreign capital. This macroeconomic stability, together with her thriving agricultural sector, enabled her to keep her domestic wages low. Thus, after early attempts to pursue import-substitution policies of domestic industrialization, she was able to switch from the expansion of labour-intensive peasant exports to the expansion of labour-intensive manufactured exports to absorb her population growth in the agricultural sector.

In contrast, Ghana broke the colonial mould of conservative fiscal and monetary policies in the latter half of the Nkrumah regime during 1959–65. Heavy budget deficits and borrowing from a newly created Central Bank were used to finance a 'Big Push' investment programme to promote domestic industrialization through import-substitution based on state enterprise. The resultant domestic inflation and balance-of-payments difficulties were controlled by tightening quantitative import controls and by heavy foreign borrowing in the form of medium-term suppliers' credit towards the end of the period. This economic débâcle and insolvency under Nkrumah paved the way of Ghana's spectacular economic decline, with the economy zigzagging downward with successive contractions of exports and national income, in the face of rampant inflation and cumulative budget deficits under a series of inept military governments. The economy reached a nadir in 1983 when inflation had so eroded the purchasing power of a contracting revenue base that the government itself became increasingly marginalized and the economic life of the country shifted out of official control into a parallel black economy and subsistence agriculture. Thus Ghana was forced into a thoroughgoing programme of trade liberalization and macroeconomic reforms with external aid under the second administration of Lieutenant Rawlings.

Over the whole period 1950–85, Thailand's GDP has grown at the rate of 6.7% a year, giving her a real rate of growth of GDP per capita of 3.9% a year, doubling income approximately every 18 years.[13] As a consequence, the proportion of her population below a fixed poverty line has been drastically reduced for the country as a whole, from 57% in 1962/3 to 33% in 1975/6 and to 24% in 1981. The breakdown of the incidence of poverty into the different regions of the country and into the urban and the rural areas also shows a clear trend towards a reduction in the inter-regional income inequalities (see Table 3.9).

Historically, the richest region in Thailand has been the central plain, which was opened up for rice exports in the late nineteenth century, followed by the rubber-growing region of the South. The poorest regions have been the north and the north-east regions, which until recent times have been only partially in the exchange economy because of poor transport and communications. Thus the opening up during the 1960s of the north and north-east regions to the new upland peasant export crops such as maize and tapioca have not only promoted economic growth but also

Table 3.9. Thailand: Incidence of poverty, 1962/3 to 1980/1 (per cent of population)

Region and area	1962/3	1975/6	1981
North-East	74	46	36
Urban	44	38	36
Rural	77	48	36
North	65	35	23
Urban	56	31	23
Rural	66	36	23
South	44	33	21
Urban	35	29	18
Rural	46	35	22
Centre*	40	16	16
Urban	40	20	24
Rural	40	15	14
Bangkok[†]	28	12	4
Whole kingdom	57	33	24
Urban	38	22	16
Rural	61	37	26

*Excludes changwats Samut Prakan, Nonthaburi, and Pathum Thani in 1975/6.

[†]Includes changwats Bangkok and Thonburi in all years and, in addition, changwats Samut Prakan, Nonthaburi, and Pathum Thani in 1975/6 and 1981.

Note: Urban areas refer to municipal areas and sanitary districts, rural areas refer to villages. The poverty line is defined in terms of household total income to be 1,981 baht/person/year in villages and 2,961 baht/person/year in municipal areas and sanitary districts in 1975/6 prices.

Source: Table 3.25 in *Thailand Study* (mimeo), ch. 3.

served to reduce regional income inequalities. This is one of the ways in which expansion of peasant exports in countries with an abundant supply of land may be expected to promote both economic growth and better income distribution without any deliberate policy on the part of the government. However, the improvements of transport and communication in the north and north-east regions, such as the Friendship Highway, had been motivated by strategic and counter-insurgency reasons. Thus both economic growth and income distribution were unintended effects (see Table 3.10).

Another important aspect of income inequality in Thailand is that which exists between the Greater Bangkok area and the rest of the country. One part of the reason for this arises from the agglomeration effects and differential access to employment opportunities in manufacturing industry in Bangkok and in the provincial towns. But the other part of the reason may be found in the bias towards Bangkok of government policies in the provision of social services. As can be seen from Table 3.11, Bangkok, with about 10% of the total population of the country, has received a disproportionately large share of social services.

Ghana's economic history from 1950 to 1983 may be described as one long failure to take advantage of her favourable initial conditions and endowment of resources. During the period 1950–8, when Nkrumah main-

Table 3.10. Thailand: Household incomes per capita as percentages of central levels, by area, 1962/3 to 1981

Area/Region	1962/3	1975/6	1981
Municipal areas and sanitary districts			
North-East	97.5	82.0	83.7
North	97.1	83.9	105.8
South	105.4	96.0	110.7
Centre	100.0	100.0	100.0
Villages			
North-East	55.7	56.6	56.7
North	62.1	67.0	78.8
South	99.0	73.9	81.8
Centre	100.0	100.0	100.0
All areas			
North-East	57.6	59.1	58.2
North	64.8	69.5	83.3
South	101.8	80.2	87.2
Centre	100.0	100.0	100.0

Note: Data for 1981 obtained from published tabulations or the data tapes.

Source: Table 3.34 in *Thailand Study* (mimeo), ch. 3.

Table 3.11. Thailand: Share of Bangkok in terms of various indicators

Indicator	Whole Kingdom	Bangkok Bangkok	% share
Population, 1980	44,824,540	4,697,071	10.5
Municipal population, 1980	7,632,916	4,697,071	61.5
Population attending school, 1980:			
Ages: 13–15	1,528,331	231,958	15.2
16–18	884,434	212,765	24.1
19–24	556,617	207,452	37.3
25–29	62,296	21,796	35.0
Number of schools	34,293	1,374	4.0
Private Schools	2,327	816	35.1
Private Students	1,119,528	432,593	38.6
Hospitals, 1977	319	92	28.8
Hospital Beds, 1977	60,045	16,399	27.3
Doctors, 1977	5,846	3,517	60.2
Nurses, 1977	15,208	8,033	52.8
Television Sets, 1979	810,000	374,172	46.2
Telephones, 1979	427,588	318,613	74.5

Source: Table 3.36 in *Thailand Study* (mimeo), ch. 3.

tained a liberal trade regime, enabling Ghana to enjoy economic growth through export expansion, Ghana showed a respectable rate of growth in GDP of 4.1% a year. During that period, the improvement in the standard of living may be judged from a rising trend in imports, from $46 million in 1950 to $78 million in 1958; three-fifths of these imports consisted of consumer goods in 1958.[14] Nkrumah's 'Big Push' shunted Ghana away from this beneficial path of growth through peasant export expansion into a disastrous attempt to promote domestic industrialization through import-substitution based on state enterprise. Apart from an unsuccessful attempt to arrest the decline during the period 1966–71, the economy zigzagged downward until it reached its lowest point in 1983.

During the periods of slow or negative rates of economic growth during the 1959–63 period and particularly during the 1972–83 period, the absolute level of poverty and malnutrition seems to have spread from the poorer to some of the less favoured sections of the middle classes. Rimmer (1992) speaks of the 'Rawlings necklaces', the nickname for the protruding collar-bones caused by malnourishment, seen among the Ghanaian university vice-chancellors who attended the Commonwealth Universities Conference in Birmingham in 1983.

In the context of a country like Ghana, perhaps the most telling index of the economic position is given by the state of migration. In the 1950s, it was believed that some 300,000 to 400,000 workers entered Ghana from the surrounding countries. By the 1970s, huge numbers of Ghanaians, both skilled and unskilled, were emigrating. When Nigeria decided, in 1983, to expel illegally resident aliens, one million of them turned out to be Ghanaians (out of Ghana's total population of 12.7 million in 1985).

In so far as one can usefully speak of changes in the relative income distribution in the Ghanaian context, two points may be mentioned. In Ghana, as in Thailand, an important element in income inequality arises from the regional differences in incomes between the cocoa-exporting regions in the southern part of the country and the drier and less fertile northern territories which had no export production.[15] While Thailand managed to reduce this source of income inequality through the diversification of peasant export crops in her north and north-eastern regions, in Ghana even the farmers in the cocoa-exporting areas of the country reverted to subsistence agriculture, due to lack of incentives for export production. The only section of farmers who gained relatively were those who shifted into food production in the face of inflation and food shortages in the country. Despite the government's attempt to create wage employment in the public sector, the real wages were already declining in the Nkrumah 'Big Push' period. The real minimum wage, which had improved in the 1950s, fell steeply from 1960 to 1983, the only interruptions in the trend occurring in 1967–8 and 1972–4. Apparently this wage fell by about 50% between 1960 and 1971, and by another 80% between 1971 and 1983. Mean wages were not greatly above the minimum and would have performed similarly. The cocoa producer price also deteriorated greatly in real value, though its retrogression was less uniform. After a substantial rise in the 1950s, the nominal price was cut by one-quarter in 1960, and the real price then fell over 60% by 1965/6. There was a recovery in the real price until 1971/2, followed by some years of stability. Between 1974/5 and 1982/3 there was another fall of 60%. The aggregate real payments to cocoa farmers move similarly, except that the last fall begins earlier—in 1972/3— and is even steeper—about 90%.

Ghana's free fall into the economic abyss, with disastrous consequences for living standards and nutrition, has been frequently blamed on the corruption of her successive ruling groups. This is not an entirely adequate explanation, since the ruling groups in Thailand were by no means free from corruption. The more interesting difference seems to be that the Thai ruling groups from Sarit (1959) onwards realized that they could more profitably pursue their rent-seeking activities in partnership with private entrepreneurs, domestic and foreign, in the context of an open economy, than by battening on inefficient state enterprises. On the other hand, Ghanaian ruling groups from Nkrumah onwards have been taken in by their own rhetoric of anti-colonialism and the 'socialist transformation of the economy' and failed to pursue a policy of enlightened self-interest for themselves and their country. Thus they tried to squeeze a larger share of a fast shrinking national income, and strangled the goose that lay the golden eggs in the form of the peasant exporters of cocoa. In contrast, the Thai peasant farmers prospered despite the vast private personal fortunes accumulated by their rulers.

V. BRAZIL AND MEXICO

Brazil and Mexico, the two largest Latin American economies, may be said to have started from similar initial conditions and to have pursued a similar mixture of policies with similar economic outcomes.

Their initial conditions are characterized by an abundant endowment of natural resources, an unequal distribution of land ownership, and the predominance of large-scale agricultural estates and mining enterprises in their primary exports production.

They have followed a mixture of import-substitution and export-expansion policies, one or other of these policies dominating in different phases of their development. Typically, an intensification of import-substitution policies to accelerate the rate of domestic industrialization tends to end up with a balance-of-payments crisis followed by trade liberalization policies to expand exports. They have also followed expansionist fiscal and monetary policies to maintain a high rate of investment, and the balance-of-payments crises have been caused not only by 'trade distortions' at the micro-economic level but also by macroeconomic imbalances, which have to be corrected by tighter fiscal and monetary policies and by an adjustment of the exchange rates to reflect the rate of domestic inflation.

Brazil and Mexico have recorded very high rates of economic growth over a long period before their economic débâcles in the early 1980s. Thus for the period 1950–80, the average rate of GDP per capita was 4.5% a year for Brazil and 3.1% a year for Mexico. These high rates of growth have contributed to a significant reduction of poverty in an absolute sense. In relative terms, however, income distribution in both countries remains highly unequal, compounded by regional income disparities. Mexico's land reform programme has arguably only slightly modified the basic income-distribution pattern. Both countries have suffered a serious balance-of-payments and debt crises in the wake of the oil shocks, the world recession, and the rise in the world interest rates. During 1980–7, Brazil's growth of income per capita declined to 0.3%, while Mexico suffered a negative growth of –1.4% a year.

We are concerned here with a longer-term comparative analysis, concentrating on the relationship between the mixed import-substitution and export-expansion policies of Brazil and Mexico with their high average growth rates.

It is possible to argue that the high rates of economic growth in Brazil and

Mexico are mainly the consequence of their abundant endowment of natural resources, which offered them obvious opportunities for expanding their agricultural and primary export production, and that their mixed policies of import-substitution and export-expansion have been pursued in a sufficiently moderate manner not to undermine the link between the expansion of primary exports and economic growth. On this view, the development of Brazil and Mexico into semi-industrial countries exporting a wide range of manufactured exports may be explained as follows. These are large countries to begin with, and the rise in their incomes per capita through the expansion of primary exports would enlarge the size of their domestic markets to allow for a natural process of import-substitution through the rise of domestic industries, which would have happened even under free-trade conditions. These domestic industries would subsequently break out into the export market, reflecting a changing pattern of comparative advantage.

This type of argument would have been rejected out of hand in the 1950s, or even much later, when 'export pessimism' concerning primary products prevailed, and domestic industrialization through import-substitution was commonly regarded as an alternative 'engine of growth'. Brazil and Mexico were then looked upon as outstanding examples of countries which had achieved rapid growth through import-substitution. Looking back, it can be agreed that in the period of rapidly expanding world trade and buoyant demand for primary products before the oil shocks and the subsequent world recession, their abundant supply of natural resources did offer countries like Brazil and Mexico obvious opportunities for rapid growth. The growth of their primary exports was important, not only as the means of promoting growth directly, but also as the means of enlarging their capacity for foreign borrowing, since the financing of their high rates of investment depended on large inflows of foreign capital.

But do the import-substitution policies necessarily conflict with export-expansion policies as depicted in textbook models, with the full employment of the 'given' resources of a country? It will be recalled that, in the Malaysian case, we have argued that the government policy of agricultural import-substitution to increase domestic self-sufficiency in rice grown in the peasant sector did not significantly retard the growth of exports from the plantation and the mining sectors, given the reserve of unused land and the availability of foreign capital for the latter sectors. Both these conditions of abundant land and the availability of foreign capital apply also to Brazil and Mexico. But there is an important difference. Malaysian policy of agricultural import substitution has not involved macroeconomic imbalances in the form of domestic inflation and over-valued exchange rates. It is the macroeconomic imbalances and the attempt to maintain over-valued exchange rates to obtain cheap imported inputs for the import-substituting manufacturing industries which have been an important cause of discouraging exports in the Latin American context. This is most clearly illustrated by the stagnation of exports in Brazil during the period 1951–64, when she went through an extreme phase of import-substitution, relying heavily on quantitative controls of foreign trade and a multiple exchange-rate system.

It is interesting to make further points of contrast between Brazil and Mexico and the Asian countries. In the land-abundant Asian countries, where traditional labour-intensive methods of cultivation prevailed in peasant agriculture, the initial sparsity of population relative to land gave rise to one or other of the following outcomes: either a considerable reserve of land was left unused, to be taken up when population and peasant exports expanded (as in Thailand); or alternatively, the abundant supply of land was used for the expansion of plantation and mining exports, bringing in low-wage immigrant labour from India and China. In either case, we start from the Asian tradition of low wages. In the Latin American type of land-abundant countries, such as Brazil and Mexico, export production is dominated by large-scale plantations and mining companies run on commercial lines; the high land-man ratio then manifested itself in a high level of wages in the modern export sector. Although capital was scarce, labour was even scarcer relatively to abundant land, and capital-intensive methods were employed, the indivisibilities being overcome by the large size of the holdings.

In the Asian countries, starting from low wage-levels, the expansion of labour-intensive peasant exports or the labour-intensive manufactured exports led to a rising trend in wages. In the Latin American countries, starting from relatively higher wage-levels, equilibrium adjustment required going through a phase of downward adjustment in wages for two reasons. First, with a given rate of capital accumulation, the rapid growth of population which occurred both in Brazil and Mexico can be absorbed only at lower wages. Secondly, there is the problem of raising the productivity of labour employed in manufacturing to bring it up to the high levels of wages established in agriculture. Given their initially higher levels of wages, the Latin American countries cannot effectively compete with the low-wage Asian countries in the highly labour-intensive type of manufactured products, and are obliged to raise their labour productivity to realize their potential comparative advantage in the less highly labour-intensive and more capital-intensive middle-level type of manufactured exports.

To make things more difficult for themselves, Brazil and Mexico have tried to promote technologically sophisticated manufacturing industries based on highly capital-intensive methods of production, making heavy demands on their savings and capacity to borrow from abroad. This is similar to Singapore's strategy of trying to climb the ladder of comparative advantage a few steps ahead in the natural evolution towards more capital-intensive types of manufactured exports. But Singapore was able to sustain this strategy without inflation, because of her ability to extract an exceptionally high rate of domestic savings. In contrast, Brazil had to impose wage freezes by military governments, and both Brazil and Mexico have had to resort to inflationary financing and heavy foreign borrowing. Thus the expansionary fiscal and monetary policies motivated by the desire to ease the political difficulties associated with a downward adjustment in wages have added to their endemic macroeconomic imbalances.

Up to 1980 Brazil maintained high rates of GDP growth: 6.6% per annum during 1950–64, 8.1% per annum during 1964–80, and 2.8% per annum during 1980–7.[16] We would expect this rapid growth to reduce poverty. This is the case, more modestly during the 1960s and more markedly during the 1970s, as can be seen from Table 3.12.

Income inequality, on the other hand, appears to have increased during the 1960s, though the trend is less obvious in the 1970s. Brazil has chosen to alleviate poverty through rapid growth rather than through income distribution policy. Brazilian levels of income inequality are high even by Latin American standards, as is the case in Mexico. Regional inequality is particularly marked and long-standing, the poorest region being the northeast, since the decline of its once prosperous sugar industry. The disparities have been aggravated by concentration of economic growth in the south and São Paulo regions, resulting in interstate income differences of 8.6 : 1 in 1980.[17] Income inequality has also arisen from the 'dualism' between small and large farms, which has not been helped by the opening up of new lands, which have mainly gone to large-scale agricultural units on the grounds of efficiency. State credit and incentives have also gone to the larger farms. The Brazilian Gini coefficient around 1970 was 0.55, and the income per capita of the top 10% was 20 times that of the bottom 20%.[18]

Average earnings of industrial employees rose by 57.3% in real terms during 1970–80. This, coupled with internal migration, eased the situation

Table 3.12. Brazil: Number of families below the poverty line, 1960–80

	1960	1970	1980
Poverty line (current new cruzeiros)	3.30	150.00	4,153.50
Deflator	1.00	45.46	1,258.64
Poverty line in 1960 prices (new cruzeiros)	3.30	3.30	3.30
Number of families (million)	5.27	7.04	5.83
Percentage of families below poverty line	38.9	37.90	21.70

Source: Maddison *et al.* (1992: table 4.11, p. 95).

a little during the 1970s, though no clear improvement in inequality is evident.[19] The centrally organized social security system (SINPAS) has grown in importance, helping significantly to improve health conditions in the country, and acting in a redistributive manner. The total impact of the tax-transfer system, however, is highly regressive. In 1975, people earning $481 a year paid 36% in taxes, and those earning $40,810 a year paid 14%.[20] The large subsidies (6.1% of GDP in 1982) and price controls have been poorly targeted, with little effect on distribution, designed more to control inflation.

Despite considerable shifts in policy emphasis between different six-yearly presidential terms, Mexico had enjoyed a sustained rate of growth generally above 6% a year from 1950 up to 1980. Since then the growth rate has declined sharply, reducing the growth of income per head to a negative rate of −1.2% a year during 1980–7.[21] By 1985 average private consumption per capita had probably risen to more than three times the 1940 level, but it is not possible to monitor this with accuracy. We do know that labour productivity in agriculture rose faster than in the rest of the economy, the productivity spreads between the richer and poorer states narrowed, and the social indicators for health and education showed substantial progress.[22]

The relative income distribution in Mexico remains highly unequal in terms of overall measures. Around 1970 the Gini coefficient for Mexican income distribution was 0.567, and this has not changed over time. The ratio of the income per capita of the top 10% of population to the bottom 20% was 25.5:1 (see Table 3.13).[23]

The authors of the study believe that income inequality is likely to be somewhat less in Mexico than in Brazil, because of Mexico's land reforms, more liberal wage policies, and higher educational expenditure, and a lesser degree of regional income inequalities. The range of inter-state income differences is estimated to be 6.3:1 compared with Brazil's 8.6:1.

Land reforms have been a way of legitimizing the Mexican revolution, and after a slow start the tempo of land redistribution to the Ejidos (common ownership of land by a whole village, with non-transferable individual holdings) quickened under President Cardenas in the 1930s and has been continued in the post-war decades. By 1970, about half of the area of arable land seemed to be cultivated under the Ejidos and communal tenure. But there are well-known limitations to the Mexican land reform, such as the communal ownership, which limits the small farmers' access to credit, and the usual differential access to government assistance in the form of subsidized inputs and technology between the large and small farmers. A large proportion of land under irrigation is cultivated by large farmers, and crop output per hectare in Ejido farms is only two-thirds that of the private farms.[24] Thus it is no wonder that Maddison et al. regard land reform as the means 'to distribute poverty'. This should also qualify the argument that

Table 3.13. Mexico: Alternative summary measures of inequality of income (Gini coefficients)

	Unadjusted for under-reporting	Adjusted for under-reporting
A. Felix (1982)		
1950	0.432	0.526
1963	0.543	0.555
1968	0.529	0.577
1975	0.570	0.579
B. Van Ginneken (1980) (post-tax income)		
1950		0.50
1963		0.55
1963		0.56
1975		0.58
C. Bergsman (1980) hypothesis B		
1963	0.527	0.584
1968	0.522	0.584
1975	0.557	0.628
1977	0.496	0.569

Source: Maddison *et al.* (1992: table 7.1, p. 186).

the rise in labour productivity in agriculture (greater in the private farms) is evidence of reduced income inequalities.[25]

VI. URUGUAY AND COSTA RICA

Uruguay and Costa Rica have been chosen as a pair of countries with highly developed social welfare systems characterized by high levels of public expenditure on health, education, social security, and food subsidies, with a high proportion of people employed in the public sector.

Uruguay and Costa Rica are small countries with comfortable levels of income per capita by Latin American standards ($1,650 and $1,300 respectively in 1985), and with populations mainly of Spanish extraction. They are land-abundant countries, but have depended on two different types of primary exports. Uruguay's main export, beef, is produced on large-scale ranches typical of the Latin American style of extensive farming using capital-intensive methods. Costa Rica's main export (before the advent of banana exports) has been coffee, produced by small farmers using relatively labour-intensive methods (contrasting with the large-scale coffee plantations of Brazil). The expansion of labour-intensive coffee exports in Costa Rica has not only promoted economic growth but also a more egalitarian distribution of income, by raising the incomes of small farmers and the wages of agricultural workers. This is thus rather similar to the effects of the expansion of peasant exports in Thailand.

Starting from these different types of export base, Uruguay and Costa Rica have pursued a similar mixture of policies, combining their social welfare policies with import-substitution policies or with export expansion policies at different phases of their history. But the time-sequence is different.

Uruguay started with a phase of combining social welfare policies with import-substitution policies, and suffered from export stagnation and a very low rate of GDP growth of less than 1% a year during the period 1955–73. This was a period of rising economic discontent and trade union militancy, with the political tensions boiling over into an urban guerrilla movement. The military take-over in 1973, pushing through trade liberalization policies and macroeconomic reforms including the exchange rate reforms, led to a recovery of Uruguay's exports and to a rise in growth rate between 4 and 5 per cent during the period 1973–81. The fact that Uruguay was able to make a recovery during this period of oil shocks and unfavourable world economic conditions suggests how severely its export production must have been distorted and repressed in the preceding period. During the 1960s and 1970s income inequalities in Uruguay seem to have been increasing, and the downward adjustment in wages to make the liberalization policies work increased income inequalities during the initial phase. But by the beginning of the 1980s, export expansion led to the expansion of employment, reversing the trend towards greater income inequality. However, during the 1982–5 period, Uruguay's growth rate has declined again.

Costa Rica, on the other hand, started with a period of combining social welfare policies with the expansion of primary exports during the period 1950–63. During this period she showed a rate of per capita GDP growth of 1.5%. In the next period, 1963–73, Costa Rica entered a phase of intensified import-substitution based on state-owned industries, coinciding with her entry into the Central American Common Market (CACM). For a time, the import-substitution policies seem to have paid off with an impressive rise of GDP to 7.2% a year, 3.9% in per capita terms. But this seems mainly to have been brought about by the 'trade diversion effect', enabling Costa Rica to export manufactured goods to the CACM behind a very heavy wall of protection. With the disintegration of the CACM in the welter of regional wars in Central America and the first oil shock, Costa Rica's position worsened rapidly. Her government budget and balance of payments came under increasing strain under the double burden of maintaining inefficient state-owned industries and increasing welfare expenditures and subsidies. During the period 1973–85, her GDP growth plunged to 2.9% a year, just barely ahead of her population growth. With rising inflation and growing budget and balance-of-payments deficits, a sharp fall in coffee prices in 1978 pushed Costa Rica over the brink into an economic collapse and a debt crisis. Income distribution, which had been improving during the period of growth, based on labour-intensive coffee exports, worsened significantly in the 1980s.

The highly developed social welfare systems of Uruguay and Costa Rica have been conventionally attributed to the 'equity-orientated' policies of their governments. But it is more instructive to look at the political economy factors behind these policies. These political economy factors can be most clearly seen in the setting of Uruguay, which embarked on social welfare policies decades before.

The production of Uruguay's export staple, meat, requires only a thin population in rural areas, and there has been an early tendency for population to be concentrated in urban areas. More than a half of Uruguay's total population of three million is concentrated in the Montevideo metropolitan region. With the passing of political power from the rural caudillos to a two-party system of government, the interest of the urban voters came to dominate government policies. The social welfare policies were brought about as a direct consequence of the political pressure of the urban population to tax the export sector for their benefit. This also went hand in hand with import-substitution policies in favour of the urban manufacturing industries, in response to powerful trade union pressures. In Uruguay, two-thirds of beef production happens to be consumed domestically, making up the budget of low-income consumers. Hence social welfare policies to subsidize consumption directly reduced the available volume of exports.

Costa Rica's coffee exports were not associated with such a concentrated degree of urbanization to begin with, but with economic development there was a similar tendency for population concentration in the San José metropolitan region, the hub of the coffee industry. The two-party political system in Costa Rica gave rise to a radical nationalist party, the PLN, with familiar ideological predilections. The social welfare policies were to be intensified in response to the demand of the urban middle classes. But there was also the reaction against the old agricultural oligarchy and the nineteenth-century liberal policies of free trade and expansion of primary exports. The country was switched towards a policy of domestic industrialization and import substitution on the basis of state-run enterprises.

The experiences of Uruguay and Costa Rica serve to emphasize not only that the economic development of small countries must depend on export expansion, but also that social welfare systems cannot be run on a sustainable basis without expanding revenues from a healthy export sector.

This can be clearly seen in the case of Costa Rica, where the relative position of the bottom 20% of households worsened after the country turned away from the earlier phase of expanding labour-intensive coffee exports to an intensification of import-substituting manufactured industries. This is readily observable after 1971. The percentage of the population classified as poor also rose from the low levels of the mid-1970s to 30% in the early 1980s (see Table 3.14).

VII. COLOMBIA AND PERU

There are obvious similarities between Colombia and Peru as two middle-sized Latin American countries, neighbouring each other, both abundantly endowed with natural resources. But it is more instructive to look at their differences.

First, there is the difference in their ethnic composition and social structure. Colombia has a more homogeneous population of mixed racial origins, sharing a common Hispanic language and culture. The oligarchy in the two ruling parties has been drawn from this mestizo population. Political power is based on regional affiliations and is not especially concentrated in Bogotá, and rich and poor people can be found in most regions.

In contrast, the Peruvian oligarchy was mainly white, and not even of Spanish origin in most cases. Political and economic power was concentrated in the Lima coastal region. A mestizo population provided the lower middle class. But there was a deep cleavage dividing these top and middle layers of society from the bottom layer, made up of the Indian population living in deep poverty in the Andean Sierras and the Amazon jungles. In 1950, the Indian population, mainly speaking Quechua, made

Table 3.14. Costa Rica: Changes in the distribution of household income, 1961–77

Percentage of households	Percentage of income			Increase in real income %	
	1961	1971	1977	1961–1971	1971–1977
10.0	2.6	2.1	0.7	11.6	−16.4
10.0	3.4	3.3	2.2	32.1	−3.8
10.0	3.8	4.2	3.4	50.8	2.5
10.0	4.0	5.1	4.6	76.3	2.5
10.0	4.4	6.2	5.8	94.0	3.3
10.0	5.5	7.5	7.2	91.2	2.3
10.0	7.1	9.3	9.2	78.7	2.8
10.0	9.3	11.7	12.2	73.3	2.9
10.0	14.0	16.2	17.3	58.3	1.7
10.0	46.0	34.4	37.4	4.3	3.7
100.0	100.0	100.0	100.0	37.5	3.3

Source: Rottenberg *et al.* (1993: combined from table 3.2, p. 46, and table 3.3, p. 49).

up some 60% of the total Peruvian population. Peru remains a 'plural society' with deep-seated conflict across the social, economic, and racial chasm.

Secondly, although Colombia and Peru are both abundantly endowed with natural resources, their economic history has been shaped by different types of staple exports. Although there are large ranches and plantations in Colombia, coffee, her major export, has been produced by small farmers using labour-intensive methods. In this, the nature of Colombia's coffee production resembles that of Costa Rica and contrasts with the Brazilian coffee exports from large-scale plantations. The small coffee farmers and coffee entrepreneurs of the Antioquia region were to play a major role at a later stage in expanding Colombia's labour-intensive manufactured exports.

In contrast, Peru's exports consist of minerals and large-scale plantation products from the coastal region. This modern export sector was owned and run by foreign investors and a small group of Peruvians, the 'agrarian oligarchy', who were foreign-orientated. The Indians from the Sierras were not involved in the expansion of this modern export sector.

Starting from these different initial conditions, the style of economic policies pursued in Colombia and Peru has been different. In the aftermath of a bitter civil war ('La Violencia'), Colombia settled down to a period of middle-of-the-road economic policies, maintaining a balance of power between two main parties, the Conservatives and the Liberals. Up to 1966, Colombia depended mainly on coffee exports and followed import-substitution policies, like other Latin American countries. The Restropo administration (1966–70) introduced economic liberalization policies, including the introduction of a 'crawling peg' system of exchange-rate adjustment. Colombia then switched to export-expansion policies, and enjoyed not only the expansion of her primary exports, such as coffee, bananas, sugar, and cotton, but also an expansion of labour-intensive manufactured exports, mainly produced by indigenous Colombian entrepreneurs on the basis of small family firms.

In contrast, there have been violent swings in the direction of economic policies in Peru, first under a right-wing military take-over by General Odría (1948–56) and next under a left-wing military take-over by General Velasco (1968–75). The Odría regime pushed through a vigorous programme of economic liberalization, and initiated a period of rapid export-expansion in economic growth during 1950–66. The left-wing military take-over by Velasco was based on a coalition of middle-class mestizo army officers, bureaucrats, and trade-unionists to overthrow the 'agrarian oligarchy' and the foreign investors dominating the export sector. The Velasco regime carried out an extensive programme of nationalization, including foreign-owned mining, banking, and fishing enterprises and large agricultural estates producing major export commodities such as sugar, rice, and cotton. In these estates and in a wide range of manufacturing industries, full-time unionized employees were given an increasing share of ownership, management, and profits as members of labour co-operatives and 'labour communities'. It is fair to say that Peru has not really recovered from the economic débâcle initiated by the Velasco regime. Under subsequent governments, the economy limped from one crisis to another, culminating in Peru's 1980s plight of hyper-inflation and a major balance-of-payments and debt crisis.

Taking the period 1950–85 as a whole, Colombia's rate of GDP growth per capita of 2% a year has been approximately twice as high as that of Peru. It has also been much steadier, since Peru's economic growth occurred mainly during the period 1950–66. Thus Colombia has been more successful than Peru in reducing poverty in an absolute sense. Both Colombia and Peru, however, started with a highly unequal distribution of income and land ownership. Colombia has to some extent been able to moderate the income inequalities by expanding the labour-intensive exports, both coffee and, later, manufactured exports. On the other hand, the Velasco revolution redistributed incomes from the top-income oligarchy to the lower middle classes, consisting of the unionized workers in urban industries and the established labour force in large estates; it has done little for the Indian population remaining outside the modern sector of the economy. The Indian population in the Sierras still live in deep poverty and economic discontent. The 'Shining Path' guerrilla movement of the Indians is rooted in this economic discontent, compounded by racial and cultural conflicts.

Although income distribution in Colombia remains unequal by international standards (see Table 3.15), the incidence of absolute poverty seems to have diminished, due to rapid economic growth and a decline in the rate of population growth and in the proportion of population living in rural areas. Using the same poverty line, the authors of the study suggest that the incidence of absolute poverty has been reduced to less than 40% of the total population by the 1980s as compared with an estimated 60% in 1950. There has also been a rise in wage levels and food consumption per capita.

Peru's income per capita (adjusted for the terms of trade) grew at the average rate of 2.8% a year during the period 1950–66 and then declined at the rate of −0.6% a year during the period 1967–85. The average income of the poorest 40% of the population grew at the rate of 1.2% a year during 1950–66 and declined at the rate of −0.1% a year during the period 1967–85. The broad picture which has emerged is of a relatively unchanged degree of absolute poverty since 1961, with a continuing rapid growth of population. (See Table 3.16.)

The author of the Peru study has also assembled the available information about the relative income distribution in Peru, but has warned that

Table 3.15. Colombia: Income distribution comparisons for the labour force, before taxes and transfers

All sectors of the economy (percentages)

		1934–6	1951	1964	1972
Share of top	5%	38.41	40.00–42.22	35.66	n.a.
	10%	48.16	51.15–53.90	47.87	49.0
	20%	60.79	64.95–67.68	63.10	62.5
	30%	70.14	74.29–77.01	73.73	73.0
	50%	83.79	86.14–88.00	86.84	85.5
Bottom	20%	3.78	2.49–3.00	3.30	3.0
Gimi coefficient		0.553	0.602–0.633	0.570	0.580

Source: *Colombia Study* (mimeo), table 4.

Table 3.16. Peru: Absolute Poverty; Income per capita of the poorest half of the population (in 1985 US $)

1950	113
1961	144
1971–2	168
1985–6	166

Source: Table 13 in the *Peru Study* (mimeo), pt. II.

the figures are not comparable across the three dates because of the different methods of calculation (see Table 3.17).

The author emphasizes that the most striking differences in income distribution in Peru arise from the large regional and urban–rural income differentials. In particular, he draws attention to economic dualism as illustrated by the extremes in income distribution between the Lima region, which has 27% of the total population, and the Sierra rural population, which makes up most of the poorest third of the population (see Table 3.18).

Despite her better economic performance, Colombia is also plagued by various radical guerrilla movements and by the rise of the drug barons, who now threaten law and order and the basic administration of justice. Peru also has her drug industry, but the coca leaves grown in the jungles by the Indians increased their cash incomes and have been a factor reducing income inequalities.

The Colombia–Peru comparison underlines two general points.

1. Two countries which at first appear similar enough to form a 'natural' pair may turn out to be rather different on a closer view, but we may learn as much from studying the differences as the similarities.

Table 3.17. Peru: Income distribution (% of total income)

Percentile	1961–72 (earners)	1985–6	
		(Household consumption)	(Household consumption per capita)
Poorest 20%	2.5	3.2	4.1
21–40	5.5	7.3	8.9
41–60	10.2	13.3	14.0
61–80	17.4	21.5	21.6
81–90	15.2	17.7	16.2
Top 10	49.2	37.0	35.2

Note: Figures are not comparable across years, due to different methods.
Source: Table 5 in the *Peru Study* (mimeo), pt. II.

Table 3.18. Peru: Income differentials

		Urban–Rural	Lima–Peru	Lima–Sierra rural
1961	Income by earner	2.7	2.0	4.3
1972	Household income	3.3	2.2	5.4
1972	Household expenditure			4.0
1981	Income by earner	2.5		
1985–6	Household per capita expenditure	2.0	1.5	2.4

Source: Table 6 in the *Peru Study* (mimeo), pt. II.

2. Given the different institutional settings, countries classified as 'land-abundant' in terms of aggregate land–man ratios may have comparative advantage in different types of primary exports, or may produce the same primary exports using different factor proportions and different scales of production. The fact that coffee is produced by small farmers using labour-intensive methods in Colombia and Costa Rica has different implications for their income distribution, as contrasted with Brazil where coffee is produced on large-scale estates.

VIII. EGYPT AND TURKEY

Apart from their geographical location and historical associations, Egypt and Turkey have a number of similarities. During much of the post-war period both countries have followed *étatiste* policies of domestic industrialization based on import-substitution. The broadly measurable outcomes in terms of growth and poverty alleviation have also been similar. During the post-war period Egypt's average growth rate was 5.4% a year compared with Tukey's 5.8% a year. Both countries have shown considerable success in poverty alleviation, and the improvements in their social indicators are similar. Yet, here again, we shall find it more instructive to look below the surface to their important differences.

First, there are the differences in resource endowments: Turkey is more abundantly endowed with agricultural land than Egypt. Despite considerable developments of irrigation, much of the economically cultivable land in Egypt had been fully cultivated in 1900, and by the 1950s Egypt was regarded as a typical example of an underdeveloped country suffering from Malthusian population pressure. In contrast, the land frontier for extension of cultivation was not closed in Turkey until the late 1950s, and Turkey's land–labour ratio is still several times higher than that of Egypt.

Secondly, the nature of the military rulers which have shaped the *étatiste* policies in the two countries is different. The Turkish military, from Kemal Atatürk to his present-day successors, have been strong rulers, while the Egyptian autocrats who came into power after the *coup d'état* in 1952 may be described as weak rulers who have had to resort to populist policies based on a network of patron–client relationships and the crony system to stay in power. The strength of the Turkish military rulers is illustrated by the way in which they have intervened to impose unpopular economic policies to control budget deficits, inflation, and balance-of-payment crises which have been beyond the capacity of civilian politicians to deal with effectively. In this the Turkish military rulers resemble the Brazilian military rulers, who have intervened off and on to impose fiscal and monetary austerity and wage freezes.

Given Egypt's abundant labour supply, the policy of trying to expand labour-intensive manufactured exports would seem to offer a promising basis for economic growth. But the necessary liberalization and decontrol of the economy, required for a switch to export-expansion policies, has been strongly resisted by the various powerful groups who have benefited from Egypt's system of sharing the political spoils. Much of the manufacturing and trading activities of the country have been run as state enterprises, subject to detailed bureaucratic controls, for the benefit of military clients and the cronies of the ruling groups.

Thus, instead of labour-intensive exports, Egypt has depended on her supply of foreign exchange from other sources; from foreign aid from America, Russia, and the oil-rich Arab countries, depending on the phase of international diplomacy; from the dues from the Suez Canal; from oil revenues, which have replaced cotton as Egypt's main export in the 1980s; and from remittances of her emigrant workers, both skilled and unskilled, in the oil-rich Middle Eastern countries. Some of these sources of foreign exchange earnings are in the nature of windfall gains and do not necessarily provide a sustainable basis for economic growth.

Up to 1980, Turkey has also followed *étatiste* policies of domestic industrialization, based on import-substitution using the proceeds from her primary exports. Turkey has also received as much foreign aid from Western sources as Egypt, and has also received remittances from emigrant workers in Western Europe, although not on the same scale as Egypt. But Turkey's economic planning, based on a series of Five Year Plans, was less subject to the corrupting influences of the crony system, although it was flawed by a misplaced emphasis on technological efficiency in the engineering sense, as distinct from economic efficiency. The different quality and calibre of the Turkish military autocrats showed themselves in 1980 when the Demeril government decided to switch from import-substitution policies to export-expansion policies. This radical switch of policies and the unpopular economic reforms involving the dismantling of the Kemalist *étatisme* could not have been carried out without the military intervention during 1980–2. Turkey then enjoyed a notable expansion of manufactured exports and a recovery of economic growth during the 1980–6 period.

Egypt has been conventionally regarded as an equity-orientated country because of her land reform programme and food subsidies. But the purpose of the land reform was to break the economic power of the royal family and the big landowners and to mobilize political support for the military junta. It has only marginally benefited the small farmers in the first quintile of land-ownership distribution; the main beneficiaries have been the medium-sized landowners in the second to the fourth quintiles of the distribution of land ownership. The revolution under Nasser and Sadat was mainly against the oligarchy consisting of a few wealthy extended families and a sizeable foreign business community, whose assets were nationalized. Apart from the ruling military groups, the main beneficiaries of the revolution were the educated urban middle classes, who gained positions of affluence and luxury as the privileged clients of the military rulers, as bureaucrats and managers of state enterprises or as 'consultants' operating in the interstices between the state and the private sectors, taking advantage of their family influence and foreign connections. The poorer classes, both in the countryside and the towns, were mainly bystanders to this 'social compact', but they were appeased by the trickling down of state largesse in the form of an almost free loaf of bread. The food subsidies, providing modest benefits in per capita terms, nevertheless amounted to a serious burden in the aggregate. Further, despite the Aswan dam, Egypt was having to import increasingly large quantities of food from abroad. Egypt ran into heavy trade deficits not only with the Western countries but also with the Communist countries in the 1979–84 period, underlining the need for a sustainable basis for social welfare policies in the form of a healthy export industry.

The distribution of land ownership (as distinct from the distribution of land holdings) is more equal in Turkey than in Egypt even after the land reforms, though this is compensated by a greater prevalence of leasing in Egypt. More generally, income distribution in relative terms seems to be more equal in Egypt than in Turkey. This is partly due to a greater degree of regional income inequality and the urban–rural income gap in Turkey than in Egypt (at least as measured in terms of the ratios of outputs per head in non-agricultural and agricultural activities). In terms of 'functional income distribution', the share of wages and salaries in the non-agricultural GDP has been higher in Egypt than in Turkey.

Indicators of the income distribution pattern are given in Tables 3.19 and 3.20. A comparison of the standards-of-life indicators in the two countries is given in Table 3.21.

But Egypt's poverty alleviation programmes are based on food subsidies, resulting in budget deficits and current-account deficits, with increasing foreign indebtedness shored up by foreign aid from various sources. In contrast, Turkey's success in poverty alleviation based on more robust economic growth seems to be more sustainable in the longer run, especially when Egypt had never gone through the necessary but unpalatable stabilization programmes which have been pushed through in Turkey.

Finally, there is an important difference between Egypt and Turkey in their approach to education as the means of spreading equal opportunities. Egypt has concentrated on higher education and universities, whereas Turkey has concentrated on primary education and the building up of a broader educational pyramid, including female education. The Egyptian approach has led to the problem of educated unemployment, compelling the government to become the employer of last resort, thereby grossly inflating the size of the bureaucracy. The Turkish approach has been more successful in raising the average educational level of the people as a whole, reducing the differences in educational and economic opportunities between different classes and between males and females. It is interesting to note that Turkey has been able to attain this superior achievement in educational improvements while spending a lower percentage of public expenditure on education than Egypt.

IX. NIGERIA AND INDONESIA

Nigeria and Indonesia are an interesting pair of countries which have responded in a very different manner to the common 'exogenous factor' in the form of huge windfall receipts from the oil booms, with dramatically contrasting economic outcomes. These different outcomes in growth, poverty alleviation, and income distribution occurred mainly after the first oil shock of 1973, but it is useful to start from the 1950s to bring out their background similarities and differences.

Nigeria and Indonesia are both very large countries in terms of area and

Table 3.19. Egypt: Indicators of household expenditure distribution, 1958/9–1982

Year	Rural areas			Urban areas	Total Egypt
	Gini coefficients		Theil's measure	Gini coefficients	Gini coefficients
	(1)	(2)	(3)	(4)	(5)
1958/59	0.34	0.37	0.16	0.40	0.42
1964/65	0.29	0.35	0.12	0.40	0.40
1974/75	0.35	0.39	0.17	0.37	0.38
1982	0.34	—	0.17	0.37	—

	Quintile					
	Lowest	2nd	3rd	4th	Top	Top 10%
Rural						
1958/59	6.7	11.0	16.6	21.9	43.9	28.0
1964/65	7.4	11.6	16.3	22.0	42.7	27.5
1974/75	5.9	11.2	15.8	21.2	45.9	30.5
1982	6.0	11.4	16.0	22.6	44.0	28.4
Urban						
1958/59	16.4		14.5	n.a.	n.a.	30.4
1964/65	16.5		14.8	n.a.	n.a.	30.8
1974/75	18.3		16.1	n.a.	n.a.	27.6
1982	n.a.			n.a.	n.a.	n.a.
Average for 9 other lower-middle-income countries						
	4.3 12.4	8.1	12.6	20.0	54.9	39.1

	Share of household expenditure, %			
	1st Quartile	2nd Quartile	3rd Quartile	4th Quartile
1981/2				
Rural	12.1	20.0	27.0	40.9
Urban	11.7	18.7	25.7	43.9

Source: Hansen (1991: tables 4.31–3, pp. 221–2).

Table 3.20. Turkey: Indicators of income distribution

Year	Gini coefficients			Lower quintile shares (%)			Upper quintile shares (%)		
	National	Agricultural	Non-agricultural	National	Agricultural	Non-agricultural	National	Agricultural	Non-agricultural
1952		0.53			5.7			60.2	
1963	0.56	0.43	0.59	4.2	6.0	3.2	61.0	49.5	65.9
1968	0.56	0.59	—	3.0	3.1	—	60.0	64.0	—
1973	0.50	0.56	0.45	3.5	2.5	5.0	55.3	60.3	51.6
1973, adjusted	0.51	0.57	0.43	2.7	2.5	5.0	55.2	61.1	48.6
1978	0.51	0.57	0.43	2.8	2.5	5.0	54.7	61.1	48.6
1978–9	—	—	0.40	—	—	6.3	—	—	46.4
1983	0.52	0.57	0.45	2.6	2.5	4.6	55.9	61.1	50.2

Source: Hansen (1991: table 6.6, p. 276). The lower figures for 1973 are adjusted for comparability from different statistical sources; see ibid. for details.

Table 3.21. Egypt and Turkey: Standards-of-life Indicators

	Egypt		Turkey	
	1960	1985	1960	1985
GNP per capita, US $ of 1985	275	610	570	1,080
Daily calorific supply per capita	2,435	3,203	2,636	3,167
Life expectancy, years at birth	46	61	51	64
Crude death rate, pro mille	19	10	16	8
Infant mortality, pro mille	109	93	194	84
Crude birth rate, pro mille	44	36	43	30
Urbanization, per cent of population	38	46	30	46
Physicians, persons per	2,560	760	3,000	1,530

Source: Hansen (1991: table 17.9, p. 491).

population. They shared a common problem after independence of trying to hold together the different parts of the country within the wide national boundaries which they have inherited from the colonial period. Nigeria was granted independence by the British on a basis of a federal constitution. Indonesia adopted a unitary constitution after a war of national independence with the Dutch. In both countries there were powerful centrifugal forces.

In each country, the politically dominant region happened to be less abundantly endowed with natural resources than the other, peripheral regions. In Nigeria the northern region gained political dominance, while the southern regions, both the Western and the Eastern, were richer. The western region was the centre of Nigeria's cocoa exports, while the discovery of oil in the eastern region triggered off a major civil war, the Biafran war, over the control of the oil revenues. In Indonesia, the central island of Java became politically dominant while the outer islands produced the bulk of the export revenues. Indonesia also had to face many secessionist wars, but was more successful in forging a coherent national unity. The constitutional revisions after the Biafran war still left Nigeria as a federation of different tribal regions, each with its own language and culture. But the Sukarno period, whatever its drawbacks, contributed to the development of an Indonesian national entity, with a national language, the Bahasa Malay, which previously had been only a lingua franca between the different dialects and languages of the Indonesian archipelago.

In the setting of countries such as Nigeria and Indonesia, the concept of equity became highly charged with the considerations of inter-regional, inter-tribal, and inter-ethnic distribution of incomes. The Nigerian Federation has always been dogged by the struggle among the regional governments to obtain a larger share of government revenues and expenditures, providing a fertile ground for corruption to bribe regional political interests.

In Indonesia the problem of inter-regional distribution of income was complicated by the hostility towards the more economically active Chinese immigrants (as in Malaysia). The Indonesian government's policies of repressing the Chinese middlemen, moneylenders, and shopkeepers in the rural areas have handicapped the earlier efforts to promote rice production during the Sukarno period. In the succeeding Suharto regime, the military leaders in charge of large state-owned enterprises pursued a more pragmatic policy of making use of the entrepreneurial and managerial capacity of the Chinese and their commercial and financial connections with Singapore and Hong Kong.

Let us now turn to some of the important background differences. Before the rise of the oil industry, Nigeria was essentially a peasant export economy based on exports such as cocoa, palm oil, and ground-nuts. The conditions were similar to those which prevailed in Ghana in the colonial period. An abundant supply of unused land was made available by a customary land tenure system to the peasant farmers to expand the cultivation of export crops, using the traditional labour-intensive methods of cultivation. Now an important feature of this pattern of peasant export expansion was that it could be carried out without reducing the production of domestic food crops. On the newly cleared land, food crops were interplanted with young cocoa trees, and as a consequence Nigeria was mainly self-sufficient in food production. The effect of the oil booms on Nigeria was not only to reduce drastically the traditional peasant exports of crops through the familiar 'Dutch Disease' phenomena[28] but also to lead to a sharp decline in Nigeria's food production.

Indonesia, on the other hand, was a mixed plantation and peasant export economy with a dominance of plantation exports. Moreover, Java is one of the most densely populated areas in South-East Asia, and since two-thirds of Indonesia's population is concentrated in Java, Indonesia has been traditionally a food-deficit country, requiring large imports of rice. One of the notable effects of the oil booms was to provide resources for investment in agriculture, increasing Indonesia's self-sufficiency in food.

Perhaps the most important difference between Nigeria and Indonesia may be found in the period preceding the oil booms when both countries were going through the phase of reacting against the colonial economic system.

In Nigeria this phase of reaction was relatively mild. The pressure for increasing public expenditure was undermining the principle of balanced budgets, and the suspension of the colonial currency-board system was permitting an expansionary monetary policy. But foreign investment in manufacturing industries was being attracted by offers of tariff protection. There were no great economic upheavals comparable to those which occurred in Indonesia under Sukarno. Nigeria was thus unprepared to cope with the impact of the oil bonanza and did not possess the administrative and management skills to absorb the huge flows of investible funds which were to accrue to the government.

In Indonesia, on the other hand, the Sukarno regime left a turbulent economic legacy which unintentionally was to stand the country in good stead in coping with the oil booms. Sukarno's government started by wholesale nationalization of foreign-owned assets and intensely inward-looking economic policies which seriously undermined export production. The resulting collapse in government revenues then paved the way for a hyper-inflation in 1965, the biggest ever experienced in South-East Asia. Thus when the Suharto regime took over after a classic IMF stabilization programme, the country was ready for pragmatic policies paying careful attention to economic imperatives. Important laws liberalizing and encouraging foreign investment were passed in 1967 and 1968, and Indonesia was already enjoying a substantial expansion of primary exports, notably timber, before the beginning of the oil boom. Underlying this shift towards outward-looking policies, there was the country's commitment to the principles of balanced budget and convertible currency, learnt at first hand through the traumatic experiences of the hyper-inflation.

Nigeria and Indonesia both received huge windfall gains from the two oil price shocks. During the first oil cycle, 1973–9, the oil revenues amounted to 19.2% of Nigeria's GDP and to 9.8% of Indonesia's GDP. During the second oil cycle, 1980–4, Nigeria obtained 17.1% and Indonesia 13.9% of GDP from oil revenues. But the policy responses of the two countries were very different.

1. Nigeria lost control of her public expenditure from the outset, and expanded public spending not only during the upswings but also the downswings of the cycles. Nigeria's budget deficits were increasing to 7% of GDP during the 1980–4 period. Indonesia's public expenditure followed the cycle, cutting it down during the downswings. She accumulated foreign exchange reserves to pay off some part of her foreign debt and maintained a stable budget deficit. Indonesia's superior macroeconomic management can be best seen when the second oil boom tapered off in 1981; she then courageously introduced unpalatable reforms of cutting subsidies on domestic fuel, pruning the growth of expenditure on the civil service, and shelving major capital projects, combined with a sizeable devaluation of 27.6%. Nigeria postponed these painful adjustments, by a combination of tightening exchange controls and increasing foreign borrowing, until 1986.

2. As might be expected, both countries pursued import-substitution policies of domestic industrialization based on heavy industries, notably steel mills. During the first oil cycle, Nigeria attempted to expand her investment in manufacturing industry well beyond her capacity to absorb capital in terms of the available managerial and technical skill. In the

second oil cycle, investment projects came to be regarded in Nigeria as the means of channelling patronage and kickbacks from government contracts, while part of the oil proceeds was directly appropriated as salary increases for politicians. Indonesia was by no means free from inefficiency and corruption, and the Pertamina crisis which broke out in 1975 after a misguided attempt to quadruple steel capacity ended with a $10 billion foreign debt. This, however, seemed to have exerted a salutary effect on the subsequent choice of investment projects. Indonesia was also more successful in increasing productive investment in social infrastructure, and in irrigation and agriculture, notably the introduction of the improved seed and fertilizer technology in rice production.

3. One of the startling effects of Nigeria's expansion of public expenditure was the massive explosion of public sector employment, approximately tripling from half a million in 1973 to one and a half million in 1981. This consisted not only of educated townspeople but also of a large number of unskilled labour from the rural areas, attracted by the wage premium obtainable in government employment. This seems to have contributed not only to the collapse of peasant exports, already suffering from high exchange rates and taxation through the Marketing Boards, but also to the reduction of food production for domestic consumption. Indonesia, by contrast, made considerable progress in increasing self-sufficiency in rice through increased rice production both in Java and in the outer islands. Furthermore, the expansion of peasant exports from the outer islands grew at only a slightly lower rate than the expansion of plantation and estate exports, keeping the 'Dutch Disease' effects of oil shocks in check.

Given these different responses to the oil shocks, the outcomes in Nigeria and Indonesia have been strikingly different. Over the whole period 1950–84, Nigeria's GDP per capita in real terms increased by only 23%, while Indonesia's increased by 146%. Poverty has been substantially reduced in Indonesia, while poverty has increased in Nigeria, since she suffered from negative rates of growth in income during the downswings of the oil cycle.

Over the whole of the period 1950–84, Nigeria has recorded a modest average rate of GDP per capita of 0.7% per annum. In terms of private consumption, Bevan et al. have estimated that, prior to the mid-1970s, average living standards were rising at around 1.5% per annum, but declined by around 7% per annum during the subsequent decade, so that average private consumption was lower by around 30% at the end of the period than at the start. They adopted two poverty lines, those which cut off the bottom 20% and 40% of the population in 1952/3, and applied these poverty lines, adjusted for inflation, to the 1983/4 income distribution. They found that 17% of the population are below the lower poverty line and 58% below the higher poverty line in 1983/4, as compared with only

40% below the higher poverty line in 1952/3.[29] These conclusions seem to be barely credible in view of the enormous windfall gains from oil. But, as the authors emphasize, the running of the Nigerian economy has been subject to an exceptionally high degree of incompetence and corruption. The authors cite the estimate of the current government that during the period of civilian rule (1979–83) capital flight and illegally held wealth abroad amounted to N $18 billion, equivalent to something over $14 billion.[30]

In the Nigerian context, the concept of equity or equality is evidently dominated by the inter-regional or inter-ethnic income distribution. The authors have pieced together information to show that in 1950 the northern region started out as the poorest, the western region (the cocoa belt) as the richest, with the eastern region occupying the middle position. They show how the northern region, particularly the northern cities, has gained relatively to the others, especially during the civilian NPN government of 1979–83 which was dominated by the northern urban interests.[31]

Another important source of inequality, the rural–urban income distribution, has been greatly influenced in Nigeria by the large inflows of rural unskilled labour. Employed in the government service sector during the oil boom, large numbers of unskilled workers returned to the food-producing areas after the subsequent lay-offs during the slumps, particularly from 1983 onwards. Bevan et al. believe that given the wage premium in government employment acting as a wage-leader in the urban sector, there was a considerable differential in favour of the urban residents during the 1950–80 period. But there has been a massive erosion in the differential during the 1980s, and, allowing for the higher cost of living in the towns, the differential may have been reversed by the mid-1980s.[32]

For Indonesia, the start of the New Order period in 1966 provides a watershed in economic growth. Before that date the growth of GDP was slow, 3% during 1953–9 and 2.1% during 1960–6, slightly below the growth of population. After 1966 the growth of GDP increased dramatically, to 6% (1966–8), 8.2% (1968–73), 7% (1973–9), and 6% (1979–84).[33]

Bevan et al. have estimated that on the basis of a common poverty line (adopted by Rao for 1970) the incidence of poverty in Indonesia has declined after 1970, very rapidly for the urban areas and more slowly but very clearly for the rural areas in the 1980s (see Table 3.22).

Bevan et al. also question the popular belief that the policy changes introduced by the New Economic Order have worsened the relative income distribution between the rich and the poor. They argue that if we use the figures for distribution of expenditures instead of distribution of incomes, the longer-term pattern in income distribution appears to be stable with a modest trend towards greater equality (see Table 3.23).

Table 3.22. Indonesia: Incidence of poverty, 1963–84 (percentage of population)

	1963	1967	1970	1976	1978	1980	1984
Urban	56.7	50.2	50.7	31.5	25.2	19.7	5.7
Rural	47.9	60.4	58.5	54.5	54.0	44.6	26.9
All	51.8	58.5	57.1	50.1	48.5	39.8	22.7

Source: table 7.4 in *Indonesia Study* (mimeo), ch. VII, p. 174, pt. II.

Table 3.23. Indonesia: The distribution of expenditures by population quintile, 1963–84

	1963	1964	1967	1970	1976	1978	1980	1981	1984
Q1	6.9	7.2	6.6	7.6	8.0	7.3	7.7	8.3	8.0
Q2	12.5	11.4	11.8	12.3	11.5	10.5	11.8	12.2	12.8
Q3	17.0	15.8	16.9	16.6	16.0	14.8	16.0	15.6	15.3
Q4	23.4	22.1	22.5	22.7	22.0	21.8	22.2	21.8	22.0
Q5	40.2	43.4	42.3	40.8	42.5	45.3	42.3	42.1	42.0

Source: Table 7.5 in *Indonesia Study* (mimeo), ch. VII.

In Indonesia (as in Nigeria), the dominant issue of income distribution is the inter-regional income distribution. Java, with two-thirds of Indonesia's population of 155 million, started out a poorer region than the outer islands, which produce the bulk of the country's exports. Over the period 1964–84 Java has gained relatively to the outer islands, so that by now the gap in the income differential has been closed, implying a considerable transfer of income from the outer islands to Java. Bevan *et al.* also find that in real terms the rural–urban income differentials, which narrowed sharply during the period of hyper-inflation, widened between 1970 and 1976 to reflect skill differentials.[34]

From a longer-run perspective, the development of the oil industry and the increase in investment (in so far as capital has been productively absorbed) may be said to have changed the initial factor proportions in Nigeria and Indonesia, increasing the endowment of natural resources and capital relative to labour. How far has this changed their potential comparative advantage in labour-intensive peasant agriculture for exports and for domestic food production? In the next chapter we shall argue against the simple textbook model in which the given resources are fully employed, implying that peasant agriculture cannot be expanded without contracting plantation exports and manufactured exports. For some time to come, there would seem to be ample scope in Nigeria to expand her peasant exports and domestic food production, provided she could remove macroeconomic imbalances and make appropriate exchange rate adjust-ments. Her policy-induced labour shortage through the expansion of public-sector employment could not be sustained over the longer run. Indonesia's success in maintaining the expansion of peasant exports from the outer islands and domestic food production both in the outer islands and in Java, provides strong support for our argument. In fact, for Indone-sia, the notion of aggregate factor proportions for the country as a whole is misleading. Java, with her high population density, is clearly a labour-abundant economy, while the outer islands are land-abundant economies. Java's potential comparative advantage may be realized by using her abun-dant supply of labour both in increasing domestic self-sufficiency in rice and in expanding labour-intensive manufactured exports. The comparative advantage in the outer islands lies in expanding resource-intensive plan-tation exports and, with an unused margin of land, in expanding both the rice production and peasant exports.

X. MALAWI AND MADAGASCAR

Malawi and Madagascar are the two poorest among the countries included in our study. Compared with Ghana and Nigeria, Malawi is less well-endowed with natural resources, besides being land-locked and dependent on a precarious transport link with the outside world. Madagascar has a larger land area but poorer soil. In both countries land is held under a customary land tenure system, but cash-crop production is less well devel-oped than in the West African countries. In both Malawi and Madagascar more than half of peasant agriculture is devoted to subsistence production, but a considerable amount of rural labour, especially in Malawi, has been drawn to work in the plantations.

At first sight, it may be thought that it does not matter whether the money economy spreads by drawing the resources from subsistence agricul-ture into cash-crop production, as in West Africa, or as wage labour, as in East Africa. But the production of cash crops and exports requires con-tinual decision-making about production and buying and selling on the part of the peasant, and thus provides him with a better opportunity for devel-oping initiative and entrepreneurial capacity than working merely as a wage labourer according to a set routine supervised by an overseer. But unfortu-nately, both under the 'African Capitalism' of Malawi and under the 'African Socialism' of Madagascar, peasant export production has suffered from discriminating government policies.

Apart from this similarity, Malawi pursued different policies from Mada-gascar and indeed from most of the newly independent African countries. This may be attributed to the unique personal influence of Malawi's Life

President, Dr Hastings Banda, who alone among the African leaders appreciated the importance of agriculture and exports and who steered his country away from the usual reaction against the 'colonial economic pattern' after independence. Thus Banda resisted the pressure to Africanize the Civil Service before suitably qualified people were available. Instead of nationalizing foreign-owned assets he welcomed foreign investment and foreign aid. He took advantage of the post-Independence euphoria to raise taxes and kept the budget in balance by strict controls on expenditure, including the application of strict commercial principles of profitability in selecting and running state enterprises.

Madagascar started with moderate economic policies under the administration of Philibert Tsiranana (1960–72). But after 1972 the country came under the radical administration of General Ramanantsoa and Didier Ratsiraka, reacting against the French 'Neo-Colonialism' and imbued with the desire to carry out a 'socialist transformation' of the economy. These policies are similar to the radical policies of Nkrumah in Ghana or the first Manley administration in Jamaica. They consisted of the familiar ingredients of the nationalization of foreign concerns in export production, commerce, and banking; the setting up of import-substitution domestic industries to be run by the government; and expansionary fiscal and monetary policies maintained by a network of government regulations and exchange controls.

Although Dr Banda was immune from the conventional belief in domestic industrialization through import substitution, he nevertheless believed in the superior efficiency of large-scale agricultural estates run on modern technology and economic management. Thus Malawi pursued a policy of 'wagering on the strong' by promoting the expansion of exports from large-scale agricultural estates at the expense of peasant exports. Peasant exports were penalized by a state monopoly agricultural marketing board paying the peasants a fraction of the world market prices for their produce, while the estates could sell their output at the going world market prices. The estates naturally had better access to credit and inputs, while the peasant producers had to meet higher transaction costs and pay higher rates of interest. This was aggravated by the fact that land held under the customary tenure could not be used as collateral for loans. As a consequence of these differential policies, estate agriculture grew at the expense of peasant agriculture, and by 1983 the estates produced 76% of the total exports of Malawi.

In Madagascar the exports both from the estate and from the peasant sectors declined sharply after 1972, penalized by the government policies of extracting the investible surpluses from agriculture to subsidize large-scale state investment projects, particularly in the modern manufacturing industry. The nationalized agricultural estates were run inefficiently by fixed-salary government managers, compounded by difficulties created by domestic inflation, over-valued currency, and foreign exchange controls. The peasant producers were penalized not only by the taxation by the state agricultural marketing board, but also by the deterioration in rural transport and communications and the suppression of private middlemen. These were mainly Chinese, Indians, and Pakistanis, who had performed the useful services of buying the peasants' produce and supplying them with credit, consumers' goods, and inputs at the farm-gate level.

Dr Banda launched Malawi into a notably high rate of economic growth and export expansion by African standards. During the period 1964–79, Malawi's GDP grew at 5.9% a year and her exports almost at the same rate. Since 1980, Malawi's growth has tapered off, partly due to external factors such as the world recession and the cutting off of the rail link by Renamo insurgents in Mozambique; the economic stagnation is also partly due to a loosening in the fiscal and monetary controls and the over-valuation of the exchange rate, and the attempt to use more *dirigiste* methods to meet the macroeconomic strains. These difficulties have been compounded by the ageing of Dr Banda and the loosening of his grip on the control of the economy.

Madagascar's GDP grew at a moderate rate of 3.1% a year during the Tsiranana period (1960–72). But after 1972 economic performance has sharply deteriorated under the radical administrations of Ramanantsoa

Table 3.24. Malawi and Madagascar: The size distribution of income (%)

Cumulative share of population arranged in order of increasing incomes	Cumulative share of gross family income					
	Malawi			Madagascar		
	1968/9		1984/5	1962		1980
	Before direct taxes	After direct taxes	Before direct taxes	Est. A before direct taxes	Est. B before direct taxes	Est. A before direct taxes
20	8.2	8.6	3.3	8.1	7.0	5.0
40	18.8	19.7	9.5	18.6	16.2	13.7
60	30.9	32.3	19.1	32.8	28.5	27.1
80	44.6	46.4	34.3	51.0	42.5	47.6
90	53.8	55.9	47.6	64.2	57.3	62.9
95	61.1	63.4	58.0	74.3	68.0	73.7
99	74.6	77.4	75.8	88.9	85.8	91.1
100	100.0	100.0	100.0	100.0	100.0	100.0

Note: A and B are limits of high and low estimates.

Source: Pryor (1990: table 16.2, p. 362).

Table 3.25. Malawi and Madagascar: Income inequality statistics

Groups of families	Number (1,000s)	Average total income*	Inequality coefficients		
			Gini	Theil	Log variance
Malawi 1968/8					
Smallholder families	885.0	86.42	0.203	0.113	0.118
Families on estates	28.0	140.31	0.187	0.093	0.110
Families in small towns	11.0	606.93	0.466	0.417	0.651
Families in four major towns	42.6	907.65	0.660	0.884	1.494
Total/average	966.5	130.03	0.448	0.796	0.317
Assuming all incomes in a group equal to mean of group	966.5	130.03	0.317	0.432	0.274
Malawi 1984/5					
Smallholder families	1,252.0	358.2	0.453	0.348	0.607
Families on estates	89.2	425.1	n.a.	n.a.	n.a.
Families in small towns	34.2	2,157.1	n.a.	n.a.	n.a.
Families in four major towns	98.5	3,235.4	0.621	0.776	1.065
Total/average	1,473.9	596.2	0.599	0.944	0.860
Assuming all incomes in a group equal to mean of group	1,473.9	596.2	0.365	0.447	0.361
Madagascar: Estimate A 1962					
Rural	1,076.2	60.9	0.290	0.194	0.220
Secondary urban centres	36.6	153.6	n.a.	n.a.	n.a.
Largest six towns	98.9	199.3	0.500	0.466	0.806
Total/average	1,211.7	75.0	0.391	0.371	0.352
Assuming all incomes in a group equal to mean of group	1,211.7	75.0	0.168	0.106	0.125
Madagascar: Estimate A 1980					
Rural sector	1,542.9	192.9	0.435	0.329	0.517
Secondary urban centres	140.5	356.2	0.487	0.399	0.747
Largest seven towns	227.3	462.7	n.a.	n.a.	n.a.
Total/average	1,910.8	237.0	0.489	0.426	0.628
Assuming all incomes in a group equal to mean of group	1,910.8	237.0	0.154	0.065	0.096

*In MK for Malawi; and 1,000 FMG for Madagascar.

Notes: All of the coefficients become larger when inequality increases. The Gini coefficient lies between 0.0 and 1.0; the others are unbounded. As noted in the discussion, the estimates for the two countries are not quite comparable. For each country, however, the results are roughly comparable over time. Sources and methods are discussed in Section I of *Malawi HS* and *Madagascar HS* (historical studies done by Pryor for the World Bank).

Source: Pryor (1990: table 16.3, p. 363).

and Ratsiraka. During the period 1972–84, Madagascar's exports on average declined by 3.8% a year and her GDP per capita fell by 2.4% a year.

Given Madagascar's spells of negative economic growth, one would expect an increase in poverty. But it is more difficult to judge whether Malawi's poverty has increased or decreased. Given her rapid economic growth before 1979, one would expect some alleviation of poverty. On the other hand, Malawi's government policies have worked adversely against the peasant agricultural sector, which moreover has suffered from increasing population pressure on limited land. Frederic Pryor, the author of the Malawi–Madagascar study, has tentatively concluded that poverty may have increased in Malawi also, but in view of the fragility of direct statistical evidence he would put a greater weight on the direction of change in the social indicators for health. Madagascar started out with a higher income per capita and a lower infant mortality rate than Malawi. Since independence, however, Malawi's infant mortality rate has declined while Madagascar's has increased, particularly from the late 1970s to the mid-1980s. The improvements in Malawi's health indicators are due to an impressive vaccination programme for children, combined with imaginative self-help and supply of equipment to provide clean water and sanitary waste disposal. It is estimated that by 1980, 79% of the urban population and 50% of the rural population in Malawi has gained access to clean drinking water.

Pryor also finds that relative income inequalities have increased both in Malawi and Madagascar since independence. Using his own recalculations of the survey data of the two countries, he suggests that in the earlier years (1968–9 for Malawi and 1962 for Madagascar) the main factor in income inequality was the urban–rural income gap. But he finds that this gap narrowed over time, and he attributes the increase in income inequality in the later years (1984–5 for Malawi and 1980 for Madagascar) to the growing income inequalities among the smallholders themselves (see Tables 3.24 and 3.25).

He explains the increased income inequality in the smallholder sector in Malawi in terms of the government's policy of a 'wager on the strong': for instance, providing technology and credit which are more suitable or accessible to the richer than the poorer farmers, and the richer farmers' privilege of selling their export crops at world auction prices and not at the lower ADMARC prices (Agricultural Development and Marketing Corporation, a monopoly agricultural marketing board). He explains the increased income inequality in the smallholder sector in Madagascar in similar terms, particularly in terms of differential access to credit, and of the more limited ability of the poorer farmers to cope with the higher transaction costs of a disintegrating transport system and the growth of black markets in agricultural inputs and consumption goods.[35]

NOTES

1. Fields (1991: ch. 1), summarized in Tables 1.2–3 above.
2. See e.g. Michaely (1977), Balassa (1978), and Krueger (1984).
3. There may be one or two exceptions to the tendency of economic growth to reduce absolute poverty. The proportion of Jamaica's labour force below a fixed poverty line increased during the period 1968–73 despite a positive rate of economic growth, but it increased more sharply during 1973–80 with a negative growth rate (Fields (1991): ch. 1, p. 22, and table 8, part B). Pryor (1991) in his study of Malawi suggests that absolute poverty may have increased in that country despite a positive growth rate, because of discriminatory policies towards peasant agriculture and population pressure on land. But he warns us against the fragility of data, and puts a greater weight on the improvements in Malawi's health indicators as a sign of poverty alleviation.
4. For a study of the earlier phase of Singapore's industrialization characterized by labour-intensive small-scale producers, see Hughes and You (1969).
5. See Bhalla and Glewwe (1986).
6. See Lal and Rajapatirana (1987).
7. See e.g. Sen (1981b).
8. Summers and Heston (1984).
9. Gavan and Chandraskera (1979).
10. Bruton (1992: 164).
11. Bhalla and Glewwe (1986). These authors emphasize the favourable indirect effects of rapid growth on poverty alleviation after the economic reforms of 1977.
12. Summers and Heston (1984).
13. Meesook et al. (mimeo: 31, table 3.8).
14. Rimmer (1992: 41 and table 4.5).
15. Ibid., table 5.8.
16. Maddison et al. (1992: 6, table 1.2).
17. Ibid. 79.
18. Ibid. 11, table 1.6.
19. Ibid. 86.
20. Ibid. 93.
21. Ibid. 6.
22. Ibid. 148–9.
23. See also ibid. 11, table 1.6.
24. Ibid. 167, table 6.21.
25. Ibid. 12, 170.
26. Urdinola et al. (mimeo: part I, tables 1–2, charts 11 and 17, pp. 8–9, 13–14, and 367–91).
27. Ibid. part II, 10, table I.
28. The term 'Dutch Disease' refers to the coexistence within the traded goods sector of booming and lagging subsectors. It was named for the adverse effects on Dutch manufacturing which appeared with the appreciation of the Dutch real-exchange rate following the discovery of natural gas in the 1960s. Similar effects of foreign exchange windfalls have occurred in economies receiving large

remittances from migrant workers (Turkey and Egypt, for instance), or aid inflows (Sri Lanka in the late 1970s), or a rise in the price of natural resources (oil in Nigeria and Indonesia, bauxite in Jamaica).

29. Bevan *et al.* (forthcoming: part I, 148 and 158–9).
30. Ibid. 140.
31. Ibid. 160–4.
32. Ibid. 165, 302–8.
33. Ibid. part II, 210.
34. Ibid. 181–7.
35. Pryor (1991: 120–1, 282–4).

4

The Role of Institutions and Organization

WE have found that in some of the countries in our study, economic growth through export expansion has been accompanied by a tendency towards a more equal distribution of incomes, while in others, income distribution tends to become more unequal. These different outcomes may be interpreted, as a first approximation, in terms of a neoclassical-type growth model combined with the Heckscher–Ohlin factor-proportions approach to comparative advantage that we have outlined in Chapter 2.

Thus our countries may be broadly classified as labour-abundant and land-abundant countries, all of them being regarded as capital-scarce countries.

The expansion of labour-intensive exports from the labour-abundant countries will raise wages relative to rental incomes on capital. Assuming that the proceeds from export expansion and economic growth are reinvested to provide a rate of capital accumulation faster than population growth, this trend will continue as these countries move up the ladder of comparative advantage from the production of the more labour-intensive to the more capital-intensive type of manufactured exports. Rents on land will also be rising due to population growth and growing land scarcity. But with the growing share of manufacturing relative to agriculture in total national output, we should expect the rising share of wages to have a dominant effect in bringing about a more equal distribution of incomes.

In the land-abundant countries, however, the expansion of resource-intensive primary exports will raise the share of rents on land relative to wages, and this tendency will be reinforced over time by population growth. Moreover, the land-abundant countries would start from a relatively higher level of wages, reflecting their higher land–man ratios compared with the labour-abundant countries. This sets them at a disadvantage in competing with the labour-abundant countries in the export markets for labour-intensive manufactures. Thus, given their initial factor endowments, the land-abundant countries would have to seek their comparative advantage in the production of the less labour-intensive and more capital-intensive type of manufactured exports from their earlier stages of industrialization. This puts a double strain on their available supply of savings, since capital accumulation has to keep up, not only with population growth, but also with equipping the growing labour force in the manufacturing sector with a larger amount of capital per head. If the rate of capital accumulation is insufficient to meet these more demanding requirements, then the land-abundant countries would have to go through a phase of downward adjustment in wages to sustain growth through export expansion. Hence their economic growth is likely to be accompanied by a tendency towards a more unequal distribution of incomes, although poverty in an absolute sense will be reduced through economic growth.

This type of analysis can, however, provide us only with a first approximation. In order to have a more satisfactory framework of interpretation, we shall have to introduce institutional and organizational factors into this skeletal framework. This is attempted in this chapter.

I. INTRODUCING A GREATER INSTITUTIONAL CONTENT

For our purpose, the 'initial conditions' of a country have to be defined more broadly to include not only the factor endowments but also the institutional and organizational factors which enter into the initial setting. We can hardly ignore the basic fact that, compared with a developed country, the initial domestic economic framework of the countries in our study is underdeveloped: that is to say, there is an incomplete development of the market systems for products and factors of production, paralleled by an underdevelopment of their administrative and fiscal systems. Their domestic systems of transport and communication and social infrastructure are also underdeveloped. Thus, in order to have a satisfactory interpretation of the longer-run economic outcomes, it is necessary to take account not only of the quantifiable magnitudes such as the rates of growth in GDP, exports, investment, and population, but also the qualitative institutional factors and changes in the underlying organizational framework, which may have an important effect on both growth and income distribution.

If we classify our countries purely in terms of their quantifiable factor endowments, as we have done in the Leamer diagram (Fig. 2.5) in Chapter 2, countries such as Brazil, Mexico, Thailand, Ghana, Colombia, and Costa Rica may all be classified as land-abundant countries. But given their different institutional settings, the primary exports from Brazil and Mexico mainly consist of plantation and mining products produced by capital-intensive technology. The expansion of this type of exports resulted in growth with a more unequal pattern of income distribution. On the other hand, the primary exports from Thailand, Colombia, and Costa Rica mainly consist of peasant exports such as rice or coffee produced by smallholders, using labour-intensive technology. Thus, despite their initial conditions of abundant land, the expansion of labour-intensive primary exports has been associated with growth with a tendency towards a more equal income distribution in Thailand, Colombia, and Costa Rica. In effect, their pattern of income distribution is similar to the one we have identified with labour-abundant countries. This is also consonant with the trends in real wages per employee in Fig. 2.6. The contrast between the mining and plantation economies, on the one hand, and the peasant export economies, on the other, can be clearly seen, and provides us with a basis for further analysis of the institutional and organizational factors in the rest of this chapter.

But before we do so, it is necessary to elaborate the concept of the underdeveloped domestic organizational framework which, we believe, should enter as an essential component in the definition of the initial conditions of an underdeveloped country in a trade-and-growth analysis. For convenient exposition, we may use as our frame of reference a simple two-sector trade-theory model. This model requires the assumption of a fully developed system of markets for products and factors of production to translate the relative scarcities of resources of a country into the relative domestic costs and prices of its tradable products. With the given international prices for these products, the country's comparative advantage is then determined by its initial resource endowments. This type of analysis is formalized by adopting the simplifying assumption of the 'perfect competition model' of the domestic economic system, which implicitly assumes that the domestic organizational framework already exists in a fully developed form.

Thus, in conventional analysis, under free-trade conditions, a country is depicted as starting from a position on its production possibility curve on the basis of its given resources and technology. Its economic growth over time is traced in terms of movements from one position to another on a series of outward-shifting production possibility curves brought about by capital accumulation, population growth, and technological change.

For our purpose of tracing the longer-run growth of a country, starting with the initial state of underdevelopment of its domestic organizational framework, it is more appropriate to start from a position inside its production possibility curve. Its given or physically available resources may not be fully employed because of the incomplete development of the market system, characterized by the prevalence of subsistence production and the use of family labour (as distinct from wage labour) in the traditional peasant sector. Similarly, imperfect knowledge or poor credit facilities may prevent the small farmers and producers from adopting the given best-practice technology. Further, in contrast to the 'frictionless' perfect competition model, the various costs of overcoming the frictions in the form of marketing and administrative costs and transport and information costs are likely to be higher in an underdeveloped economy than in a developed economy. All these would combine to hold down an underdeveloped economy to a position inside its production possibility curve in the initial situation.

It is possible to argue that any failures to attain a position on the production possibility curve may be treated as distortions in resource allocation in a broad sense. But it is useful to draw a distinction between two types of distortions, the first due to artificial restrictions in free-market forces, and the second arising spontaneously from the existing underdeveloped state of the domestic organizational framework. The first type of distortions can be corrected, in principle, by removing the artificial restrictions on free-market forces, whether due to government controls or private monopoly. The second type of distortions with which we are concerned is more deeply embedded in the underdeveloped framework and would persist even in the absence of artificial or policy-induced distortions. It can be reduced only gradually through improvements in the domestic organizational framework over time.

To isolate the symptoms of underdevelopment from the symptoms of policy-induced distortions, we may start from the initial position of an underdeveloped economy somewhere within its production possibility curve, assuming free-trade conditions. The economic forces in the form of the world market demand, capital accumulation, population growth, and technological changes would operate on our underdeveloped economy through the filter of its initial institutional conditions. But so long as we can assume the continuation of free trade and market policies, we may envisage our economy to be moving within its production possibility curve, gradually in the direction of its free-trade equilibrium position on that curve, as its domestic organizational framework develops over time.

The point about introducing this modification of the standard analysis is to enable us to allow for the interplay between the expansion of international trade and the development of the domestic economic framework, which is important for our purpose of interpreting the longer-run outcomes of growth and income distribution. In conventional analysis, the tightly specified perfect competition model of the domestic economy leaves little room for the possible impact of trade on the domestic organizational frame. Economic policies may either introduce or remove distortions without affecting the underlying organizational framework, which is assumed to be already fully developed to start with and remains invariant through the process whereby a country's production possibility curve is shifted outward through capital accumulation, population growth, and technological changes.

Our more open-ended concept of an underdeveloped domestic economic system, although it lacks formal precision, allows for some interplay between trade and domestic organization over the longer-run period with which we are concerned. As we shall see, this two-way interaction is especially important in the context of a peasant export economy, where the 'traditional' agricultural sector is less well developed or the organizational framework less fully formed than in the 'modern' export sector of the plantation and mining economy. We shall hope to show that a successful process of expansion of peasant exports in a country would not only promote its economic growth but would also develop its domestic organizational framework, easing its transition to the export of labour-intensive manufactured goods. Conversely, government policies which discourage the expansion of peasant exports would not only distort resource allocation but would also tend to repress the development of the domestic organizational framework and retard growth.

With this preliminary clearing of the ground, we may now proceed to the study of some of the organizational and institutional aspects of growth and income distribution in the countries in our study. Our analysis will be based on the distinction between the two types of land-abundant countries: the plantation and mining economies typified by countries such as Brazil and Mexico, and the peasant economies typified by countries such as Thailand and Ghana. We shall also consider the case of mixed plantation and peasant economies, such as Malaysia and Sri Lanka. We shall see that this scheme of analysis can be extended to cover other countries in our study, except the small open economies with no peasant agriculture, where the domestic economy is too small and compact to require an elaborate analysis of organizational costs.

II. PEASANT EXPORT ECONOMY AND PLANTATION AND MINING ECONOMY

We have already seen that while the expansion of exports in the plantation and mining economies is likely to lead to growth with a more unequal distribution of incomes, the expansion of exports in the peasant economies is likely to lead to growth with a more equal distribution of incomes. We shall now consider the changes in domestic economic organization which accompany a successful process of expansion of primary exports in these two types of economy.

Plantation and mining exports are produced by a relatively small number of large-scale economic enterprises in the 'modern sector', using modern capital-intensive technology. These large-scale enterprises in the modern sector can obtain their labour supply from a well-developed labour market based on a regular wage system, and have access to modern banking and financial institutions. Whether foreign or domestically owned, they can draw upon an internationally available supply of managerial and financial resources and technology. Thus, provided that the available natural resources are sufficiently abundant for profitable exploitation, exports from the modern plantation and mining sector could expand, more or less independently of the state of organizational development in the rest of the domestic economy. Even where the domestic supply of labour was insufficient, the expansion of plantation and mining exports could proceed by recruiting immigrant labour (as in the cases of Malaysia and Sri Lanka). Thus, so long as a country is willing to adopt the nineteenth-century type of liberal policies towards foreign trade, foreign investment, and immigration, a successful process of expansion of primary exports from the modern plantation and mining sector does not raise any special problems of organizational change in the rest of the domestic economy.

The situation is very different for a peasant export economy. Here the expansion of exports involves a large number of small peasant farmers widely dispersed in the traditional sector. In order to open up this traditional sector to international trade, it is necessary to introduce considerable organizational changes into the domestic economic framework. The export-import trading firms would have to set up and extend a marketing network through a chain of middlemen to reach down to potential export producers in the periphery of the exchange economy and to provide them with incentives in the form of the opportunity to buy cheap imported consumers' goods. The necessity for this more elaborate development of economic organization would at first sight suggest that the expansion of peasant exports would be more difficult and slower than the expansion of plantation and mining exports. But, historically speaking, the expansion of peasant exports from the land-abundant countries of South-East Asia and Africa in the pre-war days was very rapid.[1] Given an abundant supply of land, and improvements in law and order and in transport and communications, peasant farmers have shown a capacity to respond vigorously to economic incentives. The pre-war conditions of abundant land continued in some of the South-East Asian and West African countries in the early post-war decades. But only Thailand has shown the capacity to exploit the potential for rapid expansion of peasant exports.

For the purpose of understanding the interaction between export expansion and the development of the domestic economic organizational framework, we examine the mechanics of peasant export expansion. In the initial situation there would be many peasant households in the traditional sector who were on the periphery of the exchange economy, devoting a large proportion of their resources in the form of the family labour supply and their landholdings to subsistence production. Given an abundant supply of land, they could have produced more than their subsistence requirements, by bringing in more land under cultivation with existing agricultural techniques. But they would have no incentive to do so, for other peasant households with a similar access to abundant land could have also produced a surplus output above subsistence requirements. Given the underdevelopment of the domestic economic framework, with poor transport and communications, the size of the fragmented local markets would be too limited to absorb this potential surplus agricultural output.

In such a setting, the opening up of the traditional sector to international trade, through improvements in transport and communications and the extension of the market network, then provided a 'vent for surplus'.[2] The opportunity to buy imported consumers' goods would now provide the peasant households with the incentive to clear more land for the cultivation of cash crops for the export market, using the surplus family labour supply available during the off-seasons of current agricultural production devoted to subsistence requirements. The significance of the surplus land in this setting is that it enabled the farmers to produce export crops without reducing their subsistence output, thereby reducing their risks and costs of entering the exchange economy in the earlier stage of peasant export expansion. Had the peasant farmers been obliged to reallocate their fully employed resources from subsistence production to cash production as envisaged in the standard trade theory, the expansion of peasant exports, with unchanged agricultural techniques, would have been much slower. The significance of the surplus or off-season supply of family labour is that it enabled the peasant farmers to invest in clearing up more land with very little actual cash outlays. Thus capital formation could take place with rudimentary markets for labour and capital in the traditional sector.

We have depicted this 'vent for surplus' interpretation of peasant export expansion by locating the initial position of an underdeveloped economy within its production possibility curve, and its subsequent movement towards the production frontier. If we choose, this can be reformulated to fit in with the standard analysis in the following way. We may attach an opportunity cost to the off-season surplus agricultural labour or seasonal unemployment, by saying that it could have produced non-agricultural output or be enjoyed as leisure. Thus the cost of expanding peasant exports is a reduction in output or income elsewhere. We may also define the given land in the initial situation to include only the land actually cultivated, excluding raw natural resources or uncleared land. This will preserve the full employment assumption of the given land. Thus the expansion of peasant exports can be interpreted in the conventional way as outward shifts in the production possibility curve due to investment which increased the supply of resources of the country.

While there are no insuperable difficulties in reformulating our story in this way, much of the institutional content would have been lost.[3] The institutional vacuity of the conventional approach can be seen in another way: by explicitly recognizing the existence of the marketing, administrative, transport, and information costs usually left out in the construction of the production possibility curve based on a frictionless perfect competition model of the domestic economic system. Here a valuable insight into these neglected organization factors can be obtained from a celebrated paper by R. H. Coase.[4] Coase points out: (i) that while the market mechanism allocates resources between different firms, the allocation of resources within a firm is done by direct management or planning; (ii) that in any realistic situation, there are costs of using the market mechanism, in the form of information costs, costs of making separate short-run contracts, and other marketing costs; and (iii) that the firm exists as an economic unit because, in organizational terms, it is more efficient to carry out a certain range of its activities by direct management and planning within its own organization instead of using the outside market mechanism.

From this it follows that, in a given situation, the higher the marketing costs of using the price mechanism compared with the organizational costs of direct management, the greater will be the volume and range of economic activities, for example vertical integration, which the firm would find it advantageous to carry out within its own organization. This analysis may be applied to the peasant export economy, both to the peasant households and to the government, considered as a giant firm which seeks to extend the use of its own agencies to carry out the function of providing marketing and credit facilities to peasant farmers.

Thus the peasant families which devote a considerable part of their resources to subsistence production may be regarded as 'household firms' which find it organizationally more efficient to satisfy their wants by diversifying their activities in the production of a wide range of goods and services instead of specialization, because of the high costs and risks of using an underdeveloped market system. The greater the organizational costs of using an underdeveloped market system, the greater will be the degree of self-sufficiency within each peasant household. Thus the expansion of peasant exports, leading to the development of the market system by drawing the peasant households into the exchange economy, would be a powerful factor in reducing the marketing and organizational costs of the traditional sector. This would pave the way for further economic growth through a greater degree of specialization and division of labour along Adam Smithian lines, by widening the size of the local markets through improvements in transport and communications and joining them together into a more articulated market system extending over the whole economy.[5]

We can now apply this analysis to Thailand and Ghana, the two peasant export economies with abundant land in the 1950s. There was still room for extending the margin of cultivation in Thailand until the 1970s, and one may conjecture that Ghana still possesses some elbow-room of surplus land.

Thailand, by taking advantage of this 'easy phase' of peasant export expansion and diversification, has been able to build up the necessary organizational framework and infrastructure which helped her to adopt more cash-intensive improved agricultural methods when the surplus land was exhausted. This building up of a domestic economic organization capable of supplying the needs of a large number of small economic units for marketing, credit, transport, and information facilities, eased her transition from labour-intensive peasant exports to labour-intensive manufactured exports, following in the footsteps of Taiwan and Korea.

Ghana, in contrast, choked off the considerable potentialities for expanding peasant exports provided by her abundant land in the 1960s by heavy taxation on peasant exports. Her policies of using the State Agricultural Marketing Board and other state agencies to replace the private trading and marketing network also repressed the development of the domestic organizational framework.

In Ghana, as in many other developing countries, a popular argument for justifying government intervention in agriculture is that peasant farmers are being subjected to monopolistic exploitation by the middlemen and the moneylenders. Here, it is relevant to recall our distinction between the symptoms of distortions arising from artificial restrictions on market forces and the symptoms of underdevelopment. As is well known, the level of interest rates charged by the moneylenders in the unorganized market for loans is much higher than those charged by the banks and the financial institutions in the modern sector. But so long as there is free entry into moneylending, the higher interest rates in the traditional sector reflect the genuinely higher costs of lending money on a retail basis, including the risks of lending money to small borrowers with inadequate collateral. It may be regarded as the symptoms of an underdeveloped capital market. These high interest rates cannot be lowered by government regulations which fix the maximum ceiling rates without organizational improvements to bring down the cost of lending to small borrowers. Similarly, there is typically a wide margin between the farm-gate price received by the peasant export producers and the f.o.b. price of their export product at the point of export, which includes the costs of transport, processing, and the handling and marketing costs of conveying the peasant produce to the exporting points. The state agricultural marketing boards, which purport to reduce the 'monopolistic' middlemen's margins, have generally resulted in widening the gap between the world market f.o.b. price of the peasant exports and the farm-gate price paid to the farmers, not only because of the heavy tax element but also because of the higher administrative costs of using the government marketing agencies. Thus the government, regarded as a giant firm, would find it cheaper to use the market mechanism rather than its own administrative mechanism to perform the task of conveying the peasant produce to the exporting points. It would then be able to obtain a greater amount of revenues through an export tax than through the marketing board system, with the same burden imposed on the peasant farmers.

III. THE EFFECTS OF IMPORT-SUBSTITUTION POLICIES

It is now time to introduce the import-substitution policies into the picture. Most of the countries in our study have pursued import-substitution policies to promote domestic manufacturing industries, with the exception of Hong Kong and, at a later stage, Singapore. Some of them, such as Malaysia, Sri Lanka, and Indonesia, have also pursued agricultural import-substitution policies to help their indigenous rice farmers and to promote equity and a greater degree of domestic food self-sufficiency.

In the process of growth through the expansion of primary exports, some 'natural' import-substitution in manufactures would have occurred to reflect the changing comparative advantage of a country: that is to say, some manufacturing industries would have emerged even without tariff protection and subsidies. We may distinguish this natural import substitution from the policy-induced import substitution with which we are mainly concerned.

Theoretically, any import-substitution policy which departs from a country's comparative advantage would distort resource allocation and would be unfavourable for economic growth. But many countries seem to grow quite rapidly even where there seem to be significant distortions in their resource allocation at the microeconomic and sectoral levels. This seems to be true of countries such as Brazil and Mexico, which showed high growth rates until the 1980s. Even countries such as Thailand and Malaysia, which we would regard as countries achieving growth through successful expansion of primary exports, are not free from distortions which discriminate against agriculture.[6] Attempts to quantify the once-over static losses through trade distortions tend to come out with a small percentage of GDP which cannot hope to explain the different rates of economic growth between the successful and unsuccessful countries.[7]

To meet this difficulty we have to shift the focus of analysis from the allocation of the given stocks of resources to the allocation of the annual *flows* of investible resources. Thus, even if the once-over losses from distortions in the allocation of the given resources are small, the cumulative effect of diverting the annually available flows of investible resources into uneconomic import-substitution may be expected to be large enough to show in a slower growth rate. On the other hand, if the import-substitution policies are moderate enough to allow the expansion of exports to yield sufficient government revenues and domestic savings to subsidize the import-substitution industries, growth with import-substitution policies could proceed, although the economy might not be strictly on its efficient growth path from the standpoint of comparative advantage. The sustainability of this process then depends on maintaining a balance in allocating the annual flows of resources between export-expansion and import-substitution. If the import-substitution policies were carried too far, the export industries would be taxed too heavily and starved of investible resources to yield sufficient revenues to sustain the process. In the short run, this would lead to the balance-of-payments crises and 'stop-go' policies which interrupt growth. Over the longer run, a continuation of extreme import-substitution policies would lead to a decline of exports and growth.

The effect of import-substitution policies on income distribution may be treated in a more straightforward manner in terms of the factor-proportions analysis. Import-substituting manufacturing industries usually require more capital-intensive methods of production than the primary exports. Thus, with a given rate of investment, the promotion of import-substitution in manufacturing industry would not only tend to slow down export-expansion and growth, but would also reduce the demand for labour and employment and thus worsen income distribution. This shows itself most clearly in the wage differential between those employed in modern manu-facturing industry and those in the traditional agricultural sector and the casual labour market in the urban 'informal sector'.

There is, however, an important difference in the pattern of resource transfers under import-substitution policies in the plantation and mining economies and in the peasant economies.

In the plantation and mining economies, the resources required to sub-sidize the expansion of the domestic manufacturing industries are obtained by taxing the larger-scale export producers, who are themselves a part of the modern sector. Thus resource transfers take place within the modern sector, and incomes are redistributed to the owners of the man-made capital goods used in the protected manufacturing from the owners of natural resources used in export industries, who may be either private owners or the government. This argument is not appreciably affected by introducing foreign borrowing to finance import-substituting industries, for the resources required for debt servicing must ultimately come out of the export proceeds (or domestic savings out of the same proceeds). The traditional sector of the mining and plantation economies is not directly involved, although it of course suffers from the limited capacity of the highly capital-intensive import-substituting manufacturing industries to absorb labour from the traditional sector.

In the peasant export economies, however, the resources required to subsidize the import-substituting industries in the modern manufacturing sector have to be obtained by taxing the peasant export producers in the traditional sector. This involves a redistribution of incomes from the poorer and less developed traditional sector to the richer and more developed modern sector, with a more adverse effect on income distribution. Further, taxation levied through inefficient organizational mechanisms, such as the state agricultural marketing boards instead of export taxes, would tend to repress the development of the organizational framework in the traditional sector and worsen the longer-run prospects of economic growth.

Finally, to complete the picture, we many consider a third pattern of resource transfers, from the modern export sector consisting of plantations and mines to the traditional peasant sector. This can be seen in the 'mixed' cases of plantation and peasant economies, such as Sri Lanka, Malaysia, and Indonesia. These countries of course protect their domestic manufacturing industries in varying degrees, but they have also devoted considerable resources to agricultural import-substitution to promote a greater degree of domestic food self-sufficiency, motivated by a desire to redistribute incomes in favour of their indigenous peasant rice farmers.

Now while tariffs are widely used to protect domestic industries, their use in agricultural protection is inhibited by the fear of raising the domestic cost of living. Thus a greater reliance has to be placed on injecting subsidies into peasant agriculture, combined with greater public expenditure in improving rural transport and communications and social infrastructure. But government policies towards peasant agriculture have to operate through the filter of the underdeveloped organizational framework in the traditional sector, which includes not only the incomplete development of the market system but also the incomplete development of the government administrative system. Like the private trading firms, the government also has to operate through a series of middlemen in the form of provincial, district, and township offices to reach down to the village level. Thus the organizational and administrative costs of providing public services and subsidies to a large number of peasant farmers widely dispersed in the countryside are much higher than the costs of providing the equivalent facilities and subsidies to a small number of favoured industries in the modern sector of the economy. Public expenditure per head on social infrastructure and education and health is typically higher in the modern urban sector than in the rural sector in most developing countries, but even if the same amount per head were spent in the two sectors, the standard of facilities would be poorer in the rural sector, because of the greater administrative costs and the well-known difficulties of attracting suitable personnel to the rural areas.[8]

In the face of the underdeveloped organizational framework of the traditional sector, government policies to promote agricultural import-substitution have typically adopted three forms in varying mixtures.

First, there are the large-scale investment projects in irrigation, such as the Gal Oya project in Sri Lanka and the Muda Valley project in Malaysia. These projects are highly capital-intensive and their design and execution stretch the available supply of organizational and technical skills. They are typically financed by foreign aid, and may be regarded as the attempt to introduce islands of modern organization in the traditional agricultural sector. The estimates of their benefits and costs are uncertain, and they introduce a new factor of income inequality between the peasant farmers who are selected for inclusion and those who are left out of these 'show-case' projects.

Secondly, the government may employ its own agencies and co-operative societies to distribute subsidized credit and inputs, such as improved seeds and fertilizer, to the farmers. But these para-statal agencies tend to be highly inefficient (or corrupt) in performing the organizational tasks of distributing the subsidized inputs at the right place, in the right amounts, and at the right time to the peasant farmers. They tend to impose not only heavy administrative costs on the government but also considerable costs on the peasants themselves, because of delays and the complexities of formal procedures. This is why peasant farmers find it preferable to resort to the moneylenders or private traders at higher free-market interest rates and higher prices.

Thirdly, the government may fall back on the use of the market mechanism by offering guaranteed minimum prices to the rice peasant farmers, above the world market price of rice. In order to reduce its effect on the cost of living, countervailing measures have to be taken. In Sri Lanka, this takes the form of consumers' subsidies which distribute rice (including substantial proportions of imported rice) in fixed quantities per head at highly subsidized prices. Malaysia links the quantities of rice which private traders can import with their purchases of locally produced rice at government-guaranteed prices. This in effect combines a tariff on rice imports with subsidies on domestic rice production. Malaysia, however, manages to keep down the domestic cost of living by pursuing orthodox fiscal and monetary policies.[9]

The agricultural import-substitution policies in Sri Lanka, Malaysia, and Indonesia have reduced their rice imports and promoted a greater degree of domestic food self-sufficiency. But it is difficult to make any simple clear-cut assessment of how far they are 'economic'—that is, to what extent they involve distortions in resource allocation, and to what extent they are in line with the changes in potential comparative advantage brought about by technological changes in the form of the 'Green Revolution' and population pressure on land. They have contributed in varying degrees to the redistribution of incomes in favour of the poorer peasant farmers.

But the outcomes in terms of the sustainability of these policies have been different. Malaysia has maintained an open economy and more favourable policies towards the expansion of exports from her plantation and mining sector. This has yielded an expanding stream of government revenues to subsidize her peasant sector and redistribute incomes to her peasant farmers in a more sustainable manner. On the other hand, Sri Lanka's less favourable policies towards her plantation sector have resulted in a stagnation of her tea and rubber exports; and this, combined with the burden of her food subsidies, has resulted in stop-go policies to cope with balance-of-payments difficulties. Indonesia, by a judicious management of her windfall gains from the oil boom, has been able to siphon off her export revenues to promote a greater degree of domestic self-sufficiency in rice in an effective manner.

In sum: the pursuit of mixed policies of expanding primary exports and import-substitution, whether to promote domestic industrialization or greater domestic food self-sufficiency, has two aspects. The first is the question of how far the departures from pure free-trade policies would lead to distortions in resource allocation at the microeconomic and sectoral levels. This will be subject to qualifications by taking into account the longer-run prospects of the infant manufacturing industry and the techno-logical changes introduced by the Green Revolution. The second is the question of a sustainable balance between the tempo of export-expansion and the tempo of import-substitution. The failure to maintain a sustainable balance at the macroeconomic level results in more immediately assessable penalties and rewards. For instance, Brazil and Mexico were able to grow quite rapidly with a mixture of export-expansion and import-substitution policies during the 1960s and 1970s, until the deterioration in the world economic environment landed them in balance-of-payments and debt crises. The same analysis applies to the relative success of Malaysia and Indonesia in sustaining agricultural import-substitution policies, and the relative failure of Sri Lanka, which has been subject to balance-of-payment difficulties.

IV. THE TRANSITION TO MANUFACTURED EXPORTS

Hong Kong and Singapore, together with Taiwan and Korea, belong to the famous 'four' which achieved a spectacular success in expanding manu-factured exports in the 1960s. They were followed by the other newly industrializing countries in our group, such as Brazil, Mexico, Turkey, Colombia, Costa Rica, Thailand, and Malaysia. By the 1980s, it is not un-common to find that about one-third or more of their total exports were made up of manufactured exports.[10]

We shall now consider the transition from primary exports to manufac-turing exports in the two types of economy we have been considering. We have already stated the reasons why this transition is likely to be more difficult for the mining and plantation type of economy than for a peasant economy. Here we may introduce further considerations which are likely to make the transition more difficult for the mining and planta-tion economy when starting from the middle of an import-substitution process.

These difficulties can be most clearly seen in the context of the Latin American type of plantation and mining economy, such as Brazil and

Mexico. Here the aim of the import-substitution policies is not merely to create domestic manufacturing industry but to pass as quickly as possible from the simpler type of manufacturing, such as textiles and raw-material processing industries, to the sophisticated type of manufacturing based on highly capital-intensive methods and advanced technology to spearhead the process of domestic industrialization. Thus the structure of the import-substitution industries tends to be more capital- and skill-intensive than is warranted even by the relatively high initial level of wages. This type of plantation and mining economy would have to move a few rungs downwards on the industrial ladder, with the concomitant reduction in wages, before realizing their potential comparative advantage in the type of manufacturing appropriate to their resource endowments. Further, as is well known, import-substitution policies provide a fertile ground for 'rent-seeking' and the creation of vested interests among the entrepreneurs who benefit from protection and the urban workers employed in the protected industries. The transition process to the steady expansion of manufactured exports in line with comparative advantage has been made more difficult by the political expedients necessary to contain these powerful pressures, such as the inflationary fiscal and monetary policies, experiments with wage indexation, and the maintenance of over-valued exchange rates, which are the familiar features of many Latin American countries.

In the mean time, population would be growing rapidly. This would make itself felt in the increasing migration of labour from the rural areas to the cities, and the expansion of urban labour supply well beyond the capacity of the capital-intensive modern manufacturing sector to absorb. This leads to the rapid growth of the urban informal sector, consisting of a large number of people seeking a living in the casual labour market and in a wide variety of labour-intensive activities, such as retail trading, handicraft industries, processing and manufacturing in small workshops, market gardening, and all types of service industries. In organizational terms we now have a dualism between the modern manufacturing sector and the urban informal sector similar to the dualism between the modern sector and the traditional agricultural sector. Like the small farmers, the small-scale economic units in the urban informal sector are subject to the handicap of an underdeveloped organizational framework. Compared with the modern sector, wages will be much lower in the informal sector, and the costs of acquiring credit, information, and other inputs will be much higher.

But from the standpoint of the factor proportions approach, the growth of the urban informal sector in the Latin American countries may be interpreted as population growth leading to a change in their potential comparative advantage, increasing the scope for a natural import-substitution in a wide range of labour-intensive manufactured goods. These may be of poorer quality, but compensated for by cheaper prices geared to the consumers at the lower end of the market. In order to realize this potential comparative advantage, however, the small economic units in the urban informal sector would have to obtain access to the inputs, at free-market prices, allowing for the normal cost differentials between wholesale and retail transactions. But in a typical setting of a developing country, where the government intervenes extensively to promote import-substitution in the modern manufacturing sector, the allocation of scarce resources such as capital funds and foreign exchange would be heavily biased in favour of the large-scale capital-intensive manufacturing industries and heavily biased against the small economic units in the informal sector. Further, the urban informal sector would be subject to various controls and regulations de-signed to discourage its further growth, because of the associated problems of shanty towns, overcrowding of public services, political unrest of urban unemployment, and illegal black-market activities. Thus the organizational framework of the urban informal sector is likely to be repressed. Therefore the effect of promoting import-substitution in the modern manufacturing sector may not only discourage the expansion of primary exports but may also discourage the 'natural' import-substitution in a wide range of small-scale labour-intensive activities in the urban informal sector. The economic potential of the urban informal sector seems to be greater than is generally assumed.[11] In order to realize it, however, the trade liberalization policies would have to be extended from the foreign trade sector to the domestic economy as a whole.

Let us now turn to the transition of a peasant export economy to the production of labour-intensive manufactured exports. Thailand and Colombia are notable examples of countries which, starting from the ex-pansion of agricultural exports produced by small-scale farmers, have suc-cessfully made the transition to the labour-intensive manufactured exports, again produced on a small-scale basis. Logically, there is no necessary relationship between small-scale production and labour-intensive manufac-tured exports. Thus the labour-intensive exports from an Exports Process-ing Zone (EPZ) set up with foreign investment (e.g. in Malaysia and Mexico) are fairly large-scale. But the historical experiences of the earlier phase of development in the successful countries such as Japan, Taiwan, and Korea suggest a strong association between small-scale industries and a successful exploitation of the potential comparative advantage in labour-intensive manufactured exports.[12] This experience is repeated in Thailand, where domestic entrepreneurs engaged in the rice export trade turned to manufacturing, and in Colombia, where the Antioqueno entrepreneurs engaged in the coffee export trade turned to manufactured exports, in both cases on the basis of small family firms. The reason for this seems to be that in the earlier stages of development small family firms and workshops tend to have lower overhead costs and greater flexibility than large-scale modern-style factories. This arises not only from a fuller utilization of smaller plants but also from lower management costs, based on a greater knowledge of local conditions, including the supervision of untrained labour. In order to realize this potential comparative advantage, however, the domestic economic organization framework has to be sufficiently developed to provide a large number of small producers with the necessary marketing, credit, information, and transport facilities.

We have seen that the expansion of peasant exports from the traditional sector involves a greater degree of development of the domestic organizational framework than the expansion of plantation and mining exports from the modern sector. Similarly, the expansion of labour-intensive manufactured exports produced by domestic entrepreneurs on a small-scale basis involves a greater degree of development of the domestic organizational framework than the expansion of labour-intensive manufactured exports based on foreign investment and management in an Export Processing Zone. In fact, the EPZ is a device for taking advantage of the abundant labour supply of a country while circumventing the government regulations and the underdevelopment of organizational framework in the rest of the economy outside these specially designated 'free-trade zones'.

Thus the creation of favourable conditions for the expansion of labour-intensive manufactured exports produced by small-scale domestic entrepreneurs would require both the reduction of bias in the government policies favouring the large-scale modern enterprises, and improvements in the organizational framework. For instance, there would have to be improvements in the marketing links through the large international trading firms or through the buyers from large retail outlets in the importing countries, involving standardization and quality control. Further, there may also have to be additional institutional arrangements, such as subcontracting, which has played an important part in the expansion of labour-intensive manufactured exports in Japan and other Far Eastern countries. The development of similar institutional arrangements could contribute to the reduction of organizational dualism between the modern industrial sector and the urban informal sector in some Latin American countries and pave the way for labour-intensive manufactured exports from the urban informal sector.

The advantage of countries such as Thailand and Colombia is that, starting from the initial conditions of abundant land, they have gone through a successful phase of expansion in peasant or smallholders' exports, which contributed to the development of the domestic organizational framework which subsequently eased their transition to the expansion of labour-intensive manufactured exports on a small-scale basis.

This transition process may be traced in a stylized manner, drawing upon some of the aspects of the earlier phase of successful economic development in Japan, Taiwan, and Korea to illustrate the story.

First, we start from the initial conditions of a land-abundant peasant economy. The 'easy phase' of peasant export-expansion, bringing in more land under cultivation, generated the resources to finance the cost of setting up and improving the domestic organizational framework. This includes the extension of the network marketing, credit, and transport and communications to reach down to a larger number of small peasant exporters. The improvements in the organizational framework spread to other parts of the traditional sector, particularly to domestic food production and small-scale rural industries. This spreads the overhead costs of the organizational framework, lowering the general level of marketing and transaction costs and promoting the Adam Smithian process of division of labour and specialization, raising the productivity of the resources in the traditional sector as a whole. In contrast to the government subsidies confined to selected groups of farmers or producers, this general lowering of the organizational costs would bring out the potentialities of natural import-substitution both in domestic food production and among small-scale rural industries in the widening of the local markets. In this context it should be remembered that a substantial proportion of the resources in the rural sector of the underdeveloped countries is already employed in non-agricultural activities.[13]

Let us now go on to the next stage of development of the peasant export economy, when all its initial endowment of land has been brought under cultivation. Its future growth would then depend on its capacity to raise agricultural productivity and to switch to labour-intensive manufactured exports. Here we may draw upon the experience of countries such as Taiwan and Korea, which started in the 1950s as labour-abundant countries with high population density.

A salient feature of their rapid growth has been their success in raising agricultural productivity through the introduction of improved agricultural technology, based on high-yielding seeds and fertilizer and multiple cropping of land based on improved irrigation. This, however, involves considerable problems of improving the organizational framework of the agricultural sector: improved marketing and credit facilities to promote the new cash-intensive methods of agriculture; improved irrigation to promote multiple cropping; and improved transport and communications and the network of information to disseminate the new technology. Starting from the conditions of high population density, Taiwan and Korea have shown an outstanding capacity to solve these complex problems of organizational change. Countries which started from the initial conditions of abundant land would also have to face these problems as rapid population growth turns them into labour-abundant countries.

The transition from the easy phase of agricultural expansion based on bringing in more land under cultivation to the more difficult phase of raising the productivity of the given amount of land would be easier for countries like Thailand and Colombia, where the organizational improvements have been under way during the easy phase of peasant export-expansion, than for countries like Ghana which failed to take advantage of this easy phase.

This brings us to an essential link between labour-abundance and comparative advantage in labour-intensive manufactured exports, which is worth reiterating. In order to translate its abundant labour supply into low wage costs in manufacturing exports, a country would have to raise agricultural productivity to keep down its domestic cost of living. Without this essential condition, it would not be able to realize its potential comparative advantage. It may be noted that this argument is quite different from the argument to promote domestic food self-sufficiency on welfare grounds or to fulfil a national goal. For after a country has successfully expanded its labour-intensive manufactured exports, it may find more productive ways of using its labour, which is growing more scarce, than in domestic food production. This changing pattern of comparative advantage, in which a successful manufacturing country begins to import more agricultural imports, can be seen in a country like Taiwan. This consideration is especially relevant for a country like Malaysia, which has adopted the goal of greater domestic food self-sufficiency with a rising trend in manufactured exports.

Another notable feature of the Far Eastern style of rapid economic growth through the expansion of labour-intensive manufactured exports is the important role of small-scale entrepreneurs in improving the given technology in manufacturing by adapting it to local conditions. This contrasts with the conventional view, in which technological innovations are regarded either as exogenous changes or the result of heavy investment in research and development which only the large-scale enterprises and the government can undertake. This view, drawn from the experiences of mature industrial economies at a later stage of development, obscures the important role of small-scale entrepreneurs at the earlier stage of development. This earlier experience is encapsulated by Lockwood when he writes: 'If Japan's experience teaches any single lesson regarding the process of development in Asia, it is the cumulative importance of myriads of relatively small improvements in technology which do not radically depart from tradition or require large units of new investment?'[14] This lesson is reiterated by another writer drawing on the more recent experience of Taiwan and Korea. Chen emphasizes the importance of 'minor innovations' in the industrial development of these countries, adapting the existing technologies to local conditions to improve factor utilization, and reducing 'management slacks'.[15]

It will be seen that the thrust of our analysis has been to focus attention on the potentialities of raising productivity and growth through improvements in the domestic organizational framework, tapping the reservoir of latent entrepreneurial capacity among small peasant farmers, small traders, and small-scale manufacturers, outside the modern sector characterized by large-scale enterprises based on high capital-intensive methods and advanced technology.

Conventionally, on the assumption of a fully developed domestic organizational framework, increasing returns are assumed to be obtainable only through large-scale production by overcoming the technical indivisibilities and 'lumpiness' of investment. But in a setting of an incompletely developed domestic economic framework, where the local markets facing the small producers are small and fragmented, there may also be considerable possibilities of increasing returns by overcoming the 'indivisibilities in the small'. Thus improvements in transport and communications, by widening the size of local markets, may lead to a fuller utilization of the existing equipment of small workshops. Improvements in credit facilities may enable a small farmer or manufacturer to borrow to install capital equipment which requires investment outlays which are 'small' by ordinary standards, but are many times larger than his cash income.[16] The gains for each individual producer from overcoming these small indivisibilities may be small, but in the aggregate they may turn out to be much larger than the gains from overcoming the lumpiness of investment from a few spectacular large-scale projects.

Our argument that the latent entrepreneurial capacity among peasant farmers can be released in a free-market environment offering economic incentives goes against the once-fashionable sociological stereotype of the traditional farmers, bound by habit and custom in resisting economic change. In the light of accumulating historical experience, there is perhaps no further need to knock down this stereotype. But it is still worth pointing out that peasant farmers, like the small traders and manufacturers, are self-employed persons who have to make daily economic decisions to allocate their resources to take advantage of market opportunities. Thus they are a more promising source of entrepreneurial ability than wage labourers or salaried employees, even when these are employed in a large-scale modern manufacturing enterprise. Among our peasant export economies, there is no evidence of lack of entrepreneurial ability, not only in the successful countries like Thailand and Colombia but also in unsuccessful countries like Ghana. It is worth recalling that cocoa was first introduced into Ghana as a new export crop through the private enterprise of the Ghanaian peasant farmers. In fact cocoa, as a tree crop which yields returns only after an investment period of a few years, requires a more complex decision-making process than growing an annual crop like rice. Thus the failure of Ghana compared with the success story of Thailand may be accounted for, not in terms of the different endowments of entrepreneurial capacity, but in terms of different policies pursued by their governments.

V. REINTERPRETING THE COUNTRY STORIES

We may now round off this chapter by considering briefly how far the stories of the individual countries in our study may be fitted into our framework of interpretation, based on the contrast between the peasant export economies on the one hand and the plantation and mining economies on the other. For this purpose we may look at our countries in terms of four main groupings.

1. The Small Economies

Our framework is not relevant for the five small open economies. Hong Kong, Singapore, and Malta have no agricultural sector and as city-states, the transport, information, and other organizational costs within their domestic economy are at a minimum. Mauritius and Jamaica also do not possess a peasant agricultural sector in a significant sense. Mauritius switched from sugar plantation exports to labour-intensive manufactured exports through the introduction of an Export Processing Zone without involving small-scale producers. Jamaica still remains a plantation and mining export economy based on sugar and bauxite, without a significant development of peasant exports or labour-intensive manufactured exports. In this group without a significant peasant agricultural sector we may also include Uruguay, whose economy consists of large-scale ranching and the modern manufacturing sector. The stories of these economies also highlight the role of international migration of labour, which has been important relative to their small population base. Immigration has been important in Hong Kong and Singapore, and Malta and Uruguay have been significantly affected by out-migration and return migration, depending on the state of their economy. The rise of the oil industry has clearly increased the role of international migration of labour into the oil-rich Middle Eastern countries from Egypt and other Asian countries. There has also been a significant migration from Ghana to Nigeria during the oil boom, followed by a subsequent mass expulsion.

2. The Peasant Export Economies

Next we have the peasant export economies, which are widespread in Africa and Asia. We have devoted much attention to this type of economy for two reasons. First, the expansion of labour-intensive peasant exports tends to promote growth with more equal income distribution, and this pattern can be maintained if there is a successful transition to the expansion of labour-intensive manufactured exports. Secondly, peasant export expansion from the initial conditions of abundant land brings out most clearly the mutual interactions between foreign trade and the development of the domestic organizational framework, and helps us to have a better understanding of the organizational adaptations required in the transition from labour-intensive peasant exports to labour-intensive manufactured exports. The analysis may also be extended to the urban informal sector of the plantation and mining economies.

Thailand, Ghana, Colombia, and Costa Rica are examples of smallholder or peasant export economies with the initial conditions of abundant land. Thailand and Colombia are cases of successful peasant export expansion leading to the expansion of labour-intensive manufactured exports. Ghana is the unsuccessful case. Costa Rica followed the path of growth through export expansion, but was shunted off into capital-intensive import-substitution policies by the Central American Common Market and suffered from severe balance-of-payments problems in the 1980s, when the burden of her highly developed social welfare system became unsustainable in the aftermath of oil price shocks and the rise in interest rates.

To this group we may add Malawi, Madagascar, and Egypt, which, although they are not clear examples of peasant economies, will have to look towards the expansion of labour-intensive exports in one form or another for their future economic growth. Malawi is an interesting case in which the State Agricultural Marketing Board system has been used to tax the peasant farmers to subsidize the large-scale plantation sector—the reverse of the policy in Malaysia and Sri Lanka. While Malawi succeeded for a time in promoting growth through the expansion of plantation exports, her longer-run growth would have to depend on raising the productivity of her peasant sector, now suffering from population pressure on limited land. Madagascar, less well-endowed with natural resources than Ghana, has followed similar policies to Ghana, with similarly unfavourable outcomes in growth and income distribution. Egypt, with her high population density on usable land, would have to seek her comparative advantage in the expansion of labour-intensive manufactured exports. But so far she has relied mainly on foreign and other sources of foreign exchange earnings, such as remittances from immigrants in the oil-rich Middle Eastern countries and the rents from the Suez Canal, which have overlaid her potential comparative advantage in labour-intensive exports.

3. The Plantation and Mining Economies

Next, we have the Latin-American-type land-abundant countries, starting with comparative advantage in primary exports produced by large-scale enterprises in the modern sector. We have used Brazil and Mexico as representative examples, but should add Turkey and Peru to this group. Brazil, Mexico, and Turkey have enjoyed high rates of economic growth through a mixture of export expansion and import-substitution policies, using the proceeds of their primary exports and domestic savings to finance a highly capital-intensive pattern of domestic industrialization. They have all been successful in switching into the manufactured exports, and rank among the 'newly industrializing countries'. Their success in manufacturing exports depends on their ability to make downward adjustments in real wages to realize their potential comparative advantage in the relatively less labour-intensive and more capital-intensive middle-range type of manufactured exports. The political difficulties of cutting real wages, together with insufficient domestic savings to finance a highly capital-intensive pattern of industrialization, have contributed to their endemically high rates of domestic inflation and balance-of-payments and debt crises, punctuated by stabilization policies and bouts of economic austerity, periodically enforced by military intervention in Brazil and Turkey.

Peru enjoyed economic growth through the expansion of mining and plantation exports up to 1966, and since then she has suffered from economic decline, limping from one balance-of-payments crisis to another, culminating in a hyper-inflation and debt crisis. Peru also shares with the other Latin American countries the problem of dualism between the modern sector and the urban informal sector, which has expanded rapidly through population pressure and rural–urban migration. In Peru's case this dualism is aggravated by the existence of a large indigenous Indian population in the traditional sector which has been bypassed by the expansion of primary exports from the modern sector and the subsequent redistribution of incomes within the modern sector during the Velasco regime. The eruption of violence and insurgency among Peru's Indian population brings out acutely the need to involve the traditional sector and the urban informal sector in the development process to promote longer-run economic growth on a satisfactory basis.

4. The Mixed Cases

Finally, we come to the 'mixed' cases of plantation and mining and peasant export economies, represented by Malaysia and Sri Lanka. We may add Nigeria and Indonesia to this group, each country introducing its own variations.

Before the rise of her oil industry, Nigeria was essentially a typical land-abundant peasant export economy, a larger edition of Ghana. Much of our analysis for the peasant economy could have been applied to Nigeria, in particular her capacity to expand peasant exports without contracting domestic food production. Nigeria's mismanagement of her oil boom not only wiped out her peasant exports through the 'Dutch Disease' effect but also sharply reduced her domestic food production, due to a vast expansion of public employment which drew labour out of agriculture. Her attempts to promote highly capital-intensive domestic industries, such as the steel mills, have been abortive. It is probably true to say that, despite the macroeconomic upheavals and the debt crisis, Nigeria's underlying domestic structure organization has not been significantly changed outside the oil sector. One may visualize future growth here in terms of the recovery of her peasant exports through improvements in the infrastructure and the organizational framework in the agricultural sector, financed out of her oil revenues.

Indonesia started as a genuine mixture of plantation and peasant export economy before the oil boom. Moreover, she has a dual pattern of factor endowments, with the densely populated island of Java, which may be regarded as a labour-abundant economy, and the sparsely populated outer islands, which may be regarded as a land-abundant economy. Indonesia's economic revival began in 1967 when she adopted a more favourable policy towards foreign investment in primary exports, notably timber. She also managed her oil revenues more prudently than Nigeria at a macroeconomic level, and invested a part of these revenues in raising the productivity of peasant rice farming in Java, taking advantage of the new agricultural technology based on high-yielding seeds, fertilizer, and irrigation. Given her dual pattern of factor endowments, policies to promote domestic food self-sufficiency in Java could be carried out without affecting the expansion of plantation and mining exports from the outer islands.

Finally, we have Malaysia and Sri Lanka, both notable for their policies of subsidizing their indigenous peasant rice farmers by using the export proceeds from the plantation and mining sector. Historically, the expansion of the modern export sector in the two countries has been brought about by foreign investment and large inflows of immigrant labour from China and India. This has created a plural society consisting of different ethnic groups. In this setting, equity as perceived by their governments is not simply a more equal distribution of the rich and poor as such, but a more equal income distribution in favour of the indigenous Malay and Sinhalese population. Among the immigrant groups, the Chinese occupy an economically more dominant position in Malaysia than the Tamils do in Sri Lanka. The fear of Chinese economic domination may partly account for Malaysia's outward-looking policies towards foreign trade and foreign investment as a counterweight to the Chinese. But this friendlier attitude to foreign investment in the plantation and mining sector has generated an expanding stream of government revenues to enable Malaysia to help the peasant rice farmers in a more sustainable manner than in Sri Lanka. In contrast, Sri Lanka followed less favourable policies towards the plantation sector, leading to a stagnation of plantation exports and of government revenues. Moreover, Sri Lanka pursued a policy not only of subsidizing her rice farmers but also of subsidizing her rice consumers, requiring substantial imports of rice. Thus her government revenues and foreign-exchange earnings frequently proved insufficient to finance her policy objectives in a sustainable manner, resulting in balance-of-payments difficulties and stop–go policies in social welfare.

It is arguable how far the policies to promote domestic food self-sufficiency in Malaysia and Sri Lanka are in line with their potential comparative advantage. They have more abundant land than Java, Malaysia more than Sri Lanka. Theoretically, any departure from pure free-trade policies, whether to promote import-substitution in manufacturing or in agriculture, would lead to distortions in resource allocation. The question how far these distortions will retard growth will always be open to debate, especially by those who would appeal to the longer-run benefits of protecting infant industry. But the importance of maintaining a sustainable balance by expanding exports to generate a sufficient flow of resources to subsidize the import-substitution policies cannot be argued away. Thus the Malaysia–Sri Lanka case reinforces a general lesson on the need to maintain macro-economic stability to promote growth through export expansion without strangling the goose that lays the golden eggs.

NOTES

1. Myint (1980).
2. Myint (1958).
3. Note, however, that the mere physical existence of uncultivated land need not indicate surplus productive capacity. Land may remain uncultivated because it is uneconomic to cultivate (see Ch. 9, Sect, IV).
4. Coase (1937), reprinted in Stigler and Boulding (1953).
5. Myint (1977).
6. Krueger, Schiff, and Valdes (1988: 261–3).
7. Harberger (1959) and Corden (1975).
8. See above, Table 3.11, illustrating the bias in the provision of social services to the Greater Bangkok area. This urban bias in the provision of public services is also pronounced in the Latin American countries and is a powerful factor reinforcing the rural–urban migration of labour.
9. See Bruton (1992: 92–7 and 297–304). For an analysis of the costs, from the standpoint of the peasant farmers, of the government agencies trying to provide subsidized loans, see Adams and Graham (1981) and González-Vega (1977).
10. Maddison et al. (1992: table 13); Hansen (1992: table VII.4); Meesook et al. (mimeo: diagram 3.7). See also Ariff and Hill (1985), and Sheahan (1987: table 4.3, p. 90).
11. See especially the study on Peru (Richard Webb, mimeo: ch. IV), where the author pointed out the 'exceptional vigor' of the growth of the urban informal sector, especially in the poultry industry. See also his table on 'The Structure of the Peruvian Economy: Modern, Informal and Rural Sector' (ibid. 159–60), showing that by 1985 the urban informal sector contributed 45% of total

employment and 25% of the total net value added of the country as a whole. See also de Soto (1989).

12. See e.g. Lockwood (1954) and Galenson (1979). See also Ariff and Hill (1985: 165–76). Among the 'small economies' in our study, Hong Kong's exports are still dominated by small producers, and Singapore started with small-scale factories before moving into her policy of attracting foreign investment in the more capital-intensive and technologically sophisticated industries requiring large-scale production.

13. Thus it has been found that some 30 to 50 per cent of rural labour in the developing countries depend on non-agricultural activities and rural industries as their primary and secondary source of employment, and that this proportion tends to grow in the course of economic development. See Chuta and Liedholm (1984: 296–312).

14. Lockwood (1954: 198).

15. Chen (1989: 227–8).

16. See McKinnon, (1973: ch. 2, especially pp. 12–13 and 19–21).

5

Instability and Growth

In this chapter we proceed to the next stage in peeling the onion of the sources of differences in the growth experience of our 21 countries, by considering the comparative experience on the extent, causes, and consequences of the fluctuations in their growth rates of real GDP during the period of study (1950–85). We also examine the implications (if any) of instability in growth rates on long-run growth performance. We shall find that much of the instability of growth performance is due to loose fiscal and monetary policies. These in turn have been the result of the attempt by nearly all our countries (with the notable exceptions of Singapore and Hong Kong) to break the mould of the older colonial framework of orthodox fiscal and monetary policies. Next, we shall seek to determine any patterns in this public policy-induced macroeconomic instability.

I. DIMENSIONS OF GROWTH INSTABILITY

The stability in the growth performance of our countries has varied considerably. Annual growth rates have been very volatile,[1] and in some countries, as judged by our country study authors, growth has collapsed (see Table 5.1). From a statistical examination of the growth performance for each country in the Appendix to this chapter, it appears that there are clear cycles around deterministic trends in growth performance, and in many cases the standard deviation of growth rates was greater than 4.

As there is no rigorous way to establish what is the sustainable long-run growth rate of an economy, the economic historian's judgement (taking all the various indices of performance into account) on when and if a growth collapse occurs is unavoidable. The country studies provide the reasons which led our authors to identify a growth collapse at the relevant dates in their countries. Moreover, the Appendix provides a statistical examination of these 'break points' in our countries' GDP series, and confirms the qualitative judgements summarized in Table 5.1.

There are two striking features of this table. The first is that a number of our countries have had very volatile growth rates, as measured by a standard deviation of 4 or more. Thus all three labour-abundant countries, and a majority of the countries in our intermediate factor-endowment group, have a volatile growth performance, as do most of the relatively poor

Table 5.1. Growth instability

	Trade Orientation	GDP Growth Rate (g) 1950–85	s Std. Dev.	Cyclical	Growth Collapse	Average Annual Growth Rate Consumer Prices, P				Central Government Budget Surplus/ Deficit as % of GDP, B			Manufacturing exports as % total exports, Xm/X	
						1950–73	1973–80	1965–80	1980–85	1960	1972	1985	1960	1985
A. Labour-abundant														
Hong Kong	(SO)	8.9 (60–85)	4.47	CYCL		n.a.	n.a.	8.1	7.9	n.a.	n.a.	n.a.	80	92
Singapore	(SO)	8.3 (60–86)	4.2	CYCL		2.5 (60–73)	6	4.8	3.2	−0.4 (1963)	1.3	2.1	26	58
Malta	(MI)	5.6 (50–84)	5.74	CYCL		2.6	7.7	n.a.	3	−0.9	−4.7	−4	n.a.	
B. Land-abundant														
Malaysia	(MO)	6.9 (60–85)	2.73			1.7	6.3	4.9	4.6	1.9	−9.2	−7.4	6	27
Thailand	(MO)	6.7	2.99			3 (55–73)	11.1	6.8	4.9	0.1	−4.3	−5.5	2	35
Brazil	(MO)	6.6	3.88		1980s	26 (64–73)	43.5	31.6	148.9	−2.1	−0.3	0.9	3	41
Mexico	(MI)	5.7	3.13		1980s	5.3	20.7	13.2	60.7	−1.7 (1966)	−3	−8.7	12	28
Turkey	(SI-MO)	5.6	6.57	CYCL	1980s	8.8 (55–73)	39	20.8	38.6	−1.9 (1967)	−2.2	−7.4	3	54

Costa Rica (MO-MI)	5	4.45	CYCL	1981	2.8	12.3	11.2	34.8	-3.1	-4.3	-1.2	5	30
Colombia (MI-MI)	4.7	1.95		1976–	9.7	24.1	17.5	22.3	-0.4	-2.5	-1.1	2	18
Nigeria (MI-SI)	3.7	10	CYCL		4.1 (55–73)	18.8	14.5	18.7	-2.3 (1965)	-1.1	-3.1	3	0
Ghana (SI)	1.3 (66–86)	5.13	CYCL	1966	5.8	54.3	22.8	55.5	-6.4 (1965)	-5.7	-2.2	10	5
Uruguay (SI-MO)	1.1 (55–84)	4.28	CYCL	1980s	45.9 (68–73)	62.8	57.7	44.8	-3.8 (1965)	-2.5	-2.2	29	37
C. Intermediate													
Egypt (n.a.-MI)	5.4 (52–85)	3.1			2 (66–73)	12.1	7.5	14.3	-1.9	n.a.	-10.1	12	10
Indonesia (MO-MI)	5.3	3.64	CYCL	1960s	36.4	19.3	34.3	9.7	-0.7	-2.4	-0.3	0	11
Sri Lanka (SI-MI)	4.7 (54–86)	3.26			2.4 (68–73)	9.8	9.5	12	-6.8 (1964)	-7.7	-9.5	0	27
Malawi (n.a.-MO)	4.3	5.62	CYCL		5.4	11	7.3	13.1	0.3	-5.6	-8	n.a.	5
Peru (SI)	4.1	3.96	CYCL	1980s	10 (55–73)	41.1	20.5	102.1	1.8	-1.1	-2.3	1	11
Jamaica (MO-MI)	3.3	4.38	CYCL	1973–	4.6	22	12.6	16.6	-1	-4.1	-17.8	5	12
Mauritius (n.a.-MO)	2.9	6.93	CYCL		3.7 (63–73)	18.2	11.8	9.1	-2.2 (1966)	-3.1	-5	n.a.	31
Madagascar (MI-SI)	2 (50–86)	3.48		1978–	3.6 (64–73)	10.8	7.7	20	-1.9 (1965)	-2.5	n.a.	6	9

Note: in first column, S = strongly, M = moderately, O = outward, I = inward.

performers (in terms of average growth performance) in the land-abundant group. Perhaps these are countries which have not diversified into exports of manufactures and are still specialized in producing primary commodities, whose world prices are known to be unstable? From the data on the share of manufactures in exports of our sample of countries in 1985 (shown in the table) it is clear that such an inference is insecure. Thus Malaysia and Thailand have shares of non-manufactured exports similar to Uruguay, and yet have experienced relatively steady growth, whilst the stellar performance of the labour-abundant countries, despite cyclical growth rates, shows that instability in growth rates does not necessarily lead to poor overall growth performance.

This conclusion is confirmed by the statistical cross-country evidence examined in the Appendix, which shows that there is no relationship between the volatility of growth rates (as measured by their standard deviation) and their long-term trend.

The second noteworthy feature is that a majority of our land-abundant countries (8 out of 10), and half of our intermediate group (4 out of 8), have suffered growth collapses, whilst none of our 3 labour-abundant countries have. We will need to explore any systematic factors which explain this divergent pattern based on relative factor-endowments amongst our different countries.

II. THE CONSEQUENCES FOR GROWTH PERFORMANCE OF MACROECONOMIC INSTABILITY

There are broadly speaking two major types of source for macroeconomic instability in our sample of countries. The first can be described as exogenous. These are either internal or external shocks to national income, due for instance to climatic variability which affects agricultural output, or terms-of-trade fluctuations which have similar effects. The second can be described as endogenous, and are policy-induced. They are due to unstable monetary or fiscal policies.

1. Exogenous Shocks

Within a simple rational-expectations model of a neoclassical economy subject to stochastic shocks, it can be shown that if the shocks are independent and identically distributed over time, they will have negligible effects on growth. Output will deviate from its natural rate only because of random shocks which cannot be foreseen at the time agents form their expectations. These fluctuations in output, and hence in annual growth rates,[2] will have no effect on the long-run growth performance of the economy.[3]

A major assumption underlying this view is the 'flex-price' nature of the labour market. As is well known from rational expectations models of fixed-price labour markets (so-called 'disequilibrium' models), exogenous shocks could affect the natural rate of output and thence growth. Any actual economy will have a mix of flex-price and fixed-price labour markets. For our purposes the only relevant question is whether the mix is closer to the fixed- or flex-price end of the labour market.

What is the evidence on the nature of the labour markets in our countries? By and large our country authors have found that labour markets in all these countries behave closer to the flex-price than the fixed-price end of the spectrum. This is particularly true of their rural labour markets. Nominal wage rigidities are of importance mainly in the public sector and in some countries in the industrial sectors.

The rigidities in the labour markets which have been a principal feature of most Keynesian models of macroeconomic instability do not seem to be of any great importance in our sample of countries.[4] The fixed-price and segmented labour markets assumed in neo-Keynesian economics were also not to be found in most of our countries.[5]

A crucial difference between the labour markets in pre-industrial and industrial economies is the sustained employer–employee relationships in the latter.[6] By contrast, as the most common form of employment in pre-industrial economies is either self-employment or employment of the casual sort, their labour markets are approximately like the flex-price spot labour markets implicit in Walrasian neoclassical theory. There cannot be any 'involuntary unemployment' of the sort Keynesians worry about in such a labour market. However, in the course of development, as countries industrialize, a need will arise for specialized labour with firm-specific skills, which creates the type of fixed-wage labour markets in which there is nominal wage rigidity, and hence involuntary unemployment could occur.[7] A rough and ready guide to the likelihood of a developing country's labour market behaving in a flex- or fixed-price manner can be obtained from the proportions of the labour force in manufacturing in our various countries, given in Table 5.2.

This shows that, apart from Hong Kong and Singapore, which in 1980 had 40–50% of their labour force in industry, all the others had less than 30% of their labour force in the potentially fixed-price industrial sector. Of these, Mexico, Brazil, and Uruguay with nearly 30% in the industrial sector can be said to have some substantial fixed-price sectors, and hence their behaviour in the face of macroeconomic shocks is likely to be closer to that of industrial countries (as is confirmed by the detailed country studies). Of our two labour-abundant but relatively highly industrialized countries, Hong Kong (as our country study shows) has a highly flex-price industrial labour market, associated with the large share of family-labour-based industrial enterprises in its economy (see Findlay and Wellisz, 1993: ch. 2).

Table 5.2. Share of Labour Force in Industry (%)

Country	1965	1980
A. *Labour-abundant*		
Hong Kong	53	51
Singapore	27	38
Malta	n.a.	n.a.
B. *Land-abundant*		
Malaysia	13	19
Thailand	5	10
Brazil	20	27
Turkey	11	17
Mexico	22	29
Costa Rica	19	23
Colombia	21	24
Ghana	15	18
Uruguay	29	29
C. *Intermediate*		
Egypt	15	20
Indonesia	9	13
Sri Lanka	14	14
Malawi	3	7
Peru	19	18
Nigeria	10	12
Jamaica	20	16
Mauritius	25	24
Madagascar	4	6

By contrast, Singapore might have been expected to have the inflexibilities associated with labour markets in industrial countries. However, as our Singapore study emphasizes, Lee Kuan Yew's government has consistently pursued policies to keep the price of Singapore labour flexible in order to attract foreign investment. Our two most highly industrialized countries can therefore also be looked upon as having relatively flex-price labour markets.

Furthermore, there is some direct empirical evidence in support of the simple rational expectations view that exogenous shocks, which are typically due to fluctuating terms of trade in many primary products exported by developing countries, do not damage their growth performance.

In his important study MacBean[8] found that export instability did not impede growth. A more recent study by Knudsen and Parnes[9] found instead that export instability is positively correlated with growth of GNP and income per capita. The main reason for this is that investment, instead of being harmed by instability, was positively correlated with it. They explained these empirical findings in terms of a permanent income theory of consumption and investment for developing countries. They argue that income instability, *ceteris paribus*, reduces the average propensity to consume, and hence increases aggregate savings. If domestic investment is constrained by savings, as is usually assumed to be the case in many developing countries,[10] then export instability, which raises savings and thence investment, can also raise the growth rate. Knudsen and Parnes indeed find that the propensity to consume does decrease with higher levels of income instability in developing countries.[11]

2. Endogenous Policy-Induced Shocks

If macroeconomic instability due to exogenous shocks is not likely to damage growth performance, what of that caused by endogenous shocks in the form of unstable and unanticipated monetary and fiscal policies?

It may be noted that in most developing countries there is at best a limited market in government debt. Hence fiscal deficits (not financed through foreign capital inflows) will be financed by issuing base money. As a result, changes in monetary policy are usually the financial consequence of changes in government fiscal policy. Unstable fiscal policies are therefore likely to be the primary cause of endogenous policy-induced shocks in developing countries.

The effects of an unanticipated change in fiscal policy, say a fiscal expansion, will be to change the composition of aggregate demand. It will crowd out investment through a rise in the interest rate. This reduction in investment will affect the capital stock in the current and subsequent periods, hence future output levels, and thence growth.[12]

3. Interaction of Exogenous and Endogenous Shocks

Finally, there is an interaction between exogenous and endogenous shocks which is of some importance in various countries in our sample. Faced with fluctuations in their terms of trade, many countries have assumed that a rise in primary commodity prices is permanent, and have expanded public expenditure (both their current and future commitments) on that basis. When the boom ends, public expenditure is not cut, and the resulting fiscal deficit is then monetized.

However, there are periods in the history of some of our countries where this ratchet effect of public expenditure leading to an endogenous shock which affects growth performance was absent. These were by and large countries which maintained the old colonial currency board system.

Thus during the colonial period in Nigeria there was a phenomenal growth of tropical exports based on smallholder agriculture.[13] This was associated with great volatility in the world prices of Nigerian exports and thence in import volumes. Nevertheless, export growth was not hampered, nor economic growth (at least until the Great Depression of 1929). Under the West African Currency Board system established in 1912,[14] the Nigerian pound was backed a hundred per cent by sterling. Fiscal policy was extremely conservative, as the colony's budget had to balance. 'Hence, the colonial economy had a self-regulating system of adjustment to external shocks (much as under a gold standard). The familiar problem of a boom followed by a balance-of-payments crisis (as a result of a ratchet effect in public expenditure) simply could not occur.'[15] Nigeria's so-called macroeconomic problems (discussed below) belong to the period when it broke from this colonial system to conduct an independent monetary policy.

Similarly, Rimmer identifies Ghana's desire for monetary autonomy following independence through the abandonment of the colonial currency board system and the establishment of a Central Bank in 1957, as one of the twin 'debilitating infection(s) in Ghana's political economy'—the other being the Marketing Board system for cocoa which was established by the colonial regime. Taken together they provided the instruments for Ghana's post-1960s economic ruin. The first fiduciary issue by the Central Bank was in 1961. Comprehensive exchange control, which implied the 'domestication of the commercial banks', was imposed in the same year. These institutional changes liberated governments 'from the constraints on its outlays imposed by tax revenues and voluntary lending . . . Budget deficits had been regularly incurred in the Gold Coast since 1956. From 1962, with the external revenues mostly used up, there was recourse to the banking system to plug the deficit.'[16]

The heavy direct taxation of the good in which Ghana had comparative advantage through the Cocoa Marketing Board, and indirect taxation through the exchange control mechanism, together with the fiscal irresponsibility allowed by its breach of the colonial monetary system, set Ghana on its disastrous path of an imploding economy. 'Disregard of comparative advantage and fiscal irresponsibilities first checked and then reversed Ghana's economic growth.'[17] By contrast, though not one of our sample countries, the Ivory Coast maintained a 'hard money' monetary system because of its continuing association in the franc zone. Whilst Ghana's GDP per capita at 1975 international prices declined from $1,006 to $708 between 1960 and 1980 (taking account of terms-of-trade effects), in the Ivory Coast, 'the country most like Ghana in geographical situation, size and natural resoures', GDP per capita rose from $749 to $1,464 during this period.[18]

In our sample there are two countries, however, which (by and large) have maintained a colonial-currency-board type of monetary arrangement: Hong Kong (except for the period 1972–83) and Singapore.

Thus, in Hong Kong,

there is no Central Bank and the currency, issued by two private banks, has always been strongly backed by foreign assets or precious metals, except in the period between 1972 and 1983 . . . Neither taxation nor government expenditure has been used in a counter cyclical fashion.[19]

Annual growth rates have been volatile, ranging from highs of 17–18% to lows of between 0 and 2%,[20] but overall growth at 8.9% per annum during 1960–85 has been spectacular. Clearly the equilibrium cycles—caused by changing world economic conditions—have not affected Hong Kong's growth or poverty-redressal performance.

Similarly, Singapore has through its Monetary Authority (MAS) maintained a currency-board-type system, whilst the government has maintained a budget surplus of about 15% of GDP during 1966–80.[21] Again, its growth performance, though volatile, has been amongst the best of our countries, as has been the extent of poverty redressal.

Why did most developing countries give up the hard-money systems they had inherited? The reasons were similar to those which led rulers of many developed countries to establish central banks. This was primarily to allow them to use seigniorage[22] on issuing a paper currency to meet their chronic fiscal problems.[23]

By contrast, most of the ex-colonies in Africa and Asia considered monetary independence to be a hallmark of economic independence, and established their own central banks soon after gaining political independence in the post-war period. Monetary independence in the Latin American countries pre-dated this development in the rest of the Third World by a few decades and was in large part a response to the collapse of primary-product prices and exports in the wake of the Great Depression. Until about 1925, most Latin American countries were on a form of gold exchange standard, whose rules were periodically disobeyed whenever there was a crisis triggered by unfavourable changes in the terms of trade.[24] During these crises most Latin American countries resorted to money creation to finance public expenditure (which was the source of their chronic non-accelerating inflation) and to inconvertible or floating exchange rates to prevent capital flight.

In 1896 Uruguay had established a central bank, whilst Mexico's central bank, the Banco de México, was created in 1925. Thereafter, largely under the international pressure of financiers interested in maintaining debt service payments, central banks were established in most Latin American countries. They were by and large 'an attempt to control the power of note issue'. But with the Great Depression, the Central Bank of Argentina, created in 1935, 'was the first to depart from the conventional blueprint based implicitly on the working of the Gold Exchange Standard'.[25] It could intervene in the exchange market on behalf of the government and under the supervision of the treasury, and could engage in operations with government securities to provide short-term finance for state deficits. Other countries followed suit, and most Latin American countries were then set on the path of inflationary finance which has almost become a Latin American syndrome.

Despite differing origins, monetary independence has in effect meant that for many countries the inflation tax is now considered to be a part of their fiscal armoury. But there are countries in our sample which, either for the whole of our period or for a substantial part of it, have maintained almost Gladstonian fiscal and monetary rectitude. These include Mexico (till Echeverría), Malta, Indonesia (after Sukarno), Malaysia (till recently), and Thailand. They have shown the political self-discipline which Schumpeter realized was essential if the inflationary genie were not to be released along with their newly attained monetary independence.[26] But there are others which have been chronically inflation-prone and in which the collapse of economic growth at various times has been associated with an upsurge of acute inflationary pressures. The most notorious case in our sample of countries is Ghana (see Rimmer, 1992). The relevant question which arises—which we will address in the next chapter—is what are the political reasons why many of our countries have succumbed to the temptation of levying the inflation tax whilst some have not?

The two major conclusions of this section are, first, that cyclical instability in itself is unlikely to be harmful for growth, but that, second, if for some reason there is a fiscally induced inflationary crisis during these cycyles there could be damaging effects on growth performance. We examine the evidence on this from our country studies in the next section.

III. CAUSES OF GROWTH COLLAPSES

Most of the growth collapses in our sample of countries occurred in the 1970s and 1980s. This is not surprising. Most of our economies, despite attempts at establishing autarky in some of them, are relatively open economies, whose economic fortunes are linked to that of the world economy. Until 1973, the world economy went through what has been called its 'Golden Age' of tranquil expansion. Since the first oil price rise of 1973, however, the world economy has been buffeted by gyrating primary commodity prices, a second rise in oil prices in 1979 followed by a large fall, and large fluctuations in capital flows and their associated real interest rates. This turbulent world economic environment involved common external shocks for many developing countries. But their performance diverged sharply.

1. Trade Orientation

A summary of the extent of the shocks associated with the large changes in oil prices, commodity prices, and interest rates in the early and late 1970s,

Table 5.3. External Shocks and Adjustment, 1974–1981

Rank ordered By severity of external shock in 1974–6		External Shock as % GDP	Additional Foreign Borrowing	Policy Responses % of Shock		
				Increased Export Promotion	Increased Import Substitution	GDP Growth
1. Singapore	1971–76	20.2	87.1	−3.9	−34.0	50.6
	1979–81	34.4	36.6	89.7	−53.3	29.3
2. Jamaica	1974–76	13.6	7.3	−9.9	38.4	64.2
	1979–81	35.5	44.2	−24.7	21.2	61.3
3. Turkey	1974–76	7.5	120.2	−3.9	−11.2	−5.2
	1979–81	6.4	−11.0	10.9	52.1	48.0
4. Egypt	1974–76	7.4	296.6	−25.2	−177.7	6.3
	1979–81	6.9	47.9	−20.1	34.8	37.5
5. Uruguay	1974–76	6.6	61.6	30.3	29.7	−21.6
	1979–81	10.3	98.9	4.3	71.4	−74.8
6. Thailand	1974–76	4.5	8.2	30.3	52.1	9.4
	1979–81	7.2	78.7	39.7	−38.3	19.9
7. Mauritius	1974–76	4.2	147.1	47.1	176.5	−264.7
	1975–81	17.9	57.8	1.4	42.2	−2.0
8. Brazil	1974–76	3.9	82.6	12.4	19.8	−14.8
	1979–81	4.2	−33.5	38.4	46.2	109.0
9. Peru	1974–76	3.6	199.2	−39.8	−54.9	−4.5
	1979–81	1.3	−459.1	400.7	−74.5	32.9
10. Mexico	1974–76	1.6	177.6	−59.0	−19.3	0.8
	1979–81	1.9	315.4	562.4	−904.5	−73.3
11. Colombia	1974–76	0.9	142.7	2.1	−406.0	−4.2
	1979–81	5.0	149.1	53.0	−102.3	0.2
12. Indonesia	1974–76	−19.3	−90.3	16.0	−23.9	−1.8
	1979–81	−7.4	−118.6	16.5	7.3	−5.2
13. Nigeria	1974–76	−53.8	−60.6	−3.8	−34.4	−1.2
	1979–81	−4.1	−227.7	−28.5	27.7	128.5

Source: Balassa (1984).

and the ways in which our various countries dealt with them, is provided by a system of accounting for the 'sources of balance-of-payments disturbances and adjustments', conducted by Balassa.[27] His results for our countries are summarized in Table 5.3.

Balassa's own conclusions are based on a classification of countries as outward- and inward-looking. He concludes that outward-looking countries, despite larger shocks in both periods, performed better, because they chose output-increasing policies of export-promotion and import-substitution, whereas the inward-orientated countries adjusted to the 1974–6 shock by borrowing at often negative real interest rates to cover their balance-of-payments deficits, but then had to take savage deflationary measures in 1979–81 as their increased indebtedness and rising world interest rates limited further borrowing. Hence he concludes that economic growth rates were substantially higher in outward- than inward-orientated countries.

There is a great deal of truth in these conclusions. But they raise the question of why some countries were inward- and others outward-orientated. Also not sufficient weight is placed in this explanation on the underlying fiscal pressures which we hypothesize are most likely to lead to growth collapses, when a country is faced by some exogenous shock. No explanation is provided of what exactly it is about outward and inward orientation which makes efficient adjustment so different in the two cases; and there is the uncomfortable fact that some inward-looking countries, for example India (which is not one of our sample countries), fared much better in terms of the stability of their growth performance than, for instance, an outward-orientated country like Brazil, which suffered a growth collapse.

Table 5.1 also shows the classification of our countries by inward and outward trade orientation, as given in the *World Development Report* for 1987.[28] Of the ten countries which suffered growth collapses in the 1970s and/or 1980s (that is, excluding Indonesia), only two, Ghana and Peru, were strongly inward-orientated, whilst Nigeria and Madagascar moved to being so from being moderately inward-orientated countries during 1973–83. Two were moderately outward-orientated before 1973 and became moderately inward-orientated subsequently, namely Costa Rica and Jamaica. One, Mexico, was moderately inward-orientated, and one, Brazil, moderately outward-orientated, whilst two, Uruguay and Turkey, moved from being strongly inward-orientated to moderately outward-orientated. Clearly, neither their placement in the outward–inward orientation categories nor their movements between them can provide an explanation in itself for the growth collapses in our sample of countries.[29]

2. Inflation and Fiscal Deficits

There is a more significant relationship between the acceleration of inflation and growth collapses. Except for Uruguay, where there was a deceleration in its high inflation rate in the 1980s when growth collapsed, all the other growth-collapse countries saw an acceleration in their inflation rates. The other significant difference even amongst the growth-collapse countries is that, except for Ghana, the Latin American countries (Brazil, Mexico, Costa Rica, Uruguay, Peru) had a much higher average inflation rate than the remaining countries in the group (Turkey, Nigeria, Madagascar, and Jamaica), two of which were former British colonies.

Comparing the data on inflation rates and money-supply growth across our countries, it is clear that there is a positive relationship, but it is not tight. This is not surprising, as the inflationary impact of any money-supply increase will depend upon changes in money demand. These depend upon two counteracting influences.[30] It is well known that population and real-income growth will increase the demand for money. At the same time inflation acts as a tax on money holdings, and as with any other tax, holders of money will, *ceteris paribus*, seek to economize on their holdings, so that the demand for money will be lower in an inflationary than a non-inflationary economy. In a hyper-inflation, of course, the second factor will outweigh the first and there will be a shrinkage in the demand for real money balances.

Expanding a classification of inflationary experiences provided by Harberger,[31] we divide countries into chronic inflation and hyper-inflation categories. In the former group are countries in which consumer prices have risen by more than 20% annually over an extended period. But as, in these countries, the positive elements in the demand for money have not been swamped by the negative inflation-tax effects, the growth of the money supply can be expected to be higher than that of the price level. By contrast, in hyper-inflation countries the demand for real money balances shrinks, and the inflation rate is higher than the rate of growth of money. Using these criteria gives us Table 5.4. This shows the countries in our sample which fall into these two categories (during the 1965–80 and 1980–5 periods), as well as their inflation rates and money-supply growth rates in the relevant periods.

This table shows clearly that cases of hyper-inflation are associated with growth collapses. By contrast, chronic inflation does not necessarily lead to a growth collapse. This is just a reflection of the well-known argument that a moderate, steady, anticipated inflation is unlikely to have any real effects on growth performance.

The fairly firm connection between increased money and chronic inflation or hyper-inflation, and growth collapses in the latter group, raises the question: what are the reasons for this monetary expansion? In his 1978 study Harberger found that 'the bulk of the cases in which countries initially pursuing fixed exchange rate policies are ultimately forced to devalue their currencies, have their roots in fiscal deficits financed by recourse to the banking system'.[32] Unfortunately, the available data on fiscal deficits (particularly for Latin American countries) is very imperfect.[33] What is required is a measure of the whole public sector's borrowing requirement. As in most Third World countries, the public sector extends well beyond the 'fisc', the published figures of the central governments' deficits (shown in Table 5.1) are highly imperfect indicators both of the size and of the trends in the public sector's borrowing requirement.

An alternative, following Harberger, is to consider the connection between government borrowing from the banking system and inflation. In Table 5.5 we show the net change in the government's debt to banks expressed as a ratio of the same year's GDP, for the hyper-inflation countries in our sample which have suffered a growth collapse. For some countries (identified in the table as '1 year lag') the effects of increased

Table 5.4. Chronic Inflation and Hyper-Inflation Countries

Country	Period	Consumer prices (% p.a.)	Money supply (% p.a)	Growth collapse
I. *Chronic inflation*				
Turkey	1965–85	20.8	27.4	
	1980–85	37.1	51.9	
Brazil	1965–80	31.6	43.4	
Colombia	1980–85	22.5	27.2	
Ghana	1965–80	22.8	25.9	
Uruguay	1965–80	57.7	65.3	
Indonesia	1965–80	34.3	54.9	
Peru	1965–80	20.5	25.9	
II. *Hyper-inflation*				
Turkey	1980	110.2	54.2	Collapse
Brazil	1980–87	158.6	141.2	Collapse
	1964	91.4	86.1	
Peru	1980–85	98.6	102.5	Collapse
Mexico	1980–85	62.6	61.4	Collapse
Costa Rica	1980–85	36.4	31.1	Collapse
Ghana	1980–85	57	41.4	Collapse
Uruguay	1980–85	44.6	44.2	Collapse
	1967–68	125.3	87	
III. *Growth collapse countries without chronic/acute inflation*				
Nigeria	1965–80	14.5	28.5	
	1980–85	11.4	10.5	
Jamaica	1965–80	12.6	17.3	
	1980–85	18.3	26.5	
Madagascar	1965–80	7.7	12.0	
	1980–85	19.4	13.1	

Source: The data is from Table 1 (col. 2) and Table 25 (col. 3) of the WDR 1987 and from the IFS Yearbook 1988.

public indebtedness operated with some lag. There appears to be a link between increasing public indebtedness, rises in money supply, and accelerating inflation in the growth-collapse countries.

3. Exogenous Shocks and Misalignment of Real Exchange Rates

If deficit financing induced the inflation associated with most of the growth collapses in our countries, there are still three non-hyper- or chronic inflation countries in our sample, Nigeria, Jamaica, and Madagascar, which have suffered growth collapses. The problems of the first two are associated with the mishandling of the rents accruing from natural resource booms, and the associated problems encapsulated by the generic term 'Dutch

Table 5.5. Changes in Public Debt/GDP Ratios in Chronic Inflation and Hyper-Inflation Countries

	Country	Period	Public Debt/GDP Ratio of Previous Year (% of GDP)		Consumer Prices (% p.a.)	Nominal Money (% p.a.)
I.	Turkey	1978	(1 year lag)	4.1	45.3	34.1
		1979		0.8	58.7	54.8
		1980		1.0	110.2	54.2
		1981		1.0	36.6	37.3
		1982		0.5	30.8	27.5
		1983		−0.4	32.9	41.1
II.	Mexico	1981	(1 year lag)	−0.7	27.9	36.8
		1982		1.0	58.9	41.5
		1983		7.3	101.8	44.1
		1984		−3.2	65.5	53.2
		1985		−4.3	57.7	53.7
III.	Brazil	1979	(no lag)	0.5	52.7	46.2
		1980		0.7	82.8	76.0
		1981		0.9	105.6	65.1
		1982		−0.7	97.8	82.0
		1983		1.2	142.1	95.0
		1984		0.2	197	141.1
		1985		2.9	226.9	274.6
IV.	Costa Rica	1981	(1 year lag)	2.0	37.1	38.8
		1982		6.3	90.1	70.4
		1983		−10.1	32.6	45.3
V.	Ghana	1965	(no lag)	1.8	26.4	24.1
		1966		1.5	13.3	−0.3
		1967		6.8	−8.5	−4.3
		1975		2.9	29.8	36.6
		1976		6.4	56.1	46.1
		1977		−1.3	116.5	50.9
		1978		−0.1	73.1	74.1
		1979		−3.9	54.4	30.3
VI.	Uruguay	1980	(no lag)	0.4	63.5	34.9
		1981		−0.5	34.0	33.9
		1982		5.9	19.0	1.0
		1983		7.6	49.2	45.8
		1984		12.6	55.3	24.0
		1985		−7.3	72.2	71.8
VII.	Peru	1980	(no lag)	−1.3	59.2	71.1
		1981		0.4	75.4	43.4
		1982		−1.5	64.4	33.7
		1983		7.6	111.2	75.4
		1984		−2.5	110.2	97.3
		1985		−5.0	163.4	204.6
		1986		n.a.	77.9	175.6

Source: IFS Yearbook 1988.

Disease'. These problems are best discussed within the analytical framework of the so-called Australian or dependent-economy model of an open
economy.

This model distinguishes between three goods which are produced (by
capital and labour) and consumed in the economy: (1) an importable, (2)
an exportable, and (3) a non-traded good. The domestic prices of the two
traded goods are assumed to be set by given world prices and the nominal
exchange rate. They can thus be combined into a Hicksian composite
commodity at the given world prices, that is, a composite tradable good.
The non-traded good's price is set by domestic demand and supply. The
model thus collapses into a two-good (tradable and non-tradable) model,
where the key relative price is the real exchange rate which is defined as *the
relative price of non-traded to traded goods*.[34]

We can now examine the effects of three types of shocks which have hit
our sample of countries. Two of these are external (and exogenous)—
foreign exchange windfalls and changes in the terms of trade—and one is
internal (and policy-induced), namely unsustainable fiscal expansion.

(a) Foreign Exchange Windfalls and Fiscal Expansion

Suppose that there is a large inflow of capital, either from aid inflows (for
example, Sri Lanka after the UNP victory, or Egypt since the Camp David
Accord) or from commercial bank borrowing or other private inflows of
capital (Mexico in the 1970s, Brazil, and Uruguay) or foreign remittances
by workers from abroad (Turkey, Egypt, and Sri Lanka) or rents from
natural resources (bauxite/alumina in Jamaica, oil in Nigeria and Indonesia). In the equilibrium adjustment to the capital inflows the real exchange
rate will appreciate and there will be a trade deficit (equal to the excess
demand for the tradable good) exactly equal to the capital inflow, which in
turn will be exactly equal to the excess of domestic expenditure over
domestic output. There will be no adjustment problem.

Suppose that the government, whilst maintaining exchange control, does
not sterilize the effects of the foreign exchange inflows on the domestic
money supply, as it does not use a notion of high-powered money in its
budgetary planning. Suppose, moreover, that with the rise in foreign exchange reserves, and given the time lag between the receipt of foreign
exchange and its subsequent spending by private or public agencies, the
government is advised to use these foreign exchange reserves for development purposes by running a budget deficit, or else it decides to use the
windfall for expanding public expenditure and runs a budget deficit (for
example, in Mexico after the first oil-price rise in 1973, Sri Lanka in the late
1970s, Jamaica in the mid-1970s, Nigeria). This will lead to a secondary
trade deficit above that required to affect the capital inflow. There will also
be further excess demand for the non-traded good, leading to a rise in its
price, and hence a further real exchange rate appreciation.

The ensuing loss of reserves (which includes the use of any international credit the government might be able to muster) must entail some adjustment. A necessary part of this adjustment must be to reverse the excess absorption associated with the fiscal expansion, as well as a reversal of the excess exchange rate appreciation.

If non-traded goods prices are flexible, this latter 'switching' effect will occur automatically, as with a reduction in the fiscal deficit the excess demand will disappear for the non-traded good, putting downward pressure on its price. If, however, there are rigidities in the labour market, or price adjustments are slow, this downward movement of the non-traded good's price may be sluggish, and the requisite real exchange rate depreciation will not occur. In that case, a devaluation of the nominal exchange rate which raises the domestic price of traded goods relative to non-traded will be required to implement the switching of expenditure entailed by a real exchange rate depreciation.

It is this inability to devalue in a hard-money-type monetary system which is considered to be one of its main weaknesses. But this weakness is essentially based on the assumed downward rigidity of non-traded goods prices. As the movements in both directions in the real exchange rates for our clear-cut hard-money economies, Singapore and Hong Kong, show, even in these predominantly industrial economies this assumption is not necessarily valid. However, in some countries where the capital windfall was used in large part to expand public employment (Jamaica, Nigeria), the implicit money wage adjustment which is required for such automatic expenditure-switching was resisted. Explicit depreciation of the nominal exchange rate will then be necessary to allow the equilibrium real wage to be established (assuming that whilst nominal wages are rigid downwards, real wages are not).

Similarly, we can consider the converse case, which was relevant in many of our countries in the late 1970s. There was a sudden contraction or cessation of capital inflows (as in commercial loans to Mexico, Uruguay, and Brazil, or in natural-resource rents in Jamaica and Nigeria). With the previous level of domestic expenditure unchanged, the balance-of-payments deficit, which was previously financed by the capital inflow, becomes unsustainable. Suppose the government reduces expenditure to the new sustainable (full employment) level, but, because of sluggishness in movements in the price of the non-traded good, the real exchange rate remains unchanged. This will still leave an excess demand for tradables and a trade deficit. With the unchanged real exchange rate, the government will have to reduce expenditure further until there is no longer a balance-of-payments deficit, but now there will be excess supply and hence unemployment in the non-traded good industry. There will have been a fall in output below its potential (as happened in many of the Latin American debtor countries). But this is entirely due to the misalignment of the real exchange rate, and could be cured swiftly by a depreciation of the nominal exchange rate, or more slowly as the excess supply and unemployment in the non-traded good industry leads to a fall in the price of the non-traded good.

The cost of this real exchange rate misalignment is the forgone output following from the excessive deflation required to cure the trade deficit. Alternatively, the government may maintain real expenditure at the new full-employment level, but seek to control the accompanying trade deficit through import controls. This will lead to the dead-weight and rent-seeking costs associated with this type of intervention,[35] which will place the economy within its production possibility frontier, and hence involve a loss of potential output.

(b) Terms-of-Trade Changes

There is a third type of exogenous shock—a change in the external terms of trade—which has also affected our various countries. Some have suffered from a positive shock, as the terms of trade of some of their primary-product exports—most notably oil for Indonesia, Nigeria, and Mexico in the 1970s—have risen markedly, whilst others have seen a fall or cycles in their terms of trade—most of the other countries in our sample.

The only additional element to be noted in analysing this case, which in other aspects is similar to that discussed in the previous subsection, is that the requisite change in the real exchange rate will depend upon the relative factor intensities of the three goods.

*(i) A Geometric Three-Good Model   Suppose there is a terms-of-trade deterioration, with the foreign currency price of importables rising and the price of exportables and the nominal exchange rate unchanged.

Fig. 5.1 depicts the factor price frontier for the given product prices for the three goods. Assuming that the exportable is the most labour-intensive (least capital-intensive) of the three goods, its factor price curve will have the lowest slope at each wage–rental ratio than the other industries, of which importables are assumed to be the most capital-intensive. A rise in the price of importables shifts the C_M curve outward but leaves the C_X curve unchanged (as the price of exportables P_X has not altered). The new wage–rental equilibrium is given by the point B, with a lower wage and a higher rental rate. For this equilibrium to be sustainable the C_N curve must also pass through this point, that is, the C_N curve must shift outward, or the price of the non-traded good (P_N) must rise and the real exchange rate must appreciate. The converse would be the case if the non-traded good was more labour-intensive than the exportable. The various changes in the factor prices and the possible combination of factor intensities are set out in the table accompanying Fig. 5.1.

Data on the real exchange rates for our countries was not available, as most countries do not comply a separate index for non-traded and traded

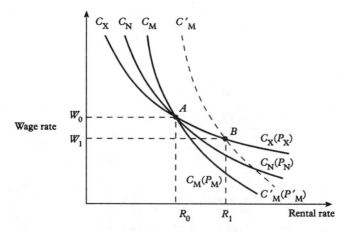

Fig. 5.1. The real exchange rate and factor prices

k_i capital–labour ratio in industry producing good

$$i = X \quad \text{exportables}$$
$$M \quad \text{importables}$$
$$N \quad \text{non-traded}$$

P_i money price of good i
w wage rate
r rental rate

Terms of trade (P_M/P_X)	If $k_M > k_X > k_N$	$k_M > k_N > k_X$	$k_X > k_M > k_N$
Improvement $(P_M/P_X)\downarrow$	$w\uparrow\ r\downarrow\ P_n\uparrow$	$w\uparrow\ r\downarrow\ P_N\downarrow$	$w\downarrow\ r\uparrow\ P_N\downarrow$
Deterioraton $(P_M/P_X)\uparrow$	$w\downarrow\ r\uparrow\ P_N\downarrow$	$w\downarrow\ r\uparrow\ P_N\uparrow$	$w\uparrow\ r\downarrow\ P_n\uparrow$

The slope of the iso-cost curve shows the capital–labour ratio at the relevant wage–rental ratio.

goods prices. *Faute de mieux*, it has become usual to use the effective real exchange rate, defined as the nominal exchange rate adjusted for the difference between domestic and world inflation rates, as a surrogate for the real exchange rate. Estimates of these effective rates are available from Wood (1988),[36] and the wage series for our countries from our country studies. During the 1970s, when most of our countries (except Indonesia and Nigeria) were hit by a negative external shock amounting to a terms-of-trade deterioration, their real exchange rate and real wage movements were determined by the relative factor intensities of their exportable goods.[37] Table 5.6 summarizes the direction of the movements in the real exchange and wage rates for our countries during the aftermath of the two oil shocks (post-1973 and post-1979), and also shows the implied factor intensities which can be deduced from the three-good model depicted by Fig. 5.1. Lacking data on the actual factor intensities of the three

Table 5.6. Changes in real wages and real exchange rates

Implied Factor Intensities		1973–5	1979–86
$k_N > k_X$	Hong Kong	$P_N\uparrow$ w$\downarrow$	$P_N\uparrow$ w$\downarrow$
$k_N > k_X$	Singapore	$P_N\uparrow$ w$\downarrow$	$P_N\uparrow$ w$\downarrow$
$k_X > k_N > k_M$	Malaysia	$P_N\uparrow$ w$\uparrow$	
$k_N > k_X$	Thailand	$P_N\uparrow$ w$\downarrow$	$P_N\uparrow$ w–
$k_X > k_N$ and then $k_N > k_X$	Turkey	$P_N\uparrow$ w–	$P_N\uparrow$ w$\downarrow$
$k_X > k_N > k_M$	Brazil	$P_N\uparrow$ w$\uparrow$	$P_N\uparrow$ w$\uparrow$
$k_X > k_N > k_M$	Mexico	$P_N\uparrow$ w$\uparrow$	$P_N\uparrow$ w$\uparrow$
$k_M > k_X > k_N$	Costa Rica	$P_N\downarrow$ w$\downarrow$	$P_N\downarrow$ w$\downarrow$
$k_M > k_X > k_N$	Columbia	$P_N\downarrow$ w$\downarrow$	$P_N\downarrow$ w$\downarrow$
$k_N > k_X$	Ghana	$P_N\uparrow$ w$\downarrow$	$P_N\uparrow$ w$\downarrow$
$k_X > k_N$	Uruguay	$P_N\uparrow$ w–	$P_N\uparrow$ w$\uparrow$
$k_X > k_M > k_N$	Egypt	$P_N\uparrow$ w$\uparrow$	$P_N\uparrow$ w$\uparrow$
$k_M > k_X > k_N$	Indonesia	$P_N\uparrow$ w$\downarrow$	$P_N\uparrow$ w–
$k_N > k_X$	Sri Lanka	$P_N\uparrow$ w–	$P_N\uparrow$ w$\downarrow$
$k_M > k_X > k_N$	Malawi	$P_N\downarrow$ w n.a.	$P_N\downarrow$ w–
$k_X > k_N$	Peru	$P_N\uparrow$ w n.a.	$P_N\uparrow$ w n.a.
$k_X > k_N$	Nigeria	$P_N\uparrow$ w–	$P_N\uparrow$ w–*
$k_N > k_X$	Jamaica	$P_N\uparrow$ w$\downarrow$	$P_N\uparrow$ w$\downarrow$
$k_N > k_X$	Mauritius	$P_N\uparrow$ w$\downarrow$	$P_N\downarrow$ w$\downarrow$
$k_N > k_X$	Madagascar	$P_N\uparrow$ w$\downarrow$	$P_N\uparrow$ w$\downarrow$

*1979–81.

types of aggregate, we cannot test the model in any meaningful way. But the implied factor intensities were judged by our country authors to be in consonance with their expectations based on their in-depth studies of their countries.

The above model shows that even if there is smooth adjustment to the terms-of-trade changes there will be 'equilibrium fluctuations' in real wages and real exchange rates. These can go either way, depending on the relative factor intensity of exportables relative to non-traded goods and importables. A rise in the real exchange rate (and in the real wage), after a country suffers an unfavourable external shock, cannot in itself be taken to be a sign of any misalignment of exchange rates or a failure of labour market policy, precipitating a growth collapse. To establish any exchange-rate misalignment the requisite equilibrium movement in the real exchange rate would have to be determined, based on information on relative factor intensities of traded and non-traded goods. Only then can it be established whether the actual real exchange rate movement is excessive. If it is, it will be usually because of an inappropriate change in fiscal and trade policy following the external shock.[38]

(ii) *Misalignment of Real Exchange Rates.* In recent work Edwards has attempted to formulate and estimate a model based on the structure depicted in the above model of misalignment of real exchange rates from their equilibrium values for twelve developing countries, which include five in our sample (Brazil, Colombia, Malaysia, Sri Lanka and Thailand).[39] He then performed a statistical test (using estimates of effective real exchange rates as surrogates for real exchange rates) to determine whether real exchange rate misalignment (as defined with reference to a model with a changing equilibrium real exchange rate) was inversely related to growth performance. He found it was.[40] Furthermore, he found that fiscal indiscipline was the main source of real exchange rate disequilibrium.

Hence we can conclude that, first, many of the facile prescriptions offered about the correct real exchange rate in the face of terms-of-trade-induced balance-of-payments crises are incorrect. Thus the common prescription that a decline in the terms of trade requires a depreciation of the real exchange rate is not generally valid.[41] Second, in the face of some exogenous shock, we cannot deduce whether the exchange rate is misaligned by merely observing the movements in the real exchange rate. Third, governments, too, will therefore find it difficult to determine the correct direction, let alone magnitude, of the required nominal exchange rate movement in the face of exogenous shocks. However, where balance-of-payments deficits have been generated by fiscal expansion, there is a presumptive need for devaluations, if non-traded goods prices adjust sluggishly. Given all these uncertainties,[42] it may be best to adopt a flexible exchange rate if there are nominal wage rigidities, or sluggishness in non-traded price movements.[43]

Fourth, and more important for our purposes, is the conclusion that output losses may occur in reversing unsustainable fiscal expansions. This is a conclusion which is supported by our country studies, and seems to be the major explanation for the growth collapses which occurred, including those in the countries without chronic or hyper-inflation, Jamaica and Nigeria. These countries suffered from the Dutch disease. They used the windfalls from rising natural resource rents to expand the public sector, in the form of unproductive government employment and the growth of inefficient and unproductive para-statal enterprises engaged in production or trade. But as the contrasting experience of Indonesia demonstrates, infection with the Dutch disease need not lead to a prolonged debilitating illness. The crucial difference was the tight control the Indonesians kept over the growth of public expenditure, which by contrast exploded in both Jamaica and Nigeria. Secondly, after the Pertamina crisis, the Indonesians reined in their public investments in heavy industry, whereas both Jamaica and Nigeria used growing shares of their windfalls to promote inefficient and unproductive import-substituting industries on familiar structuralist grounds.

It is also worth noting that the 1970s oil boom in Nigeria was not its first windfall. As Bevan *et al.* emphasize,[44] Nigeria also experienced the boom associated with the rise in commodity prices during the Korean War. Government reserves rose with the increased revenue from trade taxes. But

the policy response was largely passive, resulting in reserve accumulation . . . This was so because the marketing boards, in keeping with their stabilization role did not adjust producer prices for export crops in line with world prices. The resulting accumulation was unintentional to the extent that the boards did not foresee the boom's magnitude. . . . Adjustment during the [following] downturn was still semi-automatic (as it had been before the war) because an independent monetary policy was impossible.[45]

This example underlines the importance of the implicit or explicit monetary and fiscal constitution under which the government operates. As emphasized by Bevan *et al.*, a major reason for the Indonesian government's more successful management of the oil boom was that 'by that time the Indonesian government had constrained its own policy choices by its commitment to convertibility and budget balance'.[46]

Hence in so far as monetary independence has historically been associated with the easing of the budget constraint on the government, a rethinking of monetary and fiscal arrangements must form an essential part of designing an economic framework which prevents the growth process from being attenuated by public-policy-induced growth collapses when countries have to cope with the unavoidable volatility of a changing world economic environment. In helping to develop this framework, we next need to examine the causes of the fiscal indiscipline observed in our sample of countries.

IV. SOURCES OF FISCAL IMBALANCES

In addition to the ten countries which have suffered growth collapses, there are a few others in our sample which have more quiet crises of growth[47] stemming from incipient or actual fiscal imbalances. These are Sri Lanka[48] and Egypt.

Broadly speaking, there were two major causes of fiscal imbalances in these 12 countries in our sample of 21 countries. First, 'big push' type developmental expenditures, mainly in the public sector. Second, unsustainable social expenditures to provide income transfers and consumer subsidies. The actual or incipient fiscal crisis in Brazil, Mexico, Peru, Nigeria, Ghana, Turkey, and Madagascar (which also had a mixture of other motives) can be traced to the first type of over-expansion of developmental public expenditure, whilst that in Sri Lanka, Egypt, Jamaica, Uruguay, and Costa Rica is due to burgeoning and inflexible social expenditures which became unsustainable.

One example of each type from our country studies should suffice to delineate these two different sources of fiscal imbalances. Ghana provides the clearest case of fiscal imbalances generated by a 'big push' type of development effort, as well as a cautionary tale of the consequences. The big push in Ghana began under Nkrumah in 1959. Its purpose was to raise domestic investment financed through aid and higher domestic savings. This investment was to be channelled into import-substituting industrialization and the development of infrastructure, within the framework of a central plan. Thus gross fixed capital formation, which was about 14% of GDP, was raised to about 20% of GDP between 1960 and 1965.[49] This was achieved by an increased 'tax effort', which 'reached 16 per cent of the GDP estimate in 1964 and 1965'.[50] In addition foreign loans, mainly in the form of medium-term suppliers' credits, were contracted. 'About 2/5ths of Ghana's imports in the years 1961–65 were financed in this way.'[51] But still 'government spending ran ahead of revenues. . . . About one-third of the aggregate budget deficits of 1960–65 were covered by deficit-financing; in 1965 alone, the proportion was 85 per cent.'[52] Inflation accelerated 'from 2 per cent per annum in 1959–60 to 6 1/2 per cent per annum in 1961–63, 11 per cent in 1961 and 26 per cent in 1965.'[53] But all this pain yielded little reward. Ghana suffered the

'paradox of investment without growth'. . . . The push raised an investment rate that was already high to absorb over one-fifth of real GDP in 1963–65. Yet the estimate of aggregate real output was less than 10 per cent higher in 1965 than in 1959. Population growth in this period is believed to have been about 2.6 per cent per annum. It follows that output per head declined at an annual rate of about 1 per cent.[54]

The causes for this decline are to be found in the returns to the investments made. Estimates of the DRCs (domestic resource costs) of a sample of Ghanaian manufacturing firms that were set up during the big push showed that 67% of the output was produced by firms with DRCs greater than even a high shadow exchange rate, and 24% of the output was produced by firms 'that would have been inefficient at *any* rate of exchange since their net foreign exchange savings were negative'.[55]

We have dwelt on the Ghanaian growth disaster resulting from its big push partly because it was explicitly based on this idea, and partly as it demonstrates vividly the dangers inherent in the idea, first propounded by Rosenstein-Rodan,[56] which has recently been revived by the new growth theorists.[57] Theoretically various externalities are adduced as validating the big push. But as Rimmer notes of the DRC estimates for Ghana, 'Steel found no evidence of externalities sufficient to justify the high DRC's'.[58]

The story of the big push in Nigeria after the first oil price rise of 1973 is very similar. Whilst the stories of the big pushes in Brazil (first under Kubitschek, in the period 1956–61, and then under Delfim Neto in the military administration in the 1970s), in Mexico (under Echeverría in the early 1970s, and López Portillo in the mid- to late 1970s), and in Turkey (from 1974 onwards) are more complex, their effects in generating fiscal imbalances, accelerating inflation, and growth collapses are clear from our country studies.[59]

The second source of fiscal imbalances in the form of unsustainable social expenditures can be typified by Jamaica under the Manley government of 1972–86. Jamaican governments, despite ideological differences, shared the view that windfalls from export booms should be garnered for development purposes and to expand social expenditures. The weakness lay in a political setting in which there was unrelenting pressure on the rival political parties to increase social expenditures on education, health, low-cost housing, and creating jobs.[60] This unrelenting pressure for increased social expenditures led to growing (but not catastrophic) public indebtedness and budget deficits during the 1960s. But these pressures became especially irresistible when Jamaica imposed a levy on its bauxite production in 1974. The Jamaican government received nearly US $1.7 billion from this levy during its first ten years. But this gave free rein to the Jamaican predisposition towards expanding social expenditures. Despite the revenues from the bauxite levy, the budget deficit increased from 9.6% of GDP in 1974/5 to 23.9% in the fiscal year of 1976/7. The resulting macroeconomic imbalance, and the government's attempt to tackle it by various repressive measures rather than deal with the fundamental cause of unsustainable public expenditures, led directly to its growth collapse. Similar stories are told about the fiscal imbalances in Sri Lanka, Egypt, Uruguay, and Costa Rica by our country authors.

One striking feature of the distribution of our sample countries by these two broad categories of the causes of their fiscal imbalance is that most of the big-push-motivated excesses of public expenditure are in countries in our land-abundant group. As Peru is also pretty close to the edge of the land-abundant group in the resource endowment triangle in Fig. 2.5 (and is rich in natural resources),[61] this propensity to go for a public-sector-propelled big push would appear to be an important stylized fact about our land-abundant countries. The one major exception of a big push outside the land-abundant group is Madagascar's 'invest to the hilt' programme, which, as Pryor emphasizes, was based largely on ideological predispositions.

The second feature (which will be discussed more fully in the next chapter) is that in the group of countries where the fiscal crisis relates to excessive social expenditure, all the countries (except for Egypt) are what we will call factional states which have had some form of pluralistic democracy during fairly long periods since after World War II.

Taking these two features together, it is apparent that we need to examine the deeper political economy factors which are likely to explain the divergences in the way the public finances are managed in our sample of countries. Though in this chapter we have arrived at the importance of differences in public-sector behaviour in explaining divergent economic performance, by an examination of the comparative performance of our countries in maintaining relatively steady growth, it should be noted that some of our slow-growing countries like Sri Lanka which have not suffered obvious growth collapses have nevertheless adopted growth-retarding public policies in part because of the imperatives of public finance.

More generally, much *dirigiste* public intervention (like trade and investment controls) which creates policy-induced distortions in the economy can be looked upon as creating politically determined 'entitlements' to current and future income streams for various groups in the economy. These entitlements are implicit or explicit subsidies to certain groups, and have to be paid for by implicit or explicit taxation of other groups in the economy. In that sense, most government activity can be looked upon as equivalent to a system of taxes and subsidies, that is, a part of public finance. The winners and losers from this game will obviously depend upon whom the state chooses to favour, which in turn depends upon the objectives of the state, and the constraints it faces. In other words, we need to see if there are any explanations for the differing behaviour of governments which could provide us with a deeper explanation for the differing wealth of nations than is provided by differences of resources or technology. This is our task in the next chapter.

APPENDIX TO CHAPTER 5

Time-Series Analysis of GDP Growth Rates of 21 Countries[62]

The first task in this analysis of the structural pattern of our 21-country GDP series is to test for structural breaks in the series for the 21 countries, given the qualitative evidence from our country studies on turning-points in policies, which—sometimes wih a lag—can be expected to affect subsequent growth rates. To this end we estimate a first-order autoregressive (AR(1)) model of GDP (Y) given by:

$$Y(t) = c + a \cdot Y(t-1) + e(t) \tag{A.1}$$

and test by the use of the Chow test to see if the breaks corresponding to the years for the turning-points suggested by our country studies are statistically significant.[63] The results are given in Table A.5.1. All the breaks are statistically significant. Colombia, Hong Kong, and Malaysia had no clearly identifiable turning-points, and we would expect a simple linear trend to describe their growth process.

Table A.5.1 also shows the means and standard deviations of the growth rates before and after each break. Eight countries have two breaks, three none and the rest just one. Most of these breaks cluster around the early 1970s and 1980s, reflecting the exogenous shocks of the oil-price rise of 1973 and the debt crisis of 1981, but these led to differing policy reactions as noted in this chapter. Hence there is no obvious pattern in the changes in growth rates across countries as a result of these shocks. Nor is there any between growth rates and their volatility as measured by their standard deviations. Thus a regression of growth rates and volatility for our countries yielded no significant relationship.

Next, assuming that the growth process between breaks—or over the whole period if there were none—was one with temporary fluctuations around a linear trend, we estimated the time trends in log GDP (y) from the equation

$$y(t) = c + bT + D_{1T} + D_{2T} + e(t), \tag{A.2}$$

where T is the time trend and D_{1T} is a dummy variable to reflect a possible change in the intercept at the break point $t(b)$, and takes the value of 1 if $t > t(b)$, and 0 otherwise, and D_{2T} is a dummy variable to reflect a possible change in the slope at the break point, and takes the value $t - t(b)$ after the break point and 0 otherwise.

The resulting estimates are given in Table A.5.2, whilst Fig. A.5.1 charts the estimated trend and actual log GDP. The residuals (the difference between the two series) have conventionally been taken to be the cyclical fluctuations of GDP—its temporary deviations from a given trend.

Recently a whole new time-series econometrics has emerged for distinguishing between the permanent and cyclical elements in time series.[64] From this it was argued most forcefully by Nelson and Plosser (1982) that far from being temporary,

Table A.5.1. Properties of growth process

	Country	Period	Break	F stat. (Chow test)	Mean of Growth Rates				Std. Dev. of Growth Rates			
					Full period	Before break 1	After break 1	After break 2	Full period	Before break 1	After break 1	After break 2
(1)	Brazil	50–86	1968 1981	5.08 b	6.40	6.23	7.71	2.72	3.70	2.78	4.08	5.12
(2)	Colombia	50–85	No Break		4.59				9.85			
(3)	Costa Rica	50–85	1962 1980	6.84 a	4.89	5.22	6.03	6.03	4.35	5.33	2.20	2.20
(4)	Egypt	60–85	1975	7.88 b	6.02	4.89	7.82		2.98	2.66	2.60	
(5)	Ghana	60–84	1975	6.70 c	1.16	1.88	-1.37		5.27	5.40	6.39	
(6)	Hong Kong	60–85	No Break		8.48				4.20			
(7)	Indonesia	60–85	1968 1982	13.73 a	5.83	3.69	7.74	4.05	3.52	4.51	2.50	1.81
(8)	Jamaica	60–84	1973	12.84 a	1.71	4.33	-1.24		4.31	3.42	2.96	
(9)	Malawi	54–86	1965	3.53 b	4.21	4.44	4.77		5.39	6.41	5.80	
(10)	Malaysia	60–85	No Break		6.57				2.64			
(11)	Madagascar	50–84	1970 1979	5.31 b	1.77	2.77	1.02	0.61	3.49	2.91	3.58	5.57
(12)	Malta	60–84	1974	15.91 a	6.42	5.37	8.03		5.48	4.81	5.96	
(13)	Mauritius	60–86	1973	6.62 b	2.07	1.90	2.78		6.74	8.09	5.55	
(14)	Mexico	50–86	1980	38.93 a	5.28	6.19	1.74		3.41	2.16	5.26	
(15)	Nigeria	60–84	1969 1981	8.06 a	3.70	3.12	7.58	-4.80	9.62	11.35	9.63	1.9
(16)	Peru	50–85	1979	10.30 a	4.07	4.81	1.23		4.01	2.78	6.59	
(17)	Singapore	60–86	1982	13.51 a	7.96	8.7	4.4		4.16	3.71	4.15	
(18)	Srilanka	50–86	1957	2.45 c	4.57	2.89	5.03		3.17	4.78	2.54	
(19)	Thailand	50–85	1960 1973	3.97 c	6.19	4.98	7.31	6.41	2.90	4.53	2.02	1.74
(20)	Turkey	50–85	1967 1979	5.49 a	5.46	5.83	7.62	3.00	6.13	8.47	6.83	2.67
(21)	Uruguay	55–84	1973 1980	5.90 b	1.05	0.77	4.51	-3.10	4.32	3.13	3.48	4.84

a—significant at 1% level.
b—at 5% level.
c—at 10% level.

Table A.5.2. Estimates of time trends

	Constant	time T	D_{1T}	D_{2T}	D_{3T}	D_{4T}
Brazil	10.87	0.065		0.020	−0.16	−0.045
	(431.43)	(25.55)		(5.28)	(3.27)	(4.01)
Colombia	4.70	0.048				
	(131.21)	(26.81)				
Costa Rica	7.54	0.048		0.014		−0.067
	(406.90)	(20.37)		(4.48)		(11.73)
Egypt	7.82	0.044		0.041		
	(460.9)	(24.20)		(10.73)		
Ghana	0.01	0.025		−0.035		
	(0.55)	(10.32)		(6.73)		
Hong Kong	10.13	0.082				
	(282.21)	(36.37)				
Indonesia	0.022	0.017	0.071	0.059		−0.038
	(2.14)	(6.97)	(5.34)	(22.86)		(6.60)
Jamaica	−0.097	0.054		−0.061		
	(5.06)	(22.58)		(15.54)		
Malawi	−0.010	0.038	0.147			
	(0.13)	(8.72)	(2.70)			
Malaysia	9.404	0.069				
	(379.25)	(44.84)				
Madagascar	−0.066	0.032		−0.026	0.072	−0.022
	(5.35)	(31.24)		(8.19)	(2.24)	(2.97)
Malta	−0.19	0.064	0.273			
	(4.70)	(12.65)	(3.71)			
Mauritius	0.161	−0.005	0.211	0.024		
	(4.64)	(1.03)	(4.13)	(3.62)		
Mexico	−0.021	0.061	0.124	−0.057		
	(2.58)	(126.5)	(5.85)	(13.1)		
Nigeria	0.041	0.013	0.268	0.050	−0.09	0.11
	(0.76)	(1.13)	(3.45)	(3.66)	(0.76)	(2.72)
Peru	0.050	0.050		−0.056		
	(3.39)	(53.7)		(10.49)		
Singapore	−0.072	0.093		−0.048		
	(2.95)	(48.6)		(4.22)		
Sri Lanka	0.064	0.009		0.042		
	(2.71)	(1.85)		(8.08)		
Turkey	0.116	0.049		0.021	−0.101	−0.03
	(5.37)	(23.73)		(4.71)	(2.15)	(3.15)
Uruguay	−0.02	0.007		0.041		−0.069
	(1.28)	(4.46)		(8.23)		(6.72)

t ratios in parentheses.
$D_{1T} = 1$ if $t > t(b1)$ and 0 otherwise, where $t(b1)$ is break 1;
$D_{2T} = (t - t(b1))$ if $t > t(b1)$ and 0 otherwise;
$D_{3T} = 1$ if $t > t(b2)$ and 0 otherwise, where $t(b2)$ is break 2;
$D_{4T} = (t - t(b2))$ if $t > t(b2)$ and 0 otherwise.

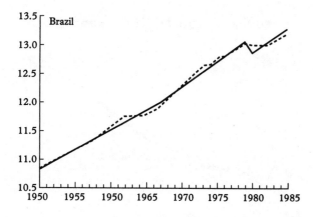

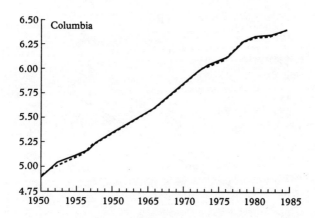

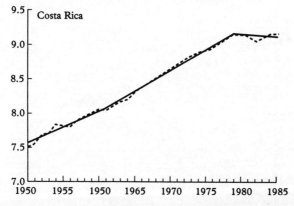

Fig. A.5.1. Growth trends and cycles. (Vertical scale shows log GDP; dashed lines show actual values, continuous lines the estimated trend or trends)

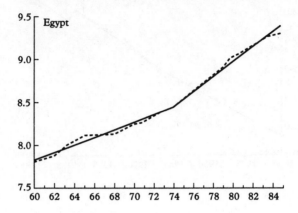

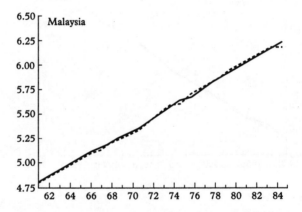

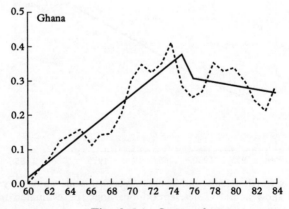

Fig. A.5.1. *Continued*

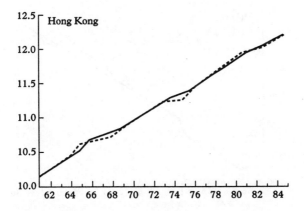

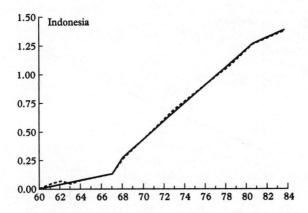

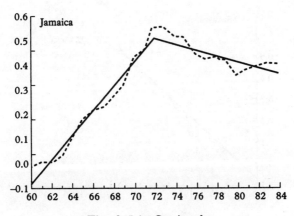

Fig. A.5.1. *Continued*

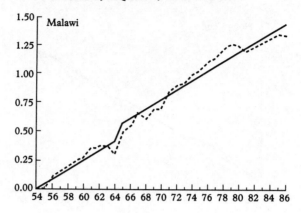

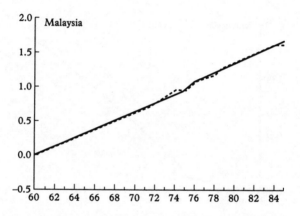

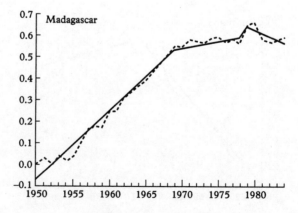

Fig. A.5.1. *Continued*

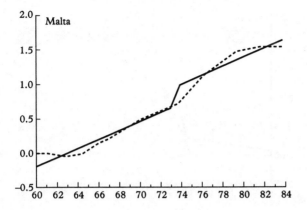

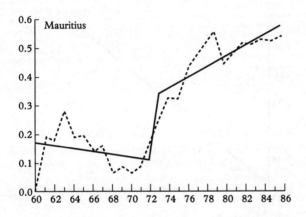

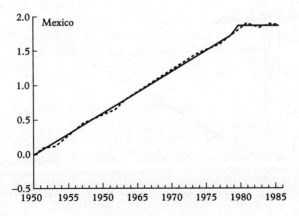

Fig. A.5.1. *Continued*

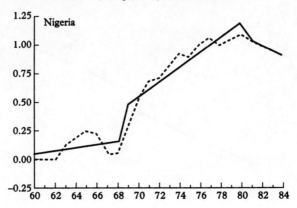

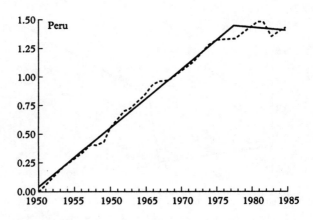

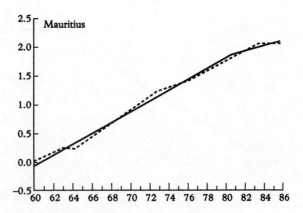

Fig. A.5.1. *Continued*

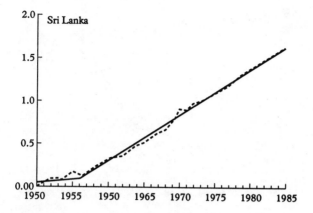

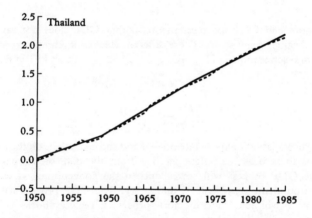

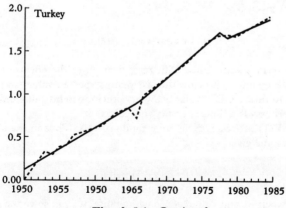

Fig. A.5.1. *Continued*

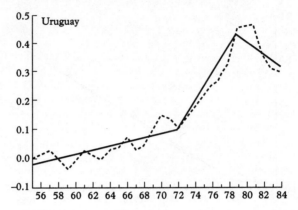

Fig. A.5.1. *Continued.*

many fluctuations in GDP are permanent, so that GDP does not revert to its previous trend value after a shock. These different viewpoints can be expressed very simply by a time-series model of log GDP, $y(t)$, which has a trend bT and a random disturbance $e(t)$:

$$y(t) = bT + \sum_{j=1}^{\infty} a(j) \cdot e(t-j).$$

(A.3)

If the error process is stationary (white noise), and the coefficient on the errors (the $a(j)$) declines to zero as the length of time from the date of the past shock j increases, the GDP process will correspond to the conventional view, and the fluctuations around the trend will be temporary. The GDP process will then be *trend-stationary*. It will be a 'short memory' process as regards shocks.[65]

If on the other hand the $a(j)$ do not decline to zero as j increases, then the effects of shocks on GDP will persist, and the GDP process will have a 'long memory'. In particular if the GDP process is generated by the simple AR(1) model of a random walk with a drift given by

$$y(t) = c + y(t-1) + e(t),$$

(A.4)

where the error term is white noise with zero mean, then the effects of any shock, say a fall in GDP by one unit below the last year's expected value (so that $e(t-1) = -1$), will lead to future GDP being below its previous trend value indefinitely by one unit. The process is a 'long memory' process.

But not all AR(1) processes generate a random walk. Thus in the simplest but general AR(1) model given by

$$y(t) = ay(t-1) + e(t),$$

(A.5)

where a lies between -1 and 1, and $e(t)$ is white noise, we can solve the equation to obtain

$$y(t) = \sum_{j=0}^{\infty} a^j \cdot e(t-j).$$ (A.6)

If $a < 1$ then the coefficient on the error term will decline at an exponential rate. The effects of past shocks will disappear. The process will have a short memory. If $a = 1$, however, then the GNP process will be a random walk (see eqns. A.4 and A.5), and all shocks, old and new, will equally effect the current value of GDP (from A.6).

Hence one way to determine whether GNP is determined by a trend-stationary process, which gives the conventional result of temporary fluctuations around a time trend, or by what is termed a *difference-stationary* process represented by a random walk with drift, is to test whether or not the value of a is significantly different from unity. This is what the so-called 'unit root' tests do.

Relaxing the assumption that the error process is white noise, and allowing both for a positive intercept and for the alternative hypothesis of a linear time trend, leads to the augmented Dickey–Fuller (ADF) procedure for testing for a unit root by estimating the regression

$$y(t) = c + bT + ay(t-1) + \sum_{i=1}^{k} c(i)y(t-1) + e(t)$$ (A.7)

and testing the t statistic using the ADF values tabulated by Mackinnon (1990), for the null hypothesis that $a = 1$, hence for the presence of a unit root and thence the absence of trend stationarity.

We applied the ADF procedure to the time series of GDP of our 21 countries[66] and found that, except for Hong Kong and Colombia, we could not reject the null hypothesis of a unit root for any of the others. However, Hong Kong and Colombia are also two of the three countries for which there was no structural break. The rejection of a unit root in their log GDP series therefore provides confirmation for our fitting a deterministic linear time trend to these series.

Moreover, we know from the qualitative evidence of our country studies, confirmed by the Chow tests summarized in Table A.5.1, that there were at least one and in some cases two 'turning-points' or 'breaks' in the GDP time trends of our countries. As Perron (1989) has shown, if there is a one-time break in the level or slope of the trend function, the standard ADF unit-root tests cannot reject the unit-root hypothesis even if the true process is trend stationary with a one-time break. He has also devised test statistics to test for trend versus difference stationarity when there is a one-time break in the time series. As these test statistics are not currently available for cases with more than one break, in applying the Perron procedures we had, *faute de mieux*, to choose, both on the qualitative evidence of the country studies and on the values of the t statistics in the 'detrending' equations presented above, the 'major' single break in those of our countries in which we have identified more than one break in Table A.5.1. Moreover, there could be three different types of break, which leads to three different regression models (see Perron, 1989):

(A) the 'crash' model, where there is change in the level of the trend at the break point, shown by a change in the intercept of the trend before and after the break; and two 'breaking trend' models,
(B) where there is a change in the trend growth rate after the break point, shown by a change in the slope of the trend, and
(C) where there is a change in both the level and growth rate of the trend after the break, shown by a change in both the intercept and the slope of the trend function.

The three resulting regression models derived by Perron are:

$$(A) \quad y(t) = c + b \cdot T + g_1 \cdot D_{1T} + d \cdot D_{0T} + a \cdot y(t-1)$$
$$+ \sum_{i=1}^{k} f(t) \Delta y(t-i) + e(t);$$

$$(B) \quad y(t) = c + b \cdot T + g_2 \cdot D_{2T} + r(t),$$
$$r(t) = ar(t-1) + \sum_{i=1}^{k} \Delta y(t-i) + e(t);$$

$$(C) \quad y(t) = c + b \cdot T + g_1 \cdot D_{1T} + h \cdot D_{ST} + d \cdot D_{0T} + a \cdot y(t-1)$$
$$+ \sum_{i=1}^{k} f(t) \Delta y(t-1) + e(t),$$

where c is a constant,
     T is a time trend,
     r is the residual,
and the following are dummy variables constructed around the break point $t(b)$:

$$D_{0T} = 1 \text{ if } t > t(b+1) \text{ and } 0 \text{ otherwise;}$$
$$D_{1T} = 1 \text{ if } t > t(b) \qquad \text{and } 0 \text{ otherwise;}$$
$$D_{2T} = 0 \text{ if } t \leqslant t(b) \qquad \text{and } = t - t(b) \text{ if } t > t(b);$$
$$D_{ST} = 0 \text{ if } t \leqslant t(b) \qquad \text{and } = t \qquad \text{if } t > t(b).$$

The dummy variable $D0T$ and the variables $y(t-1)$ and $\Sigma \Delta y(t)$ are from the null hypothesis of a unit root, and thus the regressions nest the models under both the null (difference-stationary) and alternative (trend-stationary) hypotheses.

For trend stationarity (rejection of the null hypothesis of a unit root) it is expected that

$$a < 1; \ b \neq 0; \ g_1, \ g_2, \ h \neq 0; \text{ and } d = 0.$$

Under the null hypothesis of difference stationarity we expect, for the three models,

$$(A) \quad a = 1; \ b = 0; \ g_1 = 0;$$
$$(B) \quad a = 1; \ b = 0; \ g_2 = 0;$$
$$(C) \quad a = 1; \ g = 0; \ h = 0.$$

Again using both qualitative information and the statistical time-trend estimates in Table A.5.2, we first put each of our countries into one of these three model categories. The resulting estimates of the respective models are shown in Table A.5.3.

The crucial test is the t statistic on a. Perron has derived tables for the significance levels of this statistic to reject the null hypothesis of a unit root and confirm trend stationarity. On this test, except for Ghana, all the countries pass the trend stationarity test. With Hong Kong and Colombia having passed the ADF test for

Table A.5.3. Perron tests for trend stationarity

	Malawi	Malta	Indonesia	Mauritius
t	32.00	22.00	25.00	26.00
$t(b)$	11.00	14.00	8.00	13.00
z	0.34	0.58	0.32	0.50
c	0.05	-0.068	-0.001	0.055
	(1.79)	(1.77)	(0.04)	(1.80)
b	0.004	0.023	0.005	-0.001
	(0.53)	(3.26)	(0.91)	(0.40)
g	0.137	0.031	0.104	0.124
	(2.49)	(1.24)	(3.98)	(2.05)
d	-0.06	0.74	-0.031	0.025
	(0.92)	(1.24)	(1.07)	(0.37)
k	1.00	3.00	1.00	1.00
a	0.826*	0.627*	0.899*	0.672*
	(5.16)	(6.98)	(11.99)	(4.89)

$z = t(b)/t$.
t ratios in parentheses.

Note: These estimates have been derived for model A in the text.

*significant at the 1% level from the distribution for the t statistic on the coefficient a, for values of z, for model A given in Perron (1989).

	t	$t(b)$	z	a	
Costa Rica	35.00	30.00	0.86	0.634	(4.70)***
Egypt	25.00	15.00	0.60	0.79	(4.90)***
Jamaica	24.00	13.00	0.54	0.806	(9.51)***
Peru	35.00	29.00	0.82	0.594	(4.44)***
Singapore	26.00	22.00	0.85	0.766	(6.33)***
Srilanka	36.00	7.00	0.19	0.687	(4.88)***
Thailand	35.00	10.00	0.29	0.585	(3.68)*
Uruguay	29.00	25.00	0.86	0.787	(7.04)***

***significant at the 1% level.
**at the 5% level.
* at the 10% level, from the Perron (1989) distribution for the significance of the t ratio on the coefficient a, for the given z, for model B.
t ratios in parentheses.
$z = t(b)/t$.

Notes: These estimates have been derived from model B in the text, as except for Uruguay (for which there are two breaks) the coefficients c, b, and g in model B are the same as reported for the constant, time and D_{2T} in the time trend estimates for these countries in table A.5.2. For Uruguay the value of a reported above is for the break in 1980. The values of the other coefficients are: $c = -0.089$ (3.31); $b = 0.017$ (9.03); and $g = 0.787$ (7.04). For the break in 1973 for Uruguay the estimates of the coefficients for model B are: $z = 0.62$; $c = -0.039$ (1.47); $b = 0.011$ (4.28); $g = 0.016$ (2.97); and $a = 0.79$ (5.31).***

Table A.5.3. *Continued*

	Mexico	Nigeria	Turkey	Madagascar	Brazil	Ghana
t	36.00	24.00	35.00	34.00	36.00	24.00
$t(b)$	30.00	21.00	29.00	29.00	31.00	15.00
z	0.83	0.88	0.83	0.85	0.86	0.63
c	−0.13	−0.10	0.12	0.03	2.26	−0.20
	(3.32)	(1.52)	(3.78)	(1.25)	(2.15)	(2.6)
b	0.064	0.03	0.01	0.003	0.015	0.064
	(5.35)	(2.70)	(1.09)	(0.75)	(2.04)	(3.87)
g	0.011	−0.14	0.147	−0.81	−0.50	1.29
	(0.54)	(1.58)	(4.14)	(1.64)	(0.92)	(3.73)
h	−0.063	−0.06	0.013	0.026	0.015	−0.08
	(5.78)	(1.02)	(1.06)	(1.61)	(0.89)	(3.85)
d	2.015	1.41	−0.43	−0.12	−0.05	0.02
	(5.6)	(1.00)	(1.07)	(2.11)	(1.05)	(0.22)
a	−1.029	0.554	0.68	0.88	0.79	−1.59
	(5.36)***	(3.55)*	(4.39)**	(6.77)***	(8.02)***	(2.51)

*** significant at the 1% level,
** at the 5% level, and
* at the 10% level, from the distirbution for the t ratio on the coefficient a, for values of z, for model C in Perron (1989).
$z = t(b)/t$.
t ratios in parentheses.
Note: These estimates have been derived from model C in the text.

trend stationarity, only for Ghana and Malaysia can the difference stationarity hypothesis not be rejected. But even for Ghana, though the test statistic on a does not reach the value for significance on the Perron values, all the other coefficients and corresponding significance levels of the t statistics would support the trend- rather than difference-stationarity model.

Moreover, the emerging consensus in the ongoing controversies about how best to separate trends from cycles is, first, that 'the proper handling of deterministic trends is a vital prerequisite for dealing with unit roots', and second, that 'in finite samples, any trend-stationary process can be approximated arbitrarily well by a unit root process'.[67] Or, as Miron puts it, as a result 'we will never know whether the data are difference stationary or trend stationary'.[68] So we are back to qualitative judgements—which is where we came in! But it is nice to know that these qualitative judgements are, by and large, supported by the evidence gleaned from our unit-root tests.

NOTES

1. Part of this observed fluctuation in growth rates could be due to measurement errors, particularly of GDP. These errors will be particularly serious in economies in which unorganized sectors are large, and in economies where compo-

nents of output, such as agriculture, are estimated indirectly rather than through direct measurements of market flows.

2. Slutsky (1937). The more recent mathematical theory of chaos also shows how complex cyclical patterns can be generated even in simple mechanical systems which can be represented by a one-parameter, non-linear, one-variable difference equation of the first order, say the quadratic equation $y_{t+1} = wy_t(1 - y_t)$, which yields a hill-shaped diagram. If $w > 3$, this equation will yield a complex system of oscillations, first explosive, then damped, and so forth. For an intuitive but rigorous account of chaos theory, see Baumol and Benhabib (1989). The implications of this new emerging theory are profound for economic policy. As Baumol and Benhabib note (ibid. 79):

> Where chaos occurs economic forecasting becomes extremely difficult. The two basic forecasting devices—extrapolation (of various degrees of sophistication) and estimation of a structural forecasting model—both become questionable. Extrapolation is hardly appropriate for a time path that might exhibit two-period oscillations of steadily increasing amplitude for 50 periods, with the fluctuations all but disappearing for the next 20 periods, and still another pattern abruptly emerging thereafter. Forecasting carried out with the aid of estimates of the parameters of an underlying model also runs into difficulties if an error in calculation of the third decimal place of a parameter can change the qualitative character of the forecast beyond recognition.

Moreover, some simulations by Baumol and Quandt of a chaotic time-path based on the above illustrative difference equation and of another of a deterministic time path 'subject to substantial random disturbance of moderately low probability, [showed] that standard statistical procedures may fail to determine correctly in any particular case whether the set of observations has been subject to random disturbances or whether it has been generated by a model that is perfectly deterministic but chaotic' (ibid. 95 n. 9). For an application of the theory to amend conventional growth theory, which yields 'equilibrium' but irregular growth cycles, see R. H. Day (1982, 1983).

Clearly, the so-called traditional 'optimal control' approach to economic policy, in particular stabilization policy, will be highly misleading and even counter-productive if its assumption that various time series are generated by stable linear stochastic systems is invalid, and if these series are in fact generated by deterministic non-linear systems giving rise to chaotic dynamics. However, it has recently been argued (see Parker and Stacey, 1994) that the neo-Austrian methodology and policy prescriptions can be looked upon as compatible with chaos theory.

3. There might be a case for counter-cyclical buffer stock policy (of commodities or foreign exchange). This could provide some payoff in terms of increased growth and welfare. This is the idea which lies behind the periodic desire to set up commodity stabilizing schemes, of which the most recent is that proposed under the name of the Common Fund by UNCTAD. For a critique of the infeasibility and undesirability of such schemes see Lal and Henderson (1976). For a rigorous and detailed treatment of the various issues involved in commodity price stabilization, see Newberry and Stiglitz (1981). The cocoa mar-

keting board in Ghana is the prime example of such a stabilization scheme in our sample of countries. But, as Rimmer shows at length, soon after independence in Ghana this stabilization function was subsumed in the more predatory one of extracting a surplus from cocoa farmers.

4. There is, however, the structuralist school of development economists, which merely *assumes* that such rigidities exist. See Taylor (1983). For a detailed critique of the structuralist view of the world see Little (1982) and Lal (1983).

5. For detailed studies of the labour markets of two of these countries in Latin America, see Gregory (1986) and Urrutia (1985). Two other detailed studies of labour markets in Asia and Africa are Collier and Lal (1986) and Lal (1989a).

6. Lucas (1987: 50). See the common chapters 1 in Collier and Lal (1986) and Lal (1989a), for a more detailed discussion of the differing forms of 'unemployment' in the course of development.

7. The terms 'fixed-price' and 'flex-price' are due to Hicks (1974b). More recently, a richer specification of labour contracts in both developed and developing countries has been worked out. This applies both to industrial employment and rural labour markets. For a survey of these newer theories and their application to a large Third World country, see Lal (1989a: chs. 6–9).

8. Macbean (1966).

9. Knudsen and Parnes (1975).

10. This has been empirically validated for the countries for which Little–Mirrlees shadow prices have been calculated. These normally find a premium on savings given by the divergence between the accounting and consumption rates of interest: Lal (1977b, 1979, 1980b), Powers (1981), and Scott, MacArthur, and Newberry (1976); whilst Little and Scott (1976) list many other studies (some unpublished) which have estimated Little–Mirrlees accounting prices.

11. For a formal model which incorporates the Knudsen and Parnes results and also shows their dependence on implicit labor market assumptions, see Newberry and Stiglitz (1981: ch. 27).

12. For some estimates of these effects of the crowding out of investment by public sector deficits in developing countries, see Blejer and Khan (1984).

13. See Bevan *et al.* (mimeo: 5–12), and especially their table 1.

14. An excellent and concise account of the currency board system is provided in Walters (1987: 740–2).

15. Bevan *et al.* (mimeo: 11).

16. Rimmer (1992: 205, 206).

17. Ibid. 213.

18. Ibid. 228.

19. Findlay and Wellisz (1993: ch. 2, p. 16).

20. Ibid. 19.

21. Ibid., ch. 3 by Lim *et al.*, p. 124.

22. Seigniorage refers to the excess of the face value over the cost of production of currency. With the substitution of paper money for metallic coin, the seigniorage available to governments has increased markedly because of the lower costs of producing paper instead of metallic currency.

23. The most important shortcoming of a colonial-currency-board type hard-money system for governments is that there can be no fiduciary issue of currency and hence no monetary accommodation of their budget deficits. In

this context, it may be useful to see how central banking arose in England, and the emerging role played by its discretionary monetary policy in accommodating that perennial problem of princes, the need for revenue.

The Glorious Revolution of 1688–9 which brought William of Orange and Mary to the English throne, also led to English involvement in William's Franco-Dutch wars on the Continent. To pay for these wars a series of financial measures were adopted which have come to be called a Financial Revolution. These created a system of public credit which freed the English state of its perpetual financial worries in waging war as a great power in Europe. The crucial steps in the Financial Revolution were the foundation of the Bank of England and the institution of the National Debt.

The Bank of England was founded in 1694. It was granted a monopoly advantage by being incorporated as the sole chartered joint-stock Bank in the country, 'and allowed to issue notes (which did not, however, rank as legal tender) and discount bills'. In return the Government received financial assistance of a novel sort. The Bank 'undertook to raise £1.2 million from the public—and did so in twelve days—and to lend it to the Government at 8 per cent. . . . This loan from the Bank to the Government did not have ever to be fully repaid so long as the interest was forthcoming and this is the origin of [the] present funded national debt' (Ashley, 1961). Gradually, this led to the Bank becoming not only the government's bank but the bankers' bank, with its centralization of the country's species reserves, and the ability to provide extra cash by rediscounting commercial bills. With this centralization and the gradual establishment of the monopoly of the note issue (which became the sole legal tender), the Bank monopolized the profits from the seigniorage in issuing a paper currency, which it shared with the goverment in directly or indirectly financing its public sector borrowing requirment (in modern British terminology).

In the 19th century, most European countries (for similar reasons) had also established central banks, whose aims were 'to centralize, manage and protect the metallic reserve of the country, and to facilitate and improve the payments system. While these latter functions were seen as having beneficial economic consequences, the ability to share in the profits of seigniorage and greater centralized control over the metallic (gold) reserve had obvious political attractions as well' (Goodbart, 1987).

These attractions were to multiply when all combatants in the First World War discovered that they could finance their costs of waging war through deficit finance funded by their central banks. Governments had discovered their ability to raise revenue through the (implicit) inflation tax. There were two great economists, Schumpeter and Keynes, who clearly saw this momentous change in the powers of governments to deal with their perennial problem—a shortage of revenue.

Schumpeter in a brilliant essay written in 1918 realized as Peter Drucker has noted

that World War I had brought about the monetization of the economies of all the belligerents. Country after country, including his own still fairly backward Austria-Hungary, had succeeded during the war in mobilizing the entire liquid wealth of the community, partly through taxation but mainly through borrowing. . . . In the past the inability of the State to tax nore than a very small proportion of the gross national product, or to borrow more than a very small part of the country's wealth, had made inflation self-limiting. Now the only safeguard against inflation would be political, that is self-discipline. And Schumpeter was not very sanguine about the politicians' capacity for self-discipline.   (Drucker, 1983: 55)

Keynes too recognized that the world had changed after the First World War, that money and credit had become an important lever of control in the hands of governments.

Monetary factors—deficits, money, credit, taxes—were going to be the determinants of economic activity and of the allocation of resources . . . [For] Keynes this made possible the 'economist-king', the scientific economist. The modern state, through the mechanisms of taxation and borrowing, [had] acquired the power to shift income and, through 'transfer payments' to control the distribution of the national product.   (ibid, 56)

For Keynes this was like the power flowing from a magic wand, allowing countries to achieve both social justice and economic progress with (he hoped) stability. Schumpeter was more sceptical. That the 'economist-king' would rule the earth 'he saw as pure hubris'. For 'he saw that it was not going to be economists who would exercise the power, but the politicians and generals' (ibid.).

Though some may still doubt Schumpeter's prescience as regards developed countries, there can be little doubt about its relevance and realism concerning many Third World states, not least for many in our sample of countries.

24. The following account is based on Furtado (1976: ch. 9).
25. Ibid. 97.
26. See n. 23 above.
27. See Balassa (1984: 955–72). See Fishlow's comments in the same issue of *World Development* for various criticisms of Balassa's approach. But most would agree with the broad heuristic explanations of at least the different directions in which countries responded to these shocks.
28. *World Development Report 1987* (fig. 5.1, p. 83). The few countries not listed, viz. Egypt, Malawi, Mauritius, Jamaica, and Malta, have been assigned to the relevant categories on the basis of the judgement in our country studies.
29. This is hardly surprising, as neither the World Bank's definition, nor ours (in Ch. 2), of outward and inward orientation is analytically precise.
30. See Harberger (1978: 505–21).
31. Ibid.
32. Ibid. 511.
33. See Lal and Wolf 1986.
34. Latin Americans, being upside-down, define their real exchange rate as the inverse of ours, namely the relative price of traded to non-traded goods!
35. A graphic illustration of the rent-seeking associated with import controls is provided by Rimmer for Ghana. Discussing the growth of corruption under the import control regime in the 1970s, Rimmer notes: 'As in 1964–65, the quan-

tity of import licenses became a specially notorious area for the appropriation of administratively generated rents. Kept women could be kept by the issue of licenses, so that aspirants to this status "paraded the corridors of power offering themselves for libidinal pleasures in return for favors" ' (Rimmer, 1992: 136).

36. He derived them by adjusting the nominal exchange rate of each country 'by the difference between its own inflation rate and the weighted average inflation rate of the industrial countries, measuring inflation by the rate of increase of the implicit GNP deflector' (Wood, 1988: 2). The relationship between these 'purchasing power parity real exchange rates' and the real exchange rate defined as the relative price of non-traded to traded goods is discussed in Lal (1985b).

37. Lal (1986) provides an algebraic model and econometric test of the model for a land-abundant country.

38. For an explicit exercise in this spirit, see Lal (1985b: 682–702).

39. Edwards (1988a: 311–41).

40. The estimated equation in Edwards (1988b: 46) was

$$\text{Growth of real GDP} = 0.052 - 1.050 \text{ Misalignment}$$
$$(18.440)\ (-1.929) \qquad\qquad R^2 = 0.27$$

where the figures in brackets are t statistics.

41. The same confusion surrounds the required movements in the exchange rate with trade liberalization. The correct answers are derived in Corden and Neary (1982). Also see Edwards and van Wijnbergen (1987: 458–64).

42. There are further problems concerning the dynamic path of the real exchange rate and other variables, which depend upon the relative speed of adjustments in the relevant markets, and which can lead to over- or under-shooting from their relevant equilibrium values. See Lal (1989c) for a diagrammatic account within the same framework.

43. See Lal (1980a) and Edwards (1988a) for an alternative view.

44. Bevan et al. (forthcoming: part 3, section 5).

45. Ibid. 22.

46. Ibid.

47. John Lewis (1962) devised the term 'quiet crisis' for a long-term crisis in which growth was below potential, as applicable to India.

48. It should be noted that whilst most observers would classify Sri Lanka as a growth-collapse country, the author of our country study Henry Bruton clearly does not. But see for instance Bhalla (1988); we have followed Bhalla rather than Bruton in our classification in this section.

49. Rimmer (1992: 83).

50. Ibid. 81.

51. Ibid. 82.

52. Ibid. 80.

53. Ibid. 81.

54. Ibid. 84.

55. Ibid. 90.

56. Rosenstein-Rodan (1943). For a critique of the 'big push' type of theory see Little (1982).

57. See Murphy, Shleifer, and Vishny (1989).

58. Rimmer (1992: 90).

59. Also see Lal and Maxfield (1993) for an analysis of Brazilian post-war develop-
    ment in terms of our three-factor multi-commodity model outlined in ch. 2,
    which also tries to explain the political economy impetus behind the two post-
    war Brazilian big pushes.
60. See Stone and Wellisz in Findlay and Wellisz (1993).
61. See n. 144 in ch. 2 above.
62. The research assistance of Joon-Mo Yang in the econometrics of this appendix
    is gratefully acknowledged.
63. These and the following statistical procedures were all applied using microTSP.
64. This technique for distinguishing between the permanent and cyclical elements
    of time series has been developed by Beveridge and Nelson (1981) and Nelson
    and Plosser (1982), and includes a measure of a stochastic (rather than the
    conventional purely deterministic) element in the steady-state growth trend
    (which can therefore shift up or down) of a time series. The cyclical fluctuations
    around this shifting growth path are then estimated, and will typically yield a
    smaller cyclical component in the time series. We have not used this method,
    as it has come under serious questioning (see Perron, 1989, and Cochrane,
    1988). But for an application to one of our countries (Colombia), see
    Cuddington and Urzua (1989). A useful description of the technique and its
    uses is provided by Stock and Watson (1988). For a comprehensive survey of
    the ensuing 'unit root wars', and the agnostic conclusions to be drawn, together
    with an extensive bibliography, see Campbell and Perron (1991).
65. See Engle and Granger (1991: 2).
66. The procedure is routinely available in microTSP with the UROOT command,
    and was used to apply the test to our country data.
67. Campbell and Perron (1991: 157).
68. Miron (1991: 211).

6

The Polity and
Economic Performance

IN this chapter we discuss the interactions between the polity and the economy that emerge from our country studies. The terms 'polity' and 'state' will by and large be used interchangeably in what follows. But there is one sense in which 'polity' will be used to cover wider associations of human beings than those represented by 'state'. It is only from the mid-16th century that 'state' has been used for that legal and political association of people within a defined territorial area in which the authority of a particular sovereign government is obeyed. Its spread into common usage is coterminous with that of the absolutist monarchies in Europe.[1] The older term 'polity' refers to what the Greeks called *polis*, and can stand for an association of persons, which in modern-day terms is sometimes called civil society.[2] The government (as distinguished from the state) consists of those agents who are recognized as comprising the sovereign authority which is the custodian of the law of the land, and which has the legal monopoly of coercive force in the territory.[3]

Moreover, there will be numerous mutual interactions between the polity, the government, the outside world, and the economy.[4]

Each country's interaction between its polity and economy is of course unique; detailed accounts are provided in our country studies. A more condensed account of these interactions was given in Chapter 3, in terms of our twinning framework. In this chapter we attempt to see if there are any further patterns we can discern at a more general level. Before we can do so we need some analytical schema for classifying the different polities of our countries. This is the purpose of the first section, on models of the state. Next, we classify the polities of our countries into these broad analytical categories. But we make no attempt to explain why particular countries have the polities we observe. The historical evolution of each country's polity is likely to be *sui generis*, and the result of a host of contingent historical factors. We have no desire or illusions about producing any theory of history.[5] Instead, we examine whether there is any relationship between the type of polity and the relative growth and poverty-redressal performance of our various countries. This allows an assessment of many broad popular generalizations: whether democracy is good or bad for development, and whether authoritarian or military governments promote or retard development. This is addressed in Section II.

The next section links the polity specifically to the three-factor growth framework outlined in Chapter 2. We enquire if there are any discernible patterns in the political economy of countries which fall broadly into our three categories of labour-abundant, land-abundant, and intermediate factor endowments, resulting from the different factor price evolutions of their 'stylized' development paths. This is our purpose in Section III.

In Section IV we address questions concerning changes in policy regime, that is, the political economy of reform. When and why have policy regimes changed? Is it the result of a learning process or changes in the polity? Under what circumstances is it likely that dysfunctional policies will be altered in particular types of polities and economies?

I. MODELS OF THE STATE

The essential insight from the new political economy is that we need to take an even-handed view of the motives of the state and its citizens, regarding them as being equally self-regarding. As noted in the Introduction to this book, the political form usually assumed in most of the literature is some form of majoritarian democracy. This, however, is by no means the predominant form of government in most developing countries. We therefore need some classificatory scheme to differentiate different types of government—absolutist, multi- and one-party democracies, bureaucratic-authoritarian, oligarchic, et cetera—which are likely to be found in our various countries. As we want to explain the effects of the alternative political forms on generating particular economic policies which affect growth and poverty outcomes, we need a schema in which the objectives of government and the constraints on its actions can be expressed in terms of some simple economic variables.

In devising such a system of classification, there is one broad division that readily suggests itself[6] (and which was briefly noted in the Introduction). This is between a regime or government which is *autonomous*, in the sense of having objectives of its own, and one which is a cipher for the interests of private agents who in some contingent manner succeed in capturing the state, or in which there is some form of pressure-group equilibrium. This second general type of state can be called the *factional* state. Table 6.1 also lists the possible subdivisions within these categories. We discuss each of these general types of state in turn.

1. The Autonomous State

The autonomous state, in turn, can consist of three pure types. The first, which is the staple of the economist's textbook, is the '*benevolent dictatorship*' or *Platonic guardian state*. The objective of such a state is to maximize the social welfare of its citizens. However, as Arrow has shown in his famous 'general possibility theorem',[7] it is impossible to devise a democratic social welfare function except under very restrictive assumptions, so a Platonic guardian state is unlikely to be democratic.

The conventional economist's approach to public policy has nevertheless assumed the government to be a Platonic guardian whose actions are an attempt to offset the socially undesirable actions of private agents maximizing their personal utility. It also redistributes incomes from agents with low marginal utility to those with high marginal utility, subject to constraints generated by disincentive effects. This approach is not entirely ridiculous: though governments in developing countries seldom appear to be well characterized by this description, there are likely to be occasional and unpredictable windows of benevolent rationality at various positions within a government.

The autonomous guardian may not necessarily be 'benevolent' in the rationalist sense of the economist or Plato. This type of state would also cover that heroic superman, the proclaimed Nietzschian guardian, 'who tramples down opposition, despises happiness and creates his own rules'.[8] Hitler, Mussolini, and others of that kind would also fall into this category of the 'guardian' state.

The second type of autonomous state can be described as the *(self-serving) predatory state*.[9] The objectives of the predatory state, by analogy with biological predator–prey models, involve the self-seeking extraction of the maximum continuing flow of resources (which includes intangibles such as power and prestige) for the members of the government and its associates. Predators will share an interest in the enlargement of the incomes of their prey (say, through economic growth, promoted by the provision of public goods—of which the most important is law and order) in so far as this raises the potential flow of their own income. Unlike the benevolent state, the welfare of its subjects—as conceived by economists—may at best be only a very minor direct component of a predatory state's 'objective function'. More important, however, is the likely opportunistic nature of government behaviour in the latter state, which implies that, compared with the more principled benevolent state, its choices between social objectives are likely to be fickle.

One way of characterizing the difference between the Platonic and the predatory state is that individuals in charge of the instruments of power in the Platonic state have citizens' welfare in their own objective function, whilst in the predatory state the rulers treat their citizens' welfare more as a constraint which restricts their pursuit of other objectives. In other words, citizens' welfare is an instrument rather than an objective in the hands of the rulers in the predatory state.

Moreover, two distinct types of predatory states can be distinguished. The first may be called *absolutist*. Many of the states established in Western

Europe after the Renaissance would fall into this category,[10] as would the monarchical and colonial states of many pre-independent developing countries. More generally, in the absolutist version of the predatory state, the government is assumed to be controlled by a single ruler—a monarch, a dictator, or a charismatic leader. In the first two forms of government, the monarch or dictator may change, but the form of government is not altered, as we assume the changes result from mere palace coups, and not because of any change in the interest groups controlling the state. Put differently, in this model the constellation of domestic interest groups has little direct effect on the policies of the sovereign, who is therefore more autonomous than in the following models of bureaucratic-authoritarian and factional states. The objective of the state is net revenue maximization. The model will also apply to countries ruled by a charismatic leader, who may often also be a dictator; but the model will be applicable only during his/her lifetime, unless a quasi-monarchical dynastic succession can be assured. The model will also apply to countries ruled by a colonial power which is not beholden to the interplay of domestic interest groups.

The second type of predatory state may be called *bureaucratic-authoritarian*. Its objective is to maximize the number of bureaucrats—or public employment. Many one-party states (despite democratic rhetoric and institutional trappings), as well as most Communist states, would fall into this subcategory.

If the objectives of these two subdivisions of the predatory state can be described as revenue and bureaucrat maximization respectively, what are the constraints under which the respective governments will seek to maximize these objectives? The first constraint must be economic, namely the productivity of the economy, which in turn will in part be based on the public goods the predatory state provides. This will determine the revenue available either for the absolute monarch's own purposes—courtiers, palaces, mistresses, and the accumulation of 'royal' treasure—or to increase public employment (in the bureaucratic-authoritarian version).

The second constraint concerns the danger of the government being taken over or overthrown. The third comes from expropriation-avoiding activities by private agents. To pinpoint the nature and form of these two latter constraints, it is useful to consider the fundamental question of why there should be any state at all.

The classical answer was provided by Hobbes:

Hereby it is manifest that during the time men live without a common power to keep them all in awe, they are in that condition which is called war; and such a war, as is of every man, against every man . . . In such condition, there is no place for Industry; because the fruit thereof is uncertain; and consequently no Culture of the Earth, no Navigation, nor use of the commodities that maybe imported by Sea; no commodious Building; . . . no Arts; no Letters; no Society; and which is most of all, continual fear, and danger of violent death; And the life of man, solitary, poor, nasty, brutish and short.[11]

The state is thus required at a minimum to enforce peace within its territory and to adjudicate disputes between its citizens. If an individual's property can be said to consist not merely of his material possessions but also of his person, then in the broadest sense a state is required to lay down and enforce property rights. These property rights are required as soon as men have to live together and act co-operatively. 'In a world of Robinson Crusoe property rights play no role', writes Demsetz. 'Property rights are an instrument of society and derive their significance from the fact that they help a man form those expectations which he can reasonably hold in his dealings with others.'[12] Apart from securing a man's physical person against the violence of others, such rights are therefore an essential prerequisite (as Hobbes noted) for any co-operative economic activity, as for instance in the division of labour and evolution of economic exchange.

To perform this minimalist productive function, a state must have the legal monopoly of force and some machinery for resolving disputes about the rules laid down concerning property rights, including their exchange. Such property rights must be established not only in what are called individualistic private-ownership economies, but also in socialist or Communist economies, though the rights and the rules governing their exchange will be different. Violence can generally be defined as an attempt to violate these rights by physical force within the particular territorial jurisdiction of a state. Hence the inherent and most basic characteristic of a state is its legal monopoly of the use of violence within its territory. Moreover, this violence-using and violence-controlling 'industry' is a natural monopoly, which produces at least two joint products: 'protection' and 'justice'.

This immediately suggests that the relevant economic theory to analyse the behaviour of states is likely to be provided by the theory of industrial organization—in particular that concerning the equilibrium price and output policies of a natural monopolist.

An alternative route to analysing the behaviour of states has, however, been more common. This tradition, which extends from Locke through Rawls and Buchanan and Tullock, seeks to provide a normative justification for the set of rules concerning property rights which a rational group of individuals would choose in some primeval 'state of nature' to maximize their individual gains through mutual co-operation. This idealistic contractual and constitutionalist approach to the actual and desired behaviour of states is not very useful for our purpose. Though much philosophical ink has been spilt on providing justifications for various sorts of property rights in the context of an idealized original contract setting up a state, historically many states have arisen out of the coercive (predatory) actions of individuals or groups. As North notes: 'Whether the state originated as a predatory group attacking and exploiting a peasant village (a predatory origin of the state) or developed out of the communal needs for organization of the peasant village (a contract origin of the state) cannot be resolved.'[13]

The relevant question for our purpose, therefore, is how any existing group of controllers of the natural monopoly providing 'protection' and 'justice' can maintain themselves in power, or what amounts to the same thing analytically, prevent rivals from entering and taking over the natural monopoly. For it is the height of the existing barriers to entry against rivals which will provide the second major constraint (in addition to the productivity of the economy) for a predatory state in achieving its revenue- or bureaucrat-maximizing objective. Fig. 6.1 and the starred section below provide a model of an autonomous state, in which the tax rate, public employment, and hence the level of public-goods provision are endogenously determined for the three types of autonomous state: Platonic, predatory (revenue-maximizing), and predatory (bureaucrat-maximizing). The optimal tax rate for the autonomous state is determined by the barriers to entry, that is, the contestability of the state. The level of public employment will be at the optimal level if the autonomous state is Platonic, lower than this if it is a predatory net revenue maximizer, and higher if it is a bureaucrat maximizer.

2. A Model of the Autonomous State[14]

A model which marries ideas from recent developments in the theory of industrial organization on contestability,[15] and ideas on the social productivity even of predatory states due to North,[16] as formalized by Findlay and Wilson,[17] can be used to show the differing political equilibriums of our three types of autonomous state: benevolent dictator; net-revenue-maximizing predator; and public-employment bureaucratic-authoritarian predator.

As most current developing countries as well as developed countries were primarily agrarian economies in the past, we consider a simple model of an autonomous state whose only source of revenue is a proportional tax on agricultural output.

Thus, consider a traditional peasant economy with a very favourable land–man ratio, depicted in Fig. 6.1. With traditional techniques, the existing labour force in agriculture is L_A working on a fixed quantity of land N ($N < \bar{N}$, the total land available), and through equal work and income sharing each worker receives the (net of tax) average product of labour y in agriculture as his income. There is a sovereign who imposes a fixed proportionate tax at the rate t on rural output to finance his court, army, and law-and-order institutions. Thus, part of the revenue the sovereign receives is used to hire public servants providing public goods–the police, judges, army, engineers. The rest is used for the sovereign's own purposes–

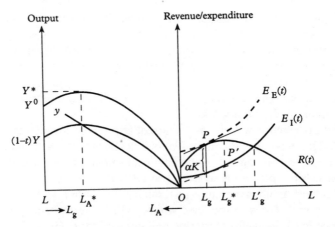

Fig. 6.1. The model of the autonomous state

courtiers, palaces, mistresses, and the accumulation of royal treasure. Following Findlay and Wilson (1987) we assume that the provision of public goods raises the productivity of the economy above the level that would exist without the state—that is in anarchy.

Thus in Fig. 6.1 we depict the total agricultural output curve of the economy with respect to the given total labour force OL, working on a given fixed acreage. If there are no government employees (L_g) then the total population is in the rural private sector (L_A) and produces output LY^0. This is the 'anarchy' level of output. With some government employees being hired to provide public goods for the rural sector, the rural labour force shrinks but total output increases until the allocation of the labour force given by $L_A^\star$ is reached, where $LL_A^\star = L_g$ workers are government employees and $OL_A^\star$ are left in the rural sector, producing the maximal output $Y^\star$ (which is higher than Y^0, because of the public goods provided by the L_g public employees).

For a given tax rate t on rural output, the vertical distance between the Y and $(1 - t)Y$ curve in Fig. 6.1 gives the total revenue available for a particular level of public (L_g) and private (L_A) employment. This revenue function $R(t)$ is plotted in quadrant I of the figure. It reaches a maximum when $L_g = L - L_A^\star$ workers are employed in the public sector. The government must pay its employees the competitive wage equal to the supply price of rural labour, which is *ex hypothesi* the net-of-tax average product in agriculture. This is given by the slope of the ray Oy when the level of rural private employment is $L_A^\star$ and public employment is L_g. Thus by a similar construction for each level of L_g, and for the given tax rate t, the variable-cost component of the public expenditure function $E(t)$ can be derived in quadrant I. In the absence of any fixed costs (on which more below), the variable-cost function and the $E(t)$ function will be the same. Let us assume that this is so.

The sovereign we have also assumed is a net-revenue maximizer. This means that for any given rate t he will seek to maximize the distance between the $R(t)$ and $E(t)$ functions, that is, equate the marginal cost of L_g public employees with the marginal tax revenue from the output produced by the remaining L_A rural workers.

The net tax revenue will rise as t is raised, as the $R(t)$ and $E(t)$ curves shift outward. The net-of-tax income of labour declines with rises in t as the $(1 - t)Y$ curve shifts downward. But there is an upper limit to t, given by the level at which the net-of-tax average product of labour is equal to subsistence income.[18] Even a revenue-maximizing predatory state is unlikely, however, to raise taxes to the level which reduces peasant incomes to the subsistence level, as well before that the current controllers of the multiproduct natural monopoly providing the public goods of law and order and security, which is the state, will find that their industry is contestable (in the sense of Baumol et al. (1982); see Lal (1988a), for this interpretation of the limits on the behaviour of the predatory state). The contestants could be either internal or external rivals. The level of taxes which will be sustainable depends upon the barriers to entry—including physical (geographical) and technological (military) as well as ideological (including religious)—which allow the maximum 'natural' rent to be extracted by any controller of the state (see Lal, 1988a).

These ideas can be formalized as follows. A large part of the costs incurred by an incumbent sovereign in capturing his/her estate will be sunk costs. Say these fixed capital costs are K, and the variable costs of providing the public goods and maintaining the sovereign in power are V. If α is the proportion of the fixed capital costs which are sunk, then the advantage the incumbent has over a new entrant is that whereas its total costs are

$$TC_I = f\big((1-\alpha)K,\ V\big), \tag{1}$$

those of the new entrant (who has access to the same military and civil technology, say) are

$$TC_E = f(K,\ V), \tag{2}$$

and as $\alpha < 1$, TC_E will lie above TC_I by the fixed amount αK.

Assume that the average variable costs, V, are incurred entirely on hiring public employees, so that total variable costs (which are the same for the incumbent and the entrant) TVC for a given tax rate are (as in Fig. 6.1)

$$TVC = y(L_g) \cdot L_g, \tag{3}$$

where y is the net-of-tax average agricultural product = public-sector wage rate, and L_g are the number of public employees hired. Then the total expenditure function for the new entrant, $E_E(t)$, for a given tax rate t, can be drawn in Fig. 6.1, quadrant I, as a vertical displacement by αK of the total expenditure function of the incumbent, $E_I(t)$.

The maximum profit the incumbent can then earn is π, given by

$$\pi = \left(TVC + K\right) - \left(TVC + \left(1 - \alpha\right)K\right) = \alpha K. \tag{4}$$

The optimal tax rate (t) for the net-revenue-maximizing predatory state will be determined by the tangency of the entrant's expenditure functions $E_E(t)$ with the revenue functions $R(t)$ for this optimal rate, as at P in quadrant I of Fig. 6.1. For suppose the tax rate were higher $(t' > t)$, then the incumbent's and entrant's expenditure functions $E(t')$ would shift downward and the revenue function $R(t')$ upwards (not drawn). The incumbent's monopoly would no longer be sustainable, as the entrant could charge a marginally lower tax rate and still make a net profit. Similarly, if the tax rate were lower $(t'' < t)$ then the revenue function would shift downward and expenditure functions would shift upwards and the incumbent would not be maximizing net revenue. Thus there will be a unique tax rate, and fiscal cum public employment equilibrium, determined by the underlying production function and the entry costs facing a new entrant.

That is, in Fig. 6.1, the vertical distance at the sustainable surplus-maximizing point between the $E_E(t)$ and $R(t)$ curves, when the $E_E(t)$ curve is tangential to the $R(t)$ curve, must equal αK. Thus in the general equilibrium model of the fiscal and employment decisions of a predatory state depicted by Fig. 6.1, quadrant I, the surplus-maximizing sovereign will set the tax rate t, such that the surplus generated at the public-employment level L_g, where the marginal costs and marginal returns (to the sovereign) from public employment are equated, is equal to the entry costs facing a new entrant coveting the state.

Next, consider the equilibrium of a bureaucrat-maximizing predatory state. Public employment will expand to L_g', well beyond the socially optimal level L_g in Fig. 6.1. At this level of public employment the budget is balanced at the entry-restricting and hence sustainable tax rate t^*. But in this process, with the increase in the provision of public goods, output could be higher than when the state is run by an absolute monarch or colonial power.

Finally, the equilibrium of a benevolent dictatorship or Platonic guardian state will be at the optimal public-employment point L_g^*. The optimal tax rate (t_g) will be such that the curve $R(t_g)$ intersects the $E(t_g)$ curve at point P' so that the optimal level of public employment is provided with a balanced budget.

3. Relevance of the Model

Though, for analytical clarity, it is useful to categorize our autonomous states in the above extreme tripartite division, most actual states will not fall into any of these pure categories. Actual states are likely to be more complex. Moreover, states may shift over time from one category into another. Of the three forms, however, the least likely is a benevolent dictatorship. The reasons for this have been well known for ages. Thus Hume clearly noted the implausibility of the psychological assumptions underlying the public interest view of the state viewed as a committee of Platonic guardians. In his essay, 'Of the Independence of Parliament', he wrote:

Political writers have established it as a maxim that, in contriving any system of government and fixing the several checks and controls of the constitution, every man ought to be supposed a knave and to have no other end, in all his actions, than private interest. By this interest we must govern him and, by means of it, make him, notwithstanding his insatiable avarice and ambition, cooperate to public good. Without this, say they, we shall in vain boast of the advantages of any constitution and shall find in the end that we have no security for our liberties or possessions except the good will of our rulers; that is, we shall have no security at all.

It is, therefore, a just political maxim that every man must be supposed a knave, though at the same time it appears somewhat strange that a maxim should be true in politics which is false in fact. But to satisfy us on this head we may consider that men are generally more honest in their private than in their public capacity, and will go greater lengths to serve a party than when their own private interest is alone concerned.

To which we may add that every court or senate is determined by the greater number of voices, so that, if self-interest influences only the majority (as it will always do), the whole senate follows the allurements of this separate interest and acts as if it contained not one member who had any regard to public interest and liberty.[19]

The predatory-state model seems to be a more credible approach for many developing countries, especially those which have recently been colonies and which thereby inherited predatory traditions. However, two hybrids of the above models seem more appropriate than any one model in isolation. First, the government may alternate between different models so that the predatory phase is temporary. We will return to this in our discussion of dynamics. Second, power may be spread between a predatory bureaucracy and rent-seeking pressure groups. The predatory nature of the bureaucracy inhibits pressure groups by extracting a proportion of revenues for its own purposes, thus raising the social cost of any transfers to powerful groups (see the Introduction). Conversely, powerful pressure groups constitute an internal take-over threat which constrains the state. As noted in the discussion of the parties–voters model versus the pressure-groups model in the Introduction, each may be pertinent to a distinct domain of policy. A bureaucracy may finance itself through debt and inflation while appeasing interest groups through market-specific interventions.

Thus, though for analytical clarity we have assumed that the autonomous state is immune to factional pressures, clearly in practice there will be some pressure that some domestic groups (even if not formally organized) will be able to exert. To the extent that this concerns the fiscal–public employment equilibrium (depicted in Fig. 6.1) and is effective, it will imply that the pressure will affect the autonomous state's perception of a change in the internal barriers to entry. But to see what factional pressures are likely to arise along the alternative development patterns of our various countries and their consequences in differing types of polities, it is necessary to look at a pure model of the factional state.

4. A Model of the Factional State

We have to some extent already outlined the types of model of the factional state that are relevant when we discussed the various public-choice theories of pressure-group equilibria in the Introduction. In this section, however, we outline a particular model of pressure-group equilibrium derived form the 'endogenous tariff formation' literature, which provides a link between the three-factor open-economy growth framework outlined in Chapter 2 and the likely behaviour of the factional state.

Unlike the absolute rulers who controlled the state in the story in the previous subsection, we now have a state which serves the interests of that coalition of pressure groups which succeeds in capturing it. The method of capturing the state need not be majoritarian democracy, even though this form of government would be compatible with our story. The interests served are narrowly defined to be the economic self-interests of the constituents of the government. The income effects induced by the economic policies adopted and hence of concern to a particular government will depend upon the returns to the primary-factor endowments of its constituents. A recent model of endogenous tariff determination in a voting polity, due to Mayer,[20] is helpful in providing an analytical framework for the behaviour of what we may call the *factional state*.

The basic idea can be explained fairly simply. Suppose that there are only two factors of production, capital (K) and labour (L), and that all individuals in the economy can be described by their respective capital/labour endowments $(k_i = K_i/L_i)$. The mean of the distribution of these individual k_i endowments will be the aggregate capital/labour endowment $K/L = k$ of the economy.[21]

Next we define the set of individuals who are decisive, in the sense that they can compete for the capture of the state and thus of economic policies subserving their interests. Suppose that initially all economic agents in the population form part of the decisive set of the polity and the political mechanism is democratic, with one man one vote, and the majority capturing the state. All voters vote their economic interests. Then, from the well-known median voter theorem, the median voter's capital/labour endowment k_m will determine the interests that will be served by the coalition of majoritarian interest groups who capture the state. If the distribution of individual factor endowments is symmetric, so that its median and the mean are the same, the median endowment will be identical to the average for the economy as a whole ($k = k_m$). Then from the law of comparative advantage we know that the income of the median individual will be maximized by free trade. If, however, the median individual's endowment is more (less) capital intensive than the average, the median voter's income-generating interests will be in a tariff (subsidy) on capital-intensive imports or a subsidy (tariff) on labour-intensive imports. Thus in this form of the pressure-group model what we need to know is the mean of the national factor endowment and the median of the distribution of the income-generating factor endowments of the set of decisive individuals.[22]

Let us next see how this model of the factional state can be linked to the three-factor, n-good open-economy growth framework we outlined in chapter 2. Recapitulating, in Fig. 2.4 we identified two (amongst many) efficient development patterns for two countries, E_L, where initial factor endowments were land-abundant, and E_A, labour-abundant.

Consider first the development path of E_A, the labour-abundant country, and ask if there are likely to be political pressures against maintaining an open trade regime in such a country. On the efficient development path, with the country developing according to its emerging comparative advantage, the returns to labour rise and those to capital fall.[23] If the factional state in such a country is captured by a group whose factor endowments are dominated by capital, there will obviously be pressures for protection. If, on the other hand, there is a majoritarian democracy, then the median voter in the population as a whole is likely to have a factor endowment which is dominated by labour, and hence will be close to the mean of the national factor endowment, and his interest will be in free trade.[24]

By contrast, consider the case of the land-abundant country depicted as E_L, and assume that the factional state is controlled initially by an oligarchy of landlords. The oligarch's median endowment of land to labour is likely to be greater than the average endowment for the economy as a whole. This implies that the interest of the median decisive individual in the oligarchic polity will be served by free trade. As the economy grows, with capital accumulating and population expanding, and if the polity is not expanded, the median endowment of the land and capital of the landed oligarchy will still be higher than the average of the economy, and so the oligarchy will still wish to maintain free trade.

However, suppose that over time, say with the introduction of manufacturing and the growth of the labour force, pressures grow for enlarging the polity, and a (populist) coalition, dominated by individuals with endowments of labour relative to capital or land greater than the mean endowment (K), comes to capture the factional state. Suppose this happens during the transition of the economy from region VI of Fig. 2.4 (where the wage was higher than in region II) to region V. During this phase, as relatively more labour-intensive manufacturing comes into the 'region of specialization', there will be inexorable downward pressures on the real wage. To prevent this outcome is in the interest of the median members of the enlarged polity (whose endowments are dominated by labour). This end may be achieved by placing a tariff on the more labour-intensive of the two goods produced in region VI, namely M_4. This will, *ceteris paribus*, raise the equilibrium capital–labour ratio in M_5, lower that in M_4, and raise the land–labour ratio in the production of the agricultural good A_2.[25] Thus the A_2 point will shift north-eastward (towards the T and K axis), the M_5 point will shift towards the K vertex, and M_4 towards the L vertex. This will enlarge the region of specialization VI, and allow the new endowment point which would otherwise have fallen in region V to remain in region VI, with a higher wage and lower rental rates on capital and land.[26]

Over time, however, for well-known reasons, the inefficiencies associated with protection will lower the efficiency of the economy. If this also leads to a lowering of the rate of capital formation relative to the labour supply, then the future transition to a lower real-wage economy will be accelerated.

Similar pressures for protection can be expected to arise in a factional state where the median individual in the ruling coalition of interests controlling the state has an endowment dominated by labour relative to capital or land, when there is a terms-of-trade improvement in a country whose exports are more capital-intensive than its imports. There will be downward pressure on the real wage, as the expanding capital-intensive sector creates an excess supply of labour, and excess demand for capital and land.[27] *Mutatis mutandis*, periods of terms-of-trade losses could also be periods where the interests of the median member of the enlarged polity would no longer be at odds with reduced protection. For the terms-of-trade decline would mean that the relative profitability of the more labour-intensive goods would rise, and this would enlarge the region of specialization in Fig. 2.4, where the more labour-intensive good would be viable at the continuing 'high' wage without protection.

This illustrates one way in which the model of the factional state can be combined with the three-factor, n-good open-economy model to analyse the deeper 'political economy' determinants of economic policies that impinge on growth and poverty redressal. Various other uses will be discussed when we synthesize the experience of our countries in later parts of this chapter.

5. Dynamic Interactions between Policies and the Polity

So far we have assumed that the policy stance of the government is coherent and that at each point in time its actions depend upon the maximization of some obvious maximand. But there is an important qualification. Many policies, however coherently conceived, may have unintended effects, which generate further policy responses which may or may not succeed in offsetting the unintended and presumably undesirable consequences. One example should suffice at this stage to clarify what we mean.[28]

Suppose the state inadvertently or because of pressure from its constituents increases its budget deficit. This can in general only be financed by foreign borrowing or by printing money. If the state increases the money supply and hence the inflation tax, it may encounter opposition from pressure groups who stand to lose from existing nominal-currency-denominated contracts. It is likely that the most vocal such group will be urban wage-earners. In response to their opposition the government may, instead of resolving its expenditure contradictions, introduce an additional policy instrument, namely price controls. Price controls have intended and unintended effects. The intended effects are to confer monopoly rents upon the interest group which motivated the intervention: those wage-earners who are able to buy goods at controlled prices are better off. The unintended effects are rent-seeking activities within commodity distribution and the emergence of grey or black markets. Agents earning (socially useless) rents in the distribution sector become a new interest group. Their interest is to maintain the controls upon which the sector depends for its existence. Thus the political pressure to maintain price controls is greater than that to introduce them. Moreover, the costs of the policy are now greater than anticipated from the intended effects. Action by a motivating pressure group (wage-earners), generates as a side-effect a new vested-interest group (rent-seekers). In turn, the black market may induce further government intervention. If the government perceives the breach of its controls as a threat to its power and prestige (or more simply as anti-state activity), then control enforcement will raise the risks, costs, and prices of black marketeers. This will both use more resources and increase monopoly rents within the black markets. The affront to honest citizens caused by rich black marketeers legitimizes continued state enforcement of price controls in addition to the support of motivating and vested-interest groups.

As an alternative to printing money, the government may borrow internationally. This temporarily sustains the exchange rate at a level which generates a matching current-account deficit. Once foreign borrowing limits are reached, the government has the choice between devaluation, which offends wage-earners and imported-input-using industrialists, and an exchange control regime. The easy way out may be to choose the latter. The effects of such a regime are well documented (Bhagwati, 1979, and Krueger, 1978). Foreign exchange often becomes used as an investment incentive, which in turn induces excessive capital intensity. As with price controls, the intervention not only rewards the motivating pressure group but creates new vested interests.

The remaining alternative to printing money or foreign borrowing, followed by some African governments, has been to raise taxation of export crops above the long-run revenue-maximizing level.[29] The subsequent tax-avoiding activity on the part of crop-producers (smuggling, reduced use of inputs, neglect of harvest) further reduces the state's options subsequently, as is vividly documented in the country study of Ghana's economic decline by Douglas Rimmer.

Enough has been said, hopefully, in this section to show both the relevance of the new political economy, and how it can be used to explain otherwise baffling public policies. We turn to the analysis of the political economy of our various countries in the following sections.

II. CLASSIFICATION OF POLITIES AND RELATIONSHIP TO OVERALL GROWTH PERFORMANCE

Table 6.1 provides the classification of countries into two broad types of polities, autonomous and factional, distinguished in the previous section. As emphasized in that section, no polity is likely to be a pure type of these different categories. Moreover, we also need to assign our countries into the even more elusive subcategories within these broader classifications. The following section provides a highly condensed justification for these classifications, based on the country studies, and also gives flesh to the nuances and the 'impurities' in the resulting rigid classification, which may otherwise seem drastically to simplify a complex reality.

Table 6.1. Typology of states

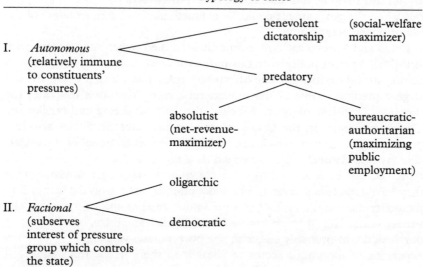

1. Classification

The classification of our three labour-abundant countries is clear. The polities of both Hong Kong and Singapore are, as Findlay and Wellisz emphasize, close to being those of a Platonic guardian state. Hong Kong is still a colony and is as close to the classical nineteenth-century ideal of a 'night watchman' state (providing essential social services and the maintenance of a system of private property rights) to be found anywhere in the world. Singapore, by contrast, though formally a democracy, has been dominated by a single party and its charismatic leader Lee Kuan Yew, who has consciously sought to act as a Platonic guardian, brooking no opposition and dismissing any pressures from factions. Finally, Malta is clearly a multi-party democracy, where the interplay of factional interests is of importance.

Amongst our group of land-abundant states, Costa Rica, Malaysia, and Uruguay are clearly democratic states, but with Uruguay going through a military break in the 1980s, which established a predatory state with elements of the authoritarian-bureaucratic state as well as some of those of a Platonic guardian state. Thailand is a mixture of the bureaucratic and revenue-maximizing predatory state, with the latter aspect predominant for much of our period, particularly during the period of Sarit's rule. More recently there seems to be a movement towards a factional state of the democratic variety. Turkey has been classified as an autonomous state of the Platonic variety largely because of the role of the Turkish military in maintaining the Platonic tradition of Kemal Atatürk. It has intervened when factionalism gets out of hand, to keep the government broadly in line within this Platonic framework. However, there have been prolonged periods when the government could be characterized as being factional of the pluralist democratic kind.

Brazil and Mexico are both primarily identified as predatory states, with Brazil falling more in line with the autocratic (revenue-maximizing) version during its substantial periods of military rule, and Mexico being by and large a predatory state of the bureaucratic type. Maddison describes the dominant political party in Mexico, the PRI, as being rather like the Communist party in the USSR in its workings. But Brazil has also had periods of government which can be categorized as factional of the oligarchic type. Colombia is characterized as a factional state of the oligarchic type, but which, according to Urdinola *et al.*, co-opts new entrants (once they have established their clout—most often by taking on the army) into the polity. Ghana is classified as a predatory state, mainly of the autocratic variety under Nkrumah and more latterly under Rawlings, but for part of our period was probably closer to the bureaucratic version, with an over-expansion of the public sector to allow it to share in the rents squeezed largely from the peasantry. Nigeria has been for the most part a factional state of the oligarchic variety, if we expand the notion of oligarchy to encompass members of dominant tribes. But, as Bevan *et al.* emphasize, it has had periods of rule by guardians, first during the first oil cycle, and most recently under Babangida.

In our intermediate-resource-endowment group of countries there are three states which are clearly factional states of the democratic variety, namely Sri Lanka, Jamaica, and Mauritius. Egypt is a fairly clear example of a predatory bureaucratic state. Madagascar, according to Pryor, is best described as a factional state of the oligarchic variety, whilst Malawi, given the predominance of Banda during our period, is best described as an autonomous state of the Platonic variety. Indonesia under Suharto is a mix of the autocratic and bureaucratic versions of the predatory state, with the autocratic element probably predominating. Finally there is Peru, which is a fairly clear example of a factional state of the oligarchic variety.

Table 6.2 lists these broad classifications of the polities of our different countries, where these countries are rank-ordered by their GDP growth rates over the 1950–85 period. The most important classification for our purpose is between autonomous and factional states. One pattern is evident. As we go down the growth rank ordering, factional states predomi-

Table 6.2. Growth and Type of Polity

Region		Growth rate	Autonomous state			Factional state	
			Platonic	Predatory		Oligarchic	Democratic
				Rev Max	Bureau Max		
As	Hong Kong	8.9	√				
As	Singapore	8.3	√				
As	Malaysia	6.9					√
As	Thailand	6.7		√			
LA	Brazil	6.6		√			
LA	Mexico	5.7			√		
ME	Malta	5.6					√
ME	Turkey	5.6	√				
ME	Egypt	5.4			√		
As	Indonesia	5.3		√			
LA	Costa Rica	5.0					√
LA	Colombia	4.7				√	
As	Sri Lanka	4.7					√
Af	Malawi	4.3	√				
LA	Peru	4.1				√	
Af	Nigeria	3.7					√
LA	Jamaica	3.3					√
As	Mauritius	2.9					√
Af	Madagascar	2.0				√	
Af	Ghana	1.3	√				
LA	Uruguay	1.1					√

Ranked in terms of growth performance. As = Asia, Af = Africa, LA = Latin America, ME = Middle East.

nate. Second, if we look at the 10 best performers with growth rates above 5% per annum and the remaining 11 countries, it appears the above-average performers are all autonomous states, with only two factional states (Malta and Malaysia) amongst them. Amongst autonomous states, as our political-economy model of the predatory state in the previous section suggested, both the benevolent Platonic guardian and the predatory-autocratic states do best of all. However, as Table 6.2 shows, of our three predatory-autocratic states (Thailand, Indonesia, and Brazil), Brazil suffered a growth collapse, as did all three of the predatory-bureaucratic states, namely Mexico, Ghana, and Egypt. Two of our oligarchic factional states, Peru and Nigeria, suffered growth collapses, whilst Madagascar had virtually no growth at all during our period. Moreover, three (Costa Rica, Uruguay, and Jamaica) out of eight of our democratic factional states suffered growth collapses.

2. Classification by Region and Resource Endowments

By region, of our seven Latin American and Caribbean states, a predominant number (five) are factional, a fact that many political scientists have noted.[30] In Asia, by contrast, four out of our seven states are autonomous. In Africa and the Middle East, autonomous states prevail (four out of seven), of which two are Platonic and two are of the predatory type.

In terms of our classification by resource endowments, two out of the three of our labour-abundant countries are autonomous states of the Platonic variety, and one, Malta, is factional. In the land-abundant category we have five autonomous and five factional states, and in the intermediate resource-endowment group three autonomous and five factional states. There does not seem to be any significant relationship between the type of state and a country's resource endowment.

Nor does a classification of states into military or non-military types provide any significant effects on relative economic performance, as documented in the detailed study by Berg and associates, in Psacharopoulos (1991).

3. Conclusion

The only conclusion at this highly general level of type of state and economic performance, therefore, seems to be that autonomous states, particularly of the Platonic and autocratic-predatory type, have had a better growth performance than bureaucratic-predatory and factional states in our sample of countries. Does this substantiate Myrdal's thesis about the different economic performance of what he termed 'hard' versus 'soft' states?[31] Myrdal defined his 'soft states' (of South Asia) as follows:

These countries are 'soft states' both in that policies decided on are often not enforced, if they are enacted at all, and in that the authorities even when forming policies, are reluctant to place obligations on people . . . [32]

or

When we characterize these countries as 'soft states' we mean that . . . national governments require extraordinarily little of their citizens. There are few obligations either to do things in the interest of the community or to avoid actions opposed to that interest.[33]

This presumably means that any state which does not fall into our autonomous state of the Platonic guardian variety would be classified as soft by Myrdal. From Table 6.2, it is apparent that three of the Platonic states are in fact amongst the above-average performers. But then so are a number of predatory and factional states. Though both theory and our empirical evidence do support the better performance of Platonic states, in practice such states cannot be willed into existence. Moreover, the successful economic outcomes in other types of polities show that a Platonic guardian state is not a prerequisite for growth and development.

We must therefore turn away from these very gross relationships to examine the more subtle interrelationships between the polity and economic performance revealed by our country studies. We begin by first discussing what may be termed the longer-term interrelationships, which are best examined within the three-factor open-economy growth framework of Chapter 2.

III. RESOURCE ENDOWMENTS, THE POLITY, AND ECONOMIC PERFORMANCE

Even the most autonomous government, whether Platonic or predatory, must take account of what we have termed the contestability of the natural monopoly—the state—which it controls. This contestability in the long run (from both internal and external contestants) will depend in part at least on the loyalty of the state's citizens. This loyalty will in turn depend partly upon ideology[34] (a factor we discuss in Chapter 7 below), but also on how the narrow material interests of the citizens are being served.

To the extent that the incomes of a country's citizens are determined by their factor endowments and factor prices, we can obtain some rough indication of the resulting pressures from the citizens on the state entailed by alternative development paths. This is turn should allow us to discern and explain some common responses by the polity to these underlying pressures from the economy. We have already provided in Chapter 2 an account of the likely path of changing factor prices for countries with initial conditions which are relatively land- or labour-intensive.

1. Land-Abundant Countries

We saw that below a critically high rate of capital accumulation in relation to population growth, the land-abundant country's growth path could (and in many of our land-abundant countries did) lead to periods of declining real wage rates. As, in the early stages of development in many countries, the majority of the population is likely to be endowed primarily with labour, this actual or incipient fall in the real wage of a majority of its constituents is likely to worry the government—whether factional or autonomous. For, if nothing else, it could portend the possibility of riots and discontent, which even if not a direct danger to the government's continuance could nevertheless be unpleasant, particularly if they take place in the capital city where those in the government reside. We would therefore expect that the governments of relatively land-abundant countries, particularly those with rapid population growth (which means that the factor-endowment path would veer less steeply towards the capital vertex in Fig. 2.4), would— irrespective of their character—tend to push public investment and capital growth well beyond their ability to finance it from domestically available sources.

Two alternatives are open to meet the budgetary shortfall. One has been foreign borrowing. This prevents current inflation. But if, as has been common in many of our growth-collapse countries, the returns to the investment financed are lower than the costs of borrowing, the seeds of a future debt crisis can thereby be sown. The other alternative is to monetize the deficit and hope that the inflation tax will bridge the financial gap. To prevent the consumption real wage from falling for some vocal constituents, partial indexation may be resorted to, the hope being that a big push in investment will eventually raise the equilibrium real product wage to equality with the (initial) disequilibrium consumption real wage. This high-wire act was attempted by Brazil in the 1970s, but failed.[35] In one way or another, land-abundant countries would thus attempt directly to engineer or indirectly to promote the big push in investment, which they rightly perceive is required to avoid the possibility of the declining-real-wage section of their incipient development path.[36] The government-mediated 'big push'-type growth policies of many of our land-abundant countries can be interpreted in these terms, whether they be the developmentalism of Kubitschek and later Neto in Brazil, or Echeverría and Portillo in Mexico, or in Turkey. By contrast, the only big push in any of our intermediate resource-endowment countries, in Madagascar, is largely explained by ideological factors.

A second characteristic of the likely development path of land-abundant countries discussed in Chapter 2 was the nature of their incremental comparative advantage, which could well be in the production of relatively capital-intensive manufactures in the early stages of development. This again is in conformity with the pattern of industrialization in some of our relatively 'large' land-abundant big-push countries, Brazil, Mexico, and Turkey. If, as is likely, these capital-intensive industries are also those which require relatively more sophisticated technological skills and lumpy investment, then a case could be made for their public promotion (though not protection)[37] on infant-industry grounds. However, the government for ideological reasons may believe that to use indirect promotional measures through the tax system will be inadequate. Also its ability to establish such promotional measures may be limited because of an underdeveloped or ineffective fiscal system (see Chapter 4). It may then choose both to protect such capital-intensive 'infants' and develop them within the public sector run by mandarins. This will lead to the well-know efficiency losses in developing capital-intensive industries in the public sector behind high tariff walls, flowing from the lack of competitive pressures and the politicizing of economic decisions. But the much larger efficiency losses arising from developing heavy industries not in line with a country's comparative advantage (as in India, for instance) may not occur. The *dirigiste* promotion of capital-intensive industrialization in such countries may therefore not damage their growth performance. This seems to be the explanation for the differing outcomes of similar *dirigiste* policies in three of our large land-abundant countries, Brazil, Mexico, and Turkey, as compared with another large but intermediate resource-endowment country, India.[38] Thus whilst India has had a rather poor growth performance, Brazil and Mexico have had a very good and Turkey a fairly good growth performance for most of the post-war period.

One other consequence of the desire for a big push to prevent real wage declines in these countries was the tendency in both Brazil and Turkey to use expansive macroeconomic policies to create 'pressure-cooker' type economies, with their endemic inflationary pressures. By contrast, Mexico, until the 1970s, maintained fairly conservative macroeconomic policies.

Finally, the inflationary policies in Brazil and Turkey can also be seen as a means of validating the real wage adjustments that were required on their development paths. Hansen shows explicitly within our three-factor open-economy framework how in Turkey a cost-push inflation was generated during the term of a democratic factional government (as part of the 'political cycle') as workers refused to accept the equilibrium real wage cut. This necessary cut in real wages was then enforced by the intervention of the Platonic guardians—the army in the 1970s.[39]

These long-run tendencies towards *dirigiste*, inflationary, and capital-intensive industrialization policies are not inevitable, however, in land-abundant countries. As the examples of two of our most successful land-abundant countries—Thailand and Malaysia—show, rapid capital accumulation (in both cases with domestic savings supplemented with large capital inflows) can allow the country to escape the declining-wage development path altogether. It can continue on a land-cum-capital-intensive path, exploiting its comparative advantage in the production of resource-intensive primary commodities, till the day when rising population shifts its endowment path (in Figs. 2.4 and 2.5) to a region where labour-intensive manufacturing becomes internationally competitive. Thailand seems to have reached this latter stage in the late 1970s, and its successful diversification into relatively labour-intensive manufactured exports is part of the reason for its successful and relatively steady growth during our period. Malaysia, by contrast, has more recently distorted its industrialization policies towards relatively capital-intensive import substitution. This is not because of the dynamic comparative advantage in capital-intensive industries of relatively high-wage land-abundant economies, but because these inward-looking policies are part of its policies of ethnic 'affirmative action' for the Malays.

Moreover, Malaysia's success (as compared with another factional but intermediate resource-endowed country, Sri Lanka) is based in large part on its having maintained an outward orientation in both foreign trade and investment despite the usual pressures of economic nationalism. This has been in part due to its pluralistic polity, in which the Malays have sought to limit the economic dominance of the Chinese by using the economic power of foreign direct investors as a counterweight. Hence, unlike the Sri Lankans, Malay economic nationalism aimed at the Chinese has not spilled over into expropriating foreign-owned natural resource investments, and thereby strangling the goose that laid the golden eggs.

Our remaining land-abundant countries, Costa Rica, Colombia, Ghana, Uruguay, and Nigeria, share the feature of still being primarily primary-product economies. Despite attempts at hothouse industrialization (except for Colombia), they have not been successful in industrializing, and at least in one case—Ghana—the big-push type of attempt at industrialization during the latter years of Nkrumah's rule was the proximate cause for its subsequent prolonged and tragic growth collapse. The predatory-bureaucratic nature of the Ghanain regime also meant that the implicit and explicit taxation of the peasant sector through the distorted pricing policies of the marketing boards, and inappropriate industrialization through the public sector, led to an implosion of the economy. In terms of our model of the predatory state depicted in Fig. 6.1, the predatory-bureaucratic state sought to meet the growing demand for public revenue to fund the needs of the burgeoning bureaucracy (including the public servants in para-statals) by raising the implicit tax rate to the point where the net-of-tax income of the rural sector falls to the subsistence level. At this stage the rural sector returns to subsistence, and the productive base and hence the source of revenue to keep the predatory-bureaucratic state going collapse. This seems to have been the story by and large of the Ghanaian post-Independence economy until the second Rawlings administration.

For the four remaining land-abundant countries, Costa Rica, Colombia, Uruguay, and Nigeria, the factional nature of their polity is of importance in explaining their economic performance. As our model of the factional state in the first section of this chapter emphasized, the crucial determinant of the long-run trends in industrialization, trade, and fiscal policies in a factional state will be the relationship of the factor proportions of the median voter in the polity to those of the economy as a whole.

In both Costa Rica and Uruguay, which have by and large been democratic states, the polity consists of the adult population. As the factor endowment of the median voter in these democratic polities has been increasingly dominated by labour relative to land, the median voters' interests were best served by policies which raised wages relative to the returns to land. Their increasing protection, and maintenance of over-valued exchange rates which implicitly taxed agriculture, can be explained in these terms.

In addition, their burgeoning welfare states, which are also in the interest of the median voter, are funded by explicit taxation of the rural 'goose that lays the golden eggs'. As such these countries can be characterized as having polities at odds with their comparative advantage, and their relatively poor economic performance (particularly in Uruguay) can be explained in these terms compared with some more successful land-abundant countries.[40]

Colombia, by contrast, is a factional state of the oligarchic kind. In the Colombian polity, the median factor endowment in its regionally diversified oligarchy has a predominance of land and capital specific to primary-product exports. This oligarchy can be expected to allow Colombia to develop successfully, as it has, in line with its comparative advantages. However, as with many other oligarchic states there is underlying pressure to expand the polity. The resulting populist pressures, apart from erupting into numerous violent episodes in the country's history, have also led the oligarchy to co-opt some of these populist interests by undertaking inward-looking trade and industrialization and welfare policies which are similar though not as extensive as in the other land-abundant fully democratic factional states of Uruguay and Costa Rica. As a result, the conflict between the polity and the economy's comparative advantage has been muted in Colombia, leading to a better economic performance than Costa Rica and Uruguay, both of which, unlike Colombia, suffered growth collapses in the late 1970s.

In the case of Nigeria, the factional nature of the polity, of an oligarchic kind but with elements of the pressures found in democratic factional states, invoked inter- and intra-tribal (largely coterminous with regional) competition for a share in the spoils of the rents accruing to the public sector from a primary-commodity boom—namely oil. The behaviour of the polity was thus very similar to that of the other factional state in which

primary-commodity rents accrued to the public sector (but in the intermediate resource-endowment group), Jamaica (which was clearly democratic). It is apparent that Nigeria behaved like other factional
land-abundant countries by going against the grain of its comparative
advantage, and that this tendency was accentuated by the disposal of the
windfall gains accruing to the public sector.

2. Labour-Abundant Countries

The most important feature of the development path of the land-poor,
labour-abundant country within the three-factor framework of Fig. 2.4, for
our purpose, it that is implies a progressive rise in wage rates and land rents.
Secondly, the comparative advantage of the country is fairly clear in moving
up the ladder of comparative advantage by successively increasing the
relative capital intensity of its exports as the capital–labour ratio in
the economy increases with capital accumulation. Except, therefore, in the
unlikely circumstance that the polity consists entirely of an oligarchy of
capitalists within a factional state, in most other cases we would expect no
inherent conflict between the polity and the economy such as has arisen in
some of our land-abundant countries. Moreover, as following the country's
comparative advantage is good not only for growth but also indirectly for
the alleviation of poverty and equity through the channel of rising real
wages, the efficient development path for such countries is likely to be a
relatively easy one. It is not surprising therefore that all three of our land-
abundant countries are amongst the top performers in terms of both growth
and equity in our sample of countries, despite differences in their polities
and ideologies.

The case of Malta is particularly instructive in this respect. A democratic
factional state, with politics and a socialist ideology similar to Manley's
Jamaica, Malta has nevertheless grown through the development of export-
oriented manufacturing industries like textiles, the growth of tourism, and
the boom in construction of homes for retired British families. Also, if its
strategic location is considered to be part of its natural endowment, the
socialist government of Dom Mintoff exploited this resource by obtaining
soft loans from Libya and Italy for capital-intensive port facilities which
provided services for China and the Soviet Union. It could thereby satisfy
the factional pressures from its powerful dock workers at low opportunity
cost. Meanwhile its labour-intensive orientation in the production of
tradables (which include the housing services for British expatriates)
yielded the same favourable development path as in our other labour-
abundant countries.

Finally, there is one other aspect of land-scarce, labour-abundant economies that should be noted. The land which exists, for instance, in Hong
Kong and Singapore is primarily urban land (real estate), and its rent

should rise (as it has) in the process of development. We would expect that if urban real estate was privately owned, and the distribution of such capital in land was unequal, then there would be a strong tendency in a factional polity to legislate rent controls. For the median voters' endowment would most likely not contain much real-estate capital, whilst if it were publicly owned there would be pressures for rent subsidies. Moreover, in a factional polity these implicit subsidies would have benefited the middle classes. Our two city-states, however, are Platonic guardian states, standing above these pressures, which have sought to equalize the effects of this implicit rise in land rents. Most of the land is publicly owned. The governments of both Singapore and Hong Kong have taken a major part in developing and leasing this land. Public investment in housing has been a major factor in equalizing what might have been strong unequalizing tendencies with rising urban land rents. In Singapore, for instance, about 84% of the population in 1985 was housed in units under the management of the public Housing Development Board; 75% of these public-housing residents had equity in the units, but 'their ownership rights are restricted, in comparison with those of owners of fully private property'.[41]

In Hong Kong, the government began to build low-cost housing estates in 1954 'and by the 1980s about half the population was housed in such estates . . . The government's housing program has gradually expanded into new town development, squatter factory resettlement and even home ownership schemes.'[42] But compared to Singapore, Hong Kong is more congested. This is due, first, to the continuance of private leases in the land in the New Territories, pre-dating the arrival of the British, which the colonial government has continued to honour. Moreover, unlike Singapore, the Hong Kong government offers no subsidy in its housing programmes. 'It has always operated under the rule that the capital costs of the program be financed out of recurrent revenue. As a consequence, tremendously high densities have been set as acceptable standards.[43]

In Malta, the third of our land-scarce countries, in the late 1960s the building boom associated with providing housing for British expatriates led to rising real-estate prices and housing costs, making it even more difficult for an ordinary Maltese family to find adequate accommodation.[44] This was a major factor in the defeat of the incumbent government and the following long reign of Dom Mintoff's Labour party, which greatly expanded welfare services—an expected outcome in a factional state, where the median endowment is dominated by labour. But as it maintained the principles of Gladstonian finance, the associated public expenditure was financed by taxation, and did not lead to the fiscal imbalances and macroeconomic crises typically found in many of our other countries which have increased social expenditures (see Chapter 5). But as the median voters' factor endowments are likely to be dominated by labour in Malta, it is not surprising that, despite its apparent *dirigisme* and the establishment of some inefficient import-substitution industries, Malta has, by and large, followed its dynamic comparative advantage very successfully through the growth of labour-intensive manufactured exports.

3. Countries with Intermediate Resource Endowments

As we have seen, the economic performance of this group of countries has been the most variable in our sample. Our three-factor growth framework would suggest two reasons for this.

First, unlike both the land-abundant and labour-abundant countries, the feasible pattern of industrialization in the intermediate countries is likely to be more flexible. Unlike the labour-abundant countries, where the limits of import-substituting, capital-intensive industrialization can become apparent fairly quickly, in these intermediate resource-endowed countries there may be some case for such industrialization—particularly if they are relatively large economies—as is the case in land-abundant countries. Thus the incremental comparative advantage of such countries may not be as self-evident as is the case for labour-abundant countries. With most states in the Third World since the Second World War having an ideological penchant for import-substituting industrialization (discussed in the next chapter), our intermediate group of countries may tend to foster inappropriate hot-house industrialization, with consequential damage to their growth and poverty-redressal performance. The very flexibility of feasible development paths in these countries make it easier to make errors in their choice.

Second, like the land-abundant countries (but unlike the labour-abundant ones), the nature of the polity could be important in determining the economic outcomes. In democratic factional states[45] where the median voter has a more labour-intensive endowment than the economy as a whole, there will be pressure for policies which artificially raise labour incomes either through protection or the expansion of the welfare state. The two prime examples of this in our sample of countries are Jamaica and Sri Lanka. Both have followed growth-retarding protectionist policies and expanded their welfare systems and bureaucracies, with damaging effects on growth performance and no marked improvement, *mutatis mutandis*, in poverty redressal. Like Uruguay and Costa Rica, these are countries in which the polity seems to be at odds with the economy (in terms of its comparative advantage). By contrast, our third democratic factional state, Mauritius, has in part escaped this trap by developing labour-intensive exports through its export processing zone. It may be useful to see how it has escaped the fate of other democratic factional states whose polity has not allowed them to develop in line with their comparative advantage. The major difference between Jamaica and Mauritius has been the (fortuitous?) establishment of the export processing zone in Mauritius at the beginning of its sugar boom in the early 1970s. The sugar planters invested their profits from the sugar boom in the EPZ; hence the basis of Mauritius's poverty-redressing and relatively efficient growth path was established. By contrast, the rents from the bauxite boom in Jamaica accrued to the public sector, where, given its factional politics, they were squandered in the promotion of inefficient import-substituting industry and the expansion of welfare services as well as public employment.[46] The major difference in the outcomes in these two democratic factional states, with similar pressures artificially to raise the labour income of the median voter, was that the major recipients of the windfall gains from the primary-commodity boom were the public sector in the poor case and the private sector in the case with the more favourable outcome.

There are two other factional states in our sample, both of the oligarchic kind—Peru and Madagascar. But Peru has strong elements of the type of pressures found in democratic factional states—at least during its 'democratic' phases. In Peru, the oligarchy of export interests which controlled the polity until the Velasco coup would, as it did, find it in its interests to maintain an open economy developing in line with its comparative advantage. However, with the enlargement of the polity, and thus with the shifting of the median voter's endowment towards a more labour-intensive bundle, we find the usual factional state's syndrome in a land-abundant country appearing. There is populist pressure towards *dirigiste* promotion of import-substituting industrialization in the public sector, as well as in the expansion of the bureaucracy and social expenditures. The resulting attempt to develop against the grain of its comparative advantage under the pressures of a populist polity has led to the expected dismal economic performance of Peru from the Velasco period onwards.

Madagascar's polity has impinged on the economy, both through ideology and interest. The socialism and nationalism espoused by Malagasy leaders is not much different from that of many other Third World leaders. However, Pryor emphasizes that the dominant interest group that in effect controlled the polity was an educated urban élite. It also came from the dominant ethnic group. As human capital was its dominant factor endowment, Malagasy policies were anti-rural, 'which skimmed off the potential agricultural profits and used them for urban investment such as the construction of universities in each province'.[47] The interests of this group were also served by the 'invest to the hilt' programme of import-substitution in industry through the public sector. The ensuing growth collapse can be looked upon, as in Ghana, as another example of killing the goose that laid the golden eggs.

This leaves us with three autonomous states—Malawi, Indonesia, and Egypt—in the intermediate resource-endowment category. Of these, Malawi is an autonomous state where Banda appears to be a Platonic guardian. Its creditable overall economic performance has been based on an outward orientation and on developing in line with its comparative advantage in agriculture. But without a sufficient voice, the smallholders have been neglected and this failure has meant that Malawi's creditable growth record has not been matched by sufficient poverty alleviation.

Indonesia, unlike Nigeria, after the initial calamitous economic perform-ance under Sukarno, has created an autonomous polity of the autocratic kind which has been successful in promoting both growth and poverty alleviation, through the successful management of the oil boom in the 1970s. This has largely been due to the influence of Western-trained technocrats who were by and large able to run the economy free from factional pressures, and in line with an implicit economic constitution which had exchange-rate convertibility and balanced budgets at its core. The resulting self-imposed fiscal and monetary constraints enabled the technocrats to resist the pressures from the polity to squander the oil windfall. Indonesia, therefore, shows by its example that a relatively autonomous state may be better able to manage oil windfalls, even if they accrue to the public sector, as compared with similar accruals in a factional state.

Finally, we have one predatory-bureaucratic state—Egypt. Hansen ar-gues that in the early 1920s Egypt's factor endowment was closer to the labour-abundant East Asian cases than the land-abundant Latin American ones.[48] Under the pluralist democracy (with more than just a touch of oligarchy) prevailing before Nasser, a combination of an agricultural (cot-ton) export-promoting and an inward-looking import-substituting industri-alization strategy was adopted and implemented. These were largely consensual (but not 'median') policies (with the voices of small farmers and workers hardly heard), initiated for reasons of economic nationalism. They were based on the early-nineteenth-century ideas of Friedrich List and the experience of Germany before the First World War, with infant-industry protection and partial state financing seen as the safe and fast road to economic development and independence. Moreover, with the 'green rev-olution' and multi-cropping having already been introduced in agriculture by the First World War, industrialization was seen as the only way to employ the growing population in the future.

These policies were continued under three sucessive autocrats after 1954, albeit with the emphasis in agriculture increasingly shifting towards import-substitution rather than exports. In this a 'basic needs' ideology played a crucial role. Post-war policies have been dominated by the massive nationalizations under Nasser, which transformed a predominantly private-enterprise economy into a mixed state-controlled one with all foreign trade and big businesses in industry, trade, transportation, and public utilities incorporated into the public sector. The pluralist system of political parties and organized interest groups was systematically destroyed and replaced with a de facto clientistic system, allocating spoils on a patron–client and crony basis. The spoils were largely based on the shortages arising from price controls. Under Nasser these spoils were largely associated with the nationalized enterprises and other public-sector activities. Under his followers they are to be found increasingly in the interstices between the public and private sectors, and domestic and foreign business, with consultancies and contract-fixing becoming a lucrative domain for resigning ministers, higher civil servants, and other dignitaries with connections. To buy off élite and popular pressures, an implicit 'social compact' was established by which the inherently weak rulers bought political acquiescence in return for consumerism, including privately financed, unlicensed consumer-goods imports, low-priced goods and services from agriculture and the public sector, heavily subsidized food, and employment guarantees in the bureaucracy for an accelerating flood of graduates from the over-expanded higher education system.

In terms of our model of the predatory state in Fig. 6.1, Egypt under autocratic rule has expanded the bureaucracy, many of whose members are little more than unemployed 'clients', way beyond the balanced-budget point. Windfalls in the form of foreign aid, rising oil prices, and emigrant remittances have for a time fortuitously saved the polity from the resulting inflationary growth collapse. If Egypt's strategic position in the Arab–Israeli conflict, and hence in the Cold War, is considered to be part of her resource endowments, then, like Malta, Egypt can be looked upon as having successfully exploited this advantage. But the *dirigisme* involved in the rent creation for clients and cronies has led to inefficiencies and an incipient fiscal crisis that only continued aid flows can avert.

Her relatively favourable economic performance until the early 1980s, which was very much based on luck, such as the windfalls and the skilful exploitation of the strategic position just mentioned, is unlikely to be sustainable in the long run, and from the mid-1980s the collapse has, according to Hansen, been lurking just around the corner. The subsidization of the urban populace and the pressures from the (skewed) 'median' interests in its polity have led to a variant of the social-expenditure expansions typical in land-abundant, factional states, as we have discussed earlier.

IV. THE POLITICAL ECONOMY OF REFORM

In this section we discuss two important questions which have been hovering in the background since our discussion of growth collapses in the last chapter.

The first concerns the movement from growth-retarding to growth- and poverty-redressing policies in many of our countries. The other side of the same coin is the failure to make this switch in some countries, or else the adoption in some of policies of economic repression. In discussing these cases of switches in policy regimes we need to identify if there is any learning process, with failed policies being ultimately replaced by better policies. If not, what is the configuration of interests and/or ideology in different types of polities which keeps the failed policies in place long after they are known to be dysfunctional by both the rulers and the ruled?

The second issue we discuss concerns the so-called 'path dependence' and unintended consequences of many policies, namely that once particular policies are in place they tend to have a momentum of their own because of the vested interests they engender. This is particularly serious in designing appropriate policies, for quite often they may have consequences which are very different from those intended by their progenitors.

1. Turning-Points

Table 6.3 lists the turning-points in policy regime that our authors have identified in our various country studies. There are in general two types of changes in overall policy regime which are apparent. First, in nearly all our countries, the first major turning-point was either at the beginning of our period, or else in the inter-war period, when most of our countries turned inwards and sought to promote import-substituting industrialization through *dirigiste* means. The second turning-point occurs at very different dates, and is usually associated with a partial or more complete switch in regime away from the *dirigiste* regime of the past to a more outward-oriented policy regime with greater emphasis on the use of the price mechanism and the private sector in resource allocation, and with reforms of the fiscal and monetary policy to secure macroeconomic balance.

A striking feature of the second set of turning-points is that they are invariably associated with macroeconomic crises. In understanding why this should be so, it is useful to seek the reasons for these macroeconomic crises, and then to ask if in the interest-based classification of our polities there are any predictable differences in how the different types of polities in our three resource-endowment categories will react. In this way we shall also be able to answer the question: how far can the turning-points be explained in terms of a learning process?

2. Crises

At its most general, a macroeconomic crisis occurs when domestic absorption is greater than domestic output. This excess absorption can be dealt with in only one of three ways. First, domestic expenditure can be cut. Second, domestic output can be increased. Third, foreign finance can be obtained to finance the actual or incipient balance-of-payments deficit that usually accompanies a crisis of excess absorption. Given the time-lags involved in raising output, the only realistic options are reductions of

Table 6.3. Turning-points in policy regimes and crises

Country	Turning-points (Nature of new regime: R = repressive, L = Liberal)		Dates of crises, if any	Nature and causes of crises (refers to period preceding the crises)
A. *Labour-abundant*				
1. Hong Kong	1950s	L	1950s	Trade embargo on PPR of China; end of entrepôt trade
2. Singapore	1965	L	1965	Break from Malaysian Federation; British withdrawal from naval base
3. Malta	1961	L	1961	Decline of British naval base
	1971	R/L	none	(election of Socialist government)
B. *Land-abundant*				
4. Malaysia	1956	L/R	none	(independence)
	1969	R/L	1969	(racial riots)
5. Thailand	1959	L	none	(Sarit's central decision)
6. Brazil	1945	R	none	(Vargas's economic nationalism)
	1964–66	L	1964	Balance-of-payments crisis
	1980s	L/R/L/R	1980s	Continuing macroeconomic and debt crisis
7. Mexico	1980s	L	1979	macroeconomic and debt crisis
8. Turkey	1929	R	none	Beginning of *étatism*.
	1960	R	1960s	Balance-of-payments crisis
	1980	L	1979/80	Macroeconomic crisis
9. Costa Rica	1959	R	none	(Entered Latin American Common Market)
	1982	L	late 70s	Balance-of-payments crisis
10. Colombia	none	L/R	throughout	
11. Nigeria	1973	R	late 60s	Civil war
	1985	L	continuing crisis	Squandering of oil rents; growth collapse
12. Ghana	1950		none	(independence)
	1959	R	none	(indeological promotion of public sector, industrialization)
	1966	L/R	periodic	balance-of-payments crises
	1983	L	1970s onward	nearly 2 decade crisis of growth collapse

Table 6.3. *Continued*

Country	Turning-points (Nature of new regime: R = repressive, L = Liberal)		Dates of crises, if any	Nature and causes of crises (refers to period preceding the crises)
13. Uruguay	1955	R	none	
	1973	L	1973	balance-of-payments crisis
C. *Intermediate*				
14. Egypt	1956	R	1956	Suez crisis followed by nationalizations etc.
	1974	L/R	periodic	Incipient fiscal crisis
15. Indonesia	1950		none	(independence)
	1956/7	R	1956/7	Balance-of-payments crisis following Korean boom; regional revolt.
	1966–7	L/R	1965	Hyper-inflation; Communist coup
16. Sri Lanka	1956	R	none	SLFP victory—*dirigiste* economic nationalism; inward-looking policies to favour Sinhalese adopted
	1977	L	periodic	Growth of unsustainable transfer state; incipient growth collapse
17. Malawi	1964	L	none	(Independence and rise of Banda)
18. Peru	1950	L	1950	Balance-of-payments crisis
	1967	R	1967	Balance-of-payments crisis; *dirigisme* under Velasco
			1975– periodic	continuing crisis of growth- and macroeconomy
19. Jamaica	1972	R	late 60s	Growing fiscal and balance-of-payments crisis
	1980	L	continuing	Growth collapse
20. Mauritius	1960	R	none	(independence)
	1971	L	none	(export boom and establishment of EPZ)
21. Madagascar	1972	R	none	Reaction against neo-colonialism; 'invest to hilt' programme leads to
	1983–4	L	1979–80	growth collapse, balance-of-payments problems

Source: Derived from the country studies.

domestic expenditure and/or access to increased foreign financing. But such finance is only likely to be made available if a credible increase in output is expected in the future. As most governments, except perhaps for the Platonic guardian type, are likely to have fairly high rates of time preference as compared with the socially optimal one (as judged by some outside neutral observer), they will attempt to cure this incipient deficit (as many in our sample of countries did) by following the third route of external financing. If the social rate of time preference is less than the cost of foreign borrowing, then time can be bought to allow a gradual reduction in expenditure or increase in output, and this gradualist approach to dealing with the crisis will be not only economically but also politically desirable. Why then have so many of our governments not been successful in following this route, and have instead been blown from their previous courses?

The reason turns on the nature of the expenditure-reducing and/or output-increasing policies that were required, and the credibility in the eyes of its foreign creditors of the government's ability to undertake these policies. There must also be a credible expectation that the rate of return on domestic assets will rise in the near future. This credibility is in turn related to the causes of the excess absorption.

In Chapter 5, we have identified an actual or incipient fiscal crisis as the proximate cause for most of the growth collapses that occurred in our sample of countries. There were also two broad types of reasons for these fiscal crises, both related to inflexibilities in public expenditure. The first were due to large developmental expenditure commitments in the pursuit of a big-push type of industrialization drive under the aegis of the public sector. The second were social-expenditure commitments which have been expanded beyond a sustainable level, either because their growth (based on demography and factional pressures) is faster than that in the explicit or implicit taxes required to finance them (Uruguay and Sri Lanka, for instance) or because the expectations of the growth of output and taxes on which they were based have been falsified (as in some of our resource boom-and-bust countries).

Cutting public expenditures of either sort raises obvious political problems for all governments, except perhaps for the rare Platonic guardian type. For, by increasing the actual or perceived unpopularity of the government, it increases the contestability of the state, as analysed in our political-economy model in Section I above. Similar problems, of course, arise with raising taxes.

But these unavoidable political costs of adjustment to the crisis have not prevented some countries from accepting them. Given their past reputation for undertaking adjustments, such governments (mainly in South-East Asia) have not had problems in obtaining foreign credit to enable them to undertake the (socially desirable) gradual domestic adjustments that are necessary to deal with the periodic adverse macroeconomic imbalances that they have faced. This is because their promises to adjust are credible. It may be thought that this is entirely due to the autonomous nature of these states. But as we have seen, we have examples of several autonomous states (including a Platonic one—Turkey) where such promises were not deemed to be credible. The question is why?

The answer must relate to deeper reasons for the fiscal crisis in most of these countries, which affect their political behaviour. These deeper sources of the fiscal crisis must also be an important part of the explanation why these 'incredible' states, often under the pressure of a lack of foreign finance, chose the radical course of a switch in their policy regime.

Most of the countries which switched policy regimes in the 1970s or 1980s had adopted varying degrees of *dirigisme* for reasons of ideology or interest. One notable effect of such *dirigisme* was the creation of politically determined entitlements[49] to current and future income streams for various groups in the economy (such as the deserving poor; industrial labour; regional interests; old-age pensioners; infant, declining, or sick industries—to name just a few). As these entitlements are implicit or explicit subsidies to particular groups, they have to be paid for by implicit or explicit taxation of other groups in the economy. However justifiable on grounds of social welfare, the gradual expansion of this 'transfer state' leads to some surprising dynamic consequences.

The gradual expansion of politically determined entitlements creates specific 'property rights'. The accompanying tax burden to finance them leads at some stage to generalized tax resistance, leading to avoidance and evasion, and to the gradual but inevitable growth of the parallel or underground economy.[50] This has been the case with both developed and developing countries in the past decade. Faced with inelastic or declining revenues but burgeoning expenditure commitments, incipient or actual fiscal deficits become chronic. These can only be financed by three means: domestic borrowing, external borrowing, or the levying of the inflation tax.[51]

Many countries, particularly those in Latin America, have tried all three—with dire consequences. Domestic borrowing to close the fiscal gap may crowd out private investment[52] and diminish the future growth of income—and thus the future tax base. The fiscal deficit may be financed by foreign borrowing for a time, particularly as in the mid-1970s, when real interest rates were low and even negative. But this form of financing is inherently unstable. The debt-service ratio can become unviable if, as in the late 1970s, world interest rates rise and the ability of the economies to generate the requisite export and fiscal surpluses to service the higher interest costs of publicly guaranteed debt is limited. This is often due to policy-induced distortions inhibiting exports—for example, the maintenance of over-valued exchange rates and high and differentiated effective rates of protection which are an indirect tax on exports—along with the difficulty in generating fiscal surpluses to match the interest on the debt. Thereupon, foreign lending can abruptly cease, leading to the kind of debt crisis which has plagued Latin America in the 1980s. The third way of financing the deficit, through the use of the inflation tax, is also unviable over the medium run, for it promotes a further growth of the parallel economy and a substitution of some indirect or direct form of foreign-currency-based assets for domestic money as a store of value. The tax base for levying the inflation tax thus shrinks rapidly.

With taxes being evaded, domestic and foreign credit virtually at an end, and private agents having adjusted to inflation to evade the inflation tax, the government finds its fiscal control of the economy vanishing. The growth of entitlements, moreover, reduces the discretionary funds available to the government, and it is discretionary funds which give the government power. It may not even be able to garner enough resources to pay the functionaries required to perform the classical state functions of providing law and order, defence, and essential infrastructure. This dynamic process, whereby the expansion of the transfer state leads to the unexpected and very un-Marxian 'withering away of the state', has rarely reached its full denouement, although in some of our countries (Peru, Ghana, perhaps Brazil) it may be close.[53]

But well before things come to such a dire pass, attempts are usually made to regain government control. Two responses by the government are possible—an illiberal and a liberal one. The former (which is rarely observed) consists of a further tightening and more stringent enforcement of direct controls. Tanzania provides an example of this response. If this tightening is effective, however, and the private utility of after-tax income received from legal productive activity declines to the level at which untaxed subsistence activities are preferable, producers may seek to escape the controls by ceasing to produce the taxed commodities altogether. The tightening and enforcement of controls could lead to an implosion of the economy.[54] The government might then find that as producers return to untaxable subsistence activities, the very production base over which it seeks control has shrunk or disappeared. This appears to have happened in Ghana.

The more usual response is to regain a degree of fiscal control through some liberalization of controls on the economy. Typically, however, these liberalization attempts are half-hearted and include some tax reform, monetary contraction, and some measure of export promotion. Their aim is to raise the economy's growth rate as well as the yield from whatever taxes are still being paid, and to improve the debt-service ratio, in the hope that this will lead to a resumption of voluntary foreign lending. But unless the underlying fiscal problem (which is largely that of unsustainable public expenditure commitments) has been tackled, these liberalization attempts have usually been aborted.[55]

Without a commitment to reducing unviable levels of entitlements, the liberalization attempts have tended to worsen the fiscal situation. With the lowering of tax rates and lags in supply response, revenues do not rise and may even fall initially. The necessary reductions in money supply to contain inflation reduce the limited seigniorage previously being extracted.[56] Government unwillingness to allow either public or private enterprises to fail entails absorbing the deficits of public enterprises as well as any newly sick units taken over, as the liberalization exerts competitive pressures on unviable firms. Moreover, where liberalization has been accompanied by large public or private capital inflows (often to finance the public-sector deficit), there has been an appreciation of the real exchange rate, sometimes accompanied by inflationary pressures arising from inappropriate nominal-exchange-rate policies (as in Sri Lanka—see Lal, 1985b). This appreciation thwarts potential export growth, so that, as capital inflows diminish, the incipient fiscal deficit is once again reflected in a chronic balance-of-payments problem, which the government then seeks to control in the old unviable ways—and the liberalization process is reversed.

The above patterns, which are observed in many of our countries, have also been observed in a large number of other countries which have attempted to liberalize in the 1980s. The major lesson to be drawn is that liberalization is often undertaken to gain fiscal control, but if nothing is done to rescind unviable public-expenditure entitlements a stabilization-cum-balance-of-payments crisis eventually emerges which undermines the attempt to liberalize the economy. It would thus seem that a *sine qua non* of a sustainable liberalization attempt must be the prior establishment of fiscal control through a reduction of unsustainable public-expenditure commitments.[57] The stabilization of the economy, no less than any prospective liberalization, also entails a willingness to overcome the resistance of those whose entitlements will be rescinded.

The political problem governments most usually face when considering economic liberalization is that the pressures from the potential losers from the liberalization tend to antedate the support which will subsequently be provided by all those who gain. As can be readily shown, under many circumstances there will be losers in the short run from the changes in relative prices and/or disabsorption flowing from the stabilization and structural adjustment programme, particularly those whose relative returns on sector-specific human and physical capital fall as a result of these changes. If the liberalization is sustained, however, it is likely to yield higher and more efficient growth in income, which will benefit most groups in the economy. Given the government's own rate of discount (which may be much higher than that of society), even if the resulting purely technocratic economic welfare integral is positive, policy-makers may still be reluctant to undertake the reforms if they feel uncertain about their ability to survive the political pressures during the transition.[58]

From the long-drawn-out (and continuing) crisis in some of our countries—for instance, Ghana, Nigeria, Jamaica, Peru, Brazil—it is evident that
the danger of economic collapse must appear to be imminent before the
bitter pill of a change in policy regime is swallowed. As most of these
countries are factional states, or autonomous ones moving towards factional ones (such as Brazil), it is the resistance to changing the factional or
pressure-group equilibrium created by past *dirigisme* which stands in the
way of what appears to everyone to be a desirable change in regime. In these
circumstances factional and non-autocratic autonomous states may not be
able to make the desired and desirable switch in policies, until the complete
breakdown of the society and economy poses the danger of an even greater
loss of future income streams than that resulting from the rescinding of
their existing entitlements. It is not surprising, therefore, that many of the
crises which have led to a lasting change in policy regime have been
accompanied by hyper-inflation (see Chapter 5).

In this context it may also be useful to note that the tolerance of different
countries to similar rates of inflation may differ. Thus it appears from our
sample of countries that the tolerance of most of our Asian and African
countries is lower than that of those in Latin America. This is likely to
reflect the longer history of chronic inflation in many countries of Latin
America, and the official or unofficial methods that economic agents have
then devised in these countries to cohabit with inflation. It may therefore
require astronomical rates of accelerating inflation before the crisis becomes
sufficiently serious for the polity to undertake the rescinding of the entitlements it has created in the past, which is the only long-lasting cure to
reverse the actual or incipient growth collapse.

The importance of acute inflationary crises as a symptom of a deeper
crisis in a country's political economy, as well as a trigger for its reform,
would thus seem to be an important empirical stylized fact that emerges
from our country studies. But there is one other important reason why only
a crisis may be able to resolve the contradictions in a *dirigiste* polity subject
to some factional pressure. It is important enough to require its own
subsection.

3. Path-Dependent Policies and Political Economic Equilibria

There are a large number of examples in our country studies of what can be
termed path-dependent policy outcomes. By this we mean that a particular
policy is implemented for some reason (whether good or bad from the
viewpoint of social utility is immaterial), and it creates entitlements for
some groups, which are then politically difficult if not impossible to rescind
if future circumstances change. This then puts an effective constraint on
future policy choices. Moreover, in reaction to these newly created group
entitlements, other interests might, if they have the characteristics of

Becker's successful interest groups discussed in the Introduction, manage to get policies adopted which in turn yield entitlements to them. As this process of obtaining entitlements favourable to oneself through the political process proceeds, the future policy choices of the government can become more and more constrained until it has no room left for manoeuvre, as any policy will hurt one or other vested interest. Moreover, it may be widely perceived that these publicly protected and often publicly financed entitlements impair the efficiency and hence growth performance of the economy, yet nothing can be done about it. In these circumstances only a crisis of the sort discussed in the previous section can resolve the resulting paralysis of the polity and the economy.[59]

As illustrations we provide a few examples from our country studies. Hansen describes how, after the Suez crisis, the 'weak' autocracy in Egypt created an *étatiste* economy, aimed at reducing the economic power of the old oligarchy. This led to the creation of a patron–client system in which the élite became privileged clients of the ruler, mainly through employment in the bureaucracy and nationalized and state industries. When the system was supposedly liberalized under Sadat, the economic system did not change, only its locus altered to the interstices of the public and private sector. At the same time, running through the whole of the post-Suez period was the social compact with the urban masses, based on providing open-ended food subsidies and public-sector employment to university graduates. The incipient fiscal crisis which the inefficiencies associated with the allocative consequences of the patron–client system entailed for future growth, and the open-ended public-expenditure commitments from the social compact, have been avoided as a result of various forms of good luck—not least the large foreign-aid inflows following the Camp David accord. But the current conjuncture is not sustainable. It may require an economic crisis of Latin American proportions to resolve the resulting paralysis in the country's political economy.

The second example is Uruguay. Starting from Batlle's establishment of a welfare state in 1904, a politico-economic system has been established in Uruguay which has created a dynamic distributional conflict (without any resolution to date) between urban and rural interests. It has promoted an expansion of public expenditure and the patronage and clientism it supports, without the ability to react to external and internal shocks in an efficient manner, as these would entail costs for urban interests. There is thus a discernible political cycle in Uruguay, which the post-1973 military intervention, according to the country authors, has not altered to any marked degree. This form of interaction between a polity and economy at odds with each other, yielding a dynamic politico-economic cycle, is to be found in many other countries.[60]

A third example is from primary-product-exporting countries with predatory-bureaucratic and factional states, which have seen an overextension of their public sectors (Sri Lanka, for example).

We now consider the model of the predatory state outlined in the first section of this chapter. Suppose that in the bureaucrat-maximizing version of this model the bureaucracy has been expanded beyond the net-revenue-maximizing point (L_g in Fig. 6.1). This may be due to the ideological preferences of the rulers, or more likely to the rent-seeking by the bureaucracy, who will seek to garner the state's surplus by exerting pressure to expand government expenditure. Findlay and Wilson (1987) describe this as the Parkinson–Niskanen law that 'Government expenditure expands to absorb all the resources available to finance it'. (Public employment will expand to L_g, well beyond the socially optimal level L_g^* in Fig. 6.1.)[61] But in this process, with the increase in the provision of public goods, output could be higher than when the state is run by an absolute monarch or colonial power.

We assume that the major source of public revenue is export taxes on primary-commodity exports. We can expect that export prices and that portion of the government's revenue derived from export taxes fluctuate. Once it has hired public servants *pari passu* with the past rise in its revenues, it will be very difficult for the government to cut either current wages or the numbers of public employees when revenues fall. It is thus likely to face a fiscal crisis with every fall in export prices (as $R(t)$ shifts downward and $E(t)$ remains unchanged in Fig. 6.1).[62]

One way for the government to insulate itself from the incipient fiscal crises that the periodic collapse in export prices generates is to put some of the revenues at good times in foreign financial assets—reserves—to be used to finance fiscal expenditures when times are bad. But for most Third World states this has proved virtually impossible because of the pressures that arise for the state to spend the windfalls, most often by hiring the relatives of its retainers.[63] To the extent that this increase in public employment also exerts upward pressure on the economy-wide wage rate, the benefits from such spending could be quite wide and hence popular. But the dangers of succumbing to these pressures is the fiscal crisis during the downside of the export cycle.

For the government to escape its fiscal bind, an alternative policy would be to insulate the financing of public employment from fluctuating export-price-induced changes in revenues. It could use the export tax proceeds in good times to import capital goods to set up import-substitute industries (beyond the natural extent that that has occurred because of the income growth associated with export-led expansion). As long as the domestic demand for the products of these industries is relatively stable, and the products can be sold at a domestic price sufficient to cover variable costs (including, above all, the public labourers employed), the government will have succeeded in providing a stable form of financing public employment from the fluctuating export-tax revenues. It should be noted, however, that as efficiency *per se* is not a goal of this net-revenue-or bureaucrat-maximizing state, there is no presumption that the government will choose to maximize the profits of these public enterprises. As far as it is concerned, the capital imports financed by the export taxes may well be a sunk cost, and as long as the public employees are paid out of the net revenues (taking account of other variable costs), the state would have achieved its predatory objectives. By conventional or social accounting criteria, however, most of these public enterprises could well be making losses.

Alternatively, the government may seek to augment its revenues by providing tariff protection to private-sector manufacturers. The revenue from the tariff supplements that from the export tax. As long as there is a subsistence sector in the economy which fixes the supply price of labour to the rest of the economy, the introduction or expansion of import-substituting industries will merely mean a reduction in output and employment in the subsistence sector, with no change in the wage rate (or in the rents accruing to landlords in the export sector if agriculture is commercially organized rather than being based on peasant household labour).[64] Thus the state may face no costs in the short run from this policy of promoting some 'hothouse' import-substituting industrialization through a combination of both public and private enterprises and the institution of some non-prohibitive revenue tariffs.

This seems to be the story (by and large) of the economic development of Thailand since 1950, of Ghana till about 1961 during the Nkrumah regime, and of Tanzania from colonial times to Nyerere's regime until the Arusha Declaration in 1967. Though introducing well-known inefficiencies in production, the mild protection to promote (in particular public-sector-based) industrialization could have been justifiable from a net-revenue- and public-employment-maximizing government's viewpoint. This is true even if account is taken of the indirect effects on government revenue from the well-known Lerner symmetry theorem, whereby an import tariff is equivalent to an export tax. The revenue tariff is likely to affect export output and hence export tax revenue adversely. But this loss in mean export revenues (in the face of fluctuating export prices) has to be balanced, from the public-employment-maximizing government's viewpoint, against the stability (reduction in the variance of tax revenues) thereby bought in the financing of public employment—essentially by substituting a more stable form of revenue generation through public-enterprise-based industrialization. There will be some optimum level of public-enterprise-based industrial-employment provision at which the costs and benefits will be equal.

Suppose, however, that on the basis of current ideas (Ghana under Nkrumah)[65] or ideology (Nyerere's Tanzania after the Arusha Declaration),[66] the state seeks to promote public-sector-based industrialization beyond this 'optimal' level (that is, in terms of Fig. 6.1, it seeks to increase public employment beyond the level L_g). As tariffs on final consumer goods become prohibitive, and most intermediate and capital goods are allowed into the country at low or zero tariffs to provide high effective protection to public-sector industries, tariff revenue is likely to fall, as is the revenue from export crops, with the increase in the direct and indirect tax burden on the sector.

Then, given the interrelationship beween export taxes, export output, the rural–urban terms of trade, and the subsistence-based supply price of peasant household labourers, there could be a complete elimination of the peasant export crop, as the peasants move to the untaxable subsistence sector. They may still be willing to exchange domestically produced manufactured import-substitutes for some subsistence output. But this reduced domestic demand for import-substitutes may no longer be sufficient to employ all the existing 'entitled' public-sector workers. Furthermore, the collapse of domestic export supply, following its increased direct and indirect taxation, will have led to a reduction in the supply of foreign exchange needed to finance even the imported intermediate inputs required by domestic industry. The state will have a fiscal, foreign-exchange, and domestic-output crisis. The predator will have a problem of surviving, as it has virtually destroyed its prey. This seems very much to be the story of Ghana after 1961, Madagascar since the late 1970s, and Tanzania in the 1970s and 1980s.[67] But this denouement is not inevitable, as the more favourable outcome in Thailand illustrates, which, however, requires a pragmatic and non-ideological state.[68]

NOTES

1. See Weldon (1953: 46), Oakeshott (1975: essay III), and Held (1983: introduction). Oakeshott (1975: 231) succinctly outlines the new 16th-century notions of state and government as follows: 'a state recognized as persons and groups of persons associated in terms of a law and of judicial decisions and administrative orders authorized by law, and government recognized as a "sovereign" authority'.

2. Weldon (1953: 50) notes:

   There really is a difference between 'State' and 'Society', but it is not philosophically important and not at all what the exponents of social solidarity would like it to be. 'Society' is used to stand for something less organized than an association. We talk more here of customs, habits and traditions and less of rights, laws and obligations . . . It is perhaps convenient to make a technical distinction of this kind between less and more highly organized groups of people, but there seems to be nothing more to it than that. We do not need the fiction of a social contract to explain the transition from society to State.

3. The identifying marks of a state and government as they appeared by the end of the 16th century in Europe are outlined by Oakeshott (1975: 70): 'A State was recognized to be a contingent, destructible association of human beings inhabiting an identified territory and joined in being the subjects of a ruler or government.'

   The status of subject was a matter of law, not of choice or chance or even territorial domicile. The ruler was a single inalienable authority without superior, partner, or competitor. He was the custodian of a 'law of the land' prescribing the rights and obligations which identified subjects, of a judicial system, of authoritative procedures for making and amending this law and for raising public revenue. He was endowed with discretionary authority to make executive decisions and to appoint officials and agents, and he was in sole command of military forces.   (ibid. 228–9)

4. See Findlay and Wellisz (1993, ch. 1, fig. 1.1, p. 5).
5. See Bauer (1971) for a trenchant critique of attempts to provide historicist accounts of economic history. Also see Popper (1957) and Berlin (1954) for more general critiques of historicism.
6. This schema was developed and applied in Lal (1989*b*); it is also adopted in Wellisz and Findlay (1988). Also see Findlay (1988).
7. Arrow (1963). Dropping Arrow's condition of 'universal domain' concerning preferences would allow majority rule to emerge. Thus if preferences are single-peaked the 'paradox of voting' of which Arrow's results are an example will not occur. See Inman (1987).
8. Sabine (1951: 721).
9. The following is based on Lal (1988*a*: ch. 13.2).
10. See Perry Anderson (1974). But as he notes (ibid. 429):

    The term 'absolutism' [is] in fact . . . technically a misnomer . . . [for] one basic characteristic . . . divided the absolute monarchies of Europe from all the myriad other types of despotic, arbitrary or tyrannical rule, incarnated or controlled by a personal sovereign, which prevailed elsewhere in the world. *The increase in the political sway of the royal state was accompanied, not by a decrease in the economic security of noble ownership, but by a corresponding increase in the general rights of private property.* The age in which 'absolutist' public authority was imposed was also simultaneously the age in which 'absolute' private property was progressively consolidated. It was this momentous social difference which separated the Bourbon, Habsburg, Tudor or Vasa monarchies from any Sultanate, Empire or Shogunate outside Europe.

11. Hobbes (1914: 64–5).
12. Demsetz (1967: 347).
13. North (1981: 64).
14. This model was developed in Lal (1984), and its fullest exposition is in ch. 13.2 of Lal (1988*a*).
15. Baumol *et al.* (1982).
16. North (1981).
17. Findlay and Wilson (1987).
18. Wellisz and Findlay (1988) show how, if the predatory sovereign is completely

unconstrained in the rate of tax he can charge, his optimum policy for maximizing his surplus is to leave the net-of-tax average product (in the model) in agriculture at the 'state of nature' level (i.e. the slope of the ray OY^0—not drawn—which is less than the slope of OY), and to employ the output-maximizing number of public servants L_g.

19. Quoted from Hendel (1953: 68).
20. Mayer (1984).
21. As Mayer notes (ibid. 974):

> It is convenient to describe capital-labor ownership ratios by k(e), where e is an index such as that $0 \leqq e \leqq 1$. All people with no capital ownership are indexed with $e = 0$, and e rises as the capital-labor ownership ratio rises; that is, $k(0) = 0$, $\delta k/\delta e > 0$, and $k(1) = k_{max}$. The proportion of factor owners with the same factor ownership is defined as $f[k(e)] \geqq 0$, where $\int_0^1 f[k(e)]\, de = 1$, as $\int_0^1 k(e)f[k(e)]\, de = K/L = k$ the economy's capital-labor endowment ratio is the mean of the factor-ownership distribution.

22. There is a well-known difficulty with the median-voter model, for in a set-up in which each voter has a negligible influence on the outcome, there is no rational basis for voting at all!
23. The rents on land will of course be rising.
24. See Findlay (1988), for various historical applications of a similar factor-endowment, open-economy model on to the polities of various countries. Also see Rogowski (1989), for an application of the Stolper–Samuelson type of theory to explain the origins of various historical cleavages in the polity.
25. This follows from the simple observation that with the tariff on M_4, producers will attempt to expand the output of M_4. As it is the most labour-intensive good being produced, an expansion in its output will create excess demand for labour, and excess supply of the land and capital used in producing the other two goods. Full employment of the three factors will only be maintained as producers switch to using more land- and capital-intensive techniques, which save on labour in producing the other two goods M_5 and A_2.
26. See Deardoff (1984: 740).
27. See Lal (1989b) for the details.
28. This is based on Paul Collier's appendix to the Myint–Lal research proposal. Also see Lal (1987b) for a schematic account of some of the unintended consequences of excessive government intervention.
29. Ghana, of course, did all three (see Rimmer, 1992).
30. Thus Wynia (1984: 30) states

> that Latin American states are weak—in large part because of the lack of any agreement on the rules of the political game. This leads to a diversity of political rules within many Latin American countries and is primarily the product of a failure to solve the fundamental problems of political legitimacy that arise in all political systems.

> This lack of consensus on a legitimate set of political rules means that 'groups and individuals who discover that the prevailing rules favour others more than themselves may prefer to undermine the rules rather than obey them' (ibid. 36).

31. Myrdal (1968), particularly ch. 18, sections 13 and 14.

32. Ibid. 895.
33. Ibid. 896.
34. North (1981) has emphasized the importance of ideology in explaining the historical evolution of states and their economic institutions in Europe.
35. See Lal and Maxfield (1993) for a discussion of this issue within the explicit three-factor Krueger–Leamer model we have adopted in this book.
36. An essential element in maintaining the consumption real wage (as distinct from the product wage) in practice has been exchange-rate manipulation, and policies of wage indexation. We take up these aspects in the later parts of this chapter.
37. The distinction between 'protection' and 'promotion' of industries is due to Little, Scitovsky, and Scott (1970). As is well known, the infant-industry argument for protection is based on a second- or third-best cure for a distortion in domestic capital markets where the private rate of discount is higher than the social. The first-best cure is a subsidy to promote investment in general. If this is infeasible for public-finance reasons, it may be desirable to protect the infant industry as a second-best measure.
38. Though this is not part of our sample of countries, see the study by one of the present authors of this case, Lal (1988a).
39. For Brazil, Lal and Maxfield (1993) show how the two big pushes there in the post-war period were motivated by the desire to prevent the incipient real wage declines on their development paths. With the resulting crisis, stabilization programmes had to be undertaken, which enforced the real wage cuts required to restore equilibrium.
40. The most dramatic case of the phenomenon of a land-abundant factional state where the median voter's endowment is dominated by labour, and hence the polity is at odds with the country's comparative advantage, is Argentina. See Lal (1989b) for a disussion of the Argentinian case.
41. Findlay and Wellisz (1993: 125).
42. Alwyn Young: *Hong Kong* (mimeo: 151).
43. Ibid. 99.
44. Findlay and Wellisz (1993: 270).
45. With a two-party system, it should be said. As is well known, in a multi-party system the median voter theorem may no longer hold.
46. Of course, the Mauritius government could have taxed the sugar planters' profits. It chose not to do so. Similarly, the Jamaican government could have chosen to hand back its bauxite rents by lowering taxes. It chose not to. So there is a difference in choices of public policy which remains to be explained.
47. Pryor (1991: 394).
48. Hansen (1992: 461).
49. The creation of politically determined entitlements which became property rights is not peculiar to developing countries. The entitlements in the US associated with Social Security and Medicare are of the same sort. See Lal and Wolf (1986) for a fuller discussion.
50. The most dramatic example in our sample of countries is Ghana (see Rimmer, 1992). A similar denouement seems to be occurring also in Peru (see Webb, mimeo, and de Soto, 1989).
51. The US has also, of course, followed these three means. Again, the contrast is

not between developing and developed countries, but in the similarities and differences in the political economy of countries which run across the rich–poor country divide.

52. See Blejer and Khan (1984).

53. For example, in Peru it is estimated (by de Soto, 1989) that in the late 1980s over 70% of the labour force in Lima worked in illegal activities, the government had no domestic or foreign credit, inflation was high and rising, and nearly 70% of the money supply was in dollar-denominated deposits.

54. See Collier *et al.* (1987), for such an interpretation of recent Tanzanian economic policy and its outcomes.

55. Some examples are the Sri Lankan 1977 liberalization episode (see Lal and Rajapatirana, 1987), the 1978 Argentina liberalization (see Nogues, 1981, and Calvo, 1986), and the latter part of the 1974 Uruguay reform episode (see Hanson and de Melo, 1985).

56. At the end of a period of hyper-inflation, however, the demand for money will increase, as will the seigniorage associated with any increase in money supply to meet this incremental demand for the newly stable money.

57. Unless, of course, there are sufficient underemployed domestic resources, so that an expenditure-switching policy such as a devaluation can rapidly increase aggregate supply and thence public revenues by the required amount.

58. The 'optimal' subsidy route for cushioning the transition for losers does not make much sense in this context, for it assumes an omnipotent and omniscient government. The political difficulties we are emphasizing arise precisely because the government does not possess these attributes. Moreover, even if the government were able to implement this gradual adjustment policy, such a policy may not be time consistent and hence feasible.

59. The recent upheavals in Eastern Europe, the Soviet Union, and to some extent China, leading to their attempts to liberalize their repressed economies, can also be interpreted in these terms.

60. The starkest example is of course Argentina; see Lal (1989*b*) for a model of this dynamic distributional conflict.

61. Thus Coulson (1982: 33) writes of the adverse effect on economic performance of the recent expansion of the bureaucracy and its *de facto* take-over of the state in Tanzania:

> The contradiction which has not been recognized is that of implementing a radical program with a 'bureaucratic bourgeoisie'—the servants of the state (with an obvious interest in expanding its services) in the paradoxical position of controlling the state. Either a section of the bureaucracy will have . . . to pursue a more ruthless capitalist accumulation or else the workers and peasants will have to use Nyerere's ideology to take control of the state through democratic organizations. . . . By 1980 it was clear that Nyerere and the Tanzanian leadership would countenance neither alternative, and that the contradictions and stagnation of the 1970s were likely to continue.

62. See Levin (1960) for a detailed discussion of this aspect of the export economy.

63. The one important exception in our sample of countries is Indonesia under Suharto.

64. See Findlay and Wellisz (1984).

65. See Killick (1978) for an interpretation of irrational *dirigiste* economic policies under Nkrumah which emphasizes that they were influenced by and based on the development economics current at that time. Rimmer, however, argues that the latter merely rationalized policies which Nkrumah had decided to undertake for reasons of economic nationalism.

66. See Coulson (1982) for a discussion of the ideological factors underlying Tanzanian policy.

67. See Rimmer (1992); also Ansu in Harberger (1984), Pryor (1991), and Collier *et al.* (1987).

68. Not seeking to expand public employment beyond the sustainable level L_g in Fig. 6.1 (quadrant I).

7

Ideas, Ideology, and Economic Policy

THE previous chapter has emphasized the long-term interactions between the initial resource-endowments of our countries and their polities. In delineating the factors which influenced long-term policy formation in this context, we have mainly emphasized the role of interests. We cannot, however, ignore the role of ideas and ideology as determinants of policy. This is our task in this chapter. It will also provide us with an explanation both for why countries have adopted seemingly dysfunctional *dirigiste* policies and for when and why they reverse them.

I. TWO RIVAL VIEWS OF THE STATE AND SOCIETY

As indigenous political traditions in most of the non-Western world have been snuffed out by those deriving from the West, it is not surprising that it is two alternative Western conceptions of the state and its relationship to society which are now in contention world-wide.

In a brilliant historical analysis of the origins of the Western state, Michael Oakeshott (1975) has argued that these two conceptions of the state have deep roots in Western thought. One view, which goes back to ancient Greece, views the state as a *civil association*. The state is seen as the custodian of laws which do not seek to impose any preferred pattern of ends (including abstractions such as the general (social) welfare, or fundamental rights), but which merely facilitate individuals to pursue their own ends. This view has been challenged by the rival conception of the state as an *enterprise association*, a view which has its roots in the Judaeo-Christian tradition. The state is now seen as the manager of an enterprise seeking to use the law for its own substantive purposes, and in particular for the legislation of morality. The classical liberalism of Smith and Hume entails the former, whilst the major secular embodiment of society viewed as an enterprise association is socialism, with its moral aim of using the state to equalize people.

Oakeshott (1993) notes that as in many other pre-industrial societies, modern Europe inherited a 'morality of communal ties' from the Middle Ages. This was gradually superseded from the sixteenth century by a morality of individuality, whereby individuals came to value making their own choices 'concerning activities, occupations, beliefs, opinions, duties and responsibilities' and also came to approve of this 'self-determined conduct' in others. This individualist morality was fostered by the gradual breakdown of the medieval order which allowed a growing number of people to escape from the 'corporate and communal organization' of medieval life. But this dissolution of communal ties also bred what Oakeshott terms the 'anti-individual', who was unwilling or unable to make his own choices. 'The counterpart of the agricultural or industrial entrepreneur of the sixteenth century was the displaced laborer; the counterpart of the free thinker was the dispossessed believer'. Some were resigned to their fate, but in others it provoked 'envy, jealousy and resentment. And in these emotions a new disposition was generated: the impulse to escape from the predicament by imposing it upon all mankind'.[1] This the anti-individual sought to do through two means.

The first was to look to the government to 'protect him from the necessity of being an individual, to make the choices on his behalf which he was unable to make for himself'. A large number of government activities, epitomized by the Elizabethan Poor Law, were devoted from the sixteenth century onwards 'to the protection of those who, by circumstance or temperament, were unable to look after themselves in this world of crumbling communal ties'.[2]

The anti-individual, secondly, sought to escape his 'feeling of guilt and inadequacy which his inability to embrace the morality of individuality provoked'[3] by calling forth a 'morality of collectivism', where ' "security" is preferred to "liberty", "solidarity" to "enterprise" and "equality" to "self-determination"': every man is recognized as a debtor who owes a debt to "society" which he can never repay and which is therefore the image of his obligation to the "collectivity".[4] Both the individualist and collectivist moralities were different modifications of the earlier communal morality, but with the collectivist morality in addition being a reaction against the morality of individualism which had emerged soon after the Middle Ages.

This collectivist morality inevitably supported the view of the state as an enterprise association. Whilst this view goes back to antiquity, few if any pre-modern states were able to do more than 'to maintain peace and order, to guard the laws and customs of the community, when necessary to organize defense, when propitious to embark upon conquest or migration, and to deal with social and economic change when they produced an emergency'. For resources were rarely available even to undertake these basic tasks of government successfully, let alone to undertake any enterprises. 'The main circumstance that prevented the activity of governing's being, or being thought proper to be, an activity of enterprise was not any abstract principle, but the conspicuous lack of power to be enterprising.'[5]

This changed with the creation of centralized 'nation-states' by the Renaissance princes and the subsequent Administrative Revolution, as Hicks has labelled the gradual expansion of the tax base and thus the span of control of the government over its subjects lives.[6] Governments now had the power to look upon their activities as an enterprise. Oakeshott (1993) identifies three versions of the collectivist morality such an enterprise association has since sought to enforce.

Since the truce declared in the eighteenth century in the European wars of religion, the major substantive purposes sought by states seen as enterprise associations are 'nation-building' and 'the promotion of some form of egalitarianism'. These correspond to what Oakeshott calls the productivist and distributionist versions of the modern embodiments of the enterprise association, whose religious version was epitomized by Calvinist Geneva, and in our own times is provided by Khomeini's Iran. Each of these collective forms conjures up some notion of perfection, believed to be 'the common good'. Of these three versions Oakeshott notes:

first a 'religious' version, where 'perfection' is understood as 'righteousness' or 'moral virtue'; secondly a 'productivist' version, where 'perfection' is understood as a condition of 'prosperity' or 'abundance' or 'wealth'; and thirdly a 'distributionist' version, where 'perfection' is understood as 'security' or 'welfare'. These three versions of the politics of collectivism succeed one another in the history of modern Europe. . . . And in our own time the politics of collectivism may be seen to be composed of a mixture in which each of these versions has its place.[7]

In the Third World the jealousy, envy, and resentment of the kind which bred the European anti-individualist were not merely based on the dissolution of the previous communal ties that industrialization and modern economic growth entails, but also, these being post-colonial societies, such emotions were strengthened by a feeling amongst the native élites of a shared exclusion from positions of power during the period of foreign domination. Gellner (1983) has argued that the resulting nationalism is a natural response in all societies moving from the cultural homogeneity of traditional, rooted and socially immobile agrarian societies, to mobile mass societies; the social mobility being both required by and promoted by industrialization.

It is not surprising therefore that the dominant ideology of the Third World came to be a form of nationalism associated with some combination of the productivist and distributivist versions of the state viewed as an enterprise association. This was moreover aided and abetted by the

crudest of all the voices of lordship, in which European mentors addressed the emergent so-called states first of South America and later of Africa. Our disposition to recognize what is going on in terms of the constitutions (not the engagements) of governments and of techniques of ruling (not modes of association) has persuaded us that our gifts to these new states have been 'liberal' constitutions and a model for an apparatus of ruling, and we are sometimes surprised at their indifference to them. But what they have learned from us is an understanding of a state as a compulsory corporate association and the notion of ruling as the management of a corporate enterprise which they call 'nationalism'. What these states have never heard is the voice of civil association because we ourselves long ago suffered it to be confused with the 'liberal' concern for constitutional devices. When the President of Malawi said 'I don't care what the world calls me, a dictator or what, my job is to develop this country', he spoke in a European voice.[8]

Historically, both the secular collectivist versions have led to *dirigisme* and the suppression or control of the market. For

in the 'productivist' version . . . individual choice was to be removed from the activity of production and . . . replaced by a cooperative activity directed and managed by a central authority; in the 'distibutivist' version, individual choice was to be removed from the activity of distributing the available wealth: the market was to be replaced by a central distributing authority, and the principle of distribution was one of 'equality'.[9]

II. ECONOMIC NATIONALISM

Not surprisingly, therefore, a common ideological feature of all our countries, with the single exception of the only colony in the sample—Hong Kong—is economic nationalism. Its economic manifestation is the common desire to industrialize, often through *dirigiste* means, which is to be found in all our countries.[10] The one exception, as emphasized by Pryor, is Malawi under Banda, who, whilst being a nationalist, has unlike most of his peers emphasized the importance of agricultural growth for his country. Haunted by memories of colonialism (as in most African and Asian countries) or their perceived inferiority with reference to the Western metropolitan powers (as in most countries in Latin America), most Third World governments considered their limited industrial base to be the major reason for their relative lack of power in their dealings with the West. Industrialization is then seen as an essential basis both for their self-respect[11] and for waging modern wars, and its promotion as the chief means to overcome that inherent military weakness which led to their subjugation in the past by superior Western arms. In this context, the *dirigiste* example of the Soviet Union was found particularly attractive (though not necessarily its Communism), since it was deemed to show how a weak and poor underdeveloped country industrialized through planning and became a great power within one generation.[12]

The nationalist desire to assert national independence is also reflected in a common suspicion of free trade and of foreign capital (Banda in Malawi and Lee Kuan Yew in Singapore being notable exceptions). The danger for the rulers is that dependence on these foreign transactions may be used to subvert or weaken, through direct or indirect pressure, the internal hold of the rulers over the ruled. This threat of direct or indirect subversion is then seen as a means of putting pressure on the medium-sized or small powers to change a course of policy 'which the national interest—or the interest of its leaders—would appear to require'.[13]

Nationalism as an idea is thus a Western import into the Third World. It arose as an ideology in Europe as the Romantic reaction to the universalist, rationalist schema of the Enlightenment, and its view that man's relationship to the surrounding world is purely manipulative.[14] It initially arose as the reaction of wounded German pride, following the French Revolution and the success of Napoleon's armies, 'against the French cultural domination of the Western world'.[15] Though nationalism, both in Europe and more recently in the ex-colonies, was in part the reaction of actual or potential élites to military defeat, this can by no means be considered a sufficient explanation for this new idea to have arisen. For as Kedourie and Berlin have emphasized, throughout history the cultural or political pride of various peoples has been wounded without entailing a nationalist response. The special ingredient which led to the nationalist response was the rapid modernization of traditional societies. This modernization was imposed by leaders who were by no means Romantics—such as Frederick the Great in Prussia, or Peter the Great in Russia—to acquire the modern material basis of economic and, more importantly, military power. The same response was elicited by the westernization imposed by colonialism or by those indigenous élites which sought to imitate the West (for instance, the Japanese after the Meiji Restoration) in our time.

This modernization disrupted traditional ways of life, and

left men, and especially the most sensitive among them—artists, thinkers, whatever their professions—without an established position, insecure and bewildered. There is then an effort to create a new synthesis, a new ideology, both to explain and justify resistance to the forces working against their convictions and ways of life, and to point in a new direction and offer them a new centre for self-identification.[16]

But as Plamenatz (1973) has emphasized, the resulting nationalism was of at least two different types, which he labels 'Western' and 'Eastern'. The former was that of the Germans and the Italians, the latter that of the Slavs, the Asians, and the Africans. The major difference was that, whereas the Western nationalists already had the cultural appurtenances and skills to put them on a par with the French and English, the 'Eastern' nationalists have had to re-equip themselves culturally with the ideas and practices of an alien civilization.

Moreover, nationalism in Asia and Africa has grown within the arbitrarily defined territorial boundaries of the colonial state. This was no accident. For it was within these colonial boundaries that the West had succeeded in erecting a state:

a legal and administrative entity which worked, an entity which the West had succeeded in identifying with the nation. As nationalists they felt secure inheriting such an entity and felt challenged to preserve this entity and make it strong, just and prosperous as the colonial power had never done ... It is perhaps fitting that nationalism which began as anti-western should end by throwing off western rule in the name of the most western institution of the new order.[17]

Thus, whereas the task as seen by German, Italian, and to some extent Slav nationalists was to create a state for a pre-existing cultural and political nation, most African and some Asian nationalists inherited and cherished states created by colonialists, within which they have since sought to create a modern nation.

As a result, Afro-Asian nationalism, unlike that of the West, has involved two sets of ambivalent rejections: 'rejection of the alien intruder and dominator who is nonetheless to be imitated and surpassed by his own standards, and rejection of ancestral ways which are seen as obstacles to progress and yet also cherished as marks of identity.'[18]

After its repudiation of the militarist attempt to challenge the West, Japan has emerged as the only country to succeed in this contorted balancing act in establishing a state with a modern identity rooted in traditional culture.[19] Many of the nationalist élites of the Third World are still struggling to find ways of achieving their primary objective of securing their power and prestige against any future challenge either from external foreign intrusions of from any internal subversion by the upholders of the traditional societies they seek to remould. They are all aware of the need both for economic progress and for the making of nations out of their subject people, so that they can better defend their sovereignty.

The economic nationalism common to most Third World governments can thus be seen as the desire to modernize, where the modernizers have often considered themselves to be a minority charged with the task of forcing the people to be free. But the nationalism and *dirigisme* they have then espoused in subserving this end, through the promotion of economic development as well as the development of a truly national consciousness, has proved to be a double-edged sword.

The process of economic development which all Third World élites seek to foster involves profound changes over time in existing patterns of income distribution, where the latter is not to be thought of in the purely statistical sense, but in terms of what happens to the incomes (and status) of particular households over time. Even without any marked change in the statistical measure of this distribution, economic growth is likely to lead to a considerable and often rapid shuffling of the relative economic position and prospects of particular individuals and households. In a genuine nation-state, the ensuing resentment of the losers may be mitigated by the solace they may find in the accompanying national gains. The resentment is, therefore, unlikely to turn into the deadly conflicts to be found in the pseudo-nation-states of the South, with their ancient and still pervasive cleavages of race, religion, or tribe, where these shufflings can be so easily identified as the humiliation of one sub-nationality by another. The nationalist rhetoric of the political élite can then rebound (as it has done quite often in the recent past) into demands to dismember the territorial state, whose preservation was the prime end for which nationalism had been conjured up in the first place.[20]

Early German and Italian nationalism was largely integrative and economically beneficial, both because of the larger common markets created out of the German and Italian principalities, and because of the partial containment of political discontent arising from the distributional shuffling involved in economic development. By contrast, 'Eastern' nationalism, seeking to build a nation out of the sub-national groups within an inherited state, can lead to a breaking up of the common market, with all its attendant economic damage. Not surprisingly, therefore, it is in the relatively ethnically homogeneous polities of East Asia that nationalism has performed the integrative emotional and economic function that it did in the West. In the more fragile and pluralistic polities of South-East Asia, South Asia, and Africa, by contrast, nationalist rhetoric used to gain independence from colonialism has created as many problems of national integration as it was hoped it would solve.

Nor has the type of *dirigisme* espoused in many Third World countries proved helpful in establishing an economically progressive nation-state. This is in part because of the Enlightenment strand in this form of *dirigisme*, which has come to be associated with the notion of planning—a term that, like 'socialism', seems to have as many different meanings as adherents. Though for some socialists planning is synonymous with Soviet practice, this form of detailed material-balance planning has not—outside India— been adopted by the South.[21] However, two aspects of Soviet practice have struck a deep chord and been embodied in the economic policies of many of these countries. The first is a suspicion of the price mechanism, accompanied by attempts to supplant or control its working. The second is a suspicion of international trade and a preference for the forced industrialization (usually termed 'self-reliance') seemingly so successfully pioneered by the USSR. This suspicion of foreign trade was not purely ideological, but the lesson drawn from the effects of the inter-war collapse of world trade on the economies of those countries most integrated into the world economy.

As a result, the economic policies of many Southern countries have involved supplanting the price mechanism by bureaucratic allocative mechanisms in the form of price controls, industrial licensing, exchange controls, and quantitative restrictions on foreign trade. These policies have now become synonymous in these countries with planning. The harm that this irrational *dirigisme* has done to the end of promoting growth as well as equity (an aim shared by all types of socialists) is documented in our country studies.[22] In practice, therefore, the type of *dirigisme* usually adopted has made promotion of the economic progress required to provide the material basis for the desired national self-autonomy all the more difficult.

However, in many of our countries, the government at some stage realized the dysfunctional nature of its past *dirigisme* and changed course in the 1960s and 1970s (Singapore, Thailand, Indonesia, Uruguay, Turkey), whilst others did not do so until much later (Sri Lanka, Ghana, Nigeria), and some only did so after the end of our period of study (1985) (Peru, Madagascar). The question then arises: What are the circumstances in which governments alter policies which experience has taught them no longer serve the twin purposes of economic development and national integration? A historical review of the rise and fall of mercantilism and the subsequent rise and fall of economic liberalism is useful in answering this question.

III. NATION-BUILDING AND THE RISE AND FALL OF MERCANTILISM

Whilst our political-economy models have by and large emphasized the importance of self-interest (of the rulers or the pressure groups, or the 'median voter') in determining the policies pursued in the Third World, the previous section has emphasized the importance of ideology, in particular the universal appeal of economic nationalism in most developing countries. The aim of this economic nationalism, we have argued, can be broadly described as 'nation-building'. This aim is very similar to that expressed by the absolute monarchies in Europe after the Renaissance. It is no accident that, like current Third World rulers, they too thought *dirigisme* was the means to build cohesive nation states.

The mercantilist system which provided the foil for Adam Smith's great work arose, as Eli Heckscher has shown (in his monumental study *Mercantilism*), from the desire of the Renaissance princes of Europe to consolidate their power by incorporating various feuding and seemingly disorderly groups, which constituted the relatively weak states they inherited from the ruins of the Roman empire, into a nation. Its purpose was to achieve 'unification and power', making the 'State's purposes decisive in a uniform economic sphere and to make all economic activity subservient to considerations corresponding to the requirements of the State'. The same nationalist motive also underlay the very similar system of mercantilist industrial and trade controls that were established in much of the post-war Third World.

In both cases the unintended consequences of these controls, instituted to establish order, was to breed disorder. As economic controls became onerous, people attempted to escape them through various forms of evasion and avoidance. In the post-war Third World, as in eighteenth-century Europe, *dirigisme* bred corruption, rent-seeking, tax evasion, and illegal activities in underground economies. The most serious consequence for the State was an erosion of its fiscal base and the accompanying prospect of the un-Marxian withering away of the state. In both cases economic liberalization was undertaken to restore the fiscal base, and thence government control over what had become ungovernable economies. In some cases the change-over could only occur through revolution—most notably in France[23]

To understand this process it is instructive to examine the rise and fall of *dirigisme* in Europe from the sixteenth to the nineteenth century.

Historians of economic thought recognize that mercantilism provided the first relatively systematic set of economic-policy prescriptions.[24] These are important for our purpose, because, as is increasingly being realized,[25] the policies of many Third World states—with their industrial regulations, state-created monopolies, import and export restrictions, price controls, at cetera—are very similar to the mercantilist policies adopted by the absolutist states of Europe after the Renaissance.[26] This is no accident.

One of the main objectives of the various mercantilist regulations was to grant trade privileges as royal favours in exchange for revenue to meet the chronic fiscal crisis of the state—a problem of the sixteenth and seventeenth centuries shared by many countries of the modern-day Third World. Another was to extend the span of government control over the economy to facilitate its integration. But the system collapsed under the administrative burden it created. As Keynes pointed out:

Above all, the ineptitude of public administration strongly prejudiced the practical man in favour of laissez-faire—a sentiment which has by no means disappeared. Almost everything which the state did in the 18th century in excess of its minimum functions was, it seemed, injurious or unsuccessful.[27]

The consequences of the regulations and controls, particularly on internal trade and industry, were similar to those observed in many developing countries—corruption, rent-seeking, tax evasion and the growth of illegal activities in burgeoning underground economies.[28] The processes that caused mercantilism to be replaced by economic liberalism for a brief period in the mid-nineteenth century are beyond the scope of this discussion. But the consequences of the new policy prescriptions are of some importance.

Paradoxically, the new-found economic liberalism (although short-lived) achieved the goal sought by mercantilism:

Great power for the state, the perpetual and fruitless goal of mercantilist endeavour, was translated into fact in the 19th century. In many respects this was the work of laissez-faire, even though the conscious efforts of the latter tended in an entirely different direction.

The result was attained primarily by limiting the functions of the state, which task laissez-faire carried through radically. The maladjustment between ends and means was one of the typical features of mercantilism, but it disappeared once the aims were considerably limited. In laissez-faire they consisted, indeed, only in certain elementary and unavoidable functions of foreign policy, defence, legislation, and the administration of justice, nicknamed by Carlyle 'Anarchy plus the Constable'. Disobedience and arbitrariness, unpunished infringements of the law, smuggling and embezzlement flourished particularly under a very extensive state administration and in periods of continually changing ordinances and interference with the course of economic life. It was because the regime de l'ordre bore this impress that disorder was one of its characteristic features.[29]

The resulting framework for economic policy can be described as economic liberalism, in the original sense of the term and not in the sense of social democracy used in the mid-twentieth century, at least in the US.[30]

But the ensuing period of economic liberalism during the nineteenth century's great Age of Reform was short-lived, in part due to the rise of another substantive purpose that most European states came to adopt—the egalitarian ideal promulgated by the Enlightenment. Governments in many developing countries also came to espouse this ideal of socialism. The apotheosis of this version of the state viewed as an enterprise association were the Communist countries seeking to legislate the socialist ideal of equalizing people. The collapse of their economies under similar but even more severe strains than those that beset less collectivist neo-mercantilist economies is now history. But the desire to promote egalitarianism through state action still lingers on as part of social-democratic political agendas in many countries.

The locus and nature of the argument of those who want to use the state to promote egalitarianism has, however, shifted in a subtle way. In the past such activists, who sought to transform society through state action, usually argued in favour of some form of revolution whereby the anointed would seize power and irreversibly transform society, if necessary by indoctrination to create a New Man.[31] With the revolutionary route at least tarnished by the hideous outcomes in Communist countries—which even fellow-travellers now concede—a new constitutional mania[32] has set in. This emphasizes substantive social and economic rights in addition to the well-known rights to liberty—freedom of speech, contract, and association being amongst the most important—emphasized by classical liberals. It seeks to use the law to enforce these rights, based partly on needs, and partly on the 'equality of respect' desired by a heterogeneity of self-selected minorities differentiated by ethnicity, gender, and/or sexual orientation. But no less than in the collectivist societies that have failed, this attempt to define and legislate a newly discovered and dense structure of rights (including for some activists those of non-human plants and animals) requires a vast expansion of the government's power over people's lives. Their implementation moreover requires—at the least—some doctoring of the market mechanism.

IV. THE RISE AND FALL OF ECONOMIC LIBERALISM

The evolution of economic thought on appropriate public policy has followed (if not led) these political tides. It is useful to outline these, to set the subsequent policy conclusions of this book in context.

Mill defined explicitly the policy prescriptions of classical economic liberalism. Thus it is useful to look at the justifiable government interventions listed in his *Principles*. He begins his chapter 'Of the Grounds and Limits of the Laissez-faire or Non-interference Principle'[33] by distinguishing two types of intervention. The first he calls *authoritative* interference, by which he means legal prohibitions on private actions. Mill argues on moral grounds that such prohibitions should be limited to actions that affect the interests of others. But even here 'the onus of making out a case always lies on the defenders of legal prohibitions. Scarcely any degree of utility, short of absolute necessity, will justify a prohibitory regulation, unless it can also be made to recommend itself to the general conscience'.[34]

The second form of intervention he calls *government agency*, which exists 'when a government, instead of issuing a command and enforcing it by penalties, [gives] advice and promulgates information . . . or side by side with their [private agents] arrangements [creates] an agency of its own for like purpose'.[35] Thus the government can provide various private and public goods, but without prohibiting competing private supply. The examples Mill gives are banking, education, public works, and medicine.

Most of the government interventions Mill allows belong to this second category. But he warns against their costs: they have large fiscal consequences; they increase the power of the government;[36] 'every additional function undertaken by government, is a fresh occupation imposed upon a body already charged with duties'. so that 'most things are ill done; much not done at all,'[37] and the results of government agency are likely to be counterproductive. In a passage that is prophetic about the structure of many public enterprises in developing countries, he writes:

The inferiority of government agency, for example, in any of the common operations of industry or commerce, is proved by the fact, that it is hardly ever able to maintain itself in equal competition with individual agency, where the individuals possess the requisite degree of industrial enterprise, and can command the necessary assemblage of means. All the facilities which a government enjoys of access to information; all the means which it possesses of remunerating, and therefore of commanding the best available talent in the market—are not an equivalent for the one great disadvantage of an inferior interest in the result.[38]

On these grounds he concludes: 'few will dispute the more than sufficiency of these reasons, to throw, in every instance, the burden of making out a strong case, not on those who resist, but on those who recommend, government interference. Laissez-faire, in short, should be the general practice: every departure from it, unless required by some great good, is a certain evil'.[39]

But Mill also provides a bridge to the ideas that were later to undermine economic liberalism. The most important of these was the socialist ideal of equality, which was later used to develop a powerful antidote to the liberal tradition through Marxism and was implemented as state socialism by the Bolsheviks. Thus Mill allows various forms of government agency, many of which echo what later came to be recognized as causes of market failure, that prima facie could justify appropriate government intervention. Such causes might be externalities in the provision of basic education and public services (like lighthouses), and the need to supervise financial institutions against fraud, or to resolve various forms of what today would be called Prisoners' Dilemmas. Mill also cited the relief of poverty (in the sense of destitution—see Chapter 1) as another possible reason for government intervention:

The question arises whether it is better that they should receive this help exclusively from individuals, and therefore uncertainly and casually, or by systematic arrangements in which society acts through its organ, the state.

Hence, he argued,

the claim to help, . . . created by destitution, is one of the strongest which can exist; and there is *prima facie* the amplest reason for making the relief of so extreme an exigency as certain to those who require it, as by any arrangements in society it can be made. On the other hand, in all cases of helping, there are two sets of consequences to be considered; the consequences of the assistance, and the consequences of relying on the assistance. The former are generally beneficial, but the latter, for the most part, injurious; so much so, in many cases, as greatly to outweigh the value of the benefit. And this is never more likely to happen than in the very cases where the need of help is the most intense. There are few things for which it is more mischievous that people should rely on the habitual aid of others, than for the means of subsistence, and unhappily there is no lesson which they more easily learn. The problem to be solved is therefore one of peculiar nicety as well as importance; how to give the greatest amount of needful help, with the smallest encouragement to undue reliance on it.[40]

This is a prescient summary of both the attractions and pitfalls of welfare programmes, which has since been validated empirically, as we shall see in Chapter 9.

Indeed, nowhere in Mill's authoritative text on nineteenth-century economic liberalism do we find any hint that its principles worked against the state, or the poor, as has been charged by modern thinkers.[41] It is important to recognize, however, that although liberalism granted these important exceptions 'to the *practical maxim*, that the business of society can be best performed by private and voluntary agency',[42] what Keynes called the 'laissez-faire dogma'[43] had become entrenched amongst the political classes. But this dogma was not without its uses. As Heckscher notes:

Free competition, individualism and the limitation of state encroachment often became pure dogmas among practical men of affairs and politicians . . . without any conscious rational foundations. That such a normative outlook existed is, in itself, by no means a criticism of laissez-faire. *Some norm or other is always behind conscious action, for every action presupposes such a conception of the norm as, in itself, is not demonstrable.* Here it was a question, in fact, not of science but of economic policy, that is not of thought but action.[44]

This liberal 'disposition towards public affairs', to use Keynes's phrase,[45] did not outlast the resurgence of economic nationalism and socialism which arose in Europe towards the end of the nineteenth century, and grew in importance after the First World War.[46]

Diverse social and intellectual trends, including important advances in scientific economics, led to the subsequent development in the post-1930s world of what one of us has labelled the *dirigiste* dogma.[47] The various forms of discretionary government intervention most cogently justified on grounds of 'market failure', within the Arrow–Debreu paradigm, provided the intellectual ballast for a new form of mercantilism, particularly in the Third World.[48] Can anyone doubt that the ensuing mercantilist view of social causation also underlies our modern-day 'optimal' tax theory, planning in its various forms, and the discretionary use of public action to correct the perceived ills of private agency? In the modern variant of mercantilism, of course, the objective of economic policy is no longer the 'welfare of the state', but the welfare of the citizens as summarized in a social welfare function *laid down by the state*. Heckscher writes: 'The underlying idea of mercantilism may be expressed as follows: people should be taken as they are and should be guided by wise measures in the direction which will enhance the wellbeing of the state. No one was more explicit in this view than Mandeville (1723).' 'Private vices', he observed, '*by the dexterous management of a skilful politician* may be turned into public benefits'.[49] The consequences of the neo-mercantilist practices that the *dirigiste* dogma has engendered in the Third World (and in its macroeconomic aspects in the First World),[50] not to mention in the wholly centralized socialist states of the Communist world, are very similar to those that helped undermine the mercantilist states of seventeenth- and eighteenth-century Europe. The contemporary reaction (as in the past) has been to move toward economic liberalism (to varying degrees), in large part to gain state control over unmanageable economies. This recent world-wide movement towards economic liberalism, embracing governments of all political complexions, has been labelled a new Age of Reform by an acute observer, David Henderson, from the vantage point of the OECD.[51] But it is still progressing half-heartedly, in part because the *dirigiste* dogma continues to have a hold on the minds of the 'thinking', or (as Mrs (now Lady) Thatcher has labelled them) the 'chattering' classes. There are a number of reasons for this state of affairs.

The first is self-interest. Enlightened government intervention (the neo-mercantilist objective) requires experts.[52] The rise of the professional classes is well documented in Britain.[53] 'It is professionals, whose power lies in expertise and in the rent they are able to extract for that, who have come to run the country . . . Its natural base was the state; its preferred model, what was later called corporatism.[54] These mandarins are for self-interested reasons supporters of the *dirigiste* dogma.

But, as we have seen, two other currents flow through the *dirigiste* dogma. The first is the belief, first propounded by Mill, that questions of allocation can be separated from those of the distribution of income:

The laws and conditions of the production of wealth, partake of the characters of physical truth. There is nothing optional, or arbitrary in them . . . It is not so with the distribution of wealth. That is a matter of human institution solely. The things once there, mankind, individually or collectively, can do with them as they like. They can place them at the disposal of whomsoever they please and on whatever terms.[55]

This view is at odds with that of the classical thinkers (including Marx), who did not believe you could separate questions concerning distribution and allocation in this manner.[56] Attempts to legislate a particular distribution of income invariably affect the productive efficiency of the economy, because of problems concerned with information and incentives. This has been borne out not only by our sample of countries, but also from the experience of many Western economies, and, most tellingly, in ex-Communist countries.

The second legacy of Mill, the neglect of the polity, has reached its apotheosis in contemporary technocratic economics, which assumes that the two so-called Fundamental Theorems of Welfare Economics derived within the Arrow–Debreu framework are applicable in practice to any polity when it comes to policy analysis. The same framework, however, provides an antidote for this problem that is increasingly recognized. According to Partha Dasgupta, one of the more distinguished theorists of this technocratic mould,

The operational appeal of the Fundamental Theorem of Welfare Economics is of course minimal. The informational requirements for the state are awesome. It is required to know the preferences, endowments and the (personalized) production set of all individuals. These observations alone suggest that individual rights to certain private decisions may not only be a moral imperative, but may at once be a necessity prompted by the fact that the state possesses incomplete information.[57]

He then summarizes the recent mathematical economics literature on 'incentive compatibility' and the problems this approach raises for a command economy run by mandarins, as Hayek and Mises pointed out at the start of the 'planning debate' in the 1930s.[58] The only feasible incentive-compatible mechanism for allocating resources in this framework is not a command economy, but one that achieves a full optimum by working through the price mechanism supplemented by optimal taxes and subsidies.

The question is, what sort of mandarins would be needed to design and administer optimal taxes? To achieve the desired outcomes, the mandarins would have to be 'economic eunuchs' (in James Buchanan's apt phrase). As Dasgupta has also pointed out,

It has been an abiding shortcoming of applied welfare economics that it has for the overwhelming part supposed a perfect government—one that faithfully goes about its tasks. But if one addresses oneself to the question of what incentives there must be to ensure that governments undertake their tasks faithfully one is, at a minimum, faced with the principal-agent problem with all its attendant difficulties.[59]

Both events (experience) and ideas have therefore undermined the post-war *dirigiste* dogma. Above all, particularly in the Third and Second Worlds, the undesirable consequences of post-World-War-II neo-mercantilism—not least for the state—have made a return towards economic liberalism possible, as did the consequences of seventeenth- and eighteenth-century mercantilism.

NOTES

1. Oakesbott (1993: 24).
2. Ibid. 25.
3. Ibid.
4. Ibid. 27.
5. Ibid. 10.
6. Hicks (1969: 99).
7. Oakeshott (1993: 92).
8. Oakeshott (1975: 296 n. 2).
9. Oakeshott (1993: 108).
10. This is based on Lal (1978, 1985a).
11. Thus Rimmer (1992: ch. x, p. 35) reports Ghana's Nkrumah as stating: 'It is precisely because we were, under colonialism, made the dumping ground of other countries' manufactures . . . that we remained backward; and if we were to refrain from building, say, a soap factory simply because we might have to

raise the price of soap to the commumity, we should be doing a disservice to the country.'

12. In fact, of course, the Soviet Union had undergone considerable industriali-
zation—particularly in heavy industry—before the Revolution. The Soviets merely perpetuated the myth that they were completely underdeveloped in order to make their subsequent achievements seem more impressive. Since the advent of perestroika and glasnost under Gorbachev, it is now recognized that the Soviet Union may have been a great military power but it was still by and large really a Third World economy.

13. Vital (1967); also see Lal (1975).

14. See Berlin (1979); Plamenatz (1973); Kedourie (1966, 1970); Wang (1973); and Stein and Stein (1970).

15. Berlin (1979: 20).

16. Ibid. 349.

17. Wang (1973: 92).

18. Plamenatz (1973: 34).

19. It is still too early to say whether, with their fledgeling democracy, the South Koreans too have entered this category.

20. In our sample of countries the violent civil wars surrounding the issues of Biafra in Nigeria and Tamils in Sri Lanka are examples, whilst the Shining Path movement in Peru can be looked upon as another civil war to assert the rights of the Andean Indians.

21. See Wiles (1967).

22. The country studies of Jamaica, Ghana, Madagascar, Egypt, Nigeria, Uruguay, and Peru in our sample of countries, for instance, provide ample evidence for these assertions.

23. See Aftalion (1990).

24. See for instance Schumpeter (1954).

25. See de Soto (1989) and Lal (1983: 108–9).

26. To ascertain the validity of this assertion the reader need only open at random the detailed account of mercantilist practices in Europe contained in the first volume of Heckscher's (1955) scholarly masterpiece to see that most of the practices described, of the regulation of both internal trade and industry and external trade and commerce, are still widespread in most Third World states.

27. J.M. Keynes (1928: 12).

28. See de Soto (1989) for a fuller elaboration and references.

29. Heckscher (1955: 325).

30. Schumpeter (1954: 394) noted: 'the term has acquired a different—in fact almost the opposite—meaning since about 1900 and especially since 1930 . . . as a supreme, if unintended compliment, the enemies of the system of private enterprise have thought it wise to appropriate its label.'

31. Sen (1973) characterizes the Chinese cultural revolution in these terms, and with some implicit approbation!

32. This term and the following argument are due to Minogue (1993).

33. Mill (1970: ch. XI of book V).

34. Ibid. 306–7

35. Ibid. 305.

36. Mill is not sanguine about the consequence that 'the public collectivity is abundantly ready to impose, not only its generally narrow views of its interests, but its abstract opinions, and even its tastes, as laws binding individuals' (ibid. 308).
37. Ibid. 309.
38. Ibid. 311.
39. Ibid. 314.
40. Ibid. 333–4.
41. This point is argued more fully in Sowell (1977).
42. Mill (1970: 345).
43. J.M. Keynes (1928).
44. Heckscher (1955: ii. 331) (emphasis added).
45. J.M. Keynes (1928: 5).
46. Keynes cites Cairnes's introductory lecture on 'Political Economy and Laissez Faire', delivered at University College, London in 1870, as 'the first by an orthodox economist to deliver a frontal attack upon laissez faire in general'. That the socialist ends had, however, grudgingly come to be accepted, is noted by Keynes, who quotes Cannan: ' "Scarcely a single English economist of repute", as Professor Cannan has expressed it, "will join in a frontal attack upon socialism in general", though, as he also adds, "nearly every economist, whether of repute or not, is always ready to pick holes in most socialistic proposals" ' (ibid. 26). Of course Keynes himself explicitly claimed in his General Theory a direct line of descent for his views from the mercantilists. For a scathing critique of Keynes's support of mercantilism, see Heckscher (1955: appendix on 'Keynes and Mercantilism').
47. Lal (1983: 25). Two books by Hirschman (1977, 1982) are important in exploring the changing fortunes of economic liberalism.
48. Two eminent theorists have in fact argued for a prima-facie case for dirigisme within this framework. See Sen (1983) and Hahn (1984, 1985); Lal (1987a) is a critique of their views.
49. Heckscher (1955: ii. 293).
50. Though in this section we are emphasizing the evolution of ideas, and relating them to changing policy regimes, this does not imply that we necessarily subscribe to the view most celebratedly propounded by Keynes, that ideas (often defunct) determine policies. On the lines of the new political economy, it is as likely that interests determine events, including changes in policy regime, and if these are far-reaching, a new set of ideas may emerge (or re-emerge) to rationalize them. That ideas lag behind events moved by interest seems to us as valid a position to take on the interaction of ideas and interests as the self-glorifying view of Keynes and many economists that ideas necessarily determine policy.

An interest-based explanation for the rise of mercantilism is provided by Ekelund and Tollison (1985); they argue for instance that the mercantilists' 'balance of trade objective was nothing more than the by product of the interplay of numerous self-interested parties who were seeking rents from monopolization in these early nation-states' (p. 5). Similarly the breakdown of the system was not caused by the victory of liberal ideas, but 'poor regulatory design on the local level and competitive rent seeking forces at the national level were the primary factors leading to the demise of economic regulation in England' (ibid. 14).

In a similar vein, Rogowski (1987), using a variant of the three-factor model we have outlined, shows how, given its relative factor endowments, Britain in the 19th century was capital- and labour-rich and land-poor, and hence the interests of the median voter (in our terms) favoured the repeal of the Corn Laws, and free trade. By contrast Germany was poor in both capital and land and rich in labour, with the polity dominated by capital and land, whose interest was in protection. Hence the emergence of the infamous 'marriage of steel and rye' in the late 19th century.

51. Henderson (1989).
52. As Keynes amongst many others recognized.
53. See for instance the recent book by Perkin (1988), and the excellent review of this book by Hawthorn (1989).
54. Hawthorn (1989).
55. Mill (1970: book II, ch. I, pp. 349–50).
56. Gray (1984: 102) notes that

> Hayek has always recognized that Mill began the 'manna from heaven' presumption of contemporary distributivist theories. It may be said that what distinguishes Mill from Hayek—and, for that matter, from Marx—is Mill's lack of any clear view of production and distribution as inseparable parts of a single economic system. We may have a choice between economic systems (though it is the burden of the Mises-Hayek-Polanyi argument about resource allocation under socialism that our freedom is far more restricted than we suppose); we do not have the freedom to mix the productive arrangements of one system with the distributive arrangements of another. This is a truth understood by all classical economists, including Marx, which Mill's influence has helped to obscure.

57. Dasgupta (1980: 112).
58. See Hayek (1935).
59. Dasgupta (1980: 119).

8

Perspective on Economic Policy

WHILST theory, as discussed in the previous chapter, may be of some relevance for the policies adopted, our country studies contain a wide range of views on the relationship between economic theory and economic policy. Some of our authors believe that the 1950s type of development theories and models, such as the 'big push' or the notion of the domestic manufacturing sector as the alternative 'engine of growth' to international trade, have influenced the policy-makers to adopt large-scale investment plans to promote, develop, and pursue import-substitution policies of domestic industrialization. Other authors have emphasized the role of ideologies, particularly economic nationalism in various forms, including 'ethnic nationalism'. Here development theories are used as rationalizations of the deeper-seated reactions against colonialism, the 'nineteenth-century pattern' of international trade, and *laissez-faire* policies. Still others have stressed the role of interest groups and have applied the new political economy of rent-seeking and the 'predatory state' to explain economic policies. On this view, economic theories are merely cloaks to lend respectability to the self-seeking efforts of interest groups.[1]

The aim of this chapter is to assess the development theories which have influenced policy in the post-war era in the light of our country studies. We shall not delve into the unsettled questions of the relative importance of 'ideas', 'ideologies', and 'interests' in influencing economic policy. For our purpose, it is sufficient to note that the fashionable development theories during the 1950s and the 1960s have been against what was regarded as orthodox neoclassical theory. While the neoclassical theory is relativist, comparing the relative advantages and disadvantages of alternative policies in a framework embracing the economy as a whole, many of these new development theories were 'fundamentalist', singling out one type of economic activity or a sector of the economy as being more important than all others and regarding policies to promote this special activity or sector as 'fundamental' for economic development. Further, while the neoclassical theory by and large tends to favour free-market and free-trade policies, the new development theories were used to justify state intervention and protection.

We shall begin by distinguishing the perspective on economic policy suggested by our more classical approach from that obtainable from the standard neoclassical approach, bearing in mind that the neoclassical approach complements the classical approach. We shall then go on briefly to examine some of the more fashionable views which have determined economic policies to promote growth and income equality in our countries. These include the fundamentalist views on the importance of capital, and the promotion of the domestic manufacturing sector or the agricultural sector as the key to economic growth. We shall conclude with a brief examination of the fundamentalist views on land reforms as the key to promoting income equality.

I. THE RELATION BETWEEN OUR APPROACH AND THE NEOCLASSICAL APPROACH TO ECONOMIC POLICY

The neoclassical argument for free-market policies is based on the removal of policy-induced distortions, defined as deviations from the optimum allocation of resources formulated in terms of the perfect-competition model. Government intervention may be required to correct various forms of 'market failure' which lead to deviations of the economy from the ideal of a perfectly competitive economy. Thus each failure is an opportunity for government intervention to make things better. But the implicit assumption that governments are omniscient, altruistic maximizers of social welfare makes much of this theory unrealistic for either formulating or analysing policy choices. Apart from this unreality of the 'market failure'-based approach to public policy, the implicit neoclassical policy model also assumes a fully developed organizational framework. Thus the neoclassical analysis concentrates on the formal conditions of the optimum, neglecting the problem of functional efficiency of the economic mechanisms which are to perform the actual task of allocating the resources. Our approach, starting from an explicit recognition of the underdevelopment of the organizational framework, concentrates on the problem of the functional efficiency of the alternative economic mechanisms. Thus we start from a typical situation of the mixed economy in an underdeveloped country, and compare the relative functional efficiency of its underdeveloped market system and its underdeveloped administrative and fiscal system in carrying out the tasks set by the government's policy objectives.

As a matter of fact, it is not possible to make any substantive case either for free-market policies or for government economic planning simply by appealing to the formal properties of the perfect-competition model. At a theoretical level, we can postulate either a market system or a planning system which behaves like the perfect-competition model. Just as private entrepreneurs equate marginal costs to prices, government bureaucrats can be instructed to follow the Lange–Lerner scheme of equating marginal costs to prices. Thus at a purely formal level, there is nothing to distinguish between a perfectly competitive market system and a perfect-planning model which can be defined as an analogue of the perfect-competition model.

But once we introduce organizational factors into this institutional vacuum, it is clear that the practical superiority of the market system to planning (or vice versa) cannot be judged in a priori terms, but has to be tested by practical experience. In a given situation, an obvious method of testing the relative efficiency of the market mechanism and the state mechanism is to allow them to compete freely with each other and let consumers' demand for the goods and services they provide decide the appropriate balance in the use of these two mechanisms as instruments of economic policy.

But would not this proposal for a competitive solution cut across the conventional demarcation line between public and private enterprise, reserving public utilities and the production of essential services to the government, and allocating the production of ordinary goods and services to private producers? On a close examination, however, no hard-and-fast demarcation line can be drawn from the standpoint of obtaining functional efficiency. It is true that some types of public utilities involve 'lumpy investments' and large-scale economies, and handing these over to private entrepreneurs might create monopolies. But given the shortage of competent managers in the public sector, it is arguable whether a state-owned monopoly would provide better service than a privately run monopoly subject to effective regulation. (A familiar example is the notoriously inefficient state-run telephone companies in many developing countries.) Further, not all social infrastructure facilities need to be produced by large-scale capital-intensive projects, unless the governments choose to have this type of prestigious 'show-case' projects for non-economic reasons. Thus, there are a whole range of social infrastructure projects, from the provision of urban bus services to the construction and maintenance of roads in rural areas, which provide scope for decentralization, subcontracting, and competition between state agencies and private producers.[2]

Concerning the government's obligation to provide socially desirable essential services, it is necessary to distinguish clearly between state intervention in the form of *financing* or subsidizing the production of these socially desirable goods and services and state intervention in the form of *producing* these goods and services by government departments and state agencies. The government must have the last word in deciding the extent of the subsidies it is willing to pay to encourage the production of the socially desirable goods and services (subject to the financial constraint of its ability to raise taxation and borrowing). But it would still be necessary to find out whether the government is getting value for money by deciding to produce the desired goods and services by its own agency instead of allowing these goods to be produced, wholly or partly, by private producers. For this purpose, it will be necessary to apply the criterion of the relative cost-effectiveness of using alternative economic mechanisms. This is the basis for the argument for allowing free entry to private producers even in the conventional sphere of providing social infrastructure and essential services so as to achieve competition.

Our general argument in favour of a greater use of the market mechanism as an instrument of economic policy may be stated as follows. Firstly, unlike in the 'frictionless' perfect-competition model, there are significant transactions and administrative costs of using the market mechanism and the state mechanism in an underdeveloped economy. Typically, the transactions costs of a market network catering for a large number of small producers and consumers widely scattered in the traditional sector are much higher than the transactions costs of catering for a small number of large economic units in the modern sector. These differential transactions costs are paralleled by the differential administrative costs of the government. Further, government departments and agencies tend to suffer from additional disadvantages for familiar reasons, such as the shortage of competent managers, the lack of incentives linked to performance, and cumbersome bureaucratic procedures. There are of course exceptions to this empirical generalization: for instance, among our countries, Singapore is noted for the high calibre of her public/government administrators.

Secondly, there is a general tendency among the governments of the developing countries to extend the scope of state intervention beyond the sphere of social infrastructure and the provision of public goods and services, into the production of ordinary goods and services, in manufacturing as well as in agriculture and export industries. The fact that this extension of state activity is functionally inefficient is evidenced by the growing financial burden of subsidizing loss-making state enterprises, rising to a significant proportion of total GDP.[3] Hence the need to shift the balance towards a greater use of the market mechanism and privatization.

Our general argument for free-market policies is derived not from the formal properties of the perfect-competition model but on empirical grounds, from experience and history. In most developing countries, there are in fact powerful causes tilting the balance in favour of greater state intervention.

(a) To begin with, the symptoms of an underdeveloped organizational framework, such as the wide wholesale–retail price margins which work against the peasant farmers, the regional and seasonal price differentials of agricultural products, and the high rates of interest in the traditional sector, have been generally attributed to monopolistic exploitation by the middlemen and moneylenders. The government usually responds to this by setting up state agencies for providing markets, credit, and the distribution of goods and services by extending state intervention by imposing price controls and using laws. The thrust of our argument is not so much against the use of state agencies as such as against the practice of claiming monopoly rights of operation, suppressing private competition and 'repressing' the development of an effective organizational network.[4]

(b) A very powerful cause contributing to the grossly inflated size of the bureaucracy in many developing countries is the pressure of interest groups within the government system—namely, politicians and civil servants—to maximize public employment in pursuit of their own objectives. This has been set out in formal terms by the model of the bureaucrat-maximizing predatory state in Chapter 6 and Fig. 6.1. This is reinforced in many countries, notably Egypt and Sri Lanka, by the over-expansion of the higher education system, impelling the government to become the 'employer of last resort' so as to defuse the politically explosive problem of educated unemployment.

(c) Another powerful reason for the expansion of state enterprises is economic nationalism and the desire to reduce foreign economic domination. Irrespective of their political or ideological leanings towards capitalism or socialism, the governments of the developing countries tend to assume that their indigenous entrepreneurs would not be able to compete on equal terms with foreign entrepreneurs and that therefore the government should intervene by setting up state enterprises to protect the country against foreign domination. This nationalistic protectionist argument is different from the usual protectionist arguments of the textbooks. It is based on the notion of comparative advantage between different groups of people and not the conventional comparative advantage between different countries as geographical units. We may mention two variants of this argument relevant for some of our countries.

(i) The reaction against the 'nineteenth-century pattern' of foreign trade and investment tends to foster the atavistic feeling that the natural resources of a country should be reserved for its own nationals and should not be allowed to be exploited by foreign investors. In some cases, this has led to the nationalization of foreign-owned mines and plantations. More generally, governments tend to reserve the right to exploit natural resources by state enterprises only. But it would be more profitable for the government to extract the maximum of economic rent from the ownership of the natural resources, and this means allowing the most efficient enterprise to exploit the resources, whether foreign investors, domestic private investors, or state-owned enterprises.

(ii) In a plural society such as Malaysia, the situation is complicated by the enterprising immigrant groups of domestic entrepreneurs, such as the Chinese. Here the government seems to have taken a more liberal attitude towards outside foreign investors as a counterweight to Chinese economic domination. However, the New Economic Policy of Malaysia in the early 1970s saw a great extension of state-

owned enterprises to redistribute incomes and assets to the indigenous Malay population (despite the government's ideological
leanings towards the free market). The shift back of priority from
'equity' to 'growth' in the early 1980s was marked by a wave of
privatization.

To sum up: we have explained how we have arrived at the familiar
neoclassical type of policy conclusions in favour of free-market policies and
outward-looking policies by an unfamiliar route. We believe that by putting
historical and institutional substance into the formal neoclassical analysis,
we have strengthened its policy conclusions. We have argued that it is
necessary to consider not only the formal conditions of efficient resource
allocation, but also the functional efficiency of the alternative economic
mechanisms which carry out the resource allocation.

II. 'CAPITAL FUNDAMENTALISM' AND 'INDUSTRIAL FUNDAMENTALISM'

Let us now turn to some of the influential 'fundamentalist' views on growth
and income-distribution policies. We may start from 'capital fundamentalism' or the view that capital formation is the key to economic growth. There
are two versions of this view which have influenced thinking and public
action on income distribution.

The first version singles out the raising of the savings–investment ratio, or
alternatively the ratio of investment to GNP, as the central problem of
economic growth. This goes back to the 1950s, when it was fashionable to
apply the simple Harrod–Domar type of growth model with constant capital–output ratios and constant propensities to save to the underdeveloped
countries. This obsolete approach to economic growth still continued to
influence thinking on the trade-off between growth and equity in the 1970s.
Thus it was argued that since economic growth could be obtained only by
raising the savings–investment ratio at the expense of current consumption
and social welfare expenditure, there would be an inevitable trade-off
between growth and equity. The Harrod–Domar type of steady-growth
model has also been extended to compare the outcome of alternative
redistributive policies, assuming fixed but different savings-investment
ratios and capital–output ratios for the different income groups affected by
the redistributive policy.[5] But these applications suffered from the same
weaknesses as the original Harrod–Domar model.

Thus we were not too surprised to find our country studies generally
sceptical about the assumption of fixed capital–output ratios. This reiter-
ates our argument that economic growth is not simply a matter of increasing the supply of investible resources; that the more important condition is
the ability to invest these resources productively, going beyond allocative

efficiency to a broader concept of productive efficiency. This is not to say that raising the level of domestic savings is unimportant. But it is likely to be more important for the short-run problem of controlling inflation and reducing budget and balance-of-payments deficits. Once a country can maintain its macroeconomic stability, however, its longer-run prospects for growth are likely to depend more on its capacity to 'absorb' capital and invest it productively than on increasing the supply of investible resources, since under these conditions domestic savings can be successfully supplemented by foreign borrowing. The debt problem of many developing countries may be said to originate not so much from lack of access to foreign capital funds as from the lack of capacity to use them productively.

The second version of capital fundamentalism arises from a narrow definition of capital as durable physical capital equipment and machinery. This leaves out circulating capital and the important concept of capital as a fund of real goods of all types necessary to sustain the economy during the waiting period before investment yields final output (for instance before an 'infant industry' grows up). There is no harm in this materialist definition of capital as such, and our factor-proportions approach has been based on this definition.[6] But if carelessly handled, the materialist definition of capital can lead to serious errors.

First, a narrow definition of capital as machines embodying modern technology frequently leads to a confusion between technical efficiency and economic efficiency in the sense of minimizing costs through the choice of appropriate techniques to suit the relative factor endowments of a country.[7] Thus governments of the developing countries tend to prefer large-scale capital-intensive methods of production based on advanced technology both in manufacturing industry—for example, the proverbial 'steel mills'—and in social overhead capital in the form of large-scale irrigation projects, preferably combined with hydroelectric plants.[8] In this policy approach they may have been frequently aided and abetted by the aid donors of this type of project, who wish to have imposing monuments to show, and by the international lending agencies, who prefer large-scale projects for ease of monitoring (for instance, perhaps, the Mahaweli project in Sri Lanka).

Secondly, the materialist definition of capital, by focusing on the technical fact that durable capital equipment physically produces goods and services, obscures the economic fact that the value of capital investment is the discounted present value of the future income-stream it is expected to generate. But there is no automatic link between the historical cost of investment in the past and the discounted value of its future income-stream: this must depend on the capacity to invest the investible resources productively.

The 'fallacy of misplaced concreteness' associated with the materialist definition of capital leads to the mistaken belief that the redistribution of

the ownership of physical assets would automatically lead to a corresponding redistribution of incomes.

Consequently, the governments of many developing countries which
have nationalized foreign-owned assets without the capacity to manage
these assets profitably have been landed with the losses from these
nationalized industries, which have strained their budgets (for instance
the nationalizations in Sri Lanka or Peru).[9] As we shall argue, it is necessary
to beware of the fallacy of misplaced concreteness in trying to carry
out land-redistribution programmes without the necessary policies to
raise the productivity of the small farmers who have received redistributed
land.

Next, we must discuss industrial fundamentalism or the belief that only
manufacturing industry can provide the necessary dynamic for sustained
economic growth. At the outset, it may be noted that this proposition does
not necessarily follow from the familiar pattern of structural change in
production, showing a decline in the share of agriculture in GDP and
increasing shares for the manufacturing and services sectors with the rise in
the income level per capita of a country.[10] This structural change is in part
a consequence of the change in the pattern of consumers' demand according to Engel's law, showing a tendency among consumers to reduce their
share of expenditure on food and agricultural products and to increase their
share of expenditure on manufactured products and services as they become better off.

The commonly employed arguments in favour of industrialization may
be summarized as follows. First, there is the argument emphasizing the
greater productivity of the modern manufacturing industry, based on modern technology and capital-intensive large-scale production, over peasant
agriculture based on traditional technology and labour-intensive small-
scale production. Here our previous distinction between technical efficiency and economic efficiency is relevant. Secondly, in a similar technical
vein, there is the argument that manufacturing industry is capable of
creating more linkages with the other sectors of the economy than the
economic 'enclaves' in the form of mines and plantations producing
primary products.[11] Thirdly, there is the well-known 'export pessimism'
of the UNCTAD economists which prevailed during the 1960s. All
these combined to produce the familiar policy conclusion of those times
that since the nineteenth-century pattern of expanding primary exports
could no longer provide an engine of growth to the developing countries,
they must seek an alternative engine in domestic industrialization through
import-substitution.

It should also be remembered that at that time there were no significant
exports of manufactured products from the underdeveloped countries,
which despaired of ever being able to compete with the developed countries
in the export markets for these. Thus it was natural for them in the 1950s

and 1960s to equate manufacturing with import-substitution and exports with primary products.

Without going into detail over the familiar story of the failure of import-substitution policies, we shall limit ourselves to a few salient policy lessons.

First, there is mounting evidence that, given appropriate economic policies, some of the developing countries can compete quite effectively with the developed countries in an increasing range of manufactured exports, including sophisticated manufactured products. Thus the goal of promoting domestic industrialization can be achieved not only by import-substitution but also, and more economically, by export-expansion.

Secondly, import-substitution policies usually fail to save foreign exchange, because of the 'import-intensity' of import-substitution and the ever-growing need to import capital equipment and other inputs as the import-substitution extends to consumer durables and capital goods. This shows up the misleading nature of the concept of the linkages, focusing attention only on the technically possible linkages between the *quantities* of inputs and outputs of different industries, while ignoring the fact that the economic realization of these linkages must depend on the *costs* and *prices* of the inputs and outputs. Thus a new industry, say a capital-goods industry, which is supposed to generate beneficial secondary rounds of economic activities inside the country, may end up by having to import large amounts of capital and intermediate goods from abroad because the locally producible products are too expensive or inferior in quality. The principle of comparative advantage must apply to the pattern of vertical international specialization between the different stages of production in the same way as it applies to the pattern of horizontal international trade in final products.

Thirdly, import-substitution policies were supposed to correct the 'dualism' and foreign economic enclaves in the form of mines and plantations producing for the export market. But it turns out that import-substitution policies have introduced a worse form of dualism between the modern manufacturing sector and the traditional agricultural sector, aggravating the income disparities between the two sectors. Primary exports, including peasant exports, are heavily taxed to support the inefficient manufacturing sector.[12]

The provision of cheap loans to the manufacturing sector not only diverts capital funds from the traditional sector but also encourages highly capital-intensive methods in manufacturing, thus reducing its capacity to absorb labour from the agricultural sector. This is aggravated by trade-union power and minimum-wage legislation, which maintains wide differentials in the earnings in the modern sector and the traditional sector, including the informal sector.[13] Price controls on agricultural products to keep down the urban cost of living turn the terms of trade against the agricultural sector. Finally, the dualism between the modern and traditional sectors is aggravated by a pattern of allocation in public expenditure and social infrastructure investment highly skewed against the traditional sector.

III. REDRESSING THE ANTI-AGRICULTURAL BIAS AND AGRICULTURAL 'FUNDAMENTALISM'

Given that the peasant agricultural sector tends to suffer from the double handicap of the distortions induced by the industrialization policies and the dualism inherent in the greater underdevelopment of the organizational framework of the traditional sector, there is a powerful case for pro-agricultural policies in the general run of the developing countries. The problem is how to redress the anti-agricultural bias without spoiling the case by tipping over into 'agricultural fundamentalism'. For instance, Indonesia's success in increasing rice production for domestic consumption through the adoption of improved seeds and fertilizer approximates to this possibility of a natural import-substitution in food production in the densely populated island of Java in accordance with potential comparative advantage. But we also have the examples of Malaysia and Sri Lanka, where the goal of greater self-sufficiency in rice has been pursued by diverting the economy probably beyond its potential comparative advantage.

The reason for these import-substitution policies for rice in both Malaysia and Sri Lanka is the desire to promote equity by redistributing incomes in favour of the indigenous Malay and Sinhalese rice farmers as distinguished from the other resident ethnic groups, namely, the Chinese and the Tamils. Some agricultural fundamentalists may be inclined to argue that policies to encourage domestic self-sufficiency in rice are justifiable, not only for political but also for economic reasons. We shall now examine the economic case for the agricultural fundamentalist argument.

The agricultural economists, in their fight against the one-sided emphasis on industrialization, have always advocated a 'balanced growth' policy between the agricultural and the manufacturing sectors. They tend to formulate their case for agricultural development by drawing up a list of contributions which it can make to industrial development:

- by releasing labour for manufacturing;
- by increasing the supply of domestic savings;
- by enlarging the size of the domestic market for the manufacturing sector; and
- by increasing the supply of foreign exchange for the manufacturing sector through expanding agricultural exports and reducing food imports.[14]

The trouble with this type of argument is that the concept of balanced growth cannot be clearly defined except in terms of a closed economy.

Once we step out into an open-economy setting, the special functions claimed for the agricultural sector can be equally performed by international trade and by the international economy.[15] Thus food and raw materials can be imported from abroad; the supply of domestic savings can be augmented by foreign borrowing; and domestic labour supply can be augmented by immigrant labour. Further, the size of the market for the manufacturing sector can be increased well beyond the narrow limits of the domestic market through exports. As for the agricultural sector's capacity to supply foreign exchange, this must depend on comparative advantage.

The root of the trouble is that the agricultural economists, in counter-attacking industrial fundamentalism based on the closed-economy model, have themselves become entrapped in the limiting framework of that model. Thus the industrial fundamentalists were fond of looking upon the manufacturing sector as the 'leading sector', whose expansion would absorb the surplus labour from the agricultural sector. The agricultural economists have countered by pointing out that, given the high rate of population growth in the developing country and the high proportion of labour employed in agriculture, the manufacturing sector would have to expand very rapidly to reduce the absolute size of population in agriculture, which determines population pressure on the land. To take an arithmetical example, if the population of a developing country is growing at $2\frac{1}{2}\%$ a year and if the proportion of agricultural employment is 70% of the total labour force, then non-agricultural employment would have to grow at more than 8.3% a year to reduce the absolute size of population in agriculture.[16]

This is true enough as far it goes and provides a useful way of illustrating the need to control population growth. But the highly pessimistic view of increasing non-agricultural employment leaves out of account the possibilities of expanding labour-intensive manufactured exports from the industrial sector and expanding labour-intensive peasant exports from the agricultural sector itself. It is not clear how far this view is due to the implicit assumption of a closed-economy model or to a recrudescence of the 1950s-type export pessimism. While it is arguable whether the world economy can return to the buoyant days of the 1960s and 1970s before the oil shock and world recession, a more balanced view would nevertheless have to include the following two considerations.

First, the limited capacity of the modern manufacturing sector to expand employment must be in part attributed to the persistence of the highly capital-intensive methods encouraged by import-substitution policies. This should not be accepted as an immutable fact of life. After all, taking an historical perspective, we have the examples of countries, such as Japan, Korea and Taiwan, which started with heavy population densities in agriculture and which have nevertheless managed to transform themselves from being labour-abundant countries into labour-scarce countries through the expansion of labour-intensive manufactured exports.

Secondly, while no one would quarrel with the need for policies which would raise the productivity of labour *in situ* in the traditional agricultural sector, one must also take into account the possibility of expanding peasant exports through the removal of crippling taxation and an over-valued currency, instead of taking the easy option of promoting a greater domestic self-sufficiency in food production. This is where we would most differ from the agricultural fundamentalist position. Our position would be coterminous with that of the neoclassicals. Import-substitution policies, whether in manufacturing or in agriculture, must ultimately be appraised in terms of potential comparative advantage.

Let us now return to the cases of Sri Lanka and Malaysia. Their policies to promote greater self-sufficiency in rice production to secure equity for their peasant farmers have involved highly capital-intensive large-scale river-valley irrigation projects and land-settlement programmes, which have turned out to be as costly and unsustainable as the more usual capital-intensive import-substitution policies in the manufacturing sector. This has led to radical revisions of policies in Sri Lanka in 1977 and in Malaysia in the early 1980s.

By the standards of many developing countries, Malaysia's irrigation projects for rice and her extensive land-settlement programmes for small-holder rubber have been carried out with a high degree of administrative efficiency. They were also better financed than Sri Lanka's projects, thanks to Malaysia's more liberal policies towards the mining and plantation export sector which provides the government revenues. But even Malaysia's impressive programmes of helping her small peasants have been able to reach only a fraction of the total Malay peasant population, leaving those excluded from these special programmes of assistance not much better off. This highlights an important point of difference between the popular approach, advocating special assistance programmes for peasant farmers, and the classical approach. Our country studies have found that, given limited resources and administrative capacity, government special assistance programmes to agriculture in the form of subsidized credit or inputs tend to reach only selected groups of farmers; and that, more frequently than not, the larger and better off farmers have benefited more from government assistance than the poorer small farmers.[17]

In contrast, on the classical approach policy should try to improve the organizational framework of the traditional sector as a whole by lowering the prevailing levels of transactions costs, which are much higher in that sector than in the modern sector. This requires not only redressing the balance in public expenditure and social-infrastructure investment in favour of the traditional sector, but also removing the government's attempt to monopolize the provision of marketing and credit and introducing competition between the state agencies and the private middlemen and money-lenders in the traditional sector. It is only through the extension of this 'competitive solution' that productivity can be raised and the marketing and credit facilities can be improved, not merely in the selective government show-piece projects but in the traditional sector as a whole.[18]

Finally, we may note that the case of promoting a greater domestic self-sufficiency simply as an insurance policy to secure a steady supply of basic consumption requirements or 'food security' is debatable. A country which is normally self-sufficient in food production may yet suffer from serious food shortages due to exceptional circumstances, such as droughts and floods. Two lessons are suggested by the recent experiences of coping with food shortages and famines in the African countries. First, the availability of food stocks in the outside world which can be drawn upon by a food-deficit country in case of need provided the most important safety net. This requires the availability of international aid and loans or the country's own foreign exchange reserves to pay for the food imports. Secondly, even if food supplies are physically available, they may fail to reach those who are in greater need because of bottlenecks in transport and communications and in the distribution channels. Here, an indirect benefit of expanding peasant exports is that it stimulates the development of a more effective transport, marketing, and credit system, which extends to domestic food production[19] and may also provide a more effective means of channelling food supplies in times of exceptional need. Thus, rather than try to promote domestic food self-sufficiency ignoring potential comparative advantage, the outward-looking policies which improve the organizational links between the outside world and the remote rural areas may provide a more effective means of obtaining food security.

From our standpoint, the most persuasive reason for subsidizing the agricultural sector is not the need to increase domestic food production as such, but the need to improve the organizational framework of the traditional agricultural sector. For instance, Brazil's attempt to increase domestic rice production on large-scale farms, using highly capital-intensive methods such as aeroplanes to broadcast seeds and apply fertilizer and pesticides, may be economically questionable and will do nothing to reduce the organizational dualism between the modern and the traditional sectors. But there may be a strong case for government investment in improving rural social infrastructure, transport, and education, to promote a 'natural' import-substitution of rice production on a small-scale labour-intensive basis in the traditional sector suffering from population pressure on land.

This leads us to the issue of land reform to redistribute land ownership to small farmers, which we shall discuss in the next section. For the moment it is important to stress the need to improve the organizational framework to raise the productivity of land and labour in a sustainable manner. Without this underpinning, the benefits of a once-over land redistribution are likely to be eroded by population growth, as seems to have happened in Mexico.[20]

IV. REDISTRIBUTIVE POLICIES AND LAND REFORM

Our approach is limited to the study of 'functional distribution' of incomes, which falls short of a full analysis of personal distribution of incomes. Our procedure has been to assume the pattern of property ownership as given as one of our initial conditions, and to consider in what direction the share of incomes accruing to wages and to the owners of property (both land and capital goods) is likely to change as a consequence of the various mixtures of inward- and outward-looking policies pursued by the countries in our study.

Obviously, the more unequal the initial distribution of property ownership, the more unequal will be the distribution of personal incomes, whatever the relative factor prices. But our approach at least provides a rough guidance on the probable direction of change in income distribution over time, irrespective of the initial pattern of property ownership. Thus a country starting from the initial condition of labour-abundance which has succeeded in expanding labour-intensive peasant exports is likely to increase the share of wages to GDP, irrespective of property ownership. It is of course true that the share of wages in GDP can provide only a crude indication of the share of income accruing to the poor, because of the well-known gap in wage and earning levels between the modern sector and the traditional sector. But as we have seen, the expansion of labour-intensive manufactured exports, in contrast to capital-intensive import-substitution policies, would tend to reduce this dualism in the labour market. Similarly, the spread of peasant exports from the central regions to the remoter parts of the country (for instance the growth of peasant exports in the North and North-East regions of Thailand) could tend to reduce regional differences in incomes. Conversely, we would expect the expansion of resource-intensive primary exports from a land-abundant country to raise the share of rents relatively to wages, irrespective of whether the natural resources are owned by the government or by private landowners. However, there are 'equity-oriented' economists who would be impatient with our type of analysis and would advocate redistributive policies designed to change the initial pattern of distribution of property ownership. We shall now briefly consider some of these redistributive policies.

Of course, some sort of income redistribution modifying the outcomes of market forces is always occurring in varying degrees in all countries through the government's fiscal and administrative system. Thus the free-market pattern of income distribution will be modified in varying degrees: by the progressiveness of the taxation system; by the proportion of government expenditure on health and education; by consumers' subsidies to promote a social welfare system; and by large-scale land-settlement programmes redistributing publicly owned land reserves (such as those carried out in Malaysia and Sri Lanka). But the advocates of land-reform programmes would like to go beyond these redistributive policies conducted through the government fiscal and administrative system to a more radical redistribution of land ownership, from large private landowners to small landless peasants.

We may look at the countries in our study in an ascending order of the degree of redistributive policies they have attempted to follow, up to the land-reform programmes.

First, there are the Asian and African countries which started from the initial conditions of fairly equal land ownership or traditional land tenure systems which provide equal access to land. In so far as these countries have been successful in achieving a labour-intensive pattern of economic growth, they have also achieved a more equal distribution of incomes by relying on the working of market forces, combined with a progressive system of taxation and an increase in public expenditure on health and education. Thailand is a successful country of this type.

Next, we may go on to a country such as Colombia which started from the Latin American type of a highly unequal pattern of land ownership. Colombia is interesting, because she has evaded the land-reform problem but has been more successful than neighbouring countries in introducing progressive taxation and increasing public expenditure on health and education.

Thirdly, we have countries which have gone beyond these ordinary fiscal reforms and have devoted a large part of their budget to consumers' subsidies to support a highly developed system of state welfare. These include countries such as Sri Lanka, Costa Rica, and Uruguay.

Finally, we have countries which have carried out land-ownership reforms in one fashion or another. These include countries such as Mexico Peru, and Egypt.

The upshot of our country studies has been to cast considerable doubt on the effectiveness of land-reform programmes as a method of redistributing income and alleviating poverty.

Mexico has gone further than other Latin American countries with land-reform programmes: by 1970 about half the area of arable land had been covered by these programmes. But the Mexican land reforms suffer from the communal system of land ownership, the Ejido system, which limited the small farmer's capacity to borrow by using his land as collateral. Further, there are the familiar problems of unequal access of small farmers compared with large farmers to subsidized inputs and technology, and unequal distribution of irrigated land between the small farmers and the large commercial farmers. Thus the productivity of the Ejido farms lagged behind the productivity of the large privately owned farms, and population pressure on the Ejido farms has eroded the benefits of land reforms.[21]

Peru under the Velasco regime nationalized large agricultural estates producing sugar, cotton, and rice for the export market. Instead of redistributing the land to small farmers, these estates were run as state-control-led labour co-operatives, the income from them being shared among the regular unionized workers who had originally worked these estates and the government. But inefficient running of these nationalized estates led to a sharp decline in Peru's primary exports and reduced the income to be shared out. Further, these land-reform programmes did nothing to improve the position of the really poor Indian peasants in the Sierras and the jungles, and they have not been able to defuse armed insurgency by the Indian peasants.[22]

Egypt's Land Reform Law of 1952, which put a ceiling on private ownership of land, only marginally benefited the small farmers (in the first quintile of land ownership distribution) and mainly benefited the medium-sized farmers (in the second to fourth quintiles). However, inequality in the size of land holdings for cultivation, as distinct from the size of land ownership, declined. According to the author of the study on Egypt, the gains accrued mainly to the small tenant farmers, who acquired security of tenure with fixed money rents, which were eroded by inflation from 1960 onwards.[23]

The political obstacles to a radical redistribution of land ownership are well known. Here we confine ourselves to some of its economic complications.

First, as borne out by the experiences of Mexico and Peru, we must beware of the fallacy of misplaced concreteness in thinking that the redistribution of property ownership would automatically redistribute incomes. In order to achieve this aim, it is necessary to pursue policies designed to raise the productivity of the land which is being redistributed. But given limited administrative capacity and possibly corruption and influence, state agencies tend to channel a larger share of the subsidized credit and inputs to the larger farmers than to the smaller farmers, with or without land reforms. This incapacity to improve the organizational framework to cater effectively to the needs of the small farmers may be regarded as the most serious obstacle to the successful implementation of the land-reform programmes, even if there is a political will.

Secondly, we must also take account of the serious repercussions of changing property rights on economic growth. In many countries, the mere threat of land reform tends to induce the big landowners to evict existing tenants (for fear of squatting) and to introduce mechanized farming involving highly capital-intensive methods, unjustified by the factor endowments of the country. It is in this sense that there is a trade-off between growth and equity: but the direction of the trade-off runs not from growth policies to income distribution, but from income distribution policies to growth. Whatever may be the rights and wrongs of the existing pattern of land ownership, policies of changing the property rights are bound to introduce uncertainty and make it difficult for individuals to make rational economic

Table 8.1. Changes in income distribution in selected countries (Kravis dollars 1970)

	Period of observation	Growth rate	
		Total	Bottom 60%
Sri Lanka	1963–73	2.0	4.6
Costa Rica	1961–71	3.2	5.1
Colombia	1964–74	3.1	4.3
Mexico	1963–75	3.2	2.4
Peru	1961–71	2.3	2.3
Brazil	1960–70	3.1	1.2

Source: Ahluwalia (1977).

plans over the longer run. *A fortiori*, some of the more radical proposals to maintain a continuous process of property redistribution to correct income inequalities would clearly have the effect of repressing economic growth.

Finally, we should remember that over the longer run the share of agriculture in total GDP would be declining with the rise of income per capita and, as a result, the land-reform issue will become relatively less important in relation to other policies of promoting income equality.

We may conclude by looking at the available data on the performance of some of the countries we have mentioned in improving their relative income distribution. The data is highly aggregative and compares the growth rate of income per capita accruing to the bottom 60% of the population in a country with the growth rate in income per capita for the country as a whole (see Table 8.1).

It will be seen that Sri Lanka and Costa Rica have been able to show a good performance in income distribution during the periods under observation. But this was achieved by devoting a very large proportion of their budget to consumers' subsidies to support a highly developed system of social welfare. This drain on the budget has, however, proved unsustainable without economic growth and export expansion. Thus Sri Lanka was obliged to change her policies in 1977, and the economic crisis brought about by the oil shocks and the world recession in the early 1980s similarly forced Costa Rica to change her policies.

It will also be seen that Colombia has been able to show a comparably good record of income distribution by pursuing ordinary middle-of-the-road policies, introducing progressive taxation and increasing public expenditure on health and education, without going too far in the direction of welfare-state policies and without a significant land-reform programme. Colombia also suffered from a decline in growth rate due to the world recession of the early 1980s, but her policies seem to be more sustainable in economic terms. She is better placed to make suitable adjustments to external shocks, and her external indebtedness, although it has grown, is still well within her capacity to manage debt servicing.

Despite land reforms and radical nationalizing policies, Mexico and Peru have shown a poor performance in income distribution. The growth rate of income per capita for the bottom 60% in Mexico was lower than the national average rate of growth in income per capita, implying a redistribution of income in favour of the top 40%. In Peru, the growth rate in income for the bottom 60% was the same as the national average. Although comparable figures are not available for Egypt, the author of that country study has pointed out the remarkable stability in income distribution in Egypt, 'despite land reforms and rent controls'.[24] Brazil's poor record of income distribution has been included in our table for comparison, although it should be noted that absolute poverty has been reduced both in Brazil and Mexico.

We may round off this section by taking a brief look at the outstandingly successful examples of land reform in countries such as Taiwan and Korea. These will help us to have a better understanding of the underlying institutional factors important for the success or failure of land-reform programmes in other countries.

Taiwan and Korea were fortunate in having a favourable conjunction of political factors, including US political pressure, which facilitated the introduction of their land reforms. But the more important lesson they have to offer is that land reforms by themselves would not be sufficient to achieve the objectives of growth with a more equal income distribution unless accompanied by appropriate economic policies and supported by an appropriate institutional framework.

Taiwan and Korea started out in the 1950s from the initial conditions of abundant labour, with heavy population pressure on land and rapid population growth. Given this, the benefits of an once-over land redistribution would have been soon swallowed by population growth. What was required was a set of continuously acting policies which would raise the productivity of resources in agriculture. Given the initial conditions of abundant labour, this meant the expansion of agricultural output based on technological improvements of a labour-using and land-saving type, combined with the expansion of a labour-intensive manufacturing industry to draw labour away from agriculture and raise the productivity of those remaining on land.

In Chapter 4, Section IV, we have already outlined the economic policies which Taiwan and Korea successfully pursued to achieve these requirements. Here we may recapitulate the salient features of these policies, concentrating on the underlying institutional factors.

First, there were their successful policies to expand agricultural output and raise agricultural productivity rapidly, by adopting a series of technological improvements based on an increasing use of high-yielding seeds and fertilizer and pesticide and the extension of multiple cropping by means of better irrigation. This was followed by agricultural diversification and the introduction of new high-value crops (such as asparagus and mushrooms in Taiwan).

Second, then there were outstandingly successful policies to expand their labour-intensive manufactured exports after their abandonment of import-substitution policies based on heavy protection and import controls.

For our present purpose, the most significant feature of the expansion of labour-intensive manufactured exports in Taiwan and Korea was that it was mainly based on small-scale industries operated by local entrepreneurs and widely dispersed in the countryside. To be sure, there were some larger-scale industries in their Export Processing Zones (EPZ) where foreign investment was attracted by the supply of cheap labour. But it is nevertheless true to say that in their earlier stages of export-expansion, manufacturing industries in Taiwan and Korea were based on a decentralized pattern of industrialization. This provided them with two great advantages. Firstly, the small factories operating in proximity with farming communities, frequently within commuting distance, were able to tap the local labour supply, cheaply and flexibly. Secondly, by adopting a decentralized pattern of industrialization, Taiwan and Korea were able to minimize the heavy social overhead capital costs (not to mention the heavy human costs) of rapid urbanization and industrial agglomeration in big cities which have crippled the other newly industrializing countries. Thus the expansion of manufactured exports from Taiwan and Korea was labour-intensive and capital-saving with regard both to the method of production and to the provision of social overhead capital.[25]

We can now bring out the institutional implications of these economic policies.

As we have seen in Chapter 4, Section IV, the successful introduction of new technologies into peasant agriculture required not only the provision of physical infrastructure, such as irrigation and the extension of transport electricity to the rural areas, but also the building up of an effective organizational network to provide marketing and credit facilities to enable the farmers to adopt the new cash-intensive methods of agriculture. It also required an improved network of communications and information to disseminate the new technologies to the small farmers widely scattered in the countryside. In Taiwan the Joint Commission on Rural Reconstruction (JCRR) did very valuable work in promoting technological innovations and institutional change by channelling the US aid funds into productive uses during 1949–53. This built on the sound foundations of rural infrastructure, including health and education, which Taiwan has inherited from the Japanese colonial period.

For our present purpose, the important thing to point out is that a very similar type of improvement in the network of marketing and credit and transport facilities is required to cater for the needs of the small industrialists producing the labour-intensive manufactured exports. Here again, Taiwan and Korea have inherited from their colonial period the Japanese flair for creating institutional arrangements favourable for the growth of efficiency of small-scale labour-intensive manufacturing industries (such as subcontracting, and quality controls for the export market). These institutional arrangements arose out of Japan's successful adaptation to her own initial conditions of abundant labour, and were readily transmitted to Taiwan and Korea with similar factor endowments.

We can now see the essential complementarity between the institutional improvements required to raise productivity in peasant agriculture and in the decentralized small-scale manufacturing industries. The remarkably rapid expansion of labour-intensive manufactured exports from Taiwan and Korea would not have been possible without the improvements in the organizational framework to support the process, and these improvements spread spontaneously to the agricultural sector. The widening of the domestic market, and the sharing of common facilities such as transport, electricity, and the marketing and credit network, between the small industrialists and the small farmers in a decentralized pattern of industrialization, would then reduce the general level of the transactions costs for the whole economy. Last but not least, the close human contacts between the small industrialists and small farmers would help to bring out latent entrepreneurial talent among the latter, stimulating a steady stream of minor technical improvements adapted to local conditions, which have contributed to the success of land reforms.

The key to the success here is not simply the expansion of labour-intensive manufactured exports as such but the decentralized pattern of industrialization based on small-scale industries. This can be clearly appreciated by looking at the countries, such as Mexico and Malaysia, which have also succeeded in expanding labour-intensive manufactured exports, but mainly of a larger-scale type by attracting foreign investment into their Export Processing Zones (EPZs). Now the expansion of labour-intensive manufacturing and processing industries in the EPZ of Mexico along the border of the United States has brought obvious benefits to Mexico in the form of greater employment and wage incomes. But no one would imagine that it could have any conceivable effect on Mexico's land-reform programmes. The expansion of labour-intensive manufacturing in Malaysia's EPZ has also shown a similar lack of spread effects, and in order to help the Malay peasant farmers the government had to pursue, on an entirely separate basis, Land Settlement programmes.

What are the implications of the Taiwan and Korea story for the prospects of successful land reform in the other countries in our study? It would appear that it is difficult to copy the success story of Taiwan and Korea for the other countries with their very different initial conditions of factor endowments and different historical and institutional settings. Land reform, however, remains a burning issue, especially in the Latin American countries with their highly unequal pattern of land ownership. Thus it may be useful to touch briefly on the institutional and organizational difficulties they would encounter, even if the opposition of big landowners could be surmounted.

The Latin American countries, typified by countries such as Mexico and Brazil, started from the initial conditions of abundant natural resources and developed a comparative advantage in primary exports produced by modern large-scale enterprises in the mining and plantation sector. They may be regarded as predominantly mining and plantation economies (before the rise of manufactured exports), for they have very little peasant exports. The institutional and organizational problems they have to solve can be better appreciated by looking first at the intermediate case of countries such as Malaysia and Sri Lanka, which produce both mining and plantation exports and peasant exports. We have seen (in Chapter 3, Section III and Chapter 4, Section III) that the Malaysian government has been more successful in helping the Malay peasants with the Land Settlement programmes than the Sri Lankan government in helping the Sinhalese peasants. We may briefly recapitulate some of the factors which have contributed to Malaysia's success, and explain why even this falls far short of the achievements of Taiwan and Korea. We shall then go on to consider the further difficulties which the Latin American countries would have to face even to achieve Malaysia's limited success.

We have seen that Malaysia and Sri Lanka are 'plural societies' made up of two main ethnic groups: the Malays and the Chinese in Malaysia and the Sinhalese and the Tamils in Sri Lanka. Ethnic nationalism has been the driving force behind the land-settlement programmes of the Malaysian government and the Sri Lankan government to help their indigenous Malay and Sinhalese peasants respectively. But the Chinese happen to be the economically dominant group in Malaysia, and to counterbalance their influence the Malaysian government has consistently pursued liberal policies towards the outside foreign enterprises in the mining and plantation sectors. The expansion of mining and plantation exports then provided the government with a steady stream of revenues to subsidize the various land-settlement programmes to help the Malay peasants. In Sri Lanka, however, the Tamils were not economically dominant and the Sinhalese nationalism was directed also towards foreign-owned plantations, discouraging exports from this sector. This reduced the government's revenues available for subsidizing the Sinhalese peasants. A further factor which has helped Malaysia's land-settlement programmes is that both the large plantations and the peasants have common export products, such as rubber and oil-palms, and this facilitated the transmission of the technological advances pioneered in the large estates (such as the cloning of high-yielding rubber trees) to the peasant exporters.

Two major factors have essentially contributed to Malaysia's land-settlement programmes. Firstly, the government agencies responsible for these programmes were exceptionally efficient. The Federal Land Development Agency (FDL) effectively planned and carried out its task of clearing vast tracts of unused land and planting them with young rubber trees and oil-palms on individual smallholdings to be handed over to selected Malay farmers on a ready-made basis, together with low-cost housing. This was accompanied by the creation of effective government agencies to carry out the follow-up action of providing the farmers with subsidized credit, inputs, and marketing and transport facilities. Secondly, the Malaysian government was able to obtain a large and expanding flow of revenues to finance not only the heavy initial capital outlays of land clearing and irrigation but also the continuing subsidies to finance the follow-up policies.

But even so, the extension of the Malaysian land-settlement programmes came to be ultimately constrained by the limitations of its financial and administrative resources, and these programmes could cater for only a limited fraction of the total Malay peasant population. This contrasts with the situation in Taiwan and Korea, where the expansion of labour-intensive manufactured exports spontaneously generated spillover effects to improve the organizational framework of the agricultural sector, reducing the transactions costs for the bulk of peasant farmers, without a continuing need for government subsidies.

We may now turn to the predominantly mining and plantation export economies of the Latin American type. Here the large-scale economic units in the modern sector, based on modern capital-intensive technology, are supporting a well-developed infrastructure and market system and have ready access to an international supply of capital, managerial resources, and technology. Thus the exports from the modern sector, whether primary products or manufactured products, could expand rapidly according to comparative advantage, unconstrained by the underdeveloped organizational framework of the traditional peasant sector, largely devoted to subsistence agriculture. Conversely, the expansion of exports from the modern sector would have very little effect on the traditional sector.

In this setting, even if the political opposition to the initial once-over redistribution of land could be overcome, it would still be extremely difficult to obtain political support to tax the powerful modern sector to obtain a continuing stream of subsidies required to finance the follow-up policies to raise the productivity of the resources in the hands of the peasant beneficiaries of the land-reform programmes. Few Latin American countries can be described as plural societies in the Malaysian sense, provided with the ethnic nationalism necessary to generate the political will to transfer a continuing stream of subsidies to help their indigenous peasants.

Peru is the closest example of a plural society in Latin America, but, as we have seen, the land-reform programmes of Velasco never seriously reached down to the Andean peasants.

Apart from this problem of maintaining an adequate stream of subsidies to support land-reform programmes, the Latin American countries have to face a further set of difficulties.

First, there are the considerable organizational and administrative problems of setting up effective government agencies to cater for the needs of small farmers. The task of providing subsidized credit and inputs to the small farmers in the right place, in the right amounts, and at the right time is difficult to perform without bureaucratic delays and inefficiency, and this may be a stumbling-block for many Latin American countries.

Secondly, in order to raise the productivity of the small farmers in the land-reform programmes, it is necessary to have a stream of technical improvements adapted to local conditions. On the other hand, the large-scale extensive farms in the Latin American countries are modelled on the highly capital-intensive American style of mechanized farming. Rather than undertake their own research and development, they find it more economical to hitch on to the stream of technological innovations from North America designed to save labour by substituting it with capital (accentuating the capital-intensive technology). This moves in a diametrically opposite direction from the type of innovations required to raise the productivity of the labour-intensive methods of agriculture employed by the small farmers. In the Latin American context, there is little scope for the possibility of transmitting technological improvements from the large estates to the small farmers which we have noted in Malaysia, let alone for the possibility of introducing a dynamic series of labour-intensive innovations like those which have contributed to the success of land reform in Taiwan. The small farmers in Latin America could of course take advantage of the general spread of the Green Revolution based on high-yielding seeds and fertilizer. But this pushes the problem back to the distribution of irrigation facilities between the large estates and the small farmers.

Thirdly, the manufacturing industries in the modern sector of the Latin American countries are not only large-scale units but also concentrated in large urban conurbations, swollen by immigration of labour from the countryside. This is not an exclusively Latin American phenomenon, but it clearly aggravates the difficulties for the land-reform policies. Rapid urbanization and the growth of huge cities has inevitably contributed in the urban bias in the allocation of social overhead investment and public expenditure, starving the rural areas of the resources needed to improve their social infrastructure. Further, since the emigration to the cities attracts the young and ambitious, the traditional agricultural sector is robbed of its potential entrepreneurial talent. But what about the growth of the 'urban informal sector' based on labour-intensive small industries which has developed in countries such as Peru? As we have suggested in Chapter 4, Section IV, this provides the Latin American country with a scope for a natural import-substitution in a wide range of labour-intensive manufactured products, in accordance with their changing comparative advantage brought about by population growth. Thus it is possible to argue that the encouragement of the growth of the urban informal sector by removing the various dis-criminatory government policies against it may be as important as land reform in promoting growth with greater income equality in many Latin American countries. But by definition, the urban informal sector is clus-tered around the big cities and cannot be expected to have much effect in improving the rural organizational framework to support the land-reform programmes.

NOTES

1. For a vigorous exposition of the interest-group approach see Findlay (1988). For a sceptical view of the rent-seeking approach, see Hansen (1992: 117–19).
2. For a well-documented survey of this matter, see *World Development Report 1983*, part II, chs. 4–8, especially boxes 5.1 and 5.4. Also see Roth (1987).
3. See *World Development Report 1983*, ch. 8 and fig. 8.1.
4. Moreover, as the recent literature on interlinked markets in rural areas has emphasized, many of the seeming imperfections in rural institutions are likely to be second-best adaptations to environmental risk and uncertainty. There is little reason to believe that public agencies will necessarily be able to overcome these environmental constraints and perform better than the traditional agents. On interrelated factor markets see Bardhan (1989a) and Basu (1984).
5. See Ahluwalia and Chenery (1974).
6. See Hicks (1974a) for an illuminating discussion of the two traditions in capital theory based on the materialist definition and on the concept of capital as a fund.
7. See e.g. Hansen (1991: 160, 361).
8. See Rimmer (1992: ch. 5, pp. 34–5), and Bruton (1992: 135–140).
9. See also *World Development Report 1983*, ch. 8.
10. For a systematic study of the pattern of structural change see Chenery and Syrquin (1975).
11. For a well-known account of the linkages, defined in terms of the size of technologically determined input–output coefficients, see Hirschman (1958: ch. 3).
12. See Krueger et al. (1988).
13. Maddison et al. (1992: 11) and Rimmer (1992: ch. 5, p. 58).
14. For a well-known formulation along these lines, see Johnston and Mellor, 1961. For a critique of this type of formulation see Myint, 1975.
15. See e.g. Little (1979: 479–80).
16. This type of calculation was first introduced by Dovring (1959: 1–11). The

arithmetical example is taken from W. A. Lewis (1979), reprinted in Meier (1984: 418–21).

17. See e.g. Pryor (1991: 103–8, 376–7).
18. For well-documented discussions of this issue in relation to the provision of agricultural credit, see Adams and Graham (1981), and Gonzalez-Vega (1977).
19. See W. O. Jones (1972: ch. 9); see also Myint (1979).
20. Taiwan's successful land-reform programme was based on improvements in rural social infrastructure and the organizational network of marketing, credit, and information, which promoted labour-intensive and land-saving technological improvements, increasing multiple cropping and diversification into new labour-intensive crops. See Fei *et al.* (1979: 45–50).
21. Maddison *et al.* (1992: 12, and table 6.21, pp. 166–71).
22. Urdinola *et al.* (mimeo: part II, 116, and summary, 16.)
23. Hansen (1991: 119).
24. Ibid. table IV, 30; summary, pp. 13–14.
25. Cf. Ranis in Galenson (1979: 221–32) and Fei *et al.* (1979: 45–50).

9

Income Transfers and
Poverty Redressal

IN Chapter 1, we distinguished between three types of poverty: structural mass poverty, destitution, and conjunctural poverty. We showed that the evidence from our country studies, as well as others, overwhelmingly supported the inference that growth does alleviate structural mass poverty. But there are some exceptions and nuances which need to be emphasized. This is done in the first section below. It has, however, been argued that this so-called indirect route to curing mass poverty needs to be supplemented (if not replaced) by a more direct route, which in effect establishes Western-style welfare states in the Third World. This question of income transfers is also of importance in dealing with what the Victorians called the 'deserving poor'—or, in our terminology, the destitute and conjuncturally poor. Most of this chapter is concerned with the desirability and efficacy of income transfers (both private and public) in alleviating all three types of poverty.

I. MASS POVERTY AND GROWTH: THE EVIDENCE
FROM THE COUNTRY STUDIES

As discussed in Chapter 1, in our country studies, lacking detailed statistical information, the authors had to make do with judgements about the initial levels of income per capita of the lowest 20–40% of the population in 1950 as a broad indicator of the initial levels of mass poverty in their respective countries. We do not have any data on the incidence of conjunctural poverty nor on destitution.[1] So we have had to rely on other studies to deal with policies for their alleviation.

Our country studies, therefore, concentrated on the relative success or failure of the economic policies of these countries to promote growth as the principal means of alleviating mass poverty. The general presumption that positive rates of growth in income per capita accompany a reduction of structural poverty has been generally supported by the findings of the country studies (see Chapter 1). There may, however, be a time-lag before economic growth shows itself in a clearly measurable sharp decline in poverty. For example, although the 'Golden Age' of economic growth in Thailand began from 1959, a sharp decline in poverty did not become clearly measurable until after 1962–3.[2] In other fast-growing countries in our group, such as Malaysia, Colombia, Brazil, or Turkey, sharp reductions in the absolute level of poverty did not become clearly visible until after 1970.[3] This may sometimes be due to statistical lags in measurement, but may also be due to genuine time-lags between growth and poverty alleviation.

We may now go a little further into what can be called the 'non-policy factors' affecting the incidence and alleviation of structural poverty. Firstly, it may be noted that the general trends in the social indicators for health, such as life expectancy and infant mortality, which are vital ingredients in the reduction of poverty, may or may not be closely related to the economic policies of a country and its record of economic growth. For instance, since the mid-1960s there has been an improving trend in life expectation and infant mortality among the low-income sub-Saharan African countries; yet during the period 1965–85 the average rates of growth in incomes per capita for these countries has been negative. Thus a considerable part of the improvement in social indicators in these countries may be attributed to exogenous factors such as the general improvements in medical knowledge and the eradication and control of disease. Moreover, simply extending the availability of safe drinking water could reduce infant mortality as well as mortality in general, and at least potentially this extension could take place in the absence of income growth. In countries such as Costa Rica and Uruguay, direct policy intervention has enabled an extensive welfare system to develop, resulting in high levels of health and education and the reduction of poverty, despite periods of low and, in Uruguay, negative growth rates of GDP per capita. Such poverty reduction, however, has not been sustainable for Costa Rica in the long run (see below). Directing resources away from her export sector to encourage the growth of a powerful welfare state at the cost of relatively low growth in the 1980s has eventually halted the progress made in the past in poverty alleviation. Uruguay, too, has been unable to sustain such a large welfare state, but had no serious problem of poverty before its collapse (see below).

Secondly, the rate of population growth of a country may be regarded as a non-policy factor in the short run, but a policy factor in the longer run. In the short run, the population growth of a country and its position in the demographic transition are carry-overs from its initial social conditions, and there is a long 'braking distance' before population-control policies take effect. But our country studies include notable examples of successful policies which have significantly reduced population growth. Thus we have Mauritius, regarded in the 1950s as a classic horror story of Malthusian over-population, dramatically reducing her birth-rate from 40 to 27 per thousand during the 1960s with the aid of birth-control policies. We also have Colombia, which has successfully reduced her population growth in contrast to Peru, Mexico, and Brazil. In Asia we have Thailand's success in bringing down her population growth. Moreover, to the extent that the trade-off between more children and increased consumption is shifted towards the latter as income increases, then growth itself will have an impact on reducing fertility.

One simple-minded approach assumes a given rate of growth in aggregate GDP and goes on to argue that, other things being equal, a reduction in population growth, by raising the rate of growth in income per capita, would tend to alleviate poverty. This, however, leaves out the possible favourable effects of population growth on economic growth through the increase in labour supply. Kuznets,[4] for instance, has assembled cross-sectional evidence showing that population growth is positively correlated with economic growth, and has stressed the importance of the organizational development of a country in enabling it to benefit from an expanding labour force. Thus he argues that the possible adverse effects of population growth on poverty may be found, not so much in the pulling down of the average rate of growth in income per capita (which cannot be treated as a constant independent of population growth), but in the differential population-growth rates between the rich and the poor and the urban and rural areas, leading to different dependency ratios. In countries like Uruguay, Costa Rica, and Mexico, the prospect of easy out-migration to neighbouring countries where employment may be more abundant relieves the poverty problem, acting as a safety-valve for the poorest sectors of the population.

The major exception to the observed result that growth alleviates structural mass poverty in our samples is that of Malawi. Here a positive growth rate of GDP per capita is accompanied by what the author concludes is rising poverty. Our country studies note that poverty is largely a rural (agricultural) phenomenon. The Malawian case guards against a conclusion that pro-agricultural policies will therefore alleviate poverty by transferring resources to the rural population. Malawi's pro-agricultural policies have largely benefited her estate sector, leaving small peasant farmers untouched. Thus she has been able to maintain her growth rates through expansion of estate-sector exports whilst squeezing smallholders through an export marketing board, taxing the poorest sector of the population. Growing population pressure in the traditional agricultural sector has also contributed to the increase in poverty.

In the plural Sir Lankan society the government has directed its efforts to raising the relative living standards of its indigenous population, the Sinhalese, transferring resources away from other ethnic groups. As the Sinhalese are one of the poorest groups in Sri Lanka, this nationalist 'equity' policy has served to reduce poverty to some extent. But this 'indirect' poverty-reduction approach has been of little help to the poorest group in Sri Lanka, the Indian Tamils, brought in as estate workers. Few serious attempts have been made to improve their living standards, and they were only recently included in the polity.[5] The Malaysian governments have followed a similar path, but have had more success in reducing poverty because the indigenous Malays are the poorest group in Malaysia.

Finally, it should be noted that poverty levels and growth rates can differ considerably within countries. Thus, although Brazil has successfully reduced overall poverty with a 3.9% growth rate of GDP per capita, poverty and a poor growth performance are concentrated in the North-East region. In Nigeria the regional concentration of poverty in the Northern region, coupled with fierce competition between the regions for resources, has made poverty-reduction policies very difficult to implement.

II. THE DIRECT METHOD OF ALLEVIATING STRUCTURAL POVERTY

It has been argued that a so-called 'direct route', based on public income transfers, should also be used to deal with what we have labelled structural mass poverty. In an influential paper Sen (1981b) argued that a number of countries (e.g. Sri Lanka, Costa Rica) had succeeded in alleviating poverty despite low growth, and beyond what could be expected with comparators with similar income levels per capita. Bhalla and Glewwe (1986) and Bhalla (1988) have contested the inferences drawn by Sen from his empirics, essentially on the grounds that Sri Lanka had already achieved high levels of poverty alleviation (based on various social indicators), before independence. Its post-independence record, they argue, was worse on both the growth and poverty-alleviation indices if this historical adjustment for its social indicators was made. The subsequent debate has shed more heat than light (see Sen's response and Bhalla's riposte in Srinivasan and Bardhan, 1988).

1. Cross-Sectional Evidence

In assessing the relative performance of our countries in terms of social indicators, Bhalla has recently suggested a simple cross-sectional statistical model[6] which allows performance to be judged relative to each country's own initial conditions (with respect to each indicator) as well as that of countries at similar levels of development or income per capita (at the base date).[7]

We have estimated this model for the 1960–86 period to see how our countries perform in terms of life expectancy and mortality. The comparators were taken to be countries in the same broad income class, low-income, middle-income, and upper-income, as defined by the World Bank. Regressions were also run taking all developing countries as the relevant comparators. Each country's initial conditions were taken into account. The results are depicted in Figs. 9.1 and 9.2 for the case when the com-

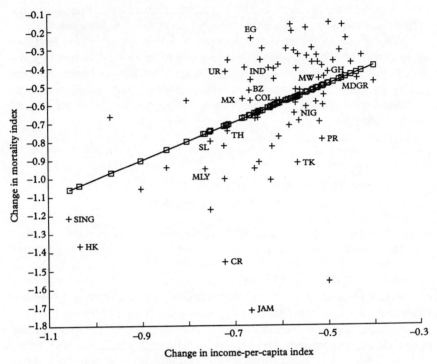

Fig 9.1. Child mortality regression

$$\Delta \ln M = -2.4\left(\frac{1}{\ln M_{60}}\right) - 0.137\left(\ln Y_{86} - Y_{60}\right).$$

plus signs show observed values for differents countries (countries in our sample are labelled); squares show corresponding values expected from the regression equation.

parator is 'all developing countries'. (The results are not very different for the individual income classes.)

Each figure shows the regression line for the relationship between the social indicator and growth rates of GDP per capita for all developing countries. The countries in our sample have been identified by self-explanatory symbols. If a country lies above (below) the line then its performance is worse (better) than its comparators.[8] In Fig. 9.1, which charts the child mortality regression (0–4 years), the performance of Egypt, Indonesia, Uruguay, and Mexico is below par, whilst that of Singapore, Hong Kong, Malaysia, Costa Rica, Jamaica, Turkey, and Peru is better than expected.[9]

Fig. 9.2 shows the results for life expectancy. The performance of Uruguay, Malawi, Brazil, and Singapore is worse than expected, whilst that

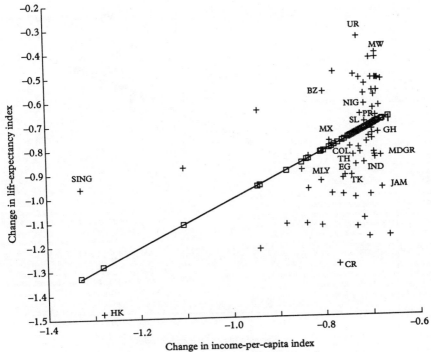

Fig 9.2. Life expectancy regression

$$\Delta \ln\left(\frac{K-H}{H}\right) = -0.686 - 0.0001\, Y_{86} + 0.00007\, Y_{60}. \text{ symbols as in Fig. 9.1.}$$

of Hong Kong, Costa Rica, Jamaica, Malaysia, Egypt, Turkey, Indonesia, and Madagascar appears to be better than expected.[10]

Finally, in Fig. 9.3 we show the results for the reduction in composite PQLI deficit (for a notional value of 100).[11] The performance of Uruguay, Brazil, Egypt, Nigeria, Malawi, and Ghana is distinctly worse, whilst that of Hong Kong, Costa Rica, and Jamaica is very much better, as is to a lesser extent that of Thailand, Colombia, Turkey, and Peru.

Taking all three figures together, it appears that Jamaica, Costa Rica, Turkey, and Hong Kong do better than expected on the social indicators, and Uruguay and Brazil worse. As the two ostensible welfare states in our example, Uruguay and Costa Rica, fall on either side of the dividing line, as do two of the relatively capitalist economies, Brazil and Hong Kong, it is apparent that the type of support such cross-section analyses can provide to those who believe that poverty redressal requires so-called direct government intervention is virtually non-existent.[12]

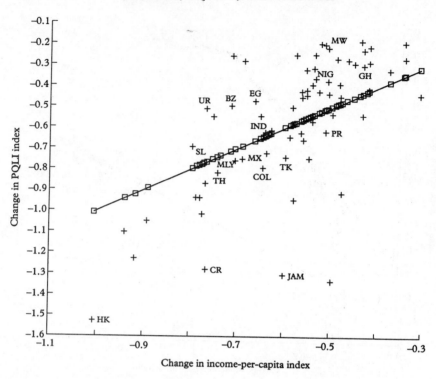

Fig 9.3. Reduction in PQL1 deficit regression

$$\Delta \ln DR = -2.13\left(\frac{1}{\ln DR_{60}}\right) - 0.203\left(\ln Y_{86} - \ln Y_{60}\right). \text{ symbols as in Fig. 9.1.}$$

2. Evidence from Country Studies

Our comparative study therefore placed more weight on the long-run analytical histories of the interactions between growth, poverty alleviation, and the political economy of policy interventions in determining the qualitative conclusions about the relative productivity of the direct and indirect routes to poverty alleviation (see Bhagwati, 1988). For it is obvious that arguing, as some proponents of the establishment of welfare states in the Third World have done, that low-growth countries with direct poverty-redressal programmes have been successful in alleviating poverty, begs a number of important questions. The first is whether the direct interventions lowered growth rates (which would have had a deleterious effect on poverty alleviation). The second is whether the resulting welfare entitlements which alleviated poverty were sustainable in a low-growth environment.

There are four countries in our sample which have established many features of a Western-style welfare state. The oldest and most notable example is that of Uruguay. It was established by Batlle at the beginning of the century and provided a code of labour legislation, unemployment compensation, old-age pensions, family allowances, workmen's compensation for injuries, and compensation for those discharged. The net effect of the welfare system (combined with the system of trade protection), according to Rottenberg, was to distort the relative prices of labour and capital, raising the former and lowering the latter.[13] More serious, however, were the fiscal consequences. As Favaro and Bension note, the tax resources available from a stagnating economy were unable to finance an explosive increase in welfare expenditures, due to demographic trends related to the ageing of the population and the increased coverage of retirement benefits. Furthermore, the social security system came to be unfunded, as its reserves, which had been used to purchase public debt (itself issued to finance fiscal imbalances), were virtually wiped out by inflation. The fiscal crisis of the Uruguayan state which was in part responsible for its growth collapse was thus largely due to these unsustainable social expenditures. Moreover, as Favaro and Bension conclude, 'Distributionally oriented policies have distorted incentives, inducing human and physical investments in activities that are highly profitable for agents in the private sector but have a low return to society as a whole.'[14]

Thus the poor growth record of Uruguay can in part be blamed on the redistributive '*immobilisme*' and inefficiencies that the combination of its welfare state and *dirigiste* trade and anti-agricultural policies entailed.

Costa Rica's development of a welfare state and its likely denouement seem to follow Uruguay's closely by about three decades. Beginning in the late 1930s and early 1940s, by the late 1970s the welfare system had been expanded to provide virtually universal social security. However, González-Vega in Rottenberg *et al.* (1993) emphasizes that most of the favourable poverty-alleviation and equity outcomes were in place by the late 1960s. They were in large part due to, first, a rapid modern-sector enlargement: 'Costa Rica was the country in Latin America with the highest rate of growth of employment in modern non-agricultural activities.' Secondly, a rapid rise in agricultural productivity promoted by infrastructural investments in the 1960s also helped to alleviate poverty in the rural areas (where poverty was concentrated).

Between the early 1960s and early 1970s, while the labor force grew by 48 per cent, the number of farmers and cattlemen grew by only 11 per cent . . . [Also] there was a substantial increase in labor productivity in agriculture, [which rose] relative to that of the whole economy . . . from 48 per cent in 1963 to about 70 per cent in the early 1980s.[15]

Poverty declined from about 50 per cent of the population around 1961 to somewhere between 20 and 25 per cent in the mid-1970s.

The welfare state was greatly expanded in the 1960s, but it only became universal with its consolidation and institutionalization in the mid-1970s *after* the decline in poverty had taken place. As González-Vega and Cespedes note:

> Economic growth and improvements in the labour market were themselves responsible for increased equality in income distribution and for alleviation of poverty. Only after the mid 1970's were explicit redistributive policies important to equity outcomes. The effects of these policies were mixed, however, because of the constraints imposed by the fiscal crisis of the early 1980's.[16]

The inflexibility in the resulting growth-reducing fiscal entitlements, together with the consequences of highly protectionist government intervention, resulted in the fiscal disequilibria which González-Vega and Cespedes conclude were at the root of its growth crisis. During the economic crisis in the 1980s poverty 'increased to about 30% of the population'.[17]

In both the Uruguayan and Costa Rican cases, therefore, whilst there was undoubtedly some poverty redressal as a result of the expansion of their welfare states, over the long run the entitlements they created damaged the growth performance of the country, on which they were predicated, and hence eventually became unsustainable.

Virtually the same story can be told about the expansion of unviable social expenditures in Sri Lanka and Jamaica, financed by taxing growth-promoting productive activities which has killed the goose that laid the golden eggs. In both cases the temporary improvement in poverty indices has not been sustainable. The essential point from these case studies which needs to be emphasized, can be brought out by noting Sen's statement that 'ultimately poverty removal must come to grips with the issue of entitlement guarantees'; and that whereas the 'growth' or 'indirect' route relies on 'successfully fostered growth and the dynamism of the encouraged labour markets', the other direct *dirigiste* route 'gives the government a more *direct* role as the provider of provisions'.[18] But as our country studies show, there are important differences in the nature of the guarantee provided by each of these alternative ways of removing poverty. Not all guarantees are equally ironclad! The security of politically determined entitlements of the poor (in, for instance, our four welfare states) has come increasingly into question as the inexorable increase in their cost confronts a fixed economic pie from which they can be financed (in part resulting from the economic stagnation that such transfers have indirectly fostered). By contrast, the alleviation of the poverty in many of our higher-growth countries (Hong Kong, Thailand, Indonesia, for instance) through the rising incomes of the poor cannot be so easily reversed by political fiat, as these 'entitlements' are really not underwritten by the state, but represent the higher returns on agents' endowments. They have been earned and are underwritten by the wealth created in the growth process.

Very similar problems are also visible in the more mature welfare states of the OECD. For though the public provision of transfers to the 'deserving poor' in the United Kingdom goes back to the Elizabethan Poor Law, it was not till the late nineteenth century that public transfers began to expand in all industrial countries. This process was in part associated with the fears of disorder arising from the growth of socialist sentiments in Europe. It began with Bismarck's introduction of social insurance against sickness, accident, and old age in Germany. It was soon followed in the United Kingdom by Lloyd George's 1911 introduction of national insurance (which in addition covered unemployment). In the US, the New Deal was the watershed. In the period after the Second World War these public transfers exploded, as in the 1960s and 1970s the coverage of health and pensions benefits was made universal and their levels increased. The share of social expenditures in total public expenditure rose from 44% to 60% between 1960 and 1980, and the share of social expenditures in GDP rose from under 14% to nearly 25% over the same period (see Hakim and Wallich, 1986). In an earlier study (see Lal and Wolf, 1986) the deleterious effects of this expansion of the welfare state on the public finances and on the economy's productivity were charted.[19] With the stagflation of the 1970s in part flowing from these trends, and with growing uneasiness about the unintended social consequences of the welfare state (on which more below), many OECD governments took measures to stem the growth of transfers. In some countries which had gone furthest down the public welfare route, the late 1980s and 1990s saw a growing questioning of the welfare state in the West, and in some cases its partial or virtual dismantling.

III. CONJUNCTURAL POVERTY, DESTITUTION, AND TRANSFERS

This still leaves problems of destitution and conjunctural poverty, which are likely to exist even if growth takes account of the alleviation of mass poverty. Unlike the classical liberals who (as we saw in Chapter 1) advocate targeted benefits to provide income and/or merit goods to these 'deserving poor', the socialist distributivist panacea is to institute Western-style welfare states with the universalization of benefits, to deal with problems like insufficient take-up and the costs of gathering information to identify beneficiaries (particularly acute in poor countries with weak administrative systems) which bedevil the targeting of benefits (see Atkinson, 1987, and Glewwe and van der Gaag, 1988).

1. Safety Nets and Welfare States

The alleviation of conjunctural poverty and destitution do require transfers—which allow the income/consumption of an individual to be higher than it would otherwise be. But in discussing such transfers it is useful to distinguish between the welfare state and a social safety net. This turns essentially upon the universality of coverage of transfers under a welfare state as opposed to the restriction of collectively provided benefits under a social safety net to those among the poor who are unlikely to benefit from economic growth or human resource development. 'The safety net includes income transfers for those chronically unable to work—because of age or handicap—and those temporarily affected by natural disasters or economic recession',[20] as it is put in a recent World Bank handbook, which also then notes two essential elements in any design of a social safety net: 'The issues concerning transfers and safety nets include identifying the groups in need of assistance, and the means of targeting assistance to those groups cost-effectively. Are these questions for public policy, or are they adequately addressed by the traditional family network?'[21]

The need for a social safety net—to be found in most economies—is not necessarily a reflection of morality, nor of public action seeking to correct market failures, but is due to the ubiquitousness of risk in men's lives and the possibility of reducing its individual burden through some kind of mutual assurance. This could take various forms: through market processes such as insurance, as well as social institutions like the family. The term 'social' needs to be clarified in this context. Though it has become coterminous with public (state) action, in its original sense it refers only to co-operative action—private or public. In this sense to say that there is a need for a 'social safety net' does not prejudge whether this should be provided through private or public action.

2. Labour-Market Risks

So what are the risks in labour markets against which mankind has sought some form of insurance through social co-operation, and how have these changed with different stages in economic development? As most economies were agrarian organic economies, in which (until fairly recently) labour was scare relative to land, there were two major types of risks that were endemic.

The first, which was a form of systemic risk, was related to the need to tie labour down to land where various forms of intensive agriculture were feasible and profitable (largely in alluvial plains, for instance the Indo-Gangetic plain in India). Without this tied labour, less intensive and productive forms of agriculture would have had to be adopted. Various institutions—feudalism in Europe (see Bloch, 1961) the caste system in India (see Lal, 1988b)—evolved to deal with this systemic risk.

More ubiquitous were the cyclical risks associated with changing climate. Various institutional arrangements like the *jajmani* system in India (see Lal, 1988b), or sharecropping or interlinked contracts in other factor markets (see Bardhan, 1989a), provided the ways to cope with these risks. More-over, in these traditional societies, unemployment and destitution as 'nor-mal' states were virtually unknown (see Garraty, 1978). Feudal societies were designed to provide a place for every member, and the local society— village, clan, or tribe—provided the requisite social safety net. The main risk, as in a famine, was of not being able to spread highly covariant risks across the local group. In traditional Indian village society, for instance, this risk was partly dealt with by acquiring relatives through marriage, in geographically distant areas whose climatic risks would not be correlated with their own. These geographically interlinked families could then expect the necessary transfers from their spatially distant relatives when they were suffering climatically induced falls in their income (see Rosenzweig (1988) for the continuing relevance of this feature in modern Indian village life).

In other parts of the world,

Among tribes, no doubt, a rough and ready concern for the sick and old marked most peoples. In settled communities, an essential part was the role played by the lord. A typical feudal provision was that of the Prussian code of 1795: the lord had to see to it that poor peasants were given education, that a livelihood for such of his vassals as had no land must be provided and, if they were reduced to poverty, he had to come to their aid.[22]

In Europe, the breakdown of medieval society and the subsequent agrarian and industrial revolutions led to major changes; not least because popu-lation expansion led, in addition to the destitution of those without any labour power (the handicapped and the old without any families), to 'the poverty of the able-bodied who lacked land, work, or wages adequate to support the dependents who were partly responsible for their poverty'.[23] They were the paupers, and, altruism apart, it was the danger to civil order from vagrancy which lent urgency to the alleviation of their poverty once the link between poverty, crime, and vice was perceived. Their numbers were also swelled by another form of conjunctural poverty arising from the Industrial Revolution's trade cycle and the unemployment that ensues in its downturns.

Finally, in most pre-industrial economies self-employment was and re-mains the dominant form of employment. A self-employed worker com-bines in his person and personal enterprise (or household) all those characteristics which, due to the division of labour, are separated in indus-trial firms. These are labour, entrepreneurship, and capital. A variation in the demand for the output produced by these factors of production will be reflected in an instantaneous change in the implicit value of the marginal products of the various factors. There cannot be any 'involuntary' unem-ployment, therefore, of the self-employed, and hence no question of un-employment insurance for them. Only the income transfers to alleviate conjunctural poverty, and those that maybe deemed necessary to provide merit goods as part of the social safety net, will be relevant for them.

3. Imperfect Information, Insurance, and the Welfare State

Classical liberals have usually advocated the targeting of benefits. Thus the indigent and the disabled are to be helped through targeted benefits. For various merit goods—health, education, and possibly housing—these involve in-kind transfers. This is very much the type of social-policy package that was implemented in Pinochet's Chile, and which not only succeeded in protecting the poor during Chile's arduous transformation to a liberal market economy, but also led to dramatic long-term improvements in its various social indicators (see Castaneda (1992) for a detailed account of these social-policy reforms and their outcome). By contrast, welfare-state advocates favour universality, as it alone in their view provides a feasible means to achieve the ends sought to be subserved by a social safety net. Some (for instance Barr, 1992a) have argued that, because of the ubiquitousness of imperfect information, markets for risk will be inherently imperfect. Hence universal welfare states are required as part of an efficient solution to deal with market failure. This argument needs to be examined, in the context of the economics of insurance.

(a) Moral Hazard

The technocratic public-economics school argues that, with imperfect information, the ideal insurance contracts which would exist in a 'complete markets' Walrasian equilibrium cannot be offered in any real-world insurance market, because of moral hazard and adverse selection. Hence, in Arrow's words (relating to health policy), 'clearly further innovation is desirable in the provision of health insurance, and I see no convincing argument that, in the absence of alternatives, it is undesirable or unnecessary for it to take the form of an increased role for the government.[24] Whilst Barr in his recent survey of the welfare state (mainly pensions, income support, and public financing or provision of medical services) states that 'a central theme is the importance of the literature on imperfect information in establishing an efficiency case for various types of state intervention'.[25] But is this normative use of the ideal Paretian optima, to judge the efficiency of how an actual market outcome copes with problems of moral hazard and adverse selection, justified?

Demsetz is devastating in his negative answer to the above question. He writes:

Moral hazard is identified by Arrow as a unique and irremedial cause of incomplete coverage of all risky activities by insurance. But in truth there is nothing at all unique about moral hazard and economizing on moral hazard provides no special problems not encountered elsewhere. Moral hazard is a relevant cost of providing insurance; ... A price can be and is attached to the sale of all insurance that includes the moral hazard cost imposed by the insured on the insurance companies. And this price is individualized to the extent that other costs, mainly costs of contracting, allow. The moral hazard cost is present, although in different amounts, no matter what percentage of the value of the good is insured. The moral hazard problem is no different than the problem posed by any other cost. Some iron ore is left unearthed because it is too costly to bring up to the surface. But we do not claim, ore mining is inefficient merely because mining is not 'complete'. Some risks are left uninsured because the cost of moral hazard is too great and this may mean that self-insurance is economic. There is no special dilemma associated with moral hazard, but Arrow's concentration on the divergence between risk shifting through insurance and risk shifting in the ideal norm, in which moral hazard is presumably absent, makes it appear as a special dilemma.[26]

In other words, much of this technocratic analysis smacks of nirvana economics. The important question, as Demsetz notes, is 'Do we shift risk or reduce moral hazard efficiently through the market place? This question cannot be answered solely by observing that insurance is incomplete in coverage. Is there an alternative institutional arrangement that seems to offer superior economizing'[27] This question is now being asked by theorists concerned with the positive economics of insurance. The answers they have come up with, in designing their so-called 'incentive-compatible' contracts in the presence of moral hazard, seem to mimic the market. Thus Laffont finds that such a contract will have both co-insurance and deductibles as essential features![28]

(b) Adverse Selection

What of adverse selection? As this is the case which Barr (1992a) uses explicitly to derive his *dirigiste* conclusions, it maybe worth spelling out the arguments within the technocratic framework more fully. This brings out both why they do not work, and also why as in the moral hazard case there is no a priori case that can be made for any necessary inefficiency of the market solution when adverse selection is an essential feature of health or any other insurance market. The general reader may wish to skip this starred section.

⋆(c) The Economics of Insurance

The argument about insurance can be summarized in one diagram (Fig. 9.4). Suppose that there are only two otherwise identical individuals (thus abstracting from distributional considerations) who differ in their probabilities of falling sick (p). The high-risk person H has a probability of falling sick (p_H) greater than that of the low-risk person L (p_L), so that $p_H > p_L$.

Next suppose that, for both people if they do not fall sick their income is y_1, and at the lower level y_2 if they are sick, and they have no way of insuring against their respective risks of falling ill. Their common no-insurance

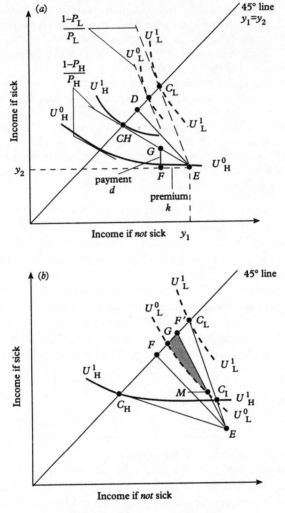

Fig 9.4. The economics of insurance

endowment in the two possible states of nature—not being sick, being
sick—can then be depicted by the point E in Fig. 9.4(a).

Given their common degree of risk aversion, both people would be
willing to trade off some of their income when they are well, to raise their
incomes above what it otherwise would be if they were sick. These preferences for trading off income from the well state to the unwell state can be
depicted by a set of indifference curves. But as the probabilities of falling ill
differ for the two individuals, who in all other respects are identical, their
indifference curves will differ. The higher-risk person will have flatter

indifference curves than the lower-risk person (the dashed ones in Fig. 9.4). This is because the high-risk person has a greater chance of having a low endowment state prevail. Hence, additional income for him will be worth more in that state than to a low-risk person with a lower chance of suffering such an adversity. That is, if we reduce y_1 at bit from E, it takes a smaller increase in y_2 to compensate the high-risk person to maintain the same level of utility than the low-risk person. Thus the high-risk indifference curves will be the flatter bold ones, and the low-risk ones the steeper dashed ones shown in Fig. 9.4.

Another feature of these indifference curves is that on the 45° line, where income in both states is the same (sometimes called 'full insurance'), they will have the same slope, equal to the probability of not being sick to that of being sick, $(1 - p)/p$. So that the slope of the high-risk person's indifference curves along the 45° full-insurance line will be $(1 - p_H)/p_H$, and of the low-risk one $(1 - p_L)/p_L$. As $p_H > p_L$, it follows that the slope of the high-risk person's indifference curves along the 45° line will be less than that of the low-risk one.

Next, introduce a competitive insurance firm which is risk-neutral, and offers to insure the two people for a given premium k, in return for a payout of d if the individual falls sick. With competition, the firm just breaks even. So for each person, the firm's zero-profit actuarily fair contract is simply

$$(1 - p)k - pd = 0. \tag{A}$$

Starting from E in Fig. 9.4(a), for the high-risk individual the insurance company can, for instance, offer a zero-profit contract given by point G. Inspection of the diagram, and the zero-profit condition stated above, then tell us that the slope of the zero-profit line of contracts will be equal to the ratio of probabilities of not being sick to being sick, $(1 - p)/p$. (This follows directly from (A), as the slope of GE is $d/k = (1 - p)/p$.) But we also know that this is also the slope of the relevant set of indifference curves at the full-insurance 45° line. Hence the zero-profit contract line from E for each risk type must be tangential to the relevant indifference curve on the 45° line. This yields the points C_H, for the high-risk individual on the zero-profit contract line EC_H, and C_L, for the low-risk individual on his zero-profit contract line EC_L. For the firm, any contracts lying above these lines will entail losses, and any points below, profits. Given the former, consumers cannot do better in terms of attainable utility than accepting the full-insurance contracts given by point C_H for the high-risk and C_L for the low-risk person.

(i) *Perfect Information*. If the firm could acquire full information about the probabilities p_H and p_L, that is if there was perfect information, and the insurance industry was competitive, then these full-insurance contracts would be the only ones to be found. For if the firm tried to choose contracts below the EC_H and EC_L lines, it could increase its profits, whilst lowering the welfare of both risky individuals (as they would be on lower indifference curves compared to C_H and C_L). But given competition, these profits would be competed away by rival insurers offering the contracts C_H and C_L. Thus it is clear that the Pareto-efficient contracts which yield the highest attainable utility to the two people with different risks would involve separating the two risk classes completely, and offering both full-insurance contracts, with the high-risk people paying higher premiums to offset their higher risks than the low-risk people. Hence, the 'cherry-picking' so often condemned in health insurance as being inefficient is in effect part of the most efficient contract!

The same diagram can also be used to show that with perfect information and competition amongst insurers a so-called 'pooling' contract, in which both risk groups are charged a common premium, would not be voluntarily chosen. Thus suppose the proportion of the low-risk people in the population is g and thence that of the high-risk ones is $1 - g$. Then the zero-profit condition can be defined in terms of the average risk of both groups, $a = g p_L + (1 - g) p_H$, as

$$(1-a)k - ad = 0. \tag{B}$$

Hence, as before, the slope of the pooling zero-contract line, $d/k = (1 - a)/a$, will now depend upon the ratio of the average risk in the population. This in turn depends upon the proportion of low-risk (g) to high-risk ($1 - g$) people in the population. The greater the former ($>g$), the lower the average risk ($< a$), which then implies that the slope of the pooling zero-profit line, $(1 - a)/a$, will be greater. This line is given by ED and must lie between EC_H and EC_L, being closer to C_L if the proportion g of low-risk people is greater, and to C_H if the converse is the case.

It is immediately apparent that, given a choice between the pooling contracts and the separating contracts, the low-risk types will always prefer the separating to the pooling contracts, because all pooling contracts lie to the left of C_L, which is on the highest attainable indifference curve for the low-risk types. Conversely, a pooling equilibrium will always be preferred by high-risk types, because it lies to the right of C_H, and hence must lie on a higher high-risk person's indifference curve. The reason is obvious—a pooling contract involves subsidizing the high-risk people at the expense of low-cost people. Thus it is clear that pooling cannot be Pareto-superior to the separating contracts C_H and C_L, remembering that a Pareto improvement requires that one person is made better off without some else being made worse off. A full-insurance zero-profit pooled equilibrium would be represented by D (or other points between C_H and C_L on the 45° line, for different ED lines representing different proportions of low-risk people g). This would correspond say to a political solution like the UK National Health Service, which charges everyone the same premium and provides them with full insurance against illness—at least in principle! In the perfect-information case, which can be taken as the bench-mark for evaluating efficiency, it is clear that the political solution is Pareto-dominated by the market solution. It is only if distributional considerations are smuggled in, and for some reason a greater weight is placed on the welfare of high-risk rather than low-risk groups, that a political solution will be necessary and desirable. But we have given reasons for eschewing egalitarianism in Chapter 1.

(ii) *Imperfect Information*. The perfect-information competitive insurance case immediately allows us to examine the more realistic case where information is imperfect. The people know their own risks (probabilities p_H, p_L) but the insurers do not. In that case, if insurers offered the same full-insurance contracts as before, but had no way of separating out the bad from good risks, all the high-risk people would choose C_L, and the insurer would make a loss.

To avoid this adverse selection, the competitive insurer will offer only two contracts. One will be the full-insurance contract at C_H, with a high premium, and the other a partial-insurance contract C_I with a lower premium (see Fig. 9.4(b)). The first contract will correspond to the contract that would be offered to high-risk people under perfect information (C_H). The second will lie on the intersection of the indifference curve U_H of the high-risk people at C_H, and the zero-profit line EC_L for the low-risk people. As a result, no high-risk person will find it in his interest to choose the partial-insurance contract C_I, whilst no low-risk person will find the full-insurance contract C_H preferable to the only other contract now available to them—the partial-insurance contract C_I. The low-risk people will clearly be worse off than if there were perfect information about the differential risks. But given the unavoidable problems of imperfect information which cause the adverse selection faced by insurers, there will (under the above assumptions) be no Pareto-superior outcome available to the low-risk people through the market.

Perhaps, there is then a political solution which can make a Pareto improvement over the market outcome? The obvious choice is a pooling equilibrium along the zero-profit line *EF*. As we have noted, its slope depends upon the relative proportion of high and low risks. Suppose this line lies to the left of *G*, the point on the 45° line where the low-risk people's indifference curve through C_I intersects it. It is obvious that, as before, no pooling zero-profit contract will be Pareto-superior to the separating zero-profit contracts C_H and C_I. There is no political solution better than the market.

If, however, the zero-profit pooling line lies to the right of *G*, say *EF'*, then there are pooling contracts between *M* and *F'* which are Pareto-superior to the separating contracts C_H and C_I, as clearly the high risks would be on a higher indifference curve than U_H^1 and low-risk types on one higher than U_L^0. (In this case there will also be no market equilibrium. But this conclusion is highly sensitive to the game-theoretic Nash behavioural assumption which underlies this type of model, and, depending upon the assumptions about the transfer of information between the insuree and the insured, various pooling and separating contracts become equilibrium contracts; see Helliweg, Laffont, Kreps.[29]) This would create an incentive for both the low-risk types and insurance companies to identify the low risks and separate them from the high risks. Attempts at what it is pejoratively defined as cherry-picking would be the market response, and the more this were successful the more the market solution would approximate the bench-mark one identified under perfect information.

Even though some pooling contracts are Pareto-superior to the separating contracts under imperfect information, it does not follow that a political solution to enforce pooling, as for instance in a national health service, would necessarily be Pareto-superior. This can be seen if, instead of the simple categorization of 'being sick' and 'not being sick' hitherto employed, we have different sicknesses with their different losses. These losses are the same, for the same sickness, for our otherwise identical individuals, as before. But there are different probabilities of occurrence of these different sicknesses for different individuals. Then for some sicknesses the distribution of risks (the g proportions, which determine the average probability of that risk and hence the slope of EF) might imply a zero-profit pooling line like EF, and for others EF'. Clearly enforcing pooling in both cases will mean that for the case of sickness with an average probability for which EF is applicable, the non-market solution will be Pareto-inferior to the market one. It is for the sickness where the proportion of high risks is low in the population, and the EF line is to the right of G, that a pooling equilibrium might be Pareto-superior. But once we move beyond unavoidably simple theoretical models, there is no reason why insurance companies which operate with a variety of contracts would not find some form of pooling for these different types of sickness profitable.

Hence there is no a priori reason to believe that with adverse selection, and/or moral hazard, there is any political solution which is Pareto-superior to that provided by a competitive market. For, as Hayek has emphasized, the market is above all a discovery process. Given uncertainty, it is unlikely that the search for more Pareto-efficient contracts through the market, which could include pooling, can be replaced by the technocratic design of an ideal system based on Walrasian general equilibrium theory.

IV. PRIVATE VERSUS PUBLIC TRANSFERS IN SOCIAL SAFETY NETS

As the risk of income shortfalls over an individual's life cycle is ubiquitous, it would be extraordinary if most societies had not found means of insurance against these risks. Historically, as noted in Chapter 1, destitution and conjunctural poverty were dealt with through five means. The first was through institutions like the Church, which took one of its primary tasks to be the care of the poor. Individual charity, most often through inter-household transfers from an extended family, provided a second means. A third was through organizations of the poor themselves: through self-help organizations (for instance rotating credit associations like the contemporary Grameen bank), and the mutually friendly societies of eighteenth- and nineteenth-century Britain discussed in Lal (1993*a*, 1994*c*). Fourth were various underworld organizations engaged in crime. Finally, various forms of insurance embodied in interlinked contracts in factor markets have historically been the major way of dealing with conjunctural poverty in traditional village economies (see Platteau, 1991).

1. Private Transfers

Of these the role of private inter-household transfers is particularly relevant. For though transfers through religious channels have probably been significant, we have not been able to find any scholarly analysis of their size or effectiveness. This is surely an area for profitable future research. Kin-based transfers, reciprocity arrangements, and interlinked factor-market contracts have been the major way that traditional societies have dealt with income risk. As Platteau concludes: 'Even though empirical evidence is scanty (but not altogether absent), the case can reasonably be made that, barring exceptionally unfavorable circumstances (such as repeated crop failures or crop diseases affecting entire communities), traditional methods for controlling the risk of falling into distress have usually enabled the people to counter natural and other hazards in a rather effective way.'[30] With the inevitable erosion of village communities it is feared that these private insurance arrangements will break down and that no private alternative will be available to counter destitution and conjunctural poverty in increasingly industrial economies.

It is in this context that the role of private inter-household transfers is of great importance. Cox and Jimenez provide evidence to show that they are of considerable quantitative importance:

For example, among a sample of urban poor in El Salvador, 33 per cent reported having received private transfers, and income from private transfers accounted for 39 per cent of total income among recipients. 93 per cent of a rural south Indian sample received transfers from other households. In Malaysia, private transfers accounted for almost half the income of the poorest households. Nearly three quarters of rural households in Java, Indonesia, gave private transfers to other households. About half of a sample of Filipino households received private cash transfers.

Moreover, since the oil price rise of the early 1970s the poor in South Asia and parts of South-East Asia have found remunerative employment in the newly rich oil states, and their remittances to their Third World relatives have helped to alleviate their poverty (see Swamy, 1981).

The motivation for these transfers is of some interest. If they were purely altruistically determined (as in Becker's famous 'rotten kid' theorem),[32] then it would imply that with inter-generational transfers between parents and children there would be dynastic families which would behave as though they were a single infinite-lived individual. Barro's famous Ricardian equivalence would then hold, with public policies such as debt financing and social security being completely neutralized by countervailing private action. Warr (1983), and Bernheim and Bagwell (1988), went further and showed that as 'propagation requires the participation of two traditionally unrelated individuals, . . . there will be a proliferation of linkages between families.' This gives rise to even stronger neutrality results:

In particular, no government transfer (including those between unrelated members of the same generation) has any real effect, and all tax instruments (including so-called distortionary taxes) are equivalent to lump sum taxes. In essence, the government can affect the allocation of real resources only by altering real expenditures. The efficiency role of government is thus severely limited, and the distributional role is entirely eliminated. More generally, . . . if all linkages between parents and children are truly operative, then market prices play no role in the resource allocation process: the distribution of goods is determined by the nature of intergenerational altruism.[33]

As these implications seem to be highly unrealistic, attempts have been made to explain private transfers as part of an exchange process involving an implicit mutually beneficial contract between, say, parents and children, who in exchange for their educational expenditure, say, are committed to looking after their parents in their old age.[34]

Lucas and Stark developed an intermediate model in which both altruism and self-interested exchange are the motives for transfers, and found that it applies satisfactorily to Botswana. They found that the prediction of the pure altruism model that lower-income households will receive higher transfers is not borne out, and that instead, as the exchange model predicts, there is 'a positive association between amount remitted and per capita income of the household from other sources'.[35] For in the exchange model the 'greater wealth of the family should increase its relative bargaining strength',[36] and thus leads to a higher demand on its migrants.

But, as Lucas and Stark recognize, their data—which is cross-sectional—does not allow the altruistic motive for transfers to be tested in a dynamic context. Rosenzweig does so. In a longitudinal study of six villages in three different agro-climatic regions in the semi-arid tropics of India, he found that 'kinship in a risky world not only tends to bond family members in a single location (in a particular way) but kinship ties are able to be sustained over time and space in implicit insurance-based transfer schemes which contribute to consumption smoothing in the face of covariant income risks'.[37] 'It is kinship, and common (family) experiences [which] induce trust, knowledge and altruism among family members, [hence] such income pooling implicit contracts may be feasible even if spread across wide areas.'[38]

Thus the empirical evidence on the motives for private transfers is mixed. As Cox and Jimenez summarize it:

Some studies find an inverse relation between recipients' resources and transfer amounts received (for instance Kaufmann and Lindauer for El Salvador, Kaufmann for the Philippines, Ravallion and Dearden for rural households in Java, and Tomes for bequests in the US). But others (Lucas and Stark for Botswana, Cox for [inter vivos transfers in] the U.S., Ravallion and Dearden for urban households in Java, and Cox and Jimenez for Peru) find a positive relation, which contradicts the altruism hypothesis.[39]

There are some empirical studies which directly estimate the crowding-out effect of public on private transfers. Most of these have been done for the US,[40] and find some small crowding-out effect. For developing countries there are only two available studies. For Peru, Cox and Jimenez (1992) found that in the absence of social security in urban Peru, private inter-household old-age support would have been higher by 20%. So there is considerable but not complete crowding out of private by public transfers. A study of the Philippines by Cox and Jimenez (1993) is probably more relevant. As they state, 'part of the reason for the low estimates of the degree of crowding out of private transfers by public ones might be due to the fact that the estimates discussed above are derived in environments [in OECD countries] where public transfers are already substantial. These transfers may have already crowded out private transfers to a large extent, rendering the small samples of private-recipients uninformative. In contrast, the Philippines has almost no public welfare payments, which makes it an ideal case study for gauging the strength of private transfers.'[41] They found that transfers were widespread and large. They used the available data to simulate the effects on these private transfers of three public policies: unemployment insurance, social security, and income grants targeted to the poor. For unemployment insurance they find: 'the reduction in private transfers is nearly as large as the boost in income that unemployment insurance gives to households. 91% of the increase in household income from unemployment insurance is offset by reductions in private transfers.[42] For retirement income they find that 'private transfers would be 37% higher' if retirement income did not exist. On a programme to eliminate poverty completely in a given area by giving each household the difference between its actual income and the poverty-line income, they find that after private-transfer adjustments, 46% of urban and 94% of rural households below the poverty line before the programme would still be below the line after the programme![43]

Moreover, they give reasons to believe that their estimates of crowding out are biased downwards. This study should certainly give anyone seeking the public-transfer route to deal with labour market risks considerable cause to pause.

These doubts are further strengthened when we consider that private transfers, by relying on locally held information (see Hayek), and in part on extra economic motivations like trust and altruism, can overcome many of the problems of adverse selection, moral hazard, and so on which have so exercised the nirvana-economics market-failure school. For as Cox and Jimenez, summarizing the empirical evidence conclude, 'private transfers equalize income' (that is, make it more equal); 'private transfers are directed toward the poor, the young, the old, women, the disabled and the unemployed'.[44]

2. Public Transfers

Perhaps public transfers can do even better, so that we should not worry if they crowd out private transfers? Public subsidization of the two merit goods—health and education—are the major public transfers in nearly all developing countries. In addition social security is important in many Latin American countries.

One question on which there is some empirical evidence is the incidence of the benefits from subsidies for merit goods. Beginning with the pioneering studies of Meerman for Malaysia and Selowsky for Colombia, a number of other studies have addressed this issue. Jimenez, summarizing the studies done till 1987, concluded:

students from the highest quartile of the income distribution profile in Chile, Colombia, Indonesia, and Malaysia receive between 51 and 83% of all public expenditures on higher education, whereas those from the lowest 40% receive between 6 and 15%. The effect is only partly counterbalanced by the concentration of primary education subsidies among poor families, which have most of a country's younger school children. The net result is a distribution of overall educational subsidies roughly proportional to each income group's population share, with the exception of the Dominican Republic where the poor's share is still less. The income bias is less for health. Health subsidies for Colombia and Malaysia are roughly proportional to each income group's population share. But in Indonesia, the poorest 40% capture only about 19% from public health centers and hospitals.[45]

The second piece of empirical evidence is contained in the survey of health and nutrition studies in developing countries by Behrman in Psacharopoulos (1991):

General food subsidies are not very effective in redistributing income to the poor, but . . . better targeted food programs may be used to shift income to some segments of the poor that depend on market purchases for food. On the other hand, targeting types of *individuals* (e.g., small children, nursing mothers) instead of households is likely to be difficult if there is much intrahousehold fungibility, as appears to be the case. However, the small nutrient elasticities with respect to income imply that nutrient intakes do not improve substantially because of the income effect of such subsidies, though welfare may be improved significantly. But the price effects may be considerable, though they may reduce nutrient intakes if subsidies are on foods other than basic staples. However some (but not all) recent studies of food subsidies and other health related input pricing policies suggest that in fact they often redistributed income *from* the poor and are not justified on the grounds of externalities, though subsidies for preventative measures for contagious diseases may be justifiable on the latter grounds and subsidies for basic staples of the poor may be justifiable on distributional grounds. Within a general equilibrium framework, the means of financing health and nutrient subsidies may change their distributional impact considerably.

UNICEF and others have made strong claims about negative multiplier effects of macroeconomic adjustment policies on health and nutrition. Careful examination of the relevant studies, however, suggests that the empirical basis for such a claim currently is quite weak. In fact the underlying studies seem to be characterized better as reflecting how well societies and people have adapted to minimize negative health and nutrition effects rather than the more negative interpretation given by UNICEF.[46]

More recent studies of the effects of health subsidies in Indonesia find that

with the sole exception of reported morbidity, all the evidence points to the children of high-expenditure households benefiting more (in terms of the marginal effects on both health utilization and health outcomes) from government health spending than the children of low expenditure households. Even in the case of reported morbidity, the greater benefits derived by the poor relative to the non-poor from government health spending is quite small.[47]

Moreover,

if government health spending largely improves publicly-provided health care opportunities for the non-poor but also crowds out private providers (say, traditional healers) that are used typically by the poor, it could reduce the total amount of medical care opportunities available to the poor. If the health outcomes of the poor are highly responsive to medical care inputs, this could have a detrimental effect on their health.[48]

Jee Peng Tan cites the conclusion from a 1990 Bank study of Asian governments' spending on health that

The findings on targeting of public expenditure on health to the poor in Asian countries are not encouraging. For the countries for which data could be assembled, there is little evidence of such targeting, either by income group or geographical area. The data suggest that the same infections and parasitic diseases that have been killing people in Asia for centuries continue to do so.[49]

For Brazil, McGreevey concludes from a 1988 Bank report that 'the poorest 19% of the population receives only about 6% of social benefits. A large share of social expenditure benefits higher-income groups. Regional inequalities are also severe'. [50]

For Costa Rica, Riboud concludes on the basis of a 1990 Bank report:

Total benefits are fairly evenly distributed among income groups. This is the result of two opposing and compensating forces: the regressiveness of the distribution of education benefits and the progressiveness of the distribution of health benefits . . . Taking account of state pensions, however, social program benefits per capita are 62% higher for the richest 20% than for the poorest 20% of the population.[50]

Further empirical evidence on the results of social security systems in alleviating low-end poverty in developing countries is provided by the surveys of Mesa-Lago and Midgley. Midgley's conclusion is that

although the development of social security in the Third World during the post-war years has been impressive these schemes have brought few, if any, benefits to ordinary people. They cater primarily for those who are already privileged by having secure jobs and steady incomes and exclude those whose needs for social security are the greatest.[52]

Meso-Largo in his survey of social security in Latin America found that there has been a dramatic increase in coverage of health and maternity care and old age and disability pensions during the last 35 years. However,

What has occurred is that social security has been extended vertically instead of horizontally, in other words, has added benefits (or covered risks) in favor of those already insured instead of extending the coverage to the population. Hence the social security principle of universality has been sacrificed and the objective of protection of the needy has not been fulfilled. Conversely, the salaried urban modern, middle income sector has accumulated benefit upon benefit. The cost of social security, has considerably increased, but not precisely to protect the most needy.[53]

He continues:

In the majority of countries social security plays either a regressive or null role. The extreme poverty group is deprived of protection (except for public health and social welfare programs) and, to add salt to injury, it contributes, through taxes and prices, to the welfare of those insured. With the latter, especially in stratified systems, the lower income groups generally receive a net social security transference inferior to that accrued by the higher income groups.[54]

Finally,

the escalating costs of social security push it into bankruptcy, [as] it is difficult to cut benefits or to tighten the conditions for acquiring rights. Inflation thus becomes a key instrument for adjusting the excessive generosity of the Social Security system to the economic reality of the nation . . . The booming costs of social security and dramatic reduction of the dependency ratio in countries with old and generous systems have depleted substantial resources for development and contributed to economic stagnation. In spite of this high price paid, extreme inequality and poverty have not been curtailed.[55]

Nor are the various public transfers indirectly targeted to help the poor, such as agricultural and food subsidies, any more effective in achieving their objectives. Thus Pamela Cox, summarizing the findings of a 1991 Bank report on the incidence of agricultural subsidies in India, found that 'benefits from agricultural input subsidies have gone overwhelmingly to wealthier and agriculturally advanced regions and to larger farmers'.[56] Whilst Liberman in World Bank (1992), summarizing a 1989 Bank report's findings on India's safety-net programmes, concluded: 'The public distribution system has high costs and weak targeting, including a strong urban bias. The national employment schemes have a small positive impact on the income of poor households, but with relatively low coverage in some very poor states.'[57]

Next, what have been the effects of social expenditures on health and education on various social indicators? The evidence again is mixed. But there is some revealing evidence that suggests that the common presumption that a rise in these social expenditures will improve literacy and life expectancy and reduce infant mortality is not secure. Thus in our country studies, Hansen finds that Turkey has a better record of educational achievement than Egypt. He finds this superior Turkish achievement 'the more remarkable as Turkey throughout the post-war period has operated its educational system at a relatively lower level of public expenditure than Egypt'.[58] Whilst Grosh, summarizing a 1990 World Bank study which

traced public social sector expenditures for nine Latin American countries in the 1980s . . . found that real per capita public social spending on health, education, and social security fell during some part of the 1980s in every country in the study. The share of health and education expenditures in total government expenditures also fell, even as that of social security rose. In spite of lower funding, and no apparent increases in equity and efficiency, social indicators generally improved in the 1980s.[59]

Apart from obvious statistical and other biases which might explain this anomaly, the most plausible explanation provided is that it might be due to 'the growing role of non-governmental organizations, and the response of the market-oriented private sector to enhanced expectations and demand'. That is, there was probably a 'crowding in' of more equitable and more efficient private transfers to replace the decline in public ones.

V. THE POLITICAL ECONOMY OF PUBLIC INCOME TRANSFERS

Even if effective public income transfers to alleviate low-end poverty were feasible, is it likely that most of the polities found in the Third World would actually implement them? In a recent review of the relevance of social security policies in the UK, the US, and France to developing countries, Atkinson and Hills stress 'the need for the analysis to range outside the purely economic and in particular to seek to understand the policy and political influences on the design of policy. The political economy of social security is of great importance.'[60]

We will be essentially concerned with the transfers that Lindbeck has labelled as constituting a vertical redistributive policy which tries 'to raise the incomes of a minority of people that are for periods at the bottom of the size distribution of factor income'.[61] Transfer payments and the subsidization or public provision of specific goods and services to low-income groups are obvious instruments within such a programme. Lindbeck sees what he calls 'altruistic paternalism' as the most likely political form to achieve such transfers, motivated partly by altruism and partly by consequential externalities, such as the private disutility of public squalor, as in seeing beggars, slums, et cetera around oneself.

The type of polity in our schema where such altruistic paternalism is most likely to occur is either the Platonic guardian or predatory-authoritarian state. For, as Lindbeck notes:

The emergence of policies according to this strategy which hails back to the charity of the church and to the old poor laws can hardly be explained by the self-interest of the *beneficiaries*, as they have often exerted very little political power, particularly before the arrival of the general franchise. Moreover, if the beneficiaries themselves had designed the policies, we would have expected these benefits to have been given as cash income rather than as selective support of specific goods and services, since cash payments would be the most valuable type of support in terms of subjective utility maximization.[62]

The altruistic paternalism of Platonic-guardian-type states is attested to by the social policies, in particular as regards housing, in two of our Platonic states, Hong Kong and Singapore. Moreover, this is the essential assumption about the nature of the state which underlies neoclassical views that seek to provide an efficiency justification for the welfare state.[63]

However, most of our polities are not Platonic guardian states. In which case, what we need to ask is: Under what circumstances in our differing polities will welfare states emerge, and what is likely to be their nature in terms of the incidence of benefits and costs? It will be easiest to take the polar opposite of our Platonic or predatory-authoritarian state, namely the factional democratic state, as the paradigm to discuss this issue. Within our sample of countries, most of the welfare states are factional states, or weak predatory-bureaucratic states subject to popular pressure.

The model of the factional state for a majoritarian democracy, outlined in Chapter 6, immediately yields the result labelled by Stigler as 'Director's Law',[64] and formally derived by Meltzer and Richard.[65] As the median voter is decisive in such a polity, the redistributive pressures for a welfare state will exist as long as the median income is below the mean, and the system that is created will redistribute income towards the median-income earners. However, because of the dead-weight costs attached to taxation, it will not be in the interests of the decisive median voter and hence of the polity to expropriate all incomes above the median, as that would also lower total income.[66] The phenomenon of 'middle-class capture' of the benefits of existing social-security systems, discussed in the previous section (and to be found in many of our sample countries), would fit this theory.

However, one implication of this theory is that, with economic development, the thrust towards redistribution ends when the median voter's income moves towards the mean. But even a cursory glance at the historical evidence suggests that, with the fall in inequality over the last hundred years in the West, there has not been a diminution in the pressures to expand their redistributive transfer systems.

A more sophisticated model has been developed by Peltzman[67] which eschews the broad income-class approach to redistribution of Meltzer and Richard, and instead uses a variant of the special-interest pressure-group model *à la* Stigler and Becker.[68] This model is applicable to countries even without majoritarian democracy, as long as the rulers are subject to some public pressure. As Peltzman puts its: 'As long as suppressing dissent is costly to a dictator, he ought to be sensitive to the popular support for his policies'.[69] This model is of some relevance, as Peltzman has applied it to 42 developing countries, of which 11 are in our sample.[70]

The major empirical implications of Peltzman's theory are that public transfers will

- increase if there is greater income equality within the beneficiary group;
- decrease if the potential beneficiaries' incomes increase relative to those of taxpayers;
- increase if there is an increase in the ability of the two groups to recognize their interests. The greater this ability amongst the beneficiary group, the more likely that the redistributive benefits will accrue to the poor.

Peltzman fitted his model to the data for a sample of 42 developing countries to explain the level and change in their share of government expenditure (which is his proxy for transfer payments) in GDP between 1960 and 1970. He found that the 'within poor group' inequality index consistently had the expected negative sign and was significant, but neither the 'between group' inequality index nor the 'ability' index was significant. He then ran a model with an interaction between ability and inequality, namely, where G = public expenditure as a share of GDP,

$$G = a.\text{ABILITY} + b_0.\text{INEQUALITY} + b_1.\left(\text{ABILITY}.\text{INEQUALITY}\right) + X.$$

We know that increased ability raises G, so that a is expected to be positive.

Peltzman argues that, despite attempts to decompose distributional data into between- and within-group measures of inequality, the two tend to be highly correlated with a summary measure of the whole distribution. In which case the proxy inequality measure he uses will absorb both the between- and within-group inequality effects, and thus the sign of b_0 is indeterminate. But if ability and inequality interact, then the theory suggests that the weight of the within-group inequality effect (which is inversely related to G) increases. Hence there would be a presumption that b_1 will be negative. When he applies this interactive model to his developing-country sample, all the coefficients have the expected signs and are significant.[71]

We have attempted to apply Peltzman's model to the available data for our sample of countries. Table 9.1 provides this data for our sample countries for public expenditure (with and without defence expenditures) and the proxies for the inequality and ability indices. Their derivations are explained in the notes to the table. Ideally we would have liked to have had data on social expenditures (which should be the dependent variable in the Peltzman model). However, like Peltzman, we were forced *faute de mieux* to use total government expenditure (non-defence) as a proxy for those social expenditures.

We found that the best fit was for changes in non-defence public-expenditure shares of GDP between 1972 and 1985 as the dependent variable, and with normalized indices of the share of the top 10% as our inequality index (I), and the (normalized) percentage of the population which is literate as our ability index (A). The normalizations being made around the means of the sample, the estimated regression, with the interaction of ability and inequality included for the 17 countries for which we had data, is

$$\Delta G = 186 + 0.813\,I + 0.64\,A - 0.006\,I.A.$$
$$\quad\quad\;\; (2.2)\quad\; (1.8)\quad\; (1.6)$$
$$R^2 = 0.46;\quad n = 17.$$

The figures in brackets are t statistics. All the signs are as expected, and the coefficient of the inequality variable is significant at the 5% level.

The tentative conclusion from this section, therefore, is that, irrespective of the efficacy of public income transfers in redressing mass poverty, their growth and level are likely to depend endogenously upon the interaction of the polity ('ability') and economy ('inequality'). Except for the Platonic state, irrespective of the social desirability of transfers targeted to the poor, such transfers are unlikely to take place in practice in most other types of polity. Most redistribution is likely to be from the poor to the rich, as well as from the poor and rich to the middle. Instead, therefore, of setting one's heart—as so many well-meaning economists and observers have done—on the necessarily zero-sum games with uncertain outcomes involved in the redistributive 'basic needs'-type programmes, it may be best to concentrate on the positive-sum game involved in rapid, efficient growth—which raises the incomes of the poor. High growth, which raises the demand for their primary endowment—their labour—still remains (as our country studies attest) the single most important feasible method of raising the incomes of the poor.

Table 9.1. Factors affecting central government expenditure

Country	G2 Central government expenditure as % GDP		Defence as% total expenditure	
	1971	1985	1972	1985
Ghana	21.9 (1972)	13.9	7.9	7.5
Hong Kong	12.1 (1974)	15.5 (1984)	10 (1974)	13 (1984)
Madagascar	20.7 (1972)	18 (1974)	3.6	n.a.
Malawi	22.3	29.8	3.1	5.7
Mauritius	23.29 (1973)	28.3	0.8	0.8
Nigeria	14.75 (1972)	18.49 (1978)	40.2	23.5 (1978)
Indonesia	14.89 (1972)	22.42	18.6	12.9
Malaysia	30.3 (1972)	32.3 (1984)	18.5	15.05 (1981)
Singapore	31.66 (1972)	36.01	35.3	20.1
Sri Lanka	26.34	33.87	3.1	2.6
Thailand	18.29 (1972)	21.61	20.2	20.2
Malta	43.2 (1972)	45.43	3.5 (1975)	2.9
Turkey	23.1	24.99	15.5	10.9
Egypt	61.5 (1975)	50.68	8.93 (1976)	17.5
Brazil	19.16	37.12	8.3	4
Columbia	12.69	14.74 (1983)	n.a.	7.8 (1983)
Costa Rica	19.67 (1972)	21.97	2.8	3
Jamaica	35.63 (1975)	44.21 (1981)	2.5 (1975)	2.6 (1977)
Mexico	13.35 (1972)	25.88	4.2	2.7
Peru	16.72	18.7 (1982)	14.8	27.6 (1982)
Uruguay	24.88 (1972)	22.91	5.6	10.8
Industrial countries	26.45	33.92	20.9	16.8

Table 9.1. *Continued*

Country	ΔG Non-defence expenditure as % GDP			Growth collapse
	Change 1985–72	1972	1985	
Ghana	−7.27	20.17	12.9	yes
Hong Kong	2.61	10.89	13.5	
Madagascar	−2.58	19.93	17.35	yes
Malawi	6.5	21.6	28.1	
Mauritius	5	23.1	28.1	
Nigeria	5.32	8.82	14.14	yes
Indonesia	7.4	12.12	19.52	
Malaysia	2.75	24.69	27.44	
Singapore	8.29	20.48	28.77	
Sri Lanka	7.46	25.52	32.98	
Thailand	2.65	14.6	17.25	
Malta	2.4	41.7	44.1	
Turkey	2.75	19.52	22.27	yes
Egypt	−14.19	56	41.81	
Brazil	18.07	17.57	35.64	yes
Columbia	1.9	11.7	13.6	
Costa Rica	2.19	19.12	21.31	yes
Jamaica	8.32	34.74	43.06	yes
Mexico	12.39	12.79	25.18	yes
Peru	−0.71	14.25	13.54	yes
Uruguay	−3.05	23.49	20.44	yes

Country	Income Distribution			WI	BI	I
	Share 4th quintile	Share 2nd quintile	4th:2nd quintiles	Top 10%	BI index normalized	
Ghana	n.a.	n.a.	n.a.	n.a.		
Hong Kong	21.6	10.8	2	31.3	78.8	
Madagascar	20.5	8.7	2.36	37.1	93.5	
Malawi	13.7	10.6	1.29	46.2	116.4	
Mauritius	17	7.5	2.3	46.7	117.6	
Nigeria	n.a.	n.a.	n.a.	n.a.		
Indonesia	23.6	7.8	3	34	85.6	
Malaysia	20.3	7.7	2.6	39.8	100.3	
Singapore	n.a.	n.a.	n.a.	n.a.		
Sri Lanka	20.3	10.1	2	34.7	87.4	
Thailand	21.1	9.6	2.2	34.1	85.9	
Malta	n.a.	n.a.	n.a.	n.a.		
Turkey	19.5	8	2.44	40.7	102.5	
Egypt	20.8	10.7	1.94	33.2	83.6	
Brazil	17	5	3.4	50.8	128	
Columbia	16.06	7.3	2.2	49	123.4	
Costa Rica	19.8	8.7	2.28	39.5	99.5	
Jamaica	19.5	8.2	2.38	43.5	109.6	
Mexico	20.4	7	2.91	40.6	102.3	
Peru	21	5.1	4.12	42.9	108.1	
Uruguay	22.5	10.31	2.2	30.17	76	

Table 9.1. *Continued*

Country	PAG % Pop in agric		L Literacy rate	A Literacy index normalized
	1965	1980		
Ghana	61	56	30	40.1
Hong Kong	6	2	90	122.3
Madagascar	85	81	34	46.2
Malawi	92	83	25	34
Mauritius	37	28	79	107.3
Nigeria	72	68	34	46.2
Indonesia	71	57	67	91
Malaysia	59	42	70	95.1
Singapore	6	2	83	112.8
Sri Lanka	56	53	86	116.8
Thailand	82	71	88	119.6
Malta	n.a.	n.a.	n.a.	n.a.
Turkey	75	58	65	88.3
Egypt	55	46	44	59.8
Brazil	49	31	74	100.5
Columbia	45	34	85	115.5
Costa Rica	47	31	90	122.3
Jamaica	37	31	96	130.4
Mexico	50	37	83	112.8
Peru	50	40	82	111.4
Uruguay	20	16	94	127.7

Sources: Central government expenditure as % of GDP: IFS Yearbook 1988, and Hong Kong from country study data.
Defence as % total expenditure: World Development Report 1987, table 23, except Jamaica (1975, 1977), Colombia (1983), Nigeria (1978), Malaysia (1981), Malta (1975, 1985), Egypt (1976), and Peru (1982), which are from the Government Finance Statistics Yearbook 1987, and Hong Kong (1974, 1984) from country study data.
Non-defence expenditure as % GDP: from first two columns.
Income distribution data—from Tilak in Psacharapoulas (1991) and country study data for Uruguay and Colombia (top 10 %). Share of 4th and 2nd quintiles for Colombia from I. Adelman and C.T. Morris, 'Society, Politics and Economic Development: A Quantitative Approach', 1971.
BI (top 10%): Index normalized around a mean of 39.7.
% population in agriculture: World Development Reports 1987, 88.
Literacy rate: from Tilak as above.
Literacy rate normalized around a mean of 73.6.
Popular pressure index: factional democratic (FD) = 100; factional oligarchic (FO) = 50; predatory bureaucratic (PB) = 50; predatory autocratic (PA) = 25; platonic (P) = 10.
AB Index from average of lit. rate and popular pressure index.

VI. UNINTENDED CONSEQUENCES OF WELFARE STATES

One final aspect of the welfare state which is relevant to our theme is its effects on what de Tocqueville in his *Democracy in America* called the 'habits of the heart'—the cultural underpinnings for both a democratic society and the market economy. The most sustained, though controversial, critique of the decadence in private habits engendered by the transfer state is in Murray's examination of the results of the US 'war on poverty'. He argues that welfare programmes associated with the war on poverty created perverse incentives, which have perpetuated the 'underclass'. This perversion was due to the objectives of the programmes seeking to ensure equality of outcomes rather than of opportunity.[72]

The cultural consequences of the welfare state may be as momentous as the economic or political ones. This, and the general subject of the relationship of culture to development—which we have abstracted from in this study—is a very large subject beyond the scope of this book.[73] But, as Lee Kwan Yew has pointed out, the Western welfare state has sapped the family bonds which provide the safety nets in East Asia.

This is of relevance, because of the oft-repeated claim that 'ageing populations, growing urbanization and the rising number of nuclear families have weakened the traditional support provided by the family and increased the need for formal provision'.[74] But are extended families in the Third World necessarily likely to be extinguished? And is the decline not only of extended but even of nuclear families in the West due to some inevitable process associated with economic growth, or, as Murray and many others maintain, is it the unintended consequence of well-intentioned welfare policies which subsidize teenage mothers, promote single-parent families, and make the type of reciprocal exchange relationships—outlined in our discussion of private transfers—more and more redundant?[75] If the family has been an institution which has to some extent been created and preserved as a form of mutual insurance against life's risks, is the transfer of these insurance functions to the state not likely to undermine the very institution whose decline politicians in all the Western welfare states are currently bemoaning? Nor can one assume that the type of individualistic as opposed to dynastic motivation for marriage which seems to predominate in the West is a universal human characteristic, nor that it is a necessary accompaniment of growth. Many Third World cultures, for instance, Indian and Chinese, seem to be relatively unaffected by these Western cultural norms. As Lee Kwan Yew suggests, the family in many Third World cultures may be relatively immune to the specifically Western social developments which have undermined it in the West.[76] But of course, as economic incentives matter, as in the West, Third World families could be undermined by similar welfare-state policies.[77] But these are all important subjects for future research.

But even the inconclusive evidence reviewed above suggests that we may still tentatively conclude that the Third World is likely to be better served by seeking ways to strengthen traditional methods of dealing with destitution and conjunctural poverty, and finding new ways to foster the civic virtues and the growth of civil associations, on which (for classical liberals) the health of sustainable democracies as well as market economies depends, than by finding arguments for a vast expansion of state provision/financing of social expenditures. For as sociologists (e.g. Nisbet) have noted, the conversion of welfare states into transfer states in the West (and some developing countries) has led to an attack on civil society from both above and below. From above, the intermediate institutions of civil society are forced to surrender their functions and authority to professional élites and the bureaucrats of centralizing states. From below, 'rights chatter'—the clamour for numerous and newly discovered individual rights (see Lal, 1993a)—undermines the authority of those traditional civil institutions, family, church, school, neighbourhood, which in the past have promoted both private benevolence and the lower-order 'vigorous virtues' (see Chapter 1). The acceptance of claims to various welfare rights substitutes public for private benevolence—sapping the latter, which for classical liberals is the highest (though scarce) virtue.

It is these longer-run, unintended, social and fiscal consequence of the welfare state, which are now leading to its partial dismantlement in many OECD countries—of which the most dramatic example is the virtual abandonment of the New Zealand welfare state by its chastened socialist party, and the most poignant is the growing reversal of that social democratic beacon of hope the Swedish 'middle way'. It is then particularly ironical that, at a time when the welfare state is coming to be repudiated by its progenitors, international institutions such as UNDP, UNICEF, and WIDER are seeking their extension in the Third World.

VII. CLASSICAL LIBERAL PRINCIPLES AND LABOUR-MARKET INSURANCE

The refurbished classical liberal principles, for public action in insuring labour-market risks leading to destitution and conjunctural poverty, then follow naturally from the above discussion.

The first is that nothing should be done which would damage the existing private institutions and channels which provide for private transfers to deal with destitution and conjunctural poverty. 'Forbear' should be the watchword for every proposed scheme which seeks to alleviate poverty through public transfers.

The second is that if, for whatever reason, public money is sought to be transferred to the needy, this is best done through private agencies. In particular, for the merit goods of primary health care and primary education, whatever the case for public financing there is hardly one for public production. As a World Bank Bolivian public-sector expenditure review noted:

in the health sector, NGOs deliver the most effective service. In education, several communities have asked the largest NGO to manage their public schooling, indicating the perceived better quality education offered, even with much higher student: teacher ratios in NGO schools . . . The public education system spends more than 10 times more per child than the largest NGO, which provides high-quality education.[78]

The third is that the very problems of moral hazard, adverse selection, and monitoring cited by 'nirvana economics' for public insurance, in fact argue for fostering the alternative private routes which capitalize on the comparative informational advantage of private agents with local knowledge.[79] These private welfare channels can be promoted by various methods of co-financing them with public funds.[80]

Fourth, in cases where for political reasons public responsibility for the needy has to be accepted, public policy should be concerned with alleviating real hardship and not with equalizing people. The socialist distributivist end must be forsworn. State help should be concentrated on the minority in absolute need, and the categories of prospective beneficiaries should not be allowed to multiply as ' "need" assumes an elastic dimension in the name of "relative poverty" '.[81]

Fifth, universal provision of welfare and social-security benefits should be eschewed. For, particularly in majoritarian democracies, such universalization will corrupt the polity, with competing politicians showing their compassion by indiscriminately buying votes with other people's money. This in turn will lead to the likely middle-class capture of the transfer state, and could lead to endemic growth and fiscal crises.

VIII. GUIDE-LINES FOR PUBLIC ACTION ON SOCIAL SAFETY NETS

If public action is considered desirable to deal with various labour-market risks what are the guide-lines for specific types of risks that the application of the above principles can provide? We deal with the various elements of the safety net in sequence.

For the merit goods of *education and health*, as noted in the last section, there maybe a case for financing the poor but not for public production. As J. S. Mill put it: 'If the country contains a sufficient number of persons qualified to provide education under government auspices, the same persons would be willing to give an equally good education on the voluntary principle under the assurance of remuneration afforded by a law rendering education compulsory, combined with state aid to those unable to defray the expense.'[82] For health it can be argued (see Lal, 1994c) that the poor are best helped by various means to allow them to purchase private care. These means include mutual-aid societies, as well as private charities and NGOs.

Matching public funds for these private institutions would be the method of channelling public funds to the poor. For both types of merit goods, if the country has an adequate administrative capacity, vouchers earmarked for purchasing these merit goods given to the preferred purchasers will be more efficient than subsidies to producers. If, *faute de mieux*, public provision of these merit goods is undertaken, then differential pricing to recover the costs of provision, whilst subsidizing the poor on the lines developed and recommended by the World Bank in the past, is desirable (see Jimenez (1989) for a powerful restatement of the case for social-sector pricing against the universalist welfarists).

Social security pensions form the other major component of social expenditures, at least in the more advanced developing and former socialist countries. As in most Western welfare states, they are pay-as-you-go schemes. In the light of demographic trends in most ex-socialist countries, they are, as in the West, an economic time bomb.[83] Given the danger, in countries where the welfare ethos has become so widespread, that it may be rational to be feckless in providing for one's old age as 'the rotten kid meets the Good Samaritan', some state compulsion in ensuring that everyone provides for a basic pension may be desirable. As in Chile (see Castaneda, 1992), this could be done through earmarked taxes that are put into fully funded and actuarially fair private pension funds.

This leaves various forms of *income support programmes*—including disability and unemployment insurance, and transfers to alleviate low-end poverty—which are common in many Western welfare states, and which are being recommended, for instance, for the transitional socialist economies (see Barr, 1992*a*, and Paull, 1991). These schemes involve unavoidable 'tax-cum-subsidy distortions', because lump-sum taxation and subsidization is normally not feasible. The econometric attempts to provide quantitative evidence of the effects on labour supply, consumption, and savings of these distortions have been inconclusive (see Atkinson, 1987)— another example of the emerging law that 'all econometric evidence is equivocal'!

Unemployment insurance is of little relevance for the majority of developing countries, in which self-employment predominates over wage employment. Even in the so-called modern sectors of these economies where wage employment is the norm, measured open unemployment rates are relatively low, and the unemployed are typically highly educated, relatively wealthy urban youth. Their unemployment reflects, in part, the availability of 'reserves' (from their relatively better-off families) to finance job search in the high-wage modern sector, and, in part, the over-expansion of higher and secondary education because of economically unjustifiable public subsidies (see Squire, 1981). In addition, relatively high institutional wages in the modern sector encourage what can be termed Harris–Todaro-type unemployment. Given these typical features of developing-country labour markets, unemployment insurance is only feasible for wage employees in the modern sector.

In an excellent overview of the literature on unemployment insurance, Hamermesh argues that the only rationale for unemployment-insurance programmes is the 'individual based goal of consumption stabilization. . . . For this goal to be valid it must be true that workers either estimate the probability of becoming unemployed correctly, but are so myopic that they do not save for the eventuality; or they underestimate the probability and thus have insufficient precautionary savings.'[84] But this still does not establish whether such programmes should be private or public. Beenstock and Brasse (1986) have argued that general private unemployment insurance would be feasible. (But see Barr (1992a), who again uses 'nirvana economics' arguments to counter this claim.) But, as Hamermesh notes:

Before the British unemployment insurance program was introduced in 1911, several private firms offered UI as an insurance option . . . The early British companies went bankrupt, and the classic argument in favor of social insurance for unemployment is that private carriers cannot insure against the common risk of a nationwide recession. A compulsory privately operated program, with very large carriers that have sufficient reserves or borrowing capacity to weather a recession, might not have such problems.[85]

If, however, for whatever reason a publicly funded programme of unemployment insurance is introduced for the urban employees in the formal sector, what should be its features? We need to minimize the side-effects in terms of the higher urban unemployment and expansion of the urban informal sector, and increased rural–urban migration, that maybe induced. These effects will depend upon how the tax to finance the benefits is raised. If the tax is levied on modern-sector employers, whilst their wage employees receive the benefits, the net effect will be to raise the effective wage of such employees, and this will through the familiar Harris–Todaro type of dynamic process lead to a reduction in modern sector employment, increase the size of the urban informal sector, and also increase rural–urban migration. If, instead, the 'tax is assessed on worker's earnings, there is no effect on the size of the urban sector, just as there is no impact on the employment or the unemployment rate. [Hence] to the extent we believe that labor-market dualism characterizes developing economies, UI benefits should be financed by taxes on the earnings of workers in the modern sector.'[86]

From a poverty viewpoint, the seasonal unemployment of landless labour in rural areas is likely to be of greater importance than urban unemployment. Rural public-works schemes like the Maharashtra Employment Guarantee scheme (see Ravallion, 1991) have been effective both in preventing famines and in dealing with problems of short-run income variability. But their success lies in the self-targeting that is made possible by offering a wage that only the truly needy will accept.

Severance payments: In many ex-socialist economies, as well as those developing countries which created over-extended and inefficient public sectors, an important part of structural adjustment is the privatization of such enterprises. In addition many bureaucracies which were set up to manage controlled economies need to be slimmed as they move towards market economies. Such structural adjustment programmes typically face political resistance from the public-sector workers, who face retrenchment and/or cuts in their real wages. Such workers can exert political pressure to prevent the rescinding of their politically determined entitlements to future income streams which are above what they would be able to obtain in the free market. The capitalized value of the difference between their expected public-sector earnings (including pension and other benefits) and those they could get in the private sector (adjusted for the probabilities of being hired and fired in the market) represent the rents public-sector workers are currently receiving. If their resistance is to be overcome they might need to be compensated for these rents. This is a political rather than an economic argument for severance payments, over and above those that might already exist in the contractual arrangements that may be in force in the respective labour markets (see Rosen (1985) for a survey of the reasons why many labour-market contracts will have various forms of severance terms built into them for efficiency reasons). How to deal with this problem will differ from country to country, depending upon the particular labour laws and the government's ability to rescind these unviable rents. If the method of adjustment is to be voluntary, however, certain common problems will be faced. The most important of these is that, given the heterogeneity of the labour force, the rents derived from public-sector jobs will differ for different workers, being highest for the bad workers whose market opportunities relative to their entitlements in the public sector are the worst. With imperfect knowledge of each worker's rents, and the difficulty in devising perfectly discriminating severance-payment schemes, if the severance compensation is set to persuade the last bad worker to leave the public sector, the intra-marginal workers will be receiving more compensation than the capitalized value of their public-sector rents. This could mean a very high cost to the fisc. But in some cases (for instance where the public enterprise is producing negative value added at world prices), shutting down the enterprise even with this high cost may lead to a gain in net GDP. In others where the enterprise might still be viable after restructuring and privatization, which involves retrenchment, the problem of tailoring a severance package remains.[87]

The most attractive plan, which would meet both the objectives of limiting political opposition and reducing the fiscal burden, would be one limited to workers not hired by the newly privatized enterprise. This tackles

the adverse selection problem, whereby the good workers take the severance package and the lemons are left with the new firm. The severance
package for those made redundant should be based on the principle of
tailoring the benefits to the median redundant worker's public-sector rents.
This would imply that if the severance package offered uniform compensation at the level of the rents to the median retrenched worker, then all those
with lower rents would be better off, and they would provide the political
support for the scheme to override those workers whose rents were greater
than the median and would be worse off. Little more can be said in
principle about the specific terms of these programmes, which need to be
tailored to local conditions, and in particular the relative bargaining power
of public-sector workers *vis-à-vis* the state.

Transfers to alleviate destitution and conjunctural poverty: We have already
discussed the reasons for preferring the strengthening of private channels
and institutions for the alleviation of low-end poverty (destitution and
conjunctural poverty), in countries where the welfare-state ethos has not
become widespread. This is best done by the co-financing of local and
international charities, as well as local mutual self-help associations. But
there are a number of countries, mainly the ex-socialist, where either
because they already have universalist welfare states, and/or because the
institutions for the private-sector option are not present, some form of
public provision for income support of the low-end poor may be necessary.
How can this best be done? A large part of the relevant group is likely to
consist of people who for identifiable reasons are incapable of earning a
living (the handicapped, the mentally ill, the old and infirm without any
families or savings). Their inability to finance their basic needs is genuinely
involuntary, and hence the problems of perverse incentives which bedevil so
many social-insurance-type programmes is not likely to arise. This category
is of people labelled the 'deserving poor' by the Victorians. In the absence
of private charity, public assistance to provide them some basic minimum
income may be justifiable. But again, for the reasons discussed in previous
sections, this public assistance is probably best channelled through local
voluntary associations.

The problems of disincentives and the creation of a dependency culture
is particularly acute for the able-bodied poor (see Murray, 1984). No
completely satisfactory scheme is available on the basis of Western experience to alleviate their poverty without the perversion of incentives. Negative
income tax, or basic income schemes (for instance those recommended by
Friedman, and in the Meade committee report), involve unacceptable tax
burdens. Thus Brittan and Webb (1990) estimate that such a scheme
which guaranteed a minimum income for all UK families at the current
income-support level would require a uniform income-tax rate of 40%,
much higher than the current basic income-tax rate of 25%. However, the
alternative of targeted means-tested benefits, which are withdrawn when

the unemployed find work or the poor move up the income ladder, leads to well-known disincentives associated with unemployment and poverty traps. There is no obvious remedy. Decentralization to local communities of the administration and monitoring of these programmes to help the able-bodied poor—as is done in Sweden and Switzerland—may be part of the answer (see Lindbeck, 1990, and Segalman, 1986). An income-maintenance scheme that distinguishes between the able-bodied poor and the deserving poor has recently been proposed for Eastern Europe by an IMF economist (see Paull, 1991). It has much to commend it. The deserving poor are means-tested and publicly assisted to bring them up to a minimum income level. The able-bodied poor are assisted through a series of training, job-search, and workfare programmes to enter or re-enter employment. The proposals are costed for Poland, and do not seem to imply unreasonable shares of GNP as compared with Polish social expenditures for 1990, or similar expenditures in developed countries. If the programmes can be decentralized so that they are administered and monitored locally, they might provide the best that can be done to deal with an intractable problem.

But in the long run, even in these ex-socialist countries the hope must lie in the creation of a civil society where private transfers and institutions arise to take care of the needy. Besides promoting the supreme moral virtue—private benevolence—extolled by classical liberalism, it would also prevent that corruption of the polity that the creation of universal welfare states has often caused.

NOTES

1. But see Lipton (1983a–c, 1985a–b). The general impression from his survey of the characteristics of the ultra-poor is the great heterogeneity of the ultra-poor in terms of location, occupation, life-cycle status, and asset ownership.
2. Edgren (mimeo: 15–16).
3. Bruton (1992: 317); Urdinola et al. (mimeo: comparative analysis, p. 7); Maddison et al. (1992: 95, table 4.11); Hansen (1991: 32).
4. Kuznets (1973).
5. Bruton (1992: 210).
6. See Bhalla (1988).
7. As Bhalla notes, ibid. 99 ff., living standards H_{it} in country i at time t can be related to income Y_{it} and other variables Z_{it}, as

$$H_{it} = f\left(Y_{it}, Z_{it}\right). \qquad (1)$$

Z in turn is a vector of all non-income determinants of H, say

$$Z_{it} = f\left(\tau_i, \alpha_t, X_{it}\right), \qquad (2)$$

where τ represents country-specific variables such as culture, tastes, etc., which are time-invariant, and α time-specific but country-invariant effects reflecting technological advances such as medical progress, etc. These technological improvements are assumed to be available to all countries. X is a vector of all other relevant variables, such as education, etc., but which, lacking independent time-series data, are assumed to be strongly correlated with Y. The basic cross-section regression equation is then of the form

$$H_{it} = \alpha_t + \tau_i + \beta Y_{it} + e. \tag{3}$$

The most appealing functional form for this equation for social indicators which have a physical limit, such as life expectancy or infant mortality, Bhalla suggests is log it. The relevant regression equation for *changes* in these social indicators is then

$$\ln\left(\frac{K - H_{iT}}{H_{iT}}\right) - \ln\left(\frac{K - H_{it}}{H_{it}}\right) = -(\alpha_T - \alpha_t) - \beta_T Y_T + \beta_t Y_t + e, \tag{4}$$

where K is the physical limit of the given indicators. If the exogenous time-impact α is not the same for all countries but a function of initial conditions, then the estimating equation becomes

$$\Delta \cdot H = (\alpha_T - \alpha_t)\frac{1}{\ln H_t} + \beta(\ln Y_{iT} - \ln Y_{it}) + e. \tag{5}$$

This is the equation we have estimated for mortality.
8. Ideally one should examine the residuals from the equations to test whether the relevant countries are outliers, by statistical techniques discussed by Bhalla. Given our gross descriptive purpose we have not conducted this refinement.
9. The regression equation estimated using Bhalla's model I,

$$\Delta \ln H = \alpha(1/\ln H_{1960}) + \beta(\ln Y_{86} - \ln Y_{60}),$$

yielded

$$\Delta \cdot \ln H = -2.4\frac{1}{\ln H_{60}} - 0.137(\ln Y_{86} - \ln Y_{60})$$

$$t = (15.04) \qquad (-2.1)$$

$$R^2 = 0.252, \quad F = 25.25 \quad (\text{significant at the 1\% level}).$$

10. The regression equation estimated was Bhalla's model II, namely

$$\Delta \cdot \ln[(K - H)/H] = \alpha_{1986} - \alpha_{1960} + \beta Y_{1986} - \tau Y_{1960}$$

(the estimated value with $K = 80$ years):

$$\Delta \cdot \ln\frac{K - H}{H} = -0.686 - 0.001 Y_{86} + 0.00007 Y_{60}$$

$$t = \qquad (-3.6) \qquad (1.33)$$

$$R^2 = 0.2099, \quad F = 9.8 \quad (\text{significant at the 1\% level}).$$

11. The regression equation estimated was Bhalla's model I, namely

$$\Delta \ln H = \alpha(1/\ln H_{1960}) + \beta(\ln Y_{1986} - \ln Y_{1960}).$$

The estimated value was

$$\Delta \cdot \ln DR = -2.13 \frac{1}{\ln DR_{60}} - 0.203 \left(\ln Y_{86} - \ln Y_{60} \right)$$

$$t = \left(-17.1 \right) \qquad\qquad \left(-3.4 \right)$$

$$R^2 = 0.411, \quad F = 50.18 \quad \text{(significant at the 1\% level).}$$

12. Sen (1981*b*) has been one of the major proponents of this line; see also his disputation with Bhalla in Srinivasan and Bardhan (1988).
13. See Rottenberg *et al.* (1993: 385).
14. Ibid. 261.
15. Ibid. 46.
16. Ibid. 128.
17. Ibid. 44.
18. Sen (1981*b*): p. 309.
19. See Lindbeck for a discussion of the productivity-damaging effects of the Swedish welfare state, which ultimately brought it to its knees.
20. World Bank, Poverty Reduction Hanbook (1992: 4-9).
21. Ibid. 2-13.
22. Thomas (1979: 577).
23. Iliffe (1987: 5).
24. Arrow (1965: 155).
25. Barr (1992*a*: 742).
26. Demsetz (1989: 8).
27. Ibid. 9.
28. Laffont (1989: 186).
29. Helliweg (1987), Laffont (1989), and Kreps (1990).
30. Platteau (1991: 156).
31. Cox and Jimenez (1990: 206). Also see Rempel and Lobdell (1978), Knowles and Anker (1981), Collier and Lal (1986), Oberai and Singh (1980), and Lucas and Stark (1985), on the significant size and effects of remittances within the rural and between the rural and urban sectors in Ghana, Liberia, Nigeria, Pakistan, Tanzania, Kenya, India, and Botswana.
32. The rotten kid theorem states that

> when one member [of a family] cares sufficiently about other members to be the head, all members have the same motivation as the head to maximize family opportunities and to internalize fully all within-family 'externalities', regardless of how selfish (or, indeed, how envious) these members are. Even a selfish child receiving transfers from his parents would automatically consider the effects of his actions on other siblings as well as his parents. Put still differently, sufficient 'love' by one member guarantees that all members act as if they loved other members as much as themselves.   (Becker, 1976: 270)

33. Bernheim and Bagwell (1988: 309–10).
34. See Kotlikoff and Spivak (1981) and Bernheim *et al.* (1985).
35. Lucas and Stark (1985: 910).
36. Ibid. 906.
37. Rosenzweig (1988: 1167).

38. Ibid. 1152
39. Cox and Jimenez (1990: 216).
40. See Lampman and Smeeding (1983), Cox and Jakubson (1989), Rosenzweig and Wolpin (1985), and Gale *et al.* (1992).
41. Cox and Jimenez (1993: 6).
42. Ibid. 19.
43. Ibid.
44. Cox and Jimenez (1990: 216).
45. Jimenez (1989: 114).
46. Behrman (1991: 152). The reference to UNICEF is to UNICEF (1984).
47. Deolalikar (1993: 26).
48. Ibid. 28. See also van de Walle (1992).
49. World Bank (1992: box 3.9).
50. Ibid., box A3.2. See also Maddison *et al.* (1992: 12–16)
51. World Bank (1992: box A3.3).
52. Midgley (1984: p. ix).
53. Mesa-Lago (1983: 89).
54. Ibid. 95.
55. Ibid. 100.
56. World Bank (1992: box 3.7).
57. Ibid. box 3.8.
58. Hansen (1992: 511).
59. World Bank (1992: box 3.4).
60. Atkinson and Hills (1991: 105).
61. Lindbeck (1985: 316).
62. Ibid. 317.
63. See in particular Barr (1987). He argues: 'The welfare state is much more than a safety net; it is justified not simply by any redistributive aims one may (or may not) have, but because it does things which private markets for technical reasons either would not do at all or would do inefficiently. We need a welfare state of some sort for efficiency reasons' (ibid. 421).
64. Stigler (1970).
65. Meltzer and Richard (1981).
66. Becker (1985), in his pressure-group model, uses this feature to argue that in the political equilibrium of a majoritarian democracy the equilibrium taxes and subsidies will correspond with the optimum taxes *à la* Ramsey favoured by economists, that is, factors and commodities in relatively inelastic supply or demand will be taxed most highly. He suggests that this also explains why relatively large countries, which can be expected to have less than infinitely elastic demand curves for their imports or exports, will have a more protectionist political equilibrium than smaller economies, for whom demand schedules for tradables are more elastic. Note that the same Ramsey optimal taxes will also be the taxes chosen by the revenue-maximizing predatory state. See Brennan and Buchanan (1980). That the recommendation of modern optimal-tax theorists serves the interests of a revenue-maximizing predatory government, and would also be the pattern of predatory fiscal exactions in pressure-group-dominated majoritarian democracies, is argued in Lal (1990).
67. Peltzman (1980).

INCOME TRANSFERS AND POVERTY REDRESSAL 391

68. Also see Demsetz (1982). The reference to Stigler is to Stigler (1970), and to Becker is to Becker (1985).

69. Peltzman (1980: 16).

70. These countries are Colombia, Costa Rica, Jamaica, Malaysia, Malta, Nigeria, Peru, Singapore. Thailand, Turkey, and Uruguay. (See ibid., table 16, n. 2, on p. 77.)

71. He also found that the model provided a good econometric fit to explain the growth of post-Depression US public expenditure.

72. Murray's basic argument (in Murray, 1984) is that the war-on-poverty programmes created incentives for the poor to undertake various actions which public policy had made privately profitable, but which also perpetuated their poverty. Thus the observed decline in the male labour-participation rates, particularly of black youths, is attributed to the rise in their reservation wage which resulted from these programmes. The increase in single-female-headed black families and the accompanying increase in illegitimate births can be traced to the incentives created by the welfare programmes for such 'optimal' behaviour. Most heinously, argues Murray, these programmes eroded the self-respect and the accompanying desire for self-improvement amongst the 'underclass'.

If the war on poverty has created perverse incentives which might have perpetuated the black underclass, by contrast the effects of economic growth and increasing black access to education, in the decades since 1940, have been identified as major sources for the remarkable advance in black economic status in the US (in the 1940 to 1980 decades). This is supported by the analysis of Welch (1989). Also see Smith and Welch (1989: 519–64).

73. But see Bruton (1992), for a thoughtful discussion of the role of the rice culture as a determinant of policies in Sri Lanka and Malaysia.

74. Ahmad (1991: 106).

75. The evidence from the US on the effects of the welfare system on incentives is summarized in Danziger et al. (1981) and Moffitt (1992). The latter also incorporates many of the findings of the former. Moffits's general conclusion (ibid. 56–7) is:

> The literature on the incentive effects of the US welfare system . . . has shown unequivocal evidence of effects on labor supply, participation in the welfare system and on some aspects of family structure. . . . Yet the review has also shown that the importance of these effects is limited in many respects. The labor supply effects, whilst statistically significant, are not large enough to explain the high rates of poverty among female heads. . . . In addition, the econometric estimates of family structure effects are not large enough to explain long-run declines in marriage rates and, in any case, are incapable of explaining recent upward trends in female headship because welfare benefits have been declining. . . . Some of the evidence assembled in the review suggests that family-structure issues appear to be at least as important in understanding the economic status of low income female heads as labor supply issues. . . . Unfortunately, the research on family structure remains in its infancy compared to the voluminous research on labor supply.

Also see Gramlich (1989), Welch (1989), and Smith and Welch (1989).

76. It is argued in Lal (1995) that the announcement of the demise of the extended family is premature, while O. Harris (1987) provides references and a summary of the literature on the extended family. As she notes, 'Some of the classic examples of large extended family households, for example, the Indian joint family, or the Japanese *dozoku*, have shown remarkable resilience in adapting to the processes of urbanization and industrialization' (p. 61).

77. See Becker and Tomas (1986). Also see the recent exchange between Becker and Goldberger on the former's economic explanation of income distribution and inter-generational mobility: Goldberger (1989) and Becker (1989).

Becker and Tomas apply their model to various specific US social-welfare programs: the effects of Head Start, welfare, and aid to poor pregnant women in the US. By and large their model predicts either nil or counter-productive effects (like those Murray finds from the available empirical evidence), largely because 'government programs that add to the resources of some members of a family and possibly take away resources from other members induce compensatory responses by altruistic parents. They spend less on members who gain resources and more on members who lose resources' (Becker and Tomas, 1986: S15). Also see Becker (1988), especially section IV, where Becker rightly emphasizes the important role historically of the family (and the inter-generational altruism of its members in meeting the risks faced by the elderly, young, sick, and unemployed). He argues that the substitution of public transfers for this inter-generational intra-family altruism occurs as the net cost of children rises—as it does with economic development.

78. World Bank (1992: box A3.1). Also see Jimenez *et al.* (1991).

79. See, for instance, the evidence on the relative efficacy of private credit agents over centralized public agencies in rural credit markets, in Binswanger *et al.* (1985), Braverman and Guasch (1989), and von Pischke *et al.* (1983).

80. Though some of the pitfalls in this public embrace of private NGOs outlined in Lal (1993*a*) should be borne in mind.

81. R. Harris (1988: 18).

82. Mill (1970: 161).

83. See Lapidus and Swanson (1988) and IMF *et al.* (1991) for socialist countries, and Lal and Wolf (1986) and Boskin (1986) for the West.

84. Hamermesh (1992: 3).

85. Ibid. 13.

86. Ibid. 35.

87. Papers by Fiszben (1992) and Diwan (1993) provide detailed analyses of the various options, as well as discussions of severance-payment schemes in a number of countries.

10

On Fostering Poverty-Redressing Growth

IT is time for a general summing up. Our country studies and this book have shown, not surprisingly, that monocausal explanations for relative growth performance, such as increased capital formation or technical progress or even 'inward' and 'outward' orientation (as usually defined), are either inadequate or vacuous 'black boxes'. This does not mean that we have been unable to discern any patterns—in terms of differing resource endowments, public policies, and political behaviour—which could help in delineating those economic environments which are most likely to foster poverty-redressing growth. The best way of summing up the lessons we have learnt from this study may be to outline the constituents of such a framework. To do so we need, first, to summarize the major patterns we have discovered in terms of our classificatory schema, encompassing differences in resource endowment, organizational structure, and the polity. We then outline and defend a classical framework for economic policy, following on from the discussion of the evolution of economic thought on policy issues over the last few centuries outlined in Chapter 7, and that in developing countries in Chapter 8.

I. SUMMARY OF FINDINGS

1. Poverty and Equity

The results can be summarized as follows. Utilizing an important distinction between mass structural poverty, destitution, and conjunctural poverty (Chapter 1) we found that, first, in all our countries, and taking account of differing growth performance within a country over time, growth in income per capita led to the alleviation of mass poverty. That this is a robust conclusion was further established in a special study by G. Fields commissioned for the project,[1] which also looked at the growth–poverty link in other developing countries. That growth does trickle down, whilst growth collapses lead to increasing poverty, is a firm conclusion from this comparative study.

Secondly, no obvious connection was found between changes in inequality (as measured, for instance, by Gini coefficients) and growth performance.

Thirdly, direct transfers and social expenditures to alleviate mass poverty were not always found to have made any appreciable dent on poverty. Those of our countries which have attempted to alleviate poverty through the creation of politically determined entitlements (Sri Lanka, Jamaica, Uruguay, Costa Rica), whilst making some dent on mass poverty, have found that these entitlements may not be sustainable. This is for three reasons. First, the countries which have sought to follow so-called 'basic needs'-type policies of direct transfers, modelled on Western welfare states, have usually financed these through natural-resource rents. In most of the cases in our sample of countries, given the nature of their factional politics, there have been pressures to expand these entitlements by bearing harder on the sector financing these rents. This has had the effect of killing the goose that laid the golden eggs, with the result that the transfer state becomes unsustainable and the over-extension of social expenditure in relation to taxes leads to the familiar fiscal and balance-of-payments crises—often accompanied by a growth collapse.

But whilst growth may be the only certain way of alleviating mass poverty, the problems of destitution and conjunctural poverty would still require some social safety net. Unlike the universalized benefits of a welfare state, those in a social safety net are targeted to the destitute and conjuncturally poor. We found much merit in rural public-works schemes which offer a wage only the truly needy will accept, and hence are self-targeting. They can be an effective means for dealing with the conjunctural poverty associated with famines and seasonal employment in agrarian economies.

We saw, however, in Chapter 9 that social safety nets are still mainly provided through private agencies—most notably the extended family—in the Third World. There is some evidence that public transfers tend to crowd out private ones (though not completely). Also private agents appear to be more efficient in both providing targeted income transfers, as well as merit goods such as education and health, than public ones. Hence our suggestion that it might be best to deal with problems of destitution and conjunctural poverty by strengthening these private channels, say by granting matching public funds to charities (local and international) to make the necessary provision.

This conclusion is strengthened by another empirical finding about so-called direct transfers, which concerns their political economy. Our study, as well as evidence from other empirical work on welfare systems in developed and developing countries, supports what has been termed 'Director's Law' by Stigler. This states that in most polities (except for the Platonic variety) public income transfers tend to be from the poor and the rich to the middle classes.

Moreover, given the unavoidable bureaucratic failure encountered in most direct means of public poverty alleviation, as well as the unintended counter-productive incentive effects of even effective poverty programmes, and their burgeoning cost to the fisc—all of which have recently come to the fore in discussions of Western welfare states—caution would dictate forbearance in extending Western-style welfare states to the Third World.

The results of the policies to promote greater income equality through the redistribution of property ownership are also not impressive, judging from the outcomes of the land-reform programmes in countries such as Mexico and Egypt. Apart from the obvious political obstacles of pushing through a land-reform programme on a significant scale, the ineffectiveness of these programmes may be traced to a failure of the complementary policies to raise the productivity of the recipients of the distributed land. In addition to the organizational problem of providing improved marketing, credit, and inputs to the small farmers, there is the problem of avoiding middle-class capture of these benefits, which are diverted to the larger and more prosperous farmers at the expense of the poorer small farmers.

There seems to be a strong case, therefore, based on both theory and experience, for relying on the established poverty-alleviating effects of rapid growth to deal with mass structural poverty, and targeting whatever public state subsidies are available to deal with problems of destitution and conjunctural poverty. As public agencies are often less efficient in such targeting than private ones, once again public co-financing of the private provision of such safety nets may be the best way to deal with an intractable problem.

2. Growth Performance

In explaining the differences in growth performance the proximate causes were found to be relative differences in both the efficiency and level of investment. A new neoclassical endogenous growth model due to Scott (1989) was found to be the most useful in explaining the divergence in growth rates in our sample of countries. We find that its three explanatory variables—the average level of gross investment to output, the (implicit) efficiency of this investment, and growth of the quality-adjusted labour force—accounted for over 90% of the variance in the 1950–85 growth rates of our sample of countries.

From the estimates of average rates of return to investment and the detailed analytical histories in our country studies, it is clear that the efficiency of investment was the crucial variable in explaining differing growth performance.

In turn, the policy regime was crucial in explaining these differences in the efficiency of investment. As many other studies have found, the most important aspect of policy was the trade regime, with better growth performance under outward orientation. Furthermore, the absence of the usual policy-induced distortions in the functioning of the price mechanism, together with the provision of an adequate physical infrastructure, were important determinants of better growth performance. But contrary to current orthodoxy, neither our country studies nor the crude statistical tests for our countries—which are similar to those currently fashionable—found differences in the educational levels or changes in them as significant determinants of growth performance. Finally, the importance of a stable monetary framework and a non-inflationary fiscal regime were also found to be as important for efficiency and sustained growth as the provision of the classical public goods of law and order.

This, however, raises the deeper question of why countries adopted the policy regimes they did, and why some of them changed these during the twenty-five years covered by our country studies. The bulk of our comparative work in this volume has been concerned with explaining differences in policy regimes and changes in them, in terms of the deeper underlying factors of initial resource-endowments, organizational structure, and the nature of the polity.

3. Stylized Patterns: Endowments, Polity, and Economic Policy

The important stylized patterns which have emerged from our country studies and this comparative study are as follows.

The first stylized pattern of some importance is that, during the first two post-war decades, the majority of our countries had increases in incomes per capita unprecedented both in relation to their past economic history, and to that of currently developed countries. This was largely due to the world-wide boom, which many observers[2] have linked to the emergence of a new liberal international economic order amongst the industrialized countries, which provided an unprecedented boost to world trade. During this period of world-wide prosperity, mild *dirigisme* towards trade and industry (of the sort found in many of our countries) did not do great damage to their growth performance. But there were some (Ghana is the major example in our sample) which by decisively turning inwards set themselves on a disastrous path of immiserization rather than growth.

It was during the more turbulent period in the world economy since 1973 that the effects of the differing policy regimes on the efficiency of investment in our countries became manifest, leading to widely divergent growth and poverty-redressal outcomes.[3] Many of our countries suffered growth collapses (as judged by our country authors). It is noteworthy that most of our land-abundant countries (8 out of 10, that is all except Thailand and Malaysia) suffered growth collapses. None of our three labour-abundant and four (Indonesia, Jamaica, Peru, and Madagascar) out of eight in our intermediate-endowment category suffered growth collapses.[4] This is the second of our stylized empirical patterns.

The proximate cause of most of the growth collapses was an inflationary-cum-balance-of-payments crisis, usually generated by unsustainable fiscal commitments. We define countries with chronic inflation as those in which consumer prices have risen by more than 20% per annum over an extended period, and those with hyper-inflation as those where the demand for real money balances is shrinking, so that the inflation rate is higher than the rate of growth of money; all our hyper-inflation countries suffered a growth collapse. Moreover, the major reason for excessive money creation was the monetization of fiscal deficits in all our growth-collapse countries. The sources of fiscal imbalances in the growth-collapse countries and in some with 'quieter crises' of growth, in turn, were twofold: (a) 'big push'-type development expenditures (in Brazil, Mexico, Peru, Nigeria, Ghana, Turkey, and Madagascar), and (b) unsustainable social expenditures to provide income transfers and consumer subsidies (in Sri Lanka, Egypt, Jamaica, Uruguay, and Costa Rica). Two features of this division of countries by source of fiscal imbalance were striking. First, most of the imbalances due to 'big push'-type fiscal expansions were in land-abundant (and natural-resource-rich) countries. Second, all the countries with unsustainable social expenditures, except for Egypt, were factional states in terms of our classification of the polity. These are our third set of stylized patterns.

The Chinese ideogram for crisis is in two parts. One represents danger, the other opportunity. All the growth-collapse countries experienced the former, but only a few seized the latter aspect of a crisis. This, we found, was due to certain patterns of political behaviour which were jointly conditioned by the country's polity and its underlying resource endowment. By and large, factional states (particularly of the democratic type) in relatively large land-abundant countries, where it was economic to have large-scale production (in either agriculture or industry or both), found it more difficult to change the policy regimes which had generated the crises in the first place until—and unless—economic ruin stared the polity in its face. This is our fourth stylized pattern.

In explaining these differing political reactions to policy-induced growth crises, we were therefore led to the deeper initial conditions—represented by differing resource endowments, organizational requirements, and polities—as the determinants of the various policy regimes which were dominant in our different countries, through most of the post-war period. We found our classification of countries into the three- by two- by five-fold categorization, outlined in Chapter 2, useful in this task.

(a) The Labour-Abundant Countries

The explicit use of the three-factor open-economy framework, which distinguishes between the differing organizational requirements of small- and large-scale production units, provides a richer menu of possible efficient development paths than the single universal development path (in terms of the movements in relative factor prices) implied by the standard 2 × 2 Heckscher–Ohlin model. The latter is mainly relevant for labour-abundant economies. For them, it implies the standard prescription of initially developing labour-intensive activities, and thence moving up the ladder of comparative advantage with capital accumulation. On this development path, real wages rise and hence there is unlikely to be any conflict between the needs of the economy and the polity (irrespective of its different forms). The major task for the government is to promote an adequate infrastructure to reduce the transactions costs of the relatively small-scale organizational units which will predominate in the earlier stages of this development path.

In a sense this growth path is the easiest to follow. This is largely because the incremental comparative advantage of the country is self-evident, as are the infrastructural requirements. Moreover, if the country is small, the limited size of the domestic market makes reliance on foreign trade inevitable. This makes it less likely that any grave departures from the free-trade resource allocation will emerge—irrespective of the degree of *dirigisme* of the government.

There seem to be two reasons for this. First, given the small size of the domestic market, any departure from the free-trade allocation is unlikely to lead to vertical import-substitution (into the inputs required by domestic industry). Hence, when the costs of inappropriate import-substitution become clear, it will be easier to switch the policy regime, by creating a quasi-free-trade regime for exporters by allowing them to obtain their inputs at world prices. With no domestic import-substitute producers of such inputs, no lobbies will exist to prevent their competitive import. By contrast, in larger countries, or those with more intermediate-resource endowments, such a switch in policy regime will be politically difficult as it would hurt the interests of inefficient import-substitute intermediate-goods producers.[5] Mistakes can thus be more easily rectified as part of a learning process in small labour-abundant countries, because the political costs of rectification are likely to be low.

A labour-abundant country's growth path is likely to be easier for a second reason. Its incremental comparative advantage is readily apparent to economic agents in both the public and the private sector. In this sense industrial winners are more obvious, and the consequences of picking losers (or policies which stimulate losers) more immediate—as with Singapore's ill-advised and ill-fated attempt to jump a few rungs on the ladder of comparative advantage through an artificial raising of wages. The propensity towards *dirigisme* of most Third World states can thus be satisfied at low cost in such countries. But as any *dirigisme* has dead-weight costs, there will still be some, though perhaps small, costs of substituting public for private action.[6] But there may be additional costs if hubris sets in and the planners depart from the obvious and seek to promote industries which do not fit the country's incremental comparative advantage.[7]

(b) The Land-Abundant Countries

Similarly, the comparative advantage of a large land-abundant country is also likely to be relatively obvious, but much more difficult to realize, for two reasons. First, with a high supply price of labour (compared with the labour-abundant countries) due to its more favourable labour–land ratios, once such a country seeks to industrialize, its incremental comparative advantage is likely to lie on the relatively capital-intensive rungs of the ladder of comparative advantage. As the development of such industries is likely to require lumpy investments, scarce skills, and imported technology, it may be difficult to develop such industries without at least some public promotion. The dangers of bureaucratic failure endemic in such promotion may then lead to a failure to realize their economic potential.

Secondly, with a growing population, if the rate of capital accumulation is not high enough, then their efficient development path could contain segments where real wages need to fall.[8] Thus, unlike the unilinear (rising wage) development path of the labour-abundant countries, land-abundant countries might find that they first have to move on to a higher rung of the ladder of comparative advantage (with high wages), then slide down a few rungs, with lower wages (if capital growth is not rapid enough), before proceeding on a similar unilinear path of rising wages to their labour-abundant cousins. This required equilibrium time-path of real wages could, however, pose some serious political problems if the polity is subject to factional democratic pressures. We could get a polity which seeks to resist the equilibrium real-wage adjustments by turning inward, and thence comes to be at odds with its comparative advantage. By contrast, as our country studies show, Platonic, oligarchic, and predatory-autocratic polities may be able to overcome the potential dissonance and hence be able to follow this politically more dangerous development path more successfully.

In polities subject to factional political pressure, policy is likely to be determined by the interests of median voters.[9] If their individual factor endowments are more labour-intensive than the economy's, the polity will seek to resist any real-wage cuts that may be required to follow a development path in line with their changing comparative advantage. The ensuing conflict between the polity and the economy can lead to political cycles in which inward-looking populist phases (seeking to resist the required wage adjustments) lead to inflationary and balance-of-payments crises. These are temporarily solved by some liberalization under a temporary Platonic, autocratic, or oligarchic regime, which in turn is eventually replaced by a populist one which restores the disequilibrium.

Given the unavoidable political imperative to avoid the falling-wage segments of their development path, irrespective of their political character, such countries will attempt big-push development programmes, often under the aegis of the public sector and usually with an important element of foreign finance. This big push often pushes them into unsustainable fiscal imbalances, debt crises, and thence into a growth collapse.

Within both the land-abundant and intermediate resource-endowment groups, however, we have also found it useful to distinguish between the differing organizational requirements of promoting peasant or plantation exports. Countries with the former type of initial conditions (for instance Thailand) found it easier to extend and expand the existing organizational framework (including most importantly entrepreneurship) developed initially for peasant exports, once the country's comparative advantage, with increasing population pressure on land and capital, shifts into the production of medium and eventually highly labour-intensive manufactures. By contrast, the plantation-type land-abundant country, going through a similar passage of changing labour–land (and labour–capital) ratios, finds it more difficult to create *de novo* the organizational infrastructure required to support the smaller-scale organizations which the realization of their incremental comparative advantage demands.

(c) Intermediate Factor-Endowment Countries

The intermediate group of resource-endowment countries have the most difficult development path. For, first, their incremental comparative advantage is not so apparent. Hence 'mistakes'[10] are not so easily recognized, nor rectified—particularly if the mistakes have been made by the public sector, which in the absence of any bankruptcy constraints resists the exit of inefficient firms. Second, like the land-abundant countries, the intermediate group are also more likely to face situations in which their polities are at odds with their comparative advantage.

We believe the delineation of alternative feasible efficient development paths (within a three-factor model of an open economy), as well as the perils to be encountered on some of them, is one of the more important and novel findings of our study. Though a moment's reflection would underline the heterogeneity of the initial conditions of the Third World, we have found it analytically useful to outline the broad common patterns on a few of the many possible alternative development paths. The relative success of our best countries in the 'difficult' resource-endowment groups (Malaysia and Thailand, and Indonesia, for instance) have been based on realizing the limits within which they can seek to deviate from their efficient growth path.

The final and perhaps most important judgement (rather than a stylized fact) flowing from the country studies was the importance of the stability of property rights (even more than their efficiency) in leading to a successful and sustainable growth outcome.[11] The stability of property rights does not mean that a 'clean' (once-for-all and well defined) redistribution of property rights is ruled out. What is harmful is uncertainty about such redistribution. Furthermore, the definition of the right to property is in effect the right to claims to the income-streams from the use of that property. Hence property rights are altered not merely through the redistribution of assets, but also through changing the implicit or explicit set of taxes and subsidies on factors and commodities, to which most public interventions are analytically equivalent, as they change the net income-stream attached to property. These taxes and subsidies must also include the changes in property rights that occur from the levying of the inflation tax. A stable fiscal and monetary constitution was thus also found to be an important part of a growth-promoting economic framework.

4. Nationalism, Dirigisme, and Liberalization

Finally, we have briefly (in Chapter 7) examined the role of ideology, in particular economic nationalism (which is ubiquitous), in the evolution of *dirigiste* policy regimes in most developing countries. These policy regimes were very similar to the mercantilist regimes set up by the nationalist absolute monarchies in Europe after the Renaissance. The liberalization of current Third World regimes (and in many First and Second World countries), like that of the European mercantilist regimes of the seventeeth and eighteenth centuries, was shown to lie in the realization by the polity that the nationalist objective is better served by a liberal economic order through sustained liberalization. The disorder created by *dirigisme* (through the growth of black markets, tax evasion, et cetera) leads paradoxically to the state losing control over the economy. There is a growing realization that reversing this un-Marxian withering away of the state, as well as the restoration of the order necessary for national integration, requires economic liberalization (see Lal, 1987b). This has led in the 1980s to a new world-wide Age of Reform.

II. TOWARDS A LIBERAL ECONOMIC FRAMEWORK FOR POLICY

What would be a liberal economic framework for policy in this new age? A succinct modern restatement of the case for economic liberalism, and what it does and does not entail, has recently been provided by David Henderson:

The objections to economic liberalism and the market economy centre round the role of governments and states, both nationally and internationally. For many people liberalism goes with *laissez-faire*, which in turn is viewed as outdated, negative, unconcerned with what happens to weaker members of society and *de facto* favouring the stronger, and uncompromisingly negative in its attitude to the state. This rests on a double misconception. First, it distorts the message of *laissez-faire*.

Second, it wrongly identifies belief in a market economy with an extreme interpretation of the *laissez-faire* principle.

As to the first point, *laissez-faire* gets an undeservedly bad press. The message it conveys is not that governments should be inert or indifferent. Its emphasis is a positive one. It is concerned with economic freedom, including the freedom of individuals and enterprises to enter industries or occupations, to choose their place of residence or operation within a country, and to decide their own products, processes and markets. There is nothing outdated about these principles, nor do they operate against the weak. To the contrary, they enable opportunities to be opened up more widely, and thus operate against special privileges within an economic system. It is no accident that outside the communist world the economy which most conspicuously departs from *laissez-faire* is that of the Republic of South Africa.

In any case, liberalism is not to be identified with hostility to the state, nor with a doctrinaire presumption that governments have only a minor role in economic life. On the contrary, the liberal view of the role of the state, both internal and external, is strongly positive.[12]

More importantly, the widespread acceptance of economic liberalism as a practical maxim (one important aspect of an ideology—see Chapter 7) would, in all likelihood, put a stop to the ubiquitous rent-seeking predatoriness of many Third World states, as it did briefly in the liberal phase in Europe. It would provide some internalized commitments against those neo-mercantilist interventions of the state that have impaired growth performance and thus reduced the chances of alleviating poverty in many countries.

As we have argued, the main springs of growth (entrepreneurship, productivity, and thrift) can best be fostered within an economic framework that maintains relatively stable property rights. Various forms of *dirigiste* intervention upset the stability of these rights and hence increase the fog in which economic agents undertake their actions. The uncertainty-based, externality-creating form of investment which Scott has emphasized as a major source of growth is considerably more difficult to undertake in such an environment.

Many economic historians[13] have argued that the European growth miracle of the eighteenth and nineteenth centuries is directly related to the creation of property rights broadly associated with a market economy. These property rights made it possible to curb the inherent predatory power of the state—historically, through various forms of taxation based on representation. The resulting liberal economic framework gave freer rein to the entrepreneurial talents and instincts of private agents. The classical thinkers and their modern-day successors, the neo-Austrians, have always emphasized that the entrepreneur plays an important role in an economic environment characterized by *ignorance*—which *faute de mieux* is characteristic of the forward-looking investment decisions that typically fuel the growth process. Investment efficiency depends just as much on free entry by potential competitors as it does on the exit of unviable firms. This freedom of entry and exit by entrepreneurs must not be impaired, as it most often is by *dirigiste* interventions.

These classical and neo-Austrian insights[14] are not available to the technocratic tradition that now dominates public-policy discussions, as the entrepreneur[15] is redundant in neoclassical economics, which assumes an environment of purely actuarial Knightian risk. But he is at the centre of the neo-Austrian stage—creating and searching out investment opportunities and gambling on the future. The liberal economic framework allows this entrepreneurial function (which, even though unquantifiable, is undeniably at the heart of the growth process) its fullest play. The neo-mercantilist policies of most Third World countries divert these entrepreneurial talents and resources away from productive activities into the zero-sum redistributive games involved in wasteful lobbying and rent-seeking. By contrast, the liberal economic framework provides the necessary incentives for entrepreneurship, productivity, and thrift. These qualities (and their determinants) are only dimly understood by economists in a formal sense. But at bottom they are, as our country studies amply demonstrate, the mainsprings of sustained and sustainable economic growth.

The two most important features of the liberal economic framework are its emphasis on Gladstonian finance and sound money. The requirements of the latter are self-evident. The nature of the former is less well-known and more contentious. Schumpeter lists three basic principles of Gladstonian finance:[16]

1. *Retrenchment*, which meant that 'the most important thing was to remove fiscal obstructions to private activity. And for this, it was necessary to keep public expenditure low.'[17]
2. *Neutrality*, which implies 'raising the revenue that would still have to be raised in such a way as to deflect economic behavior as little as possible from what it would have been in the absence of all taxation'.[18]
3. *Balance*, where Schumpeter refers to the principle of the balanced budget, or rather, since debt was to be reduced, 'the principle that Robert Lowe . . . embodied in his definition of a minister of finance: "an animal that ought to have a surplus"'.[19]

A recent OECD study[20] concludes that the present-day concerns and objectives of most OECD countries, irrespective of their political complexion, seem to revolve around re-instituting the principles of Gladstonian finance in their economies. Nevertheless, many mainstream economists are advocates of the highly sophisticated and interventionist 'optimal tax' theory of Frank Ramsey and his followers.[21]

This theory assumes, as one recent application to developing countries notes, that 'the government has coherent, unified and largely benevolent objectives, captured in the social welfare function, and we search for ways in which the tools available to it can be used to improve the measure of welfare'.[22] That the theory does not apply to most developing countries is patently obvious, as most of their polities do not even come close to these assumptions about their character.

Once a predatory state or rent-seeking society is accepted as the norm, however, the pattern of optimal taxes à la Ramsey, even from the point of view of a neutral outside observer, is no longer desirable. Thus

the well known inverse elasticity rule which calls for concentrating excise taxation on inelastically demanded commodities in order to minimize the social cost for acquiring a given amount of tax revenue is altered by the existence of rent-seeking. Rent-seeking increases the marginal social cost of excise taxation across commodities in such a way as to confound the traditional result. It can easily follow that the correct pattern of excises is to tax relatively more elastic demand curves first.[23]

An important distinction to make concerning the 'neutrality' of taxation is that in the optimal-tax tradition this means minimizing the dead-weight costs of taxation, whereas in Gladstonian finance the term refers to the generality or uniformity of a tax.[24] A number of arguments (apart from rent-seeking) can be made against the former (neoclassical) and in favour of the latter (classical) prescription of neutrality.

First, Ramsey's optimal taxation is based on the assumption that, even though non-uniform taxation tends to encourage individuals to shift their demands and supplies from taxed to non-taxed goods and activities, such leakages will be small. It is only if tastes are given, as optimal-tax theorists assume, that such counter-productive behaviour, from their viewpoint, will not arise.

Second, Harberger has argued:

Economic theory assumes that the dominant source is substitution. . . . There is thus a very strong presumption that broadening the coverage and lowering the rate of a uniform tax will reduce the deadweight loss. . . . One can build policy on this basis without having any detailed knowledge of the parameters of supply and demand, without any particular hope of gaining anything more than a very patchy knowledge about them in the future, and indeed *with* an almost absolute assurance that wherever the relevant parameters might be now, they will undergo substantial changes in the future. If one believes that these conditions come close to describing our present and likely future state of knowledge about the relevant parameters he will likely be predisposed toward uniform as against Ramsey-rule taxation.

Finally, Harberger notes that 'to tax salt more heavily than sugar' on Ramsey-optimal lines 'simply and solely because it has a lower elasticity of demand is at least as capricious (from the standpoint of equity) as taxing people differently according to the color of their eyes'.

The main difference between the two approaches to neutrality in taxation, according to Harberger, is their different philosophies of government, one of which corresponds to the classical liberal view, the other to the neo-mercantilist 'social engineering' view,[25] or between the state seen as a civil or enterprise association (see Chapter 7). We have hopefully drawn attention in this study to the importance of using the former and the perils of relying on the latter as a framework for public policy geared towards poverty-alleviating growth in the Third World.

The burden of our conclusions therefore is simply this. To understand the differing wealth of nations we need to return to the concerns and perspectives of the classical thinkers, but without abandoning our more powerful theoretical and statistical tools. Mercantilism, in its various guises, still remains the dominant impediment to the attainment of that poverty-redressing growth that many of our countries have shown to be feasible, for all the countries of the Third World. In fighting mercantilism—old or new—these countries should make it their top priority to establish a policy framework that emphasizes economic freedom (misleadingly called *laissez-faire*) in the classical sense.

But there will still be important tasks for the state, as the classics realized.[26] The clearest modern statement of the content of economic liberalism has been set out by Hayek in *The Constitution of Liberty*.[27] Hayek notes that the cornerstone of the liberal position is non-discrimination. This means that

The range and variety of government action that is, at least in principle, reconcilable with a free system is thus considerable. The old formulae of *laissez-faire* or non-intervention do not provide us with an adequate criterion for distinguishing between what is and what is not admissible in a free system.[28]

Like Mill, he distinguishes between coercive activities and pure service activities of the state. In the latter group, state enterprises would be permissible (if their costs are not outweighed by their benefits), but, like Mill, Hayek argues that they should not be state monopolies. The most important political reason against setting up such enterprises, Hayek notes, is that the government will 'use its coercive powers, and particularly its powers of taxation, in order to assist its enterprises, [and so] it can always turn their position into one of actual monopoly'.[29]

He also argues that 'a free system does not exclude on principle all those general regulations of economic activity which can be laid down in the form of general rules specifying conditions which everybody who engages in a certain activity must satisfy'.[30] Though the resulting general non-discriminating interventions may be perverse as they 'reduce overall productivity', they will not infringe that stability of property rights which is engendered 'by a permanent legal framework which enables the individual to plan with a degree of confidence and which reduces human uncertainty as much as possible'.[31] Also in practice, as the empirical evidence from our countries testifies, many of these general interventions have impaired overall productivity.

What are particularly ruled out are discretionary price controls and that regulation of prices and quantities which creates instability in property rights. These are

[G] overnmental measures which the rule of law excludes in principle because they cannot be achieved by merely enforcing general rules but, of necessity, *involve redistributory discrimination between persons*. . . . the exercise of all controls of quantities [and prices] must, of necessity, be discretionary, determined not by rule but by the judgement of authority concerning the relative importance of particular ends. . . . To grant such power to authorities means in effect to give it power arbitrarily to determine what is to be produced, by whom and for whom.[32]

This arbitrary state control over production decisions was of course a mercantilist end, which is also desired by many of our contemporary neo-mercantilist states.[33]

In summing up the resulting classical viewpoint on the appropriate public policies for the Third World, we can do no better than quote the leading contemporary votary of the classical viewpoint on Third World development, Peter Bauer. He wrote:

Criticism of central planning or of the policies pursued in its name must not obscure the importance of the essential tasks of government. The adequate performance of these tasks is indeed helpful to the effective operation of the market, if not necessary for it. The tasks include the successful conduct of external affairs, notably the defence of the country, and also the preservation and encouragement of external communications and contacts; the maintenance of public security; the effective administration of the monetary and fiscal system; the promotion of a suitable institutional framework for the activities of individuals; and the provision of basic health and education services and of basic communications.[34]

We need only to substitute 'possible finance' for 'provision' in the last sentence. This should be enough to be getting on with to promote poverty-alleviating growth in much of the Third World.

NOTES

1. This is published in Psacharopoulos (1991).
2. See, for instance, Blackhurst *et al.* (1978), Lal (1978), and Little (1982).
3. It could be argued that the slow-down in growth in industrial countries since 1973 is the basic explanation for the poor performance of many developing countries. But as this is a general change in the environment affecting *all* development countries, it would not explain the marked divergence in performance amongst our sample of countries in the turbulent 1970s and 1980s.
4. These, except for Madagascar, are also natural-resource-rich countries (for which our measure of land abundance is only an imperfect measure), and hence their political economy is likely to be closer to the land- than the labour-

abundant category of countries. Moreover, Indonesia, after its growth collapse under Sukarno, reversed policies, which led to one of the better growth performances subsequently amongst our sample of countries. So, like the genetic endowment of individuals, whilst resource endowments may predispose countries to certain policies, this is by no means inevitable!

5. For a discussion of the relative difficulties of India adopting Korean tactics to switch trade regimes, see Lal (1988*b*).

6. Thus *dirigiste* Singapore has incurred a much higher cost in terms of consumption foregone to achieve a growth rate comparable to the *laissez-faire* Hong Kong. See Findlay and Wellisz (1984).

7. An example is the promotion of inappropriate heavy industry in South Korea in the 1970s. See K. W. Kim (1981) and Little (1994).

8. Of our land-abundant countries, except for the best performers (Thailand and Malaysia), all the rest had a U or inverted U-shaped time-path of real wages.

9. But see for instance Inman (1987) for a discussion of the limitations of the median-voter theorem.

10. The reason for putting the term in inverted commas is that if incremental comparative advantage is not apparent, then the mistakes cannot be *ex ante* ones. They can only be identified with hindsight, and so it becomes doubtful if they are mistakes!

11. The importance of the evolution of different property-rights systems in explaining the historical growth outcomes in Europe is emphasized by North and Thomas (1973).

12. Henderson (1986: 98–9).

13. Hicks, North, and Braudel, for instance.

14. See Lal (1987*a*) for a fuller discussion.

15. For the importance of entrepreneurship, see the detailed analysis by Young of Hong Kong summarized in Findlay and Wellisz (1993). For a study which questions the usual pessimistic view about entrepreneurship in Africa, see Elkan (1988), and for the importance of entrepreneurship in the growth process see Schultz (1990).

16. Schumpeter (1954: 403). Also see Henderson's lecture to the Institute of Fiscal Studies, Henderson (1989).

17. Schumpeter (1954: 403).

18. Ibid. 404.

19. Ibid. 405–6.

20. OECD (1989).

21. A technically sophisticated and comprehensive application of these principles to developing countries is to be found in Stern and Newbery (1987). But the authors themselves acknowledge (p. 14):

> The book is silent on the positive theory of public finance. The reason is not that we regard the study of ways in which policies are actually determined as uninteresting. . . . Rather we think it is important to discover what would be desirable even when it may be currently politically infeasible or when prudence cautions against creating an institutional framework to administer proposed taxes.

22. Ibid. 653.

23. Lee and Tollison (1988: 349).
24. See Harberger (1987: 645-7) for a lucid and important discussion of these traditions of neutrality in public finance, one classical, the other neoclassical, if we may so term them. The following discussion draws heavily on this source.
25. Thus he writes (ibid. 646):

> Consider the philosophy of government that assigns to governments the role of creating a framework of laws and regulations within which the private sector then is encouraged to operate freely. Under this philosophy a positive value is placed on the authorities not caring what private agents do. . . . It is a positive desideratum to create a tax system that is robust against changes in risks and technology. . . . On the other side of the coin we have a philosophy of social engineering in which the detailed tastes and technology of the society enter as data into a process by which the policy makers choose parameters such as tax rates and coverage so as to maximize some social measure of social benefit.

26. As Mill (1970: 345) noted:

> At some times and places, there will be no roads, docks, harbours, canals, works of irrigation, hospitals, schools, colleges, printing presses, unless the government establishes them; the public being either too poor to command the necessary resources, or too little advanced in intelligence to appreciate the ends, or not sufficiently practised in joint action to be capable of the means. This is true, more or less, of all countries inured to despotism, and particularly of those in which there is a very wide distance in civilization between the people and the government: as in those which have been conquered and are retained in subjection by a more energetic and more cultivated people. In many parts of the world, the people can do nothing for themselves which requires large means and combined action: all such things are left undone, unless done by the state. In these cases, the mode in which the government can most surely demonstrate the sincerity with which it intends the greatest good of its subjects, is by doing the things which are made incumbent on it by the helplessness of the public, in such a manner as shall tend not to increase and perpetuate, but to correct, that helplessness. A good government will give all its aid in such a shape, [so] as to encourage and nurture any rudiments it may find of a spirit of individual exertion.

27. Hayek (1960); see in particular ch. 15.
28. Ibid. 231.
29. Ibid. 224.
30. Ibid.
31. Ibid. 222.
32. Ibid. 227-8.
33. That an economic liberal opposes the resulting *dirigisme* is clearly stated by Hayek (ibid. 231):

> A government which cannot use coercion except in the enforcement of general rules has no power to achieve particular aims that require means other than those explicitly entrusted to its care and, in particular, cannot

determine the material position of particular people or enforce distributive or 'social' justice. In order to achieve such aims, it would have to pursue a policy which is best described—since the word 'planning' is so ambiguous—by the French word *dirigisme*, that is, a policy which determined for what specific purposes particular means are to be used. This, however, is precisely what a government bound by the rule of law cannot do.

34. Bauer (1984: 28).

REFERENCES

Adams, D. W., and Graham, D. H. (1981): 'A Critique of Traditional Credit Projects and Policies', *Journal of Development Economics*, 8.

Adelman, I., and Morris, C. T. (1988): *Comparative Patterns of Economic Development, 1850–1914*, Johns Hopkins University Press, Baltimore.

Aftalion, F. (1990): *The French Revolution—An Economic Interpretation*, Cambridge.

Agarwala, R. (1983): *Price Distortion and Growth in Developing Countries*, World Bank Staff Working Paper no. 575, Management and Development Subseries, no. 2.

Ahluwalia, I. J. (1985): *Industrial Growth in India: Stagnation Since the Mid 1960's*, Oxford University Press, Delhi.

Ahluwalia, M., Carter, N., and Chenery, H. (1979): 'Growth and Poverty in Developing Countries', *Journal of Development Economics*, b/3: 299–341.

—— and Chenery, H. B. (1974): 'A Model of Distribution and Growth', in Chenery (ed.), *Redistribution with Growth*, World Bank and Oxford University Press, New York.

Ahmad, E. (1991): 'Social Security and the Poor: Choices for Developing Countries', *World Bank Research Observer*, 6/1: 105–27.

—— Dreze, J., Hills, J., and Sen, A. K. (eds.) (1991): *Social Security in Developing Countries*, Clarendon Press, Oxford.

Akerloff, G. (1984) *An Economic Theorist's Book of Tales*, Cambridge University Press, Cambridge.

Alchian, A., and Demsetz, H. (1972): 'Production, Information Costs, and Economic Organization', *American Economic Review*, 62 (Dec.), 777–95.

Almond, G. A., and Verba, S. (1963): *The Civic Culture: Political Attitudes and Democracy in Five Nations*, Princeton University Press, Princeton N.J.

Alt, J. E., and Chrystal, K. A. (1983): *Political Economics*, University of California Press, Los Angeles.

Amsden, A. H. (1989): *Asia's Next Giant*, OUP, New York.

Anderson, D. (1990): 'Investment and Economic Growth', *World Development*, 18/8 (Aug.), 1057–79.

Anderson, P. (1974): *Lineages of the Absolutist State*, Verso, London.

Ariff, M., and Hill, H. (1985): *Export-Orientated Industrialization: The Asian Experience*, Allen and Unwin, Sydney and London.

Arndt, H. W. (1988): 'Market Failure and Underdevelopment', *World Development*, 16/2, 219–29.

Arrow, K. J. (1962): 'The Economic Implications of Learning by Doing', *Review of Economic Studies*, 29/3: 155–73.

—— (1963): *Social Choice and Individual Values*, 2nd edition, Yale University Press, New Haven.

—— (1963a): 'Uncertainty and the Welfare Economics of Medical Care', *American Economic Review*, 52: 941–73.

—— (1965): 'A Reply', *American Economic Review*, 55: 154–8.

—— (1974): *The Limits of Organization*, Norton, New York.

—— (1983): *General Equilibrium: Collected Papers*, vol. i, Harvard University Press.

—— and Hahn, F. H. (1971): *General Competitive Analysis*, Holden Day, San Francisco.

Ashley, M. (1961): *England in the 17th Century*, 3rd edn., Pelican, London.

Atkinson, A. B. (1969): 'The True Scale of Economic Models: How Long is the Long Run?', *Review of Economic Studies*, 51/106, 137–52.

—— (1970): 'On the Measurement of Inequality', *Journal of Economic Theory*, 2: 244–63.

—— (1987): 'Income Maintenance and Social Insurance', in A. J. Auerbach and M. Feldstein (eds.): *Handbook of Public Economics*, vol. ii, North Holland, Amsterdam, 779–908.

—— and Hills, J. (1991): 'Social Security in Developed Countries: Are There Lessons for Developing Countries?', Development Economics Research Programme, Discussion Paper no. 16, London School of Economics; reprinted in Ahmad *et al.*

—— and Micklewright, J. (1991): 'Unemployment Compensation and Labor Market Institutions: A Critical Review', *Journal of Economic Literature*, 29/4 (Dec.), 1679–727.

Balassa, B. (1971): *The Structure of Protection in Developing Countries*, Johns Hopkins Univ. Press, Baltimore.

—— (1978): 'Exports and Economic Growth: Further Evidence', *Journal of Development Economics*, 5/2: 181–90.

—— (1982): *Development Strategies in Semi-Industrial Economies*, Oxford University Press.

—— (1984): 'Adjustment Policies in Developing Countries: A Reassessment', *World Development*, 12/9 (Sept.), 955–72.

Baldwin, R. E. (1969): 'The Case Against Infant Industry Tariff Protection', *Journal of Political Economy*, 77 (May/June), 295–305, reprinted in Lal (1992).

—— (1992): 'Are Economists' Traditional Policy Views Still Valid?', *Journal of Economic Literature*, 30 (June), 804–29.

Baldwin, R. and Krugman, P. (1988a): 'Market Access and International Competition', in R. C. Feenstra (ed.), *Empirical Methods for International Trade*, MIT Press, Cambridge, Mass.

—— —— (1988b): 'Industrial Policy and International Competition in Wide Bodied Jet Aircraft', in R. E. Baldwin (ed.), *Trade Policy Issues*. University of Chicago Press, Chicago.

Bardhan, P. (1980): 'Interlocking Factor Markets and Agrarian Development: A Review of Issues', *Oxford Economic Papers*, 32/1.

—— (1989a): *Land, Labor and Rural Poverty*, Columbia University Press, New York.

—— (1989b): 'The New Institutional Economics and Development Theory: A Brief Critical Assessment', *World Development*, 17/9, reprinted in Lal (1992).

Barr, N. (1987): *The Economics of the Welfare State*, Weidenfeld and Nicholson, London.

—— (1992a): 'Economic Theory and the Welfare State: A Survey and Interpretation', *Journal of Economic Literature*, 30/2 (June), 741–803.

—— (1992*b*): 'Income transfers and the Social Safety Net in Russia', *Studies of Economies in Transition*, Paper no. 4, World Bank, Washington DC.

Barro, R. J. (1991): 'Economic Growth in a Cross-Section of Countries', *Quarterly Journal of Economics*, 106 (May), 407–43.

—— (1994): 'Economic Growth and Convergence', *Occasional Paper* no. 46, International Center for Economic Growth, San Francisco.

—— and Sala-i-Martin, X. (1991): 'Convergence Across States and Regions', *Brookings Papers on Economic Activity*, 1: 107–58.

—— —— (1992): 'Convergence', *Journal of Political Economy*, 100 (April), 223–51.

Barry, B. (1978): *Sociologists, Economists and Democracy*, University of Chicago Press, Chicago.

—— (1989): 'Claims of Common Citizenship', *Times Literary Supplement* (1989), 20–6.

Barzel, Y. (1989): *Economic Analysis of Property Rights*, Cambridge University Press.

Basu, K. (1984): *The Less Developed Economy*, Blackwell, Oxford.

Bauer, P. T. (1954): *West African Trade*, Cambridge University Press, Cambridge. 1954.

—— (1980): *Reality and Rhetoric: Studies in the Economics of Development*, Weidenfeld and Nicolson, London.

—— (1971): 'Economic History as Theory', *Economica*, 38/150 (May).

Baumol, W. J, and Benhabib, J. (1989): 'Chaos: Significance, Mechanism and Economic Applications', *Journal of Economic Perspectives*, 3/1 (Winter), 77–105.

—— Panzar, J., and Willig, R. (1982): *Contestable Markets*, Harcourt Brace Jovanovic, New York.

Becker, G. S. (1974): 'A Theory of Social Interactions', *Journal of Political Economy*, 82/6: 1063–91: reprinted in his *The Economic Approach to Human Behaviour*, Chicago.

—— (1976): *The Economic Approach to Economic Behavior*, Chicago Univ. Press, Chicago.

—— (1983): 'A Theory of Competition among Pressure Groups for Political Influence', *Quarterly Journal of Economics*, 18/3 (August), 371–400.

—— (1985): 'Public Policies, Pressure Groups and Deadweight Costs', *Journal of Public Economics*, 28/3 (Dec.), 329–48.

—— (1988): 'Family Economics and Macro Behavior', *American Economic Review*, 78/1 (March). 1–13.

—— (1989): 'On the Economics of the Family: Reply to a Skeptic', *American Economic Review*, 514–18.

—— (1991): *A Trealise on the Family*, 2nd revised edn. Harvard Univ. Press, Cambridge, Mass.

—— and Murphy, I. C. M. (1988): 'The Family and the State', *Journal of Law and Economics*, 31 (April), 1–18.

—— and Tomas, N. (1986): 'Human Capital and the Rise and Fall of Families', *Journal of Labor Economics*, 4 (July), S1–S39.

Beenstock, M., and Brasse, V. (1986): *Insurance for Unemployment*, Allen and Unwin, London.

Behrman, J. (1990): 'Thoughts on Human Resource Led Development Possibilities', mimeo, Univ. of Pennsylvania.

Bell, M., Ross-Larsen, B., and Westphal, L. E. (1984): 'Assessing the Performance of Infant Industries', *Journal of Development Economics*, 16/1–2 (Sept./Oct.), 101–28.

Berg, A. (1973): *The Nutritional Factor*, Brookings Institution, Washington, DC.

Berlin, I. (1955): *Historical Inevitability*, Oxford University Press, London.

—— (1979): *Against the Current: Essays in the History of Ideas*, Hogarth Press, London.

Bernheim, B. (1986): 'On the Voluntary and Involuntary Provision of Public Goods', *American Economic Review*, 764 (Sept.), 789–93.

—— and Bagwell, K. (1988): 'Is Everything Neutral?', *Journal of Political Economy*, 96/2 (April). 308–38.

—— Shleifer, A., and Summers, L. (1985): 'The Strategic Bequest Motive', *Journal of Political Economy*, 936 (Dec.), 1045–76.

Beveridge, S., and Nelson, C. R. (1981): 'A New Approach to Decomposition of Economic Time Series into Permanent and Transitory Components with Particular Attention to Measurement of the "Business Cycle"', *Journal of Monetary Economics*, 7: 151–74.

Bhagwati, J. N. (1979): *Anatomy and Consequences of Trade Control Regimes*, NBER and Ballinger, Cambridge Mass.

—— (1982): 'Directly Unproductive Profit Seeking (DUP) Activities', *Journal of Political Economy*, 90/5: 988–1002.

—— (1988): 'Poverty and Public Policy,' *World Development*, vol 16, no. 5, May, no. 539–55, reprinted in Lal (1992).

Bhalla, S. (1988): 'Is Sri Lanka an Exception? A Comparative Study of Living Standards', in T. N. Srinivasan and P. Bardhan (eds.), *Rural Poverty in South Asia*, Columbia University Press, New York.

—— and Glewwe, P. (1986): 'Growth and Equity in Developing Countries: A Reinterpretation of the Sri Lankan Experience', *World Bank Economic Review* (Sept.) 35–63, reprinted in Lal (1992).

Binswanger, H. P., Balaramaiah, T., Rao, V. B., Bhende, M. J., and Kashirsagar, K. V. (1985): 'Credit Markets in Rural South India: Theoretical Issues and Empirical Research', Agricultural and Rural Dept., Research Rpt. No. 45, World Bank, Washington, DC.

—— and Rosenzweig, Mark R. (1986): 'Behavioral and Material Determinants of Production Relations in Agriculture', *Journal of Development Studies*, 22/3 (Apr.), 503–39, reprinted in Lal (1992).

Birdsall, N. (1989): 'Economic Analyses of Rapid Population Growth', *World Bank Research Observes*, 4/1 (Jan.) 23–50, reprinted in Lal (1992).

Black, D. (1958): *The Theory of Committees and Elections*, Cambridge University Press, Cambridge.

Blackhurst, R., Marian, N., and Tumlir, J. (1978): *Adjustment, Trade and Growth in Developed and Developing Countries*, (Sept.), GATT, Geneva.

Blaug, M. (1980): *The Methodology of Economics*, Cambridge University Press, Cambridge.

Blejer, M., and Khan, M. (1984): 'Government Policy and Private Investment in Developing Countries', *IMF Staff Papers*, 31/2 (June).

Bloch, M. (1961): *Feudal Society*, Routledge, London.

Bodie, Z. (1990): 'Pensions as Retirement Income', *Journal of Economic Literature*, 28/1 (Mar.), 28–49.

Boskin, M. J. (1986): *Too Many Promises: The Uncertain Future of Social Security*, Dow Jones–Irwin, Homewood, Ill.

Braudel, F. (1982): *Civilisation and Capitalism, ii. The Wheels of Commerce*, London.

Braverman, A., and Guasch, J. L. (1989): 'Rural Credit in Developing Countries', Population, Planning and Research Paper no. 219, World Bank, Washington, DC.

Brennan, G., and Buchanan, J. (1990): *The Power to Tax: Analytical Foundations of the Fiscal Constitution*, Cambridge University Press.

—— —— (1985): *The Reason of Rules: Constitutional Political Economy*, Cambridge.

Brittan, S., and Webb, S. (1990): 'Beyond the Welfare State', *Hume Paper no. 17*, David Hume Institute, Aberdeen University Press.

Bruce, N., and Waldman, M. (1990): 'The Rotten Kid Theorem Meets the Samaritan's Dilemma', *Quarterly Journal of Economics*, 105 (Feb.), 155–66.

Bruton, H. J. and associates (1992), *The Political Economy of Poverty, Equity, and Growth: Sri Lanka and Malaysia*, Oxford University Press, New York.

Buchanan, J. (1987): 'Constitutional Economics', in *The New Palgrave: A Dictionary of Economics*, Macmillan, 1: 585–8.

—— and Stubblebine, W. C. (1962): 'Externality', *Economica*, 29: 371–84.

—— Tollison, R. D., and Tullock, G. L. (1980): *Toward a Theory of the Rent-Seeking Society*, Texas A&M University Press, College Station, Texas.

—— and Tullock, G. (1962): '*The Calculus of Consent, Logical Foundations of Constitutional Democracy*, Michigan University Press, Ann Arbor.

Caldwell, B. (1982): *Beyond Positivism in Economics*, Allen & Unwin, London.

Calvo, G. A. (1986): 'Fractured Liberalism: Argentina Under Martinez de Hoz', *Economic Development and Cultural Change* 34/3, 511–34.

Campbell, J. Y., and Perron, P. (1991): 'Pitfalls and Opportunities: What Macroeconomists should Know about Unit Roots', in Blanchard and Fischer (eds.), *NBER Macroeconomics Annual*, MIT, Cambridge, Mass.

Castaneda, T. (1992): *Combating Poverty*, International Center for Economic Growth, ICS Press, San Francisco.

Chakravarti, A. (1972): 'The Social Profitability of Training Unskilled Workers in the Public Sector in India', *Oxford Economic Papers*, 24/1 (March), 111–23.

Chen, E. C. K. (1989): 'The Changing Role of the Asian NICs in the Pacific Region towards the Year 2000', in Shinohara and Lo (eds.), *Global Adjustment and the Future of Asian Pacific Economy*, P. M. C. Publications, Tokyo.

Chenery, H., Ahluwalia, M., Bell, C. L. G., Duloy, J. H., and Jolly, R. (1974): *Redistribution with Growth*, Oxford University Press.

—— Robinson, S., and Syrquin, M. (1986): *Industrialization and Growth: A Comparative Study*, Oxford University Press, New York.

—— and Syrquin, M. (1975): *Patterns of Development 1950–70*, World Bank and Oxford University Press.

Cheung, S. N. (1969): *The Theory of Share Tenancy*, Chicago University Press.

—— (1987): 'Economic Organization and Transaction Costs', *The New Palgrave: A Dictionary of Economics*, vol. ii, Macmillan, 55–7.

Chow, G. C. (1985): *The Chinese Economy*, Harper and Row, New York.

Chuta, E., and Liedholm, C. (1984): 'Rural Small-Scale Industry: Empirical Evidence and Policy Issues', in Eicher Staatz (eds.), *Agricultural Development in the Third World*, Johns Hopkins University Press, Baltimore.

Cline, W. R. (1982): 'Can the East Asian Model of Development be Generalized?', *World Development*, 10/2: 81–90.

—— *et al.* (1978): *Trade Negotiations in The Tokyo Round: A Quantitative Assessment*, The Brookings Institution, Washington, DC.

Clower, R. W. (1972): 'The Ideas of Economists', Sixth Monash Economics Lecture, Monash University, reprinted in Klamer, McCloskey, and Solow (eds.): *The Consequences of Economic Rhetoric*, Cambridge, Mass., 1988.

Coase, R. H. (1937): 'The Nature of the Firm', *Economica* reprinted in Coase: *The Firm, the Market and the Law*, Univ. of Chicago Press, Chicago, 33–55.

—— (1960): 'The Problem of Social Cost', *Journal of Law and Economics*, 1–44.

Cochrane, J. H. (1988): 'How Big is the Random Walk in GNP?', *Journal of Political Economy*, 96: 893–920.

—— (1991): 'Comment', in Blanchard and Fischer (eds.), *Macroeconomics Annual*, MIT, Cambridge, Mass.

Collier, P. and Lal, D. (1986): *Labor and Poverty in Kenya 1900–1980*, Clarendon Press, Oxford.

Collier, P., D. L. Bevan, and J. Gunning: *The Political Economy of Poverty, Equity, and Growth: Nigeria and Indonesia*, Oxford University Press.

Collier, P., Bigsten, A., Bevan, D., and Gunning, J. W. (1987): *East African Lessons on Economic Liberalization*, Thames Essays no. 48. Trade Policy Research Center, Gower, London.

Corden, W. M. (1974): *Trade Policy and Economic Welfare*, Clarendon Press, Oxford.

—— (1975): 'The Cost and Consequences of Protection: A Survey of Empirical Work', in P. B. Kenen (ed.), *International Trade and Finance: Frontiers for Research*, Cambridge University Press.

Corden, W. M., and Neary, J. P. (1982): 'Booming Sector and De-Industrialization in a Small Open Economy', *Economic Journal* (Dec.), 825–48.

Coulson, A. (1982): *Tanzania: A Political Economy*, Clarendon Press, Oxford.

Cox, D. (1987): 'Motives for Private Income Transfers', *Journal of Political Economy*, 95/3 (June), 508–46.

—— 'Intergenerational Transfers and Liquidity Constraints', *Quarterly Journal of Economics*, 105/1 (Feb.), 187–218.

—— and Jakubson, G. (1989): 'The Connection between Public Transfers and Private Interfamily Transfers', mimeo, Boston College, Boston.

—— —— (1990): 'Achieving Social Objectives through Private Transfers: A Review', *World Bank Research Observer*, 5/2 (July), 205–18.

—— and E. Jimenez (1992): 'Social Security and Private Transfers in Peru', *World Bank Economic Review*, 6/1 (Jan.), 155–69.

—— —— (1993): 'Private Transfers and the Effectiveness of Public Income Redistribution in the Phillipines', mimeo, World Bank Conference on Public Expenditures and the Poor: Incidence and Targetting.

Crafts, N. (1984): 'Patterns of Development in 19th Century Europe', *Oxford Economic Papers*, 36/3 438–58.

—— (1985): *British Economic Growth during the Industrial Revolution*, Clarendon Press, Oxford.

—— (1987): 'Economic History', *The New Palgrave*. vol. ii, Macmillan, 41.

Cuddington, J. T. and Urzua, C. M. (1989): 'Trends and Cycles in Colombia's Real GDP and Fiscal Deficit', *Journal of Development Economics*, 30/2 (Apr.), 325–43.

Danziger, R., Haveman, R., and Plotnick, R. (1981): 'How Income Transfers Affect Work, Savings and Income 'Distribution', *Journal of Economic Literature*, 19 (Sept.), 975–1028.

Darratt, A. F. (1986): 'Trade and development: The Asian Experience', *Cato Journal*, 6/2: 695–9.

Dasgupta, P. (1980): 'Decentralization and Rights', *Economica*, 47 (May), 107–23.

Day, R. H. (1982): 'Irregular Growth Cycles', *American Economic Review*, 72: 406–14.

—— (1983): 'The Emergence of Chaos from Classical Economic Growth', *Quarterly Journal of Economics*, 98: 201–13.

Deardoff, A. (1984): 'An Exposition and Exploration of Krueger's Trade Model', *Canadian Journal of Economics*, 17 (Nov.), reprinted in Lal (1992).

—— (1988): 'Popper and the LSE Economists', in de Marchi (ed.) (1988), 139–66.

de Marchi, N. (1988) (ed.): *The Popperian Legacy in Economics*, Cambridge.

Demsetz, H. (1967): 'Toward a Theory of Property Rights', *American Economic Review* (May), 347–59.

—— (1968): 'Why Regulate Utilities?' *Journal of Law and Economics* (Apr.), 55–65.

—— (1982): *Economic, Legal and Political Dimensions of Competition*, De Vries Lectures no. 4, North Holland, Amsterdam.

—— (1988): 'The Control Function of Private Wealth', ch. 14 in Demsetz, *The Organisation of Economic Activity*, vol. i, Blackwells, Oxford.

—— (1989): *The Organization of Economic Activity: vol. 2, Efficiency Competition and Policy*, Blackwells, Oxford.

—— (1992): 'Economic Development and the Corporate Control Problem', mimeo, UCLA Dept. of Economics, (May).

Denison, E. (1985): '*Trends in American Economic Growth, 1929–1982*, Brookings Institution, Washington, DC.

Deolalikar, A. B. (1993): 'Does the Impact of Government Health Spending on the Utilization of Health Services by Children and on Child Health Outcomes Differ by household Expenditure: The Case of Indonesia,' mimeo, paper for World Bank conference on Public Expenditures and the Poor: Incidence and Targetting.

Desai, P., and Martin, R. (1983): 'Efficiency Loss from Resource Misallocation in Soviet Industry', *Quarterly Journal of Economics*, 98/3 (Aug.), 441–56.

Diaz-Alejandro, C. (1970): *Essays on the Eonomic History of the Argentine Republic*, Yale University Press, New Haven, Conn.

—— (1975)., in P. B. Kenen (ed.), *International Trade and Finance: Frontiers for Research*, Cambridge University Press.

Dickson, P. G. M. (1967): *The Financial Revolution in England: A Study in the Development of Public Credit, 1688–1756*, London.

Diwan, I. (1993): 'Efficient Severance Payment Schemes', mimeo, World Bank (May).

Dixit, A. (1973): 'Models of Dual Economies', in Mirrlees and Stern (eds.), *Models of Economic Growth*, Macmillan, London.

—— (1988): 'Optimal Trade and Industrial Policy for the U. S. Automobile Industry', in R. C. Feenstra (ed.) *Empirical Methods for International Trade*, MIT Press, Cambridge, Mass.

Dollar, D. (1992): 'Outward Oriented Developing Economies really do Grow More

Rapidly: Evidence for 95 LDCs, 1976–1985', *Economic Development and Cultural Change*, 40/3: 532–44.

—— and Sokoloff, K. (1990): 'Patterns of Productivity Growth in S. Korean Manufacturing Industries, 1963–79', *Journal of Development Economics*, 33: 309–27.

Donges, J. B. (1976): 'A Comparative Survey of Industrialization Policies in 15 Semi-Industrialized Countries', *Weltwirtschaftliches Archiv*, 112/4.

Dornbusch, R. (1980): *Open Economy Macroeconomics*, Basic Books, New York.

Dovring, F. (1959): 'The Share of Agriculture in a Growing Population', *Monthly Bulletin of Agricultural Economics and Statistics* (Aug.–Sept.), 1–11.

Downs, A. (1957): *An Economic Theory of Democracy*, Harper and Row, New York.

—— (1967): *Inside Bureaucracy*, Little Brown, Boston.

Drèze, J. (1988): 'Famine Prevention in India', Development Economics Research Program Discussion Paper no. 3, London School of Economics.

—— and Sen, A. K. (1989): *Hunger and Public Action*, Clarendon Press, Oxford.

Drucker, P. (1983): 'Schumpeter and Keynes', *Imprint* (Dec.), 54–7.

Dworkin, R. (1977): *Taking Rights Seriously*, Duckworth, London.

Edgren, G. (1987): 'Ghana and Thailand: The Twin Study', mimeo, World Bank, Washington, D.C.

Edwards, S. (1988a): 'Real and Monetary Determinants of Real Exchange Rate Behavior: Theory and Evidence from Developing Countries', *Journal of Development Economics*, 29/3 (Nov.), 311–41, reprinted in Lal (1992).

—— (1988b): *Exchange Rate Misalignments in Developing Countries*, World Bank Occasional Papers, NS 2, Johns Hopkins University Press, Baltimore.

—— (1992): 'Trade Orientation, Distortions and Growth in Developing. Countries', *Journal of Development Economics*, 39/1 (July), 31–57.

—— and van Wijnbergen, S. (1987): 'Tariffs, the Real Exchange Rate and the Terms of Trade: Two Popular Propositions in International Economics', *Oxford Economic Papers*, 39/3 (Sept.), 458–64.

Ekelund, R. E., and Tollison, R. J. (1985): *Mercantilism as a Rent-Seeking Society*, Texas A&M University Press.

Elkan, W. (1988): 'Entrepreneurs and Entrepreneurship in Africa', *World Bank Research Observer* 3/2 (July). 171–88.

Elster, J. (1983): *Explaining Technical Change*, Cambridge University Press.

Eltis, W. (1973): *Growth and Distribution*, MacMillan, London.

Engle, R. F., and Granger, C. W. J. (eds.) (1991): *Long-Run Economic Relationships*, Clarendon Press, Oxford.

Feder, G. (1983): 'On Exports and Economic Growth', *Journal of Development Economics*, 12/1–2: 59–74.

Feeny, D. (1988): 'The Development of Property Rights in Land: A Comparative Study', in R. H. Bates (ed.), *Toward a Political Economy of Development*. California Studies on Social choice and Political Development, vol. 14, University of California Press.

Fei. J. C. H., Ranis, G., and Kuo, Shirley W. Y. (1979): *Growth with Equity: The Taiwan Case*, World Bank and Oxford University Press, New York.

Fields, G. (1991): 'Growth and Income Distribution', ch. 1. in Psacharopoulos.

Findlay, R. (1988): 'Trade, Development and the State', in G. Ranis and P. Schultz (eds.), *The State of Development Economics*, Blackwell Oxford.

—— and Wellisz, S. (1984): 'Protection and Rent-Seeking in Developing Countries', in D. C. Colander (ed.), *Neoclassical Political Economy*, Ballinger, Cambridge, Mass.

—— (ed.) (1993), *The Political Economy of Poverty, Equity, and Growth: Five Small Economies*, Oxford University Press.

—— and Wilson, J. (1987): 'The Political Economy of Leviathian', in A. Razin and E. Sadka (eds.), *Economic Policy in Theory and Practice*, Macmillan, London.

Fischer S. (1981): 'Towards an Understanding of the Costs of Inflation', *Carnegie-Rochester Conference Series on Public Policy*, 15: reprinted in his *Indexing, Inflation and Economic Policy*, MIT Press, 1986.

Fisher, I. (1930): *The Theory of Interest*, Macmillan, New York.

Fiszben, A. (1992): 'Labor Retrenchment and Redundancy Compensation in State Owned Enterprises: The Case of Sri Lanka', South Asia Region Internal Discussion Paper, Report No. IDP 121, World Bank, Dec.

Frey, B. D. (1978): *Modern Political Economy*, Martin Robertson, Oxford.

Friedman, D. (1987): 'Law and Economics', *The New Palgrave: A Dictionary of Economics*, 3: 144–8.

Friedman, M. (1953): 'The Methodology of Positive Economics', in his *Essays in Positive Economics*, Chicago University Press.

—— (1962): *Capitalism and Freedom*, Chicago University Press.

Furtado, C. (1976): *Economic Development of Latin America*, 2nd eds., Cambridge University Press.

Galbraith, J. K. (1973): 'Power and the Useful Economist', *American Economic Review*, 63/1 (March).

Gale, W., Maritato, N., and Scholtz, J. K. (1992): 'Effects of Public and Private Transfers on Income Variability and the Poverty Rate', mimeo, University of Wisconsin, Madison.

Galenson, W. (ed.) (1979): *Economic Growth and Structural Change in Taiwan*, Cornell University Press Ithaca, NY.

Galton, F. S. (1886): 'Regression towards Mediocrity in Hereditary Stature', *Journal of the Anthropological Institute of Great Britain and Ireland*, 15: 246–63.

Garraty, J. A. (1978): *Unemployment in History*, Harper & Row, New York.

Gavan, J. D., and Chandraskera, I. S. (1979): *The Impact of Public Food Grain Distribution on Food Consumption and welfare in Sri Lanka*, Research Report 13, International Food Policy Research Institute, Washington, DC.

Gellner, E. (1983): *Nations and Nationalism*, Blackwells, Oxford.

Gerschenkron, A. (1962): *Economic Backwardness in Historical Perspective*, Harvard, Cambridge, Mass.

Gillis, M. (1984): 'Episodes in Indonesian Economic Growth', in A. C. Harberger (ed.), *World Economic Growth*, Institute for Contemporary Studies, San Francisco.

Glewwe, P., and van der Gaag, J. (1988): 'Confronting Poverty in Developing Countries: Definitions, Information and Policies', *Living Standards Measurement Study*, WP no. 48, World Bank (June).

Goldberger, A. S. (1989): 'Economic and Mechanical Models of Intergenerational Transmission', *American Economic Review*, 79/3: 504–13.

González-Vega, C. (1977): 'Interest Rate Restriction and Income Distribution', *American Journal of Agricultural Economics* 59/5.

Goodhart, C. (1987): 'Central Banking', in *The New Palgrave*, 1: 386.

Graaf, J. de V. (1957): *Theoretical Welfare Economics*, Cambridge University Press.

Gramlich, E. M. (1989): 'Economists' View of the Welfare Sate', *American Economic Review*, 79/2 (May) 190–6.

Gray, John (1984): *Hayek on Liberty*, Blackwell, Oxford.

Gregory, P. (1986): *The Myth of Market Failure: Employment and the Labor Maket in Mexico*, Johns Hopkins University Press, Baltimore.

Grossman, G., and Helpman, E. (1991): *Innovation and Growth in the Global Economy*, MIT Press, Cambridge, Mass.

Hahn, F. (1984): *Macroeconomics and Equilibrium*, Blackwell, Oxford.

—— and Matthews, R. C. O. (1965): 'The Theory of Economic Growth: A Survey' in American Economic Association, *Surveys of Economic Theory*, vol. ii, Macmillan, London.

Hakim, L., and Wallich, C. (1986): 'OECD Deficits, Debt and Savings; Structure and Trends 1965–81: A Survey of Evidence', in Lal and Wolf, (1986).

Hamermesh, D. S. (1992): 'Unemployment Insurance for Developing Countries', Policy Research Working Paper no. 897, World Bank, (May).

Hansen, B. (1991): *The Political Economy of Poverty, Equity, and Growth: Egypt and Turkey*, Oxford University Press.

—— and de Melo, J. (1985): 'External Shocks, Financial Reforms, and Stabilisation Attempts in Uruguay 1974–83', *World Development*, 13/8, 917–39.

Harberger, A. C. (1959): 'Using the Resources at Hand more Efficiently', *American Economic Review Proceedings*, 49/2, 134–46.

—— (1978): 'A Primer on Inflation', *Journal of Money, Credit and Banking*, 10/4 (Nov.), 505–21. reprinted in Lal (1992).

—— (1984): 'Basic Needs verous Distributional Weights in Social Cost-Benefit Analysis', *Economic Development and Cultural Change*, 32: 455–74.

—— (1987): 'Neutral Taxation', in *The New Palgrave*, 3: 645–7.

Harris, O. (1987): 'Extended family' in *The New Palgrave*, I: 251–3.

Harris, R. (1988): *Beyond the Welfare State: An Economic, Political and Moral Critique of Indiscriminate State Welfare and a Review of Alternatives to Dependency*, Institute of Economic Affairs, Occasional Paper no. 77, London.

Hausman, D. M. (1989): 'Economic Methodology in a Nutshell', *Journal of Economic Perspectives*, 3/2, 115–27.

—— (1992): *The Inexact and Separate Science of Economics*, Cambridge University Press.

Hawthorn, G. (1989): 'A Triumph of Self-Interest', *Times Literary Supplement* (14–20 July), 266.

Hayami, Y., and Ruttan, V. W. (1985): *Agricultural Development*, 2nd edn., John Hopkins University Press, Baltimore.

Hayek, F. A. (ed.) (1935): *Collectivist Economic Planning*, Routledge, London.

—— (1945): 'The Use of Knowledge in Society', *American Economic Review*, 35/4 (Sept.), 519–30.

—— (1949): *Individualism and Economic Order*, Routledge and Kegan Paul, London.

—— (1952a): 'Scientism and the Study of Society', in his *The Counter revolution of Science*, Chicago University Press.

—— (1952b): *The Sensory Order*, Chicago University Press.

—— (1960): *The Constitution of Liberty*, Routledge, London.

—— (1967): *Studies in Philosophy and Economics*, Routledge, London.

—— (1976): *Law, Legislation and Liberty*, ii. *The Mirage of Social Justice*, Routledge, London.

—— (1988): *The Fatal Conceit*, Routledge, London.

—— (1994): *Hayek on Hayek*, Routledge, London.

Hazari, R. K. (1966): *The Corporate Private Sector*, Asia Publishing House, New York.

Heckscher, A. (1955): *Mercantilism*, 2 vols.; revised 2nd edn., Allen and Unwin, London.

Held, D. (ed.) (1983): *States and Societies*, Open University, Robertson, Oxford.

Helliner, G. (1985): 'Industrial Organization, Trade and Investment', paper for Conference on Industrial Organization, Trade and Investment in North America, Merida, Mexico.

Helliweg, M. (1987): 'Some Recent Developments in the Theory of Competition in Markets with Adverse Selection', *European Economic Review*, 31: 319–25.

Helpman, E. (1981): 'International Trade in the Presence of Product Differentiation, Economies of Scale and Monopolistic Competition: A Chamberlin–Heckscher–Ohlin Approach', *Journal of International Economics*, 11/3 (Aug.), 305–40.

—— and Krugman, P. (1985): *Market Structure and Foreign Trade*, MIT Press, Cambridge, Mass.

—— (1989): *Trade Policy and Market Structure*, MIT Press, Cambridge, Mass.

Hendel, C. (ed.) (1953): *David Hume's Political Essays*, New York, cited in B. Barry: *Political Argument*, Routledge, London, 1965.

Henderson, P. D. (1986): *Innocence and Design: The Influence of Economic Ideas on Policy*, Blackwell, Oxford.

—— (1989): 'A New Age of Reform?' Annual lecture to the Institute for Fiscal Studies, London.

Hicks, J. R. (1940): 'The Valuation of Social Income', *Economica* (May); reprinted in *Wealth and Welfare*, Blackwell, Oxford, (1981).

—— (1958): 'The Measurement of Real Income', *Oxford Economic Papers;* reprinted in *Wealth and Welfare*, Blackwell, Oxford, 1981.

—— (1965): *Capital and Growth*, Clarendon Press, Oxford.

—— (1969): *A Theory of Economic History*, Clarendon Press, Oxford.

—— (1974a): 'Capital Controversies: Ancient and Modern', *American Economic Review* (May); reprinted in his *Economic Perspectives*, Clarendon Press, Oxford, 1977.

—— (1974b): *The Crisis in Keynesian Economics*, Blackwell, Oxford, 1974b.

—— (1979): *Causality in Economics*, Blackwell, Oxford.

—— (1981): 'The Scope and Status of Welfare Economics', in *Wealth and Welfare*, Blackwell, Oxford.

Himmelfarb, G. (1983): *The Idea of Poverty*, Knopf, New York.

Hirschman, A. O. (1958): *Strategy of Economic Development*, Yale University Press, New Haven.

—— (1977): *The Passions and the Interests: Political Arguments for Capitalism before its Triumph*, Princeton University Press.

—— (1982): *Shifting Involvements: Private Interest and Public Action*, Princeton University Press.

Hobbes, T. (1914): *Leviathan*, Everyman edn. ed. J. M Lindsay, J. M. Dent, London.

Howarth, T. E. B. (1985): *Prospect and Reality: Great Britain 1945–1955*, Collins, London.

Hughes, H., and You, P. S. (eds.) (1969): *Foreign Investment and Industrialization in Singapore*, Australian National University, Canberra.

Hume, D. (1975): *An Enquiry Concerning Human Understanding* (first published 1748). Clarendon Press, Oxford.

Hutchinson, T. (1938): *The Significance and Basic Postulates of Economic Theory*, Macmillan, London.

—— (1977): *Knowledge and Ignorance in Economics*, Blackwell, Oxford, 1977.

—— (1978): *On Revolution and Progress in Economic Knowledge*, Cambridge University Press.

Iliffe, J. (1987): *The African Poor*, Cambridge University Press, Cambridge.

ILO (1976): *Employment, Growth and Basic Needs*, ILO, Geneva.

—— (1977): *The Basic Needs Approach to Development*, ILO, Geneva.

IMF: *IFS Yearbook* (1988), Washungton, D.C.

Jasy, A. de (1985): *The State*, Blackwell, Oxford.

—— (1989): *Social Contract, Free Ride*, Clarendon Press, Oxford.

Inman, R. P. (1987): 'Markets, Governments and the 'New' Political Economy, in A. J. Auerbach M. Feldstein` (eds.): *Handbook of Public Economics*, vol. ii, North Holland, Amsterdam, 647–777.

Jimenez, E. (1989): 'Social Sector Pricing Revisited: A Survey of some Recent Contributions', *Proceedings of the World Bank Annual Conference on Development Economics*, 109–38.

—— Lockheed, M. E., and Paqueo, V. (1991): 'The Relative Efficiency of Private and Public Schools in Developing Countries', *World Bank Research Observer*, 6/2 (July), 205–18.

Johnson, C. (1992): *MITI and the Japanese Miracle: The Growth of Industrial Policy*, Stanford University Press, Stanford Calif.

Johnson, H. G. (1954): 'Optimum Tariffs and Retaliation', *Review of Economic Studies*, 2,/2/55 (1953–4), 142–53.

—— (1964): 'Towards a Generalized Capital Accumulation Approach to Economic Development,' in OECD: *The Residual Factor and Economic Growth*, Paris.

—— (1967): 'The Possibility of Income Losses from Increasing Efficiency or Factor Accumulation in the Presence of Tariffs', *Economic Journal*, 77: 30–5.

Johnson, W. A. (1966): *The Steel Industry of India*, Harvard, Cambridge, Mass.

Johnston, B. F. and Mellor, J. W. (1961): 'The Role of Agriculture in Economic Development,' *American Economic Review*, 51/4.

Jolly, R., and Cornia, G. A. (eds.) (1984): *The Impact of World Recession on Children*, Pergamon, Oxford.

Jones, R. (1971): 'A Three-Factor Model in Theory, Trade and History', in J. Bhagwati *et al.* (eds.), *Trade, Balance of Payments and Growth*, Amsterdam, North Holland.

Jones E. L. (1981): *The European Miracle: Environments, Economies and Geopolitics in the History of Europe and Asia*, Cambridge University Press.

—— (1988): *Growth Recurring. Economic Changes in World History*, Clarendon Press, Oxford.

—— and Manuelli, R. (1990): 'A Convex Model of Equilibrium Growth: Theory and Policy Implications', *Journal of Political Economy*, 98/5, pt. 1 (Oct.), 1008–38.

Jones, W. O. (1972): *Marketing Staple Food Crop: in Tropical Africa*, Cornell University Press, Ithaca, NY.

Jung, W. S., and Marshall, P. J. (1985): 'Exports, Growth and Causality in Developing Countries', *Journal of Development Economics*, 18/1: 1–12.

Kakwani, N. (1980): *Income Inequality and Poverty*, Oxford University Press.

Kaldor, N. (1957): 'A Model of Economic Growth', *Economic Journal*, 67/268: 591–264.

—— and Mirrlees, J. (1962): 'A New Model of Economic Growth', *Review of Economic Studies*, 29/3: 174–92.

Kaufmann, D. (1982): 'Social Interaction a Strategy for Economic Survival among the Urban Poor: Theory and Evidence', Ph. D. Diss., Harvard University, Cambridge, Mass.

—— and Lindauer, D. (1986): 'A Model of Income Transfers for the Urban Poor', *Journal of Development Economics*, 22 (July), 337–50.

Kedourie, E. (1966): *Nationalism*, Hutchinson, London.

—— (ed.) (1970): *Nationalism in Asia and Africa*, Weidenfield and Nicholson, London.

Keynes, J. M. (1928): *The End of Laissez Faire*, Hogarth Press, London.

Keynes, J. N. (1890): *The Scope and Method of Political Economy*, Macmillan, London.

Killick, T. (1978): *Development Economics in Action: A Study of Economic Policies in Ghana*, Heinemann Educational Book, London.

Kim, K. W. (1984): 'South Korea', in Saunders (ed.), *The Political Economy of New and Old Industrial Countries*, Butterworth.

Kindleberger, C. (1962): *Foreign Trade and the National Economy*, Yale University Press, New Haven.

King, R. G., and Rebelo, S. T. (1993): 'Transitional Dynamics and Economic Growth in the Neoclassical Model', *American Economic Review*, 83/4 (Sept.), 908–31.

Knowles, J. C., and Anker, R. (1981): 'An Analysis of Income Transfers in a Developing Country', *Journal of Development Economics*, 8 (April), 205–6.

Knudsen, O., and Parnes, A. (1975): *Trade Instability and Economic Development*, Heath Lexington, Lexington, Mass.

Kotlikoff, L. J., and Spivak, A. (1981): 'The Family as an Incomplete Annuities Market', *Journal of Political Economy*, 89 (April), 372–91.

Kravis, I. (1970): 'Trade as a Handmaiden of Growth: Similarities between the 19th and 20th Centuries', *Economic Journal* 80 (Dec.), 850–72, reprinted in Lal (1992).

—— Heston, A., and Summers, L. (1978): *International Comparisons of Real Product and Purchasing Power*, Johns Hopkins University Press, Baltimore.

Kreps, D. (1990): *A Course in Microecnomic Theory*, Harvester Wheatsheaf, Hemel Hempstead.

Krueger, A. O. (1974): 'The Political Economy of the Rent-Seeking Society', *American Economic Review*, 64/3: 481–7, reprinted in Lal (1992).

—— (1977): *Growth, Distortions and Patterns of Trade among Many Countries*, Princeton Studies in International Finance, no. 40, Princeton University.

—— (1978): *Liberalization Attempts and Consequences*, NBER and Ballinger, Cambridge, Mass.

—— (1984): 'Comparative Advantage and Development Policy 20 Years Later', in *Economic Structure and Performance*, Academic Press, New York.

—— and Tuncer, B. (1982): 'An Empirical Test of the Infant-Industry Argument', *American Economic Review*, 72 (Dec.), 1142–52, reprinted in Lal (1992).

—— Schiff, M., and Valdes, A. (1988): 'Agricultural Incentives in Developing Countries: Measuring the Effect of Sectoral and Economy Wide Policies', *World Bank Review* (Sept.), 255–71, reprinted in Lal (1992).

Krugman, P. (1987): 'Is Free Trade Passé?' *Journal of Economic Literature*, 2.

—— (1992): 'Toward a Counter Counter-Revolution in Development Theory', *Proceedings of the World Bank Annual Conference on Development Economics*, 15–38.

Kuznets, S. (1973): *Population, Capital and Growth*, Heinemann, London.

Laffont, J. (1989): *The Economics of Uncertainty and Information*, MIT Press, Cambridge, Mass.

Lal. D. (1975): *Appraising Foreign Investment in Developing Countries*, Heinemann Educational Books, London.

—— (1976): 'Distribution and Development: A Review Article', *World Development*, 4/9: 725–38, reprinted in Lal (1993*b*).

—— (1977*a*): 'Distributional Weights, Shadow Wages and the Accounting Rate of Interest: Estimates for India', *Indian Economic Review* (Oct.).

—— (1977*b*): 'Estimates of Shadow Prices for Korea', mimeo, *Discussion Papers in Public Economics*, no. 10, University College, London.

—— (1978): *Poverty, Power and Prejudice*, Fabian Research Series, no. 340, London (Dec.), reprinted in Lal (1994*a*).

—— (1979): 'Accounting Prices for Jamaica', *Social and Economic Studies* (Sept.).

—— (1980*a*): *A Liberal International Economic Order: The International Monetary System and Economic Development*, Princeton Essays on International Finance, no. 139 (Oct.), reprinted in Lal (1993*b*).

—— (1980*b*): *Prices for Planning*, Heinemann Educational Books, London.

—— (1983): *The Poverty of Development Economics*, IEA, London, and Harvard, University Press, Cambridge, Mass. 1985.

—— (1984): *The Political Economy of the Predatory State*, DRD Discussion Paper no. 105, World Bank mimeo.

—— (1985*a*): 'Nationalsim, Socialism and Planning: Influential Ideas in the South', *World Development*, 13/6 (June), 749–59, reprinted in Lal (1993*b*).

—— (1985*b*): 'The Real Exchange Rate, Capital Inflows and Inflation: Sri Lanka 1970–1982', *Weltwirtschaftliches Archiv*, 121/4: 682–702, reprinted in Lal (1993*b*).

—— (1986): 'Stolper-Samuelson-Rybczynski in the Pacific: Real Wage and Real Exchange Rates in the Philippines, 1956–1978', *Journal of Development Economics*, 21/1 (April), 181–204, reprinted in Lal (1993*b*).

—— (1987*a*): 'Markets, Mandarins and Mathematicians', *Cato Journal*, 7/1 (June), 43–70, reprinted in Lal (1994*a*).

—— (1987*b*): 'The Political Economy of Economic Liberalization', *World Bank Economic Review*, 1/2 (Jan.), 273–99, reprinted in Lal (1993*b*).

—— (1988*a*): *The Hindu Equilibrium* i: *Cultural Stability and Economic Stagnation*, *India c. 1500BC–1980*, Clarendon Press, Oxford.

—— (1988b): 'Ideology and Industrialization in India and East Asia', in H. Hughes (ed.) *Achieving Industrialization in East Asia*, Cambridge University Press.

—— (1989a): *The Hindu Equilibrium ii: Aspects of Indian Labour*, Clarendon Press, Oxford.

—— (1989b): 'The Political Economy of Industrialization in Primary Product Export Economies', in N. Islam (ed.), *The Balance Between Agriculture and Industry*, vol. 5, Macmillan, for the International Economic Association, reprinted in Lal (1993b).

—— (1989c): 'A Simple Framework for Analyzing Various Real Aspects of Stabilization and Structural Adjustment Policies,' *Journal of Development Studies* (Apr.): 291–313, reprinted in Lal (1993b).

—— (1990): *Fighting Fiscal Privilege: Towards a Fiscal Constitution*, Social Market Foundation, Paper no. 7, London, reprinted in Lal (1994a).

—— (ed.) (1992): *Development Economics*, 4 vols., Edward Elgar, Aldershot.

—— (1993a): 'Participation, Markets and Democracy', HRO WP20, World Bank.

—— (1993b): *The Repressed Economy*, Edward Elgar, Aldershot.

—— (1994a): *Against Dirigisme*, ICEG, ICS Press, San Francisco.

—— (1994b): 'In Praise of the Classics', in G. Meier (ed.), *From Classical Economics To Development Economics: Essays in Honor of Hla Myint*, Macmillan, London.

—— (1994c): 'The Role of the Public and Privake Sectors in Health Financing', HROWP 33, June 1994, World Bank, Washington DC.

—— (1995): 'Poverty, Markets and Democracy', The 1995 Nestlé Lecture on the Developing World, Nestlé UK, London.

—— and Henderson, P. D. (1976): 'UNCTAD IV: The Commodities Problem and International Economic Reform', *ODI Review*, 2: 11–30.

—— and Maxfield, S. (1993): 'The Political Economy of Stabilization in Brazil,' in R. Bates and A. O. Krueger (eds.), *Political and Economic Interactions in Economic Policy Reform*, Blackwell, Oxford reprinted in Lal (1993b)

—— and Rajapatirana, S. (1987): 'Foreign Trade Regimes and Economic Growth', *World Bank Research Observer* (July): 189–217, reprinted in Lal (1993b).

—— and Wolf, M. (eds.) (1986): *Stagflation, Savings and the State*, Oxford.

Lampman, R. J., and Smeeding, T. (1983): 'Interfamily Transfers as Alternatives to Government Transfers to Persons', *Review of Income and Wealth*, 29 (March), 45–66.

Lapidus, G. W., and Swanson, G. E. (1988): 'State and Welfare USA/USSR,' Institute of International Studies, Berkeley.

Leamer, E. (1984): *Sources of International Comparative Advantage*, MIT press, Cambridge, Mass.

—— (1985): 'Vector Autoregressions for Causal Inference?', *Carnegie Rochester Series on Public Policy*, no. 22, North-Holland, Amsterdam.

—— (1987): 'Patterns of Development in the Three-Factor n-Good General Equilibrium Model', *Journal of Political Economy*, 95/5 (Oct.): 961–99.

—— (1988): 'Measures of Openness', in R. E. Baldwin (ed.), *Trade Policy Issues and Empirical Analysis*, Chicago University Press.

Lecaillon, J., Paukert, F., Morrison, C., and Gesmidis, C. (1984): *Income Distribution and Economic Development*, ILO, Geneva.

Lee, D. R., and Tollison, R. D. (1988): 'Optimal Taxation in a Rent-Seeking

Environment', in C. K. Rowley, R. D. Tollison, and G. Tullock (eds.) *The Political Economy of Rent-Seeking*, Kluwer Academics, Boston.

Leff, N. H. (1978): 'Industrial Organization and Entrepreneurship in Developing Countries: The Economic Groups', *Economic Development and Cultural Change*, 26/4: 661–75.

—— (1979): 'Entrepreneurship and Economic Development: The Problem Revisited', *Journal of Economic Literature*, 18/1 (Mar.), 46–64.

Leibenstein, H. (1968): 'Entrepreneurship and Development', *American Economic Review*, 68 (May), 72–83.

Letwin, S. (1992): *The Anatomy of Thatcherism*, Fontana, London.

Letwin, W. (ed.) (1983): *Against Equality*, Macmillan, London.

Levin, J. V. (1960): *The Export Economics*, Harvard University Press, Cambridge, Mass.

Levine, R., and Renelt, D. (1992): 'A Sensitivity Analysis of Cross-Country Growth Regressions', *American Economic Review*, 82/4 (Sept.), 942–63.

Lewis, J. P. (1962): *The Quiet Crisis in India.*, Brookings Institution, Washington, DC.

Lewis, W. A. (1954): 'Economic Development with Unlimited Supplies of Labor', *Manchester School of Economic and Social Studies*, 22 (May), 139–91.

—— (1955): *The Theory of Economic Growth*, Allen and Unwin, London.

—— (1979): *Development Strategy in a Limping World Economy*, Elmhurst Lecture, reprinted in Meier (1984), 418–21.

Lin, J. (1990): 'Collectivisation and China's Agricultural Crisis in 1959–61', *Journal of Political Economy*, 98 (Dec.), 228–52.

Lindbeck, A. (1976): 'Stabilization in Open Economies with Endogenous Politicians', *American Economic Review*, 66/2 (May.), 1–19.

—— (1985): 'Redistribution Policy and the Expansion of the Public Sector', *Journal of Public Economics*, 28/3 (Dec.), 309–28.

—— (1990): 'The Swedish Experience', Institute for International Economic Studies, Seminar Paper no. 482, Stockholm.

Lipset, S. M. (1959): *Political Man*, Heinemann, London.

—— (1967): 'Political Sociology', in N. Smelser (ed.): *Sociology: An Introduction*, Wiley, New York.

Lipsey, R. E. : *An Introduction to Positive Economics*, 2nd edn., Weidenfeld and Nicholson, London.

Lipton, M. (1983a): *Poverty, Undernutrition and Hunger*, World Bank Staff Working Paper no. 597, April.

—— (1983b): *Labor and Poverty*, World Bank Staff Working Paper no. 616, Oct.

—— (1983c): *Demography and Poverty*, World Bank Staff Working Paper no. 623, Nov.

—— (1985a): *Land Assets and Rural Poverty*, World Bank Staff Working Paper no. 741.

—— (1985b): *The Poor and the Poorest: Some Interim Findings*, World Bank Discussion Papers no. 25, April.

Little, I. M. D. (1957): *A Critique of Welfare Economics*, 2nd edn., Oxford University Press.

—— (1979): 'An Economic Reconnaissance', in Galenson.

—— (1982): *Economic Development*, Basic Books, New York.

—— (1994): 'Trade and Industrialisation Revisited', Iqbal memorial lecture, Pakistan Institute of Development Economics, April.

—— Scitovsky, T., and Scott, M. (1970): *Industry and Trade in Some Developing Countries*, Oxford University Press.

—— and Mirrlees, J. A. (1974): *Project Appraisal and Planning for Developing Countries*, Heinemann Educational Books, London.

—— and Scott, M. F. (1976): *Using Shadow Prices*, Heinemann Educational Books, London.

Lockwood, W. W. (1954): *The Economic Development of Japan*, Princeton University Press.

Lucas, R. E. Jr. (1987): *Models of Business Cycles*, Blackwell, Oxford.

—— (1988): 'The Mechanics of Economic Development', *Journal of Monetary Economics*, 33 (July), 3–42.

Lucas, R. E. and Stark, O. (1985): 'Motivations to Remit: Evidence from Botswana', *Journal of Political Economy*, 93 (Oct.), 901–18.

MacBean, A. (1966): *Export Instability and Economic Development*, Harvard University Press, Cambridge, Mass.

McCloskey, D. M. (1983): 'The Rhetoric of Economics', *Journal of Economic Literature*, 31 (June), 434–61.

—— (1985): *The Rhetoric of Economics*, University of Wisconsin Press, Madison, Wis.

—— and Solow, R. (eds.) (1988): *The Consequences of Economic Rhetoric*, Cambridge University Press.

McCombie, R. (1990): 'Review of Scott: A New View of Economic Growth', *Economic Journal*, 100/399 (March), 271–4.

McKinnon, R. (1973): *Money and Capital in Economic Development*, Brookings Institution, Washington, DC.

Machlup, F. (1982): 'Operationalism and Pure Theory in Economics', in his *Methodology of Economics and other Social Sciences*, Academic Press, New York.

Maddison, A. (1991): *Dynamic Forces in Capitalist Development*, Oxford University Press, Oxford.

—— and associates (1992): *The Political Economy of Poverty, Equity, and Growth: Brazil and Mexico*, Oxford University Press.

Markusen, J., and Melvin, J. (1984): 'The Gains from Trade Theorem with Increasing Returns to Scale', in H. Kierzkowski (ed.), *Monopolistic Competition and International Trade*, Clarendon Press, Oxford.

Mayer, W. (1984): 'Endogenous Tariff Formation', *American Economic Review*, 74/5 (Dec.), 970–85.

Meade Committee (1978): *The Structure and Reform of Direct Taxation*, Institute for Fiscal Studies, Allen and Unwin, London.

Meerman, J. (1979): *Public Expenditure in Malaysia: Who Benefits and Why*, Oxford University Press, New York.

Meesook, O. (1987): 'The Political Economy of Poverty, Equity, and Growth: Thailand', mimeo, to be published by Oxford University Press.

Meier, G. M. (1984): *Leading Issues in Economic Development*, Oxford University Press.

Meltzer, A., and Richard, S. F. (1981): 'Tests of a Rational Theory of the Size of Government', *Journal of Political Economy*, 89 (Oct.), 914–27.

Mesa-Lago, C. (1983): 'Social Security and Extreme Poverty in Latin America', *Journal of Development Studies*, 12: 83–110.

—— (1989): *Ascent to Bankruptcy: Financing Social Security in Latin America*, Pittsburgh.

Michaely, M. (1977): 'Exports and Growth: An Empirical Investigation,' *Journal of Development Economics*, 4/1: 149–53.

Midgley, J. (1984): *Social Security, Inequality and the Third World*, John Wiley, New York, 1984.

Mill, John Smart (1843): *A System of Logic*, J. W. Parker, London.

—— (1970): *Principles of Political Economy*, ed. Winch, Penguin Books, London.

Minogue, K. (1993): 'The Constitutional Mania', Centre for Policy Studies, Policy Study no. 134, London.

Miron, J. A. (1991): 'Comment', in Blanchard and Fischer (eds.), *NBER Macroeconomics Annual*, MIT, Cambridge, Mass.

Mirrlees, J. A. (1969): 'The Evaluation of National Income in an Imperfect Economy', *Pakistan Development Review* (Spring).

Mitchell, O. S. (1993): 'Trends in Retirement Systems and Lessons for Reform', Policy Research Working Paper 1118, World Bank, Washington, DC.

Moffitt, R. (1992): 'Incentive Effects of the U. S. Welfare System: A Review', *Journal of Economic Literature*, 30/1: 1–61.

Morishima, M. (1973): *Marx's Economics*, Cambridge University Press.

Morris, D. (1979): *Measuring the Conditions of the World's Poor: The Physical Quality of Life Index*, Pergamon, Oxford.

Mosley, P., Harrigan, T., and Toye, J. (1991): *Aid and Poverty*, vol. i, Routledge, London.

Moykr, J. (1988): Review of Chenery *et al.* (1986), *Journal of Economic Literature* (Dec.), 1755–6.

Mueller, D. C. (1979): *Public Choice*, Cambridge University Press.

—— (ed.) (1983): *The Political Economy of Growth*, Yale University Press, New Haven.

Muller, J. Z. (1992): *Adam Smith in His Time and Ours*, Free Press, New York.

Mundell, R. A. (1957): 'International Trade and Factor Mobility', *American Economic Review* 67 (June), 321–35.

Murphy, K. M., Shleifer, A., and Vishny, R. W. (1989): 'Industrialization and the Big Push', *Journal of Political Economy*, 97/5 (Oct.), 1,003–26.

—— —— —— (1991): 'The Allocation of Talent: Implications for Growth', *Quarterly Journal of Economics*, 106/2 (May), 503–30.

Murray, C. (1984): *Losing Ground: American Social Policy 1950–1980*, Basic Books, New York.

Muth, J. (1961): 'Rational Expectations and the Theory of Price Movements', *Econometrica*, 29/6: 315–35.

Myint, H. M. (1971): *Economic Theory and the Underdeveloped Countries*, Oxford University Press, New York.

—— (1958): 'The Classical Theory of International Trade and the Underdeveloped Countries', *Economic Journal* 68 (June): 317–37.

—— (1975): 'Agriculture and Economic Development in the Open Economy', in G. Reynolds (ed.), *Agriculture in Development Theory*, Yale University Press, New Haven, Conn.

—— H. (1977): 'The Place of Institutional Changes in International Trade Theory in the Setting of the Underdeveloped Economies', in B. Ohlin *et al.* (eds.), *The International Allocation of Economic Activity*, Macmillan, London.

—— (1979): 'Exports and Economic Development of LDC's' in I. Adelman (ed.), *Economic Growth and Resources*, iv: *National and International Policies*, International Economic Association, Macmillan, London.

—— (1980): 'Comparative Analysis of Taiwan's Economic Development with Other Countries', *Taipei Academic Papers*, 10/1 (Mar.).

—— (1984): 'Inward- and Outward-Looking Countries Revisited: The Case of Indonesia', *Bulletin of Indonesian Economic Studies* (Aug.).

—— (1985): 'Organizational Dualism and Economic Development', *Asian Development Review*, 3/1 reprinted in Lal (1992).

—— and Lal, D. (1985): 'The Political Economy of Poverty, Equity and Growth: A Research Proposal', World Bank mimeo, July.

Myrdal, G. (1968): *Asian Drama*, 3 vols., Pantheon, New York.

Nadiri, I (1972): 'International Studies of Factor Inputs and Total Productivity: A Brief Survey', *Review of Income and Wealth* (June).

Nelson, C. R., and Plosser, C. I. (1982): 'Trends and Random Walks in Macroeconomic Time Series', *Journal of Monetary Economics*, 8: 129–62.

Newbery, D. M., and Stiglitz, J. (1981): *The Theory of Commodity Price Stabilization*, Clarendon Press, Oxford.

Nisbet, R. (1971): *The Quest for Community*, Oxford University Press, New York.

Niskanen, W. (1971): *Bureaucracy and Representative Government*, Chicago University Press, Chicago.

Nogues, J. (1981): 'Politica commercial Y cambiaria: Uña evtluición Cuantitativa de la politica argentina durante 1961–1981', Technical Study 52, Banco Central de la Republice Argentine.

Nordhaus, W. D. (1975): 'The Political Business Cycle', *Review of Economic Studies*, 42 (Apr.) 169–90.

North, D. C. (1981): *Structure and Change in Economic History*, Norton, New York.

—— (1990): *Institutions, Institutional Change and Economic Performance* Cambridge University Press.

—— and Thomas, R. D. (1973): *The Rise of The Western World*, Cambridge University Press.

Nozick, R. (1974): *Anarchy, State and Utopia*, Blackwell, Oxford.

Oakeshott, M. (1975): *On Human Conduct*, Clarendon Press, Oxford.

—— (1993): *Morality and Politics in Modern Europe*, Yale University Press, New Haven Corn.

Oberai, A. S., and Singh, H. K. M. (1980): 'Migration, Remittances and Rural Development', *International Labor Review*, Mar-Apr.

OECD (1989): *Economies in Transition*, Paris.

Ofer, G. (1987): 'Soviet Economic Growth 1928–1985', *Journal of Economic Literature*, 25/4 (Dec), 1767–833.

Okochi, A. and Yasuoka, S,. (eds.) (1984): *Family Business in the Era of Industrial Growth*, International Conference in Business History, University of Tokyo Press.

Olivier, R. (1987): 'Review of Iliffe', *Times Literary Supplement*, 27 May.

Olson, M. (1965): *The Logic of Collective Action*, Harvard University Press.

—— (1967): 'The Relationship of Economics to the Other Social Sciences: The Province of a "Special Report"', paper delivered at the Annual Meeting of the American Political Science Association.

—— (1982): *The Rise and Decline of Nations*, Yale University Press, New Haven Conn.

Pack, H. (1994): 'Endogenous Growth Theory: Intellectual Appeal and Empirical Shortcomings', *Journal of Economic Perspectives*, 8/1: 55–72.

—— and Westphal, L. E. (1986): 'Industrial Strategy and Technological Change: Theory versus Reality', *Journal of Development Economics*, 22 (June), 87–128, reprinted in Lal (1992).

—— and Page, J. (1994): 'Accumulation, Exports and Growth in High Performing Asian Countries', *Carnegie Rochester Papers on Public Policy* (Winter).

Papageorgiou, D., Choksi, A., and Michaely, M. (1991): *Liberalization of Foreign Trade in Developing Countries: The Lessons of Experience*, Blackwell, Oxford, 1991.

Parker, D., and Stacey, R. (1994): *Chaos, Management and Economics*, Hobart Paper no 125, Institute of Economic Affairs, London.

Park, C. H. (1963): *The Country, the Revolution and I*, Trans. L. Sinder, Seoul: n.p.

Parsons, T. (1937): *The Structure of Social Action*, Free Press, New York.

Paull, G. (1991): 'Poverty Alleviation and Social Safety Net Schemes for Economies in Transition', IMF WP/91/14, Research Dept., IMF, Washington, DC.

Peltzman, S. (1975): 'The Effects of Automobile Safety Regulations', *Journal. of Political Economy*, 83/4: 672–725.

—— (1970): 'Toward a More General Theory of Regulation', *Journal of Law and Economics*, 19/2 (Aug.), 211–40.

—— (1980): 'The Growth of Government', *Journal of Law and Economics*, 23 (Oct.), 209–87; reprinted in Stigler (1988).

Pendle, G. (1963): *A History of Latin America*, Pelican, London.

Perkin, P. (1988): *The Rise of Professional Society: England since 1880*, Routledge, London.

Perron, P. (1989): 'The Great Crash, the Oil Price Shock, and the Unit Root Hypothesis', *Econometrica*, 57/6 (Nov.), 1361–401.

Pigou, A. C. (1932): *The Economics of Welfare*, 4th edn., Macmillan, London.

Pischke, J. D. von, Adams, D. W., and Donald, G. (1983): *Rural Financial Markets in Developing Countries*, Johns Hopkins University Press, Baltimore.

Plamenatz, J. (1973): 'Two Types of Nationalism', in E. Kamenka (ed.): *Nationalism*, Arnold, London.

Platteau, J. -P. (1991): 'Traditional Systems of Social Security and Hunger Insurance: Some Lessons From the Evidence Pertaining to Third World Village Societies', in E. Ahmad (et al.).

Pocock, J. Q. A. (1975a): 'Early Modern Capitalism: The Augustan Perception.' in Kamenka and Neale (eds.) :*Feudalism, Capitalism and Beyond*, Edward Arnold, London.

—— (1975b): *The Machiavellian Moment*, Princeton University Press.

Popper, K. (1957): *The Poverty of Historicism*, Routledge, London.

—— (1959): *The Logic of Scientific Discovery*, Basic Books, New York.

Posner, R. A. (1975): 'The Social Costs of Monopoly and Regulation,' *Journal of Political Economy*, 83/4 (Aug.), 807–27.

—— (1981): *The Economics of Justice*, Harvard University Press.

Pryor, F. (1990): *The Political Economy of Poverty, Equity, and Growth: Malawi and Madagascar*, Oxford University Press.

Psacharopoulos, G. (1973): *Returns to Education: An International Comparison*, Elsevier, Amsterdam.

—— (1984): 'The Contribution of Education to Economic Growth.' International Comparisons', in D. Kendrick (ed.), *International Comparisons of Productivity and Causes of the Slowdown*, Ballinger, Cambridge.

—— (1988): 'Education and Development: A Review', *World Bank Research Observer*, 3/1 (Jan.), 99–116.

—— (ed.) (1991): *Essays on Poverty, Equity and Growth*, Pergamon, Oxford.

—— and Tilak, T. B. G. (1991): 'Schooling and Equity', in Psacharopoulos (1991).

Ranis, G. (1985): 'Can the East Asian Model of Development be Generalised? A Comment', *World Development* 13/4: 543–5, reprinted in Lal (1992).

—— and Fei, J. (1961): 'A Theory of Economic Development', *American Economic Review*, 51 (Sept.), 533–65, reprinted in Lal (1992).

Ravallion, M. (1991): 'Reaching the Poor Through Public Employment: Arguments, Evidence and Lessons From Southeast Asia', *World Bank Research Observer*, 6/2 (July), 153–76.

—— (1992): *Poverty Comparisons: A Guide to Concepts and Methods*, Living Standards Measurement Study Working Paper no. 88, World Bank, Washington, DC.

—— and Dearden, L. (1988): 'Social Security in a "Moral" Economy: An Empirical Analysis for Java', *Review of Economics and Statistics*, 70 (Feb.), 36–44.

—— and Subbarow, K. (1992): 'Adjustment and Human Development in India', *Journal of Indian School of Political Economy*, 4/1: 55–79.

Rawls, J. (1972): *A Theory of Justice*, Clarendon Press, Oxford.

Raz, J. (1986): *The Morality of Freedom*, Clarendon Press, Oxford.

Rempel, H., and Lobdell R., (1978): 'The Role of Urban-to-Rural Remittances in Rural Development', *Journal of Development Studies*, 14 (April), 324–41.

Reutlinger, S., and Selowsky, M. (1976): *Malnutrition and Poverty; Magnitude and Policy Options*, World Bank Staff Occasional Paper no. 23, Johns Hopkins. University Press, Baltimore.

Reynolds, L. G., (1985): *Economic Growth in the Third World 1980–1985*, Yale University Press.

Ricardo, D. (1951): *On the Principles of Political Economy and Taxation*, ed. P. Sraffa vol. i, Cambridge University Press.

Richardson, J. D. (1989): 'Empirical Research on Trade Liberalization with Imperfect Competition: A Survey', *OECD Economic Studies*, 12 (Spring).

Riedel, J. (1995), 'Strategies of Economic Development', in Grilli and Salvatore (eds.), *Handbook of Economic Development*, North Holland, Amsterdam.

Rimmer, D.: *Staying Poor: Ghana's Political Economy 1950–1990*, Pergamon, Oxford.

Robbins, L. (1932): *An Essay on the Nature and Significance of Economic Science*, Macmillan, London.

—— (1938): 'Live and Dead Issues in the Methodology of Economics', *Economica*, 5 (1938).

Rogowski, R. (1989): 'Political Cleavages and Changing Exposure to Trade', *American Political Science Review*, 81/4 (Dec.), 1121–137.

—— (1989): *Commerce and Coalitions*, Princeton Univ. Press, Princeton NJ.

Romer, P. M.(1986): 'Increasing Returns and Long Run Growth', *Journal of Political Economy*, 94/5 (Oct.), 1002–36.

—— (1989): 'Capital Accumulation in the Theory of Long-Rum Growth' in R. Barro (ed.): *Modern Business Cycle Theory*, Harvard Univ. Press, Cambridge, Mass, 51–127.

—— (1990a): 'Endogenous Technical Change', *Journal of Political Economy*, 98 (Oct.), S71–102.

—— (1990b): 'Human Capital and Growth', *Carnegie-Rochester Series on Public Policy*, 32 (Spring), 251–86.

Rosen, S. (1985): 'Implicit Contracts: A Survey', *Journal of Economic Literature*, 23: 1144–75.

Rosenstein-Rodan, P. (1943): 'Problems of Industrialisation of Eastern and South-Eastern Europe', *Economic Journal*, 53: 202—11.

Rosenzweig, M. (1988): 'Risk, Implict Contracts and the Family in Rural Areas of Low Income Countries', *Economic Journal*, 98 (Dec.), 1148–70.

—— and Wolpin, K. (1985): 'Specific Experience, Household Structure, and Intergenerational Transfers: Farm Family Land and Labor Arrangements in Developing Countries', *Quarterly Journal of Economics*, Supplement, 100: 961-87.

Rostow, W. (1960): *The Stages of Economic Growth*, Cambridge University Press.

Roth, G. (1987): *The Private Provision of Public Services in Developing Countries*, Oxford University Press, for the World Bank, New York.

Rottenberg, S. (ed.): *The Political Economy of Poverty, Equity, and Growth: Costa Rica and Uruguay*, Oxford University Press.

Rungta, R. S. (1970): *Rise of Business Corporations in India*, Cambridge University Press.

Ryan, A. (ed.) (1973): *The Philosophy of Social Explanation*, Oxford University Press.

Sabine, G. H. (1973): *A History of Political Theory*, 4 th edn., Holt, Reinhart, and Winston, Fort Worth, Texas.

Sala-i-Martin, X. (1994): 'Cross-Sectional Regressions and the Empirics of Economic Growth', *European Economic Review*, 8/3–4 (April), 739–47.

Sampson, G. P., and Yeats, A. T. (1977): 'An Evaluation of the Common Agricultural Policy as a Barrier Facing Agricultural Exports in the EEC', *American Journal of Agricultural Economics*, 59.

Samuelson, P. A. (1948): 'International Trade and the Equalization of Factor Prices', *Economic Journal* 58 (June), 163–84.

—— (1952): 'Economic Theory and Mathematics: An Appraisal', *American Economic Review*, 42 (May), 56–66.

—— (1958): 'Evaluation of Real National Income', *Oxford Economic Papers* (Jan.), 1–29.

—— (1974): *Foundations of Economic Analysis*, 2nd. edn., Atheneum, New York.

Sato, K. (1966): 'On the Adjustment Time in Neo-classical Growth Models', *Review of Economic Studies*, 33/95: 263–8.

Schultz, T. (1990): *Retoring Economic Equilibrium*, Blackwells, Oxford.

Schumpeter, J. A. (1918): *Die Krise des Steuerstaats*, Zeitfragen aus dem Gebiete der Soziologie, Graz and Leipzig, English translation by W. F. Stolper and R. A. Musgrave as *The Crisis of the Tax State*, in *International Economic Papers*, no. 4.

Schumpeter, J. (1954): *A History of Economic Analysis*, Oxford University Press, New York.

Scitovsky, T. (1954): 'Two Concepts of External Economies', *Journal of Political Economy*, 17: 143–51, reprinted in K. J. Arrow T. Scitorsky (ed): *Readings in Welfare Economics*, Allen and Unwin, London, 1969.

—— (1990): 'Economic Development in Taiwan and S. Korea 1965–1981', in L. J. Lau (ed.), *Models of Development*, ICEG, ICS Press, San Francisco.

Scott, M. F. (1976): 'Investment and Growth', *Oxford Economic Papers*, 28/3: 317–63.

—— (1989): *A New View of Economic Growth*, Clarendon Press, Oxford.

—— and Little, I. M. D. (eds.) (1976): *Using Shadow Prices*, Heinemann Educational Books, London.

—— MacArthur, J. D., and Newbery, D. M. G. (1976): *Project Appraisal in Practice*, Heinemann Educational Books, London.

Segalman, R. (1986): *The Swiss Way of Welfare: Lessons for the Western World*, New York.

Selden, T. M., and Wasylenko, M. J. (1992): 'Measuring the Distributional Effects of Public Education in Peru', mimeo, World Bank Conference on Public Expenditures and the Poor: Targeting and Incidence.

Selowsky, M. (1979): *Who Benefits from Public Expenditure? A Case Study of Colombia*. Oxford Unversity Press, New York.

Sen, A. K. (1973): *On Economic Inequality*, Oxford, Clarendon Press.

—— (1976): 'Poverty: An Ordinal Approach to Measurement', *Econometrica*, 44 (Mar.), 219–31.

—— (1979): 'The Welfare Basis of Real Income Comparisons: A Survey', *Journal of Economic Literature* (Mar.), 1–45.

—— (1981a): *Poverty and Famines*, Clarendon Press, Oxford.

—— (1981b): 'Public Action and the Quality of Life', *Oxford Bulletin of Economics and Statistics*, 43/1 (Feb.), 287—321, reprinted in Lal (1992).

—— (1982): 'Equality of What?' in *Choice Welfare and Measurement*, Blackwell, Oxford.

—— (1985a): *Commodities and Capabilities*, North Holland, Amsterdam.

—— (1985b): 'A Sociological Approach to the Measurement of Poverty: A Reply to Professor Peter Townsend', *Oxford Economic Papers* (Dec.), 669–70.

—— (1987a): 'Social Choice', *The New Palgrave: A Dictionary of Economics*, Macmillan, London.

—— (1987b): *The Standard of Living*, Cambridge.

—— (1992): *Inequality Reexamined*, Harvard University Press, Cambridge, Mass.

—— and Williams, B. (ed.) (1982): *Utilitarianism: For and Against*, Cambridge University Press.

Sheahan, J. (1987) *Patterns of Development in Latin America*, Princeton University Press.

Sheehy, E. J. (1990): 'Exports and Growth: A Flawed Framework', *Journal of Development Studies*, 27/1 (Oct.), 111–16.

Skopcol, T. (1979): *States and Social Revolutions*, Cambridge University Press.

Slutsky, E. (1937): 'The Summation of Random Causes as the Source of Cyclic Processes', *Econometrica*, 5: 105–46.

Smith, A. (1910): *The Wealth of Nations*, Everyman edn., J. M. Dent and Sons, London.

Smith, J. P., and Welch, F. R. (1989): 'Black Economic Progress after Myrdal', *Journal of Economic Literature*, 28/2 (June), 519–64.

Solomon, S. (1990): *Phases of Economic Growth 1950–1973*, Cambridge University Press.

Solow, R. (1957): 'Technical Change and the Aggregate Production Function', *Review of Economics and Statistics*, 39 (Aug.), 312–20.

—— (1985): 'Economic History and Economics', *American Economic Review* (May), 328–31.

—— (1988): 'Growth Theory and After', *American Economic Review*, 78/3 (June), 307–17.

—— (1994): 'Perspectives on Growth Theory, *Journal of Economic Perspectives*, 8/1 (winter), 45–54.

Sosa, E. (ed.) (1975): *Causation and Conditionals*, Oxford University Press.

Soto, H. de. (1989): *The Other Path: The Invisible Revolution in the Third World*, Harper and Row, New York.

Sowell, T. (1977): *Classical Economics Reconsidered*, Princeton University Press.

Spence, M. (1974): *Market Signaling*, Harvard University Press.

Squire, L. (1981): *Employment Policy in Developing Countries*, Oxford University Press.

—— (1993): 'Fighting Poverty, *American Economic Review*, 83/2 (May), 377–82.

—— and Tak, H. van der (1975): *Economic Analysis of Projects*, Johns Hopkins, University Press, Baltimore.

Srinivasan, T. N. (1977): 'Development, Poverty and Basic Human Needs', *Food Research Institute Studies*, 16/2: 11–28, reprinted in Lal (1992).

—— (1981): 'Malnutrition: Some Measurement and Policy Issues', *Journal of Development Economics*, 8/1.

—— (1986): 'The Costs and Benefits of being a Small, Remote Island, Landlocked, or Ministate Economy', *World Bank Research Observer*, 1/2: 205–18.

—— (1989): 'Recent Theories of Imperfect Competition and International Trade: Any Implications For Development Strategy', *Indian Economic Review*, 24/1 (Jan.), 1–23; reprinted in Lal (1992).

—— (1994): 'Database for Development Analysis: An Overview', *Journal of Development Economics*, 44/1 (June), 3–27.

—— and P. Bardhan eds. (1988): *Rural Poverty in South Asia*, Columbia University Press, New York.

Staniland, M. (1985): *What is Political Economy?* Yale University Press.

Stark, O., and Levhari, D. (1982): 'On Migration and Risk', *Economic Development and Cultural Change*, 31/1: 191–6.

Stein, S. J., and Stein, B. H. (1970): *The Colonial Heritage of Latin America*, Oxford.

Stern, N. (1991): 'The Determinants of Growth', *Economic Journal*, 101 (Jan.), 122–33; reprinted in Lal (1992).

—— and Newbery, D. (1987): *The Theory of Taxation for Developing Countries*, Oxford University Press.

Stewart, F. (1982): 'Recent Theories of International Trade: Some Implications for the South', in H. Kierzkowski (ed.), *Monopolistic Competition and International Trade*, Blackwell, Oxford.

Stewart, I. M. T. (1979): *Reasoning and Method in Economics: An Introduction to Economic Methodology*, McGraw Hill, London and New York.

Stigler, G. J. (1970): 'Director's Law of Public Income Distribution', *Journal of Law and Economics*, 13 (Apr.), 1–10.

—— (1971): 'The Theory of Economic Regulation', *Bell Journal of Economics*, 2/1 (Spring), 1–21.

—— (ed.) (1988): *Chicago Studies in Political Economy*, Chicago University Press.

—— and Boulding, K. E. (eds.) (1953): *Readings in Price Theory*, American Economic Association, Allen and Unwin, London.

Stiglitz, J. (1986): 'The New Development Economics'. *World Development*, 14/2 (Feb.), 257–65.

—— (1987): 'Principal and Agent (ii)', *The New Palgrave: A Dictionary of Economics*, Macmillan, London, iii. 966–92.

—— (1989): 'The Role of Institutions in Economic Development', *World Development*, 17/9 (Sept.).

Stock, J. H., and Watson, M. W. (1988): 'Variable Trends in Economic Time Series', *Journal of Economic Perspectives*, 2/3 (Summer), 147–74.

Stokey, N. (1991): 'Human Capital, Product Quality and Growth', *Quarterly Journal of Economics*, 106 (May), 587–616.

Streeten, P. (1982): 'A Cool Look at "Outward-Looking" Stategies for Development', *The World Economy*, 5/1 (Mar.), 159–70.

—— and associates (1981): *First Things First*, Oxford University Press.

—— and Lall, S. (1977): *Foreign Investment, Transnationals and Developing Countries*, Macmillan, London.

Sugden, R. (1982): 'A Review of Inequality Re-examined by Amartya Sen', *Journal of Economic Literature*, 31/4 (Dec.), 1947–86.

—— (1982): 'On the Economics of Philanthropy', *Economic Journal* 92: 341–50.

—— (1983): *Who Cares? An Economic and Ethical Analysis of Private Charity and the Welfare State*, Occassional Paper 67, Institute of Economic Affairs, London.

Summers, R., and Heston, A. (1984): 'Improved International Comparisons of Real Product and its Composition', *Review of Income and Wealth* (March).

—— —— (1988): 'A New Set of Interational Comparisons of Real Product and Price Level Estimates for 130 Countries, 1950–85.' *Review of Income and Wealth* (Mar.), 1–25.

—— —— (1991): 'The Pen World Table (Mark 5: An Expanded Set of International Comparisions, 1950–1988). *Quarterly Journal of Economics*, 106/2, (May), 327–68.'

Swamy, G. (1981): 'International Migrant Workers' Remittances: Issues and Prospects', World Bank Staff Working Paper no. 481, World Bank, Washington, DC.

Taylor, L. (1983): *Structuralist Macroeconomics*, Basic Books, New York.

Thomas, H. (1979): *A History of the World*, Harper and Row, New York.

Timberg, T. (1978): *The Marwaris*, Vikas Publishing House, New Delhi.

Tocqueville, A. de (1835): *Democracy in America*, Paris.

—— (1968): 'Memoir on Pauperism', reprinted in Drescher (ed.) *De Tocqueville and Beaumont on Social Reform*, New York.

Tomes, N. (1981): 'The Family, Inheritance, and the Intergenerational Transmisson of Inequality', *Journal of Political Economy*, 89 (Oct.), 309–22.

Trewartha, G. T. (1943): *An Introduction to Weather and Clinate*, McGraw Hill, New York.

Tullock, G. (1965): *The Politics of Bureaucracy*, Public Affairs Press, Washington, DC.

—— (1967): 'The Welfare Costs of Tariffs, Monopolies and Theft', *Western Economic Journal*, 5/3: 224–32.

—— (1987): 'Public Choice', in *The New Palgrave: A Dictionary of Economics*, vol. iii, Macmillan, London, 1041.

UNICEF (1984): *The State of the World's Children 1984*, Oxford University Press.

Urdinola, A., Carrizosa Serano, M., and Wett, R. (1987): *The Political Economy of Poverty, Equity, and Growth*, mimeo, World Bank, Washington, D.C.

Urrutia, M. (1985): *Winners and Losers in Colombia's Economic Growth in the 1970s*, Johns Hopkins Press, Baltimore.

Viner, J (1931): 'Cost and Supply Curves', *Zeitschrift fur Nationalekonomie*, 3; reprinted in Stigler and Boulding (1953). 331–51.

Vital, D. (1967): *The Inequality of States*, Clarendon Press, Oxford.

von Mises, L. (1962): *The Ultimate Foundation of Economic Science*, van Nostrand, Princeton, NJ.

Wade, R. (1990): *Governing the Market*, Princeton University Press.

Walle, D. van de (1992): 'The Distribution of the Benefits from Social Services in Indonesia, 1978–87', Policy Research Working Paper, Country Economics Dept., World Bank, Washington, DC.

Walters, A. (1989): 'Currency Boards', in *The New Palgrave*, 1: 740–2.

Wang, Gungwu (1973): 'Nationalism in Asia', in Kamenka (ed.), *Nationalism: the Nature and Evolution of an Idea*, Arnold, London.

Warr, P. G. (1983): 'The Private Provision of a Public Good is Independent of the Distribution of Income', *Economic Letters*, 13: 207–11.

Welch, F. (1989): 'The Employment of Black Men', *Journal of Labor Economics*.

Wellisz, S., and Findlay, R. (1988): 'The State and the Invisible Hand', *World Bank Research Observer*, 3/1 (Jan.), 59–80.

Whynes, D. (ed.) (1984): *What is Political Economy?*, Blackwell, Oxford.

Wiles, P. (1967): 'Power without Influence: The Economic Impact', in Royal Institute of International Affairs: *The Impact of the Russian Revolution 1917–1967: The Influence of Bolshevism on the World Outside Russia*, Oxford.

Williamson, O. E. (1975): *Markets and Hierarchies*, Free Press, New York.

Wood, A. (1988): *Global Trends in Real Exchange Rates, 1960–1984*, World Bank Discussion Papers no. 35, World Bank, Washington, DC.

World Bank: (1983, 1984, 1987, 1991), *World Development Report*, Oxford University Press, New York.

World Bank (1980): *World Tables*, World Bank, Washington, DC.

—— (1992): *Poverty Reduction Handbook*, Washington, DC.

—— (1993): *The East Asian Miracle*, Oxford, New York.

Wrigley, E. A. (1988): *Continuity, Chance and Change: The Character of the Industrial Revolution in England*, Cambridge University Press, Cambridge.

Wu, Y. L., and Wu, C. H. 1980: *Economic Development in South East Asia: The Chinese Dimension*, Hoover Institution, Stanford, Calif.

Wynia, G. (1984): *The Politics of Latin American Development*, 2nd edn., Cambridge University Press.

Yasuoka, S. (1984): 'Capital Ownership in Family Companies', in Okochi and Yasuoka (1984).

Young, A. (1991): Learning by Doing and the Dynamic Effects of International Trade', *Quarterly Journal of Economics*, 106: 369–405.

—— (1992): 'A Tale of Two Cities: Factor Accumulation and Technical Change in Hong Kong and Singapore', in Blanchard and Fischer (eds.), *NBER Macroeconomics Annual 1992*, MIT Press, Cambridge, Mass.

—— (1993): 'Invention and Bounded Learning By Doing', *Journal of Political Economy*, 101/3 (June), 443–72.

—— (1987): *Hong Kong*, Study for the Project on 'The Political Economy of Poverty, Equity and Growth', mimeo, World Bank, Washington, DC.

INDEX OF SUBJECTS

INDEX OF NAMES